Twenty Questions for the Writer

A Rhetoric with Readings

Fourth Edition

Twenty Questions for the Writer

A Rhetoric with Readings

Fourth Edition

Jacqueline Berke

Drew University

HBJ **Harcourt Brace Jovanovich, Publishers**

San Diego   New York   Chicago   Atlanta   Washington, D.C.
London   Sydney   Toronto

*To the students in my writing courses
at Drew University, who helped me
through four editions.*

Preface

*T*hat *Twenty Questions for the Writer* has served students and instructors well enough to warrant a Fourth Edition is gratifying indeed. Even more important, a new edition has enabled me to make further improvements (such as a new emphasis on the "process approach") that were possible only with time, continued classroom testing, and helpful suggestions from colleagues throughout the country. Above all, I have tried again to preserve readability and teachability in this edition. The text is still a reader-rhetoric-research-guide-handbook all in one, complete and ready for instructors and students to use without any additional resources other than a good dictionary. The twenty questions themselves, each used as a probing instrument to generate a different type of essay, have remained the heart of the text and, by all reports, its most distinguished and distinguishing feature.

The twenty questions, then, continue to provide not only a point of departure for writing assignments, but also a frame for the course, a step-by-step procedure for moving through the weeks of the semester. Each unit is self-contained, with precise instructions on writing in a given form, plus ample illustrative readings, warm-up exercises, and suggested writing assignments. Of course, instructors may organize segments into whatever sequence best suits individual needs and preferences.

Beyond the twenty questions, I have made six major improvements in this edition which substantially expand the perspectives of the book.

1. *Reorganization to conform to a process approach*
   The parts of *Twenty Questions* now reflect a more realistic picture of the writing process as it has emerged in current composition research (and as professional writers have long recognized). Consequently, the parts of the text now follow the sequence of *prewriting, writing,* and *rewriting.* Even

though we know that this process is not simply sequential (not linear but recursive), we can benefit from a reminder—embedded in the very structure of the text—of the stages of writing and their cyclical character: we rewrite as we write, and frequently we prewrite in order to get the words flowing, to overcome inertia, stir memory, clear cobwebs, redefine purpose, or rediscover direction. The final section of the text includes specific directions on how to revise—three steps to successful revision, plus five specific strategies, and a "case study" of the revision process behind John F. Kennedy's Inaugural Address. Similarly, I have provided a step-by-step account of a student essay as it moved through a first, a second, a third, and finally a fourth draft—a finished *product* infinitely enhanced by the persistence of *process*.

2. *Addition of an introductory section on prewriting*
An added, substantial introductory section describes such prewriting warm-up strategies as freewriting, brainstorming, clustering, and journal writing.

3. *Thirty-six new readings*
Drawn from across the curriculum, on subjects as far-ranging as food and philosophy, new class-tested essays and articles bring the total number of readings in this edition to 114. Still functioning as models and inspiration for writing assignments, they now include such engaging short pieces as Roger Angell's descriptive "The Baseball," George Orwell's warmly reflective "Some Thoughts on the Common Toad," Russell Baker's vividly evoked "The Prim Mr. Fleagle," a tribute to a favorite English teacher, and Maxine Hong Kingston's "Uncle Bun," a haunting portrait from *China Men*. For instructors who stress more factual and analytical exposition, I have added a number of models that embody careful research and systematic organization: "Sylvia Plath: A Short Life," "The Sweet Truth About Sugar," Martin Luther King, Jr.'s monumental "Letter from Birmingham Jail," and others.

4. *Lively new exercises*
Because students can improve their style and their work habits only by practice—the actual running of neural pathways—I have included many new exercises throughout the text, particularly in Part One, Prewriting. Shirley Weissenborn, graduate student in English at Drew and a writer of rare liveliness and ingenuity, devised most of these. Designed for use in class as well as outside, these exercises, which include prewriting throughout the book, serve a variety of purposes: they break down writing blocks; they tap deeper levels of concentration and imagination; they help to reinforce rhetorical principles and, at the same time, develop the student's confidence. At their best, these exercises—always ungraded and therefore free of pressure—will introduce students to the simple pleasures of writing as well as the pervasive anxieties.

5. *Focus on audience and the reader-writer relationship*
This edition gives writers specific instructions about how to establish a successful relationship with their readers by visualizing them: by beginning

with self-confrontation, moving through identification of context and occasion, and ending with clear definition of purpose.

6. *Close analysis of "the long paper"*

In this edition, for the first time, I have "anatomized" the long paper, showing that just as the short essay represents an answer to a single question, so the long paper represents a complex reply to many questions. To make this demonstration, I chose Martin Luther King, Jr.'s "Letter from Birmingham Jail" because this remarkable human document, written under the most extraordinary circumstances, remains one of the most brilliantly argued "position papers" ever written—a model for all who aspire to speak out more movingly and convincingly in behalf of their chosen subjects.

By specific design, the resources of this text exceed what any instructor might actively use in any one semester. Such abundance enables an instructor to shape the syllabus differently from class section to class section or year to year, to keep the course fresh and "in motion," an ever-changing configuration or process, like the act of writing itself. For those who wish to give students a sense of the dimensions of expository prose plus a representative sampling of the types, I have found (and colleagues have confirmed) that the following distribution of assignments provides both flexibility and reasonably full coverage—with emphasis on the analytical.

	General Category of Writing	*Questions Generating Specific Essays*	*Types of Essays*	*Suggested Number of Assignments from Each Group*
Group I	Imaginative	1. How can X be described?	Description	1–2
		2. How did X happen?	Narration	
		3. What kind of person is X?	Characterization	
		4. What is my memory of X?	Reminiscence	
		5. What is my personal response to X?	Response	
Group II	Informative	6. What are the facts about X?	Information	1–2
		7. How can X be summarized?	Summary	
Group III	Analytical	8. What does X mean?	Definition	4–6
		9. What is the essential function of X?	Functional Definition	
		10. What are the component parts of X?	Simple Analysis	
		11. How is X made or done?	Process Analysis	

General Category of Writing	Questions Generating Specific Essays	Types of Essays	Suggested Number of Assignments from Each Group
	12. How should X be made or done?	Directional Analysis	
	13. What are the causes of X?	Causal Analysis	
	14. What are the consequences of X?	Casual Analysis	
	15. What are the types of X?	Classification	
	16. How does X compare to Y?	Comparison	
	17. What is the present status of X?	Comparison	
Group IV Critical	18. How should X be interpreted?	Interpretation	1–2
	19. What is the value of X?	Critical Evaluation	
	20. What case can be made for or against X?	Argumentation	
		Total	7–12 Short Essays Plus *One Long* Paper

Although you will find many changes in this Fourth Edition, you will find no change in its basic commitment to writing as an essentially *moral* activity, a way to foster human understanding, a way to achieve what Carl Rogers calls "consensus" and Kenneth Burke calls "social cooperation in the human jungle." This humanistic perspective has remained my "star to steer by," more important today than ever, as our technology continues to expand at a dazzling and dizzying pace. How can we expect to interact creatively and productively with this technology if we do not make it our own, if we do not remind ourselves at every opportunity that *writing is a uniquely human activity designed to fulfill uniquely human ends*? No matter what our means or methods of writing—calligraphic pen and parchment, chalk and blackboard, typewriter, word processor, or fine fading lines of smoke against a blue sky—writing is still an exclusively, sometimes excruciatingly, human process. Only people read; only people write; only people program remarkable machines that give an uncanny imitation of these activities, even "talking back" to us as though they, too, were people. We know better. We know that students and teachers alike—all of us "programmers" of our own thoughts and ideas—must struggle constantly to convey our thoughts and ideas to others. We also know (if we stop to think about it) that no single impulse leads more surely to clear communication than genuine concern and compassion. Propelled by such feelings, we automatically make clarity our major objective, even as simplicity and economy become forms of courtesy and kindness as well as craft. Thus for this Fourth Edition, as for earlier editions, I have chosen as epigraph to the text a simple but compellingly human and illuminating observation from F. L. Lucas's *Style:*

> And how is clarity to be acquired? Mainly by taking trouble
> and by writing to serve people rather than to impress them.

To Bill McLane, who launched this Fourth Edition, and to members of the extraordinarily competent and conscientious editorial team at Harcourt Brace Jovanovich who "carried the ball" all the way, I want to express deep appreciation. First, foremost, and forevermore I am beholden to Marlane Y. Agriesti, associate editor, College Department. To me, of course, she is simply *my* editor—and a wonderful editor at that.

Similarly, I admire and salute the expertise of Gene Lettau, manuscript editor; Rick Roehrich, production editor; Cathy Reynolds, designer; Tricia Griffith, senior art editor; and Eleanor Garner, permissions editor.

I am also indebted to colleagues across the country who read and reviewed earlier editions of this book: Jim Vandergriff, Central Missouri State University; Linda P. Young, University of California, Davis; George Miller, University of Delaware; Janet L. Larson, Rutgers University; Virginia Oram, Southern Methodist University; Ben Vasta, Camden County Community College; Jo Koster Tarvers, The University of North Carolina at Chapel Hill; and Peggy Pryzant, Modesto Junior College.

Finally, I want to thank the following for providing helpful input along the way: William Sartoris, Camden County Community College; William Ballard, Becone College; Martha Ravits, University of Oregon; John Teague, The University of North Carolina at Chapel Hill; Harvey Kassebaum, Cuyahoga Community College; Joseph Flory, Eastern Kentucky University; Maureen Hong, Wichita State; and Linda Haskins, Delaware State College.

I also want to thank Richard Costner, Tennessee Temple University; Betty Boling, Bacon College; Anthony Spatola, Camden County Community College; Susan Betts Landstrom, The University of North Carolina at Chapel Hill; Ralph St. Louis, University of Evansville; Sandra Vekasy, Evangel College; Allen Ramsey, Central Missouri State University; and Kathy Reuter, University of North Carolina at Chapel Hill.

And in addition I want to thank Loris Galford, McNeese State University; Jayne Menich, University of Wisconsin; Walter Everett, Indiana State University at Evansville; Ruth Foreman, South Dakota State University; Jennifer Ginn, The University of North Carolina at Chapel Hill; Roy McAuley, Central Missouri State University; and Margaret Bretschneider, Lakeland Community College.

Jacqueline Berke

Contents

Part One

THE PREWRITING PROCESS   13

Part Four

WRITING A LONG PAPER: ANSWERING THE TWENTY QUESTIONS

Twenty Questions for the Writer

A Rhetoric with Readings

Fourth Edition

Introduction

And how is clarity to be acquired? Mainly by taking trouble; and by writing to serve people rather than to impress them.

—F. L. Lucas, *Style*

WRITING AS A HUMAN ACTIVITY

*O*nly when we view writing in the broadest perspective—as a means by which human beings reach across both time and space, transmitting their accumulated culture to one another and to subsequent generations—can we see how vital our written language is not only to the life of the individual but to the total life of the community. "Greece and Rome [were] civilized by language," Ezra Pound tells us.

The classical meaning of "rhetoric"—and the meaning insisted on by modern rhetoricians and sustained throughout this book—is the art of using language to its best possible effect: to teach, to delight, to move an audience to considered and significant action. This view of rhetoric as issuing from shared principles and common aims is best expressed in Kenneth Burke's deeply moral definition of rhetoric as "the use of language to promote social cooperation in the human jungle." Thus the modern rhetorician—dedicated to the effective and forceful use of language—shuns verbal trickery, sophistry, and all forms of sensationalism and harangue, leaving these to the demagogue, the professional agitator, the propagandist. As citizens in a democracy—and particularly as members of a college community, where our special task is to search out truth—we are expected to make our appeals to reason rather than merely emotion: to inform and explain by indicating precisely *how* and *why*; to organize material in logical patterns; to support, illustrate, demonstrate, amplify, and wherever possible *prove* our points; to express ourselves clearly and accurately. These are the touchstones of responsible writing.

Only responsible writing makes an exchange of views possible: once "B" understands what "A" means, "B" can reply to "A" and "A" can then, in turn, reply to "B." If both sides treat this exchange with respect and what psychotherapist Carl Rogers calls "empathetic understanding" (understanding *with* and not merely *about* the other person), the resulting dialogue may progress to "mutual communication." This may well be our only hope for the future. Rogers (quoted in Young, *Rhetoric*) says:

> Mutual communication tends to be pointed toward solving a problem rather than toward attacking a person or group. It leads to a situation in which I see how the problem appears to you, as well as to me, and you see how it appears to me, as well as to you. Thus accurately and realistically defined, the problem is almost certain to yield to intelligent attack, or if it is in part insoluble, it will be comfortably accepted as such.

In Question 20, "What case can I make for or against X?" we shall explore further implications of consensus-producing argument; here I shall simply say that writing clearly, cogently, and compellingly is imperative. We must build bridges to one another with our written discourse; we must use it to unite and not divide us. Thanks to twentieth-century technology, we may well live in a global village where electronic media connect even the most remote areas of the world, but we are still tied to the written word as the basic means of human communication and interaction. On a personal and political level we still write *to* and *for* one another, as the increasing number of newspapers, magazines, and books demonstrates. We are still tied to written communication for conducting the business of the world. Machine makers and button pushers follow written instructions. Radio and television programs originate in written proposals, recommendations, and scripts. Statesmen negotiate—endlessly—in formal correspondence (witness the huge collections of presidential materials in the Truman, Eisenhower, Kennedy, and Johnson libraries). In short, supplemented by film, tape, and record, the written document still provides the copious details that constitute the archives of our civilization.

DEVELOPING THE ABILITY TO WRITE

Certainly, then, the skill to write cogently and persuasively is a basic need in our time. Unfortunately, this need goes largely unfulfilled. Most people write poorly—and thus with great reluctance. As one student complained, pointing first to his head and then to the paper in front of him, "It's all up here; I just can't get it down there." Although he thought this was *his* unique problem, this student was actually voicing everyone's problem. Writing is the act of transmitting thoughts, feelings, and ideas from "up here" in the head to "down there" on paper. "Putting black on white," as one author described his work, is very exacting.

When it is done well, writing is very exciting work that requires many composite skills: (1) *mental*—you must be able to think clearly and to organize your ideas in an orderly, logical sequence; (2) *psychological*—you must feel free and sufficiently relaxed so that ideas will in fact move from head to hand; (3) *rhetorical*—you must know the fundamentals of the craft: the various ways you can put sentences together to make a smoothly flowing, readable composition; (4) *critical*—once you have written something, you must be able to judge it, to know whether it is good or bad, and, if it is bad, to improve it.

Students often admit they realize a paper is poor when they turn it in, but they do not know how to improve it. They do not know *specifically* what is weak, or *specifically* how it can be strengthened. Unless we can evaluate our writing in a concrete and constructive way, unless we learn to be patient and painstaking almost to the limits of endurance, we cannot hope to reach a level of excellence or even competence. Professional writers who recognize that "hard writing makes easy reading" resign themselves to drudgery. Dorothy Parker complained that "I can't write five words but that I change seven." And James Thurber, a witty, urbane, and seemingly facile writer, said:

> There is no writing, only re-writing....The first or second draft of everything I write reads as if it was turned out by a charwoman....For me it's mostly a question of rewriting....A story I've been working on—"The Train on Track Six"...was rewritten fifteen complete times....It's part of a constant attempt on my part to make the finished version smooth, to make it seem effortless.

To make the finished version seem effortless: this is the mark of a supremely good style. Good style is *unobtrusively* good; it does not call attention to itself. In fact, readers are barely aware of *how* the writer has written; they are aware only of *what* has been written; the subject matter alone stands out, not the writing. The writing flows smoothly, like a river moving onward with the current.

Many people who must write are simply not aware of what is involved in the writing process. For this process involves thinking, planning, assembling, classifying, organizing—in short, the *prewriting* necessary for a clear presentation (not to mention the rewriting that comes later). Other people do realize what they need to do but stubbornly refuse to take the necessary pains. Their writing is obscure and hard to read because they will not submit to the demands of the discipline. Unfortunately, we sometimes have to read the work of such authors. They surround us and they sometimes even write textbooks. Reading their writing means reading and rereading, for their prose is like an obstacle course through which we wind our uncertain way—as in the following passage:

> In conformity with the preceding point, if all the interacting parties in marriage, in minority-majority groups, in different occupational, religious, political, economic, racial, ethnic, and other interacting groups and persons view the given overtly similar (or dissimilar) traits: A, B, C, D, N (physical, biological, mental, socio-cultural) as negligible values or as no values at all, as compromising even no similarity (or dissimilarity), such overt similarities-dissimilarites are innocuous in the generation of either solidarity or antagonism (cited in Kitzhaber, 129).

Whenever possible, of course, the sensible reader refuses to read such gibberish, just as the sensible person refuses to visit a doctor who is careless or a lawyer who is incompetent. To begin with, the writer's thoughts are addled (we wonder, "Does *he* know what he is talking about?"). One phrase tumbles out after another in no discernible order, and excessive parentheses interrupt the flow of thought. The endless abstract words, curiously hyphenated words, jargon, and unnecessary coding (A, B, C, D, N) make the reader's head spin. We cannot follow or even *guess* at the writer's meaning.

Of course, you cannot hope that a basic writing course—or even a four-year college education—will make you a first-rate writer, a master of the craft. But you can expect to gain important insights into the art of writing. You will learn how to analyze a page of prose and to recognize how a piece of writing works. You will understand why some writing succeeds as a unit of communication and why some writing projects reveal only a distorted notion of the intended meaning. Most important, you will gain greater control of your own writing; you will learn to find and develop ideas in a systematic way and put them down on paper with greater fluency and flexibility.

The Qualities of Good Writing

Even before you prepare to write, your own instinct and intuition help you to make certain judgments about what is "good." Take, for example, the following familiar sentence: "I know not what course others may take, but as for me, give me liberty or give me death." Do you suppose Patrick Henry's thought would have come ringing down through the centuries if he had expressed it not in one tight, rhythmical sentence but as follows?

> It would be difficult, if not impossible, to predict on the basis of my limited information as to the predilections of the public, what the citizenry at large will regard as action commensurate with the present provocation, but after arduous consideration I personally feel so intensely and irrevocably committed to the position of social, political, and economic independence, that rather than submit to foreign and despotic control which is anathema to me, I will make the ultimate sacrifice of which humanity is capable—under the aegis of personal honor, ideological conviction, and existential commitment, I will sacrifice my own mortal existence.

How does this "high-flown" paraphrase measure up to the bold "Give me liberty or give me death"? Who will deny that something is "happening" in Patrick Henry's rousing challenge that not only fails to happen in the paraphrase but is actually negated there? Would you bear with this long-winded speaker to the end? If you were to judge this statement strictly on its rhetoric (its choice and arrangement of words), you might aptly call it more boring than brave. Perhaps a plainer version will work better:

> Liberty is a very important thing for a person to have. Most people—at least the people I've talked to or that other people have told me about—know this and therefore are very anxious to preserve their liberty. Of course I can't be absolutely sure about what other folks are going to do in this present crisis, what with all these threats and everything, but I've made up my mind that I'm going to fight because liberty is really a very important thing to me; at least that's the way I feel about it.

This flat, "homely" prose is weighted down with what the French author Gustave Flaubert called "fatty deposits." As in the pompous paraphrase, every verb agrees with its subject, every comma is in its proper place; nonetheless it lacks the qualities that make a statement—whether short or long—pungent, vital, and memorable.

Let us isolate these qualities and briefly describe them. (They are described in greater detail in the Style Guide at the end of this volume.)

ECONOMY

The first quality of good writing is *economy*. An appropriately slender volume on style by William Strunk, Jr. and E. B. White presents the case for economy concisely:

> A sentence should contain no unnecessary words, for the same reason that a drawing should have no unnecessary lines and a machine no unnecessary parts. This requires not that the writer make all his sentences short or that he avoid all detail . . . but that every word tell.

Economical writing is *efficient* and *aesthetically satisfying*. While it makes a minimum demand on the energy and patience of readers, it returns to them a maximum of sharply compressed meaning. This is one of your basic responsibilities as a writer: to inflict no unnecessary words on your reader—just as a dentist inflicts no unnecessary pain, a lawyer no unnecessary risk. Economical writing avoids strain and promotes pleasure by producing a sense of form and proper proportion, a sense of words that fit the ideas the words embody. Terse writing has no "deadwood" to dull the reader's attention, no useless phrases to clog the free flow of ideas, which the author expresses swiftly and clearly.

SIMPLICITY

Another basic quality of good writing is *simplicity*. Here again you do not have to make all your sentences primerlike or reduce complexities to the bare bone, but do avoid embellishment and embroidery. A natural, unpretentious style which signifies sincerity is best. When people say what they *really mean*, they tend to say it with disarming simplicity. Paradoxically, simplicity or naturalness does not come naturally. By the time they are old enough to write, most people have grown so self-conscious that they stiffen, sometimes to the point of rigidity, when they have to make a statement in speech or in writing. It is easy to offer the kindly advice "Be yourself". But many people change when they take a pencil in hand or sit down at a typewriter. During the early days of the Second World War, when citizens feared air raids in New York City and instituted blackouts, an anonymous writer—probably a young civil service worker at City Hall—produced and distributed the following poster:

> *Illumination*
> *Is Required*
> *to be*
> *Extinguished*
> *on These Premises*
> *After Nightfall*

What this meant, of course, was simply "Lights Out After Dark." But apparently that direct imperative—clear and to the point—did not sound "official" enough. The writer resorted to long Latinate words and involved syntax (note the awkward passives "*Is* Required" and "*to be* Extinguished") to establish a tone of dignity and authority. In contrast, how beautifully simple are the words of the translators of the King James Version of the Bible, who felt no need for flamboyance or grandiloquence. The Lord did not bombastically proclaim that universal illumination was required to be instantaneously installed. The simple but majestic translation reads, "And God said, Let there be light: and there was light.... And God called the light Day, and the darkness he called Night."

Most memorable declarations have been spare and direct. The French author Andre Maurois noted that Abraham Lincoln and John F. Kennedy seemed to "speak to each other across the span of a century." Both men embodied noble themes in eloqently simple terms. Lincoln, in his second Inaugural Address, said: "With malice toward none, with charity for all, with firmness in the right as God gives us to see the right, let us strive on to finish the work we are in...." One hundred years later President Kennedy made his Inaugural dedication: "With a good conscience our only sure reward, with history the final judge of our deeds, let us go forth to lead the land we love...."

CLARITY

A third fundamental element of good writing is *clarity*. Some people question whether it is always possible to be clear. After all, certain ideas are inherently complicated and inescapably difficult. True enough. But the responsible writer recognizes that writing should not add to the complications nor increase the difficulty: It should not set up an additional roadblock to understanding. If writers understand their own ideas and want to convey them to others, they are obliged to render those ideas in clear, orderly, readable, understandable prose—or why bother writing in the first place? Actually, obscure writers are usually confused themselves, uncertain of what they want to say or what they mean; they have not yet completed that process of thinking through and reasoning into the heart of the subject.

Whatever the topic, whatever the occasion, expository writing should be readable, informative, and, wherever possible, engaging. At its best it may even be poetic.

Even in technical writing, where the range of styles is necessarily limited, you must always be aware of "the reader over your shoulder." Topics such as how to follow postal regulations for overseas mail, how to change oil in an engine, or how to produce aspirin from salicylic acid require technical descriptions that defy a memorable turn of phrase. Such writing is of necessity cut and dried, dispassionate, and bloodless. But it need not be tedious, or confusing to readers who want to find out about mailing letters, changing oil, or making aspirin. Readers who are looking for such information should have reasonably easy access to it. Written instructions should be clear, spare, direct, and, most of all, *human*: No matter how technical the subject, human beings write for other human beings. Writing, like language itself, is a strictly human enterprise. Machines may stamp letters, measure oil, and convert acids, but only human beings talk and write about these procedures so that other human beings may better understand them. Therefore, being human in the way you write is always appropriate.

"COURTSHIP" DEVICES

The writer should draw upon those personal and aesthetic effects that enhance a statement without distorting it and that "delight"—or at least sustain—the reader's attention. "One's case," said Aristotle, "should, in justice, be fought on the strength of the facts alone." This would be ideal: mind speaking to mind. The truth is, however, that people do not react solely on rational grounds, or, to quote Aristotle in a more cynical mood, "External matters do count much, because of the sorry nature of the audience." Facing the realities, then, you should try to "woo" the reader through a kind of "courtship." You should try, as Carl Rogers reminds us, to break down the natural barriers and fears that separate people, whether their encounters are face to face or on the printed page.

You must personalize your relationship with the reader by using those rhetorical devices that enable you to emerge from the page as a human being, with a distinctive voice and, in a broad sense, a personality. When the writer and reader come together, the occasion should be special, marked by a common purpose and an element of pleasure.

Rhetoric provides a rich storehouse of "courting" devices, and I shall present these in Part Three. For example, the pleasant rhythm of a balanced antithesis is evident in President Kennedy's immortal statement, "... ask not what your country can do for you; ask what you can do for your country." The lilting suspense of a periodic sentence (one that suspends its predication until the end) appears in Edward Gibbon's delightful account of how he came to write the famous *Decline and Fall of the Roman Empire*:

> It was at Rome, on the 15th of October 1764, as I sat musing amidst the ruins of the Capitol, while the barefooted friars were singing vespers in the temple of Jupiter, that the idea of writing the decline and fall of the city first started to my mind.

Simeon Potter, a modern scholar, has observed that the word picture Gibbon draws, although brief, is "artistically perfect":

> The rhythm is stately and entirely satisfying. The reader is held in suspense to the end. Had he wished, and had he been less of an artist, Gibbon might have said exactly the same things in a different way, arranging them in their logical and grammatical order: "The idea of writing the decline and fall of the city first started to my mind as I sat musing amidst the ruins of the Capitol at Rome on the 15th of October 1764, while the barefooted friars were singing vespers in the temple of Jupiter." What has happened? It is not merely that a periodic sentence has been re-expressed as a loose one. The emphasis is now all wrong and the magnificent cadence of the original is quite marred. All is still grammatically correct, but "proper words" are no longer in "proper places." The passage has quite lost its harmonious rhythm.

In addition then to economy, simplicity, and clarity—the foundation of sound, dependable rhetoric—include this marvelous dimension of "harmonious rhythm," of proper words in proper places. If you are sensitive to these "strategies," you will delight as well as inform your reader, and in delighting, reinforce your statement.

The Student Writer

Erich Fromm, a well-known psychologist, has said of the child, "He must grow until finally he becomes his own father." So too I can say to the student writer: You must grow until you become your own teacher, your own critic, and your own editor. Slowly you will cultivate a sensitivity to clear, unpretentious prose. At the same time you will develop a negative sensitivity—an intolerance—to diffuse, pompous, or jargon-ridden prose. You will be able to view your own or someone else's writing with a critical eye. You will be able to see what skill has gone into creating it and to judge the finished piece.

Most important, when you have reached maturity as a writer, you will know how to go about the job of writing, no matter what your assignment. Your material will not overwhelm or intimidate you any more than the unworked wood for a desk or a bookcase overwhelms or intimidates a cabinetmaker. You will act on your raw material and shape it in accordance with your will and plan, in much the same way as the cabinetmaker does. You will know what you want to say, just as a cabinetmaker knows before picking up a saw what the final product is to be. You will organize your ideas in a logical, orderly sequence, just as a cabinetmaker assembles the tools and maps out the steps by which he or she transforms raw wood into smooth, polished furniture.

Like the artisan or artist, you will always be in control, and you will experience a sense of creativity. For, in truth, you *will be* creating. Indeed, we should not limit the term "creative writing" to poetry, short stories, and novels as we often do. *All* writing is creative when the writer forges out of his or her raw material (poetic images, anecdotes, statistics, a set of facts) a new whole: a poem, an expository article, an essay, or a term paper. Proficient writers understand language as a medium of expression and shape it in a deliberate and disciplined way to address a chosen audience. Whether writing fiction or exposition, they work creatively and produce creative writing. You, too, should regard all writing, expository or otherwise, as a creative challenge; you create out of isolated, separate elements (facts, feelings, memories, ideas, and so on) a new whole that is, as John Stuart Mill described a chemical compound, "more than the sum of its parts."

EXERCISES

1. As a reader, respond to the following passages, indicating whether you think they are well written or poorly written and why. Try to be specific as to which features you like and which you find difficult and clumsy.

   a. The data, in general, suggest that neither similarity nor complementarity of needs appears to be particularly meaningful in the determination of adolescent friendships beyond the suggested importance of similarity in a case where an extreme difference in friendship choices exists. However, both of these need patterns are internally consistent phenomena and perhaps are related to other factors. Similarities in perceptual and cognitive phenomena appear to be promising leads for future research in this area.
      —From a doctoral dissertation in education, cited in
      Albert Kitzhaber, *Themes, Theories, and Therapy*

   b. Of the two types of crime, namely crime as deviant behavior and crime as learned behavior, the theory of deviant behavior is implicit or explicit in most predictive studies. Also, personality differences which are ignored or considered unimportant in the cultural approach to crime are considered relevant in most prediction instruments, whether devised by clinicians or by sociologists. For example, studies have emphasized that delinquent recidivism is the result of failure of personal and/or social controls, whether in the family or in the local community. But from a learning viewpoint of delinquency the emphasis would have been upon accessibility to delinquent associates and upon the continued influence by delinquents as against conventional persons.

   According to this paragraph, studies in the prediction of crimes emphasize —.
   Fill in the correct letter, choosing from the following answers.

      A. Complete reliance on measurable community factors in terms of continued relations with delinquent or criminal types.
      B. Deviations from conventional behavior as key clues in prediction.
      C. Personality factors as more significant than cultural factors.
      D. Primarily the direct linkages between learned behavior and crime incidents.
      E. The relationships between persons outside the home rather than inside the family.
      —From a New York City Civil Service Exam

c. I suspect that we have a good deal to learn from the 18th-century travelers. First, they saw that their books were printed with dignity, with fine type and wide margins on paper that had some texture to it. Second, they took with them an attitude of mind that delighted in the extravagance and eccentricities of the people they met on their journeys; they were far from being moralists. Third, they had a fine feeling for monuments, by which they meant palaces and castles, towers, churches and gateways, and all carved stonework and woodwork wherever it met the eye. Finally, they were in no hurry.

—Robert Payne, "Florence Was Exciting, Venice Overrated"

d. Once upon a time, we had a writer on the magazine whose breezy motto was, "Don't get it right, get it written!" He didn't stay with us long. His careless practices but not his high spirits were shared by another writer of a good many years ago, a man whom I think of as the classic loser among the many losers who have worked their way, nearly always by means mysterious to me, into and then away from the not very turbulent whirlpool of *The New Yorker*, vanishing after a while as if they were so much foam. But they were not foam, or not altogether, and it is often the case that ten or twenty years after their departure from the magazine, an obituary of one or another of them will appear in *The New York Times*—an obituary whose importance the *Times* evidently will have judged according to the dead man's connection with the magazine. It may turn out that few of us who read the obituary will be able to remember a word of what the dead man wrote, or even perhaps what he looked like: was he the hawk-faced little man who used to flatten himself like the crushed corpse of a crow against the wall of a corridor when anyone passed him, though the corridor was wide enough for two big men to pass in comfort? Or was he the sour blond boy who spent much of the day in the nearby Cortile bar, writing his pieces in cramped wheels of words along the circumference of innumerable cardboard beer coasters, which he would gather up at nightfall and deposit in the storm-sewer on the corner of Forty-fourth Street and Fifth Avenue?

—Brendan Gill, *Here at The New Yorker*

e. Out on Safaris, I had seen a herd of Buffalo, one hundred and twenty-nine of them, come out of the morning mist under a copper sky, one by one, as if the dark and massive, iron-like animals with the mighty horizontally swung horns were not approaching, but were being created before my eyes and sent out as they were finished. I had seen a herd of Elephant travelling through dense Native forest, where the sunlight is strewn down between the thick creepers in small spots and patches, pacing along as if they had an appointment at the end of the world. It was, in giant size, the border of a very old, infinitely precious Persian carpet, in the dyes of green, yellow, and black-brown. I had time after time watched the progression across the plain of the Giraffe, in their queer, inimitable, vegetative gracefulness, as if it were not a herd of animals but a family of rare, long-stemmed, speckled gigantic flowers slowly advancing. I had followed two Rhino on their morning promenade, when they were sniffing and snorting in the air of the dawn—which is so cold that it hurts in the nose—and looked like two very big angular stones rollicking in the long valley and enjoying life together. I had seen the royal lion, before sunrise, below a waning moon, crossing the grey plain on his way home from the kill, drawing a dark wake in the silvery grass, his face still red up to the ears, or during a midday-siesta, when he reposed contentedly in the midst of his family on the short grass and in the delicate, spring-like shade of the broad Acacia trees of his part of Africa.

—Isak Dinesen, *Out of Africa*

f. Pagination! I have always loved the word and been sorry that it doesn't mean all the things I think it ought to mean. Its sound wafts me to romantic or faraway worlds. I think of the great voyages that paginated the Indies. I watch the moonlight playing across the pagination on the Taj Mahal. I hear glorious music (Lully's pagination for trumpets). I savor gourmet meals (mussels paginated with sage). I see beautiful women—the pagination on their bodice catches my eye—and dream of the nights we will spend in torrid pagination. The wine that we sip will be exquisitely paginated—dry, but not too dry—and as the magical hours slip away we will...

But why torture myself? The fact is that it's a dumb word that means just one thing: the process of arranging pages in their proper sequence and getting them properly numbered. It's something we all do, every day, almost without thought. We paginate every time we scribble a shopping list on a few scraps of paper. So much for the romance of pagination.

—William Zinsser, *Writing with a Word Processor*

g. Childhood is not a time of innocence, it is not a time of unmitigated pleasure, it is not a time of easy joys and carefree days. It is so only in the nostalgia of adults. Childhood is a time of difficult inquiry, of trying discovery, of hard quests and unfulfilled desires. It is a time of bumping into limits that seem to have no reason, of enduring meaningless ceremonies, and also of striking out into exciting visions. It is a time of pain and yet a time of ecstasy, because so much is new and discovery of the new is always filled with both a wonder and a hurt.

—Jean Karl, *From Childhood to Childhood*

2. Here are two samples of writing freshmen submitted at a large state university: One sample was judged as acceptable, the other unacceptable. The students were asked to describe one characteristic of Lady Macbeth and to show the importance of that characteristic in the whole play. Which form do you find acceptable? Explain your decision.

Lady Macbeth's Fierceness

The dominant impression one receives of Lady Macbeth is her fierceness. She gives her husband the spiritual strength to kill Duncan and take the throne. Without her urging and her help on the night of the murder it is doubtful whether he could have done the deed by himself. She is the one who first mentions the idea of killing the king. Macbeth is horrified just to think of killing their royal guest. She prepares the plot, tells Macbeth exactly what he must do, and then practically scolds him into murdering Duncan. When he comes back with bloody hands after doing the deed, she takes the daggers that he has absent-mindedly brought with him and plants them near the sleeping grooms so that they will be blamed for the murder.

But after she has forced her husband to screw his courage to the sticking point, all her fierceness seems to vanish. After the knocking at the gate, the entrance of Macduff and Lennox, and the confusion that follows the discovery of the murder, she faints and has to be carried off the stage. She never appears to be forceful with her husband again. Once she has shown him the way, he seems to be able to plan his own murders. He plans to murder Banquo without even telling her, and she doesn't seem to care. She seems to be in a daze and has trouble sleeping at night. We learn later in the play that she walks in her sleep. The doctor who is called to take care of her realizes that there is something on her conscience. This comes out in the sleepwalking scene when she walks and goes through the events of the night of the murder. She keeps trying to wash her hands and remove the blood that she imagines is there. It is evident that her fierceness on the night of the murder has taken its toll on her spirit.

Lady MacBeth

Lady Macbeth is a virile and manic female type personage that plays the leading roll in Shakespeares play, Macbeth. Her husband, Macbeth and she decides to kill the king, they want to seize that of the throne and to rule Scotland together.

As in Dante's "Inferno," everyperson has a strong ambition and Lady Macbeths ambition is ruling over Scotland. Being of a cruel and ambitious nature, her plan to rule over Scotland by killing the king comes naturally to her perverted mind.

She and McBeth do alright in their plan to kill the king and seize the reigns of Scot. until the latter begins to get cold feet after they have done the deed; hideous, bloody, and sanguine. Then there is a knocking at the door. they are sure they have been caught in the Act. Murder will out they think and both begins to get scarred. So we can see why Lady M. Fails in her plan to rule Scotland, because she was weak. Shakespeare wrote this play in 1606 and the womans parts were acted by boys. A boy acted the cruel Lady B. and a boy also assumed the other womans roles in the play, "Macbeth." I liked the play especially the part when the old porter scares Lady, knocking on the door. I did not like the way Shakespeare however, beats over the bush. The flowery discriptions makes the play more boring to the reader

Shakespere gets his affects across. He is a truly invincable masterpiece.

Part One

THE PREWRITING PROCESS

Finding a Subject

Developing a Subject:
  Prewriting Strategies and Exercises

Gathering Information

Organizing a Subject

Finding a Subject

FACING THE BLANK PAGE

*I*t is not true—as many people think—that professional writers have something vital and compelling to say that drives them to the typewriter so that they can say it and be *done* until another idea comes along to drive them to the typewriter again. More often, writers are people who have chosen to write because they find writing to be a delight, a disease, or some of both. But once they have made this decision, they are not perennially brimming over with subjects or topics to write *about*.

Like all writers who do not work on given assignments (as reporters do), you the student writer are periodically faced with a blank page and an equally blank mind. From the "booming buzzing confusion" of the world around you, you must somehow locate and concentrate on one particular, self-contained topic. You must, as Cicero, the classical Roman orator and writer said, "hit upon what to say." Once you have done this, you can go on to "manage and marshal" your materials and finally "to array them in the adornments of style" (Cicero, again). But first—and you cannot get around this—*first you must hit upon what to say*. Until the recent revival of rhetoric, writing courses ignored this obvious first step as an integral part of the composition process. The assumption seemed to be that getting an idea was a writer's own private problem. Seek, and ye shall find. Somehow.

Of course, finding an idea is indeed a private, inner process; and if you wish to find, you certainly have to seek. But *how* to seek? Where to find? Answering these questions is not easy, because in the beginning you don't even know exactly *what* you are seeking—just a good idea. "I wasted the entire week trying to decide what to write about," says a discouraged freshman. True enough: he spends hours at his desk staring into space in morose silence, lamenting his fate, moaning, groaning, and chewing erasers off pencils (a pleasantly self-pitying approach, but not especially productive). Unwillingly, he submits the finished paper; he wrote it between midnight and 4 A.M. and proofread on the way to class. He knows it is not very good, but at least it is *done*. How he hates to write! If only he could think of things to write about....

This student needs an introduction to what classical Greek and Roman rhetoricians called the art of invention—finding something to write about. He needs to see that his first step in the composition process is an art in itself that he consciously and conscientiously cultivates. Briefly, the art of invention is the skill of knowing how to "invent" or "discover" (classical rhetoricians used both terms) the subject of a discourse by actively searching out stimulation, the kind of stimulation that will actively generate ideas and produce a specific topic and things to say about the topic.

The two main aspects of the art of invention are finding a subject and developing it. Like every other stage of the composition process, the writer can deal with this first stage of finding something to write about actively and systematically. Even more important, the writer can and must deal with this stage *creatively* because finding an idea and preparing to mold it into a new and original whole is a distinctly creative process.

The aim of this section, then, is to explain how to go about the creative process of invention with appropriate creative energy and purpose. To help accomplish this aim we shall draw upon basic principles of rhetoric[1] and concentrate on common-sense techniques like trying to find an idea by *looking* for it and by using simple, easily accessible guides such as the dictionary, which is a rich source of ideas.

CHECKLIST OF SUBJECTS

Here, then, are twenty subjects chosen from the most familiar and available of all reference works, the dictionary. (An encyclopedia, reader's guide, or any alphabetically arranged subject index will do as well.) The procedure is simple: Thumb through the pages starting with A and move on through the alphabet, jotting down whatever terms catch your eye and your interest—whatever you *respond* to. You can be certain that an unconscious as well as a conscious process of selection is at work here, guiding you to one or another term that appeals to you and that will therefore provide a good starting point for the invention process.

1. American Indian	8. Intellectual	15. Prejudice
2. Assassination	9. Language	16. Propaganda
3. Books	10. Literature	17. Science
4. Creativity	11. Nature	18. Symbol
5. Education	12. Patriotism	19. Women
6. Family	13. Poetry	20. Writing
7. Holocaust	14. Poverty	

LIMITING THE SUBJECT

Let us begin with the first item on the subject list—American Indian. Surely we cannot approach this subject as such, for it is as vast and formless as the Great Plains the Indians once inhabited. Where should we begin? How can we hope to cover the American Indian in less than a volume? Clearly, the only sensible procedure is to *limit the subject*, to concentrate on one or another of its many aspects. For instance, we

---

[1] In "Gathering Information" (pages 47–75), we shall deal with methods of probing the mind to gather information for an essay, using the insights of depth psychology; for it is from the psychologist rather than the rhetorician that we can learn how to reach into the "inner psyche" and thereby activate a stubborn memory or stimulate a seemingly empty mind. In this process we must learn how to probe our own ideas and feelings; how to concentrate deeply; how to be receptive to images that are "not thought out but beheld" (cited in Progoff, 236).

could consider one particular tribe in one particular place (Navajos of New Mexico). We could limit the subject still further (Navajos living in New Mexico *at the present time*). The subject is now more manageable in scope, more suitable for the essay form, although we have still not focused sharply on what we will say *about* the Navajos living in New Mexico at the present time. The specific content will come later (as we shall see), when we address a specific question to the limited topic; only then will we arrive at the *real* topic—the thesis, or *point of the piece*.

Let us move on to the third item on the subject list—books. Here again, we cannot reasonably expect to write a short, coherent piece about books in general. Why not reduce the subject numerically, then, to *one particular* book? E. M. Forster once wrote a delightful and engaging essay on "A Book That Influenced Me"; William Golding wrote nostalgically and vividly of his response to one childhood favorite, *The Swiss Family Robinson*.

We are not concerned at this point with the actual finding of a specific topic, but rather with the preliminary process of narrowing down a subject to some aspect of it that we can encompass in a single essay of approximately 500 to 750 words (the average weekly paper in a college writing course). This conscious, deliberate narrowing-down process is an imperative first step in invention; without it we are likely to wander over a vast, amorphous field, and never get our bearings. Only if we resist such overwhelming subjects as "Science" and consider a limited subject such as three specific characteristics of the scientific spirit (consider Robert Millikan, "The Spirit of Modern Science," pages 283–85 can we achieve a unified and coherent unit of discourse.

To summarize: In selecting a topic for a paper, we should try to view it in terms of such limiting factors as the following:

1. a specific *kind*	not music in general, but new wave music
2. a specific *time*	not music in all periods, but the last decade of twentieth-century music
3. a specific *place*	not universal music, but music in America or England
4. a specific *number*	not all new wave musicians, but representative new wave musicians
5. a specific *person*	Boy George, a well-known new wave musician in the group, "Culture Club"
6. a specific *type*	not all kinds of new wave music, but modern love songs
7. a specific *aspect*	not music as a whole, but music as communication
8. a specific *example*	not all new wave songs, but Culture Club's "I'll Tumble For Ya"
9. A specific *experience*	the first time you went to a new wave concert

Admittedly, we may have times when the normal processes of invention seem to telescope, as if by miracle, into a sudden flash of inspiration ("Ah, *this* is what I want to say!"), followed by a few hours of pouring forth what we do in fact *want to say at a particular moment*. This "inspiration" is an exhilarating experience, but we cannot *depend* on it. We must proceed by plan and regular procedure, as writers did throughout the centuries when rhetoric was taught as a formal discipline.

THE CLASSICAL TOPICS

Having found and limited our subject, we go on to the second stage of invention: finding something to say about our subject and developing it. Let us turn to the classical rhetoricians, for although they were concerned largely with writing speeches to be delivered in public, they recognized that the full sweep of the composition process begins with the mind looking *out* on its subject matter and *in* on itself. The orator read widely and studied conscientiously to "stock" the mind with subject matter. Cicero specified that the ideal orator was a person of vast learning and liberal education, trained in techniques to set the mind in motion, to entreat thinking, to stir memory, and to coax imagination. Through these concrete procedures the orator avoided the torments of the blank page, the frustration of just sitting back and waiting for a topic to present itself. Aristotle codified the invention procedure by reducing all possible topics to four categories:

1. what is possible or impossible
2. what happened or did not happen
3. what will happen
4. questions of degree (greatness or smallness)

Aristotle's list may seem oversimplified, but notice that these four categories are excellent places to begin thinking about what a writer might want to say about any topic (thus the ancient designation *topoi*: a place or region of thinking where an argument might be located and developed). Take an example of *topoi*—or, as we now say, topic—1 (what is possible or impossible): "By mining the sea, we can derive more than sufficient foodstuff to feed the hungry people of the world." The writer asserts that something is possible—a familiar type of proposition. Topic 2 (what happened or did not happen) also provides a familiar type of proposition: "The Treaty of Versailles laid the groundwork for the Second World War." Either this *did* or *did not* happen; the writer who asserts either position must prepare an argument. Topic 3 (what will happen) characterizes all prophetic writing, from the simple weather forecast to full-scale analyses of future developments in any sphere: why candidate X will win the election, why urban areas are heading for decentralization. The possibilities are endless. Finally there is topic 4 (questions of degree): "Human organ transplants are too widely and sensationally publicized, thereby creating a circuslike atmosphere around a serious new medical specialty." The proposition stands as an argument for *less* of something, and, by implication, *more* of something else—privacy, dignity.

Aristotle's four basic categories plus certain other modes of analysis recognized by the classical rhetoricians—cause-effect (X causes Y); similarity (X is like Y); dissimilarity (X is unlike Y); example (X illustrates Y); consequence (X is a result of Y)—provided a kind of checklist of mental acts orators might perform when investigating and collecting arguments on a subject. Having this checklist available, classical orators were never at a loss; on the contrary, they always had before them the prescribed "discovery procedures" they could confidently follow to locate their arguments and line up their proofs.

ASKING THE RIGHT QUESTIONS

Actually, we can sum up the substance of this approach in a single phrase: asking the right questions. By using the question as a probing instrument—turned inward to the mind (a repository of dormant ideas) and outward to the subject matter (a source of data and information)—we are able to make discoveries and ultimately to generate a sharply focused idea. In every case, as we shall see, *the question, posed and answered, is at the heart of any single piece of discourse*. For what else does the writer do but ask questions and then answer them?

The writer may be telling newspaper readers who robbed which house and what was stolen; explaining in a magazine advertisement why Brand X cosmetic cream will prevent "crow's feet" around the eyes; or describing in a controversial book the death of a president or the reasons for violence in American cities. Whatever the subject, whatever the temper and tone of the piece, the writer forever answers questions. "And a writer cannot answer a question," as one journalist pointed out, "unless he has first asked it" (Lobsenz 15). Nor can the writer achieve a sharp focus or a unified thrust in a piece of writing unless he or she is aware of exactly what the question or questions are. The writer must make certain to hold firmly to a steady line of development so that the finished piece answers precisely that single question or those several questions.

Like journalists, then, applying to all events the perennial "who-what-when-where-why," writers must always be prepared with the right set of questions if they expect to find a way into a topic, to stimulate thinking, to stake out a special area of interest. They need the right questions to glean enough information about the topic and to make a new whole—a unified piece of writing that has a distinctive identity.

What are the right questions specifically? We shall consider them and elaborate on the many ways they may generate and focus a piece of discourse. But first it will be well to caution against viewing a modern set of *topoi* with the same complacency Aristotle felt toward the "commonplaces," that is, the common places where one may go in order to invent an argument. The seeming completeness of Aristotle's survey of topics was, as we now know, largely illusory. The number of topics or of topic categories is not fixed; the number is endless. *Discourse is a process; one idea generates another in ongoing, open-ended progression.* As we proceed through this text, you will also proceed through the successive and overlapping, interacting stages of this most complex and challenging of all human activities—writing.

CHECKLIST OF TWENTY QUESTIONS

In this cycle of question generating idea, idea generating question, and further questions generating further ideas, we have compiled the following twenty basic questions. Although we have stripped them of all concrete subject reference, their faceless aspect should not put you off: We have referred to the topic as "X" to keep the discussion on an abstract level. These twenty questions present ways of *observing* or *thinking about* a subject. They are "thought starters" intended to set the wheels of invention turning. As such they apply to any subject matter.

Suppose, for example, your instructor has asked you to write a paper on anything that interests you. *Where* will you find a wedge into *what* subject? We have already considered ways of locating and limiting a subject; now let us examine this checklist of questions, each of which can provide the final, focal point of departure for your essay. These fit into four categories (left column), which characterize them generally. Each question generates the type of essay listed in the right-hand column.

Imaginative	1. How can X be described?	Description
	2. How did X happen?	Narration
	3. What kind of person is X?	Characterization
	4. What is my memory of X?	Reminiscence
	5. What is my personal response to X?	Response
Informative	6. What are the facts about X?	Information
	7. How can X be summarized?	Summary
Analytical	8. What does X mean?	Definition
	9. What is the essential function of X?	Functional Definition
	10. What are the component parts of X?	Simple Analysis
	11. How is X made or done?	Process Analysis
	12. How should X be made or done?	Directional Analysis
	13. What are the causes of X?	Causal Analysis
	14. What are the consequences of X?	Causal Analysis
	15. What are the types of X?	Classification
	16. How does X compare to Y?	Comparison
	17. What is the present status of X?	Comparison
Critical	18. How should I interpret X?	Interpretation
	19. What is the value of X?	Critical Evaluation
	20. What case can I make for or against X?	Argumentation

Before we put flesh and bone on X by referring to specific subjects, we should look at a few important points about the questions themselves. First, as you can see, they are not comprehensive. There are more questions you can ask of a subject than we have indicated here. Even the newest discovery procedures do not pretend to cover *all* possible approaches. In this case your imagination can fill in any gaps you may encounter. You may, in other words, invent your own questions or frame them somewhat differently if that helps you to focus your idea more precisely.

Furthermore, some overlapping occurs within the twenty questions themselves. This is inevitable, as every list compiler ultimately discovers, whether the list contains principles, rules, regulations, or questions. (Even the Ten Commandments overlap to some extent, as do the Seven Deadly Sins.)

Admittedly, then, these questions are only suggestive of the way the mind regularly and automatically goes about its business of thinking and exploring the universe. Like Aristotle's "commonplaces," these questions represent some of the common places the mind naturally travels to when it encounters a person, object, event, or idea in the outside world, or an experience, thought, feeling, or sensation within. "What is it?" we wonder. "How does it work?" "Why?" We are forever wondering about things and searching for answers and explanations using the natural, ongoing processes of the human mind.

APPLYING QUESTION TO SUBJECT = TOPIC

As we have said, the special job of invention is to start up a specific line of questioning *at a given time* when the mind may not necessarily be ready to perform; when it may be tired or simply lazy; but when it must, nonetheless, think up something to write about. For by asking a question we find a topic, and by answering the questions about this topic we compose our paper.

The selections reprinted in the first five sections in this book illustrate answers to the twenty questions. For example, in response to question 1, "How can X be described?" John V. Young produces an essay, "Moonrise Over Monument Valley" (pages 149–50), that is a narrowed-down, sharply focused presentation of the broad subject area "Nature" (subject 11 on the checklist):

Nature:	limited to one type of habitat	the desert
	limited to one country	United States
	limited to one state	Arizona
	limited to one place in that state	Monument Valley
	limited to one time	when the moon rises

To this narrowed-down aspect of his subject area Young addresses the question, "How can X be described?" He gives his answer in the very striking and evocative description of the moon rising over "a limitless expanse of tawny desert."

BEYOND TWENTY QUESTIONS

Note that Young binds all the descriptive details together with what rhetoricians call a "thesis," a central or controlling idea that pervades the parts, binding them together into a unified whole. What *about* the moon rising over Monument Valley makes it worth an essay in the *New York Times*?

"What's the *story*?" the travel editor may well have asked the reporter when giving the assignment, posing a key twenty-first question to encompass all the others:

"What single main point do I want to make here?" The *story,* as the writer-reporter would discover in the act of covering the story, is that the moon rising over Monument Valley produces more than a series of separate and spectacular images; it produces an overwhelming total impression: a magical, almost mystical experience.

This perception charges the description with a life of its own, a distinct personality that is more than the sum of its parts. Without it—without some such central perception or insight or "thesis" (call it what you will)—the essay would lack what one rhetorician called "the big idea" that should activate and animate every piece of writing, giving it a single unifying *point* and a sharply focused *purpose.*

Beyond the twenty questions that generate a topic, then, the student writer—indeed every writer—will profit from pressing a topic still further to wring from it (at the earliest possible stage of writing) an answer to the additional question: What is the main point of this piece? "What's the story?" as the journalist puts it. What—as we might put it, asking the question in the most profound sense—is the big idea?

At this point we do not need to review the many ways in which a writer *invents* or *locates* a topic by addressing a pertinent question to some aspect of a subject area. The table of contents provides abundant illustrations of how this heuristic (art of invention or discovery) works. Suffice it to say here that the art of invention or discovery itself is not so much a formal technique as it is plain common sense. But it is common sense *applied in a deliberate and disciplined manner* to help you fulfill a particular assignment at a particular time and to make you relatively independent of "inspiration"; to show you how to *find* something to write about when you *need* something to write about, not merely when the spirit moves you.

This heuristic combines a disciplined and ordered method of invention or discovery with the question procedure, an essentially intuitive process; you have been asking similar questions and inventing topics all your life. The aim of the discovery and development procedure we describe here is to help you invent and develop topics "on call," with more precision, originality, and ease. Eventually you will come to feel toward this heuristic something of the confidence and assurance that the classical orators felt toward Aristotle's "commonplaces." Eventually the question procedure will serve you in the same efficient and dependable way.

EXERCISES

1. Using a dictionary or any reference work of comparable scope, make up a list of twenty subjects that interest you. They may be fields of study (astronomy, astrology); hobbies (glassblowing, raising guppies); sports (rugby, ice hockey, tennis). Almost any subject area—provided you are interested in it or know something about it—will offer a good starting point for the invention process.
2. Using the list of limiting factors cited on page 18, narrow each of your subjects to one aspect of itself (one specific kind, time, place, experience).
3. Select five of your twenty subjects and carry them through progressive stages of limitation (as on page 18). Formulate your *real* topic by posing a specific question chosen from the list on page 21 to some aspect of your limited topic. For example: "What is my memory of a new wave concert?" "What are the facts about new wave music?" "What kind of person is Boy George?" (Title: "Boy George: A Popular New Wave Star.")

Developing a Subject: Prewriting Strategies and Exercises

FREEWRITING

TALKING TO YOURSELF

TALKING TO OTHER PEOPLE

BRAINSTORMING

CLUSTERING

CONJURING UP MEMORIES

KEEPING AN INTENSIVE JOURNAL

SUGGESTED JOURNAL ENTRIES

SHARPENING POWERS OF OBSERVATION

VISUALIZING YOUR AUDIENCE

ESTABLISHING A READER-WRITER RELATIONSHIP

*R*ecent research on the composing process has shown that even after locating a subject, the writer is wise not to approach the subject "cold." Like the runner who limbers up before the race, the writer needs to do a variety of stretching and bending exercises before setting out. Researchers have observed that prewriting strategies not only help to make the writer feel more comfortable about the subject but also help to generate new ideas or new perceptions of old ideas.

Professional writers have long been aware of the importance of a prewriting period during which they can probe corners of their own minds and explore feelings and attitudes that may not rise to the surface without conscious and conscientious stirring up. One of the most helpful of these prewriting strategies comes from Peter Elbow, the lively author of *Writing Without Teachers* (Oxford University Press, 1973). As a warming-up exercise he advocates preparatory "self-confrontation." This is especially helpful for students who may be blocked or uptight about their writing, afraid to make the first move. It also helps those who are afraid to make mistakes, the most common fear of all writers.

FREEWRITING

Such people can loosen up by trying a form of "freewriting," also called "automatic writing," or simply "babbling and jabbering exercises." According to Elbow, these should be done at least three times a week.

> The idea is simply to write for ten minutes (later on, perhaps fifteen or twenty). Don't stop for anything. Go quickly without rushing. Never stop to look back, to cross something out, to wonder how to spell something, to wonder what word or thought to use, or to think about what you are doing. If you can't think of a word or a spelling, just use a squiggle or else write, "I can't think of it." Just put down something. The easiest thing is just to put down whatever is in your mind. If you get stuck it's fine to write "I can't think what to say, I can't think what to say" as many times as you want; or repeat the last word you wrote over and over again; or anything else. The only requirement is that you *never* stop.

There are those, says Elbow, who accuse freewriting "of being an invitation to write garbage." Actually freewriting serves a very important function by setting the wheels of the mind turning and getting words on paper. As Elbow suggests and as recent studies have confirmed, the advantage of prewriting is that you always produce something in the assigned time period. This writing is free and unstructured and may be a mere string of seemingly unrelated sentences, or even only fragments or phrases. No matter. Whatever you do is fine. As Hegel once said of history, "Whatever is is right." Of course, his claim is erroneous when applied to history, but it has real merit in terms of rhetoric principle. By accepting unconditionally what you are writing, by refusing to pause for spelling or grammar checks or any other correction along the way, you gather momentum, focus on the act of writing itself, and lose yourself in the process. You feel no pressure or concern about grades because this writing is ungraded and for your eyes alone if you choose. It remains unedited, unrevised—*as is* (whatever is is OK). Freewriting exists only to put you in closer touch with yourself and with the special rhythm, texture, and tone of your own natural voice. As Elbow points out, and as many professional writers agree, your "natural voice is the main source of power in your writing...the force that will make a reader listen to you."

By making regular entries in a freewriting diary, you put yourself on more intimate terms with this natural voice. You get to know what "sounds right" in your writing and what "rings false," even when you are factually correct. Professional writers have long been practitioners of freewriting, turning to their diaries routinely for prewriting warm-ups. Short story writer Katherine Mansfield, for example, described a process that is clearly comparable: "Looking back," she reported, "I imagine I was always writing. Twaddle it was too. But far better write twaddle or anything, anything, than nothing at all."

Still another benefit to be gained from freewriting is that it often provides the seed of an idea that you can later develop further and polish into a full-length finished piece. Take, for example, the following passage of freewriting, this one set off by a suggested topic, "Depressing Things":

OK—it's now 11:30 and I'm supposed to write for fifteen minutes—just let my mind wander along paths suggested by this title "depressing things." That's what she told us to do so I'm going to try to see how far I get by free-associating. She said that was a good idea so I'll try that. I never did it before but here goes—depressing/heavy/hot/lead/bread. How did "bread" get in? Well, that's a rhyme, I wonder if that's OK—to rhyme—fine. That's almost a rhyme again: fine/shine/wine/spine/mine. Better get back to depressing words like sadness, death, breath. Gee, I'm rhyming again. Maybe because when I think of death I try to return to life again with breath. Now I'm trying to be a psychologist. Forget it, forget it. Go back to free associating again, back to "depressing." I wonder if I can come up with any more words or ideas that are "depressing." Let's see, let's see: there's a notebook filled with a whole semester's notes left on the train. All that work, exam coming up, no way to get the notebook back. That's not just depressing—that's disgusting, a disaster, panic. Awful, awful, awful. What else can I write about now, I still have more time. Oh yes, I can see where my mind travels with the word "things." I guess that's what I decided to do when I started out—to take up one word at a time, try to get more mileage that way. Not a bad idea, let's see where it takes me. What do I think of that's a "thing." Well, first of all a thing is different from a person, a human being. Things are inanimate objects without sense or feeling. They can't feel pleasure or pain, can they? Of course not. So things in and of themselves can't really be said to be depressing or heartening either. This is a strange assignment then, the two words of the title don't work together sensibly. The more I think about it the more I realize that people can be depressed but things can't. Things can only be associated with something that's depressing and in that way they can create depression in the person doing the associating (things don't associate, either; only people associate one thing with another). I guess I'm saying that depression isn't a quality of a thing; it's not *in* the thing, that is, only in the person who encounters or experiences the thing and by a process of association becomes depressed by it. Like an old Valentine card from an old boyfriend who now has a new girlfriend. Or something like that. The card becomes a depressing reminder (a reminder that makes you depressed) of happier times. Sniff, sniff, you fool. The point I think I'm making is that the card itself is not depressing, it just *is*, it exists. But it's a reminder of what might have been—and so it is by a process of association a depressing thing in that it's a thing that can create depression in a person. I said that before, I said that before. I'm beginning to repeat myself, repeat myself, because it isn't time to stop yet, it isn't time to stop, time to stop ... Time.

In rereading this passage of "self-confrontation," you discover some interesting things about the way this writer's mind works and also about the way she responds to words as words—very playfully. Note her tendency to rhyme, for example. Obviously she *hears* words in her inner ear as she is writing; she is clearly sensitive to sound. More than that, as this passage reveals, she just doesn't *think* as she writes; she *feels* as well. We can see this strong feeling component in the way she sets the word *breath* against *death*, perhaps as a kind of rescue effort. Whatever the psychological explanation (and of course all free associating moves by psychological process), the freewriting passage obviously involves thinking and reasoning as well as feeling. Note the analytical distinction the writer makes between depressing *things* and depressing *people*. Having established that things in and of themselves cannot be depressing, the writer points to a phenomenon that could be the germ of an essay: the way "things," which are inherently neutral, become associated with happy and unhappy circumstances. If the student then decides to sharpen her focus by addressing leading questions to this observation, she may develop a suitable topic. The kind of internal dialogue that may take place when you follow freewriting with intensive "talking to yourself" appears in the "Talking to Yourself" exercise in the assignments. As Thoreau pointed out long ago, "A writer must first speak to himself."

EXERCISES

1. Try a relatively free and unfocused freewriting exercise which begins with Peter Elbow's words, "I think I'll write what's on my mind." Give yourself ten minutes.
2. Recall a recent dream. What did you *feel* afterward? Freewrite for ten minutes.
3. Select one of the following topics, using it as the point of departure for fifteen minutes of freewriting:

   splendid things
   incredible things
   appearance and reality
   an experience
   the stars
   the sound of a voice
   happiness
   social success
   somewhere

4. Freewrite for fifteen minutes. Just GO.

TALKING TO YOURSELF

Question: Now think about this: what kinds of things make you happy? What objects do you like? What comes to mind right off as having pleasant associations?

Answer: Well, right off, I think about my stamp collection.

Question: Ah, so you like stamps. What do you like about them—specifically?

Answer: Well, they're beautiful, for one thing.

Question: Beautiful? What's beautiful about them?

Answer: They're like miniature works of art—lots of them. Especially the American commemorative stamps that I save.

Question: What are those?

Answer: Those are stamps that are issued in honor of certain historic events like the freeing of the slaves; or certain people like Harriet Beecher Stowe; or certain features of American life, like state flowers or birds. These stamps aren't just beautiful either; they're meaningful.

Question: Would you say, then, that that's another thing you like about stamps? Another thing that makes your stamp collection enjoyable? The fact that they are associated with American history?

Answer: Definitely. My stamp collection is like a history book—I learn all sorts of important things about how this country grew and the people who helped to make it grow.

Question: That sounds like a third pleasant aspect of stamp collecting—it's educational.

Answer: Absolutely. I've learned a tremendous amount about geography, science, art, sports, business, exploration, women's suffrage; I've found commemorative stamps for nearly every subject imaginable.

Question: Would you say, then, that you have "hit upon" something to write about, a personal essay, perhaps?

Answer: Yes, I would certainly enjoy writing about my stamp collection. Every time I buy a new stamp or put it into my album, I feel just great. So I could write about that: why I collect stamps.

Question: Maybe that could be your title: "Why I Collect Commemorative Stamps."[1]

Answer: Perfect. Now why don't you try out that idea on other people, see how they react to it, hear what they have to say.

---

[1] For a discussion of ways to structure an essay in "causal analysis" see Question 13, "What are the causes of X?". (pp. 313–31). For a consideration of audience and tone of voice, see Question 5, "What is my personal response to X?". (pp. 211–24).

TALKING TO OTHER PEOPLE

Although writing is notoriously and necessarily an isolated and independent activity, you can and should collaborate during the process. When your idea is still in the germinating stage—before you have begun to write—you should approach other people and ask them to share their knowledge with you and to tell you how they feel and what they have observed. Follow this common sense principle of *listening* and *learning*, confine your side of the conversation to questions, and you will not run the risk of "having your say" too early. You want to save your presentation for your final writing. By listening to what others have to tell you, you open yourself to different points of view and to new and perhaps unexpected insights that may never otherwise occur to you. Interestingly, the most unlikely people may have excellent ideas about your subject, so don't confine your conversations to people you know are knowledgeable. Sometimes the "quiet ones" have more expertise and general background than you suspect.

Here again prepare a set of questions to serve as a starting point. Avoid conversation stoppers like "Tell me all you know about stamps." Just as you yourself need precise probes into a subject, so do the sources you turn to. So be specific whenever possible and always be provocative enough to elicit a response.

BRAINSTORMING

After you talk to yourself and to others, and after you jot down notes for further use later on, you may think you are ready to dash off a quick first draft. But before you begin to write, give yourself an opportunity to conjure up still other details you may not be aware of. One good method is "Brainstorming." (Business executives originated this problem-solving procedure. Imaginative breakthroughs using this method have saved companies from bankruptcy and put new million-dollar products on the market.) The goal of brainstorming is imaginative thinking that goes beyond conventional categories. Using this technique can help you to tap deeper levels of imagination and creativity.

Think of brainstorming as another discovery procedure or another path to "self-confrontation." To brainstorm, write down a key word and allow this word to lead you to free associate with another, as you do in freewriting. But with brainstorming you don't compose sentences. Just let one word follow the one before with a key word serving as starting point. Let's use *stamps* again as an example, since we have already "warmed up" on that subject. Look at the figure on page 31.

You can see that each of the terms easily gives rise to another term that then serves as the point of departure for still other terms which continue branching off in other directions. Let yourself think wild thoughts—about how expensive stamps can be, for example. Is there a stamp worth thousands of dollars? What is the world's most expensive stamp? Is that stamp a freak or are there many stamps that are fantastically, prohibitively expensive? Have stamps in general become costly? Has stamp collecting gone the way of many hobbies that were once within the reach of young boys and girls who built collections by saving nickels, dimes, and pennies from their weekly allowance? (Today even a single baseball trading card, originally sold with bubble gum and included in the price of the package—five cents in the old days—might now sell for hundreds of dollars—even more if it's rare and in mint condition.)

Some other topics may be fun to brainstorm. Are there any hobbies left that young people can afford? Which ones? A professional free-lance writer would instantly spot a potential story here and begin getting ideas (how about kite flying?). A tentative title might come to mind: "Hobbies You Can Still Afford." Or maybe "Hobbies You and I Can Still Afford." Or "Hobbies We Can All Afford." In trying to come up with a good title, feeling free and uninhibited is especially important. Risk sounding silly and foolish, way "off the track"—wherever and whatever the "track" may be. Only when you allow yourself the privilege of making new tracks (seven attempts will lead nowhere; the eighth will take you where you want to go); only when you persistently demand that your mind yield its hidden potential and that it be active rather than passive can you get the best from your own resources. Conduct brainstorming sessions routinely and regularly, on your own or with others in small groups. Let your mind supply ideas, some of which will appear on the page as if written by some other hand (the contribution of a deeper level of thinking). As one researcher concluded, all writing begins with some tuning in, by whatever means, to "that great ongoing inner panorama that William James called 'the stream of consciousness'" (Moffett 231).

EXERCISES

Get together with three or four friends or classmates for a brainstorming session, basing it on one of the topics at the top of page 32.

seat belts	divorce	feminists
drunk driving	hairdryers	chauvinists
dropouts	nuclear war	movie stars
God	the devil	presidents
marriage	hats	politicians

If possible, tape record your session or have someone write down the ideas generated while the brainstorming is going on. Otherwise, much of what "happens" tends to be lost or forgotten.

CLUSTERING

One particularly effective and innovative way of tuning into your own "stream of consciousness" is through a form of brainstorming developed by Gabriele Rico called *clustering*. Like freewriting and other kinds of brainstorming, clustering releases the profusion of ideas and images, language and sound patterns, feelings, observations, and sensations all of us unconsciously respond to Rico says we must

> begin with the whole, with the fundamental human desire for giving shape to experience, for expressiveness, for creating form and structure out of the confusion that constitutes both our inner and outer worlds. . . . Natural writing depends on gaining access to a part of your mind we normally do not associate with writing skills (16).

Rico explains that just as certain fruits (such as grapes) and certain flowers (such as lilacs) come in clusters, "thoughts and images, when given free rein, seem to come in clusters of associations" (29). By following the lead of these associations, you often move through stages of chaos and uncertainty until you gradually begin to see the outlines of a pattern or design, the emergence of a *shape* that can then serve as basis for a piece of writing—an essay, story, character sketch, or editorial.

Where do you begin? As in freewriting or other kinds of brainstorming, you begin the clustering process with a word—any word. Rico quotes the literary critic Northrop Frye, who originally pointed the way to this approach by indicating that any word can become "a storm center of meanings, sounds, and associations radiating out indefinitely like ripples in a pool" (29).

You begin with a word or word phrase, using that as a stimulus for setting down—as quickly and spontaneously as possible—all the associations that spring *naturally* to your mind. Speed is important here in helping you organize ideas into clusters as you set them down on paper. This grouping of ideas and images into "sets" distinguishes clustering from other forms of brainstorming.

Let's begin with the nucleus word SNOW as shown in the following illustration to see how the clustering process works. The central term provides the center or nucleus from which branches spread out in all directions. Each can later serve as a separate part or passage of an emerging piece of writing.

The setting down of a cluster design such as the above should take an average of five to ten minutes. Given another fifteen to twenty minutes, a writer—using the

Christmas trees for sale

smell of pine

stores along Main St.

darkness gathering

Christmas week

slush piled along streets

wet

white

cold

snow

small child

seven or eight

wearing leather jacket

walking alone

crispness in air

gift for mother

surprise

people rushing by

shoppers

shopping days

gifts

brightly colored

various cluster-balloons as source and stimulus for a short story or sketch—came up with the following:

> It is almost dark along Main Street. It's cold but getting warmer so that the snow, half-melted on the street, makes for slush underfoot. The stores are brightly lit and open late this week for Christmas shoppers, all of them rushing, rushing, clutching gifts wrapped in bright red tissue paper, tied with gold and green ribbons, sealed with Santa stickers; clutching shopping bags filled with Christmas ornaments: bulbs and figurines and long strips of aluminum foil for tossing on the tree where they will hang on branches like snow—silent, silver snow. Icicles really.
>
> Christmas trees: hundreds are lined up against the high wood fence on the corner, in front of the empty lot. The smell of pine is deep and dank and thick, as if the air itself had turned to pine. The world is pine for a little girl of seven, snugly warm in her fleece-lined leather jacket, hurrying home from her Christmas shopping in the local department store. It is getting much too dark; she has never been out alone this late. But she is not frightened, only excited because she has made her big Christmas purchase, a calendar for her mother, a huge picture calendar showing the seasons of the year. Not one day of this coming year will be equal in pleasure and excitement to this day, this moment of deepening darkness and cold and wetness underfoot and the fragrance of pine everywhere and the spectacle of huge Christmas trees disappearing into the backs of large station wagons, deposited there after long family discussions. This moment as she crosses the street with her own secret purchase under her arm, she thrills to the certainty that no one will ever be able to guess what it is—not until the paper is ripped off—ah, *only then* will they know!
>
> On Christmas morning she will say to her mother, handing her this mysterious gift: "You'll never guess what I bought you."
>
> "Is it a calendar?" her mother will ask.

It is clear that this vignette is more than the sum of its parts, for the writer has forged from the parts a short description-narration that has a unity and coherence and purpose beyond what is contained in the separate clusters. How did this happen? How did the writer create from the scattered balloons one single, self-contained piece?

The aim of the writer should be to achieve "creative interaction" between the two sides of the self: the irrational and spontaneous on one side, the rational and disciplined on the other. As each plays a part in the conduct of human life, so each plays a part in the composing process. In phase one we should try to generate ideas in as free and unrestricted a setting as possible. We should swirl our ideas into freehand circles and clusters of circles and not worry about literal meanings or logical sequences or even about making sense. Later, we enter what Rico calls the "conscious, critical phase, which edits, refines, and revises" what we have conjured up during the previous stage of mental and emotional abandon.

EXERCISES

The following adaptations of Rico's exercises give you a sense of the energy and spontaneous flow of ideas that clustering produces—a toning-up of both sides of the brain, a recognition of the "two persons" writers must confront in themselves.

Remember that surprise is one of the rewards of clustering. As one thought prods another, your mind moves toward a creative "burst" which usually produces enough material for a good beginning and an equally good ending. *Important reminder*: work quickly and don't worry about results. You can fit your "sets" together when you write your vignette.

1. Select five of the words below and for each one create a cluster of associations. Let the words and phrases spring from the nucleus word. If you wish, choose five words of your own.

star	breaking free	wired	pickle
dream	lonely	bottle	razor
slipper	barefoot	frost	whiskers
storm	glitter	orphan	warm
time	stone	crop	cuddle
pain	blessing	turnip	raid
clown	attic	fierce	kindness
dark	echo	time out	trigger

Now give yourself twenty to thirty minutes to write a vignette on each of the five words you have clustered.

2. Choose as your nucleus word the name of someone you care for and create a cluster of the things that come to mind about that person: strengths, weaknesses, quirks, sayings, appearance, attitudes—whatever "flows" when you think about the person you choose. Write a vignette (twenty to thirty minutes).

3. Select one of the following emotions and use it as the basis of a cluster:

joy
fear
pain
panic
love
laughter

4. Choose a saying, such as "All that glitters is not gold," or "Marry in haste, repent in leisure," or "Idleness is the Devil's workshop." Write a short explanation of what the saying *means*. Then cluster it in single words, whole phrases, or both. Be as loose in your clustering as you were tight in your explanation. This exercise brings both sides of the brain into play.

5. Cluster the phrases "I really like ..." and "I really hate ..." for about five minutes each and see what you come up with. Avoid the obvious; you may be surprised at what emerges. From each, write a short vignette, allowing yourself twenty to thirty minutes.

6. Quickly cluster the word COLOR and see what happens. Then choose a color you particularly like. Cluster it, setting down as many images as you can. Be open to associations from the past. "Grandma's yellow tablecloth" or "Aunt Lena's chipped pink nail polish." Continue until you know where you are going. Then in twenty to thirty minutes write a vignette using the images you have conjured up.

CONJURING UP MEMORIES

Novelist Thomas Wolfe could remember with shattering clarity events of his childhood and early youth: they came back to him unsolicited in their minutest, most vivid detail (see page 200). Because most of us do not have this gift of total recall, we must make a conscious and sustained effort to conjure up the past so that we can reproduce it on paper with a degree of reality and vividness.

Take a typical memorable event; for example, let us say you once almost drowned. That should provide the ingredients for an exciting narrative account—but maybe not. It depends on how accurately you can recall specific details. If you are a careful writer, you will strain to remember and render in vivid images the specific sensations and impressions associated with the original experience. You may remember how the water bubbled in your ears as you went down... down... or the *exact* way voices sounded in the distance. You know that you can make your experience live again on paper only if you activate those small, telling details that capture its essence. As you spend many hours at various prewriting strategies such as freewriting, brainstorming, and clustering, you will recover information from the deepest recesses of memory. You know the facts are all buried there somewhere. If you persist in your digging, you will recover them. Although this is a formidable discipline, you will find it rewarding, for you will recapture your own past.

Interestingly, people who want to prod their memories have worked out many other psychological procedures and even rituals. Two of these are worth mentioning here, for you may adapt them to the writing process. They arise from creativity and "direct experience" workshops conducted by psychotherapist Ira Progoff.[2] These workshops have a larger than literary purpose. "They are designed," says Progoff, "to expand awareness and evoke the unlivened creative potential of the individual." But you can apply these methods to retrieving your past experience so that you may recreate it realistically on paper. In his workshop sessions, Progoff tries "to help the individual extend the *time* dimensions of his personality so that he can feel the movement and direction of his life from the outside." Thus at one workshop session Progoff addressed the group as follows:

> Let's put ourselves in adolescence... make it early adolescence, pre-sexual awareness. Ask yourself "How did I feel then? Were there any special experiences that stand out in my mind? Funny? Sad? Strange? How did I feel about myself? About life? About my relation to life? What was my image of myself in those days?" Let yourself be carried back... relax and think... try to remember... people... images... events... Just speak out when you *do* remember.... Tell us what it was like.

You can simulate a creativity workshop by assembling a small group of people, five or six classmates, who systematically set out to evoke memories, their own and one another's. Actually you can conduct such sessions in many ways. The participants may take turns free associating, letting their minds wander at will and telling their stories as they think of them, or as other people's stories remind them of their own. Or you may structure the session by having one person present a problem, like the following:

---

[2] Dr. Progoff, formerly a special lecturer of depth psychology at Drew University and now director of Dialogue House in New York City, has conducted such workshops at universities and study centers across the country.

There's an intersection: two roads going in different directions; one road is taken, one is not. Relax and think of yourself on the road, any kind of road that will lead into a crossroad. Get the feeling of being there, walking along, thinking, feeling, coming to the intersection, trying to decide which way to go....*which way will it be?* What happens? What is there on the road you finally take? *Why* do you take it? Just speak out as it comes to you on that road....

KEEPING AN INTENSIVE JOURNAL

Still another way student writers may adapt workshop methods to their own purpose is by keeping an intensive journal (as workshop members call it), a psychological notebook in which they enter significant images or thoughts, flashes of memory, dreams, ideas, feelings, fears. "The purpose of the notebook," says Dr. Progoff, "is to give the individual a tangible procedure by which he can enter the depth of himself and [thereby] reexperience his existence from an inward point of view." This tangible procedure of reexperiencing one's existence *inwardly* can be most helpful to you as a writer. You should make daily entries in your notebook; then, after a few days, read the entries at your leisure, ponder their significance, and try to recover those half-forgotten details that are often the key to a whole experience.

Take that most trite of trite topics, for example, which students and teachers alike ridicule as a nonsubject—"My Summer Vacation." Everyone expects a paper written under this heading to be slapdash and dull, *but does it have to be?* Is a visit to the Grand Canyon dull if you have really looked and really seen? If you have experienced it genuinely in your own person and remembered not only the familiar outward spectacle but your own inward response as well? When approached in this way—with a sense of the self at the center of the experience ("Let me tell you, reader, what it was like; I have a purpose in writing this piece")—an account of your summer vacation at the Grand Canyon, or anywhere, will not be a bore to yourself or your readers. (For solid proof of this, see "The Latest Fashion in Travel," pages 378–79.)

I should mention one last point in this section. Writing an essay that *authentically* recreates one of your own experiences not only gains the instructor's commendation but also, and more importantly, gains for *you* a portion of your own life seen again from a deeper and more meaningful perspective. In doing this you are, in a sense, *extending* your life; for it may be that you will see your experiences for the first time in their true shape; it may be that you will recognize for the first time their true and full significance.

Suggested Journal Entries

1. Think about an experience you had in the past week that affected you emotionally. Who was involved? What was the setting? The situation? What was said? Describe the experience in detail. How did you feel? Does the experience remind you of anything similar that happened in the past? Do any images come to mind? Write a one-page journal entry.

2. Choose a twenty-four hour period—beginning tomorrow morning from the moment you awaken. Did you dream during the night? Describe your dream. Describe your morning mood. Enter the events of the entire day in your journal and force yourself to observe and interpret.

3. For one week, try to record your nightly dreams, even if you can recall only fragments. These constitute "dream data." Do not make judgments about the dreams, simply record them. At the end of the week, try to interpret this "script" your subconscious has written. Does it suggest anything to you about the way you feel about your life—hidden attitudes, anxieties, frustrations, or desires? Write a page in your journal.

4. In a one-page paper, try to recall your earliest dream, and explain that dream in the light of the person you are at present.

SHARPENING POWERS OF OBSERVATION

Just as you can probe and prod your memory, so you can extend and sharpen your powers of observation by making a conscientious and deliberate effort to gain more than a general impression of something—a place, event, person, object. Anyone can get a general impression merely by being present at an event. But this is not enough for the writer; in fact, merely to look is not enough. Looking must be *purposive*; all your senses must be alert to precise details: the exact color, texture, shape, smell, temperature, or tactile sensation of a place or an object; the exact appearance of a person—facial expressions, hand gestures, body movements, tones of voice; the exact event as it occurred and the way people reacted to it and to one another. These raw materials must register in your consciousness if you are to gather facts from observations and write a realistic account of how something happened, or what someone or something was like. Not everyone is a highly sensitive receptor, to be sure, but you can at least *try* to see more than you would ordinarily see if you made no special effort.

Actually, observation, like charity, begins at home, in our immediate surroundings. Because professional writers realize this, they are—in an important sense—always "on duty," always gathering information, making mental notes, noticing this or that detail that might provide material at some future time. Your regular prewriting activities of brainstorming, clustering, and outlining will help you to observe your environment more carefully, because unconsciously you will always be preparing to prewrite.

Perhaps you have decided to write a piece about a single special place—the campus library. Since you are a regular visitor and pass it daily, you regard this as a relatively simple, straightforward assignment. Are you ready, then, to sit down and start writing? Not at all. Not until you have looked at it with the conscious intention of seeing the library with fresh eyes, as if you had never seen it before. Only then will you discover that in truth *you have never seen it before* in any richness or sharpness of detail. Chances are that on each previous visit—numerous as they were—you only glossed over its general contour and main features. In just this way New Yorkers observe their own huge New York Public Library on Fifth Avenue at Forty-second Street. Naturally, everyone notices the stately white columns that frame the entrance and the famous reclining stone lions. But how many observers note that there are precisely *six* columns and that the lions are *angled* slightly toward each other? How many of those who look, look still more closely—over the heads of the lions—at the maxim engraved on the building itself: BUT ABOVE ALL THINGS TRUTH BEARETH AWAY THE VICTORY (on the right), and BEAUTY OLD YET EVER NEW, ETERNAL VOICE AND INWARD WORD (on the left). The careful observer will note still another detail: over the revolving doors of the main entrance are three plaques pointing out that this library is in actuality *three separate libraries* housed in one building, a fact that most New Yorkers are unaware of, even though it appears in bold lettering on the face of the building that many thousands of them pass every day of the week.

A famous teacher of the art of observation was Louis Agassiz, the great nineteenth-century naturalist, who began his course in zoology by presenting his students with a dead fish, insisting that they *look at it*. And so they would for an entire morning. Agassiz would then return, asking "Well, what is it like?" As the students recited what they had seen (fringed gill-arches, fleshy lips, lidless eyes), Agassiz's face would reflect disappointment. "Keeping looking," he would finally say—and leave them to their observations for the afternoon. One student who had been looking for days and days and days, later described the experience as follows:

> I was piqued. I was mortified. Still more of that wretched fish! But now I set myself to my task with a will, and discovered one new thing after another, until I saw how just the Professor's criticism had been. The afternoon passed quickly; and when, towards its close, the professor inquired:
> "Do you see it yet?"
> "No," I replied, "I am certain I do not, but I see how little I saw before."
> "That is next best," said he, earnestly, "but I won't hear you now; put away your fish and go home; perhaps you will be ready with a better answer in the morning."

For eight solid months Agassiz would entreat his pupils to "look at your fish"; he had them compare it with other fish in the same family, note resemblances and differences, detect the orderly arrangement of parts, and finally see the parts in relation to the whole and the whole in relation to an overall principle or law. The lesson in looking ended only after Agassiz had warned his students never to be satisfied with isolated observations, no matter how apt they might be. Agassiz believed that "Facts are stupid things until brought into connection with some general law."

In order to see a "general law" behind a set of particular details, you must carry the process of observation a step further: you must go beyond looking to *thinking*; you must observe and analyze each particular, and then move on through a chain of reasoning to a valid and correct inference about the nature of the whole. To draw an inference, to see one truth as following from another, is still another way of gathering information for a piece of writing.

Not everyone is equally adept at formulating original interpretations, but as I suggest in the section on argumentation, everyone of normal intelligence is capable of moving in a logical progression from one thought or observation to another. William Blake aspired to see the world in a grain of sand—an essentially poetic insight, to be sure, but also a *cerebral* one, which he arrived at through rigorous thinking and through a leap or inference from the facts as observed in a grain of sand to a larger truth of nature.

EXERCISES

Make the invisible visible (try to see with the seeing eye) by looking at the things you see around you every day as if you were seeing them for the first time.

> Select a place on campus that you know well such as the coffee shop, pub, reading room, or a classroom.

OR

> Find a familiar place in town, a store, a landmark, or a park.

OR

> Select an object from your pocket or handbag.

Using the prewriting techniques you have learned before, write a paragraph in which you answer the following questions:

1. What are the physical characteristics (size, shape, color, composition)?
2. Does it remind you of anything you have seen before?
3. In what ways is it the same?
4. In what ways different?
5. Who produced or constructed it?
6. For what reason?
7. Who uses it?
8. What purpose does it serve?
9. How efficiently does it function?
10. If it were not there or did not exist, would it be missed and why?

VISUALIZING YOUR AUDIENCE

A fundamental principle of rhetoric is that *you should never write anything in a vacuum.* You should try to identify your audience, hypothetical or real, so that you may speak to it in an appropriate voice. A student, for example, should never "just write" but should always include in the prewriting process a visualizing of definite groups of readers.

Unless your instructor suggests otherwise, the audience you would do best to invent—*invention* is the accurate term here since many researchers have observed that the writer's audience is always a fiction—is the educated community at large: intelligent nonspecialists.

If this seems too general you could invent a more specific group of readers—such as your college classmates, or still more specifically, the members of your composition course. If your instructor runs your class as a workshop, as many do, you will periodically present your papers to your fellow writers who are all struggling to improve their writing.

Of course, members of the class may feel competitive toward your work, but will be supportive. In any case, they are there to respond to you and to provide the feedback you need to determine how successfully you have achieved your goals. Have you stated your arguments effectively? (Have you convinced everyone? Anyone?) Are your witty asides in fact witty? (Do people laugh? Or at least smile?) Are your narratives interesting? (Do your listeners listen attentively?) Are your analyses clear and understandable? Study facial expressions, and don't ignore signs of confusion or puzzlement. Without feedback, you can never be certain that you conveyed your intended meaning accurately.

Listeners may send negative responses back to the speaker (shifting in seats, whispering, looking at wristwatches for the time), or they may give positive reinforcement (smiles, nodding of heads, applause). Writers receive no such clues, no face-to-face confrontation. Writers must therefore take far greater pains; they must plan ahead and try to anticipate the readers' needs. Some writers are more successful at this than others. The writers who will try hardest to meet the needs of that collective entity called "the audience" recognize that writing is a human activity (see Introduction); they respect the essential fragility and ambiguity of language itself (see "The Limits of Language," pages 511–21), and view writing as a way "to serve people rather than impress them" (see epigraph, page 1). Such writers let good will and common sense guide them.

Good writers will be sensitive to E. B. White's keen observation that whatever the educational level or cultural background, "... most readers are in trouble about half of the time." Thus White's compassionate exhortation on behalf of "... clarity, clarity, clarity.... Even to a writer who is being intentionally obscure or wild of tongue we can say, 'Be obscure clearly! Be wild of tongue in a way we can understand.'" The editor of a large metropolitan daily must have shared White's dedication to clarity, for he posted the following sign in the news room: "Never underestimate the intelligence of your readers, but never overestimate their information."

No one is more sensitive to the requirements of readers than the writer of advertising copy whose very livelihood depends on motivating readers to think, feel, and respond in a given way. Note, for example, what is "going on" in the advertisement on page 42.

First, the picture sends its own nonverbal message: an attractive young couple dressed in handsome cable-knit sweaters beam upon their young son (who is drinking apple juice), while the mother cuddles a contented baby (also drinking apple juice, as is father). Does the writer want to tell you that drinking apple juice will make your family healthy and happy?

Well, just look at the picture and then read the text, explicitly addressed to mothers "who care about wholesomeness." (Would any mother claim otherwise?)

The writer provides only two complete sentences in this message; the others are fragments ("Nor water. Nor sugar...."). Such liberties with conventional sentence structure are not usually permissible in formal or academic situations but they serve the copywriter's purpose because they are easy to read, emphatic, and they get the reader's attention.

Note the "homey" reassuring tone of the writing: A voice from the past reminds us of how lovingly and painstakingly Grandma pressed juice from five different kinds of apples to make one wonderful drink with a "one of a kind quality."

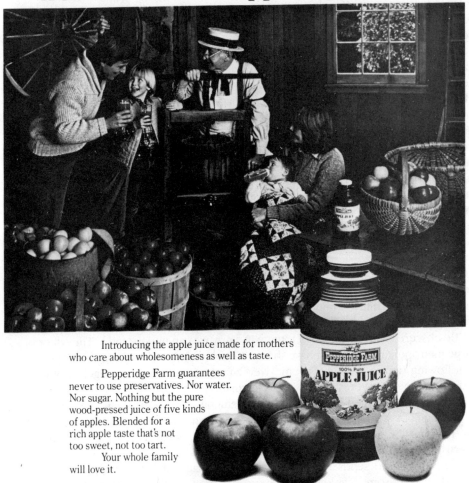

**Finally, wholesome apple juice
from the Farm...Pepperidge Farm™**

Introducing the apple juice made for mothers who care about wholesomeness as well as taste.

Pepperidge Farm guarantees never to use preservatives. Nor water. Nor sugar. Nothing but the pure wood-pressed juice of five kinds of apples. Blended for a rich apple taste that's not too sweet, not too tart.

Your whole family will love it.

Five kinds of apples. One of a kind quality.

EXERCISES

1. Study the ad on the following page:
    Note that this ad presents a very different kind of beverage. To what audience does the advertiser direct this ad? What age group? Economic group? Men or women—or both? Describe the time. Paraphrase the text: What does it state? What does it imply? What emotion does it try to arouse? Do you consider this ad effective? Explain.

Two unquestioning eyes. Wherever they look, they learn.
Whatever they behold, they believe in. Two shining reasons for
every father to exercise judgment, wisdom, and moderation in
all things…including the use of the products we sell.

Nineteenth in the series of Father's Day messages from THE HOUSE OF SEAGRAM *Fine Whiskies Since 1857*

2. Imagine you are a copywriter. Your agency has just assigned you a new client—a restaurant. You must write an ad for the Grand Opening. Decide what kind of restaurant it is: fast food chain, Chinese, vegetarian, a pizza parlor, a steak house, or haute cuisine. Then you must decide whom you want to attract to the restaurant: high school or college students, middle- or upper-income patrons. Present the restaurant, its atmosphere, its cuisine, and its particular appeal in such a way that your readers will storm the doors on opening night.

3. Let's say you want to open a video arcade on Main Street. Certain people in the town fear that your operaton will corrupt the town youth. You want to allay their fears and turn their opinion in your favor as well as convince the undecided to lend you their support. Write a letter. Decide who your readers are from among the following:

> The town council
> The school board
> The clergy
> Parents
> Merchants
> School students

ESTABLISHING A READER-WRITER RELATIONSHIP

A good way to begin connecting with readers whom you visualize as your chosen audience is by letting them know you are someone they can trust, and you *are* someone they can trust, someone who is on their side. By making this kind of "ethical appeal," as classical rhetoricians called it, you can establish a solid and enduring reader-writer relationship. Here again the process begins with self-confrontation, or a series of considerations that you should always include in the prewriting procedure:

1. *Your own identity as a writer:* How do you see yourself in relation to the reader and to the subject matter? "Who am I this time," asks a character in a Kurt Vonnegut short story. He is comfortable only when he is playing a well-defined role that he knows he can handle. You as a writer should ask yourself the same question whenever you undertake a new assignment: *Who am I this time?* What special role is best suited to the needs of this particular piece? How can I best project myself as "persona"? Am I the calm, confident advocate of civil rights, certain that ultimately "we shall overcome"? Or am I an outraged, up-in-arms defender of increasing civil rights violations, fearful that they are whittling away at freedom? Or am I a dispassionate onlooker, taking no sides, letting the facts I present objectively speak for themselves? Each identity requires its own carefully worked out presentation and its own appropriate voice which you should maintain consistently throughout (see "Consistency of Tone" pages 116–18).

2. *The identity of your readers:* Beyond seeing them as fellow human beings struggling to decipher and make sense of your message, you should try to estimate, as best you can, their specific age group, educational and economic level, cultural context, and special needs. We know that professional writers submitting an article or story to a particular publication have received a profile of the "average reader" of that publication (including age group, occupation and profession, and education). Having a good idea, then, of the readers' backgrounds and capabilities, their literacy level, their preferences and special interests, professional writers can speak in an appropriate

voice and write in an acceptable style: in lively, slickly sophisticated, highly compressed, fast-moving prose for readers of *Time* or *Newsweek*; in a slower, more leisurely style for readers of *Scientific American*, with its more technical, in-depth coverage of specialized scientific subjects. More specifically, the writer can make more intelligent and successful decisions as to choice of words, sentence structure, and level of usage.

A word of caution: Whoever your readers are and however you try to satisfy their distinctive needs and abilities, you should guard against the two futile and offensive extremes of aiming "over their heads" or "talking down" to them.

3. *The context or occasion for a given piece of writing:* This third vital prewriting consideration is closely related to consideration of the readers themselves. Who are they, we ask, and what is the occasion for addressing them? All of us make adjustments automatically and naturally to occasion and context when we are using language orally in face-to-face encounters. We explain a problem one way to our friends over lunch, another to a formal committee assembled to hear an official report. Audience and occasion are intimately related and can often be "checked out" together. If you are going to address a student group, for instance, on the occasion of a campus wide election, you might test your speech on a representative member of your audience, asking for a candid reaction. "Does my use of a colloquialism in this context trivialize or obscure an issue? Might it offend some people?"

Careful study of conventional contexts, such as the "Letters to the Editor" column in your local newspaper will give you clues on general usage in that context. You can get a sense of how others writing on the same occasion handled the assignment.

4. *The purpose of a piece of writing:* As obvious as this consideration may sound, many inexperienced writers never consciously ask before they write—What am I trying to achieve? At the earliest possible time you should decide whether you are trying to entertain or instruct your readers. Do you wish to persuade them to think a certain way? Do you want the reader to take a particular side on a controversial issue and take action in its behalf by voting for or actively supporting a given candidate? Will you shed new light on an old problem?

In order to win assent from your readers—probably the most challenging of all purposes—you must first establish your own credibility; second, you must keep the reader reading. You can implement both goals by making certain that you present sufficient facts along with convincing supporting data, examples, and lively anecdotes (everyone likes a story). Touches of humor are also helpful and may win the day over a deadly grim and dull presentation that leaves readers bored and indifferent.

Some rhetoricians say that the writer's purpose is *always* to win assent or agreement from readers (yes, that candidate deserves to win the election; yes, this essay is funny; yes, I understand DNA now; yes, I can now bake a blueberry pie; and so on). Whatever *your* purpose is, you must train yourself to see your subject from the readers' point of view. Why should they see things your way? How do they stand to benefit? What are their expectations to begin with? Are you aware of these and are you fulfilling them? Here again, if your purpose is *genuinely* to serve people and not merely to impress or convince them, then you will make the necessary effort to demonstrate in an orderly and animated manner *why* your purpose will work on their behalf as well as your own. In fact, you will convince them that you share a single or similar purpose and that you stand on common ground.

EXERCISES

Visualize and be prepared to *discuss* a reader-writer relationship growing out of the following topics:
1. Hunting black bear with a bow and arrow
2. New treatment for the hyperactive child
3. What's new in stereo equipment?
4. Suggestions for getting into the college of your choice
5. Shopping for the perfect retirement home
6. The hidden perils in vitamins
7. Trekking through a rain forest
8. Adjusting to stepparents

In each of these situations, work out the four basic aspects of the reader-writer relationship:
1. Your own identity as a writer
2. The identity of the reader
3. The context or occasion of the piece
4. The purpose of the piece

Once you have answered these questions, you will be able to decide on answers to additional questions, such as: What tone should you use? How technical or detailed should your presentation be? How can you best capture and keep your audience?

Gathering Information

*H*aving considered prewriting strategies you will need, we now move on to consider systematic techniques for gathering information. No technique is more important, for as poet John Ciardi pointed out in an article entitled "What Every Writer Must Learn," all "good writers deal in information." Certainly writers and students who want their writing to have substance and texture will build upon solid data, facts, figures, statistics—whatever they need to document as well as demonstrate and explicate their ideas.

Notice, however, that even while you are gathering information, you may look backward toward your original idea and modify it when you turn up some new fact in your research. And while you look backward, you may also look ahead and begin to map out an outline, a first rough draft, or even an opening paragraph that suddenly seems ripe for the writing.

For we now know what professional writers have long been aware of—that the stages of writing do not proceed in a neat linear sequence: first find a subject, then develop it, prewrite, gather information, organize, outline, and so on. The chapters of a book about writing must be organized in some such sequential manner, but the *act* of writing is not nearly as tidy. In actual experience, the stages of writing "overlap and interact" so that the writer is always doing many things at the same time. Having found an idea and thought about it, the writer begins to talk to other people, to collect information, and to modify the original idea. The writer thinks about the idea further, jots down notes, and gathers still more information. This leads the writer to think further about the idea, to sharpen the focus, and to modify again. The whole process keeps moving toward the finished piece at one level while at another level it keeps circling back on itself as the writer constantly reviews and revises the original idea in the light of new evidence.

MAJOR REFERENCE SOURCES

To be a good researcher you must be part scholar, part reporter: you must be able to locate printed and manuscript sources that contain the facts you need within the libraries accessible to you. You must have a kind of nose for news. You should develop the ability to see which of the facts you encounter in your reading best serve your purpose and which you must discard because they do not contribute to the special thesis of your piece. This screening process is evidence that invention does not end when research begins. Even as you are gathering the special information that will constitute the substance of your paper, you are rounding it out and reshaping it. You may even revise your original thesis somewhat in the light of the materials you collect during this active research period.

Most often you will gather more information for a research paper than you use. This may seem wasteful, but it is really a necessary part of the research procedure because you are learning about your subject, developing a perspective on your materials and an awareness of the context from which they are drawn. Without this broader view, you may not be able to distinguish what is relevant from what is not. Furthermore, all the facts that you know about your subject, even those that do not appear in the finished piece, contribute to its total impact, for they give you confidence in your knowledge of your subject and authority in your writing.

At the same time, you must not allow yourself to get bogged down in research. There is a point at which you must decide "this is enough"—even if it does not seem *quite* enough. In most cases, no matter how conscientiously you have explored your subject, there will be some aspect of it you would like to pursue further, something else you would like to know. Arbitrarily but firmly you must call an end to research and move on to the writing. In most cases, of course, you will begin writing (however tentatively) while you are still doing research—setting up a possible beginning, a strong conclusion, or some self-contained middle section.

Charles Schulz, creator of the famous "Peanuts" comic strip has commented aptly on the necessity of limiting research to what is feasible within the allotted time. Because Schulz believes that a comic strip should constantly introduce the reader to "new areas of thought and endeavor," which "should be treated in an authentic manner," he is constantly engaged in research:

> I never draw about anything unless I feel I have a better than average knowledge of my subject. This does not mean that I am an expert on Beethoven, kite-flying, or psychiatry, but it means that as a creative person, I have the ability to skim the surface of such subjects and use just what I need (73–74).

To skim the surface of a subject and dip down only where and when there is usable information pertinent to your purpose is a skill you should learn so that you can cope with the thousands of pages you will consult during your college years.

We shall now move into the library itself to see what major reference sources are available and how you can find the precise source you need when you need it. An important aspect of research technique is being able to find what you want as quickly as possible without wasting time looking up unusable information. Library materials are roughly of two kinds: primary and secondary. "Primary" refers to firsthand sources: original manuscripts, letters, diaries, journals, notebooks, research reports written by researchers themselves, statistics issued by the people who compiled them, reports of interviews, and so on. Articles and books are considered primary if the content is essentially original with the authors. Secondary materials are largely derivative. They are assembled from a variety of outside sources. Thus all major reference works such as encyclopedias and almanacs are secondary; so are essays, articles, and books whose major purpose is to report on, analyze, or interpret the findings of original researchers.

I shall make a brief survey here of the major reference sources[1] you are likely to need during the academic years ahead—and in later years as well. Your professional work or your duties as a citizen (determined to *write* that letter to the editor, and not just talk about it!) may send you to the reference room of your local library or a university library to gather information.

First, one source gives this definition of a reference book: A reference book, as generally understood, is a book to be consulted for some definite information rather than for consecutive reading. In such books, the facts are usually brought together from a vast number of sources and arranged for convenient and rapid use.

Reference tools serve the inquirer in two ways. They may supply the information directly, as in encyclopedias, directories, almanacs, and similar works, or they may point the way to the place where the information is found, the function of the many ingenious bibliographies and indexes now available (Barton and Bell 7).

A reference book, then, differs from an ordinary book in that you do not read it sequentially. You turn to it with a special purpose in mind, thumbing as quickly as possible to the place that will provide the information you need.

In the sections that follow, I have grouped reference materials under seven main headings:

1. Card Catalog
2. General Reference Books
    A. Encyclopedias
    B. Biographical Works
    C. Dictionaries
    D. Yearbooks and Almanacs
    E. Atlases and Gazetteers
    F. Books of Curious Facts
3. Special Reference Books
4. General Bibliographies
5. Periodical Indexes and Abstracts
    A. General Indexes
    B. Special Subject Indexes
    C. Abstracts

[1] The main emphasis in the following discussion is on *categories* of reference works, with only representative examples of the works themselves, since a listing of all reference sources would occupy a whole volume. Indeed, such a volume is available in all libraries as the standard, annotated guide to reference materials:

Constance M. Winchell, *Guide to Reference Books*, 8th ed. (Chicago: American Library Association, 1967). First Supplement, 1965–1966. Second Supplement, 1967–1968.

For a handy, quick guide suitable for your own reference shelf, you should buy one of the following inexpensive paperbacks:

Barton, Mary Neill, and Marion V. Bell. *Reference Books: A Brief Guide for Students and Other Users of the Library*. 6th ed. Baltimore: Enoch Pratt Free Library, 1966.

Galin, Saul, and Peter Spielberg. *Reference Books: How to Select and Use Them*. New York: Random House, 1969.

Gates, Jean Key. *Guide to the Use of Books and Libraries*. New York: McGraw-Hill Book Company, 1969.

McCormick, Mona. *Who-What-When-Where-How-Why Made Easy. A New York Times Book*. Chicago: Quadrangle Books, 1971.

Morse, Grant W. *A Concise Guide to Library Research*. New York: Washington Square Press, Inc., 1967.

Murphy, Robert W. *How and Where to Look It Up*. New York: McGraw-Hill Book Company, 1958.

6. Government Publications
7. Pamphlets

The definition on page 50 points out two broad types of reference works: those that give information about a subject and those that tell you where to find information. The logical place to begin research is the card catalog, followed by general and special reference books which in most instances contain direct sources of information exclusively.

Card Catalog

The card catalog[2] is exactly that: a catalog of 3 × 5 index cards, filed alphabetically in pull-out drawers in the main circulation room in your library. This catalog is the index to the library, for each card represents a library holding—a book, a booklet, or a periodical—and contains such vital facts as author, title, subject, publisher, place and date of publication, number of pages. For each library holding there are usually three cards: one indexed under the author's name, one under the title of the book, the third under the subject. Two typical cards are shown. One illustrates the Dewey Decimal System of indexing, still in use in many college libraries (page 52); the other illustrates the more prevalent Library of Congress system (page 53).

The card catalog is extremely important because it tells you not merely what has been published on your subject but what your own library actually has available.

Learning how to use the card catalog is not difficult. It requires no special sleuthing to turn to the "Man-Mut" drawer to locate books on the subject of "Money"; or the "Gut-Hil" drawer for a novel by "Hemingway"; or "Fez-Fos" if the title of the novel you want is *For Whom the Bell Tolls*.

What does take some thought, however, is tracking down *all* the material in the library that pertains to your subject, for this is not always evident from a first quick look under the obvious main headings. Here again you must be aware of various subheadings under which the catalog may list relevant works. Some subheadings are indicated on the main entry card itself as illustrated on page 52 ("Anthropology—Addresses, essays, lectures"). For further information you can refer to these subject cards. In addition to being ingenious about subheadings, you must be imaginative and knowledgeable enough about your subject to figure out alternate designations. If it is "cinema techniques" you want to know about, for example, then you should surely think of turning to "Motion Pictures," "Film," or perhaps "Movies." By referring to *Subject Headings . . . of the Library of Congress*, a large volume owned by most libraries and installed near the card catalog, you will get an idea of the variety of cross-references possible for most subjects.

One of the main limitations of the card catalog is that it generally includes only the main subject matter of a book, but not all the subjects discussed in the book. Thus, as one librarian-author reminds us, "a book on North American Indians might contain a very useful discussion of wampum, but few card catalogs would have a subject card for

---

[2] Some libraries now have catalogs on Microfiche or in book form. Using these catalogs is similar to using a card catalog.

The Dewey Decimal System

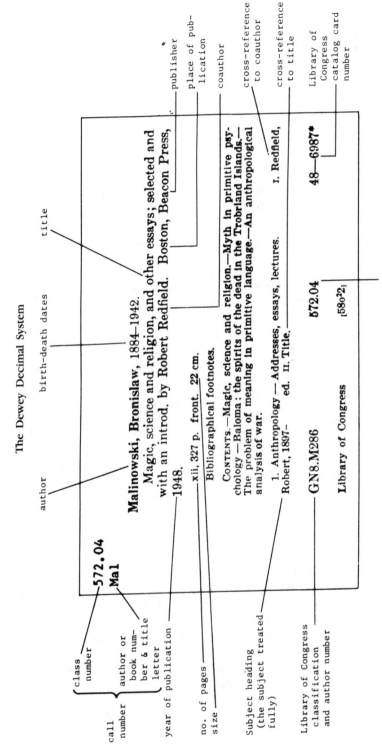

call number

class number

author or book number & title letter

year of publication

no. of pages
size

Subject heading (the subject treated fully)

Library of Congress classification and author number

author   birth–death dates   title

publisher

place of publication

coauthor

cross-reference to coauthor

cross-reference to title

Library of Congress catalog card number

572.04
Mal

Malinowski, Bronislaw, 1884–1942.
 Magic, science and religion, and other essays; selected and
with an introd. by Robert Redfield. Boston, Beacon Press,
1948.
 xii, 327 p. front. 22 cm.
 Bibliographical footnotes.

 CONTENTS.—Magic, science and religion.—Myth in primitive psychology.—Baloma: the spirits of the dead in the Trobriand Islands.—
The problem of meaning in primitive language.—An anthropological
analysis of war.

 1. Anthropology — Addresses, essays, lectures.   I. Redfield,
Robert, 1897–   ed. II. Title.

GN8.M286   572.04

Library of Congress   [580²²]

Dewey classification

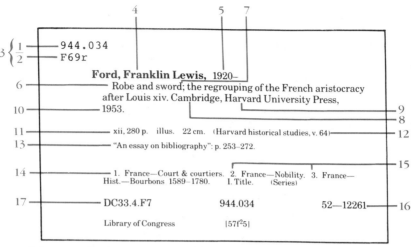

The Library of Congress System

Author card or main entry: (1) class number; (2) author or book number and title letter; (3) call number; (4) author's name, inverted; (5) author's date of birth; (6) title of book; (7) subtitle; (8) place of publication; (9) publisher; (10) date of publication; (11) collation; (12) series note; (13) bibliographical note; (14) subject heading (the subject treated fully); (15) other subjects treated; (16) Library of Congress catalog card number; (17) Library of Congress classification and author number (Gates, *Guide*).

this book indexed under wampum" (Murphy, *How and Where* 33). What to do, then, to tap resource material *within* books themselves?

> There are a number of other guides to a library's contents which you should learn to use. For example, you may find that your reference librarian has his own card catalog, developed out of his own experience. That is, he will have carded for his own use the best sources of information on many different subjects. These may include subjects which are important but about which few or no special books have been written. Through his years of answering people's queries he has found sources containing the needed information, and he has carded these sources. Most librarians will be glad to let you use their special card files.
>
> In addition ... most special collections in libraries have their own card catalogs, both complementing and supplementing the main catalog. In a number of such catalogs the index of subjects is considerably more detailed than it is in the main library catalog (Murphy 33).

Helpful as it is to become aware of special catalogs, you should concentrate on the regular catalog, especially that single main entry card, which generally provides you with enough information to decide whether or not a book is worth fetching from the stacks. *Note date of publication:* Maybe the work is too old to be useful. *Note author:* Is he or she known to you? Is he or she reputable? Is the book likely to be a trustworthy treatment of the subject? *Note publisher:* Is it a reputable press or a fly-by-night, pay-for-publication-yourself "vanity" press that publishes anything? *Note the number of pages:* Maybe the book is too long or too short for your purposes. *Note the exact wording of the title and subtitle:* Maybe the tone of the book is all wrong.

A final note: Having become acquainted on your own with the main resources of the library, you need not feel guilty about addressing difficult questions to the reference librarian, whose job is to guide researchers in areas where they cannot find their own way. Indeed, reference librarians are themselves repositories of vast information concerning the resources of the particular library in which they work, and of the resources to be found locally as well as in the nation at large. When necessary, they can help you obtain materials through interlibrary loan, or, if this is not possible, they may suggest alternate materials.

General Reference Books

When you have finally found your topic and are ready to gather information, you would be wise to turn at the outset to the most general sources available, for they will provide a helpful overview of the subject, a description of its essential nature and its scope. More than that, they will verify whatever facts you have on hand and fill in further details, thereby bringing you up-to-date on your subject and either reinforcing your interest in it or (equally helpful) discouraging you, if your preliminary study shows that the subject is not as promising as it seemed.

A. ENCYCLOPEDIAS

The best—and best-known—all-around reference work is the encyclopedia, which provides background materials for almost any field of knowledge. Do you want to know about white supremacy in Africa? the fiscal crisis of Catholic parochial education? the world's consumption of raw materials? All these questions call for initial consultation with a broad treatment of the subject. This is exactly what the encyclopedia offers in the form of a relatively short, condensed article, in many cases written by a specialist and signed.

The best general encyclopedias include the following:

> *The New Encyclopaedia Britannica: A Survey of Universal Knowledge.* 30 vols. Chicago: Encyclopaedia Britannica, Inc., 1974.
> Supplemented annually by the *Britannica Book of the Year.*
> *Encyclopedia Americana* (International Edition). 30 vols. New York: Encyclopedia Americana Corp., 1975.
> Supplemented annually by the *Americana Annual.*
> *Chambers's Encyclopaedia.* New rev. ed. Oxford and New York: Pergamon Press, 1967.
> Supplemented annually by Chambers's *Encyclopaedia World Survey.*
> *Collier's Encyclopedia.* 24 vols. New York: Crowell-Collier, 1970.
> Supplemented by *Collier's Year Book.*

Special Note:

Whatever encyclopedia you use, several facts are worth remembering:

1. Although the major encyclopedias are not thoroughly revised each year, most of them undergo a process of continuous revision whereby each printing embodies some changes. In most cases, therefore, the information gathered from a reputable

encyclopedia is relatively up-to-date. For up-to-the-minute information, however, you must consult a periodical—an abstract, article, or news report. (I describe these under "Periodical Indexes and Abstracts.")

2. Every encyclopedia contains an explanation of its own code: its abbreviations, a key to the initials on the signed articles, index conventions, and so on. You should consult this code at the outset of research so that you can understand the information you gather.

3. The major encyclopedias contain bibliographies (lists of other works on a given subject or other places where you may find information), plus a detailed index, usually located in the last volume. Researchers are not always aware of these supplementary aids; students often ignore the main index, in particular, because they hurriedly turn to the main entry where they can usually—but not always—find most of the needed information. But proper use of the encyclopedia also involves cross-referencing. If your topic is the chateau country of France, for example, you should follow each of the suggested cross-references to individual chateaux as they are mentioned in the main entry (Amboise, Chenonceaux). Then you should proceed—on your own—to look up other entries that *might* provide more information: you might investigate individual kings, for example, who built or restored chateaux (Charles VIII, Louis XII, Francis I), or you might turn to the individual towns in which chateaux are located. Your ingenuity at cross-referencing may determine whether your paper contains simply the usual and expected information or that extra dimension that raises it above the ordinary.

B. BIOGRAPHICAL WORKS

If your topic involves a prominent person or persons (an historical character, an inventor, a literary figure), then you must begin your research by compiling biographical data. General biographical works may be universal in scope (like the first two in the following list) or they may be limited to individuals of a particular nationality, geographical location, or professional position. For our purposes—in fact for most purposes—the main distinction is whether the person in question is living or dead.

Persons Living

Current Biography, 1940–date. New York: Wilson, 1940–date.
  Published monthly and gathered into annual volumes, each of which contains lively profiles of about 400 new personalities.

Who's Who, 1849–date. London: Black, 1849–date.
  Published annually, this famous dictionary of notable living Englishmen and a few distinguished persons of other countries gives brief facts and addresses.

Who's Who in America, 1899/1900–date. Chicago: Marquis, 1899–date.
  This American counterpart of the British *Who's Who* is published every other year, along with a supplementary *Who's Who of American Women*, 1958–date. (See also separate volumes of *Who's Who* that cover different regions of the United States: *Who's Who in the East*, *Who's Who in the South and Southwest*, *Who's Who in the Midwest*, and so on. See also volumes covering various other nations such as *Who's Who in Australia*, *Who's Who in Modern China*, *Who's Who in Latin America*.)

Other contemporary biographical sources are organized according to profession and include such volumes as the following:

American Men and Women of Science
The Directory of American Scholars
Twentieth Century Authors
Contemporary Authors
Who's Who in American Politics
Dictionary of Scientific Biography

Persons No Longer Living

Dictionary of American Biography. 20 vols. New York: Scribner, 1927–1972.

Also includes Index and Supplements I–IV.

Long, detailed articles, written by prominent scholars and accompanied by a bibliography of sources (most of them primary), chronicle the lives and accomplishments of distinguished Americans. See also *Facts About the Presidents, American Authors* (1600–1900), and *Notable American Women, 1607–1950.*

Dictionary of National Biography. Ed. Leslie Stephen and Sir Sidney Lee. London: Smith, Elder and Co., and Oxford University Press, 1885–date.

The British counterpart of (and model for) the *Dictionary of American Biography* (D.A.B.), the D.N.B. is the most complete and accurate guide to the lives of important Britons of the past.

(See also such helpful sources as *Who Was Who, British Authors of the Nineteenth Century, British Authors Before 1800, European Authors, 1000–1900,* and *World Authors: 1950–1970.*)

Persons Living and Dead

Webster's Biographical Dictionary. Springfield, Mass.: Merriam, 1969.

Chambers's Biographical Dictionary. Rev. ed. New York: St. Martins, 1969.

(See also entries under individual names in the general encyclopedias and see *Biography Index,* described below under "Periodical Indexes and Abstracts.")

C. DICTIONARIES

At the outset of research, look up key terms to find out their conventional boundaries of meaning. Will you want to stay within these boundaries or will you want to use certain terms in an unorthodox sense, either more or less restricted than usual? As we shall see in Question 1, "What does X mean?" you can vary word usage provided you indicate at the outset that you are using the term in a special sense, one that meets the particular needs of the paper.

Before you can make any such statement, however, you must see what the dictionary—preferably an unabridged dictionary—has to say. You may even find it necessary to discover how the meaning of a particular word has changed over the years: maybe a past meaning will be specially relevant to your purpose; maybe it will be worth adopting or adapting. Four good standard dictionaries provide information of this kind: three are general, one historical.

Webster's Third New International Dictionary of the English Language. 3d ed. unabridged. Ed. Philip Gove. Springfield, Mass.: Merriam, 1961.

One of the great English dictionaries—the first to be published under the direct and commanding influence of modern linguistic science—*Webster's Third* contains almost half a million words, 100,000 of which are new entries or new meanings for older entries. Some early critics maintained that this dictionary would never replace Webster's more traditional Second Edition (1934), but it has.

The Random House Dictionary of the English Language. Unabridged ed. Ed. Jess Stein. New York: Random House, 1966.

A computer-produced, highly legible dictionary containing 260,000 words.

The American Heritage Dictionary of the English Language. Ed. William Morris. New York: American Heritage Publishing Co., Inc., and Boston: Houghton Mifflin Co., 1969.

An entirely new and highly readable dictionary, copiously illustrated.

New English Dictionary on Historical Principles. Ed. Sir James A. H. Murray. 10 vols. and supplement. Oxford: Clarendon Press, 1888–1933. Reissued, 1933, in 13 vols. under the title *Oxford English Dictionary* (OED).

(See also the one-volume *Oxford University Dictionary*, 3d ed., revised with addenda and corrections. Oxford: Clarendon Press, 1959.)

This great dictionary, the most scholarly lexicographical achievement in the English language, which took years of cooperative scholarship to complete, was compiled on a different plan and serves a different purpose from that of the ordinary dictionary. It traces the history of every word in the language (its meaning, spelling, pronunciation) from the time it first appeared as an English word (perhaps 800 years ago) to the present, giving illustrations of its usage at the various stages of its career.

D. YEARBOOKS AND ALMANACS

Yearbooks and almanacs, published each year, contain a wealth of general information and statistics, much of it based on primary materials from government bulletins and abstracts.

Facts on File, A Weekly Digest of World Events with Cumulative Index. New York: Facts on File, Inc., 1930–date.

An extremely helpful, time-saving weekly digest of the news, arranged under such headings as world affairs, arts, economy, science, education, religion. It has been said that *Facts on File* is a *current* encyclopedia, keeping the reader abreast of the latest developments in all fields, particularly in the United States.

(See also *Keesing's Contemporary Archives*, a weekly diary of world events, published in London but worldwide in scope.)

The New York Times Encyclopedic Almanac. New York: The New York Times, 1970–date.

Comprehensive and reliable, this recently introduced encyclopedic almanac offers all the useful features of an almanac (statistics on every phase of American life, from the Supreme Court to sports) based on the research and educational resources of the *New York Times.* Issued annually.

The World Almanac and Book of Facts. New York: Newspaper Enterprise Association, 1868–1876, 1886–date.

Statesman's Year-Book: Statistical and Historical Annual of the States of the World. London: Macmillan, 1864–date.

An exceptionally useful manual containing information and statistics on the governments of the world—their rulers, constitutions, forms of government, population, commerce, state finance, defense, production, industry.

(See also thè Worldmark *Encyclopedia of the Nations* (1971), which provides supplementary materials to the *Statesman's Year-Book* and presents helpful information on the newer countries and on famous persons in each country's history. See also yearbooks for individual countries and continents, such as *Europa Year Book: A World Survey, Canadian Almanac and Directory, South American Handbook.*)

E. ATLASES AND GAZETTEERS

There are general and special atlases, some of which are listed below:

General

> *Hammond Medallion World Atlas*
> *Rand McNally Commercial Atlas*
> *Rand McNally Cosmopolitan World Atlas*
> *McGraw-Hill International Atlas*
> *The Times Atlas of the World*

Special

> *Atlas of American History*
> *Atlas of World History*
> *Atlas of the Historical Geography of the United States*
> *Atlas of the Sky*

A gazetteer is a dictionary of places that provides information about history, population, trade, industry, cultural institutions, natural resources. See, for example:

> *Columbia-Lippincott Gazetteer of the World*
> *Webster's New Geographical Dictionary*
> *The Times Index-Gazetteer of the World*

F. BOOKS OF CURIOUS FACTS

You can locate odd bits of out-of-the-way information in such books of "curious facts" as those listed below:

> Douglas, George William. *The American Book of Days*. Rev. ed. New York: Wilson, 1948.
> An account of the history and observance of American holidays, local festivals, and anniversaries of such events as the world's first balloon ascension. (For the British equivalent see Chambers, Robert. *Book of Days, A Miscellany of Popular Antiquities.* 2 vols. Edinburgh: Chambers, 1863–64.)
> Kane, Joseph Nathan. *Famous First Facts*. 3d ed. New York: Wilson, 1964.
> Records famous "firsts" in the United States: events, discoveries, inventions, etc.
> *Funk & Wagnalls Standard Dictionary of Folklore, Mythology and Legend*. Ed. Maria Leach. New York: Funk & Wagnalls, 1972.

A vast and comprehensive work dealing with all aspects of world culture: gods, heroes, tales, customs, beliefs, songs, dances, demons, folklore of animals and plants.

Walsh, William Shepard. *Curiosities of Popular Customs and of Rites, Ceremonies, Observances, and Miscellaneous Antiquities.* Philadelphia and London: Lippincott, 1898.
Descriptions of popular customs and celebrations in different countries of the world.

Walsh, William Shepard. *Handy Book of Curious Information Comprising Strange Happenings in the Life of Men and Animals, Odd Statistics, Extraordinary Phenomena and Out-of-the-Way Facts Concerning the Wonderlands of the Earth.* Philadelphia and London: Lippincott, 1913.
(See also *Walsh's Handy Book of Literary Curiosities,* 1909.)

Wheeler, William Adolphus. *Familiar Allusions: A Handbook of Miscellaneous Information.* 5th ed. Boston: Houghton, 1890.

Radford, E., and M. A. Radford. *Encyclopedia of Superstitions.* Ed. and rev. by Christina Hole. London: Hutchinson, 1961.
(See also *A Treasury of American Superstitions.*)

Special Reference Books

In addition to general references, many special reference works are devoted to individual fields such as history, political science, and literature. Each of these fields has its own body of materials—encyclopedias, handbooks, indexes, abstracts, almanacs, yearbooks, dictionaries, and so on—that you can locate through a general reference guide like Constance Winchell's standard *Guide to Reference Books* or one of the smaller "pocket guides." These overall subject guides are your single most helpful research aid, for they acquaint you with the major writings in your chosen field and list not only encyclopedias and handbooks but also bibliographies, abstracts, and periodical indexes that tell you where you can find further information (discussed below under "Periodical Indexes").

How many subject areas have their own reference shelf of special materials? It would be impossible to list them all here, for there are separate reference works devoted to almost every discipline, activity, profession, occupation, and recreation; handbooks and encyclopedias are available for you in every field and every field-within-a-field you can imagine. I can suggest only some of the more common subject headings under which special reference works are likely to be listed:

Subject Heading	Representative Reference Works
Philosophy	*Encyclopedia of Philosophy*
Psychology	*Annual Review of Psychology*
Religion	*Encyclopedia of Religion and Ethics* (See separate encyclopedias for Catholic, Jewish, etc.)
Social Sciences	*Sources of Information in the Social Sciences* *International Encyclopedia of the Social Sciences* *Dictionary of Sociology* *Biennial Review of Anthropology* (See separate reference works in political science, economics, law, education, etc.)

Physical Sciences	*The Harper Encyclopedia of Science* *McGraw-Hill Encyclopedia of Science and Technology* *A Guide to the Literature of Chemistry* *The International Dictionary of Applied Mathematics* *Encyclopaedic Dictionary of Physics* *Glossary of Geology and Related Sciences*
Natural Sciences	*The Encyclopedia of Biological Sciences* *Gray's Manual of Botany* *Mammals of the World* *Glossary of Genetics and Other Biological Terms*
Technology	*McGraw-Hill Encyclopedia of Science and Technology* *A Guide to Information Sources in Space Science and Technology* (See separate reference works under medical science, engineering, agriculture, business, etc.)
Fine Arts	*Encyclopedia of World Art* *A Guide to Art Reference Books* *Grove's Dictionary of Music and Musicians* *Encyclopedia of Jazz*
Literature	*The Reader's Adviser: A Guide to the Best in Literature* (See also bibliographies, dictionaries, directories, handbooks, biographies, criticism, history, drama, poetry, fiction, etc.; see also national literatures: English, American, French, etc.)
Language and Linguistics	*The World's Chief Languages* *Language in Culture and Society* *A History of the English Language* [3] *Dictionary of Linguistics*
History	*An Encyclopedia of World History* *Oxford Classical Dictionary* (See under historical periods: ancient, medieval, etc.; see also national histories: English, American, etc.)

General Bibliographies

Formal bibliographies are very much like subject guides in that they also list books and other written materials according to author and subject. Thus Winchell's *Guide to*

---

[3] This book, by scholar-historian Albert Baugh, is an example of a textbook so comprehensive that it may be regarded as a reference work.

Reference Books also functions as an annotated bibliography, for it includes brief notes and comments about each title listed. A formal bibliography (one that is published independently, not merely appended to a scholarly article or an encyclopedia entry) is an end in itself, a rigorously and systematically organized listing of the literature on a given subject.

A bibliography, then, is a list and nothing but a list. As such it is extraordinarily useful, for it indicates how much material exists on a subject and where it is available. It also suggests—either implicitly in the title of the work listed or explicitly in an annotation—which articles and books bear most directly on a topic. Thus a good bibliography saves you time and effort, for it helps you to begin your research with the most useful and pertinent works. Equally important, it enables you to check the literature on your subject so that you will know what has already been done and what remains to be done.

There are several master bibliographies that you should be familiar with and refer to early in your research.

> *Bibliographic Index: A Cumulative Bibliography of Bibliographies.* New York: Wilson, 1938–.
> > An indispensable tool for anyone compiling a bibliography in a particular subject, especially if the subject is somewhat obscure.
>
> *World Bibliography of Bibliographies.* 4th ed., rev. and enl. Ed. Theodore Besterman. Geneva: Societas Bibliographica, 1965–66.
> > A monumental work that includes 117,000 separately published bibliographies arranged according to subject.
>
> *Subject Guide to Books in Print: An Index to the Publishers' Trade List Annual.* New York: Bowker, 1957–. Annual.
>
> *United States Catalog.* 4th ed. New York: Wilson, 1928. Supplemented by *Cumulative Book Index*, 1928–date. New York: Wilson, 1933–date.
>
> *Library of Congress Catalog.* Washington, D.C.: Library of Congress, 1955–.

Periodical Indexes and Abstracts

When you want to find out the latest information on a given subject (the influence of drugs on mental alertness, critical opinion of a current production of *King Lear*, or new facts about the moon), you must turn to periodical indexes that list articles, reports, reviews, essays, news stories, speeches, bulletins, and editorials that have appeared in periodicals—journals, magazines, and newspapers. In some cases, you may want to turn to this resource immediately, for what is new about your subject may be the most important thing you need to learn; it may be the core of your paper and your reason for writing it.

You can expect the periodical indexes, then, to put you in touch with the most recent and up-to-date information. In that special type of index known as an "abstract," you will also find a brief summary of what the articles and essays contain.

Major periodical indexes can be divided into general and specialized (according to subject areas).

A. GENERAL INDEXES

Readers' Guide to Periodical Literature. New York: Wilson, 1905–date.
Social Science Index and *Humanities Index.* New York: Wilson, 1974–date. Formerly known as *Social Sciences and Humanities Index*, 1965–1974.
New York Times Index. New York: New York Times Corp., 1851–date.
Essay and General Literature Index. New York: Wilson, 1900–date.
Book Review Digest. New York: Wilson, 1905–date.
Book Review Index. Detroit: Gale Research, 1965–date.

B. SPECIAL SUBJECT INDEXES

Here again, it is impossible to list all the separate indexes devoted to particular subjects. To locate the particular one most useful to your purpose, consult one of the general guides to the literature such as Winchell's *Guide to Reference Books* (mentioned earlier), or the less formal but eminently readable *How and Where to Look It Up*.

A few representative subject indexes are:

Applied Science and Technology Index. New York: Wilson, 1958–date. Formerly *Industrial Arts Index*, 1913–58.
Art Index. New York: Wilson, 1929–date.
Business Periodicals Index. New York: Wilson, 1958–date.
Education Index. New York: Wilson, 1929–date.
Film Literature Index, 1973–date.
Index of Religious Periodical Literature. Ed. American Theological Library Assn. Princeton, N.J.: Princeton Theological Seminary, 1953–date.
The Music Index. Detroit: Information Service, Inc., 1949–date.
Public Affairs Information Service Bulletin. New York: Public Affairs Information Service, 1915–date.
Psychological Index, 1894–1935. 42 vols. Princeton, N.J.: Psychological Review Co., 1895–1936. (Continued by *Psychological Abstracts*)

C. ABSTRACTS

Abstract of English Studies
America: History and Life: A Guide to Periodical Literature (with abstracts)
Biological Abstracts
Chemical Abstracts
Historical Abstracts
    Now being published in two parts: *Modern Abstracts*, 1775–1914; and *Twentieth Century Abstracts*, 1914–date.
Mathematical Reviews
Mineralogical Abstracts
Psychological Abstracts
Religious and Theological Abstracts
Science Abstracts (physics and electrical engineering)
Sociological Abstracts

Government Publications

The United States government is probably the largest and most versatile publisher in the world, printing and processing in a single year more books, booklets, periodicals, newsletters, leaflets, films, and filmstrips; more annual reports, research documents, transcripts (of Congressional hearings, for example), manuals, handbooks, bibliographies, indexes, dictionaries, catalogs, checklists, and statistical compilations than any single commercial publisher or any foreign government.

Few people are aware of the enormous amount of information available through the Government Printing Office, either free or at very low cost. A brief listing of recent titles suggests how far-ranging this information is: *Science and the City, Mini-gardens for Vegetables, Family Budgeting, The Nature of Ocean Beds, Raising Raccoons, Home Construction, Space, National Parks, Living Death: The Truth About Drug Addiction, FDA* (Food and Drug Administration) *on Oral Contraceptives, Story of the Mississippi Choctaws, Pocket Guide to Japan, Fables from Incunabula to the Present.* In truth, government publications touch on nearly every field, especially in the areas of history, travel, and the social, physical, and biological sciences.

To tap this rich source of authoritative and up-to-date primary source material, you should be familiar with the main bibliographies and indexes issued by the government and some of the more recent and important guides.[4]

U.S. *Superintendent of Documents. Monthly Catalog of United States Government Publications.* Washington, D.C.: Government Printing Office, 1895–date.
Price Lists of Government Publications. Washington, D.C.: Government Printing Office, 1898–date.
U.S. Bureau of the Census. *Statistical Abstract of the United States.* Washington, D.C.: Government Printing Office, 1878–date.

This matchless compendium of statistics covers the political, social, economic, and industrial organization of the country, including vital statistics, and figures on population, immigration, finance, employment, etc. It is the basic source of statistical information of all kinds from which most other sources (yearbooks, almanacs) get their information.

Jackson, Ellen. *Subject Guide to Major United States Government Publications.* Chicago: American Library Association, 1968.

Covers important government publications from the earliest period to the publication date, arranged by subject.

Leidy, W. Philip. *A Popular Guide to Governmental Publications.* 4th ed. New York: Columbia University Press, 1976.

Covers the most popular government publications issued 1961–66, arranged by subject.

Schmeckebier, Lawrence F., and Roy B. Eastin. *Government Publications and Their Use.* 2d rev. ed. Washington, D.C.: Brookings Institute, 1969.

Contains descriptions of catalogs and indexes, bibliographies, Congressional publications, constitutions (federal and state), court decisions, presidential papers, etc.

[4] Libraries organize their government materials differently: some catalog them in the regular card catalog, as they would any other library material; others keep them in a separate file, or official United States government depository, classifying them as "Government Documents" or "Government Publications." The reference librarian can explain the system used in the individual library.

Pamphlets

Pamphlets deserve to be treated in a separate category because, like government publications, student researchers who are unaware of their importance or even their existence often ignore them. Pamphlets serve the important function of bridging a time gap until researchers can gather current information on a given topic into book form.

Many reputable organizations and institutions, such as the Mental Health Association, the public affairs offices of colleges and universities, and the American Civil Liberties Union, regularly publish pamphlets in order to keep the public abreast of their activities and achievements.

The best way to locate a pamphlet dealing with a given subject is through the Pamphlet or Vertical File of the library or, if your library integrates pamphlets into its general collection, in the regular card catalog under the appropriate subject heading. You can expect to find materials on current and controversial subjects such as racial conflicts, drug addiction, alcoholism, civil disobedience, and pollution.

In working with pamphlets, you should be particularly alert for evidence of bias. Extremist political groups, for example, often distribute pamphlets that seem to be informative but are really propagandist. You should view these with appropriate suspicion.

Titles of some of the more noteworthy pamphlet series follow.

Public Affairs Pamphlets
    Published by the nonprofit Public Affairs Committee to keep the American public informed on vital economic and social problems.
Headline Series
    Published by the nonprofit, nonpartisan Foreign Policy Association to stimulate wider interest in world affairs.
Editorial Research Reports
    Individual monographs dealing with vital contemporary issues.
National Industrial Conference Board
    This nonprofit fact-finding board publishes studies on scientific research in the fields of business economics and management.
American Universities Field Staff Publications
    A continuing series on current developments in world affairs issued by the nonprofit American Field Staff, Inc.
National Bureau of Economic Research
    Publishes scientific reports on current economic problems.
Center for the Study of Democratic Institutions
    A nonprofit, nonpartisan educational institution, the Center publishes articles dealing with basic problems in a democratic society.

GATHERING INFORMATION FOR SHORT PAPERS

The weekly, biweekly, or semiweekly writing assignment that usually runs from 500 to 1,000 words often requires library research. Let us take an average 500–750-word paper (two to three pages) and call it a "short" paper. You can gather information for this average writing assignment in approximately three to four hours of library re-search. You should allow an equal amount of time for writing the paper and revising. Thus the average writing assignment requires from six to eight hours of total effort. Since virtually all writing assignments have a deadline, they are self-limiting: what you need to do, in other words, becomes a function of what you *can* do within the prescribed time. You should keep this in mind, for it puts the paper in perspective and helps you make a realistic assessment of how much you can hope to cover and what you can accomplish.

Let us consider how you might go about gathering information for four possible topics, each an answer to a specific question.[5]

1. How does X compare to Y?
   Title: The Peace Corps—Then and Now

LIST OF POSSIBLE SOURCES:
Encyclopedia Americana
Government publications (See "Federal Depository" in college library, which contains recent government reports, pamphlets, bulletins, programs, etc.)
Public Affairs Information Service Bulletin (PAIS)
New York Times Index
Readers' Guide to Periodical Literature

2. What is the present status of X?
   Title: A New View of the Soul[6]

LIST OF POSSIBLE SOURCES:
Encyclopedia of Philosophy
The Dictionary of Religious Terms
Encyclopedia of Religion and Ethics
The New Schaff-Herzog Encyclopedia of Religious Knowledge
Handbook of Denominations in the United States
Religious and Theological Abstracts

3. How is X made or done?
   Title: How Artificial Snow Is Made

LIST OF POSSIBLE SOURCES:
Science News Yearbook (annual)
Encyclopaedia Britannica

---

[5] You do not need to consult all references listed in each instance; sometimes one or two provide sufficient information. Should you want to extend the piece to a long paper, however, these bibliographies would represent the bare essentials. Although it is obvious, in most cases you should also look into the card catalog under appropriate headings. Even if you do not have time to read a whole book on a subject, you may find separate chapters directly pertinent to your purpose.

[6] You could easily extend this topic, in particular, into a long piece dealing with different concepts of the soul at different periods in history or among different religions. See *Handbook of Denominations in the United States* and encyclopedias and dictionaries of the various religions.

McGraw-Hill Encyclopedia of Science and Technology
  (see supplementary yearbooks)
    or
Van Nostrand's Scientific Encyclopedia
Weather and Climate
Applied Science and Technology Index
Readers' Guide to Periodical Literature

4. What case can be made for or against X?
  Title: The Case Against Multiple Choice Tests

LIST OF POSSIBLE SOURCES:
Encyclopedia of Educational Research
Mental Measurements Yearbook
Psychological Abstracts
Education Index
Readers' Guide to Periodical Literature
Card catalog (under "Educational Tests," "Testing," etc.)

GATHERING INFORMATION FOR LONG PAPERS

Long papers take not merely three or four hours but perhaps as much as thirty or forty hours in the library. You may not be able to devote that much time to a term paper assignment, but you should plan on at least fifteen to twenty hours of research for a paper that will run between 3,000 and 5,000 words. It is impossible, of course, to set exact specifications; the demands of the subject vary, along with the background knowledge of the writer.

Following is a list of possible sources for projected term paper topics. They give an indication of the extent of research necessary for a typical term paper.

Term Paper 1: Description-Narration

Title: The Assassination of Malcolm X
  (Since this event occurred in 1965, you will need to use recent references.)

1. Biographical sources

   Current Biography
   Who Was Who in America
   Biography Index

2. Newspaper and magazine accounts

   New York Times Index
   Readers' Guide to Periodical Literature

3. Essays and commentaries in journals, anthologies, etc.

   Essay and General Literature Index
   Social Science and Humanities Index
   America: History and Life: A Guide to Periodical Literature

4. Card catalog

   See under Malcolm X: Biography, Bibliography.

5. Reference books

   Black American Reference Book
   Encyclopedia of Islam

Term Paper 2: Extended Characterization-Interpretation

Title: The World of Pablo Picasso

1. Biographical sources

   Chambers's Biographical Dictionary, rev. ed.
   Webster's Biographical Dictionary

2. Encyclopedias and dictionaries

   Encyclopedia of World Art
   Encyclopedia of Modern Art
   Dictionary of Art and Artists
   Dictionary of Art
   Dictionary of Modern Painting

3. Bibliographies and indexes

   Readers' Guide to Periodical Literature (for articles in national magazines)
   New York Times Index
   The Art Index
   A Guide to Art Reference Books

4. Picasso's artistic development—some specific works

   Ashton, Dore. *Picasso on Art*. New York: Viking Press, 1972.
   Barr, Alfred H., Jr. *Picasso: Fifty Years of His Art*. Rev. and enl. ed. New York: Museum of Modern Art, 1974.
   Chevalier, Denis. *Picasso: Blue and Rose Periods*. New York: Crown, 1969.
   Gallwitz, Klaus. *Picasso at 90: The Late Work*. New York: Putnam, 1971.
   Schiff, G., ed. *Picasso in Perspective*. Englewood Cliffs, N. J.: Prentice-Hall, 1974.

5. Card Catalog

   For individual biographies, check under "Picasso, Pablo." For background information, check under "Art History," "Modern Art," "Twentieth-Century Art."

Term Paper 3: Extended Factual Article

Title: The Latest Facts About Twins

  1. Basic background reference

> *Encyclopaedia Britannica* (See under "Genetics-Human")
> *McGraw-Hill Encyclopedia of Science and Technology*
> *International Encyclopedia of Psychiatry, Psychology, Analysis, and Neurology*

  2. Bibliographies and indexes

> *Index Medicus*
> *Social Sciences Index*
> *Sociological Abstracts*
> *Psychological Abstracts*
> *Readers' Guide to Periodical Literature*
> *New York Times Index*

  3. Card catalog

> See under Twins; also Birth (Multiple), Brothers & Sisters, Diseases in Twins, Human Genetics, Heredity

Term Paper 4: Extended Argument

Title: The Case Against Capital Punishment

  1. Basic reference

> *International Encyclopedia of the Social Sciences*

  2. Bibliographies and indexes

> *Readers' Guide to Periodical Literature*
> *New York Times Index*
> *Public Affairs Information Service Bulletin (PAIS)*
> *Social Sciences Index*
> *Sociological Abstracts*
> *CIS/INDEX: Index to Congressional Publications and Public Laws*

  3. Government document

> *Monthly Catalog*

  4. Reference pamphlet collection

  5. Card catalog

NOTE-TAKING

I cannot overemphasize the importance of familiarizing yourself with the library's major reference tools, but at the same time the vast resources of the Library of Congress itself are of little use if you do not know how to extract from them the information you need. In order to develop your particular topic into a sound and informative paper, you must know how to take good notes, for they are obviously the foundation on which you will construct the paper itself. When the time comes to sit down and write the paper—when you must make certain points or provide certain data—if you have taken good notes you need simply thumb through them and the needed information will be there. *The writing process is a lot easier when you have taken accurate, ample, and well-organized notes.* If you have not, you are in serious trouble, for without good notes you will not be able to write a good research paper, just as a bricklayer cannot build a strong and attractive building if the individual bricks are not themselves strong and attractive.

It is worthwhile, then, to devote special attention to note-taking, a skill closely related to writing, for the good note-taker does not mindlessly copy a paragraph of text, word for word. On the contrary, you must actively *think* about what you read and try to figure out exactly what it means and how it may contribute to your topic. Only after you have figured out its possible usefulness to your purpose are you ready to put pencil to pad—preferably a small 3 × 5 or 5 × 8 pad (or cards) where you can enter separate points on separate pages, saving yourself the trouble later on of leafing through dense, cluttered, and unclassified sheets of a notebook.

You should write each note in your own words (unless the passage deserves to be quoted verbatim) and carefully label it (in the upper right-hand corner of the page, or wherever you choose—according to the special category of information that it deals with). Thus a note card or page might read like the sample cards on pages 70–71.

By classifying your notes as you go along, you create order out of the mass of materials that confronts you. You cannot take it *all* down. You need only what relates to your topic. Presumably you have made at least a tentative decision about your topic and its main headings. Your notes pick up these headings and perhaps even break them down into smaller subheadings (for example, Poe/Early years/Relationship with mother), so that later you can sort related page headings into separate groups (an "early years" group subdivided into "relationship with parents," "school," "early influences"; a "theory of poetry" group; a "marriage" group; a "drinking problem" group; a "financial reverses" group). When you organize notes this way, you can see the total paper taking shape, even before you have begun writing. You can also judge your materials more easily. You are able to see where you have enough information (on Poe's theory of poetry, let us say) and where you may want to do further research to avoid confusing "gaps" (Was Poe a dipsomaniac or a drunkard? Is there a difference between the two?). So, simply by examining a particular grouping of notes you can see that in one area you need more information whereas in other areas your research is complete. If you take notes conscientiously you will probably end up with more notes than you actually use, but if you are reasonably selective along the way, you will not pile up an insurmountable mountain of information.

Beyond what I have already said about being a thoughtful rather than a passive note-taker, here are a few more principles of note-taking:

1. Avoid taking notes too soon—during the preliminary background reading period in encyclopedias, for example. You may want to get down certain

basic facts, figures, and dates about your subject, but beyond this you should generally hold your pencil until you have the overall feel of your subject. More specialized references, which you may turn to later, probably provide more timely and profound information; *then* you *begin* note-taking in earnest, but not before. (See sample card 1.)

2. Read reference materials at different rates and levels of intensity, depending on how promising they seem. You may merely have to skim page after page of a book, without taking a single note; then you may come upon a section or a separate article so relevant and reliable that you must pause two or three times per page to take notes.

Card 1

Poe / Early Years

The only major American writer of his time to spend part of childhood at school in England. Apparently healthy: a good athlete; boxer; represented his school at racing competition; story often told of how he could swim up to six miles, against the tide and under a hot June sun. Also a top student with a "keen disciplined mind." Yet as reminiscences from schoolmates indicate, he was "not popular in the usual sense of the word." (p. 84)

Quinn's **EAP**, pp. 65-85

Card 2

Poe / Personal Appearance

Neat and tidy, nervous in manner. Slender and dark: "His hair was dark as a raven's wing. So was his beard--which he always kept shaved." (p. 53) Broad forehead; long slender neck which "made him appear, when sitting, rather taller than he really was." (p. 54) Slender arms and hands, gracefully tapered: "In fact, his hands were truly remarkable for their roseate softness and lily-like, feminine delicacy." (p. 56) Oval face, violet eyes with long lashes, strong chin, even white teeth: "really handsome...especially when he smiled." (p. 57) Strange smile: "...there was this peculiarity about his smile...it did not appear to be the result of gladness of heart altogether...but ...of that apollonian disdain which seemed to say, what you 'see through a glass darkly, I behold through the couched eyes of an illuminated Seer.'"

- Chivers' Life of Poe, pp. 53-58

Card 3

```
                        Poe / Theory of Poetry

Poe saw "Beauty" as the proper province of the poem and
"Sadness" as the proper tone:
                 Beauty of whatever kind, in its supreme
                 development, invariably excites the
                 sensitive soul to tears.  Melancholy
                 is thus the most legitimate of all the
                 poetical tones.

                          Philos. of Comp., p. 198
```

3. Just as you deal with different types of references, so you must take different types of notes: you may simply record relevant facts or ideas, summarizing them in your own words (card 2); another type of note may be a direct word-for-word copy of a quotation you would like to use (cards 2 and 3); still another may include not only the data gleaned from reading, but your own comment on it, your own responses and observations as they strike you during your reading. It is wise to jot these down immediately, while the thought is with you; it is also wise to set off your own remarks in brackets, or in some other way, so that you can distinguish later between what your authority said and what you said.

4. In general, try to compress and summarize information you take down from a reference source so that when you are ready to use this information, you will have no alternative but to fill out the idea in your own words. This reduces the possibility of inadvertent plagiarism (see the next section, "Avoiding Plagiarism").

5. Very important: the first time you use a new source, make out a complete citation card on which you enter *all* the documentary information you will need for endnotes and bibliography (for example, "Davidson, Edward H. *Poe: A Critical Study*. Cambridge, Mass: Harvard University Press, 1957"). Having done this, you need not repeat all the information about the work on each page of notes; in fact, some simple code like "Davidson, p. 8" or "David., p. 8" or "David/8" or even "D/8" is sufficient—so long as you can understand your own abbreviations later.[7]

6. Finally, a suggestion that may seem trivial but is actually important: never take notes on both sides of the paper. Unfailingly, when you are at the writing stage, looking for a specific point of information, it will be on the *other* side of the page you are looking at—where you cannot find it. To avoid a frustrating shuffle from one side of a sheet to the other, write on only one side of a note page.

[7] Note that on each sample card on pages 70 and 71, the source is cited in shorthand form. The full citations for Cards 1, 2, and 3 would be noted on separate 3 × 5 bibliography cards. See the top of page 72.

```
Quinn, Arthur Hobson.  Edgar Allen Poe, A Critical
Biography.  New York:  Appleton-Century-Crofts,
1941.
```

```
Chivers' Life of Poe.  Ed. Richard Beale Davis.
New York: E. P. Dutton & Co., 1952.
```

```
Poe, Edgar Allen.  "The Philosophy of Composition,"
Graham's Magazine (Apr. 1846), rpt. in James A.
Harrison, ed., The Complete Works of Edgar Allen
Poe.  Vol. XIV.  New York: AMS Press, Inc., 1965,
pp. 193-208.
```

AVOIDING PLAGIARISM

Plagiarism is an ugly practice, which most students try to avoid, but may inadvertently commit if they are not aware of what plagiarism *is*. You should have no uncertainties on this score, however, for the offense is serious. Plagiarism is literally a crime, a form of theft in which one person steals the words of another—in ignorance, perhaps, of the fact that "phraseology, like land and money, can be individual personal property, protected by law" (Williams and Stevenson, *Research* 126). Plagiarism can also involve ideas: you might take someone else's ideas, put them into your own words, and say they are yours. But they are *not* yours, and courtesy as well as honesty requires that you acknowledge this fact with a simple phrase such as "according to":

> *According to Northrop Frye*, the writer's ability to shape life into a literary form comes not from life but from previous contact with literature. Frye makes this point in his essay "Nature and Homer."

Even if it seems to you, after having read it, that you could have thought of that idea yourself, remember that *you did not* and that you therefore owe a credit line to Mr. Frye, whether you have used his exact words or not. You have borrowed his idea. As a conscientious writer, you must always be on guard against violations of this kind. You should be aware, for instance, that it was not anybody-at-all or nobody-in-particular, but *specifically* H. L. Mencken who maintained that "No quackery has ever been given up by the American people until they have had a worse quackery to take its place." This observation, with its fine cynical edge, was passed along by Gilbert Seldes in *The Stammering Century*, a history of quacks and cultists in nineteenth-century America. Seldes credited Mencken with the statement even though it is not a direct quotation and Seldes was not even certain whether Mencken made the remark in print or in private conversation.

Another subtle and often unwitting form of plagiarism involves *slightly changing* someone else's statement (substituting a different word here and there, shifting phrases, inverting clauses) and then presenting the passage as one's own. Here again it is important to recognize that this is not permissible. A paraphrase in your own language and style still deserves your credit.

Most students realize they must use quotation marks when they pick up an exact sentence or two, but they may not realize that this holds true even for a simple phrase or even for a single word: if that word is significant, you should place it in quotes. It was the critic Gilbert Murray, for example, who wrote an essay called "Literature and Revelation." If you were to follow Murray in this—that is, to treat literature as "revelation" and introduce the term as such into your writing, with all the richness of meaning that accompanies it, you should credit Murray: "Another way to view literature, as Gilbert Murray has pointed out, is as 'revelation.'" (An endnote or a footnote should indicate precisely in what article Murray said this.)

Of course, you can arrive independently at an idea such as Murray's. "I just thought up that idea myself," you might say. "I wrote about literature as revelation because that's the way I saw it. I don't even know who Gilbert Murray is." The point is that you *should* know; you should know who has written on your chosen subject before you did; you should have read Murray's essay as part of a routine check of the literature in the *Essay and General Literature Index* or one of the literary bibliographies listed according to topic. After all, it stands to reason: very few ideas are totally original. The honest and conscientious writer, student and professional alike, realizes this and therefore always begins a piece of writing by searching the literature to see what has already been said on his or her projected subject. By conducting this preliminary search of the literature, you gain two advantages: you stimulate your own thinking and possibly learn something new; you also find out what has already been written. Knowing this, you will not naively present as new and original an idea that is, in fact, old and familiar (as many seemingly fresh ideas turn out to be). This does not mean that no one can write about literature as revelation because Murray has already done so. It *does* mean that anyone writing on the subject should know what Murray said at an earlier date, and go on from there.

To summarize: credit should be given in the following instances—either in an endnote or in the body of text:

1. When you directly quote someone else.
2. When you use someone else's ideas or opinions (unless they are common knowledge).
3. When you use someone else's examples.
4. When you cite statistics or other facts someone else gathered.
5. When you present evidence or testimony taken from someone else's argument.

DOCUMENTATION

Footnotes or their more convenient equivalent, in-text notes, and bibliographies provide a set procedure for crediting your sources, telling readers exactly where you obtained information on your subject. In order to simplify and standardize the process of documentation, most writers use one of two established forms, either the form in *The Chicago Manual of Style* or that in the newest 1984 *MLA* (Modern Language

Association) *Handbook*. The writer simply chooses the one that serves his or her purpose better (writers in the sciences tend toward the University of Chicago style, those in the humanities toward the MLA). You should determine which one you want to use (or are required to use) and use it consistently throughout. This book uses the latest MLA in-text style. As I pointed out in the section on plagiarism, you should document all information taken from sources; whether summarized, paraphrased, or quoted.

In-Text Notes

The MLA in-text system is very simple. You simply give the reference within parentheses immediately following the material you are quoting or referring to. You include the author's last name, an abbreviated title of the work you are documenting, and the appropriate page number. If you mention any of these items in the text, you leave them out of the reference. If you are using only one work by an author, you omit the title of the work from your reference. You will find ample examples of these parenthetical references in this book.

Notes

You may also use notes for explanations and additional comments you wish to include but that interrupt the continuity of thought in your text. You are free to develop your own style for this kind of note. We refer to these notes with consecutive superscript numbers in the text. We place the information, also numbered, either at the bottom of each page or all together at the end of the chapter or paper.

List of Works Cited

At the end of your paper you include a list of works you have cited with the author's last name first, followed by the first name, the title of the book or article, volume number (if there is one), the title of the publication (if the work cited is from a periodical), the city of publication, the publisher's name, and the date of publication. You will find such a list at the back of this book. For more detailed information about documentation, you should consult the appropriate style manual for your subject area.

EXERCISES

1. Preparing Bibliographies
   a. Prepare a bibliography of general references you would consult in order to write a short essay (500–750 words) on one of the following topics:
      Why the Taj Mahal Was Built
      A Brief History of the Alligator

Four Types of American Prisons
Carrie Nation: A Character Study
The Facts About Smoking
The Function of the Pituitary Gland
The Present Status of Pop Art
What Is Propaganda?
The Poverty Program: Then and Now
A Critical Estimate of Edward Albee

b. Prepare a bibliography of eight to twelve reference works you would consult in preparation for writing a term paper on one of the following:

1. The Case Against (or for) Capital Punishment
2. A Critical Estimate of Tennessee Williams
3. Hiroshima in Retrospect (an analysis and evaluation of causes and consequences)
4. The Lincoln and Kennedy Assassinations: A Comparative Study

2. Take notes on the following essays, treating them as if they were source materials for a paper you are writing on a related subject:

Jonathan Spence, "The Earthquake"
David Randolph, "Five Basic Elements of Music"
George Stade, "Football—The Game of Aggression"
I. Bernard Cohen, "Isaac Newton"

Organizing a Subject

*H*aving found your topic, brainstormed and gathered sufficient information, you face your next and in some ways most bedeviling challenge, *how to handle your materials*: how to sort, select, and classify categories of information; how to isolate main points and weave in supporting details; how to determine what should go where—and why. (You may have accomplished some of this in the clustering process.) Classical rhetoricians referred to this stage of the writing process as "disposition" or "arrangement," the organization of the whole into an orderly sequence of parts. Whether you organize on paper in carefully worked out detail or only roughly in your head, you must plan your paper so that it flows smoothly and logically from one point to another, moving steadily in its intended direction.

NATURAL ORDER

In examining the twenty questions that generate topics, you saw that some kinds of writing are, in a sense, self-organizing. A simple analysis, for example, breaks a subject down into its component parts or types, which are then quite naturally listed in a series (part one, part two, and so on). Similarly an analysis of a process (how something is done or made) is inevitably organized chronologically (first this, then this, then this). A description is usually arranged according to space (left to right, north to south), and narration naturally organizes itself according to time (chronological sequence, flashback, and so on). In such cases the materials determine how you should develop them. You need only recognize the imperatives of your topic and fulfill them; the piece organizes itself.

LOGICAL ORDER

This is not always the case, however. In constructing a comparison, for example (Question 6, "How does X compare to Y?"), you must make a conscious decision about its structure: Should you compare the totalities X and Y (comparison of wholes)? Should you break them down and systematically examine elements of each (comparison of parts)? Should you compare likenesses or contrast differences? The decision rests on your own logical determinations: Which ordering principle will exhibit your points in their clearest and sharpest light and best achieve your purpose?

Presenting a portrait of Isaac Newton (pages 137–40), the author organizes his materials chronologically, focusing from the beginning on Newton as a "strange, solitary figure" who seemed himself to be an embodiment of the forces of Nature that he would later study and illuminate.

Introduction: The "great powers" of Newton were recognized but their source, like that of the Nile, "had not been discovered."

I. Childhood
   A. Family background
   B. Political setting
   C. Personality

II. College and Early Career
   A. Trinity College
   B. Seeds of scientific work: the golden 18 months
      1. mathematics
      2. celestial mechanics
      3. physical optics
   C. Public recognition

III. Triumphs and Controversies
   A. Theory of light and colors
   B. Teaching at Cambridge
   C. *Principia*

IV. Declining Years
   A. Position at Warden
   B. Speculations and hypotheses

Conclusion: Quotation from Pope provides a "cyclical return" to the idea that Newton was himself a force of Nature, his special power being to illuminate Nature's Laws (though Newton, curiously, remains mysterious to the end).

In this essay, as in most exposition and all argumentation, the author orders parts in a purely logical way. The writer works out his or her own pattern of ideas—establishing causal connections, making inferences, drawing conclusions. If the reasoning process is sound, then the essay seems as inevitably ordered as the steps of a natural process.

INTUITIVE ORDER

Still another method of organizing a piece of writing is by intuition, according to an internal "voice" and rhythm that dictates how to treat a subject. What should come first, second, third? What are the proper points of view, the appropriate tone, the right word? The structure of such a piece follows the contours of the writer's musings, which may have their own natural logic. Similarly, the writer establishes the mood not with any premeditated plan, but simply by following feelings and setting them down as felt, with no conscious organization. Approached in this way, as critic Herbert Read wrote, an essay is an informal "attempt at the expression of an idea or a mood or feeling lurking unexpressed in the mind ... an attempt to create a pattern in words which shall correspond with the idea, mood or feeling" (*Modern* 66).

Read wrote further that this process is comparable to musical improvisation; it is also "the counterpart of the lyric in poetry." The writer's intimate relationship to the subject and his or her desire to explore with readers an essentially "inner experience" make an intuitive ordering of materials not only appropriate but inevitable. In such cases, as in the writing of a poem, in the act of writing itself the writer discovers what he or she wants to say.

Of course, only certain subjects and certain informal types of writing lend themselves to this approach; a term paper, for example, usually does *not* fall into this category.

GETTING STARTED

Many students complain that getting started is the most difficult job in writing. After you have used the prewriting strategies we have discussed, you will probably have a much easier time. However, the opening section is least likely to come naturally. This is an important section, however, for here the writer must capture the attention of readers. A provocative introduction that arouses curiosity or establishes the importance of the subject encourages them to read on into the body of the piece. Provided it is not a mere trick to entice readers—provided it creates an honest and appropriate expectation of what will follow—a provocative introduction may be a valid and valuable rhetorical device.

There are many types of introductions. Note that each of the following examples prepares readers for the piece by raising a central issue, making a meaningful observation, creating a mood, or defining a key term.

1. A quotation or meaningful allusion:

> "I have traveled a good deal in Concord," said the stationary pilgrim Henry Thoreau. Today his descendants move from country to country instead, some seeking wisdom, some seeking academic credit, some only fun. Indeed, a latter day Children's Crusade is upon us. No crusaders are sold into slavery, but nobody can say whether any will reach Jerusalem.
>
> —Hans Rosenhaupt, "The New Children's Crusade, or Going to Jerusalem on a Grant"

> William Congreve's opinion that hell has no fury like a woman scorned can fairly be expanded by the alteration of a word. For "woman" read "author"; the cries of exasperation from aggrieved writers come shrieking down the centuries.
>
> —Ivor Brown, "Critics and Creators"

> Pascal once remarked that the entire face of the world was changed by the shape of Cleopatra's nose. Almost two thousand years later the entire face of history was nearly changed by the shape of another nose. In the fall of 1831 the twenty-two-year-old divinity student, Charles Darwin, was about to sail as an unpaid naturalist on his Majesty's ship, the *Beagle*. But Captain Fitzroy, who commanded the *Beagle*, hesitated to take Darwin along because he judged, from the shape of Darwin's nose, that the young man had "neither the mentality nor the energy" to become a good scientist.
>
> —Henry Thomas and Dana Lee Thomas, "Charles Robert Darwin"

2. A short narration:

> Nine days before his death Immanuel Kant was visited by his physician. Old, ill and nearly blind, he rose from his chair and stood trembling with weakness and muttering unintelligible words. Finally his faithful companion realized that he would not sit down again until the visitor had taken a seat. This he did, and Kant then permitted himself to be helped to his chair and, after having regained some of his strength, said "Das Gefühl für Humanität hat mich noch nicht verlassen"—"The sense of humanity has not yet left me." The two men were moved almost to tears. For, though the word *Humanität* had come, in the eighteenth century, to mean little more than politeness or civility, it had, for Kant, a much deeper significance, which the circumstances of the moment served to emphasize: man's proud and tragic consciousness of self-approved and self-imposed principles, contrasting with his utter subjection to illness, decay and all that is implied in the word "mortality."
>
> Historically the word *humanitas* has had two clearly distinguishable meanings....
>
> —Erwin Panofsky, "The History of Art as a Humanistic Discipline"

> A young medical student at Pisa was kneeling in the Cathedral. There was silence over the vast auditory save for the annoying rattle of a chain. A sacristan had just filled a hanging oil lamp and had carelessly left it swinging in the air. The tick-tack of the swinging chain interrupted the student's prayer and started him upon a train of thought that was far removed from his devotions.
>
> Suddenly he jumped to his feet, to the amazement of the other worshipers. A flash of light had descended upon him in the rhythm of the swinging lamp. It seemed to him that this rhythm was regular, and that the pendulum of the rattling chain was taking exactly the same time in each of its oscillations although the distance of these oscillations was constantly becoming less and less.
>
> Was this evidence of his senses correct? If so, he had hit upon a miracle. He must rush home and find out immediately whether he had suffered an illusion or discovered one of the great truths of nature.
>
> When he arrived home, he hunted up two threads of the same length and attached them to two pieces of lead of the same weight. He then tied the other ends of the threads to separate nails and was ready for his experiment. He asked his godfather, Muzio Tedaldi, to help him in this experiment. "I want you to count the motions of one of the threads while I count the motions of the other."
>
> The old man shrugged his shoulders. "Another of Galileo's crazy ideas," he mumbled to himself. But he agreed to help.
>
> Galileo took the two pendulums, drew one of them to a distance of four hands' breadth and the other to a distance of two hands' breadth from the perpendicular, and then let them go simultaneously. The two men counted the oscillations of the two threads, and then compared notes. The total was exactly the same—one hundred counts in each case. The two threads, in spite of the great difference in their starting points, had arrived at the same point at the same time.
>
> And thus, in the swinging motion of the cathedral oil lamp, Galileo had discovered the rhythmic principle of nature which today is applied in the counting of the human pulse, the measurement of time on the clock, the eclipses of the sun and the movement of the stars.
>
> —Henry Thomas and Dana Lee Thomas, "Galileo Galilei"

3. A provocative question, observation, or line of dialogue:

The attitude of some citizens is like that of a mother who said to her son, "Why do you want to be a physicist, John? Isn't there enough trouble in the world already?"
—Joel H. Hildebrand, "The Care and Feeding of Creative Young Minds"

"Now tell me," said the lady, "all about yourself."
—J. B. Priestley, "All About Ourselves"

4. A definition of a key term:

"Alienation," a term once confined to philosophy, law, psychiatry and advanced literary criticism, has entered the daily vocabulary. Newspaper editorials refer without quotes or elucidation to the alienation of the slum dweller, the drug addict, the vanguard painter; popular fiction writers rely on readers to recognize the symptoms of alienation as a motive for adultery or murder. Alienage, or strangeness, is understood to be not only a condition (as of foreigners) but a process. As they say in the health drives, it can happen to anyone.
—Harold Rosenberg, "It Can Happen to Anyone"

5. A striking contrast:

Not often in the story of mankind does a man arrive on earth who is both steel and velvet, who is as hard as rock and soft as drifting fog, who holds in his heart and mind the paradox of terrible storm and peace unspeakable and perfect.

Here and there across centuries come reports of men alleged to have these contrasts. And the incomparable Abraham Lincoln, born 150 years ago this day, is an approach if not a perfect realization of this character.
—Carl Sandburg, "Lincoln, Man of Steel and Velvet"

6. A direct statement:

Where readers may be assumed to have interest in and some knowledge of the subject, writers may announce their purpose directly, with no preparation or buildup:

The film "Hiroshima, Mon Amour," which is getting a good deal of attention in this country, deserves to be viewed—and reviewed—from a number of perspectives. But I have noticed that reviewers have all tended *not* to explore its moral substance, what the vernacular would call its "message." This is remarkable when a film's message is expressed as urgently as this one's is, and even more remarkable when it is expressed with success *cinematically*, when it is perfectly fused with a web of images and sounds. Here is a film that contradicts the widely-held assumption that messages and good esthetics are incompatible.
—Amitai Etzioni, "Hiroshima in America"

It might well dismay the intelligent reader to be informed at the outset that the years 1600–60 were an age of transition. But while every period in history deserves, and doubtless has received, that illuminating label, there are some periods in which disruptive and creative forces reach maturity and combine to speed up the normal process of change. In the history of England, as in that of Europe at large, the seventeenth century is probably the most conspicuous modern example, unless we except our own age, of such acceleration.
—Douglas Bush, "The Background of the Age"

Critics permit themselves, for this or that purpose, to identify literature with great books, with imaginative writing, with expressiveness in writing, with the non-referential and non-pragmatic, with beauty in language, with order, with myth, with structured and formed discourse—the list of definitions is nearly endless—with verbal play, with uses of language that stress the medium itself, with the expression of an age, with dogma, with the *cri de coeur*, with neurosis. Now of course literature is itself and not another thing, to paraphrase Bishop Butler; yet analogies and classifications have merit. For a short space let us think of literature as sentences.

—Richard Ohmann, "Literature as Sentences"

THE WORKING OUTLINE

A practical approach to organization is apparent in such reminders as E. B. White's, "Before beginning to compose something, gauge the nature and extent of the enterprise and work from a suitable design." White's reasoning is simple and convincing:

> Design informs even the simplest structure, whether of brick and steel or of prose. You raise a pup tent from one sort of vision, a cathedral from another. This does not mean that you must sit with a blueprint always in front of you, merely that you had best anticipate what you are getting into (*Style* 63).

Journalist John Gunther also believed in anticipating "what you are getting into." Before he had written a single page of his voluminous *Inside Asia*, he had projected thirty-five chapters; he ended up with thirty-six. "It is always a good thing," he suggested, "to have a firm structure in mind." This is helpful advice, for without a structure or goal in mind, the writer resembles the harried gentleman who reportedly jumped on his horse and rode off in all directions.

Let us face a deeper truth about organization: a writer does not accomplish it, as some people think, with a strict outline that establishes once and for all the shape of the final paper. "One's plan is one thing," said Henry James, "and one's result another." As mentioned earlier, invention is an ongoing process. It spills over into the research stage and the organizing and writing stages as well. The writer continues to make discoveries. Writing itself is discovery, and the outline, to cite James again, is but "the early bloom of one's good faith." You must allow for, indeed expect, later blooms as well. In this sense, you should view the outline not as a permanent form but as a working guide, pointing the way in a given direction but amenable to change when you happen on new and better possibilities.

Keeping this in mind, let us see how you could draw up an outline for a representative term paper topic—an extended analysis of hypnosis that includes information on its function, present status, and value. Whether the paper is to be 2,000 or 10,000 words, certain inevitable categories suggest themselves:

1. definition (What constitutes the hypnotic state?)
2. history (the phenomenon of hypnosis as observed through the centuries)
3. hypnotic technique
4. hypnotic behavior

5. uses of hypnotism (medicine, dentistry, psychotheraphy)
6. abuses and dangers of hypnotism (unqualified hypnotists)
7. autohypnosis
8. individual susceptibility to hypnosis
9. recent experimental evidence
10. posthypnotic suggestion
11. misconceptions about hypnosis
12. current scientific opinion of hypnosis

Certainly these twelve categories are useful during the note-taking stage when you group your information under specific headings. Later on, however, when you organize your material, you will undoubtedly find twelve categories unwieldy and repetitious. Thus you have to condense the categories into three or four main headings under which you list various subheadings. Thus the working outline may look something like this:

Tentative title: "What Is Hypnotism? or The Continuing Mystery of Hypnosis"

Thesis statement or "Headnote":   Hypnotism, a subject that has intrigued people for centuries and that remains mysterious despite the probings of modern science, has many uses in modern medicine and psychotherapy.

  I. What hypnotism is (brief description of psychological and physiological state)

 II. History
     A. Ancient observations, superstitions
     B. Eighteenth and nineteenth centuries: beginning of scientific study (Mesmer, Charcot)

III. Hypnotism today: what we know
     A. The hypnotic trance
        1. How induced
           a. Classical techniques (gazing at fixed object)
           b. Drugs (sodium pentothal)
           c. Autohypnosis
        2. How subject reacts (*cite examples*)
           a. Hypnotic anaesthesia (insensitivity to pain)
           b. Hallucinations
           c. Age regression
           d. Unusual muscular strength and rigidity
           e. Organic effects (blisters)
           f. Social behavior
        3. Posthypnotic suggestions
     B. Hypnotic subjects
        1. Variations in individual susceptibility
        2. Variations in "how far" people go under hypnosis
           a. Antisocial acts (crime)
           b. Destructive acts

    C. Uses of hypnotism
        1. Medicine (*weave in evidence from recent scientific studies*)
        2. Dentistry
        3. Psychotherapy (*cite examples*)
    D. Abuses and possible dangers (*weave in stories to illustrate*)
        1. Hypnotism as "entertainment"
        2. Unqualified hypnotists (unable to awaken subject)

Conclusion: Summary of significance of hypnotism; speculation on possible future applications

A working outline helps you to channel your ideas as you write and gives you a chance to check beforehand on their logical progression. Does section three logically follow section two, or should you reverse the order? Should you transfer part of the introduction to the conclusion? Is the first part of the middle section too long in comparison to the second part? And so on. By studying the outline carefully, much as an architect studies a blueprint, you can see whether the structure is likely to hold together: whether you have related the parts clearly and consistently and whether you have developed them soundly and strategically, each in its proper proportion. By checking and improving a paper in the outline stage you can save yourself hours of reworking and rewriting later on.

ENDING THE PAPER

At one point in her adventures in Wonderland, Alice is advised to "begin at the beginning, keep going until you get to the end, and then stop." In some cases it is possible for you to do exactly the same thing: to stop when you have finished saying what you want to say. Your piece (especially if it is a short paper) ends where your last thought ends, creating its own sense of completeness and finality. However, usually a long paper needs a formal conclusion of some kind: a recapitulation of the main points; a heightened restatement of the thesis or argument (what the ancients called a "peroration"); a summing-up quotation; a reference to an idea or event mentioned earlier. Any one of these devices (and there are many other suitable equivalents) signals readers that the piece is coming to an end: *Pay close attention; here are my final words on the subject.*

Unquestionably the end is an emphatic position, for the final words impress themselves more forcibly on readers' minds than any others. Similarly, the mood at the end of a piece strongly influences and may even determine readers' final feeling about what they have read.

Since there are no standard endings, you must depend on your own judgment in ending your paper. You must compose a conclusion that is appropriate to the subject and purpose of your piece. One helpful procedure is to set aside, at an early stage of research or writing, some information or a passage of quoted material that might serve as a concluding statement. This ending should not open up a whole new aspect of the subject (it is too late for that), nor should it raise additional questions that you cannot answer. Rather, the ending should tie the paper together so that readers experience a sense of closure where the unit of discourse has reached a logical conclusion and the end *feels* like the end.

EXERCISES

1. Indicate in outline form the structure of the following essays:
   Bruce Catton, "Grant and Lee" (page 360)
   A. M. Rosenthal, "No News from Auschwitz" (page 274)
   George Stade, "Football—the Game of Aggression" (page 384)
   Allen H. Gilbert, "College Lectures Are Obsolete" (page 419)
   I. Bernard Cohen, "Isaac Newton" (page 137)

2. Evaluate the opening and closing paragraphs of the above essays. What special devices for opening and closing are used? Are they effective? Can you suggest alternate opening and closing paragraphs that would be equally, or perhaps even more, effective?

FORCES FOR WRITING

As the writer passes through the many states of thinking, prewriting—freewriting, clustering, reading, researching, talking to people and establishing an audience, and then researching and organizing—pressures begin building to get a first draft down on paper, "to get black on white" as de Maupassant put it. According to writer-researcher Donald M. Murray (375–81), these pressures act as positive, often urgent "forces for writing." (Only one force is negative, the universal Law of Delay, familiar to every writer who has ever sharpened a pencil three times before finally getting down to work).

The four positive forces Murray describes are well known to professional writers. The first arises from the increasing information writers collect on their subjects. At some point the "urge to impart" this information, to share it with others, makes itself felt. The writer then feels the urge to start writing. A second impetus reinforces this first impulse: The writer feels increasingly committed to the subject. For the more you know about something, the more interested and involved you become, the more eager you will be to convey it accurately and clearly to those who are not yet informed or committed. Winston Churchill explained that the forces for writing could build to such strength that they could sweep the writer away in the current. "Writing a book was an adventure," he said. "To begin with it was a toy, an amusement. Then it became a mistress, and then a master. And then a tyrant" (Charlton, *Companion* 37).

And, as you have already learned, the third force moving the writer—particularly the professional writer—is the sense of a waiting audience, of readers "out there" who will respond in various ways to the finished piece. That these responses will be largely favorable and sympathetic is, of course, the chief fantasy: that readers will smile at amusing passages; that they will glower with indignation or feel appropriate alarm or suitable conviction, as the subject matter and the writer's handling of it dictate. If a good reader is to become one with the writer, as Virginia Woolf advises, then the good writer at this stage must try to become one with the readers, anticipating their support, sparing them possible disappointments.

In place of a large audience, the student can look forward to a single reader—the instructor, plus a group of classmates in the workshop situation. Surprisingly, this audience may provide comparable and sufficient stimulation and challenge. Will the instructor respond as expected and desired? How will the class react? Curiosity itself urges the writer to complete the piece and to find out how the members of the audience will receive it. What will *they* think?

The final force for writing is the impending deadline, coming closer with each passing day. Would anyone ever complete a piece of writing without benefit of deadline? Possibly not. Only a firm deadline enables the writer to overcome a natural tendency to take more time and still more time—especially when a writing assignment is not moving as smoothly as expected. The deadline sets limits to fuming and fussing and making the kind of last-minute changes that can go on endlessly. What a critic once said of a work of art—that it is never finished but abandoned—applies as well to many kinds of efforts. After doing *just so much*, writers must end the task, even if they are not "finished" in the deepest and most satisfying sense. They must just quit.

REWRITING: A CASE STUDY OF FOUR DRAFTS

At the other end of the spectrum, there are writers—generally beginning writers—who quit too soon, as in the following example of a student effort that was clearly all too effortless. Applying to medical school, the student submitted the following reply to the question: "What are your reasons for wanting to become a doctor?"

> Becoming a doctor is by no means a recent notion, it is a goal which has lingered with me since high school. I am not interested in going into a field of research or teaching, although I am quite aware that without these professions, medicine would not have progressed much from Hippocrates' time. My purpose for obtaining an M.D. is to go into the practice of medicine. To treat patients with the best equipment at my disposal and to establish a personal patient-physician relationship. To me being a doctor is not a five day a week job, one's work is not completed after office hours. A good doctor will be available when he is needed. I want to become a doctor so I can instill a feeling of security and trust in my patients and to convey to them that a doctor can be more than just one who prescribes medication. He can be someone to trust and turn to in time of crisis—a healer in the broadest sense of the word.
>
> A doctor holds an admirable position in today's society and being a physician offers security for the future. There is no worry about having a job for next year or that a bad winter will cause financial difficulties. I am certainly looking forward to having a family some day and expect to send my children through school. As a doctor I would be assured the ability to send my children through school and establish a happy life for my family.
> —Student application to medical school

What is wrong with this statement? Since this is a case study, let's trace its history step by step.

Background

While reviewing the professional school applications of graduating seniors at this college—to make sure all questions had been answered, all necessary information provided—an alert counselor in the counseling center spotted this "embarrassment" as she called it. Turning it over to members of the English Department, she attached the following note: "Putting this student's worst enemy on the Admissions Committee could not do more damage to his chances than this carelessly tossed off essay on why he wants to be doctor. The student is far from stupid and he does have something to say, no question. Buy why must he say it so poorly? Couldn't he have taken the time to reread and rewrite so that sentence errors could be corrected, and the ideas developed more fully?"

I agreed that this student's writing did not do justice to his application (to say the least); that it did not reflect his academic ability or his own best thinking; and that his problem, as I see it, was in submitting hastily scribbled notes on his subject rather than a carefully worked over, properly revised, and polished final draft. Clearly, the statement had potential which the student could (and ultimately *would*) fulfill once he settled down to work. For curiously, this student *was* a worker who had earned straight A's in his science courses. "Well," he explained, "I really *work* at those."

"Fine," a member of the English Department told him. "Now let's see you *work* at your writing." The instructor implemented the suggestion with a quotation from Sinclair Lewis which all students (and many professionals) should tack up on their bulletin boards:

> Writing is just work—there's no secret.
> If you dictate or use a pen or type or write with your toes—it is still just work.

With a new no-nonsense approach, then, and with the instructor's help, this student finally went to work. Step number one was to review his writing situation.

Review of Writing Situation

As I indicated earlier, every writer needs to consider at the outset the specific context out of which a piece of writing originates. Thus this student needed to answer for himself the four crucial questions which define every writing situation:

1. *What is my identity as writer?*
   The answer is very clear: He is a graduating college senior aspiring to enter medical school.

2. *Who are my readers?*
   Here again the answer is clear: The readers are members of the medical school Board of Admissions. As doctors of high position and distinction, they review applications and make judgments as to who should be accepted, who rejected.

3. *What is the occasion?*
   Still no ambiguity here: The student is "making his case" before the board, submitting his credentials, his "argument" in his own behalf.

4. *What is my purpose?*
   A form of that most common writing purpose—winning assent guides him; in this case, he wants to convince the medical board to admit him to the medical school.

Critical Analysis: Content/Organization/Style/Mechanics

With this clear picture of the writing situation—a situation which involved the writer's entire future—the instructor had no difficulty deciding that this student needed to do considerable revision. In preparation, the instructor tried to help him come to a better understanding of what he himself had written, to see more clearly and judge more critically the implications and ramifications of certain statements he had made. He would have to examine his own ideas more seriously, more attentively, more respectfully.

Under the heading of *Content*, the instructor asked the student to reread and reevaluate the points he had presented: Had he made the best selection? Had he explored his answer, first from one angle, then from another? Most important, had he meant what he said, said what he meant? Had he tapped deep and honest levels of thought and feeling within himself? Had he dealt with these clearly and convincingly? The instructor called attention to certain jarring aspects of his statement, such as the seeming contradiction between idealistic motives ("to be a healer") and materialistic motives ("security for the future"). Did he realize that he had slipped in a self-serving reason at the end? Was it, in fact, a "slip?" Or had he consciously decided to be completely candid? If so, was such candor appropriate? Was it strategic? Would it help or hinder his purpose?

Organization: Had the student paid careful attention to every detail of organization, the kind of attention to detail required in all aspects of medical study and practice? On the contrary, the student seems to have set down the piece haphazardly—idea following idea, as they flashed into his mind. This procedure, appropriate to freewriting and prewriting warm-ups, cannot produce a final draft suitable for submission to an official admissions committee. The occasion clearly required a more carefully worked out organization which reflected the writer's ability to shape his materials methodically and to speak in a tone of voice that was neither stiff and formal nor overly familiar.

Specifically, the instructor suggested that the student examine samples of Christensen's "coordinate sequence" as one possible organizational pattern (see pages 121–23; see also Question 13, "What are the causes of X?").

Style: A first editing showed that in addition to poor organization, problems included poor word choice, broken parallelism, and shifts in tone (see edited copy which follows). Here again, the problems create a damaging impression of the writer's character and personality since they suggest carelessness, imprecision, and failure to pay attention to details ("Ah, if that's the way he writes, will he diagnose and treat patients in the same nonchalant, offhand manner?")

Concern for coherence (sticking together) raises the question of transitions. In this case a graceful transition could not only resolve the seeming contradiction between idealism and materialism within the essay but could also show that both motives are legitimate: To serve others and to serve oneself may be shown as consistent with reason, good will, and human nature. Such a resolution even reflects a healthy attitude toward the profession. For no one today, not even the poets, would say that starving in an attic serves any useful or "purifying" purpose. Thus, the applicant who stressed *only* the idealistic and altruistic aspects of medicine might be dismissed as patently insincere, "too good to be true." *What* the student has said about promoting his own interests (content) is acceptable then; *how* the student has said it (style) is not acceptable.

Mechanics: To the student's credit, this essay contains no spelling errors, no grammatical violations. Punctuation is a problem, however, as is basic sentence construction.

In summary, you can see that the medical school applicant would have saved himself time and anxiety if he had treated his assignment—from the beginning—in terms of a process, a series of steps, beginning with freewriting and brainstorming to generate ideas and prod his memory. This exploratory and generating stage would have ended in a rough draft which he could have shown to friends or classmates, a trusted instructor, someone competent and interested who could have provided helpful comments and corrections where necessary. On the basis of responses from others and continued thinking and studying of the first draft, a second and third draft might be in order, incorporating the writer's best thoughts and soundest advice. Yes, this is a tedious process, one that is familiar to all professional writers. In fact, it almost defines the writer, for as novelist John Hersey has pointed out, "To be a writer is to throw away a great deal, not to be satisfied, to type again, and then again, and once more, and over and over...."

Since the future career of the medical school applicant depended to a considerable extent on how successfully he projected himself in his written application, he would have been wise to emulate the painstaking role of writer, for his reward was no less than "winning assent" to his application—getting into medical school.

Draft Number One: With corrections and editorial comments[1]

[Handwritten annotations surround the typed text below:]

deadwood

Isn't this word too casual?

Becoming a doctor is by no means a recent notion, it is a goal which

comma splice

has lingered with me since high

gap in thought here: a big leap from one aspect of the subject to another.

school. I am not interested in going into a field of research or teaching, although I am quite aware that without these professions, medicine would not have progressed much from Hippocrates' time. My purpose for obtaining an M.D. is to go into the practice of medicine.

Is this a word? Does a serious goal "linger" or does a melody "linger", a memory "linger"?

---

[1] Criticism of content and organization (as described in this draft) was discussed with the student during a private conference.

Is this a full sentence or a fragment?

To treat patients with the best equipment at my disposal and to establish a personal patient-physician relationship. To me being a doctor is not a five day a week job, one's work is not completed after office hours. A good doctor will be available when he is needed. I want

comma splice: use ⊙ ⊙ or ⊙

wordy, repetitious—unnecessary shift in structure: broken parallelism

to become a doctor so I can instill a feeling of security and trust in my patients and to convey to them that a doctor can be more than just one who prescribes medication. He can be someone to trust and turn to in times of crisis--a healer in the broadest sense of the word.

This is not badly stated, but then it is dropped!

A doctor holds an admirable position in today's society and being a physician offers security for the future. There is no worry about having a job for next year or

transition needed to bridge gap between these two points

broken parallelism

that a bad winter will cause financial difficulties. I am certainly looking forward to having a family some day and expect to send my children through school. As a doctor I would be assured the ability to send my children through school and establish a happy life for my family.

diffusely stated; not in tone

--Student application
to medical school

Draft Number Two: An improved version of Draft Number One follows. The organization is now somewhat tighter and no longer slipshod. The statement now lends itself to more intricate editing, deeper analysis of how the student has positioned ideas and how—in the interest of logic and grace—he or she might reposition these ideas more effectively. At this point the instructor could make still other editorial observations about possible redundancies, transitions, and the appropriateness of particular words. Draft Number Two incorporates changes suggested on the first draft. The retyped draft can be edited again and further suggestions made for improvement:

Becoming a doctor is not a new
idea for me; but a dream I have had
since high school. My (focus) is not
research or teaching (although without those professions, medicine
would not have progressed beyond ___
Hippocrates) but the actual practice
of medicine.

My interest in becoming an M.D.
is twofold. First, I want the
opportunity to treat patients with
the best equipment and (knowledge) at
my disposal and [to establish a
personal patient-physician relationship.] To really offer the patient
the best care, I feel that the
practice of medicine is a twenty-four
hour a day job. The dedicated
physician must be available when he
is needed. I want to [instill a
feeling of security and trust in my
patients,] assuring them that my concern goes beyond simply prescribing

Handwritten margin notes:

Is "focus" the word you want?

No - you need "time" - or something!

nicely stated

Do you treat people with "knowledge"? What you say here shows promise - but have you ordered your statements properly? Think about some reorganizing

Don't these two points belong together?

medicine. ✓ I want to be a healer in
the broadest sense; someone to turn
to in time of crisis; concerned with
the spirit as well as the body.

Transition term: "In summary" perhaps?

well said here - a good point

My second interest is less
idealistic and more practical. Being
a physician offers two <u>attractive</u>
<u>rewards</u>; social prestige and financial
security. A doctor need not worry
about being out of work if the crops
fail or the recession worsens.
Therefore, he can relax <u>in his</u>
<u>ability</u> to provide for his family.

redundant?

Does one relax "in an ability"?

For me, the opportunity to study
medicine is the opportunity to
fulfill my dream of the past and
work toward my dream of the future.

excellent ending

Draft Number Three incorporates the additional suggestions made on Draft Number Two. What emerges here is a much improved version, almost ready to submit except for a few fine points of polishing and still further probing of motives: Has the student resolved his apparent confusion?

For me, becoming a doctor is
not a new idea, but a dream I have
had since high school. Although I
respect research and teaching (for
without these professions there
would have been no progress since
the time of Hippocrates) my special
interest is in the actual day-by-day
practice of medicine.

Comma not needed

Basically I have two goals.
First ~~of all~~, I want to be a really
dedicated doctor: I want to offer
my patients the best care I can give
them, even if it means working
twenty-four hours a day. I want to
establish the kind of personal
patient-physician relationship that
will instill a feeling of security
and trust in my patients. They will
know that my concern goes beyond
simply prescribing medication. For
I will always <u>endeavor</u> to treat   *try?*
them with the best equipment avail-
able and keep up to date with
medical findings. In essence, I
want to be a healer in the broadest

note
punctuation sense;⊙someone to turn to in time of
                          someone
crisis; ∧concerned with the spirit   *parallelism*
        ⊙
as well as the body.

My second goal is less ideal-   *Are you*
istic and <u>more practical</u>. Being a   *suggesting*
                                           that it is
physician offers two additional   *impractical to*
rewards that appeal to me: social   *be idealistic?*
position and financial security. A   *Are they*
doctor need not worry about being   *necessarily*
                                        opposed to
out of work if the crops fail or the   *one another?*
recession worsens. Therefore, he   *I'd like to*
                          s   *see you*
~~can relax and~~ know∧that he will   *think this*
always be able to provide for his   *through*
                                        still further.

family, ~~to~~ give his children a good
education and a good life.

    I feel that the opportunity to
study medicine is the opportunity to
fulfill my dream of the past and to
work toward my dream of the future.

Draft Number Four is ready for submission.

    For me, becoming a doctor is not a new idea but a
dream I have had since high school. Although I respect
research and teaching (without these professions there
would have been no progress since the time of
Hippocrates), my special interest is the actual
day-by-day practice of medicine.
    Basically I have two goals. First, I want to be a
really dedicated doctor. I want to offer my patients
the best care I can give them, even if it means working
twenty-four hours a day. I want to establish the kind
of personal patient-physician relationship that will
instill a feeling of security and trust in my patients.
They will know that my concern goes beyond simply
prescribing medicine. For I will always try to treat
them with the best equipment available and to keep
up-to-date with medical findings. In essence, I want to
be a healer in the broadest sense: someone to turn to
in times of crisis, someone concerned with the spirit as
well as the body.
    My second goal is admittedly more selfish. Being a
physician offers two additional rewards that appeal to
me: social position and financial security. I feel
that doctors earn their social position because it grows
out of the respect people have for their many years of
training and their medical skills. Financial security--
or at least freedom from anxiety about earning a living
or holding a job--seems to be an imperative if a doctor
is to do good work. Even if the crops fail or the
recession worsens, he will go on practicing medicine; he
knows he'll also be able to provide for his family, give
his children a good education and a good life.
    As I see it, the study of medicine will give me the
opportunity to fulfill my dream of the past and to work
toward my dream of the future.

EXERCISES

1. In your own words, describe the progression from drafts number one to four. Evaluate the quality of change in each one.

2. Using the prewriting steps you have learned, write a one-page essay of your own in which you explain to a graduate or professional school of your choice why you want to enter a particular discipline or field. Seek editorial response and assistance and incorporate suggestions into successive drafts (as many as you find necessary).

GENERATING FURTHER IDEAS

Asking Subquestions

Once you have identified your audience or have some sense of who your readers are, you can begin to explore your subject still further, focusing now on more tangible criteria. What do you know about your subject that would interest your readers? Do you have any special or specific ideas that are particularly suitable? The popular TV essayist, Andy Rooney, has pointed out that "our brains have a way of jumping around a lot, thinking of one thing for a few seconds and then flitting off to think of another." Very true. Unless you make a deliberate and determined effort to focus your mind on a given subject and make an orderly exploration of its many aspects, first from one point of view, then from another, you will have trouble moving ahead toward a finished piece.

How apt, then, that Rooney would indicate further that "for me as a writer, it's always been fun to see if I could stop one subject in my head long enough to take a good look at it." *To stop a subject in one's head in order to take a good look at it:* this is precisely what he does in the following essay. It is characteristic of Rooney, a kind of Everyman to his large TV following, that he has chosen a familiar subject, something we see around us every day. "I was thinking about fences," he says very simply. Note how he proceeds from there, generating ideas as he goes along by answering a series of questions on his announced topic.

Because the questioning procedure is as helpful in generating subject matter as it is in finding a subject, you should concentrate on this phase of prewriting, asking many subquestions as you move along. The best sets of questions will be those you devise yourself, using the twenty questions as points of departure for further questions. Use the twenty questions as basic probes which lead to further probing and more precise analysis.

Fences

Andy Rooney

What kind of fences are there? How many? What size? What are the differences between fences? What purposes	Our brains have a way of jumping around a lot, thinking of one thing for a few seconds and then flitting off to think of another. For me as a writer, it's always been fun to see if I could stop one subject in my head for long enough to take a good look at it.

do fences serve? To whom are fences helpful? Any examples? Why are fences built? Where are fences built? Usually? Sometimes? Is it ever hard to tell how a fence is functioning? What is confusing? What do you suspect? What personal response do certain fences elicit? Why? Which fences are most beautiful? What can they be compared to? What makes them beautiful? Which fences are ugliest? What are they made of? Which fences do the best job? What is a "minimal" fence? What message do fences send? How would you define a fence? How does it compare to similar structures such as a wall? A barrier? What adds to the confusion? In what sense are fences like people? What are the types of fences? How do they differ? Do they generate special attitudes or feelings? In what ways? How do people react to fences? What are some of the perils of being a fence? Do fences influence other fences? In what ways? What do people want of fences? What final response do you have toward fences? What is the future of fences? How do fences influence the world? What would happen if all fences disappeared?

For instance, I was thinking about fences. There are as many kinds of fences in this country as there are people. You couldn't *count* all the kinds of fences there are. There are big fences, small fences, teeny-tiny fences.

The biggest difference between one fence and another fence is whether the fence was built to protect what's inside from what's outside or to protect what's outside from what's inside. To protect the people outside, for instance, a mean dog has to be fenced in.

It's a mystery why some fences are ever built at all. Most cemeteries have fences, even though no one outside really wants to get in and no one inside ever tries to get out.

Sometimes you can't tell what a fence is keeping in—or keeping out. You can't tell what a fence is protecting from what. You suspect that sometimes people just put up fences from habit, or as a show of strength or wealth. I hate anyone who has a fence that cost more than my house cost.

The best-looking fences are often the simplest. A simple fence around a beautiful home can be like a frame around a picture. The house isn't hidden; its beauty is enhanced by the frame. But a fence can be a massive, ugly thing, too, made of bricks and mortar. Sometimes the insignificant little fences do their job just as well as the ten-foot walls. Maybe it's only a string stretched between here and there in a field. The message is clear: don't cross here.

There's often a question about whether a barrier is a fence or a wall. Fences, I think, are thinner than walls. And, of course, there are people who confuse us further by building fences on top of walls.

Every fence has its own personality and some don't have much. There are friendly fences. A friendly fence takes kindly to being leaned on. There are friendly fences around playgrounds. And some playground fences are more fun to play on than anything they surround. There are more mean fences than friendly fences overall, though. Some have their own built-in invitation not to be sat upon. Unfriendly fences get it right back sometimes. You seldom see one that hasn't been hit, bashed, bumped or in some way broken or knocked down.

One of the phenomena of fences is their tendency to proliferate. Note, if you will, how often one fence brings on another fence. People often seem to want their own fence, even if it's back to back, cheek by jowl with the neighbor's fence, almost as though the fence was put up to keep the fence out.

The other thing I thought about fences: I thought maybe the world wouldn't be very much changed if tomorrow morning ... every fence was gone.

BURKE'S PENTAD

Someone observed that the best questioning procedure " .... will have all of the elegant simplicity of a profound mathematical formula." Certainly the "Pentad" composed by Kenneth Burke meets that description. It consists of five key questions we must apply to any dramatic event as we attempt to describe it, analyze motives of characters, action, and so on.

1) What was done?	(the *act*; that which took place in thought or deed)
2) When or where was it done?	(the *scene*; the background of the act, the situation in which it occurred)
3) Who did it?	(the *agent*; the person or kind of person who performed the act)
4) How was it done?	(the *agency*; what means or instrument was used)
5) Why was it done?	(the *purpose*)

According to Burke (xvii) the Pentad reflects the absolute bare and indispensable minimum of any dramatic event. For as he explains:

> Men may violently disagree about the purposes behind a given act, or about the character of the person who did it, or how he did it, or in what kind of situation he acted; or they may even insist upon totally different words to name the act itself. But be that as it may, any complete statement about motives will offer some kind of answers to these five questions: what was done (act), when or where it was done (scene), who did it (agent), how he did it (agency) and why (purpose).

As we shall see in Question 2 (How did X happen?), these five questions can help student writers make their way confidently through the several stages of telling a story.

EXERCISES

1. Read the following essays carefully and reconstruct the subquestions that lie behind the data presented and that you may infer from it (as in Rooney's essay on "Fences"):
   a. "Uncle Bun" (page 183)
   b. "A Social Evening with the Woolfs" (page 206)
   c. "The Postcard: Count Your Miseries" (page 275)
   d. "College Lectures Are Obsolete" (page 419)

2. *Burke's Pentad*
   Read the essay "A Hanging," in Question 2, "How did X happen?" (pages 159–76) indicate how the writer has dealt with the questions contained in Burke's Pentad.

Part Two

WRITING PARAGRAPHS

The Paragraph as a Cage of Form

Applying Principles of Good Paragraphing

The Paragraph as a Cage of Form

AN OVERVIEW

When I talk about writing the paragraph, I am talking about the actual at-the-desk, ⸱word-by-word, sentence-by-sentence writing situation. How can you commit your ideas to paper, capture them, as Archibald MacLeish said, in a "cage of form"? MacLeish's image refers to poetry, but it applies equally to the paragraph. For in the paragraph—the major message unit of the piece—you unfold your ideas, one by one, as your mind dictates and your pen flows once you have used your prewriting techniques.

In this sense we write in paragraphs. True, the writing process proceeds sentence by sentence, but we never write a sentence in isolation; we write within the context of the paragraph. Certainly we think in paragraphs, or units of thought that we block out as we write, indenting every so often when it seems "time" to do so. Interestingly, this intuitive approach works well, for studies have shown that most people instinctively begin a new paragraph at the right place: where there is a change or turn of thought, a shift from one phase of the subject to another.

In its basic function, the paragraph is both a convenience and a convention. Visually it breaks up a solid mass of print that would otherwise tire readers' eyes and tax their patience.

The paragraph is a logical and rhetorical unit as well as a mechanical structure. Marjorie Boulton describes the paragraph as "a small group of thoughts that hang together" (*Prose* 41). Although part of a larger whole, they generally constitute a self-contained unit that makes sense by itself. Each paragraph or series of paragraphs marks a stage in the development of the writer's thought. Thus we can justify each paragraph in a well-written essay as such: The writer made it a paragraph because it is a meaningful unit of the total discourse. Paragraph indentations, then, help readers by indicating the organization and development of the writer's thought as it moves from one aspect of the subject to another.

PARAGRAPH DIVISION

Many paragraphs dictate their own boundaries, especially if the writer is working from an outline. In a short paper each heading often turns out to be one or two paragraphs; in a longer paper the subheadings frequently constitute or at least suggest paragraph divisions. Of course the topic itself generally determines paragraph breaks. In fact it is a common and generally wise practice to open a paragraph with a *topic sentence*— such a sentence announces the main or base idea on which the writer constructs the entire paragraph, the idea that determines what belongs and what does not belong in the paragraph. Both writer and reader benefit from topic sentences, for they keep the discourse moving in a single, logical line of development.

In the short essay that follows, note that the first sentence is, in fact, an introductory (topic) paragraph listing the three elements that will make up the whole; the writer then embodies each of these elements in a topic sentence of its own, serving as a base for further amplification and illustration within the paragraph. The essay ends with a fifth paragraph containing a summing-up statement.

Studying Music in India

Ravi Shankar

Guru, vinaya, sadhana—these three words form the heart of the musical tradition of India.

Guru, as many people now know, means master, spiritual teacher, or preceptor. We give a very important place to the *guru,* for we consider him to be the representation of the divine. There is a saying—

> Pani piye chhanke
> Guru banaye janke

—which means that one should drink water only after it has been filtered, and one should take a *guru* only after one feels sure of the decision. The choice of the *guru,* to us, is even more important than choosing a husband or a wife. A potential disciple cannot make a hasty decision to take just any teacher as his *guru,* nor should he break the bond between *guru* and *shishya,* once the *ganda* or *nara* ceremony, the initiation, which symbolically binds the two together for life, has taken place.

Vinaya means humility; it is the complete surrendering of the self on the part of the *shishya* to the *guru.* The ideal disciple feels love, adoration, reverence, and even fear toward his *guru,* and he accepts equally praise or scoldings. Talent, sincerity, and the willingness to practice faithfully are essential qualities of the serious student. The *guru,* as the giver in this relationship, seems to be all-powerful. Often, he may be unreasonable, harsh, or haughty, though the ideal *guru* is none of these. Ideally, he should respond to the efforts of the disciple and love him almost as his own child. In India, a Hindu child, from his earliest years, is taught to feel humble toward anyone older than he or superior in any way. From the simplest gesture of the *namaskar,* or greeting (putting the hands palm to palm in front of the forehead and bowing), or the *pranam* (a respectful greeting consisting of touching the greeted person's feet, then one's own eyes and forehead with the hands held palm to palm) to the practice of *vinaya* or humility tempered with a feeling of love and worship, the Hindu devotee's vanity and pretension are worn away....

The third principal term associated with our music is *sadhana,* which means practice and discipline, eventually leading to self-realization. It means practicing with a fanatic zeal and ardent dedication to the *guru* and the music. If the student is talented, sincere, faithful to his *guru* and devoted in his practicing, and if the *guru* is teaching with utmost dedication and not being miserly with his knowledge, there is a distinct pattern for learning Indian music. The student must begin by acquiring the most basic techniques of the voice or instrument. In vocal music, this skill is achieved by assiduously practicing first one note, trying to produce correct breathing, voice, and pitch control. Students both of vocal and of instrumental music then learn scales and *paltas* (also called *alankars*). *Paltas* are short melodic figures performed in sequential order with a scale and *tala* framework in different tempi. Then, the *sargams* must be learned—the various fixed compositions sung to the note-names. In some fixed compositions *talas* and tempi can be varied, and in others no *tala* is used at all. The student also learns various other fixed compositions called *bandishes*, which include songs in different styles sung to a meaningful text, slow or fast instrumental pieces (*gats*), or some melodic phrases in a variety of melodic motions and tempi (*tans*).

This elementary training, for a talented and persevering student, should last not less than five years, very much like the elementary training for any Western musical discipline. This means the student should practice every day for at least eight hours .... Starting from the very beginning, I would estimate that it requires at least twenty years of constant work and practice to reach maturity and a high standard of achievement in our classical music.

Paragraphing does not always correspond so neatly to joints in the structure of thought, for in addition to logic many considerations enter into the division of prose into paragraphs. Indeed, "thought movement itself," as rhetorician Paul C. Rodgers has pointed out, "submits to very flexible partitioning; hence the size of a given logical paragraph frequently reflects secondary influences" (cited in *Composition*, 5). The narrow-column format of a newspaper, for example, and readers' demand that they be able to skim the page and get the news almost at a glance, require short, varied paragraphs. (They should all be short but not *equally* short.) Normally, however, you should not fragment your ideas by chopping them up into a series of consistently short paragraph units. We can see immediately that a typewritten page containing four or more paragraphs needs reworking: The writer either has not developed his or her ideas sufficiently or has failed to respect their unity and flow.

Strictly formal considerations may also enter into paragraph division, "as when paragraphs are paired off for contrast or comparison or knit into some larger pattern involving paragraphs as units" (Rogers 5).

Similarly, you may set off a paragraph for a particular purpose: as an introduction, a conclusion, or a transition from one aspect of thought to another. Such paragraphs may contain only one or two sentences, but they nonetheless deserve to stand alone.

Finally, we must consider emphasis, rhythm, and tone. A short paragraph, for example, isolates a piece of information and thereby stresses it; it may also contribute to the rhythmic sweep of your essay and the particular tone you hope to establish. A philosophic essay may contain relatively long, detailed paragraphs that reinforce the unity, flow, and continuity of thought. A light essay may embody its scattered and tentative ideas in shorter, less formally structured paragraphs. As always, you must consider not only your subject but your readers as well. Will a demandingly long and bulky paragraph discourage them? If so, you may want to divide a normal unit of thought into two units—that is, to develop one topic sentence over two paragraphs. The writer of the following narrative has done this to increase readability:

In any journey there are three separate and recognizable stages. First there is the setting-out, the more-or-less anxious business of organizing the expedition and getting it off complete and on time. Then there is the journey itself, with its satisfying sense of achievement in each mile travelled. This is the most peaceful stage for the travellers, since we hand ourselves over as so much baggage to be passively transported. Even in a motor-car which we drive ourselves we are only a part of the steering-wheel: we have only to propel the car; and even driving across London in the rush hour is wonderfully soothing, for instance, compared with getting a family off on summer holiday.

The third stage of the journey is less definite and more variable. It begins imperceptibly as we near the end, and we recognize the transition by a growing impatience to arrive. We are no longer travelling, but impatiently covering the distance which still separates us from where we want to be. However it is not the number of miles remaining which decides our impatience: it is their proportion of the whole. On a journey of a hundred miles, at forty-nine we are still placid travellers.

—Nan Fairbrother, *The House in the Country*

THE PARAGRAPH AS MINIATURE ESSAY

One helpful way to study paragraphs—and to gain practice in writing them—is to view them as miniature essays. Often writers can expand the well-organized paragraph to an essay, just as they can reduce the well-organized essay to a paragraph.

Let us take a second, closer look at the Ravi Shankar essay. Its impeccable organization and clean paragraph divisions enable us to see the expansion-compression process at work. As I have already noted, the introductory paragraph provides a one-sentence summary of the entire piece, a "thesis statement," as it is sometimes called:

> *Guru, vinaya, sadhana*—these three words form the heart of the musical tradition of India.

Obviously this introduction gives us the kernel idea, or *thesis*, which the writer will develop throughout the rest of the essay. Standing alone, for emphasis, this one-sentence paragraph might easily be expanded into a self-contained longer paragraph. Below is this hypothetical paragraph—an expanded form of the introductory sentence and a compressed form, as you will see, of the essay as a whole:

Topic sentence	*Guru, vinaya, sadhana*—these three words form the heart of the musical tradition of India. Guru, as many people now know, means master, spiritual teacher, or preceptor. We give a very important place to the *guru,* for we consider him to be the representative of the divine. *Vinaya* means humility; it is the complete surrendering of the self on the part of the disciple or *shishya* to the *guru*. The ideal disciple feels love, adoration, reverence, and even fear toward his *guru*. The third principal term associated with our music is *sadhana*, which means practice and discipline, eventually leading to self-realization. It means practicing with a fanatic zeal and ardent dedication to the *guru* and to the music. Starting from the very beginning, it requires at least twenty years of constant work and practice to reach maturity and a high standard of achievement in our classical music.
Developing details	
Closing comment	

Clearly the compression of this essay into a paragraph robbed it of its rich texture and substance. The paragraph provides only the essential facts about studying music in

India; it fails to offer many of the telling details, the nuances, the overall tone. Such failure is inevitable, however, for the paragraph in its limited space must necessarily serve a limited purpose.

Reread the Shankar essay once again and you will see how skillfully Shankar developed the skeletal structure of his piece by expanding each section with additional details, examples, and reasons, thereby adding texture and substance to his discussion. This expansion procedure is necessarily carried out paragraph-by-paragraph, for at each stage of exposition the writer must be sure to say *enough*, that is, to give readers a sense of inclusiveness, a clear, well-rounded, and reasonably complete picture of the subject under consideration. As Edgar Allan Poe said of the poem and short story, so may we say of any piece of prose writing, that "a certain degree of duration" is necessary to produce a given effect.

Paragraph Duration

I cannot generalize about how much you should tell your readers at any given stage of exposition. You yourself must decide, paragraph by paragraph, how best to amplify a unit of meaning so that you do not leave readers with unanswered questions and gaps in thought and reasoning. To avoid these problems, you must provide supporting data that fill in the boundaries of an idea: examples, illustrations, details, reasons, and other elements, such as facts, quotations, analogies, and anecdotes. These supporting materials of paragraph development which provide for sufficient duration may be grouped roughly under five headings.

Examples

Examples support a generalization with concrete information and thereby illuminate it. Nothing is more encouraging to the reader plowing through difficult material than the two words "for example," since the example frequently clarifies the straight exposition that preceded it. In the paragraph below the writer develops the point made in the topic sentence (that many people in Hiroshima were indifferent about the ethics of using the bomb) by citing examples of two "typical" people.

> A surprising number of the people of Hiroshima remained more or less indifferent about the ethics of using the bomb. Possibly they were too terrified by it to want to think about it at all. Not many of them even bothered to find out much about what it was like. Mrs. Nakamura's conception of it—and awe of it—was typical. "The atom bomb," she would say when asked about it, "is the size of a matchbox. The heat of it is six thousand times that of the sun. It exploded in the air. There is some radium in it. I don't know just how it works, but when the radium is put together, it explodes." As for the use of the bomb, she would add, "Shikata ga nai," a Japanese expression as common as, and corresponding to, the Russian word "nicheve": "It can't be helped. Oh, well. Too bad." Dr. Fujii said approximately the same thing about the use of the bomb to Father Kleinsorge one evening, in German: "Da ist Nichts zu machen. There's nothing to be done about it."
>
> —John Hersey, *Hiroshima*

Illustrations

An illustration is a little story, a narrative example or an anecdote that embodies an idea in an action. In illustration, something happens (the distinguishing mark of all narration). The writer may develop his or her point with a one-paragraph illustration or with several shorter ones.

"Omit needless words!" cries the author on page 17, and into that imperative Will Strunk really put his heart and soul. In the days when I was sitting in his class, he omitted so many needless words, and omitted them so forcibly and with such eagerness and obvious relish, that he often seemed in the position of having shortchanged himself—a man left with nothing more to say yet with time to fill, a radio prophet who had outdistanced the clock. Will Strunk got out of this predicament by a simple trick: he uttered every sentence three times. When he delivered his oration on brevity to the class, he leaned forward over his desk, grasped his coat lapels in his hands, and, in a husky, conspiratorial voice, said, "Rule Thirteen. Omit needless words! Omit needless words! Omit needless words!"

—William Strunk, Jr., and E. B. White, *Elements of Style*

Never in the history of English letters has there been a more dedicated participant in the literary feuds of his day than the great and cantankerous Dr. Samuel Johnson, who stomped noisily through eighteenth-century London, demolishing arguments and smashing reputations with enormous vigor and gusto. Usually his verbal abuse was enough to smite the unworthy, but sometimes the impatient Doctor resorted to physical violence. ("There is no arguing with Johnson," the novelist, Oliver Goldsmith, said, "for when his pistol misses fire he knocks you down with the butt end of it.") Once, when a waiter used his dirty fingers instead of the proper tongs to drop a lump of sugar into the Doctor's tea, Johnson tossed the glass through the window and was about to do the same with the waiter, when a friend appeared and calmed him. On another occasion, the manager had placed a chair on a side stage especially for Dr. Johnson's use. Another man, finding the seat empty, sat in it, and then made the unpardonable error of failing to relinquish it to its rightful holder. Faced with this effrontery, the powerful Dr. Johnson simply picked up the chair, with the man still in it, and threw both chair and occupant into the pit.

—Myrick Land, *The Fine Art of Literary Mayhem*

Details

Details are the component parts that make up a whole—the individual steps in a procedure, the particular aspects of an image or impression. Details include factual data of all kinds: statistics, evidence, direct quotations, analogies. They answer the questions "How?" and "What?" In the following description of Ho Chi Minh, the writer supports his judgment that the Vietnamese leader "had altered" by citing specific details of his alteration. Similarly, the writer of the second paragraph below supports his statement—that scientists have learned to supplement the sense of sight in numerous ways—by citing five specific ways in which this has been done.

He had altered. His eyes had lost a little of the brilliance which used to strike one so forcibly, and his face was no longer ascetically thin. His hair had turned white, or course, and this made his beard look less sparse. The body covered by the sand-colored tunic was as frail as ever; but his cheeks had filled out and taken on a pinkness which gave him a somewhat artificial air. There was still a strong hint of mischief in his expression, however, and his dry laugh supplied the finishing touch—he looked and sounded like some old scholar whose wisdom had led him to discover the virtues of poverty....

—Jean Lacouture, *Ho Chi Minh*

Scientists have learned to supplement the sense of sight in numerous ways. In front of the tiny pupil of the eye they put, on Mount Palomar, a great monocle 200 inches in diameter, and with it see 2000 times farther into the depths of space. Or they look through a small pair of lenses arranged as a microscope into a drop of water or blood, and magnify by as much as 2000 diameters the living creatures there, many of which are among man's most dangerous enemies. Or, if we want to see distant happenings on earth, they use some of the previously wasted electromagnetic waves to carry television images which they re-create as light by whipping tiny crystals on a screen with electrons in a vacuum. Or they can bring happenings of long ago and far away as colored motion pictures, by arranging silver atoms and color-absorbing molecules to force light waves into the patterns of the original reality. Or if we want to see into the center of a steel casting or the chest of an injured child, they send the information on a beam of penetrating short-wave X rays, and then convert it back into images we can see on a screen or photograph. Thus almost every type of electromagnetic radiation yet discovered has been used to extend our sense of sight in some way.

—George R. Harrison, "Faith and the Scientist"

Reasons

Reasons answer the question "Why?" Reasons are acceptable and respectable only if the writer founds them on established fact, close observation and experience, or logical analysis. In the following paragraph Pusey provides a list of reasons to back up his contention that the life of the student in India is extraordinarily difficult.

The life of a student in India is much more difficult than anything we know in this country. Lack of material resources hampers most of the students at every turn. An overwhelming majority of them live at home, if they have homes, in conditions—by any standards we know—of miserable poverty. Often they have too little to eat, very little to wear, almost never any money to spend on the small things which we take so much for granted in our country. More serious is the fact that they can rarely afford to buy books for study, nor do their libraries have resources remotely comparable with those of our institutions. Beyond this, instruction is frequently anything but inspiring, and study is constrained and limited because the student is required by law to pass an annual examination which puts a high premium on memory work—an examination, set by an outside examining authority, to which each year many more are called than can possibly be chosen. And if a student persists in the face of repeated difficulty and finally in time earns a degree, there is the further debilitating consideration that his chances of finding an appropriate job are frighteningly slim. Yet so great is his inner drive and so bright his hope that the Indian student desires education beyond all else, and perseveres.

—Nathan M. Pusey, *The Age of the Scholar*

Mixed Materials

Not all paragraphs are neatly representative of a type, of course. Many writers mix supporting examples, reasons, and details, as in the following paragraph. In it Norman

Podhoretz explains, through a series of vividly recounted details, presented anecdotally, precisely why he finds Norman Mailer "extraordinary."

> The better I got to know Mailer personally—and we became very close friends—the more extraordinary I found him. He was, as the saying goes, a walking bag of contradictions: pugnacious in temperament and yet of a surpassing sweetness of character; foolish beyond belief about people, and yet unbelievably quick to understand the point of what anyone was up to; obsessed with fame, power, and rank, and yet the freest of any man I had ever encountered of snobbishness in any of its forms. Like most famous writers, he was surrounded by courtiers and sycophants, but with this difference: he allowed them into his life not to flatter him but to give his radically egalitarian imagination a constant workout. He had the true novelist's curiosity about people unlike himself—you could see him getting hooked ten times a night by strangers at a party—and his respect for modes of life other than his own was so great that it often led him into romanticizing people and things that might legitimately have been dismissed as uninteresting or mediocre. He would look into the empty eyes of some vapid upper-class girl and announce to her that she could be the madam of a Mexican whorehouse; or he would decide that some broken-down Negro junkie he had met in a Village dive was a battalion-commander at heart. Mailer assumed in the most straightforward way that everyone was out for all the power he could get at every minute of the day, and that from the most casual confrontation between two people, one emerged with a victory and the other with a defeat; he even had a hypochondriacal theory involving the birth and death of cells to cover for the assumption. He himself wanted everything: he would "settle for nothing less" than making a revolution in the consciousness of his time, *and* earning millions of dollars, *and* achieving the very heights of American celebrityhood. He respected the position of celebrityhood precisely as he respected people, sometimes romanticizing a particular "office," but never making the more common and worse mistake of underestimating how much it took to get anywhere big in America or pooh-poohing the qualities of mind and character required for staying on top (*Making It*).

Similarly, the following paragraph mixes its supporting materials by incorporating into an extended illustration a mass of statistical data that would be dull if presented directly. When presented within the frame of a story, however, the facts and figures come alive. It is the concreteness and specificity of the illustrative story—dealing with a family in a specific place, paying a stated amount of money for a prefabricated ranch house—that demonstrate the truth of the general observation.

> Investigating home-buying habits in the Midwest, I found that most home buyers do not compute the burden they are undertaking when a home is offered to them on a long-term mortgage. In Toledo, Ohio, a salesman and his wife proudly showed me their customized pre-fab ranch house which they said they had just bought for $19,500. Did they have a mortgage? Yes, it was a thirty-year kind for $17,000. How much was their interest rate? The husband said, "Gosh, I don't know... $4\frac{1}{2}$ per cent I think." His wife thought it was 6 per cent. Their difference in guesses could make a difference of nearly $6,000 in the total cost. Actually, it turned out, they were paying $5\frac{1}{2}$ per cent interest. The one thing they did know was that their monthly payment was $96.53. We quickly multiplied that figure by the 360 months they had committed themselves to pay it, and added on the $2,500 cash down payment. The result was a figure that plainly dismayed them: $37,250.80. That was the real price of their home, not $19,500.
>
> —Vance Packard, *The Waste Makers*

PARAGRAPH DEVELOPMENT

Unity

The substance of the paragraph (like the substance of the total piece) should be about what it is supposed to be about; it should make the points you set out to make and not some other points that happen to occur to you as you are writing. It should, in other words, stick to its subject and not wander off into irrelevant side issues. A paragraph is unified when it contains only those elements that contribute to the realization of its main idea.

No quality is more central to good exposition than *unity*. For only through a series of unified paragraphs, clearly and systematically related to one another, can a good piece of writing—whether a short essay or a long book—result.

You achieve unity in a paragraph when you recognize and respect the thrust of your own idea, whether it is explicitly stated or only implied. The following passage demonstrates vividly how every detail in a unified paragraph contributes to the total effect—in this case an image of "disgust." Note that the topic sentence is the third sentence of the paragraph; the first two sentences serve as an introduction.

Whoever writes about his childhood must beware of exaggeration and self-pity. I do not want to claim that I was a martyr or that Crossgates was a sort of Dotheboys Hall. But I should be falsifying my own memories if I did not record that they are largely memories of disgust. The overcrowded, underfed, underwashed life that we led was disgusting, as I recall it. If I shut my eyes and say "school," it is of course the physical surroundings that first come back to me: the flat playing-field with its cricket pavilion and the little shed by the rifle range, the draughty dormitories, the dusty splintery passages, the square of asphalt in front of the gymnasium, the raw-looking pinewood chapel at the back. And at almost every point some filthy detail obtrudes itself. For example, there were the pewter bowls out of which we had our porridge. They had overhanging rims, and under the rims there were accumulations of sour porridge, which could be flaked off in long strips. The porridge itself, too, contained more lumps, hairs and unexplained black things than one would have thought possible, unless someone were putting them there on purpose. It was never safe to start on that porridge without investigating it first. And there was the slimy water of the plunge bath—it was twelve or fifteen feet long, the whole school was supposed to go into it every morning, and I doubt whether the water was changed at all frequently—and the always-damp towels with their cheesy smell: and, on occasional visits in the winter, the murky sea-water of the local Baths, which came straight in from the beach and on which I once saw floating a human turd. And the sweaty smell of the changing-room with its greasy basins, and, giving on this, the row of filthy, dilapidated lavatories, which had no fastenings of any kind on the doors, so that whenever you were sitting there someone was sure to come crashing in. It is not easy for me to think of my schooldays without seeming to breathe in a whiff of something cold and evil-smelling—a sort of compound of sweaty stockings, dirty towels, faecal smells blowing along the corridors, forks with old food between the prongs, neck-of-mutton stew, and the banging doors of the lavatories and the echoing chamber-pots in the dormitories.
—George Orwell, *Such, Such Were the Joys*

The most common violation of unity is the inclusion of material in one paragraph that should either occur in a separate paragraph or not be used at all. You should always reread the first draft of each paper to make certain that you have not allowed any extraneous material to creep in during the writing stage. You must be very critical at this time, and examine each point of information and each turn in the development of thought to make sure that they belong where they are and that each point picks up the preceding point and leads to the next in a natural, logical movement.

Every well-written structural element (sentence, paragraph, essay, chapter, book) is never a haphazard concourse of ideas but rather "a careful record of mind moving toward a preconceived goal." This principle in action, the meticulous development of a single idea through its various stages, gives a work its essential unity, the oneness of aim in all its parts.

Coherence

Coherence literally means "sticking together." Thus a piece of writing is coherent when all its parts stick together, when the writer arranges and connects the individual words, phrases, and sentences so that a clear *pattern* of thought emerges.

Readers, who are "always in trouble," as E. B. White once noted, have no time and certainly no inclination to play games, to reassemble verbal parts; they must accept the writer's composition as they read it. If important pieces are missing so that the elements do not interlock (such as gaps in thought or puzzling jumps from one idea to another), then readers cannot see the shape of the writer's thought.

As a conscientious writer, then, you must try to communicate more than the basic raw material of your ideas. You must try to communicate relationships: Why does point three follow point two and not vice versa? Does the example cited at the end of the paragraph illustrate the whole paragraph or only the last point? Is the second point the cause or the effect of the first? And what does reason three have to do with reason two? Are they of equal importance, or is one subordinate to the other? You should allow for no guesswork. You should make certain not only that your readers can share the main idea of your paragraph (unity), but also that they can follow your particular train of thought from beginning to end (coherence).

You can achieve coherence in your writing in three basic ways:

1. By arranging materials according to an appropriate ordering principle.
2. By providing transitions from one idea to another.
3. By maintaining a consistent tone and point of view.

Let us look at each of these in turn.

Ordering Principles

TIME

You can arrange material according to *when* it happened (past to present, early to late, old to new), or in what order the reader should accomplish the process (first do this, then that, and finally this). You should present narration, historical accounts, the steps in a process, directions or instructions in the order in which they happen or should happen.

An example of this type of ordering is an account of the final moments in the life of Mary, Queen of Scôts. The writer (Froude, *History of England*) takes us to the scaffold and allows us to witness the event minute by minute:

> She laid her crucifix on her chair. The chief executioner took it as a perquisite, but was ordered instantly to lay it down. The lawn veil was lifted carefully off, not to disturb the hair, and was hung upon the rail. The black robe was next removed. Below it was a petticoat of crimson velvet. The black jacket followed, and under the jacket was a body of crimson satin. One of her ladies handed her a pair of crimson sleeves, with which she hastily covered her arms; and thus she stood on the black scaffold with the black figures all around her, blood-red from head to foot.

Chronological order does not necessarily imply an uninterrupted movement forward in time. You may begin with an important or exciting event and weave in background by interrupting the ongoing development of the story to dip into the past for some crucial or illuminating details. You may organize your material in whatever time sequence best suits the subject and purpose of your paragraph (or essay), as long as the presentation proceeds in an orderly manner readers can follow.

SPACE

Just as some material lends itself to a presentation in time, other material calls for a presentation in space. Again no rigid rules prescribe one spatial pattern over another. Writers should visualize the effect they are trying to achieve and then set about achieving that effect in a systematic manner. They should be clear in their own minds where the narrator stands (point of view), and proceed according to a natural or logical principle of progression (left to right, far to near, bottom to top). In the following paragraph from *The Adventures of Huckleberry Finn*, Mark Twain blends a time and space pattern. Huck is a stationary observer, describing what he sees as the day breaks over the water.

> The first thing to see, looking away over the water, was a kind of dull line—that was the woods on t'other side; you couldn't make nothing else out; then a pale place in the sky; then more paleness spreading around; then the river softened up away off, and warn't black any more, but gray; you could see little dark spots drifting along ever so far away—trading-scows, and such things; and long black streaks—rafts; sometimes you could hear a sweep creaking; or jumbled-up voices, it was so still, and sounds come so far; and by and by you could see a streak on the water which you know by the look of the streak that there's a snag there in a swift current which breaks on it and makes that streak look that way; and you see the mist curl up off the water, and the east reddens up, and the river, and you make out a log cabin in the edge of the woods, away on the bank on t'other side of the river, being a wood-yard, likely, and piled by them cheats so you can throw a dog through it anywheres; then the nice breeze springs up, and comes fanning you from over there, so cool and fresh and sweet to smell on account of the woods and the flowers; but sometimes not that way, because they've left dead fish laying around, gars and such, and they do get pretty rank; and next you've got the full day, and everything smiling in the sun, and the song-birds just going to it!

ORDER OF IMPORTANCE

As I mentioned earlier, when presenting a series of items or ideas, arranging them in ascending order of importance or value is generally most effective. The rhetorical justification rests on what appears to be a law of human nature: We intuitively build to a climax, passing from the least to the most, with the last-mentioned item impressing itself most forcibly on our minds. If a third or fourth item is weak, we say that it is anticlimatic; we have built up to something and then fallen off. Attempting to order your materials emphatically, you might begin by embedding a specific fact or situation in your topic sentence which you then unfold by degrees, working steadily toward a culmination or resolution. Or you might simply move from what your readers expect and find obvious to what they don't and find surprising—as in the following paragraph:

> As Americans are drawn more into overseas travel and service abroad, we are advised to be ready for something called "culture shock." Culture shock, roughy defined, is the total psychological discomfort one feels in foreign situations where every human function is dealt with somewhat differently. Big differences, such as language, are obvious; it is not too hard to make allowances for them and adjust to them. But the many, many tiny differences between life in the United States and life abroad—like the taste of the coffee, the value of time, or the smells—are more insidious. Bit by bit, their effects pile up in the pit of the emotions until they all become too much to be endured. Suddenly, unexpectedly, we have had it.
>
> —Donald Lloyd, "The Quietmouth American"

The building-up order of climax is not always suitable. Sometimes one item is so obvious and all-important that you must state it at the outset—directly after the topic sentence—just as you must present an overwhelmingly strong reason in support of an argument first if you do not want to distract your readers, who may keep wondering why you do not say the obvious. Thus in the following paragraph, the writer quite properly presents his most important explanation first:

> Some people are astonished to find that such primitive transportation as dog traction is still used. Why? Probably the most important reason is economy. A dog team can be assembled without expenditure of too much money. Pups appear in the normal course of events. The team becomes self-supporting since it enables the owner to become a more efficient hunter, especially of seals and caribou. The environment furnishes food for the team and food and clothing for the hunter and his family. A vehicle such as a weasel, snow-buggy, or motor toboggan requires cash capital for the initial investment and for spare parts, gasoline, and oil. Most Eskimos are relatively wealthy in meat and animal products but desperately poor in money. A recent comparison of motor toboggans and dog teams in the Canadian Arctic showed that, considering weight only of food or fuel needed per mile, the dog teams were more efficient. And—very important—a team can be started in thirty-below-zero weather without preheating, using explosive ether for starting fluid, or "burning" one's hands on the cold steel.

Transitional Devices

The word "transition" means passing over. Thus transitional guides are connectives (symbols, words, phrases; sometimes whole sentences and paragraphs) that make possible a smooth "passing over" from one idea to the next. You make transitions by referring to what you have said before, establishing cause-and-effect connections, looking ahead to what you will say, referring to the present, marking time and place, qualifying, comparing, contrasting. These and other common transitional devices appear here in categories that necessarily overlap to some extent.

Referring back: as we have seen, on the whole, as mentioned above, as stated previously, as I have said, it seems then

Looking ahead: then, later, next, after, afterward, thereafter, finally, now, consequently, to sum up

Establishing causal connections: the result, in conclusion, to conclude, because, for, since, consequently, accordingly, hence, thus, therefore

Time markers: now, then, later, soon, before, next, afterward, finally, meanwhile, thereafter, at the same time

Place markers: here, there, at this point, below, beside, next to, behind, in front, outside, inside

Comparing and establishing degree: and, similarly, in like manner, in the same way, just as, so . . . that, also, more than, less than, beyond this

Qualifying, conceding, or contrasting: but, nevertheless, on the other hand, however, despite this, still, on the contrary, conversely, if, as if, granted that, unless, whether, anyhow, although, even though, yet

Adding and intensifying: first, second, third; a, b, c; 1, 2, 3; to repeat, in addition, moreover, and, also, still, again, similarly, furthermore, finally, really, indeed

Introducing an illustration: thus, to illustrate, for example, for instance

Repeating a key word: This device keeps the main idea before the reader and carries the thread of meaning throughout a passage.

Using synonyms: Instead of repeating a key word so that it becomes monotonous, you may use suitable synonyms that continue the same thought.

Using proper pronoun reference: Another substitute for the repetition of key nouns and another way of connecting ideas is to use pronouns in place of nouns.

Maintaining same subject throughout paragraph: You can often continue the same subject from sentence to sentence, thereby maintaining a steady focus throughout the paragraph.

Establishing repetitive or parallel sentence patterns: In addition to repeating key words and ideas, you may repeat the grammatical structure of your sentences to reinforce the unity of your thoughts and promote their flow.

Linking of last sentence of one paragraph with first sentence of next: This natural, frequently intuitive method maintains coherence between paragraphs. Sometimes you may need connecting words (such as "then again" or "on another occasion"), but often the direction of the thought provides its own continuity.

Let us examine a passage of prose and observe how the writer has included many transitional signals (thirty-five) to keep readers moving steadily from beginning to end in a straight line of connected statements, each following logically from the one preceding it, and each telling readers accurately what they can expect next (an "and" suggesting another item of equal value, a "however" suggesting contrast, a "because" anticipating a reason).

Place marker   But the plays we are concerned with *here pursue*

       ends quite different from those of the conventional   Pronoun reference

Causal connection   play and *therefore use* quite different methods.   Parallel (to "pursue")

Pronoun reference   *They* can be judged only by the standards of the

       Theatre of the Absurd, which it is the purpose of

Demonstrative adjective   *this* book to define and clarify.

       It must be stressed, *however*, that the dramatists   Contrast

Place marker   whose work is *here* presented and discussed under

       the generic heading of the Theatre of the Absurd do

       not form part of any self-proclaimed or self-conscious

Synonym (for "dramatists")   school or movement. *On the contrary*, each   Contrast

       of the *writers* in question is an individual who

       regards himself as a lone outsider, cut off and

Pronoun reference   isolated in his private world. *Each* has his own   Parallel structure

       personal approach to both subject matter and

       form; his own roots, sources, and background. *If*   Qualifying condition

Additives   they *also*, very clearly *and* in spite of *themselves*,   Reflexive pronoun

Causal connection   have a good deal in common, *it* is *because their*   Pronoun reference

Comparison of degree   work *most* sensitively mirrors and reflects the   Additive "and's" plus parallel structure

       preoccupations and anxieties, the emotions and

       thinking of an important segment of their contem-

Transitional phrase (looking back)   poraries in the Western World.

       This is not to say that their works are representa-   Pronoun reference tive of mass attitudes. It is an oversimplification to assume that any age presents a homogeneous pattern. *Ours* being, *more than most others*, an age of transition, *it* displays a bewilderingly stratified picture: medieval beliefs *still* held and overlaid by eighteenth-century rationalism and mid-nineteenth-century Marxism, *rocked* by sudden volcanic eruptions of prehistoric fanaticisms and primitive tribal cults. *Each of these* components of the cultural pattern of the age finds *its* characteristic artistic expression. The Theatre of the Absurd, *however*, can be seen as the reflection of what seems the attitude most genuinely representative of our own time's contribution.

The hallmark of *this attitude* is its sense that the certitudes and unshakable basic assumptions of former ages have been swept away, that they have been tested and found wanting, that they have been discredited as cheap and somewhat childish illusions. The decline of religious faith was masked until the end of the Second World War by the substitute religions of faith in progress, nationalism, and various totalitarian fallacies. *All this* was shat-

Margin annotations (left):
Pronoun reference
Pronoun reference
Pronoun reference
Contrast
Parallel "that" clauses

Margin annotations (right):
Comparison of degree
Additive and time marker
Parallel (to "held and overlaid")
Pronoun reference
Demonstrative adjective plus repetition of "attitude"
Pronoun reference

tered by the war. By 1942, Albert Camus was calmly

putting the question why, since life had lost all

meaning, man should not seek escape in suicide. (Esslin,

Theatre).

Consistency of Tone

Simply stated, tone is a function of your attitude toward your subject and your readers. How do you want them to take your statement: as a formal explanation, a personal impression, an emotional attack, a lament, a joke? Not merely what you say but the *way* that you say it enters into the total meaning of a piece of writing and either reinforces or violates its coherence.

To maintain a consistent tone and point of view, you must begin with mechanical decisions concerning who is speaking (a first-person "I"? an impersonal "one"? an unbiased "he or she"?) and then consider whether the statement should be made in the present or past tense, the active or passive voice. On a deeper level, you must consider who your readers are; having visualized them, you will know what kind of usage is most appropriate (should you say "conflagration" or fire"?). On a still deeper level you must define the particular effect you are trying to create with your words (should you call a woman "thin," "skinny," or "scrawny"?). You need to accompany these mechanical and semantic considerations with a searching of your own mind to ensure that you have a clear idea of how *you* feel about what you are saying and how you want your readers to feel and think.

In the following scatterbrained account of New York City the writer fails to maintain consistency either in tone or point of view: the person shifts from "I" to "one" to "you"; tenses and voice change throughout; the writer gasps colloquially over a "hunk of engineering" and then comments pompously on what is "therapeutically preferable." The writer has done poorly on many counts, not the least of which is failure to establish and maintain an appropriate tone.

Although I was born and raised in New York, it still seems to me an exciting city. One can see beautiful sights no matter where you travel, especially up the West Side Highway where I saw the George Washington Bridge eloquently span the Hudson River from New York to New Jersey. What a hunk of engineering! All kinds of recreational activities are offered by New York: at Madison Square Garden you could be a spectator of almost any sport one is interested in: basketball, hockey, boxing. As for participating sports (which are, psychiatrists maintain, therapeutically preferable), I can't imagine any that you wouldn't be able to take up: bowling, tennis, horseback riding, ad infinitum. A veritable cornucopia of cultural activities also awaits the visitor to New York: theatres where thespians from all over the country—nay, the globe—exhibit their talents in plays that rival the splendor of the glorious age of Greek drama; museums which I had the opportunity to visit all my life and were always educational and are also interesting;

concerts which are always well-attended by New Yorkers as well as a multitude of outsiders who will be eager to see their favorite artists in the flesh. No kidding, New York is an exciting city.

As a more successful example of tone, examine the following paragraph, also about New York City. That it works at all is a "miracle," says E. B. White, who then goes on to describe this miracle. Note how skillfully his details are held together by a sustained and pervasive tone of affectionate incredulity.

> It is a miracle that New York works at all. The whole thing is implausible. Every time the residents brush their teeth, millions of gallons of water must be drawn from the Catskills and the hills of Westchester. When a young man in Manhattan writes a letter to his girl in Brooklyn, the love message gets blown to her through a pneumatic tube—pfft—just like that. The subterranean system of telephone cable, power lines, steam pipes, gas mains and sewer pipes is reason enough to abandon the island to the gods and weevils. Every time an incision is made in the pavement, the noisy surgeons expose ganglia that are tangled beyond belief. By rights, New York should have destroyed itself long ago, from panic or fire or rioting or failure of some vital supply line in its circulatory system or from some deep labyrinthine short circuit. Long ago the city should have experienced an insoluble traffic snarl at some impossible bottleneck. It should have perished of hunger when food lines failed for a few days. It should have been wiped out by a plague starting in its slums or carried in by ships' rats. It should have been overwhelmed by the sea that licks at it on every side. The workers in its myriad cells should have succumbed to nerves, from the fearful pall of smoke-fog that drifts over every few days from Jersey, blotting out all light at noon and leaving the high offices suspended, men groping and depressed, and the sense of world's end. It should have been touched in the head by the August heat and gone off its rocker.
>
> —E. B. White, *Here is New York*

No simple or single formula will help you maintain an appropriate tone throughout a unit of writing; your own sensitivity plus a keen awareness of rhetorical stance (your relation to your subject and your audience) must be your guides. However, the tone of modern prose style is, on the whole, natural and informal, for as I mentioned earlier, most expository writers use the rhythms of normal, everyday speech.

Using these principles as a general guide, you must check for violations of tone in the paragraphs of the piece you are writing. If a flippantly irreverent term—ill-suited to the context of your subject—slips into a sentence during the writing stage, you should delete it during a later rewriting or revision. So too you should eliminate ponderous or overly elaborate phrases from a light informal piece and tone down strongly emotional outbursts in a serious argument.

Choice of words and phrases, levels of usage, length and rhythm of sentences, juxtaposition of details, and other such rhetorical devices combine to produce the special tone of the paragraph. You are responsible for forging the tone you feel is appropriate, and, having forged it, you should—in the name of coherence—maintain that tone throughout.

Applying
Principles of
Good Paragraphing

WRITING PARAGRAPHS

*T*he following procedure will help you apply the principles of good paragraphing. Follow these three steps:

> *First:* Observe the workings of some recurrent paragraph patterns drawn from the work of established writers.
>
> *Second:* Practice these patterns until you have mastered them.
>
> *Third:* Go on to more complex and innovative forms as skill and inclination dictate, and as your instructor suggests.

You should recognize a truth at the outset—a truth every professional writer is aware of and every student writer should be aware of—that paragraph patterns (indeed all units of prose discourse) are infinitely various. Writers are entitled to create any pattern they are capable of creating, provided it works, fulfills the purpose for which it was designed, and does what the writer wants it to do. This is the ultimate practical test of all writing.

However, beginning writers start with what they know will work—what has worked in the past and what is still working for contemporary prose writers. After mastering these fundamental forms, the beginner, of course, is no longer a beginner. The forging of an individual, personal, perhaps powerful style lies ahead for those who continue to polish their prose. Expanding their knowledge of the infinite resources of language, they will see options open at every level: word, sentence, paragraph.

This presentation is modeled on the "generative" approach of Francis Christensen whose study of the paragraphs of established writers is especially valuable because it is *inductive*. That is, it is based on what writers actually do to make their writing effective, rather than on what prescriptive "experts" *think* they do or think they *should* do. Furthermore, Christensen shows us realistically and specifically how writers achieve their purposes.

PARAGRAPH PATTERNS:
COORDINATE AND SUBORDINATE SEQUENCES

Christensen's method of diagramming paragraphs is the one we shall follow here. He positions the sentences of the paragraph one under the other (like the lines of a poem), numbering them to indicate their level of generalization. Number one is the "top" (or topic) sentence, the sentence "... on which the others depend, the sentence whose assertion is supported or whose meaning is explicated or whose parts are detailed by the sentences added to it" (*A New Rhetoric*).

First, let us look at a basic type of paragraph, familiar to us all. It moves in a straight line from the general to a series of specifics.

1 Many of the Founding Fathers were passionate lovers or practitioners of music.

2 Jefferson used to rise at five in the morning to practice the violin; his expense books record many a purchase of "the latest minuets" and of fiddle strings for string quartet sessions, and he was well acquainted with the technique and construction of various instruments.

2 Samuel Adams organized the people of Boston into secret singing clubs to stir up enthusiasm for independence.

2 And Thomas Paine wrote at least two fine songs, "The Liberty Tree" and "Bunker Hill."

2 In addition to having made a famous ride, Paul Revere might go down in history as having been the engraver of the first volume of original hymns and anthems ever published in this country.

2 And Benjamin Franklin–most versatile of all—not only was a writer of ballad verses and a music publisher, but even invented a new musical instrument—the glass Armonica, for which Gluck, Mozart, and Beethoven composed a number of pieces.

—Elie Siegmeister, "Music in Early America"

Coordinate Sequence

Christensen calls patterns of this type a *coordinate sequence* because all sentences following the topic sentence are coordinate; that is, they are equal in rank to one another, all serving the same function. In this case each of the Founding Fathers (Jefferson, Adams, Paine, Revere, and Franklin) provides an example of the same general category: They are all "lovers or practitioners of music."

At the same time, as you may have already figured out yourself, the coordinate sentences in this paragraph are all *subordinate* to the topic sentence; that is, they are all at lower levels of generality.

Thus within the boundaries of each separate sentence, the writer presents each Founding Father as grammatical subject followed by an appropriately active verb:

Jefferson used to rise...
Samuel Adams organized...
...Thomas Paine wrote...
...Paul Revere might go down in history...
...Benjamin Franklin...not only was a writer...but invented...

It is not difficult to perceive the advantages of making all subordinate sentences in a coordinate sequence structurally alike (like things said in like ways): The construction of the sentences reinforces the likeness of their meaning and function and indicates at each step that the author is about to present another item in the series. In the paragraph above, for example, the parallel construction announces at the start of each sentence that the writer is about to present another Founding Father (note the transitional "and's" used in the third and fourth sentences). Of course some variation is necessary to prevent monotony; thus we see the writer shifting in sentence five to a modifying prepositional phrase as sentence opener ("In addition to making a famous ride, Paul Revere . . ."). Writers must use common sense and instinct here: the best of devices, used too frequently or mechanically, become obtrusive and irritating.

Note, finally, that the writer signals us at the end of the paragraph to let us know that we are coming to the last entry. Obviously he assigns Benjamin Franklin to this most emphatic final position because Franklin was—of all the Founding Fathers—the "most versatile." The writer clearly organizes his paragraph according to order of climax.

The simple structure of the coordinate sequence makes a significant and ultimately profound point about the nature of orderly writing and the ordered mind behind such writing. In the following paragraph, for example, the writer tells us in the topic sentence that "There are three kinds of analytic group therapy." Only a very careless writer, insensitive to the expectations created in a reader, would not then proceed to list the kinds (development by details). Note that here again the writer lists like things in like ways, using parallel construction to introduce each item in the coordinate series. Note also that the last sentence is subordinate to the next-to-the-last sentence in this otherwise coordinate series.

1 There are three different kinds of analytic group therapy.

   2 One concerns itself with the psychoanalysis of the individual in groups, as represented by Alexander Wolf.

   2 The second variety of analytic group therapy is psychoanalysis of the entire group as a whole, as represented by the technique of Jacob Moreno.

   2 The third variation of analytic group therapy is analysis by the group as developed by Michael Foulkes, DeMare, James Anthony and others.

     3 It is this type of analytic group therapy with which I identify.
        —Martin Grotjahn, *The Art and Technique*
of Analytic Group Therapy

The paragraph below provides another example of the coordinate sequence in which like things are said in like ways.

1 This is the essence of the religious spirit—the sense of power, beauty, greatness, truth infinitely beyond one's own reach, but infinitely to be aspired to.

   2 It invests men with pride in a purpose and with humility in accomplishment.

2 It is the source of all true tolerance, for in its light all men see other men as they see themselves, as being capable of being more than they are, and yet falling short, inevitably, of what they can imagine human opportunities to be.

2 It is the supporter of human dignity and pride and the dissolver of vanity.

2 And it is the very creator of the scientific spirit; for without the aspiration to understand and control the miracle of life, no man would have sweated in a laboratory or tortured his brain in the exquisite search after truth.

--Dorothy Thompson (cited in Christensen, *Notes* 59)

The simple coordinate sequence—a topic sentence followed by a series of coordinate sentences with like things put in like ways—"is a natural point for starting to master paragraph structure," says Christensen. "It is a simple kind of structure, but you may have to fight an ingrained habit of putting down just what comes naturally" (*A New Rhetoric* 164).

You will find, if you give it a fair try, that the form itself provides discipline and direction, helping you guard against digressions, careless non sequiturs, or gaps in thought. The form also helps to sort and order your ideas both in the prewriting stage and while you are writing. Indeed, once you have assimilated the form, your memory and imagination will more easily dredge up old ideas and dream up new ones. The approach is appropriately described as "generative": One idea generates another in an ongoing sequence.

Subordinate Sequence

Thus far we have reviewed the coordinate sequence, the paragraph in which all added sentences have the same structural relationship to the topic sentence: That is, they are all direct comments on the topic sentence. Now let us examine a second main paragraph pattern, the subordinate sequence.

In a subordinate sequence the added sentences have different structural relationships to the topic sentence. They do not comment directly on the topic sentence. Instead, each succeeding sentence is a direct comment on its immediate predecessor. In such a paragraph—as you will see in the example below—the topic sentence serves essentially as a point of departure from which every succeeding sentence moves further and further away. Each sentence is then seen to be *subordinate* to its predecessor and is numbered accordingly:

1 The process of learning is essential to our lives.

2 All higher animals seek it deliberately.

3 They are inquisitive and [they] experiment.

4 An experiment is a sort of harmless trial run of some action which we shall have to make in the real world...whether it is made in the laboratory by scientists or by fox cubs outside their [den].

5 The scientist experiments and the cub plays; both are learning to correct their errors of judgment in a setting in which errors are not fatal.

6 Perhaps this is what gives them both their air of happiness and freedom in these activities.

—J. Bronowski (cited in Christensen, *Notes* 60)

To draw an analogy, one might say that sentences in a coordinate sequence—all relating back in the same way to the topic sentence—are children of the same parent; whereas sentences in a subordinate sequence—each relating back to its immediate predecessor—represent succeeding generations of the same parent. They are descendants, as it were; or, in rhetorical terms, they *descend* progressively to lower and lower levels of generalization, each providing a still more specific comment on the generalization contained in the original "top" or topic sentence.

You must be careful in a subordinate sequence to establish connecting links among the descendants. Indeed you must guard against digression at each and every point. In the subordinate sequence the question of coherence—the sticking together of parts—may become a problem.

Let us look at the Bronowski paragraph cited above to see how he avoided this problem, how he provided the links that keep his main thought moving in a straight and steady line of development, moving toward the progressively more specific. His topic sentence provides a general base on which a block of thought takes shape:

Level 1: The process of learning is essential to our lives.

He announces the subject simply and directly. Even though the succeeding sentences of the paragraph will move away from this general statement, he scrupulously maintains a connecting thread throughout.

Level 2: All higher animals seek it deliberately.

This sentence is a comment on the first, an amplification or development of it at a more specific level since it *specifies who* seeks the process: "all higher animals" (a detail) and *how* they seek it: "deliberately" (another detail). The writer has provided two added specifics within the frame of a sentence connected to the preceding sentence by the pronoun "it," which clearly refers back to "the process of learning."

Level 3: They are inquisitive and [they] experiment.

Although this sentence moves the reader still further from the topic sentence, it is not confusing. The pronoun "they" clearly refers back to "higher animals," explaining *why* they seek to learn: "They are inquisitive" (a specific reason); and *how* they seek to learn: "they experiment" (a specific detail). Note how skillfully Bronowski weaves in the basic materials of paragraph development.

Level 4: An experiment is a sort of harmless trial run of some action which we shall have to make in the real world ... whether it is made in the laboratory by scientists or by fox cubs outside their [den].

He joins this sentence to its predecessor by repetition of the key word "experiment." As the last word of sentence three and the first word of sentence four, "experiment" provides an unmistakable link in the ongoing progression. True, this sentence departs further and further from the topic sentence, but note how closely connected the departing steps are to one another. *Specifically*, the level four sentence *defines* a key word in level three. Level four also tells who experiments: "scientists" and "fox cubs" (specific examples); and *where* each experiments: "in the laboratory" or "outside their [den]" (specific details).

> *Level 5:* The scientist experiments and the cub plays; both are learning to correct their errors of judgment in a setting in which errors are not fatal.

Here again repetition of key words serves as a connecting link. The writer now describes the actions of the previously mentioned "scientist" and "fox cub" more specifically in terms of *what* they do: "the scientist experiments and the fox cub plays" (specific examples); *what* they are learning: to "correct their errors" (additional detail); and *where* they are learning: in a nonfatal setting (final detail).

> *Level 6:* Perhaps this is what gives them both their air of happiness and freedom in these activities.

With the opening word "perhaps" the writer clearly speculates on what he has just said before. Three pronoun references ("this," "them," and "their") plus one demonstrative adjective ("these") bind this last sentence in the paragraph to its predecessor. The earlier description of the setting as one in which errors are not fatal implies the new detail that both scientist and fox cub enjoy an "air of happiness and freedom." This same detail might well serve as transition to a new paragraph dealing with the pleasures of learning under controlled conditions.

As you can see, a subordinate sequence achieves unity and coherence when the writer makes judicious use of transitions: repetition of key words, pronoun reference, and so on (see pages 113–16 for discussion of transitional devices). Even in a simple narrative—and narrative paragraphs are often subordinate—transitions are what keep the story *moving*. Note how the pattern works in the following paragraph.

1 *Starlings* are notoriously difficult to "control."

Repetition of key word

2 The story is told of a man who was bothered by *starlings* roosting in a large sycamore near his house.

Pronoun references

3 *He* said he tried everything to get rid of *them* and finally took a shotgun to three of *them* and killed them.

Pronoun references, synonym

4 When asked if *that* discouraged the *birds*, he reflected a minute, leaned forward, and said confidentially, "*Those three* it did." (Dillard, *Pilgrim*).

Demonstrative adjective, repetition of key word

By viewing the paragraph as a linked sequence of sentences—as in the above examples—Christensen provides a quick and useful test of paragraph unity, one which we can easily apply to our own writing. As we reread the first draft of a paragraph we have written, we can ask, "Does every sentence (that is, every link in the sequence) connect with the sentence that precedes it and the sentence that follows?" If not, if a sentence is neither coordinate with any sentence before it nor subordinate to the sentence immediately preceding it, then it does not belong in the paragraph (it breaks the sequence) and we should either move it elsewhere or set if off in parentheses. In these cases, as Christensen puts it, "the paragraph has begun to drift from its moorings, or the writer has unwittingly begun a new paragraph."

In the properly unified paragraph, then, all the sentences deal with the same subject but at various levels of generality. A comment, for example, will be subordinate to the sentence on which it is commenting; an explanation or example of the comment will be subordinate to the comment, and so on. The paragraph moves and takes shape in terms of how each added sentence relates—either coordinately or subordinately—to the sentence that precedes it.

Mixed Sequences

Purely coordinate or subordinate sequences are not, as we might expect, as common as those in which the sequence is mixed, although one form or the other usually dominates.

Note, for example, that in the paragraph (page 122) dealing with different types of analytic group therapy, the topic sentence ("there are three different kinds of analytic group therapy") suggests that the paragraph will provide a series of three coordinate sentences. Having provided these, the writer wants the reader to know that he will discuss only the last item in the coordinate series further. To tell us this, he shifts downward from a level-two sentence to a final level-three.

Similarly in the paragraph below, the writer—having committed himself at the outset to a coordinate sequence—shifts regularly within that sequence of level-two sentences to level-three's, which provide specific examples of the points made at level two. The paragraph provides a perfect example of that subtler movement—that ebb and flow between the general and specific—which characterizes the more complex paragraphs of our best writers.

Mixed sequence, based on coordination

1 The atmosphere that stirs expectation, that tantalizes the secret hunches that all theater-goers have, is composed of many things, some tangible and some not so very.

2 Titles count.

3 ("Sixth Finger in a Five Finger Glove" is not a good title; "The Strong Are Lonely" is not a good title; "Bells Are Ringing" is a good title.)

2 Personalities count.

3 (I've always liked that nice Walter Pidgeon.)

2 Subject matter counts.

3 (Do I want to see a play tonight about treachery in a prison camp?)

2 Timing counts.

   3 (I may want to see a play about treachery in a prison camp next year, or I may have wanted to see one last year, but—tonight?)

2 Circumstances count.

   3 (Is it Eugene O'Neill's last play, and what did he say about his family?)

2 Curiosity counts.

   3 (What in heaven's name can "The Waltz of the Toreadors" be like?)

2 The curve of the moon counts.

—Walter Kerr, "How to Beat the Critics"

You can see how the alternating of level-two with level-three examples in the above paragraph rounds it out so that it offers more than a laundry-list itemization. Similarly in the next paragraph the writer pauses at one point—and only at one point—to develop his level-two item with a specific example and further details.

Mixed sequence, based on coordination .

1 It is commonplace that most artists of outstanding originality and creative power have met lack of appreciation or abuse in their lifetimes.

  2 We know that Beethoven's latest and finest works seemed to his contemporaries to be meaningless meanderings of senility aligned with deafness, that Rembrandt's paintings were judged to be "Gothic and crude" by the autocrats of good taste in France.

  2 We know the obloquy which the Post-Impressionist painters were required to face.

    3 Even in 1925 Cézanne was described by one American critic as "commonplace, mediocre, and a third-rate painter," and in 1934 his work was characterized by another as "meager and unfulfilled art," while an English critic of some prominence has published his judgement that when you have seen one you have seen them all.

  2 We know the indignation which was aroused at the beginning of the century by the new enthusiasm for African sculpture.

  2 We remember the bewildered ridicule of "modern" music—Stravinsky and Bartók, even of Scriabin and Sibelius—which is now accepted and "placed."

  2 We remember the controversies aroused by D. H. Lawrence and James Joyce, the repudiation of Eliot, Pound, Auden.

[Summing-up] This is not a new thing in critics who have led the vociferous opposition to the new.

—Harold Osborne, *Aesthetics and Criticism*

Now note in the following paragraph how a writer introduces a coordinate series into a subordinate sequence; in this case the coordinate elements come at the end of the paragraph.

Mixed sequence, based on subordination

1 The timing of New York's entry into casino gambling raises another, basic question: Can it really provide significant economic stimulus to decaying localities?

  2 Officials assume favorable answers, but with little evidence.

    3 Unless casinos bring a flood of visitors to the state, they will simply reshuffle local assets.

      4 Does Mayor Koch believe that Manhattan casinos will increase tourism?

      4 Will new hotels rise here for gamblers when Atlantic City and Las Vegas are already in the business and further competition impends?

      4 Would such gambling drain other city entertainments, such as theaters and restaurants?
         —*New York Times* Editorial, "Gambling on the Facts in New York"

Mixed paragraphs such as these are especially interesting and worthy of close study, for as Christensen says, they suggest "careful calculation of what could be left to the reader and what must be made more explicit." Obviously the writer treats those points that contain several subordinate sentences at greater length because he feels that they need clarification or emphasis. The inclusion of further information (details, examples, illustrations, and so on) provides the additional "mass" that tells the reader "take note: this is difficult; it needs further explaining" or "this is important, and therefore I want to linger over it."

Thus in the mixed sequence below, the writer stops the subordinate thrust of the sequence at two points, moving on to complete the sequence only after the "pauses" have achieved their purpose.

Mixed sequence, based on subordination

1 Whether we like it or not, ours is an Age of Science.

  2 It is also like every other epoch of history, an Age of Private Experience.

    3 In this second half of the twentieth century what can a writer do about these inescapable historical facts?

    3 And what, as a conscientious literary artist and a responsible citizen, ought he to do about them?

      4 His first duty, of course, is to write as well as he can.

        5 Much of our experience comes to us, so to say, through the refracting medium of art.

    6 If that art is inept, our experience will be vulgarized and corrupted.

    6 Along with unrealistic philosophy and religious supersition, bad art is a crime against society.

  4 The writer's next duty is to learn something, if only superficially and in patches, about the methods and results of advancing science.

    5 This knowledge should then be correlated with private experience and the shared traditions of culture, and the amalgam should be treated as a new kind of raw material for the creation of new varieties of the familiar literary forms.

— Harper's

Strictly speaking, the well-constructed, well-developed paragraph may assume an indefinite number of forms: it is impossible to encompass all possible paragraphs in a single description. But basically, as Christensen (*Notes* 57) has written, the paragraph is "a sequence of structurally related sentences," that is,

> ... sentences related to one another by coordination and subordination. If a first sentence of a paragraph is the topic sentence, the second is quite likely to be a comment on it, a development of it, and therefore subordinate to it. The third sentence may be coordinate with the second sentence ... or subordinate to it. The fourth sentence may be coordinate with either the second or third (or with both if they themselves are co-ordinate ...) or subordinate to the third. And so on.

  The determination of how much the writer must tell the reader at any point—where an added subordinate sentence is necessary or where another coordinate statement might clarify or emphasize an important idea—is up to the judgment of the individual writer. There is no formula that spells out the proper proportions of a paragraph. Even so, the writer can benefit enormously by familiarity with the "additive" approach, for very often all that is necessary to improve a passage of prose is further development or amplification at a given level. Thus, says Christensen, addressing this remark to the teacher of writing; "there is nothing arbitrary or unnatural about urging the student to add levels, usually of a lower order of generality, in order to produce a texture rich enough to contain and display his subject" (*Symposium* 60–88). John Lord reinforces this idea when he tells us in his study of the paragraph that "all good writing is a constant weaving up and down between the concrete and the abstract, as well as a constant forward movement from a beginning through a middle to an end" (*Paragraph* 73).

Placement of Topic Sentence

Note that a paragraph may have no introductory topic sentence, that is, no announced statement of its theme, as in the following paragraph. Note also, however, that a topic sentence does indeed lurk in the second level-two sentence, beginning with "In Italy . . . ."

2 In Spain, where I saw him last, he looked profoundly Spanish.

   3 He might have passed for one of those confidential street dealers who earn their living selling spurious Parker pens in the cafés of Málaga or Valencia.

      4 Like them, he wore a faded chalk-striped shirt, a coat slung over his shoulders, a trim, dark moustache, and a sleazy, fat-cat smile.

      4 His walk, like theirs, was a raffish saunter, and everthing about him seemed slept in, especially his hair, a nest of small, wet serpents.

   3 Had he been in Seville and his clothes been more formal, he could have been mistaken for a pampered elder son idling away a legacy in dribs and on drabs, the sort you see in windows along the Sierpes, apparently stuffed.

2 In Italy he looks Italian; in Greece, Greek: wherever he travels on the Mediterranean coast, Tennessee Williams takes on a protective colouring which melts him into his background, like a lizard on a rock.

2 In New York or London he seems out of place, and is best explained away as a retired bandit.

   3 Or a beach comber: shave the beard off any of the self-portraits Gauguin painted in Tahiti, soften the features a little, and you have a sleepy outcast face that might well be Tennessee's.

         —Kenneth Tynan (cited in Christensen, *Notes* 71–72)

Very often the structure and impetus of an idea may carry over from paragraph to paragraph so that the paragraph needs no formal transition or topic sentence. In fact, a writer may promote readability by distributing a single idea over several paragraphs. In the following selection, for example, the topic sentence—"Sebastiana was devoted to Tanguy in a silent inarticulate way"—controls four relatively short paragraphs, each bringing out a different aspect of her devotion, and each serving as a kind of level-two sentence. The final three sentences serve as a concluding commentary or "terminator."

    Sebastiana was devoted to Tanguy, in a silent, inarticulate way. She watched over him and took care of him. Every day, during the midday break, everyone saw her arrive with "the kid's" dinner. She had a half-hour's walk each way to bring him his food, but she was determined he must get something hot inside him. She always managed to get something which she considered a "luxury"— a slice of ham, perhaps, or a little cheese. She arrived proudly carrying her bundle and sat on a big stone, in the shade, beside Tanguy. Other workers used to have jokes at her expense, and tell her she was "past the age for that kind of thing." She let them talk, and did not even take the trouble to reply. She was desolate at seeing Tanguy so ill and dejected, and she continued to look after him with extraordinary tenderness.

    She spent a great deal of time finding classical music for him in the radio programs, pretending to adore Bach and Beethoven. In the evening, after Tanguy had come home, they would sit before dinner in the little courtyard and chat. When he was reading the paper or listening to music, she sat quietly, without moving or speaking.

    They never expressed their affection openly. Sebastiana's love remained dumb; like Gunther, she never gave external reality to her tender feelings except through the unimpeachable eloquence of her actual behavior. She lived for Tanguy as she would have lived for her own son, watched over him while he slept, took care of his clothes, gave him the kind of food he liked best (as far as she could), and tried to find amusements for him. On Sundays they sometimes picnicked on the beach, well away from the crowd.

He told her about everything. She listened in silence and smiled at him tenderly. All her understanding came from her heart, for she was the maternal instinct personified. Tanguy, on his part, loved and admired her because she was fair and honest. He loved her uncalculating generosity and her tranquil expression. She was sensible rather than clever, but she almost always knew what was right (del Castillo, *Child*).

Although the topic or "top" sentence does generally lead off the paragraph, it may also wind it up. In the following paragraph, Willa Cather deliberately saves her topic sentence for the end of the paragraph so that the reader—having been offered a series of vivid images—can arrive with the writer at a summing-up generalization.

> 2 Ivy's red skin was flecked with tiny freckles, like rust spots, and in each of his hard cheeks there was a curly indentation, like a knot in a treehole —two permanent dimples which did anything but soften his countenance.
>
> 2 His eyes were very small, and an absence of eyelashes gave his pupils the fixed, unblinking hardness of a snail's or a lizard's.
>
> 2 His hands had the same swollen look as his face, were deeply creased across the back and knuckles, as if the skin were stretched too tight.
>
> 1 He was an ugly fellow, Ivy Peters, and he liked being ugly.
>
> —Willa Cather, *The Lost Lady*

To summarize this most crucial subject of development, each paragraph unit (or each series of units) should have its appropriate pattern and sufficient "duration" to do full justice to its subject; it should also develop its thought (answer its question) systematically, with a variety of materials that give the paragraph substance and texture (levels of generalization); and it should not drop the thought (leave that aspect of the answer) until, as Herbert Read wrote, it has been "seen in all profitable lights." Furthermore, the writer should develop these thoughts at a steady, reasonably accelerated pace so that the writing *flows*. To quote Read (61) again:

> There is about good writing a visual actuality. It exactly reproduces what we should metaphorically call the contour of our thought. The metaphor is for once exact: thought has a contour or a shape. The paragraph is the preception of this contour or shape.
>
> The writer has toward his materials, words, the same relation that an artist, say a modeller, has toward his material, clay. The paragraph is a plastic mass, and it takes its shape from the thought it has to express: its shape *is* the thought.

DISCUSSION AND EXERCISES

1. Coordinate Sequence

1. Students wrote both paragraphs below using the same topic sentence, "Sweet are the uses of adversity." Christensen commended one paragraph, and criticized the other. Analyze the paragraphs and distinguish between the two, explaining your choice. Note that even in the

"commendable" paragraph Christensen observes that "the shape is faulty at ... one point" (*New Rhetoric* 164–65). See if you can locate that point and comment.

a. "Sweet are the uses of adversity," for it is in misfortune that a man is truly revealed. Adversity gives rise to dreams and hopes which prosperity might never incite. Adversity educates and strengthens the mind, eliciting talents which under more fortunate circumstances might have lain dormant. Adversity following prosperity challenges a comeback, giving the future a purpose and placing a new value on the lost success. Without experiencing adversity it is difficult to appreciate prosperity. Finally, it is in adversity that the truly noble spirit shines brightest—both that of the afflicted and that of his loyal friend who stands by in spite of everything.

b. "Sweet are the uses of adversity." The poet, John Keats, struggled with sorrow and adversity experienced in the finite world. Keats searched for the ideal, but came to the conclusion sorrow and suffering must be accepted as part of the human experience. Beauty must die in order to have existence, for beauty fixed would be cold and inhuman. Alluding to his two poems, "To Autumn" and "Ode to a Nightingale," Keats resolved that autumn, too, has its song. Adversity is a part of living that makes one's human experiences more complete.

2. Use each of the following topic sentences as the basis for a coordinate sequence paragraph (add three or four sentences to each topic sentence). Try to order your materials appropriately, say "like things in like ways," use transitions where needed, and employ slight variations in structure where they will improve the flow and avoid monotony.

a. Sweet are the uses of adversity.
b. There are many things I like about my generation.
c. There are at least three different types of love.
d. There are countless ways to improve the quality of life on this campus.
e. I have several favorite books.

3. Write ten more coordinate sequences using the following quotations as topic sentences and adding as many sentences as you need to develop the idea.

a. It never rains but it pours.
b. Politics does indeed make strange bedfellows.
c. What's in a name?
d. There is no place more delightful than home.
e. The pen is mightier than the Saturday Night Special.
f. Knowledge is power.
g. Nothing is so much to be feared as fear itself.
h. Forsake not an old friend, for the new is not comparable to him.
i. Second thoughts are best.
j. The heroes, the saints, and the sages—they are those who face the world alone.

2. Subordinate Sequence

1. Write subordinate sequences using the following quotations as "points of departure": add as many levels as you need to complete your idea. Remember that in developing a subordinate sequence you do not refer back directly to the topic sentence, but only to the preceding one. Your idea should move forward steadily.

a. A man's reach should exceed his grasp.

b. It is better to have loved and lost than never to have loved at all.

c. Variety is not always the spice of life.

d. A classic is something that everybody wants to have read and nobody wants to read.

e. I laughed till I cried.

f. False words are not only evil in themselves, but they infect the soul with evil.

g. Nothing great was ever achieved without enthusiasm.

h. The reward of a thing well done is to have done it.

i. He ... thought the moon was made of green cheese.

j. The mass of men lead lives of quiet desperation.

2. Even topic sentences which might initially suggest a coordinate series may generate a subordinate series. If the writer wants to, he or she may use a second sentence to focus on only one aspect of the topic. Let us begin this assignment with one such example.

> 1 Sweet are the uses of adversity.
>
> *2 I remember the day I discovered the truth of this famous line from Shakespeare.*

Note that the second sentence now enables you to narrate the events of that particular day. Add a comparably limiting second sentence to each of the following.

a. There is one book I'll never forget.

b. The sense of greatness keeps a nation great.

c. According to an old song title, "Saturday Night Is the Loneliest Night of the Week."

3. Mixed Sequence

1. Use the topic sentences below to write mixed sequences, following the pattern indicated for each paragraph.

a. The atmosphere that stirs expectation, that tantalizes the secret hunches that all movie-goers have, is composed of many things, some tangible and some not so very. (1, 2, 3, 2, 3, 2, 3, 2, 3, 2: See paragraph "How to Beat the Critics," pages 126–27).

b. There are many things I like about my generation. (1, 2, 2, 2, 3, 4, 5)

c. Whether we like it or not, ours is an Age of Anxiety. (1, 2, 3, 3, 4, 5, 6, 6, 4, 5: See paragraph on "Age of Science," pages 128–29).

d. He had changed. (1, 2, 2, 3, 3, 4, 5) or (1, 2, 3, 4, 4, 4, 4)

e. Some people simply don't learn from experience. (1, 2, 3, 3, 2, 3, 2, 3, 4, 5)

2. Number the following paragraphs to determine their pattern (mixed sequences based on coordination or subordination); then write a paragraph following the same pattern, using a topic sentence of your own, or selecting one of the quotations provided in the exercises above.

a.   Never in the history of English letters has there been a more dedicated participant in the literary feuds of his day than the great and cantankerous Dr. Samuel Johnson, who stomped noisily through eighteenth-century London, demolishing arguments and smashing reputations with enormous vigor and gusto. Usually his verbal abuse was enough to smite the unworthy, but sometimes the impatient Doctor resorted to physical violence. ("There is no arguing with Johnson," the novelist, Oliver Goldsmith, said, "for when his pistol misses fire he knocks you down with the butt end of it.") Once, when a waiter used his dirty fingers instead of the proper tongs to drop a lump of sugar into the Doctor's tea, Johnson tossed the glass through the window and was about to do the same with the waiter, when a friend appeared and calmed him. On another occasion, the manager had placed a chair on a side stage especially for Dr. Johnson's use. Another man, finding the seat empty, sat in it, and then made the unpardonable error of failing to relinquish it to its rightful holder. Faced with this effrontery, the powerful Dr. Johnson simply picked up the chair, with the man still in it, and threw both chair and occupant into the pit.

—Myrick Land, *The Fine Art of Literary Mayhem*

b.   A surprising number of the people of Hiroshima remained more or less indifferent about the ethics of using the bomb. Possibly they were too terrified by it to want to think about it at all. Not many of them even bothered to find out much about what it was like. Mrs. Nakamura's conception of it—and awe of it—was typical. "The atom bomb," she would say when asked about it, "is the size of a matchbox. The heat of it is six thousand times that of the sun. It exploded in the air. There is some radium in it. I don't know just how it works, but when the radium is put together, it explodes." As for the use of the bomb, she would add, "Shikata ga nai," a Japanese expression as common as, and corresponding to, the Russian word "nicheve": "It can't be helped. Oh, well. Too bad." Dr. Fujii said approximately the same thing about the use of the bomb to Father Kleinsorge one evening, in German: "Da ist Nichts zu machen. There's nothing to be done about it."

—John Hersey, *Hiroshima*

4. Identifying Paragraph Patterns

1. Characterize the following paragraphs as coordinate, subordinate, or mixed. Number the various "levels of generality."

a.   The English language has not begun its life entirely devoid of Greek and Roman influence. Far back in the Dark Ages it drew in Latin and Greek words to cover activities which were not native to its people—religious, social, political—and even the names of foreign foods and drinks. *Church* and *kirk* come from the Greek; so do *bishop, monk, priest,* and *wine.* Many Latin words entered indirectly at the Conquest, through Norman-French. Then, as the Middle Ages flowed towards the Renaissance, English began to grow in the same way, and for the same reasons, as French: very largely under the influence of French. Chaucer was the chief figure in this process.

—Gilbert Highet, *The Classical Tradition*

b.   What are qualities that make language live? *Feeling* is one. A writer's ability to feel life deeply, to be responsive to it. Then *power over language,* the gift to use words significantly and to form them in ways to give them meaning and impact. Also the quality of *style,* a writer's personal way with words, as intimate a part of a good writer as the size and shape of his nose. *Knowledge* is another quality that elevates writing into literature, so that the reader is memorably informed and made aware of new worlds. *Insight* is still another quality—a writer's ability to illuminate experience, to light up the dark places so that the reader sees life more clearly. And lastly what Dobie calls *perspective,* so that in reading one is aware of relationships both in space and time.

—Lawrence Clark Powell, *The Little Package*

c.   "There is hardly any activity, any enterprise, which is started with such tremendous hopes and expectations, and yet which fails so regularly, as love," wrote Erich Fromm. I think that part of the reason for this failure rate is that too often people are speaking different languages when they speak of love. The problem is not how much love they feel, but which kind. The way to have a mutually satisfying love affair is not to find a partner who loves "in the right amount," but one who shares the same approach to loving, the same definition of love.

—John Alan Lee, "The Styles of Loving"

d. As I said earlier, the average writer sets out to commit an act of literature. He thinks that his article must be of a certain length or it won't seem important. He thinks how it will look in print. He thinks of all the people who will read it. He thinks that its style must dazzle. No wonder he tightens: he is so busy thinking of his awesome responsibility to the finished article that he can't even start!

—William Zinsser, "On Writing Well"

e. [There is]... that recurrent Dickens figure, the Good Rich Man. This character belongs especially to Dickens's early optimistic period. He is usually a "merchant" (we are not necessarily told what merchandise he deals in), and he is always a superhumanly kind-hearted old gentleman who "trots" to and fro, raising his employees' wages, patting children on the head, getting debtors out of jail and, in general, acting the fairy godmother. Of course he is a pure dream figure, much further from real life than, say, Squeers or Micawber. Even Dickens must have reflected occasionally that anyone who was so anxious to give his money away would never have acquired it in the first place. Mr. Pickwick, for instance, had "been in the city," but it is difficult to imagine him making a fortune there. Nevertheless this character runs like a connecting thread through most of the earlier books. Pickwick, the Cheerybles, old Chuzzlewit, Scrooge—it is the same figure over and over again, the good rich man, handing out guineas.

George Orwell, *Dickens, Dali and Others*

f. Her doctor had told Julian's mother that she must lose twenty pounds on account of her blood pressure, so on Wednesday nights Julian had to take her downtown on the bus for a reducing class at the Y. The reducing class was designed for working girls over fifty, who weighed from 165 to 200 pounds. His mother was one of the slimmer ones, but she said ladies did not tell their age or weight. She would not ride the buses by herself since they had been integrated, and because the reducing class was one of her few pleasures, necessary for her health and free, she said Julian could at least put himself out to take her, considering all she did for him. Julian did not like to consider all she did for him, but every Wednesday night he braced himself and took her.

—Flannery O'Conner, "Everything That Rises Must Converge"

g. The chronicler of Petrarch's life must record high hopes coupled with bitter disappointments. The poet spent a lifetime lyricizing an idealized and unattainable love, finally concluding that "Commerce with women, without which I had sometimes thought I could not live, I now fear more than death....When I reflect on what woman is, a temptation quickly vanishes." He worked for the restoration of an imperial Rome, only to decide that it was a city which sold for gold the blood of Christ. He wanted an ivory tower in which to write masterpieces, but wandered restlessly through a dozen towns on a lifetime odyssey, which Bishop retraced in preparing his book. (Mrs. Bishop's pen impressions of these towns illustrate and enhance the volume.) He sought to emulate Virgil by rallying Italy to greatness with an epic poem on Scipio Africanus, only to have contemporaries hoot at it and tempt him to burn it. He strove for immortality through erudite works in Latin, but he won it with Italian rimes to a woman he had never touched.

—Robert J. Clements, "Laurels in Lieu of the Lady"

h. In his function as a finder, the critic may be called the scientist of the unsuspected and the cartographer of the uncircumscribed. He returns from the realms of gold with a relief map of the hills and valleys. He must accept the role of John Keats' Cortez, toiling up the landward slope of some masking range to stand finally upon the peak, seeing for the first time perhaps a broad and heaving expanse whose existence has been known, but whose islands and archipelagos, whose shoals and depths, had not hitherto been adequately charted. He must be prepared for change: what once loomed as a considerable mountain on the horizons of its own epoch may since have been eroded to a minor protuberance by the weathering of successive ages. Like Robert Frost's oven bird, the critic must have some idea of "what to make of a diminished thing."

—Carlos Baker, "What Are Critics Good For?"

i. Out on Safaris, I had seen a herd of Buffalo, one hundred and twenty-nine of them, come out of the morning mist under a copper sky, one by one, as if the dark and massive, iron-like animals with the mighty horizontally swung horns were not approaching, but were being created before my eyes and sent out as they were finished. I had seen a herd of Elephant travelling through dense Native forest, where the sunlight is strewn down between the thick creepers in small spots and patches, pacing along as if they had an appointment at the end of the world. It was, in giant size, the border of a very old, infinitely precious Persian carpet, in the dyes of green, yellow, and black-brown. I had time after time watched the progression across the plain of the Giraffe, in their queer, inimitable, vegetative gracefulness, as if it were not a herd of animals but a family of rare, long-stemmed, speckled gigantic flowers slowly advancing. I had followed two Rhino on their morning promenade, when they were sniffing and snorting in the air of the dawn—which is so cold that it hurts in the nose—and looked like two very big angular stones rollicking in the long valley and enjoying life together. I had seen the royal lion, before sunrise, below a waning moon, crossing the grey plain on his way home from the kill, drawing a dark wake in the silvery grass, his face still red up to the ears, or during a midday-siesta, when he reposed contentedly in the midst of his family on the short grass and in the delicate, spring-like shade of the broad Acacia trees of his part of Africa.

—Isak Dinesen, *Out of Africa*

j. Have you noticed us? We scuttle through the halls in sensible shoes, bent double with the weight of our books and purses. We wear serious expressions because we *are* serious. (Laughter is for the young; it's simply not our style.) We always sit in clusters, usually in the front seats of the classroom. Who could miss us! And we love to answer questions because we are convinced that our two cents is worth at least twenty. We are (have you guessed it?) the CUE[1] students at Drew University. And we are having a wonderful time.

—Shirley Weissenborn

k. In its days of glory, Hollywood was much more than a symbol. It was a power, a velvet-gloved tyranny exerted over most of the globe. And it could show its despotism in whimsical ways. When, around 1910, the movies began their trek westward to California, actors found the celluloid collars that were conventional wear at the time too hot; so they affected soft-collared shirts. Men across the world aped the new screen style so obediently that within a year or two the celluloid-collar industry was finished forever. A quarter of a century later, the male-underwear business experienced a similar crisis when Clark Gable removed his shirt in *It Happened One Night* to reveal that he wore no undershirt. In women's style the tyranny was inevitably even more severe and continuous. Gloria

---

[1] Continuing University Education

Swanson's gowns, the length of Mary Pickford's hair, Theda Bara's mascara or Clara Bow's rouge, Jean Harlow's peroxide, Joan Crawford's shoulders, Veronica Lake's peekaboo, Jane Russell's profile, Marilyn's wiggle. Taken together, these women affected the look of an entire generation.

—David Robinson, "The Movies"

2. Analyze the paragraph sequences in the following essay, "Isaac Newton," noting the patterns of the paragraphs and their movement from beginning to end:

Isaac Newton

I. Bernard Cohen

The mind and personality of Isaac Newton challenge any historian. Newton was a strange, solitary figure, and the wellsprings of his behavior were hidden even from his contemporaries. A biographer of his time compared Newton to the River Nile, whose great powers were known but whose source had not been discovered. Nevertheless, the few facts we have about his early life do allow some speculation about Newton's character and development.

He was born prematurely, a physical weakling. It is said that he had to wear a "bolster" to support his neck during his first few months, that no one expected him to live. Newton later was fond of saying that his mother had said he was so tiny at birth that he could have been put into a quart mug.

Newton's father died three months before he was born. When the boy was less than two years old, his mother remarried, and he was turned over to his aged grandmother. He lived on an isolated farm, deprived of parental care and love, without the friendly companionship and rivalry of brothers and sisters. The late Louis T. More, author of the best-known modern biography of the man, held that much of Newton's "inwardness" could be attributed to his lonely and unhapply childhood.

Born in 1642, Newton grew up in an era when England was still tasting the "terrors of a protracted and bitter civil war." Raiding and plundering parties were common. His grandmother was "suspected of sympathy to the royal forces." In the face of these real terrors and "the frights of his imagination," he could not have received much comfort from his grandmother or the hired laborers on the farm. Naturally enough, as More observed, the boy turned to "the solace of lonely meditation" and developed a strong habit of self-absorption. A girl who knew him in his youth described him as a "sober, silent, thinking lad" who "was never known scarce to play with the boys abroad, at their silly amusements."

He evidently overcame his physical weakness by the time he reached school age, for a schoolmate reported that Newton challenged a bully who had kicked him in the belly to a fight and "beat him till he would fight no more"—winning out because he had "more spirit and resolution." The bully stood high in the class, and Newton was so determined "to beat him also at his books" that "by hard work he finally succeeded, and then gradually rose to be the first in the school."

When Newton was 14, his mother took the boy back into her home, her second husband having died. She conceived the idea of making him a farmer, but the experiment proved an unqualified failure. Newton found farming totally distasteful. Instead of attending properly to his chores, he would read, make wooden models with his knife, or dream. Fortunately for science, his mother gave up the attempt and allowed him to prepare for Cambridge University.

At the age of 18, Newton entered Trinity College. In his early years at the University he was not outstanding in any way. Then he came under the influence of Isaac Barrow, a professor of mathematics and an extraordinary man. He was an able mathematician, a classicist, an astronomer and an authority in the field of optics. Barrow was one of the first to recognize Newton's genius. Soon after his student had taken a degree, Barrow resigned his professorship so that Newton might have it. Thus at 26 Newton was established in an academic post of distinction and was free to pursue his epoch-making studies.

He had already sown the seeds of his revolutionary contributions to three distinct fields of scientific inquiry: mathematics, celestial mechanics and physical optics. After his graduation from the University he had returned to his home at Woolsthorpe for 18 months of work which can fairly be described as the most fruitful 18 months in all the history of the creative imagination. Newton's subsequent life in science consisted to a large degree in the elaboration of the great discoveries made during those "golden" months. What Newton did at Woolsthorpe is best stated in his words:

"In the beginning of the year 1665 I found the method for approximating series and the rule for reducing any dignity [power] of any binomial to such a series [i.e., the binomial theorem]. The same year in May I found the method of tangents of Gregory and Slusius, and in November [discovered] the direct method of Fluxions [i.e., the elements of the differential calculus], and the next year in January had the Theory of Colours, and in May following I had entrance into the inverse method of Fluxions [i.e., integral calculus], and in the same year I began to think of gravity extending to the orb of the Moon . . . and having thereby compared the force requisite to keep the Moon in her orb with the force of gravity at the surface of the earth, and found them to answer pretty nearly. . . ."

As a by-product of his analysis of light and colors, which he had shyly kept to himself, Newton invented a reflecting telescope, to free telescopes from the chromatic aberration of refracting lenses. He made a small version of his new telescope for the Royal Society of London, and was shortly elected, at the age of 30, as a Fellow of the Royal Society, the highest scientific honor in England.

Newton was understandably overwhelmed by his sudden public recognition. He had been loath to announce his discoveries, but within a week after his election to the Society he asked permission to communicate an account of the "philosophical discovery" which had induced him "to the making of the said telescope." With a disarming lack of false modesty, he said that in his judgment he had made "the oddest, if not the most considerable detection, which hath hitherto been made in the operations of nature."

Newton's letter to the Royal Society, "containing his new theory of light and colours," was sent to London on February 6, 1672. This paper can claim a number of "firsts." It was Newton's initial publication; it founded the science of spectroscopy, and it marked the beginning of a sound analysis of color phenomena. Briefly, what Newton showed is that a prism separates white light into its component colors, associated with specific indices of refraction, and that a second prism can recombine the dispersed light and render it white again. These magnificent experiments provided a new departure for the formulation of theories about the nature of color. Yet the paper did not win for Newton the universal applause that he had sought. The Royal Society was bombarded with letters disputing Newton's conclusions. Some of the objectors were unimportant, but others were men of stature: Christian Huygens, Robert Hooke. With astonishing patience, Newton wrote careful letters answering each objection. But he won over only one of his opponents— the French Jesuit Father Pardies.

The controversy had an acid effect on Newton's personality. He vowed that he would publish no further discoveries. As he wrote later to Leibnitz: "I was so persecuted with discussions arising from the publication of my theory of light, that I blamed my own imprudence for parting with so substantial a blessing as my quiet to run after a shadow." And yet he did later continue to publish; he wanted the applause of the scientific world. This ambivalence was not overlooked by Newton's enemies. The astronomer John Flamsteed, who broke with Newton, described him as "insidious, ambitious, and excessively covetous of praise, and impatient of contradiction.... I believe him to be a good man at the bottom; but, through his nature, suspicious."

At Cambridge Newton was the very model of an absent-minded professor. His amanuensis, Humphrey Newton (no relative), wrote that he never knew Newton "to take any recreation or pastime either in riding out to take the air, walking, bowling, or any other exercise whatever, thinking all hours lost that were not spent in his studies." He often worked until two or three o'clock in the morning, ate sparingly and sometimes forgot to eat altogether. When reminded that he had not eaten, he would go to the table and "eat a bite or two standing." Newton rarely dined in the college hall; when he did, he was apt to appear "with shoes down at heels, stockings untied, surplice on, and his head scarcely combed." It was said that he often delivered his lectures to an empty hall, apparently with as much satisfaction as if the room had been full of students.

After the controversy, Newton withdrew from the public eye as a scientist. He served the University as its representative in Parliament and worked away in private at chemistry and alchemy, theology, physics and mathematices. He became acquainted with Leibnitz, but refused to give his great contemporary any exact information about his discoveries in mathematics. Today it is generally agreed that the calculus was discovered more or less independently by both Newton and Leibnitz, but the two men and their partisans quarreled acrimoniously over priority, and Newton accused Leibnitz of plagiarism. Newton conceived a jealous proprietary interest in every subject he studied, and almost every achievement of his creative life was accompanied by some quarrel.

In 1684 came the famous visit to Newton by the astronomer Edmund Halley. He had a problem concerning the gravitational attraction between the sun and the planets. Halley and Hooke had concluded from Johannes Kepler's accounting of planetary motions that the force of attraction must vary inversely with the square of the distance between a planet and the sun. But they had been unable to prove their idea. "What," Halley asked Newton, "would be the curve described by the planets on the supposition that gravity diminished as the square of the distance?" Newton answered without hesitation: "An ellipse." How did he know that? "Why," replied Newton, "I have calculated it." These four words informed Halley that Newton had worked out one of the most fundamental laws of the universe—the law of gravity. Halley wanted to see the calculations at once, but Newton could not find his notes. He promised to write out the theorems and proofs. Under Halley's insistent urging he completed a manuscript for the Royal Society. Thus was born the *Philosophiae Naturalis Principia Mathematica,* known ever since simply as the *Principia.*

Just before its publication a crisis arose when Hooke laid claim to the inverse-square law. Newton threatened to withdraw the climactic chapters of his work, but Halley mollified him and the great classic went to press intact. Halley's credit in this enterprise is enormous. He not only got Newton to write the work but also saw it through the press and paid the costs of publication, although he was not a wealthy man.

The *Principia* is divided into three "books." In the first Newton laid down his three laws of motion and explored the consequences of various laws of force. In the second he explored motion in various types of fluids; here he was somewhat less successful, and much of his work had to be revised in the succeeding decades. In the third he discussed universal gravitation and showed how a single law of force explains at once the falling of bodies on the earth, the motion of our moon or of Jupiter's satellites, the motions of planets and the phenomenon of tides.

One of the most vexing problems for Newton was to find a rigorous proof that a sphere acts gravitationally as if all its mass were concentrated at its center. Without this theorem, the whole theory of gravitation would rest on intuition rather than precise calculation. For instance, in the simple case of an apple falling to the ground—the occasion of the central idea of gravitation according to Newton's own account—what is the "distance between" the earth and the apple? Here the calculus came into play. Newton considered the earth as a collection of tiny volumes of matter, each attracting the apple according to the inverse-square law of gravitation. Then he summed up the individual forces and showed that the result was the same as if the earth were a point mass, as if all the matter of the earth were shrunk into a tiny region at its center.

Newton suffered some kind of "nervous breakdown" after the completion of the *Principia*. He complained that he could not sleep, and said that he lacked the "former consistency of his mind." He wrote angry letters to friends and then apologized; he protested bitterly to John Locke, for example, that the philosopher had attempted to "embroil him with women."

In 1696 Newton abandoned the academic life for the position of Warden, later Master, of the Mint. Honors for his scientific achievements continued to come to him: he was knighted in 1705 and served many years as president of the Royal Society. But the last quarter century of his life produced no major contributions to science. Some say that his creative genius had simply burned out. Others argue that after having founded the science of physical optics, invented the calculus and shown the mechanism of the universe, there just wasn't anything left for him to do in the realm of science.

Although he made no important discoveries, Newton's last years were not barren of ideas. Now famous and honored, he felt secure enough to offer many public speculations on scientific problems. He suggested various possible hypotheses as to the "cause" of gravitation and speculated on the nature of the "ether," the size of the constituent units of matter, the forces of electricity and magnetism, the cause of muscular response to the "commands of the will," the origins of sensation, the creation of the world, the ultimate destiny of man. In the century after Newton, physical experimenters followed up many of his bold speculations.

Newton is often described as the inaugurator of the "Age of Reason." Alexander Pope expressed the sentiment of his time in the famous lines:

> Nature and Nature's laws lay hid in night:
> God said, Let Newton be! and all was light.

Part Three

WRITING A SHORT PAPER: ANSWERING THE TWENTY QUESTIONS

1. How Can X Be Described?
2. How Did X Happen?
3. What Kind of Person Is X?
4. What Is My Memory of X?
5. What Is My Personal Response to X?
6. What Are the Facts About X?
7. How Can X Be Summarized?
8. What Does X Mean?
9. What Is the Essential Function of X?
10. What Are the Component Parts of X?
11. How Is X Made or Done?
12. How Should X Be Made or Done?
13. What Are the Causes of X?
14. What Are the Consequences of X?
15. What Are the Types of X?
16. How Does X Compare to Y?
17. What Is the Present Status of X?
18. How Should X Be Interpreted?
19. What Is the Value of X?
20. What Case Can Be Made for or Against X?

1. How Can X Be Described?

*F*or the student who reportedly said that he would "have to run out and get run over by a truck in order to find something to write about," there is a simpler and safer alternative. The student can ask the question "How can I describe it?" He can look at some aspect of the environment—a person, a place, an object, or an event. This student—or you—can look at the sky and the stars; look at the school gymnasium and the used-car lot at the edge of town (the subject need not be poetic). You can look up from your desk, look across the room, look at the window, look *out* the window, look out and *beyond*. Look and then answer the question "What does it look like?" Describe what you see, hear, smell, feel. Describe your sensations and impressions. Is the night dark and eerie (scary?); is the day gray and bleak (depressing?); or is the day sunny and warm, alive with people and laughter? Whatever is happening out there, take careful note; for as poet John Ciardi has said, whatever we look at carefully is worth looking at—and, he might have added, worth writing about as well.

A description may be an essay in itself or part of a longer work (short story, essay, novel, article, biography). Description is a necessary adjunct to all types of writing, because it reconstructs for the reader how something or someone *appears*. Remember this above all, then, in writing description: You must have a keen eye; in fact, all your senses must be alert if you are to take in the scene and then reproduce it in a verbal picture that will come alive for the reader.

EFFECTIVE SELECTION OF DETAIL

Clearly, a good description must evoke sensory impressions, for only then can the reader begin to respond totally. Although a particular piece of writing may call several senses into play, the visual will usually predominate, since most of us use our eyes as a primary guide and as a check or verifier of our other senses. (Thus Shakespeare, in *A Midsummer Night's Dream*, has Bottom rush into the woods "to see a noise that he heard.") It is not surprising, then, that most descriptions focus on how something or someone looks.

For example, take Henry Fielding's description of Sophia, the lovely heroine of his novel, *Tom Jones*.

> Sophia ... the only daughter of Mr. Western, was a middle-sized woman; but rather inclining to tall. Her shape was not only exact, but extremely delicate; and the nice proportion of her arms promised the truest symmetry in her limbs. Her hair, which was black, was so luxuriant that it reached her middle, before she cut it to comply with the modern fashion; and it was now curled so gracefully in her neck that few could believe it to be her own. If envy could find any part of the face which demanded less commendation than the rest, it might possibly think her forehead might have been higher

without prejudice to her. Her eyebrows were full, even, and arched beyond the power of art to imitate. Her black eyes had a lustre in them which all her softness could not extinguish.

Fielding does not give all the details of Sophia's appearance; an overly detailed listing would be tedious and dull. Instead he selects those precise physical characteristics that enable us to see her in our mind's eye: she is tall, with nice proportions (the relationship of the parts of the body); she is delicate (the texture or "aura" of her); her black hair curls gracefully on her neck; she has a relatively low forehead (perhaps a slight imperfection to make her seem more human); she has lovely arched eyebrows and lustrous black eyes (proverbially "the windows of the soul").

Clearly, Fielding had a long list of subquestions in mind when he drew this verbal portrait, questions concerning size, shape, coloring, posture, proportion, expression, style, and manner. For all practical purposes, Sophia stands before us as if in a photograph.

So too does the schoolroom which Dickens describes in *David Copperfield*. Here Dickens selects details with the express purpose of creating a dominant mood or impression. It is a "forlorn and desolate place," we are told in the opening sentence of the paragraph, and the following specific details paint a picture which supports that judgment: the floor is "dirty" and littered (the room looks "forlorn and desolate"); the birds make a "mournful rattle" (the room sounds "forlorn and desolate"); the air itself is "unwholesome" (the room smells "forlorn and desolate").

> I gazed upon the schoolroom into which he took me, as the most forlorn and desolate place I had ever seen. I see it now. A long room, with three long rows of desks, and six of forms, and bristling all around with pegs for hats and slates. Scraps of old copy-books and exercises litter the dirty floor. Some silkworms' houses, made of the same materials, are scattered over the desks. Two miserable little white mice, left behind by their owner, are running up and down in a fusty castle made of pasteboard and wire, looking in all corners with their red eyes for anything to eat. A bird, in a cage very little bigger than himself, makes a mournful rattle now and then in hopping on his perch, two inches high, or dropping from it, but neither sings nor chirps. There is a strange unwholesome smell upon the room, like mildewed corduroys, sweet apples wanting air, and rotten books. There could not well be more ink splashed about it, if it had been roofless from its first construction, and the skies had rained, snowed, hailed, and blown ink through the varying seasons of the year.

Dickens's first impression, that the schoolroom was "the most forlorn and desolate place" he had ever seen, leads him to recreate it for his readers. We see it now, just as he saw it then. He piles detail upon detail in this stirring passage. They appeal to all our senses: we *see* the "long room," the "scraps of old copy-books," the "two miserable little white mice," and the "bird"; we *hear* the bird's "mournful rattle"; we *smell* "mildewed corduroys, sweet apples wanting air, and rotten books." Every detail suggests abandonment and decay—the very opposite of what should happen in the classroom: intellectual and physical growth. It all speaks, as Dickens no doubt intended it to, for a country whose educational system is in a horrifying state of disrepair.

As Dickens well understood, a good verbal description, like a good drawing or painting, rivals the most accurate photograph. In urging students to develop what she called "fresh seeing," artist Emily Carr observed that "we may copy something as faithfully as the camera, but unless we bring to our picture something additional—something creative—something of ourselves—our picture does not live." (*Seeing* 11). The same is true of verbal pictures: they too must be animated by a creative vision—by "fresh seeing."

In contrast to the preceding writers, John Updike in the following essay is not a fixed gazer but a moving observer recording a vivid list of images as he walks through Central Park on the first day of spring. We the readers are at his side, sharing those images:

> ...great black rocks...with craggy skins....
> ...four boys...throwing snowballs at each other....
> ...water murmuring....
> Two pigeons feeding each other.
> One red mitten lying lost under a poplar tree.

Each image is rendered with such sharp particularity that as they succeed one another, they build into a total impression. Like the pieces of a jigsaw puzzle when finally assembled, these images emerge into a wonderful picture: a special day in Central Park.

Central Park

John Updike

On the afternoon of the first day of spring, when the gutters were still heaped high with Monday's snow but the sky itself was swept clean, we put on our galoshes and walked up the sunny side of Fifth Avenue to Central Park. There we saw:

Great black rocks emerging from the melting drifts, their craggy skins glistening like the backs of resurrected brontosaurs.

A pigeon on the half-frozen pond strutting to the edge of the ice and looking a duck in the face.

A policeman getting his shoe wet testing the ice.

Three elderly relatives trying to coax a little boy to accompany his father on a sled ride down a short but steep slope. After much balking, the boy did, and, sure enough, the sled tipped over and the father got his collar full of snow. Everybody laughed except the boy, who sniffled.

Four boys in black leather jackets throwing snowballs at each other. (The snow was ideally soggy, and packed hard with one squeeze.)

Seven men without hats.

Twelve snowmen, none of them intact.

Two men listening to the radio in a car parked outside the Zoo; Mel Allen was broadcasting the Yanks-Cardinals game from St. Petersburg.

A tahr (*Hemitragus jemlaicus*) pleasantly squinting in the sunlight.

An aoudad absently pawing the mud and chewing.

A yak with its back turned.

Empty cages labelled "Coati," "Orang-outang," "Ocelot."

A father saying to his little boy, who was annoyed almost to tears by the inactivity of the seals, "Father (Father Seal, we assumed) is very tired; he worked hard all day."

Most of the cafeteria's out-of-doors tables occupied.

A pretty girl in black pants falling on them at the Wollman Memorial Rink.

"BILL & DORIS" carved on a tree. "REX & RITA" written in the snow.

Two old men playing, and six supervising, a checkers game.

The Michael Friedsam Foundation Merry-Go-Round, nearly empty of children but overflowing with calliope music.

A man on a bench near the carrousel reading, through sunglasses, a book on economics.

Crews of shinglers repairing the roof of the Tavern-on-the-Green.

A woman dropping a camera she was trying to load, the film unrolling in the slush and exposing itself.

A little colored boy in aviator goggles rubbing his ears and saying, "He really hurt me." "No, he didn't," his nursemaid told him.

The green head of Giuseppe Mazzini staring across the white softball field, unblinking, though the sun was in its eyes.

Water murmuring down walks and rocks and steps. A grown man trying to block one rivulet with snow.

Things like brown sticks nosing through a plot of cleared soil.

A tire track in a piece of mud far removed from where any automobiles could be.

Footprints around a KEEP OFF sign.

Two pigeons feeding each other.

Two showgirls, whose faces had not yet thawed the frost of their makeup, treading indignantly through the slush.

A plump old man saying "Chick, chick" and feeding peanuts to squirrels.

Many solitary men throwing snowballs at tree trunks.

Many birds calling to each other about how little the Ramble has changed.

One red mitten lying lost under a poplar tree.

An airplane, very bright and distant, slowly moving through the branches of a sycamore.

EFFECTIVE ARRANGEMENT OF DETAILS

As we have just seen, the first basic principle of description is that it should involve the senses or evoke sensory impressions through the selection of details. Maintaining a consistent point of view or arranging details not in random fashion but in an order either inherent in the subject or dictated by the context is the second basic principle. To maintain a consistent point of view, writers describe subjects as they observe them and include only what they can observe. The organization of a descriptive essay or other writing, then, depends on the way in which the writer—and the reader—perceive the subject. For instance, if you are describing a room, you would move from right to left, or from top to bottom (spatial organization). If you were describing an event, you would move from beginning to end (chronological organization). If you were describing a series of related actions, you would move from cause to effect (causal organization). We will examine each of these in turn.

In spatial organization, point of view—or angle of vision as it is sometimes called—is especially important because it determines what writers can see, how they see what they do, how what they see makes them feel, and so on. In Updike's essay, which is spatially organized, the writer is—as I pointed out above—a moving observer, passing from one point in Central Park to another, describing, item by item, what he observes as he goes along. In the selection which follows, a passage from Dr. Seuss's famous children's story, *The 500 Hats of Bartholomew Cubbins*, the observer is "fixed"—anchored in one spot. First he looks up; then he looks down, each direction creating not only a different sense of place but a different sense of self in relation to place.

The Kingdom of Didd

Dr. Seuss

The Kingdom of Didd was ruled by King Derwin. His palace stood high on the top of the mountain. From his balcony, he looked down over the houses of all his sub-jects—first, over the spires of the noblemen's castles, across the broad roofs of the rich men's mansions, then over the little houses of the townsfolk, to the huts of the farmers far off in the fields.

It was a mighty view and it made King Derwin feel mighty important.

Far off in the fields, on the edge of a cranberry bog, stood the hut of the Cubbins family. From the small door Bartholomew looked across the huts of the farmers to the houses of the townsfolk, then to the rich men's mansions and the noblemen's castles, up to the great towering palace of the King. It was exactly the same view that King Derwin saw from his balcony, but Bartholomew saw it backward.

It was a mighty view, but it made Bartholomew Cubbins feel mighty small.

In the following vivid description—also a spatial organization—we watch the moon rise over Monument Valley with the writer, John V. Young. We share Young's campsite and, more important, his point of view—facing east "across the limitless expanse of tawny desert." With him, we are turned toward the rising moon, and never—from the opening to the closing paragraph—do we turn away. Our position in relation to the subject is fixed throughout, even when we are momentarily distracted from the scenery by the appearance of "a Navajo girl wearing a long, dark, velvet dress gleaming with silver ornaments."

Actually, the order of this piece is both *chronological* and spatial; it begins "before the sun was fully down" and ends when "the moon had cleared the tops of The Mittens"; the camp faces east, "toward the rising sun and the rising moon." As the scene unfolds, with its sense of the "mysterious and lonely," Young probes beneath the surface of the event to create an underlying mood or atmosphere. The slow passing of time, marked by changes in the natural scenery and the sky, contributes to this effect. So do the many details: we see the colors; we hear the rustle of the night wind; we feel the texture of the surrounding sandstone; we sense in our own muscles the movement of the land upward toward the sky where, soon, the moon will rise.

Moonrise Over Monument Valley

John V. Young

We were camped here in early spring, by one of those open-faced shelters that the Navajos have provided for tourists in this part of their vast tribal park on the Arizona-Utah border, 25 miles north of Kayenta. It was cool but pleasant, and we were alone, three men in a truck.

We were here for a purpose: to see the full moon rise over this most mysterious and lonely of scenic wonders, where fantastically eroded red and yellow sandstone shapes soar to the sky like a giant's chess pieces and where people—especially white strangers—come quickly to feel like pretty small change indeed.

Because all Navajo dwellings face east, our camp faced east—toward the rising sun and the rising moon and across a limitless expanse of tawny desert, that ancient sea, framed by the towering nearby twin pinnacles called The Mittens. We began to feel the magic even before the sun was fully down. It occurred when a diminutive wraith of a Navajo girl wearing a long, dark, velvet dress gleaming with silver ornaments drifted silently by, herding a flock of ghostly sheep to a waterhole somewhere. A bell on one of the rams tinkled faintly, and then its music was lost in the soft rustle of the night wind, leaving us with an impression that perhaps we had really seen nothing at all.

Just then, a large woolly dog appeared out of the gloom, seeming to materialize on the spot. It sat quietly on the edge of the glow from our camp-fire, its eyes shining like mirrors. It made no sound but when we offered food, it accepted the gift gravely and with much dignity. The dog then vanished again, probably to join the girl and her flock. We were not certain it was not part of the illusion.

As the sun disappeared entirely, the evening afterglow brush tipped all the spires and cliffs with magenta, deepening to purple, and the sand ripples stood out like miniature ocean waves in darkening shades of orange. Off to the east on the edge of the desert, a pale saffron glow told us the moon was about to rise behind a thin layer of clouds, slashed by the white contrail of an invisible jet airplane miles away.

We had our cameras on tripods and were fussing with light meters, making casual bets as to the exact place where the moon would first appear, when it happened—instant enchantment. Precisely between the twin spires of The Mittens, the enormous golden globe loomed suddenly, seeming as big as the sun itself, behind a coppery curtain on the rim of creation.

We were as totally unprepared for the great size of the moon as we were for its flaming color, nor could we have prepared ourselves for the improbable setting. We felt like the wizards of Stonehenge, commanding the planets to send their light through the magic orifices in line at the equinox. Had the Navajo medicine men contrived this for our benefit?

The massive disk of the moon seemed to rise very fast at first, an optical effect magnified by the crystalline air and the flatness of the landscape between us and the distant, ragged skyline. Then it seemed to pause for a moment, as if it were pinioned on one of the pinnacles or impaled on a sharply upthrusting rocky point. Its blazing light made inky shadows all around us, split by the brilliant wedge of the moon's path between the spires. The wind had stopped. There was not a sound anywhere, not even a whisper. If a drum had sounded just then, it would not have been out of place, I suppose, but it would have frightened us half to death.

Before the moon had cleared the tops of The Mittens, the show was over and the magic was gone. A thin veil of clouds spread over the sky, ending the spell as suddenly as it had come upon us. It was as if the gods had decided that we had seen enough for mere mortals on one spring night, and I must confess it was something of a relief to find ourselves back on mundane earth again, with sand in our shoes and a chill in the air.

The causal organization of a piece of descriptive writing occurs most commonly in technical composition. For instance, if the designer of a new piece of equipment wants to describe how its various parts work together, a causal organization would be the most logical. In the following selection, causal combines with a chronological ordering of actions. The parts of an event describe an "ongoing process"— specifically, an earthquake which strikes in the evening, with "the moon just rising." As the writer describes the destructive effects, one leading to another in a deadly causal chain, he makes us painfully conscious that from the first "frightening roar" this ongoing process is irreversible.

The Earthquake

Jonathan Spence

The earthquake struck T'an-ch'eng on July 25, 1668. It was evening, the moon just rising. There was no warning, save for a frightening roar that seemed to come from somewhere to the northwest. The buildings in the city began to shake and the trees took up a rhythmical swaying, tossing ever more wildly back and forth until their tips almost touched the ground. Then came one sharp violent jolt that brought down stretches of the city walls and battlements, officials' yamens, temples, and thousands of private homes. Broad fissures opened up across the streets and underneath the houses, jets of water spurted up into the air to a height of twenty feet or more, and streams of water poured down the roads and flooded the irrigation ditches. Those people who tried to remain standing felt as if their feet were round stones spinning out of control, and were brought crashing to the ground.

Some, like Li Hsien-yü, fell into the fissures but were buoyed up on underground streams and able to cling to the edge; others had their houses sheared in half and survived in the living quarters as the storage rooms slid into the earth. Some watched helplessly as their families fell away from them: Kao Te-mou had lived in a household of twenty-nine with his consorts, children, relatives, and servants, but only he, one son, and one daughter survived.

As suddenly as it had come the earthquake departed. The ground was still. The water seeped away, leaving the open fissures edged with mud and fine sand. The ruins rested in layers where they had fallen, like giant sets of steps.

It was, wrote Feng K'o-ts'an, who in 1673 compiled the *Local History of T'an-ch'eng*, as if fate were "throwing rocks upon a man who had already fallen in a well."

DESCRIBING TO INFORM AND DELIGHT

Roger Angell's description of a baseball, which follows, contains more information about physical characteristics than you might think a writer could amass about one single, relatively small item: such as its size, weight, texture, composition, and even its history.

So much for the informative detail, Angell seems to be saying, as the paragraph suddenly turns from painstakingly itemized *facts* to personal *feelings*. "But never mind," he says; presumably "never mind" that the baseball is "made of a composition—cork nucleus encased in two thin layers of rubber." Never mind such details, for what is more significant is that the baseball—any baseball—"is beautiful . . . it is a perfect object for a man's hand." Once he pronounces this aesthetic judgment (and we may assume that there are some women who would share this judgment: See Susan Jacoby's "The First Girl at Second Base," pages 376–77), the writer goes on to support his feelings by drawing the reader into a relationship with a baseball. Pick it up, he suggests, feel it, throw it. The baseball depicted in the second half of this piece is a "spare and sensual object" that fascinates Angell and involves him so emotionally that by simple contagion, as well as by his extraordinary craft, he involves the reader as well.

The Baseball

Roger Angell

It weighs just over five ounces and measures between 2.86 and 2.94 inches in diameter. It is made of a composition-cork nucleus encased in two thin layers of rubber, one black and one red, surrounded by 121 yards of tightly wrapped blue-gray wool yarn, 45 yards of white wool yarn, 53 more yards of blue-gray wool yarn, 150 yards of fine cotton yarn, a coat of rubber cement, and a cowhide (formerly horsehide) exterior, which is held together with 216 slightly raised red cotton stitches. Printed certifications, endorsements, and outdoor advertising spherically attest to its authenticity. Like most institutions, it is considered inferior in its present form to its ancient archetypes, and in this case the complaint is probably justified; on occasion in recent years it has actually been known to come apart under the demands of its brief but rigorous active career. Baseballs are assembled and hand-stitched in Taiwan (before this year the work was done in Haiti, and before 1973 in Chicopee, Massachusetts), and contemporary pitchers claim that there is a tangible variation in the size and feel of the balls that now come into play in a single game; a true peewee is treasured by hurlers, and its departure from the premises, by fair means or foul, is secretly mourned. But never mind: any baseball is beautiful. No other small package comes as close to the ideal in design and utility. It is a perfect object for a man's hand. Pick it up and it instantly suggests its purpose; it is meant to be thrown a considerable distance—thrown hard and with precision. Its feel and heft are the beginning of the sport's critical dimensions; if it were a fraction of an inch larger or smaller, a few centigrams heavier or lighter, the game of baseball would be utterly different. Hold a baseball in your hand. As it happens, this one is not brand-new. Here, just to one side of the curved surgical welt of stitches, there is a pale-green grass smudge, darkening on one edge almost to black—the mark of an old infield play, a tough grounder now lost in memory. Feel the ball, turn it over in your hand; hold it across the seam or the other way, with the seam just to the side of your middle finger. Speculation stirs. You want to get outdoors and throw this spare and sensual object to somebody or, at the very least, watch somebody else throw it. The game has begun.

DESCRIBING TO CREATE MOOD AND MEANING

In its creation of mood and its suggestion of a larger meaning (the meaning of life itself), James Agee's description of "Shady Grove, Alabama" is a small classic. It combines place (a southern cemetery) and natural event (death); more than that, it provides "data" which are so strange as to be barely believable. Yet we are moved to belief because the painstakingly rendered details and the matter-of-fact tone give the piece a documentary solidness. On the one hand, the description provides objectively verifiable, measurable facts ("The graveyard is about fifty by a hundred yards . . ."); on the other hand, it provides vivid sense impressions rendered in poetic images ("It is heavily silent and fragrant and all the leaves are breathing slowly . . ."). For many reasons, and on many levels, this essay in description will repay your close study.

Shady Grove, Alabama, July 1936

James Agee

The graveyard is about fifty by a hundred yards inside a wire fence. There are almost no trees in it: a lemon verbena and a small magnolia; it is all red clay and very few weeds.

Out at the front of it across the road there is a cornfield and then a field of cotton and then trees.

Most of the headboards are pine, and at the far end of the yard from the church the graves are thinned out and there are many slender and low pine stumps about the height of the headboards. The shadows are all struck sharp lengthwise of the graves, toward the cornfield, by the afternoon sun. There is no one anywhere in sight. It is heavily silent and fragrant and all the leaves are breathing slowly without touching each other.

Some of the graves have real headstones, a few of them so large they must be the graves of landowners. One is a thick limestone log erected by the Woodmen of the World. One or two of the others, besides a headpiece, have a flat of stone as large as the whole grave.

On one of these there is a china dish on whose cover delicate hands lie crossed, cuffs at their wrists, and the nails distinct.

On another a large fluted vase stands full of dead flowers, with an inch of rusty water at the bottom.

On others of these stones, as many as a dozen of them, there is something I have never seen before: by some kind of porcelain reproduction, a photograph of the person who is buried there; the last or the best likeness that had been made, in a small-town studio, or at home with a snapshot camera. I remember one well of a fifteen-year-old boy in Sunday pants and a plaid pull-over sweater, his hair combed, his cap in his hand, sitting against a piece of farm machinery and grinning. His eyes are squinted against the light and his nose makes a deep shadow down one side of his chin. Somebody's arm, with the sleeve rolled up, is against him; somebody who is almost certainly still alive: they could not cut him entirely out of the picture. Another is a studio portrait, close up, in artificial lighting, of a young woman. She is leaned a little forward, smiling vivaciously, one hand at her cheek. She is not very pretty, but she believed she was; her face is free from strain or fear. She is wearing an evidently new dress, with a mail-order look about it; patterns of beads are sewn over it and have caught the light. Her face is soft with powder and at the wings of her nose lines have been deleted. Her dark blonde hair is newly washed and professionally done up in puffs at the ears which in that time, shortly after the first great war of her century, were called cootie garages. This image of her face is split across and the split has begun to turn brown at its edges.

I think these would be graves of small farmers.

There are others about which there can be no mistake: they are the graves of the poorest of the farmers and of the tenants. Mainly they are the graves with the pine headboards; or without them.

When the grave is still young, it is very sharply distinct, and of a peculiar form. The clay is raised in a long and narrow oval with a sharp ridge, the shape exactly of an inverted boat. A fairly broad board is driven at the head; a narrower one, sometimes only a stob, at the feet. A good many of the headboards have been sawed into the flat simulacrum of an hourglass; in some of these, the top has been roughly rounded off, so that the resemblance is more nearly that of a head and shoulders sunken or risen to the waist in the dirt. On some of these boards names and dates have been written or printed in hesitant letterings, in pencil or in crayon, but most of them appear never to have been touched in this way. The boards at some of the graves have fallen slantwise or down; many graves seem never to have been marked except in their own carefully made shape. These graves are of all sizes between those of giants and of newborn children; and there are a great many, so many they seem shoals of minnows, two feet long and less, lying near one another; and of these smallest graves, very few are marked with any wood at all, and many are already so drawn into the earth that they are scarcely distinguishable. Some of the largest, on the other hand, are of heroic size, seven and eight feet long, and of these more are marked, a few, even, with the smallest and plainest blocks of limestone, and initials, once or twice a full name; but many more of them have never been marked, and many, too, are sunken half down and more and almost entirely into the earth. A great many of these graves, perhaps half to two thirds of those which are still distinct, have been decorated, not only with shrunken flowers in their cracked vases and with bent targets of blasted flowers, but otherwise as well. Some have a line of white clamshells planted along their ridge; of others, the rim as well is garlanded with these shells. On one large grave, which is otherwise completely plain, a blown-out electric bulb is screwed into the clay at the exact center. On another, on the slope of clay just in front of the headboard, its feet next the board, is a horseshoe; and at its center a blown bulb is stood upright. On two or three others there are insulators of bluegreen glass. On several graves, which I presume to be those of women, there is at the center the prettiest or the oldest and most valued piece of china: on one, a blue glass butter dish whose cover is a setting hen; on another, an intricate milk-colored glass basket; on others, ten-cent-store candy dishes and iridescent vases; on one, a pattern of white and colored buttons. On other graves there are small and thick white butter dishes of the sort which are used in lunch-rooms, and by the action of rain these stand free of the grave on slender turrets of clay. On still another grave, laid carefully next the headboard, is a corncob pipe. On the graves of children there are still these pretty pieces of glass and china, but they begin to diminish in size and they verge into the forms of animals and into homuncular symbols of growth; and there are toys: small autos, locomotives and fire engines of red and blue metal; tea sets for dolls, and tin kettles the size of thimbles: little effigies in rubber and glass and china, of cows, lions, bulldogs, squeaking mice, and the characters of comic strips; and ... what two parents have done here for their little daughter: not only a tea set, and a cocacola bottle, and a milk bottle, ranged on her short grave, but a stone at the head and a stone at the foot, and in the headstone her six month image as she lies sleeping dead in her white dress, the head sunken delicately forward, deeply and delicately gone, the eyes seamed, as that of a dead bird, and on the rear face of this stone the words:

We can't have all things to please us,
Our little Daughter, Joe An, has gone to Jesus.

DISCUSSION AND EXERCISES

1. Study the selection and organization of details in the following paragraphs and answer the following questions:

   a. Is there a topic sentence, and if so, how does it function?
   b. Is the observer fixed or moving?
   c. List the individual details in each paragraph and indicate in what ways they are judiciously chosen. Which does the author present with camera-like objectivity and which does he render subjectively and *feelingly*? Which senses does he appeal to (sight or sound)?
   d. Contemplate the spatial pattern of the paragraph; trace its movement from first to last sentence, indicating what point of view and principle of organization govern the arrangement of details. Does the writer move from left to right; from top to bottom; in order of prominence ("the first thing one sees on entering the room …")? Analyze and explain.
   e. Does the paragraph convey a dominant mood or impression? If so, how does the writer create it? Consider such matters as choice of words, sense images, projection of feeling.

> One November evening, in the neighbourhood of Lyndhurst, I saw a flock of geese marching in a long procession, led, as their custom is, by a majestical gander; they were coming home from their feeding-ground in the forest, and when I spied them were approaching their owner's cottage. Arrived at the wooden gate of the garden in front of the cottage, the leading bird drew up square before it, and with repeated loud screams demanded admittance. Pretty soon, in response to the summons, a man came out of the cottage, walked briskly down the garden path and opened the gate, but only wide enough to put his right leg through; then, placing his foot and knee against the leading bird, he thrust him roughly back; as he did so three young geese pressed forward and were allowed to pass in; then the gate was slammed in the face of the gander and the rest of his followers, and the man went back to the cottage. The gander's indignation was fine to see, though he had most probably experienced the same rude treatment on many previous occasions. Drawing up to the gate again he called more loudly than before; then deliberately lifted a leg, and placing his broad webbed foot like an open hand against the gate actually tried to push it open! His strength was not sufficient; but he continued to push and to call until the man returned to open the gate and let the birds go in.
>
> It was an amusing scene, and the behaviour of the bird struck me as characteristic.   —W. H. Hudson, *Birds and Man*

> Fog everywhere. Fog up the river, where it flows among green aits and meadows; fog down the river, where it rolls defiled among the tiers of shipping, and the waterside pollutions of a great (and dirty) city. Fog on the Essex marshes, fog on the Kentish heights. Fog creeping into the cabooses of collier-brigs; fog lying out on the yards, and hovering in the rigging of great ships; fog drooping on

the gunwales of barges and small boats. Fog in the eyes and throats of ancient Greenwich pensioners, wheezing by the firesides of their wards; fog in the stem and bowl of the afternoon pipe of the wrathful skipper, down in his close cabin; fog cruelly pinching the toes and fingers of his shivering little 'prentice boy on deck. Chance people on the bridges peeping over the parapets into a nether sky of fog, with fog all round them, as if they were up in a balloon, and hanging in the misty clouds.

—Charles Dickens, *Bleak House*

2. a. Evaluate the effectiveness of the separate items or images in Updike's "Central Park," pages 146–47. Note the choice of adjectives (*craggy* skins), adverbs (*ideally* soggy), nouns (a *tabr*). What advantage does Updike gain by using sentence fragments rather than complete sentences?

   b. Write a one-paragraph description of the room in which you are now sitting. Begin the paragraph as follows: "As I look around the room, this is what I see." Be sure to follow a principle of organization that best fulfills the purpose you set for yourself. Begin by using prewriting techniques.

3. Write a paragraph in which your spatial relationship to your subject affects your feelings about yourself (as in the Dr. Seuss passage).

4. In a paragraph (150–250 words) describe a *person, place, setting,* or *event* in such a way that you project one of the following moods or atmospheres:

bustling activity	poverty	loneliness
calm and quiet	beauty	despair
sloppiness	luxury	gaiety
cleanliness	fear	ugliness
deprivation	suspicion	

5. In a paragraph (150–250 words), describe a season of the year, an aspect of a season, or a particular mood or emotion associated with a particular month ("April is the cruelest month," wrote T. S. Eliot, "mixing memory and desire"). Try to place your topic sentence at the beginning of the paragraph.

6. As in Andy Rooney's essay on "Fences," (pages 96–97) there are many subquestions that Jonathan Spence was compelled to ask—consciously or unconsciously—before he could write "The Earthquakes": When did it happen—day or night? Was it expected? What happened first? From what direction did it originate? What specific objects were involved (buildings, trees, walls)?

   a. What other subquestions can you infer that the writer posed to himself in preparing this description?

   b. How does the writer create a sense of impending catastrophe from which there is no escape (note the adverb "helplessly"; note also imagery depicting forces beyond control such as water spurting and stones spinning, both of which suggest inevitability)?

   c. Think about a natural disaster such as Spence's "The Earthquake": a tornado, hurricane, volcanic eruption, flood, violent storm or fire (something you have experienced, seen on television, heard of or read about). Create a cluster around the nucleus word (such as "fire"); then write a 250-word paragraph (one page) drawing on memory and/or imagination.

d. Think about an unnatural or man-made disaster like a bomb explosion, traffic accident, plane crash, nuclear attack, or village massacre (one of the horrors we read about in the newspaper or see on television). Create a cluster; then write a paragraph of 250 words (one page).

7. Contemplate Angell's "The Baseball" in terms of the following:

   a. Physical description:
      Make a list of the physical data Angell has provided about the baseball. Is the opening effective? Consider the matter-of-fact tone: Does it prepare you for what follows? Or is there a shift in tone? Explain.

   b. Historical background:
      Make a list of historical information that Angell gives us regarding the baseball. Does it increase your interest in the subject? Does it increase your involvement?

   c. Subjective description:
      Where does Angell become less objective and more subjective? How does he personally feel about the baseball? What does he mean by "perfect object for a man's hand" or the baseball being a "sensual object"?

   d. Audience:
      Who would find this essay interesting? Sport fans? Those indifferent to sports? Men only? Women? A special audience or a general audience? On what do you base your opinion?

   e. Select an object comparable to the baseball—perhaps another type of ball used in sports (a football, basketball, golf ball, soccer ball, or tennis ball) or any other type of object that interests or delights you. For instance, you might look at a book closely and ask such questions as: What is its size, weight, color, feel, even its smell (old books have a musty smell, new pages can smell of ink, old pages sometimes feel soft, new pages have a certain stiffness). Other suggested objects:

pen	pencil	money	shoe
stone	apple	egg	shell

8. Write a one-paragraph (150–250 words) description of a room, a building, a street, a lake, or a mountain, from two different physical points of view: Regard your subject first from a fixed position (as in "Moonrise Over Monument Valley"), and then move through your subject (as in "Central Park").

9. a. Evaluate the description of Shady Grove cemetery in the following terms:

      1. technical elements that give the piece documentary solidness
      2. sensory images, personal impressions, judgments
      3. point of view
      4. selection, arrangement, and significance of details
      5. organization
      6. dominant mood or atmosphere
      7. choice of words and images
      8. tone
      9. aptness of subject (Do you agree with poet John Ciardi that anything looked at carefully is worth looking at?)

   b. Do you think this cemetery is worth looking at? Why?

   c. Write a one-paragraph answer (150–250 words) to the following question: Do you think Agee is making a comment ("thematic statement") on human nature and life in general in this essay? State your position in an opening topic sentence; then support that position with concrete details.

ESSAY SUGGESTIONS

1. Write your own essay version of John Updike's "Central Park" (500–750 words) depicting a walk through a park or comparable site in your area. Remember, you are a "moving observer"; your essay will reflect your passage from one point to another.
2. In the manner of "Moonrise Over Monument Valley," write a descriptive essay (500–750 words) of a natural event as you watch it happen or as you imagine it; organize your material chronologically.
3. Use your cluster of a "disaster" as the basis for an essay of 500–750 words. Try to organize the sequence of events both chronologically and causally, as Spence does in "The Earthquake."

OR

Read John Hersey's account of *Hiroshima*. Using his data, write a 500–750 word essay in which you identify yourself as a surviving witness. Be sure to develop a list of subquestions here which can help you to take more detailed and relevant notes on the Hiroshima account.
4. Write a descriptive essay (500–750 words) in which you combine physical data and human interest, as in "The Baseball" and "Shady Grove, Alabama, July 1936."

2. How Did X Happen?

When you ask the question "How Did X Happen?" you are preparing to write narration, a report about how something happened. We shall confine our attention here (as elsewhere in this book) to what *actually did happen*—not in the imagination of the writer but in real life; that is, we shall deal with factual rather than fictional narrative. In both kinds of narrative there are characters and ongoing actions: a series of events unfolding against a specific setting, causally related and moving steadily forward in time and through stages of action. Unlike analysis, which merely *explains* an event, narration attempts to *recreate* it by putting readers in the very flow of the happening so that they may see and hear and feel exactly what it was like; so that they may vicariously *have* the experience, not merely learn about it. To achieve this, the narrator must present the events in the form of a story; there must be both a teller and a tale. For a piece of writing to qualify as narrative it requires no more and no less than this.

STRUCTURE IN NARRATION

A narrative begins at a specifically designated point in time ("Once upon a time" is the best-known fictional opening) and ends at an equally specific time. In the following episode by Nikos Kazantzakis, the action of the narrative begins at nightfall and ends the next morning. In between, the author provides us with "markers" indicating where we are located in the progression of the incident ("almost nightfall," "suddenly," "finally," "as soon as"). Note how at the outset Kazantzakis establishes a mood of tension, anxiety, and suspense by describing the deserted streets, bolted doors, and atmosphere of enveloping gloom. The narrator is preparing us for a conflict he fearfully anticipates, and we follow him with mounting suspense as he moves into danger—or is it danger? The narrative unfolds quietly toward its gentle climax, revealed in the last line.

A Night in a Calabrian Village

Nikos Kazantzakis

It was almost nightfall. The whole day: rain, torrents of rain. Drenched to the bone, I arrived in a little Calabrian village. I had to find a hearth where I could dry out, a corner where I could sleep. The streets were deserted, the doors bolted. The dogs were the only ones to scent the stranger's breath; they began to bark from within the courtyards. The peasants in this region are wild and misanthropic, suspicious of strangers. I hesitated at every door, extended my hand, but did not dare to knock.

O for my late grandfather in Crete who took his lantern each evening and made the rounds of the village to see if any stranger had come. He would take him home, feed him, give him a bed for the night, and then in the morning see him off with a cup of wine and a slice of bread. Here in the Calabrian villages there were no such grandfathers.

Suddenly I saw an open door at the edge of the village. Inclining my head, I looked in: a murky corridor with a lighted fire at the far end and an old lady bent over it. She seemed to be cooking. Not a sound, nothing but the burning wood. It was fragrant; it must have been pine. I crossed the threshold and entered, bumping against a long table which stood in the middle of the room. Finally I reached the fire and sat down on a stool which I found in front of the hearth. The old lady was squatting on another stool, stirring the meal with a wooden spoon. I felt that she eyed me rapidly, without turning. But she said nothing. Taking off my jacket, I began to dry it. I sensed happiness rising in me like warmth, from my feet to my shins, my thighs, my breast. Hungrily, avidly, I inhaled the fragrance of the steam rising from the pot. The meal must have been baked beans; the aroma was overwhelming. Once more I realized to what an extent earthly happiness is made to the measure of man. It is not a rare bird which we must pursue at one moment in heaven, at the next in our minds. Happiness is a domestic bird found in our own courtyards.

Rising, the old lady took down two soup plates from a shelf next to her. She filled them, and the whole world smelled of beans. Lighting a lamp, she placed it on the long table. Next she brought two wooden spoons and a loaf of black bread. We sat down opposite each other. She made the sign of the cross, then glanced rapidly at me. I understood. I crossed myself and we began to eat. We were both hungry; we did not breathe a word. I had decided not to speak in order to see what would happen. Could she be a mute, I asked myself—or perhaps she's mad, one of those peaceful, kindly lunatics so much like saints.

As soon as we finished, she prepared a bed for me on a bench to the right of the table. I lay down, and she lay down on the other bench opposite me. Outside the rain was falling by the bucketful. For a considerable time I heard the water cackle on the roof, mixed with the old lady's calm, quiet breathing. She must have been tired, for she fell asleep the moment she inclined her head. Little by little, with the rain and the old lady's rhythmical respiration, I too slipped into sleep. When I awoke, I saw daylight peering through the cracks in the door.

The old lady had already risen and placed a saucepan on the fire to prepare the morning milk. I looked at her now in the sparse daylight. Shriveled and humped, she could fit into the palm of your hand. Her legs were so swollen that she had to stop at every step and catch her breath. But her eyes, only her large, pitch-black eyes, gleamed with youthful, unaging brilliance. How beautiful she must have been in her youth, I thought to myself, cursing man's fate, his inevitable deterioration. Sitting down opposite each other again, we drank the milk. Then I rose and slung my carpetbag over my shoulder. I took out my wallet, but the old lady colored deeply.

"No, no," she murmured, extending her hand.

As I looked at her in astonishment, the whole of her bewrinkled face suddenly gleamed.

"Goodbye, and God bless you," she said. "May the Lord repay you for the good you've done me. Since my husband died I've never slept so well."

Although the action of Kazantzakis' narrative is low-keyed and essentially leisurely, it moves steadily toward its culmination. A basic element of good narration is that the narrative must move steadily forward. It should never slacken or bog down in unessential details or issues not directly related to what it is primarily about. Some beginning writers deliberately try to "draw the story out," on the mistaken notion that this creates suspense. On the contrary, the skillful writer creates suspense—indeed, interest—when the narrative has pace, when it moves without undue interruption toward its climax—the revelation of what happened.

John Steinbeck provides an interesting contrast to what happened in a Calabrian village in his account of his experience in a Maine motel. The two narratives are similar in structure and general movement: in both cases a man is on the road looking for shelter, a simple overnight stop; in both they encounter a woman. But in Steinbeck's case, the woman is a totally different type of person (almost a different species) than the simple peasant woman who inspired Kazantzakis. Notice that both writers use dialogue to support the impression that straight description and narration create.

A Night in a Maine Motel

John Steinbeck

Not far outside of Bangor I stopped at an auto court and rented a room. It wasn't expensive. The sign said "Greatly Reduced Winter Rates." It was immaculate; everything was done in plastics—the floors, the curtain, table tops of stainless burnless plastic, lamp shades of plastic. Only the bedding and the towels were of natural material. I went to the small restaurant run in conjunction. It was all plastic too—the table linen, the butter dish. The sugar and crackers were wrapped in cellophane, the jelly in a small plastic coffin sealed with cellophane. It was early evening and I was the only customer. Even the waitress wore a sponge-off apron. She wasn't happy, but then she wasn't unhappy. She wasn't anything. But I don't believe anyone is a nothing. There has to be something inside, if only to keep the skin from collapsing. This vacant eye, listless hand, this damask cheek dusted like a doughnut with plastic powder, had to have a memory or a dream.

On a chance I asked, "How soon you going to Florida?"

"Nex' week," she said listlessly. Then something stirred in that aching void. "Say, how do you know I'm going?"

"Read your mind, I guess."

She looked at my beard. "You with a show?"

"No."

"Then how do you mean read my mind?"

"Maybe I guessed. Like it down there?"

"Oh sure! I go every year. Lots of waitress jobs in the winter."

"What do you do down there, I mean for fun?"

"Oh, nothing. Just fool around."

"Do you fish or swim?"

"Not much. I just fool around. I don't like that sand, makes me itch."

"Make good money?"

"It's a cheap crowd."

"Cheap?"

"They rather spen' it on booze."

"Than what?"

"Than tips just the same here with the summer."

Strange how one person can saturate a room with vitality, with excitement. Then there are others, and this dame was one of them, who can drain off energy and joy, can suck pleasure dry and get no sustenance from it. Such people spread a grayness in the air about them. I'd been driving a long time, and perhaps my energy was low and my resistence down. She got me. I felt so blue and miserable I wanted to crawl into a plastic cover and die. What a date she must be, what a lover! I tried to imagine that last and couldn't. For a moment I considered giving her a five-dollar tip, but I knew what would happen. She wouldn't be glad. She'd just think I was crazy.

I went back to my clean little room. I don't ever drink alone. It's not much fun. And I don't think I will until I am an alcoholic. But this night I got a bottle of vodka from my stores and took it to my cell. In the bathroom two water tumblers were sealed in cellophane sacks with the words: "These glasses are sterilized for your protection." Across the toilet seat a strip of paper bore the message: "This seat has been sterilized with ultraviolet light for your protection." Everyone was protecting me and it was horrible. I tore the glasses from their covers. I violated the toilet-seat seal with my foot. I poured half a tumbler of vodka and drank it and then another. Then I lay deep in hot water in the tub and I was utterly miserable, and nothing was good anywhere.

POINT OF VIEW IN NARRATION

In narration as in description, you must clearly establish your point of view, the vantage point from which you are narrating. What is your relation to the events? How much do you know? What is your purpose? As a narrator, you may assume any one of several points of view. You may be an outsider, narrating in the third person and knowing everything that is happening, including what goes on in everybody's head. This is called the *omniscient* point of view, and has generally been used by writers of fiction rather than nonfiction (obviously, since no one is really omniscient). Within the last two decades, however, a group of "new nonfiction" writers such as Tom Wolfe in *The Right Stuff* and Truman Capote in *In Cold Blood* (which he called a "nonfiction novel") have borrowed the techniques of the novelist and short story writer in order to give their reportage a deeper vitality and reality. Thus they either speculate on what various persons are thinking, or find out (usually through intensive interviews) what they actually were thinking and feeling during the time of a reported happening.

You may also narrate from the viewpoint of one character, seeing and knowing only what that character sees and knows. This is called the *limited* point of view. Or, as we have seen, you may narrate in the first person. Or you may move like a sound camera, recording only what you can see and hear, never delving into anyone's mind or heart—the *objective* or *dramatic* point of view.

In Pete Hamill's lively rendition of a boy-meets-girl plot, we see how effectively the objective point of view allows the facts to speak for themselves. Offering a minimum of explanation as to motives and emotions, Hamill *dramatizes* the characters; that is, brings them alive through their enactment of themselves—what they say, and even more important, what they do.

Boy Meets Girl, Boy Loses Girl,
Man Gets Woman

Pete Hamill

They called her Big Red from the day that she first showed up at the Copa, in the spring of 1944. She was nineteen years old then, with clean, peach-colored skin, legs that started at her rib cage, and a mane of flaming red hair that made grown men walk into lampposts. On that first day, Jules Podell, who ran the place, didn't even rap his pinkie ring against a table when he saw her, or scream from the darkness of the banquettes, or demand an audition. He took one look at the hair and the legs and the skin and he hired her on the spot.

And for a year, Big Red was one of the glories of New York. The waiters loved her; the dishwashers politely bowed their hellos; and Frank Costello, when he came around, always called her Miss Red.

Her secret was a kind of clumsy innocence. Big Red couldn't dance much, although she could kick her legs higher than her chin; her voice was as frail as a sparrow in traffic; she didn't go to acting classes, didn't dream of a niche in the Hollywood solar system. She was just a great big girl who bumped into things—doors, waiters, and other dancers— and was always forgiven because she was so beautiful and so nice. Podell, who usually punished his enemies by screaming them deaf, never raised his voice to her. And the hoodlums protected her. Whenever an armed citizen visiting from Detroit would try to drag her into the Burma Road, a dim purgatory of seats against the back wall, he would be strongly advised to lay off. Big Red was different. Big Red went to grammar school in a convent. Big Red was a nice girl.

"I want the redheaded broad," one underwear buyer shouted one night. "I'd like to give her a boff."

"If ya open ya mout about da red-headed broad again," said a gentleman in an elegant sharkskin suit, "you will never talk for da rest of your life."

A few such choice words usually settled the matter, although it was rumored that several citizens, including the pudgy son of a Caribbean dictator, had to be deposited with force on the cement of East Sixtieth Street before they got the point.

Then Sal came into her life. Sal was from Bensonhurst, and he was only 5 foot 4 and 21 years old. He had clean, perfect features, like a wonderful miniature painting, and he wanted to be a singer. Well, not just a singer. He wanted to be Frank Sinatra.

He came to audition one day and stood next to a piano, held a cigaret in his right hand and loosened the bow tie of his rented tux with his left. He sang "This Love of Mine," "I'll Never Be the Same," "Just One of Those Things" and "Nancy, With the Laughing Face." He was tender like Frank, and he swaggered like Frank, and he bent the notes the way Frank did, holding the high ones, and reaching down into the lower register when he was hurting the most. Just like Frank.

But in those years, the Copacabana already had one Frank Sinatra. The real one. They didn't need another, particularly one who was only slightly taller than a mailbox. So Jules Podell told the kid to grow six inches and learn to sing like himself, and in the meantime he should try the "Ted Mack Amateur Hour," maybe he could get work at the RKO Prospect in Brooklyn. Sal was destroyed.

He walked out of the frigid darkness of the club into the warm afternoon air, just as Big Red was arriving for a rehearsal. Big Red bumped into him, almost knocking him down, and then realized that tears were streaming down his face.

"Oh, you poor little thing," Big Red said. "You're gonna get your tuxedo wet."

That started it. She put her long arms around him and hugged him, and he leaned into her largeness, and she patted his head, and told him everything was going to be all right—don't you worry, Sal, everything'll be fine. And for a while it was. Three days later, Sal moved into Big Red's place in Chelsea, and when she wasn't working they went everywhere together. She had the money from the Copa; he had his dream.

But as the months went by, Sal started going a little crazy. His pride started to eat away at his brain; would Frank Sinatra let a girl pay the bills? Would Frank let his girl work every night, half-naked in front of a bunch of drunks? Big Red woke up one day about noon and saw Sal looking out the kitchen window into the backyard. His body was shaking as if he couldn't control his laughter. She smiled, tip-toed over to him and leaned down to kiss him on the head, and then realized that he was crying.

It all came pouring out: the bruised pride, the sense of being a leech or worse, his need to make it on his own. And he told her he wanted to go to Vegas, where Bugsy Siegel had built the Flamingo, and where a lot of new joints were opening up. He was sure he could get work there as a singer. He was sure he could get the big break. All he needed was enough money for a car and the trip west. He was sure he could get the money from an uncle on Eighty-six Street and Fourteenth Avenue. And he wanted Big Red to go with him.

So Big Red gave her notice, and that was the closest anyone had ever come to seeing Jules Podell cry. He just sat there, like a museum director who had just lost the Mona Lisa. That Saturday night, all the regulars gave Big Red a farewell party after the last show. They gave her phone numbers in Vegas, certain well-connected parties to call. And they gave her a necklace, a set of luggage and a big cake, among other things.

But when she went outside, carrying all the gifts, Sal was not there waiting as he was supposed to be. Sal was in the squad room of a police station in Brooklyn, and two homicide cops were typing up forms charging him with murder. Sal had borrowed a gun and walked into a saloon to get the money for the Vegas trip. There was a fight, the gun had gone off and a bartender was dead. Sal was on his way to Attica.

A few days later, one of the Copa regulars called Big Red. One of the hoodlums. He told her Sal would be gone for a long time. She was welcome to come back to the Copa, but when she said no, that the Copa would only remind her of Sal, this party said that an airline ticket to Vegas would be waiting for her at Idlewild. And a job would be waiting for her when she got there. She cried for two days and then went west. She never heard a word from Sal.

She worked at the Dunes and did the Lido de Paris Show for a couple of years; she married and divorced an Oklahoma oil man, then married a beauty parlor operator who later died in a car crash. Her three children grew up, went to school, married, went away. She settled in Santa Monica in a small house two blocks from the Pacific. She planted a garden, watched TV, talked a lot to her children on the phone and started going to Mass. Every day, to stay in shape, she spent an hour in the ocean.

One morning, she came back from the beach and the phone was ringing. The operator asked her name, and said she had a person-to-person call from New York.

"Okay, that's me. Go ahead, operator."

"I have your party on the line," the operator said, in a metallic voice.

"Oh, great, great, operator, thank you. Thanks."

The voice was familiar.

"It's me, Sal," the voice said. "They just let me out."

She turned around quickly, bumped into the table and knocked the toaster to the floor.

"Sal? That's really you, Sal?"

"Yeah. I have been tryin' for three days to find a number for you. I called everywheres. Vegas. Texas. Jules Podell's dead, you know?"

"Yeah, I heard that, Sal."

"I must of missed it somehow. I didn't know it. New York sure ain't the same, is it?"

"I guess not. That was too bad about Jules."

"Hey, listen, I gotta ask you something."

"Yeah, Sal?"

"Are you married?"

"No."

She could hear him breathe out hard in relief. "Well, I'd like to come out there," he said. "I'd like to get a job out there, start over."

There was a long pause. "I don't look the way I used to look," she said, her voice trembling.

"Neither do I," Sal said, his voice dropping into the lower register.

"I've got grown-up kids and all. I have a garden. I even go to church. I'm really boring."

"So am I."

"Uh, when were you, uh, thinking of coming out?"

"Tonight," he said.

"Tonight?" She turned, tangled in the phone wire, and reached for the toaster. She knocked over a chair. "Uh, well, gee, that'd be...what flight?"

He gave her the number. She wrote it on the wall beside the phone.

"I'll be there," she said. "I'll be at the gate. I'll be wearing, uh, black slacks and a white blouse. I'll be there, Sal. I'll be there. I'm big, remember? With red hair."

She hung up, stood there for a moment and then kicked a leg higher than her chin.

IMMEDIACY IN NARRATION

Narration clearly enables you to do more than talk about your subject. Through a well-chosen illustration you can embody your points in a dramatic presentation far more meaningful and memorable than simple analysis. The pain and poignancy of the lives of human beings come through powerfully.

In much the same way, George Orwell in the following essay says more about the inhumanity of capital punishment by presenting his point in a brief narrative account than he might have said in a long treatise on the subject. Similarly, the essay indicts the dehumanizing effect of colonialism on the colonizers as well as on the subjugated colonials, an effect that finds devastating expression in the irritable complaint of the supervising army doctor anxious to get on with the execution (then to breakfast). "For God's sake," he says to his lackey, "the man ought to have been dead by this time."

A Hanging

George Orwell

It was in Burma, a sodden morning of the rains. A sickly light, like yellow tinfoil, was slanting over the high walls into the jail yard. We were waiting outside the condemned cells, a row of sheds fronted with double bars, like small animal cages. Each cell measured about ten feet by ten and was quite bare within except for a plank bed and a pot for drinking water. In some of them brown silent men were squatting at the inner bars, with their blankets draped round them. These were the condemned men, due to be hanged within the next week or two.

One prisoner had been brought out of his cell. He was a Hindu, a puny wisp of a man, with a shaven head and vague liquid eyes. He had a thick, sprouting moustache, absurdly too big for his body, rather like the moustache of a comic man on the films. Six tall Indian warders were guarding him and getting him ready for the gallows. Two of them stood by with rifles and fixed bayonets, while the others handcuffed him, passed a chain through his handcuffs and fixed it to their belts, and lashed his arms tight to his sides. They crowded very close about him, with their hands always on him in a careful, caressing grip, as though all the while feeling him to make sure he was there. It was like men handling a fish which is still alive and may jump back into the water. But he stood quite unresisting, yielding his arms limply to the ropes, as though he hardly noticed what was happening.

Eight o'clock and a bugle call, desolately thin in the wet air, floated from the distant barracks. The superintendent of the jail, who was standing apart from the rest of us, moodily prodding the gravel with his stick, raised his head at the sound. He was an army doctor, with a grey toothbrush moustache and a gruff voice. "For God's sake hurry up, Francis," he said irritably. "The man ought to have been dead by this time. Aren't you ready yet?"

Francis, the head jailer, a fat Dravidian in a white drill suit and gold spectacles, waved his black hand. "Yes sir, yes sir," he bubbled. "All iss satisfactorily prepared. The hangman iss waiting. We shall proceed."

"Well, quick march, then. The prisoners can't get their breakfast till this job's over."

We set out for the gallows. Two warders marched on either side of the prisoner, with their rifles at the slope; two others marched close against him, gripping him by arm and shoulder, as though at once pushing and supporting him. The rest of us, magistrates and the like, followed behind. Suddenly, when we had gone ten yards, the procession stopped short without any order or warning. A dreadful thing had happened—a dog, come goodness knows whence, had appeared in the yard. It came bounding among us with a loud volley of barks, and leapt round us wagging its whole body, wild with glee at finding so many human beings together. It was a large woolly dog, half Airedale, half pariah. For a moment it pranced round us, and then, before anyone could stop it, it had made a dash for the prisoner and, jumping up, tried to lick his face. Everyone stood aghast, too taken aback even to grab at the dog.

"Who let the bloody brute in here?" said the superintendent angrily. "Catch it, someone!"

A warder, detached from the escort, charged clumsily after the dog, but it danced and gambolled just out of his reach, taking everything as part of the game. A young Eurasian jailer picked up a handful of gravel and tried to stone the dog away, but it dodged the stones and came after us again. Its yaps echoed from the jail walls. The prisoner, in the grasp of the two warders, looked on incuriously, as though this was another formality of the hanging. It was several minutes before someone managed to catch the dog. Then we put my handkerchief through its collar and moved off once more, with the dog still straining and whimpering.

It was about forty yards to the gallows. I watched the bare brown back of the prisoner marching in front of me. He walked clumsily with his bound arms, but quite steadily, with that bobbing gait of the Indian who never straightens his knees. At each step his muscles slid neatly into place, the lock of hair on his scalp danced up and down, his feet printed themselves on the wet gravel. And once, in spite of the men who gripped him by each shoulder, he stepped slightly aside to avoid a puddle on the path.

It is curious, but till that moment I had never realized what it meant to destroy a healthy, conscious man. When I saw the prisoner step aside to avoid the puddle I saw the mystery, the unspeakable wrongness of cutting a life short when it is in full tide. This man was not dying, he was alive just as we are alive. All the organs of his body were working—bowels digesting food, skin renewing itself, nails growing, tissues forming—all toiling away in solemn foolery. His nails would still be growing when he stood on the drop, when he was falling through the air with a tenth-of-a-second to live. His eyes saw the yellow gravel and the grey walls, and his brain still remembered, foresaw, reasoned—reasoned even about puddles. He and we were a party of men walking together, seeing, feeling, understanding the same world; and in two minutes, with a sudden snap, one of us would be gone—one mind less, one world less.

The gallows stood in a small yard, separate from the main grounds of the prison, and overgrown with tall prickly weeds. It was a brick erection like three sides of a shed, with planking on top, and above that two beams and a crossbar with the rope dangling. The hangman, a grey-haired convict in the white uniform of the prison, was waiting beside his machine. He greeted us with a servile crouch as we entered. At a word from Francis the two warders, gripping the prisoner more closely than ever, half led half pushed him to the gallows and helped him clumsily up the ladder. Then the hangman climbed up and fixed the rope around the prisoner's neck.

We stood waiting, five yards away. The warders had formed in a rough circle round the gallows. And then, when the noose was fixed, the prisoner began crying out to his god. It was a high, reiterated cry of "Ram! Ram! Ram! Ram!" not urgent and fearful like a prayer or cry for help, but steady, rhythmical, almost like the tolling of a bell. The dog answered the sound with a whine. The hangman, still standing on the gallows, produced a small cotton bag like a flour bag and drew it down over the prisoner's face. But the sound, muffled by the cloth, still persisted, over and over again: "Ram! Ram! Ram! Ram! Ram!"

The hangman climbed down and stood ready, holding the lever. Minutes seemed to pass. The steady, muffled crying from the prisoner went on and on, "Ram! Ram! Ram!" never faltering for an instant. The superintendent, his head on his chest, was slowly poking the ground with his stick; perhaps he was counting the cries, allowing the prisoner a fixed number—fifty, perhaps, or a hundred. Everyone had changed color. The Indians had gone grey like bad coffee, and one or two of the bayonets were wavering. We looked at the lashed, hooded man on the drop, and listened to his cries—each cry another second of life; the same thought was in all our minds: oh, kill him quickly, get it over, stop that abominable noise!

Suddenly the superintendent made up his mind. Throwing up his head he made a swift motion with his stick. "Chalo!" he shouted almost fiercely.

There was a clanking noise, and then dead silence. The prisoner had vanished, and the rope was twisting on itself. I let go of the dog, and it galloped immediately to the back of the gallows; but when it got there it stopped short, barked, and then retreated into a corner of the yard, where it stood among the weeds, looking timorously out at us. We went round the gallows to inspect the prisoner's body. He was dangling with his toes pointed straight downwards, very slowly revolving, as dead as a stone.

The superintendent reached out with his stick and poked the bare brown body; it oscillated slightly. "*He's* all right," said the superintendent. He backed out from under the gallows, and blew out a deep breath. The moody look had gone out of his face quite suddenly. He glanced at his wrist-watch. "Eight minutes past eight. Well, that's all for this morning, thank God."

The warders unfixed bayonets and marched away. The dog, sobered and conscious of having misbehaved itself, slipped after them. We walked out of the gallows yard, past the condemned cells with their waiting prisoners, into the big central yard of the prison. The convicts, under the command of warders armed with lathis, were already receiving their breakfast. They squatted in long rows, each man holding a tin panikin, while two warders with buckets marched round ladling out rice; it seemed quite a homely, jolly scene, after the hanging. An enormous relief had come upon us now that the job was done. One felt an impulse to sing, to break into a run, to snigger. All at once everyone began chattering gaily.

The Eurasian boy walking beside me nodded toward the way we had come, with a knowing smile: "Do you know, sir, our friend [he meant the dead man] when he heard his appeal had been dismissed, he pissed on the floor of his own cell. From fright. Kindly take one of my cigarettes, sir. Do you not admire my new silver case, sir? From the boxwalah, two rupees eight annas. Classy European style."

Several people laughed—at what, nobody seemed certain.

Francis was walking by the superintendent, talking garrulously. "Well, sir, all hass passed off with the utmost satisfactoriness. It was all finished—flick! like that. It iss not always so—oah, no! I have known cases where the doctor wass obliged to go beneath the gallows and pull the prissoner's legs to ensure decease. Most disagreeable!"

"Wriggling about, eh? That's bad," said the superintendent.

"Ach, sir, it iss worse when they become refractory! One man, I recall, clung to the bars of hiss cage when we went to take him out. You will scarcely credit, sir, that it took six warders to dislodge him, three pulling at each leg. We reasoned with him. 'My dear fellow,' we said, 'think of all the pain and trouble you are causing to us!' But no, he would not listen! Ach, he wass very troublesome!"

I found that I was laughing quite loudly. Everyone was laughing. Even the superintendent grinned in a tolerant way. "You'd better all come out and have a drink," he said quite genially. "I've got a bottle of whisky in the car. We could do with it."

We went through the big double gates of the prison into the road. "Pulling at his legs!" exclaimed a Burmese magistrate suddenly, and burst into a loud chuckling. We all began laughing again. At that moment Francis' anecdote seemed extraordinarily funny. We all had a drink together, native and European alike, quite amicably. The dead man was a hundred yards away.

AUTOBIOGRAPHICAL NARRATION

In the following selection Dick Gregory, comedian and civil rights activist, tells how hate and shame entered his life. Note how this effective narrative flows smoothly and easily—as if the events were taking place at the very moment of telling—and how the dialogue rings true: the easy, colloquial speech of the narrator, the cold, unbending tones of the teacher, the flustered repetitions of the child.

Not Poor, Just Broke

Dick Gregory

I have never learned hate at home, or shame. I had to go to school for that. I was about seven years old when I got my first big lesson. I was in love with a little girl named Helene Tucker, a light-complected little girl with pigtails and nice manners. She was always clean and she was smart in school. I think I went to school then mostly to look at her. I brushed my hair and even got me a little old handkerchief. It was a lady's handkerchief, but I didn't want Helene to see me wipe my nose on my hand. The pipes were frozen again, there was no water in the house, but I washed my socks and shirt every night. I'd get a pot, and go over to Mister Ben's grocery store, and stick my pot down into his soda machine. Scoop out some chopped ice. By evening the ice melted to water for washing. I got sick a lot that winter because the fire would go out at night before the clothes were dry. In the morning I'd put them on, wet or dry, because they were the only clothes I had.

Everybody's got a Helene Tucker, a symbol of everything you want. I loved her for her goodness, her cleanness, her popularity. She'd walk down my street and my brothers and sisters would yell, "Here comes Helene," and I'd rub my tennis sneakers on the back of my pants and wish my hair wasn't so nappy and the white folks' shirt fit me better. I'd run out on the street. If I knew my place and didn't come too close, she'd wink at me and say hello. That was a good feeling. Sometimes I'd follow her all the way home, and shovel the snow off her walk and try to make friends with her Momma and her aunts. I'd drop money on her stoop late at night on my way back from shining shoes in the taverns. And she had a Daddy, and he had a good job. He was a paper hanger.

I guess I would have gotten over Helene by summertime, but something happened in that classroom that made her face hang in front of me for the next twenty-two years. When I played the drums in high school it was for Helene and when I broke track records in college it was for Helene and when I started standing behind microphones and heard applause I wished Helene could hear it, too. It wasn't until I was twenty-nine years old and married and making money that I finally got her out of my system. Helene was sitting in that classroom when I learned to be ashamed of myself.

It was on a Thursday. I was sitting in the back of the room, in a seat with a chalk circle drawn around it. The idiot's seat, the troublemaker's seat.

The teacher thought I was stupid. Couldn't spell, couldn't read, couldn't do arithmetic. Just stupid. Teachers were never interested in finding out that you couldn't concentrate because you were so hungry, because you hadn't had any breakfast. All you could think about was noontime, would it ever come? Maybe you could sneak into the cloakroom and steal a bite of some kid's lunch out of a coat pocket. A bite of something. Paste. You can't really make a meal of paste, or put it on bread for a sandwich, but sometimes I'd scoop a few spoonfuls out of the paste jar in the back of the room. Pregnant people get strange tastes. I was pregnant with poverty. Pregnant with dirt and pregnant with smells that made people turn away, pregnant with cold and pregnant with shoes that were never bought for me, pregnant with five other people in my bed and no Daddy in the next room, and pregnant with hunger. Paste doesn't taste too bad when you're hungry.

The teacher thought I was a troublemaker. All she saw from the front of the room was a little black boy who squirmed in his idiot's seat and made noises and poked the kids around him. I guess she couldn't see a kid who made noises because he wanted someone to know he was there.

It was on a Thursday, the day before the Negro payday. The eagle always flew on Friday. The teacher was asking each student how much his father would give to the Community Chest. On Friday night, each kid would get the money from his father, and on Monday he would bring it to school. I decided I was going to buy me a Daddy right then. I had money in my pocket from shining shoes and selling papers, and whatever Helene Tucker pledged for her Daddy I was going to top it. And I'd hand the money right in. I wasn't going to wait until Monday to buy me a Daddy.

I was shaking, scared to death. The teacher opened her book and started calling out names alphabetically.

"Helene Tucker?"

"My Daddy said he'd give two dollars and fifty cents."

"That's very nice, Helene. Very, very nice indeed."

That made me feel pretty good. It wouldn't take too much to top that. I had almost three dollars in dimes and quarters in my pocket. I stuck my hand in my pocket and held onto the money, waiting for her to call my name. But the teacher closed her book after she called everybody else in the class.

I stood up and raised my hand.

"What is it now?"

"You forgot me."

She turned toward the blackboard. "I don't have time to be playing with you, Richard."

"My Daddy said he'd..."

"Sit down, Richard, you're disturbing the class."

"My Daddy said he'd give ... fifteen dollars."

She turned around and looked mad. "We are collecting this money for you and your kind, Richard Gregory. If your Daddy can give fifteen dollars you have no business being on relief."

"I got it right now, I got it right now, my Daddy gave it to me to turn in today, my Daddy said..."

"And furthermore," she said, looking right at me, her nostrils getting big and her lips getting thin and her eyes opening wide, "we know you don't have a Daddy."

Helene Tucker turned around, her eyes full of tears. She felt sorry for me. Then I couldn't see her too well because I was crying, too.

"Sit down, Richard."

And I always thought the teacher kind of liked me. She always picked me to wash the blackboard on Friday, after school. That was a big thrill, it made me feel important. If I didn't wash it, come Monday the school might not function right.

"Where are you going, Richard?"

I walked out of school that day, and for a long time I didn't go back very often. There was shame there.

Now there was shame everywhere. It seemed like the whole world had been inside that classroom, everyone had heard what the teacher had said, everyone had turned around and felt sorry for me. There was shame in going to the Worthy Boys Annual Christmas Dinner for you and your kind, because everybody knew what a worthy boy was. Why couldn't they just call it the Boys Annual Dinner, why'd they have to give it a name? There was shame in wearing the brown and orange and white plaid mackinaw the welfare gave to 3,000 boys. Why'd it have to be the same for everybody so when you walked down the street the people could see you were on relief? It was a nice warm mackinaw and it had a hood, and my Momma beat me and called me a little rat when she found out I stuffed it in the bottom of a pail full of garbage way over on Cottage Street. There was shame in running over to Mister Ben's at the end of the day and asking for his rotten peaches, there was shame in asking Mr. Simmons for a spoonful of sugar, there was shame in running out to meet the relief truck. I hated that truck, full of food for you and your kind. I ran into the house and hid when it came. And then I started to sneak through alleys, to take the long way home so the people going into White's Eat Stop wouldn't see me. Yeah, the whole world heard the teacher that day, we all know you don't have a Daddy.

HISTORICAL NARRATION

All historical accounts are, in a sense, answers to the question "How did it happen?" But only some historical accounts can be called "narrative." Only certain writers present history not merely as a record of the past (wars, treaties, dates) but as an unfolding drama, a direct presentation of human experience. One master of historical narrative was Winston Churchill, whose four-volume *A History of the English-Speaking Peoples* moves with novel-like rapidity across the centuries, to describe the sweep and flow of events that shaped the English nation.

In the passage below, reprinted from the first volume, Churchill describes the Battle of Hastings (1066). He brings the climax of William the Conqueror's invasion to life through the steady accumulation of concrete details that dramatize the butchery of battle; the slyness of William's feigned retreat; the terrible bloodiness of Harold's defeat; the pathos of his death as his naked body is "wrapped only in a robe of purple," and as his grief-stricken mother pleads in vain for permission to bury her son in holy ground. Note also a masterful touch: Churchill opens the battle scene by focusing (as in a movie close-up) on the fate of one man — Ivan Taillefer, "the minstrel knight who had claimed the right to make the first attack." With the "astonished English," we watch this impetuous adventurer fling his sword into the air and catch it again with all the jauntiness of a juggler performing before a wide-eyed audience. As he charges into the English ranks, they immediately slay him. Thus, in a four-line vignette, Churchill creates an unforgettable paradigm of human pride and futility.

In the Battle of Hastings

Winston Churchill

At the first streak of dawn William set out from his camp at Pevensey, resolved to put all to the test; and Harold the Saxon King, eight miles away, awaited him in resolute array.

As the battle began Ivan Taillefer, the minstrel knight who had claimed the right to make the first attack, advanced up the hill on horseback, throwing his lance and sword into the air and catching them before the astonished English. He then charged deep into the English ranks, and was slain. The cavalry charges of William's mail-clad knights, cumbersome in manoeuvre, beat in vain upon the dense, ordered masses of the English. Neither the arrow hail nor the assaults of the horsemen could prevail against them. William's left wing of cavalry was thrown into disorder, and retreated rapidly down the hill. On this the troops on Harold's right, who were mainly the local "fyrd," broke their ranks in eager pursuit. William, in the centre, turned his disciplined squadrons upon them and cut them to pieces. The Normans then reformed their ranks and began a second series of charges upon the English masses, subjecting them in the intervals to severe archery. It has often been remarked that this part of the action resembles the afternoon at Waterloo, when Ney's cavalry exhausted themselves upon the British squares, torn by artillery in the intervals. In both cases the tortured infantry stood unbroken. Never, it was said, had the Norman knights met foot-soldiers of this stubbornness. They were utterly unable to break through the shield-walls, and they suffered serious losses from deft blows of the axe-men, or from javelins, or clubs hurled from the ranks behind. But the arrow showers took a cruel toll. So closely were the English wedged that the wounded could not be removed, and the dead scarcely found room in which to sink upon the ground.

The autumn afternoon was far spent before any result had been achieved, and it was then that William adopted the time-honoured ruse of a feigned retreat. He had seen how readily Harold's right had quitted their positions in pursuit after the first repulse of the Normans. He now organised a sham retreat in apparent disorder, while keeping a powerful force in his own hands.

The house-carls around Harold preserved their discipline and kept their ranks, but the sense of relief to the less trained forces after these hours of combat was such that seeing their enemy in flight proved irresistible. They surged forward on the impulse of victory, and when half-way down the hill were savagely slaughtered by William's horsemen. There remained, as the dusk grew, only the valiant bodyguard who fought round the King and his standard. His brothers, Gyrth and Leofwine, had already been killed. William now directed his archers to shoot high into the air, so that the arrows would fall behind the shield-wall, and one of these pierced Harold in the right eye, inflicting a mortal wound. He fell at the foot of the royal standard, unconquerable except by death, which does not count in honour. The hard-fought battle was now decided. The last formed body of troops was broken, though by no means overwhelmed. They withdrew into the woods behind, and William, who had fought in the foremost ranks and had three horses killed under him, could claim the victory. Nevertheless the pursuit was heavily checked. There is a sudden deep ditch on the reverse slope of the hill of Hastings, into which large numbers of Norman horsemen fell, and in which they were butchered by the infuriated English lurking in the wood.

The dead king's naked body, wrapped only in a robe of purple, was hidden among the rocks of the bay. His mother in vain offered the weight of the body in gold for permission to bury him in holy ground. The Norman Duke's answer was that Harold would be more fittingly laid upon the Saxon shore which he had given his life to defend. The body was later transferred to Waltham Abbey, which he had founded. Although here the English once again accepted conquest and bowed in a new destiny, yet ever must the name of Harold be honoured in the island for which he and his famous house-carls fought indomitably to the end.

DISCUSSION AND EXERCISES

1. Evaluate Dick Gregory's "Not Poor, Just Broke."
   a. Why does Gregory use this title? Does "Broke" have more than one meaning here?
   b. How do the two opening sentences function in the story?
   c. Does Gregory draw the characters convincingly? Quote specific details.
   d. Outline the "plot." What is the central conflict? What additional conflicts does the author imply in the story?
   e. How does the writer establish and maintain an element of suspense?
   f. How does the third paragraph function? What rhetorical device unifies the second sentence? What rhetorical purpose does it serve?
   g. List descriptive details that seem to you especially well-selected and evocative in helping you to see, hear, feel, and understand what is going on.
   h. Does the crucial event or climax of the story have sufficient impact? Explain.
   i. Where and how does the mood of the story change? Is there a reversal?

2. We can easily see how the narration in Kazantzakis's "A Night in a Calabrian Village" fits into the context of Burke's Pentad:

   1. What do the characters do? — The main "act" consists of an encounter in which two people exchange warmth and trust.
   2. Where does the action take place? — The "scene" or setting is a little village in Italy—Calabria.
   3. Who does it? — A traveler and an old lady are the main "agents."

| 4. How do they accomplish it? | The "agency" is a chance meeting and wordless communication. |
| 5. Why do they do it? | His "purpose": to find shelter. Her "purpose": to assuage loneliness. |

Apply the Pentad to other narratives in this section, showing how each of them applies—and replies—to Burke's five basic questions.

3. Compare the Steinbeck and Kazantzakis narratives on the basis of the following:

   a. point of view (voice, tone, rhetorical stance)
   b. setting (locale, atmosphere)
   c. characters (compare their respective moods at the beginning and end of the narrative)
   d. action (sequence and development of events, climax)
   e. theme (suggestions about human nature, economic values, and the impact of chance encounters)
   f. style (sentence structure, choice of words, images)

4. Write a one-paragraph comparison (150–250 words) of the women in the Kazantzakis and Steinbeck essays. Use prewriting techniques you have learned.

5. Consider Pete Hamill's "Boy Meets Girl, Boy Loses Girl, Man Gets Woman."

   a. Indicate in what ways the following passages contribute to the development of character, plot, and the main action of the story:
   1. He took one look at the hair and the legs and the skin and he hired her on the spot.
   2. Her secret was a kind of clumsy innocence.
   3. Podell ... never raised his voice to her. And the hoodlums protected her.
   4. He had clean, perfect features, like some wonderful miniature painting, and he wanted to be a singer. Well, not just a singer. He wanted to be Frank Sinatra.
   5. She had the money from the Copa; he had his dream.
   6. Sal was on his way to Attica.
   7. She cried for two days and then went west.
   8. "I've got grown-up kids and all. I have a garden. I even go to church. I'm really boring."
   9. She ... stood there for a moment and then kicked a leg higher than her chin.

   b. How are Big Red and Sal like one another? In what ways are they different? What is their appeal for each other?
   c. Although Hamill does not delve into the mind and heart of his characters, the reader comes to *know* what they are thinking and feeling. Indicate specific places where the dramatic point of view makes this deeper understanding possible.
   d. Approximately twenty years are telescoped in one paragraph. In what sense is this a fair proportion? What is the writer saying about these twenty years—beyond the recounting of events?
   e. Can you project ahead and imagine what happens to the characters in the next twenty years of their lives?

6. a. Show how the following images from "A Hanging" contribute to the total effect and thesis of the piece:
   1. A "sickly light" slants into the jail yard.
   2. The prisoner is held as if he were "a fish which is still alive and may jump back into the water."
   3. "... a bugle call, desolately thin in the wet air, floated from the distant barracks."
   4. The dog ("half Airedale, half pariah") licks the prisoner's face.
   5. The prisoner cries "Ram! Ram! Ram! Ram!"
   6. The superintendent examines the body and says, *"He's all right."*
   7. "... everyone began chattering gaily."

b. Why do you suppose Orwell does not indicate what crime the prisoner committed? Is it important?

c. How effective is the one paragraph of explicit protest against capital punishment? How appropriate is this paragraph in the middle of the narrative? Does it contribute to the horror of what is happening?

d. What did you feel when you read about the laughing and drinking that follow the hanging? Explain.

7. Study the picture below and compose a short narrative (150–250 words) explaining what happened.

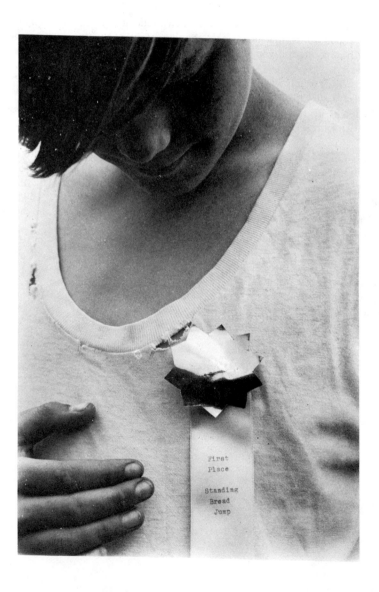

ESSAY SUGGESTIONS

1. Write a narrative essay (750–1,000 words) in which you describe how some dimension of feeling or understanding entered your life (as in Dick Gregory's "Not Poor, Just Broke"). Make certain your description is cast within the frame of a narrative in which there is a specific setting, characters (let them speak in normal, natural tones), and action. You may wish to follow the general structure of Gregory's essay:

> Introduction
> Background situation described (conflict)
> Crucial incident (climax)
> Long-term effect (resolution)

Be sure to choose an appropriate tone for your narrative and use a prewriting plan.

2. Write an essay (750–1,000 words) in which you tell the story of your encounter with another person, describing how it affected you, for either good or ill (as in the Kazantzakis and Steinbeck narratives).
3. Write a journalistic narrative in the manner of Pete Hamill's "Boy Meets Girl . . ." (500–750 words). Try to invent a switch on the old boy-meets-girl formula.
4. Write a dramatization (750–1,000 words) of an event you have witnessed in which you suggest rather than explicitly state your judgment of its meaning and moral significance (as in "A Hanging").
5. Write a narrative essay (750–1,000 words) in which you describe a historical event, using the panoramic point of view as Winston Churchill does in "The Battle of Hastings." He sweeps across the battlefield, moving from one event to another, closing in briefly here and there for a close-up, then moving on again.

a. Historic incidents:

> Boston Tea Party
> Chicago Fire
> Signing of the Declaration of Independence
> Pocahontas saves John Smith (fact and fiction)
> Francis Scott Key composes the "Star-Spangled Banner"
> The first humans walk on the moon
> Charlemagne is crowned emperor of the Holy Roman Empire
> Napoleon dies
> Balboa views the Pacific Ocean
> Fulton takes his steamboat up the Hudson River
> The Wright brothers fly at Kitty Hawk

b. Battles:

Gettysburg	Crecy	Bunker Hill
Bull Run	Poitiers	Themopylae
Shiloh	Waterloo	Dunkirk

3. What Kind of Person Is X?

*M*any artists can create the "sense" of a person by simply setting down on their sketch pads a few swift, well-placed lines to pictorially answer the question, "What kind of person is X?" So it is with writers. By concentrating on a few well-selected, representative characteristics of their subject—a few broad brush strokes—they give a character sketch, a word-picture, of what those persons essentially are from the writers' point of view.

As Boswell told us, the aim of the biographer is to present the person so that readers can "...see him live, and 'live o'er each scene with him, as he actually advanced through the several stages of his life.'" Clearly, essayists cannot do as much, although they must obviously try to bring the subject to life on the page. The character essay can merely point to the thread that runs through a life and that thereby defines it or to the single quality that seems to sum it up—to what Mary McCarthy calls (in reference to her fictional characters) the "key" that turns the lock.

A MEMBER OF THE FAMILY

No one has recreated the "sense of a person" on paper with greater warmth and wisdom than the late newspaper editor, William Allen White. His quiet, lyric tribute to his sixteen-year-old daughter Mary, killed in a riding accident, has become an American classic. We come to know this dauntlessly athletic young woman whose sheer will and grit had transformed her from a delicate and sickly child to a strong, muscular young woman. Though it is a loving portrait, White does not idealize her. Mary was "as full of faults as an old shoe," her father concedes, going on to particularize her even more emphatically by reversing normal word order to say of her: "No angel was Mary White, but an easy girl to live with, for she never nursed a grouch five minutes in her life." Few people reading this portrait will be able to forget it. Surprised himself by its wide acclaim, White told an interviewer:

> "My baggage for the short trip into posterity which I may possibly take will probably consist of one article less than a thousand words. It would please Mary that she and I should go hand in hand together in our little visible journey before our road turned into oblivion."

Mary White

William Allen White

The Associated Press reports carrying the news of Mary White's death declared that it came as the result of a fall from a horse. How she would have hooted at that! She never fell from a horse in her life. Horses have fallen on her and with her—"I'm always trying to hold 'em in my lap," she used to say. But she was proud of few things, and one was that she could ride anything that had four legs and hair. Her death resulted not from a fall, but from a blow on the head which fractured her skull, and the blow came from the limb of an overhanging tree on the parking.

The last hour of her life was typical of its happiness. She came home from a day's work at school, topped off by a hard grind with the copy on the High School Annual, and felt that a ride would refresh her. She climbed into her khakis, chattering to her mother about the work she was doing, and hurried to get her horse and be out on the dirt roads for the country air and the radiant green fields of the spring. As she rode through the town on an easy gallop she kept waving at passers-by. She knew everyone in town. For a decade the little figure with the long pig-tail and the red hair ribbon has been familiar on the streets of Emporia, and she got in the way of speaking to those who nodded at her. She passed the Kerrs, walking the horse, in front of the Normal Library, and waved at them; passed another friend a few hundred feet further on, and waved at her. The horse was walking and, as she turned into North Merchant street she took off her cowboy hat, and the horse swung into a lope. She passed the Tripletts and waved her cowboy hat at them, still moving gaily north on Merchant street. A Gazette carrier passed—a High School boy friend—and she waved at him, but with her bridle hand: the horse veered quickly, plunged into the parking where the low-hanging limb faced her, and, while she still looked back waving, the blow came. But she did not fall from the horse; she slipped off, dazed a bit, staggered and fell in a faint. She never quite recovered consciousness.

But she did not fall from the horse, neither was she riding fast. A year or so ago she used to go like the wind. But that habit was broken, and she used the horse to get into the open to get fresh, hard exercise, and to work off a certain surplus energy that welled up in her and needed a physical outlet. That need has been in her heart for years. It was back of the impulse that kept the dauntless, little brown-clad figure on the streets and country roads of this community and built into a strong, muscular body what had been a frail and sickly frame during the first years of her life. But the riding gave her more than a body. It released a gay and hardy soul. She was the happiest thing in the world. And she was happy because she was enlarging her horizon. She came to know all sorts and conditions of men; Charley O'Brien, the traffic cop, was one of her best friends. W. L. Holtz, the Latin teacher, was another. Tom O'Connor, farmer-politician, and Rev. J. H. J. Rice, preacher and police judge, and Frank Beach, music master, were her special friends; and all the girls, black and white, above the track and below the track, in Pepville and Stringtown, were among her acquaintances. And she brought home riotous stories of her adventures. She loved to rollick; persiflage was her natural expression at home. Her humor was a continual bubble of joy. She seemed to think in hyperbole and metaphor. She was mischievous without malice, as full of faults as an old shoe. No angel was Mary White, but an easy girl to live with, for she never nursed a grouch five minutes in her life.

With all her eagerness for the out-of-doors, she loved books. On her table when she left her room were a book by Conrad, one by Galsworthy, "Creative Chemistry" by E. E. Slosson, and a Kipling book. She read Mark Twain, Dickens and Kipling before she was 10—all of their writings. Wells and Arnold Bennett particularly amused and diverted her. She was entered as a student in Wellesley in 1922; was assistant editor of the High School Annual this year, and in line for election to the editorship of the Annual next year. She was a member of the executive committee of the High School Y.W.C.A.

Within the last two years she had begun to be moved by an ambition to draw. She began as most children do by scribbling in her school books, funny pictures. She bought cartoon magazines and took a course—rather casually, naturally, for she was, after all, a child with no strong purposes—and this year she tasted the first fruits of success by having her pictures accepted by the High School Annual. But the thrill of delight she got when Mr. Ecord, of the Normal Annual, asked her to do the cartooning for that book this spring, was too beautiful for words. She fell to her work with all her enthusiastic heart. Her drawings were accepted, and her pride—always repressed by a lively sense of the ridiculousness of the figure she was cutting—was a really gorgeous thing to see. No successful artist ever drank a deeper draught of satisfaction than she took from the little fame her work was getting among her schoolfellows. In her glory, she almost forgot her horse—but never her car.

For she used the car as a jitney bus. It was her social life. She never had a "party" in all her nearly seventeen years—wouldn't have one; but she never drove a block in the car in her life that she didn't begin to fill the car with pick-ups! Everybody rode with Mary White—white and black, old and young, rich and poor, men and women. She liked nothing better than to fill the car full of long-legged High School boys and an occasional girl, and parade the town. She never had a "date," nor went to a dance, except once with her brother, Bill, and the "boy proposition" didn't interest her—yet. But young people—great spring-breaking, varnish-cracking, fender-bending, door-sagging carloads of "kids"—gave her great pleasure. Her zests were keen. But the most fun she ever had in her life was acting as chairman of the committee that got up the big turkey dinner for the poor folks at the county home; scores of pies, gallons of slaw; jam, cakes, preserves, oranges and a wilderness of turkey were loaded in the car and taken to the county home. And, being of a practical turn of mind, she risked her own Christmas dinner by staying to see that the poor folks actually got it all. Not that she was a cynic; she just disliked to tempt folks. While there she found a blind colored uncle, very old, who could do nothing but make rag rugs, and she rustled up from her school friends rags enough to keep him busy for a season. The last engagement she tried to make was to take the guests at the county home out for a car ride. And the last endeavor of her life was to try to get a rest room for colored girls in the High School. She found one girl reading in the toilet, because there was no better place for a colored girl to loaf, and it inflamed her sense of injustice and she became a nagging harpie to those who, she thought, could remedy the evil. The poor she had always with her, and was glad of it. She hungered and thirsted for righteousness; and was the most impious creature in the world. She joined the Congregational Church without consulting her parents; not particularly for her soul's good. She never had a thrill of piety in her life, and would have hooted at a "testimony." But even as a little child she felt the church was an agency for helping people to more of life's abundance, and she wanted to help. She never wanted help for herself. Clothes meant little to her. It was a fight to get a new rig on her; but eventually a harder fight to get it off. She never wore a jewel and had no ring but her High School class ring, and never asked for anything but a wrist watch. She refused to have her hair up; though she was nearly 17. "Mother," she protested, "you don't know how much I get by with, in my braided pigtails that I could not, with my hair up." Above every other passion of her life was her passion not to grow up, to be a child. The tom-boy in her, which was big, seemed to loath to be put away forever in skirts. She was a Peter Pan, who refused to grow up.

Her funeral yesterday at the Congregational Church was as she would have wished it; no singing, no flowers save the big bunch of red roses from her Brother Bill's Harvard classmen—Heavens, how proud that would have made her! and the red roses from the Gazette force—in vases at her head and feet. A short prayer, Paul's beautiful essay on "Love" from the Thirteenth Chapter of First Corinthians, some remarks about her democratic spirit by her friend, John H. J. Rice, pastor and police judge, which she would have deprecated if she could, a prayer sent down for her by her friend, Carl Nau, and opening the service the slow, poignant movement from Beethoven's Moonlight Sonata, which she loved, and closing the service a cutting from the joyously melancholy first movement of Tschaikowski's Pathetic Symphony, which she liked to hear in certain moods on the phonograph; then the Lord's Prayer by her friends in the High School. That was all.

For her pallbearers only her friends were chosen; her Latin teacher—W. L Holtz; her High School principal, Rice Brown; her doctor, Frank Foncannon, her friend, W. W. Finney; her pal at the Gazette office, Walter Hughes; and her brother Bill. It would have made her smile to know that her friend, Charley O'Brien, the traffic cop, had been transferred from Sixth and Commercial to the corner near the church to direct her friends who came to bid her goodbye.

A rift in the clouds in a gray day threw a shaft of sunlight upon her coffin as her nervous, energetic little body sank to its last sleep. But the soul of her, the glowing, gorgeous, fervent soul of her, surely was flaming in eager joy upon some other dawn.

In writing about close relatives, detachment is rarely possible, for in viewing them the writer often sees and feels the edges of his or her own life. Thus, a character sketch of a parent or grandparent is likely to be emotional—a paean of praise, perhaps, as in the E. E. Cummings piece that follows; or a projection of past miseries, as in W. B. Yeats's essay about his grandfather. Interestingly and typically, both essays tell us something about the writers as well as the persons about whom they are writing.

Notice that Cummings writes his piece in one virtuoso sentence as though a child were spilling out countless details without pausing to take a breath. In fact, Cummings achieves something of that same breathless, headlong intensity here by creating a new form which combines the structure of the sentence with that of the paragraph and—at the same time—unites the paragraph and gives to prose something of the compression and power of poetry.

My Father

E. E. Cummings

My father ... was a New Hampshire man, 6 foot 2, a crack shot & a famous fly-fisherman & a firstrate sailor (his sloop was named The Actress) & a woodsman who could find his way through forests primeval without a compass & a canoeist who'd still-paddle you up to a deer without ruffling the surface of a pond & an ornithologist & taxidermist & (when he gave up hunting) an expert photographer (the best I've ever seen) & an actor who portrayed Julius Caesar in Sanders Theatre & a painter (both in oils & watercolors) & a better carpenter than any professional & an architect who designed his own houses before building them & (when he liked) a plumber who just for the fun of it installed all his own waterworks & (while at Harvard) a teacher with small use for professors—by whom (Royce, Lanman, Taussig, etc.) we were literally surrounded (but not defeated)—& later (at Doctor Hale's socalled South Congregational really Unitarian church) a preacher who announced, during the last war, that the Gott Mit Uns boys were in error since the only thing which mattered was for man to be on God's side (& one beautiful Sunday in Spring remarked from the pulpit that he couldn't understand why anyone had come to hear him on such a day) & horribly shocked his pewholders by crying "the kingdom of Heaven is no spiritual roofgarden: it's inside you" & my father had the first telephone in Cambridge & (long before any Model T Ford) he piloted an Orient Buckboard with Friction Drive produced by the Waltham watch company & my father sent me to a certain public school because its principal was a gentle immense coalblack negress & when he became a diplomat (for World Peace) he gave me & my friends a tremendous party up in a tree at Sceaux Robinson & my father was a servant of the people who fought Boston's biggest & crookedest politician fiercely all day & a few evenings later sat down with him cheerfully at the Rotary Club & my father's voice was so magnificent that he was called on to impersonate God speaking from Beacon Hill (he was heard all over the common) & my father gave me Plato's metaphor of the cave with my mother's milk.

Grandfather

William Butler Yeats

Some of my misery was loneliness and some of it fear of old William Pollexfen my grandfather. He was never unkind, and I cannot remember that he ever spoke harshly to me, but it was the custom to fear and admire him. He had won the freedom of some Spanish city, for saving a life perhaps, but was so silent that his wife never knew it till he was near eighty, and then from the chance visit of some old sailor. She asked him if it was true and he said it was true, but she knew him too well to question and his old shipmate had left the town. She too had the habit of fear. We knew that he had been in many parts of the world, for there was a great scar on his hand made by a whaling-hook, and in the dining-room was a cabinet with bits of coral in it and a jar of water from the Jordan for the baptizing of his children and Chinese pictures upon rice-paper and an ivory walking-stick from India that came to me after his death. He had great physical strength and had the reputation of never ordering a man to do anything he would not do himself. He owned many sailing ships and once, when a captain just come to anchor at Rosses Point reported something wrong with the rudder, had sent a messenger to say "Send a man down to find out what's wrong." "The crew all refuse," was the answer, and to that my grandfather answered, "Go down yourself," and not being obeyed, he dived from the main deck, all the neighbourhood lined along the pebbles of the shore. He came up with his skin torn but well informed about the rudder. He had a violent temper and kept a hatchet at his bedside for burglars and would knock a man down instead of going to law, and I once saw him hunt a party of men with a horsewhip. He had no relation for he was an only child and, being solitary and silent, he had few friends. He corresponded with Campbell of Islay who had befriended him and his crew after a shipwreck, and Captain Webb, the first man who had swum the Channel and who was drowned swimming the Niagara Rapids, had been a mate in his employ and a close friend. That is all the friends I can remember and yet he was so looked up to and admired that when he returned from taking the waters at Bath his men would light bonfires along the railway line for miles; while his partner William Middleton whose father after the great famine had attended the sick for weeks, and taken cholera from a man he carried in his arms into his own house and died of it, and was himself civil to everybody and a cleverer man than my grandfather, came and went without notice. I think I confused my grandfather with God, for I remember in one of my attacks of melancholy praying that he might punish me for my sins, and I was shocked and astonished when a daring little girl—a cousin I think—having waited under a group of trees in the avenue, where she knew he would pass near four o'clock on the way to his dinner, said to him, "If I were you and you were a little girl, I would give you a doll."

Yet for all my admiration and alarm, neither I nor any one else thought it wrong to outwit his violence or his rigour; and his lack of suspicion and something helpless about him made that easy while it stirred our affection. When I must have been still a very little boy, seven or eight years old perhaps, an uncle called me out of bed one night, to ride the five or six miles to Rosses Point to borrow a railway-pass from a cousin. My grandfather had one, but thought it dishonest to let another use it, but the cousin was not so particular. I was let out through a gate that opened upon a little lane beside the garden away from ear-shot of the house, and rode delighted through the moonlight, and awoke my cousin in the small hours by tapping on his window with a whip. I was home again by two or three in the morning and found the coachman waiting in the little lane. My grandfather would not have thought such an adventure possible, for every night at eight he believed that the stable-yard was locked, and he knew that he was brought the key. Some servant had once got into trouble at night and so he had arranged that they should all be locked in. He never knew, what everybody else in the house knew, that for all the ceremonious bringing of the key the gate was never locked.

Even to-day when I read *King Lear* his image is always before me and I often wonder if the delight in passionate men in my plays and in my poetry is more than his memory. He must have been ignorant, though I could not judge him in my childhood, for he had run away to sea when a boy, "gone to sea through the hawse-hole" as he phrased it, and I can but remember him with two books—his Bible and Falconer's *Shipwreck*, a little green-covered book that lay always upon his table.

No more bizarre character can be imagined than the "round and bald," compulsively talkative "Uncle Bun," vividly evoked in Maxine Hong Kingston's *China Men*. The name itself may be a pun, she tells us, for "Uncle Stupid." "He's crazy," Kingston's mother says of this frequent, uninvited guest at the family laundry where he regales the children—and any adult who will listen—with long speeches on food phobias and his paranoid conviction that some nameless enemy is trying to poison him. He was so obsessively repetitious, Kingston tells us, that inevitably "some of what he said seeped into the ears." More often, though, the children would just stare at him, transfixed and revolted by "the spit foam at the corners of his mouth."

Something about Uncle Bun was obviously unforgettable to Kingston, for after many years she could still see him clearly in her mind's eye, still hear his long ramblings and wild imaginings. For her little sister, however—as we see at the end of the essay—Uncle Bun did not leave quite so indelible an impression.

Uncle Bun

Maxine Hong Kingston

We had an uncle, a second or third cousin maybe, who went back to China to be a Communist. We called him Uncle Bun, which might have been his name, but could also be a pun, Uncle Stupid. He was a blood relative and not just a villager. He was very talkative. In fact, he hardly ever stopped talking, and we kids watched the spit foam at the corners of his mouth. He came to the laundry and sat, or if it was very hot, he stood near the door to talk and talk. It was more like a lecture than a conversation. He repeated himself so often that some of what he said seeped into the ears. He talked about wheat germ. "You ought to eat wheat germ," he said, "because wheat germ is the most potent food in the world. Eat it and you'll stay young for a long time; you'll never get sick. You'll be beautiful and tall and strong, also intelligent. The reason for so much unhappiness and strife is that people have been eating wrong. Meat turns them into animals. Wheat germ, which we can digest easier, can help us evolve into better people. Wheat germ is full of vitamins (*why-huh-ming*), and it is very cheap. A, C, thiamine, riboflavin, niacin, calcium, carbohydrates, fats, iron (*eye-yun*)." He was a scientific and up-to-date man who used English scientific terms. In two weighty syllables, both equally accented, a spondee, he said "Wheat Germ." Wheat germ would fatten up my father and also fatten up all the skinny children. Unlike the rest of the men in the family, who were thin and had white hair, this uncle was round and bald with black hair above his ears and around the back of his head. He wore a pearl gray three-piece suit and a necktie with a gold tiepin, the gold chain of his pocket watch linking one vest pocket to the other, the last button of his vest open over his prosperous paunch. He opened his eyes wide to see everything through his round gold-framed eyeglasses.

"Wheat germ—you can put it into any food," he said. "Sprinkle it on the rice and strew it on all the accompaniments. Stir it into milk and juices. Drink it in soups and beverages; it melts right in. Mix it with ice cream and strawberries. Combine it with flour. Combine it with rice. Beat it into cakes and pancakes. Scatter it on fried eggs for a crunchy texture. You can eat it by itself. Eat it by the handful, cooked or raw. Add it to cold food or hot food, sauces and gravies. Rain it on vegetables. Coat fish, meat, and fowl with it. Use it as a binder in meatballs and fishcakes. It goes with anything." Wheat germ. I could not imagine this miracle food, whether it was sweet or salty, what size it was, what it was, what color, whether it tasted good. Was it a liquid or a solid? Was *germ* the same germ as in bacteria? "Wheat germ is golden brown," he said, "though the color blends with whatever you're cooking. A pinch of it changes regular food into a medicine." It sounded like a fairy-tale elixir, fairy food. "You cannot taste or detect its presence in other foods," he said. "Yet you can eat it by itself like cornflakes," which he also pronounced spondaically in his accent, *Coon Flex.* "Wheat germ is the heart of the wheat," he said, "the heart of bread and wheat, which is more nutritious in the first place than rice. It repairs broken parts and tissues."

"Hum," said my father and mother.

"We ought to buy some, don't you think?" I asked my parents, hating to ask them to spend more money, but we might be wasting away from the lack of a vital food.

"He's crazy," my mother said. "Anything that necessary has to have been invented long ago."

He brought us some sample wheat germ, which tasted like raw peas or raw oats.

Although he was about my father's age, Uncle Bun, like many of the old men, did not appear to have a job and was able to afford entire mornings, afternoons, days, and evenings sitting and chatting while we worked. Maybe his sons sent money from Chicago. My father did join him talking politics, a man's topic as gray as newspapers....

"We have to examine the causes of poverty," said Uncle Bun. "The world has never experimented to find out if it is rich enough and big enough to support all its people. It probably is. Look at all the rich people who own too much, and you can see there's extra food, land, and money. And certainly, there's always work enough. Only the distribution is wrong; we have to divide up the goods evenly." We kids divided every five-cent candy bar and all the chores. "Who really owns the land?" he asked. "The man who farms it with his sweat and piss or the man whose name is on the paper? And shouldn't the worker on the assembly line own his labor and the results of his labor?"...

"Actually these aren't dreams or plans," Uncle Bun said. "I'm making predictions about ineluctabilities. This Beautiful Nation, this Gold Mountain, this America will end as we know it. There will be one nation, and it will be a world nation. A united planet. Not just Russian Communism. Not just Chinese Communism. World Communism."

He said, "When we don't need to break our bodies earning our daily living any more, and we have time to think, we'll write poems, sing songs, develop religions, invent customs, build statues, plant gardens, and make a perfect world." He paused to contemplate the wonders.

"Isn't that great?" I said after he left.

"Don't get brainwashed," said my mother. "He's going to get in trouble for talking like that. He's going to get us in trouble; the barbarians think that Communists and Chinese are the same."

Even when the uncles were killed during the Revolution and the aunts tortured, Uncle Bun did not change his mind about Communism. "We have to weigh the death of a few against the lives of millions of poor workers and the coming generations," he said.

"A fermentation of dreams," said my father. Uncle Bun should not have said such Communist things against our dead relatives....

"Ah, sad, sad America, which does not respect the poor," he said. "The poor are important. And look, look, even if we distribute everything, and it's spread so thin that we're all poor—that's good. Consider the culture we poor have invented— vegetarianism and fasting, pencil sketches, pottery, singing without instruments, mending, saving and reusing things, quilting, patchwork, the poetry written on leaves, rocks, and walls, acrobatics, dancing, and kung fu, which doesn't require expensive sports equipment. Oh, let's value the poor, who in a way are all of us. Even with money, the rich can't buy good food. They eat white bread and poisoned food. What they ought to do is eat wheat germ."

Amazing! His two big ideas—wheat germ and Communism—connected....

"He's gone crazy," my mother diagnosed. "He's getting crazier. When he comes to the house, and we're at the laundry, you kids don't let him in."...

He did come to our house one day when neither of our parents were home. Unfortunately, the front door was wide open, so we couldn't hide and pretend we were out. It would be embarrassing to tell him why he couldn't come in. Being the oldest, I decided that we children would go outside and talk to him on the porch. It was pleasant out there under the grapevines. We stood between him and the red door and asked him questions to distract him. He usually walked right in. "What exactly is wheat germ?" we asked, but he seemed not as interested in wheat germ as before. "How's shopping at the new grocery store?" "Fine. Fine," he said. "May I have a drink of water?" he asked. "We'll get it," we said, some of us blocking his way while one ran inside, very rude, a guest having to ask for refreshments. He drank the entire glassful quickly. "You must finish all your water," he advised us. "When you have milk, finish all of it. Finish your food. Eat everything. Don't leave scraps. Scraps turn into garbage. Food one moment, garbage the next. Same with paper. Don't blotch it, and if you do, save it for scratch paper. Cross out the mistakes rather than crumple the paper. Make every page count." He did not go berserk, did not break into the house and throw himself against the sofa like a padded cell, did not act like a maniac at all. He sounded like other adults, advising this, advising that, advising eat.

At the laundry, where it would be dangerous to run amok among the hot machines, he announced: "*They* are not *only* hiding the poison in my food. I am on the verge of discovering the *real* plot. Have you noticed—oh, surely, you must have been alarmed by it—you must have seen how many garbage demons there are in this country?" "Yes, there are," said my mother. "Do you see," he asked, "how the white demons are very careful with garbage? And how much garbage there is?"...

A few days later he again came running into the laundry. He was highly excited and frightened, as if he were being chased. "I've discovered what they do with the garbage." He was sweating. "They're collecting it for me. They're going to feed it to me. They'll capture me and tie me down and shovel it into my mouth. They're going to make me eat it. All of it. It's all for me. You must see what a big plot it is. Everybody is manufacturing garbage constantly, some knowing the purpose and some just because everyone else is doing it. It all ties in with the poisoning, don't you see? The newspapers and radios are in on it too, telling them to buy, buy, and then they turn everything they buy into garbage as fast as they can. They're preparing and saving for the day when they'll shovel it into my mouth. They've been collecting for years, and I didn't see the plot till now. That day is coming soon. They'll make me eat it."

"Why should they do that to you?" asked my mother.

"Because of my talk about Communism," he said.

"The garbage is not for you," said my father. "The garbage isn't that important. You're not that important. Forget the garbage."

"You should go to a mind doctor," said my mother.

He got offended and left. "You'll be sorry when the day arrives, and you see it all come true. Feeding day."

His stomach got thinner. He refused most food; he ate only greens and browns, leaving not a scrap, not contributing to the garbage that "they" would feed him later. "Paper garbage too," he said. "Paper cups, paper plates, paper napkins, Kleenex, gum and gum wrappers."

At last he said, "I'm going back to China. I've outsmarted them. I know which day the feeding will be on, and I'll leave before then. It was not like this in China. Remember? In fact, they couldn't poison your milk and bread because we didn't drink milk; only babies drank milk. And we didn't eat much bread. We used everything thoroughly in China. Remember? There was hardly any garbage. We ate all the food. Remember how we could see with our own eyes that the hogs ate the peelings? If the human beings didn't eat rinds, the animals did, and the fish bones got plowed into the fields. Remember how paper gatherers collected paper that had writing on it and burned it in wood furnaces? Remember we saved the bags and boxes? Why, this—" he picked up a cornflakes box—"we would have treasured a pretty box like this, such bright colors, such sturdy cardboard. We would have opened the flaps carefully and used it to store valuable and useful things in. We'd have taken good care of it, made it last, handed it down. I'm going back to New Society Village." . . .

From that decision on, he acted saner and saner, happier, and stopped talking about the garbage except to say, "I'm returning to China before feeding day." "Returning" is not to say that he necessarily had ever been there before. . . .

The day he left, he spoke to my youngest sister, who was about three years old. He bent over so that she could hear and see him very well. "Don't forget me, will you?" he asked. "Remember I used to play with you. Remember I'm the man who sang songs to you and gave you dimes. What's my name?" She laughed that he would ask her such a silly, easy question. Of course, she knew his name. He coaxed her to say it several times for him. "You won't forget? Tell me you won't forget."

"I won't forget," she said. He seemed satisfied to leave, and we never saw him or heard from him again.

For a while I reminded my sister, "Do you remember Uncle Bun, the bald fat man who talked a lot? Do you remember him asking you not to forget him?"

"Oh, yes, the funny man. I remember."

I reminded her periodically. But one day, I noticed that I had not asked her for some time. "Do you remember the funny man who talked a lot, the one who smuggled himself into Red China?"

"Who?" she asked.

"Uncle Bun. Remember?"

"No," she said.

A FAMOUS WOMAN

The following essay on Sylvia Plath, described as "pretty" and "all-American," a brilliant student in her youth, a "priestess of poetry" later on, draws on biographical and other material for background information. Carefully researched and documented, this essay provides a brief overview for the reader who knows little or nothing about the life and work of Sylvia Plath. By supplementing the vital passages from her poems, her letters, her posthumous novel, the writer adds an emotional dimension to her portrait, a poignant sense of the young woman whose ordeals were finally too overwhelming to struggle against.

Sylvia Plath: A Short Life

Katinka Matson

Dying
Is an art, like everything else,
I do it exceptionally well.

I do it so it feels like hell.
I do it so it feels real.
I guess you could say I've a call.[1]

Sylvia Plath. American poet. She was a pretty, all-American girl with bright red lips and a pageboy haircut. After her suicide, a manuscript of poems was discovered and published. Critics called the book, *Ariel*, terrifying, visionary, terrible and strange. Sylvia Plath attained cult status. She became a priestess of poetry, a category unto herself.

> I saw that my body had all sorts of little tricks, such as making my hands go limp at the crucial second, which would save it, time and again, whereas if I had the whole say, I would be dead in a flash.
> I would simply have to ambush it with whatever sense I had left or it would trap me in its stupid cage for fifty years without any sense at all.[2]

[1] Plath, 'Lady Lazarus', *Ariel*.

[2] Plath, *The Bell Jar*.

Sylvia Plath was born in Boston, Massachusetts, on 27 October 1932. Her father, Otto Emil Plath, was a German emigré and professor of entomology at Boston University; his specialty was bumble-bees. He was twenty-one years older than Plath's mother, Aurelia Schober, a woman of Austrian parentage whom he met in one of his German classes. Sylvia was their first child. Her brother, Warren, was born exactly two and a half years later. When Plath was eight years old her father died.

> Daddy, I have had to kill you.
> You died before I had time—
> Marble-heavy, a bag full of God,
> Ghastly statue with one grey toe
> Big as a Frisco seal
>
> And a head in the freakish Atlantic
> Where it pours bean green over blue
> In the waters off beautiful Nauset.
> I used to pray to recover you.
> Ach, du.[3]

Aurelia Plath went to work teaching secretarial skills at Boston University. The children were left in the care of her parents, who moved into their home in Winthrop. Soon after, the entire family moved to Wellesley, an upper-middle-class college town with good schools for the children.

Aurelia made a 'tireless effort to see that her children had all the advantages given their much-better-off contemporaries. These included summer camps, Scouting, sailing, piano and viola lessons, dance "assemblies", painting and watercolour lessons, and numerous other, frequently expensive, extracurricular activities.'[4]

> Mother, you sent me to piano lessons
> And praised my arabesques and trills
> Although each teacher found my touch
> Oddly wooden in spite of scales
> And the hours of practising, my ear
> Tone-deaf and yes, unteachable.
> I learned, I learned, I learned elsewhere,
> From muses unhired by you, dear mother.[5]

A model student with a 'genius' IQ, Plath's high-school years were highlighted by rows of straight As, honour roll, special awards and achievement certificates (even one for punctuality). She had a story published in *Seventeen* magazine and a poem in the *Christian Science Monitor*. She was editor of the yearbook in her senior year and wrote a column for the town paper. She was also growing up tall and slender, with long brown hair, and a lovely smile.

To Aurelia Plath:
It was one of those cartoon and personality write-ups titled 'Teen Triumphs'. There was a sketch of a girl s'posed to be me—writing, also a cow. It said, and I quote: 'BORN TO WRITE! Sylvia Plath, seventeen, really works at writing. To get atmosphere for a story about a farm she took a job as a farmhand. Now she's working on a sea story.' Then there's another sketch of me saying, 'and I get a job

[3] Plath, 'Daddy', *Ariel*.

[4] Butscher, *Sylvia Plath: Method and Madness*.

[5] Plath: 'The Disquieting Muses', *The Colossus*.

on a boat'. Not only that. 'A national magazine had published two of her brain children, the real test of being a writer.'[6]

At Smith College, where Plath had a partial scholarship, she continued to excel. In her sophomore year she won a $1,500 *Mademoiselle* prize for college fiction. In her junior year she won a guest editorship to the same magazine, and headed for New York City.

> I knew something was wrong with me that summer, because all I could think about was the Rosenbergs and how stupid I'd been to buy all those uncomfortable, expensive clothes, hanging limp as a fish in my closet, and how all the little successes I'd totted up so happily fizzled to nothing outside the slick marble and plate-glass fronts along Madison Avenue.
>
> I felt very still and very empty, the way the eye of a tornado must feel, moving dully along in the middle of the surrounding hullabaloo.[7]

Plath returned to Wellesley after her month in New York to learn that she had not been accepted for Frank O'Connor's summer writing course at Harvard. She had been counting on the class to occupy her during the long summer and had no alternative plans. Suddenly, she was at loose ends. She became insomniac and was unable even to read. Obviously disturbed, Plath saw a psychiatrist and was given shock treatments. She refused to return to him. On 24 August her mother found a note from her daughter: 'Have gone for a long walk. Will be home tomorrow.'[8] She was discovered three days later lying in a crawlspace under the house—her brother had heard her faint cries.

> The second time I meant
> To last it out and not come back at all.
> I rocked shut
>
> As a sea shell.
> They had to call and call
> And pick the worms off me like sticky pearls.[9]

Plath spent six months at McLean Hospital in Belmont, Massachusetts, an expensive psychiatric institution, where she underwent insulin therapy and shock treatments. She was pronounced 'cured' in time to return to Smith for the second semester. She bleached her hair blonde and pursued a social life with her old determination to succeed, seeing many different men and experimenting with sex. She began to write poetry again, and won a scholarship for her final year at Smith.

Gordon Lamayer (friend):
Life was always full to the brim for Sylvia at Smith in those days and cresting over the brim, 'overflowing'. If she had been a Marlovian heroine, she would have been an 'over-reacher', because she could not stick by the golden mean, nothing too much, but was always anxious to experiment *in extremis*, with Blake, to find out what 'enough' was by indulging herself 'too much'. Her letters were filled with purple passages. In retrospect, I would say that at times she was whistling Dixie, telling herself she was extremely happy in an effort to mask her anxiety.[10]

In 1955, her last year at Smith, she dyed her hair back to its natural brown, and deliberately subdued her 'healthy bohemianism' to concentrate on her studies, her

---

[6] Aurelia Schober Plath, *Letters Home*.

[7] Plath, *The Bell Jar*.

[8] Aurelia Schober Plath, *Letters Home*.

[9] Plath, 'Lady Lazarus', *Ariel*.

[10] Butscher, *Sylvia Plath: The Woman and the Work*.

writing, and the ever-present question of her future. Ever striving, she made a clean sweep of the poetry prizes, graduated summa cum laude, and won a Fulbright scholarship to study at Cambridge.

> If only England would by some miracle come through, I would be forced shivering into a new, unfamiliar world, where I had to forge anew friends and a home for myself, and although such experiences are painful and awkward at first, I know, intellectually, that they are the best things to make one grow—always biting off just a slight bit more than you chewed before.[11]

At Cambridge, Plath continued to succeed, both academically and socially. In March she met Ted Hughes at a party and fell in love with the 'brilliant ex-Cambridge poet . . . the only man I've met yet here who'd be strong enough to be equal with'.[12] Hughes was a tall, lanky, handsome man, the son of a Yorkshire carpenter, a 'large, hulking, healthy Adam'.[13] Most important, Hughes was a serious and dedicated poet. Since it was against the rules for Plath to be married while a student at Cambridge, she and Ted were married secretly in London in June, her mother in attendance.

> The last thing I wanted was infinite security and to be the place an arrow shoots off from. I wanted change and excitement and to shoot off in all directions myself, like the coloured arrows from a Fourth of July rocket.[14]

Plath and Ted spent the summer in a rented house in Spain, rising at seven each morning to write. Besides doing her own work, she typed Ted's poems for submission to magazines. To her mother, she described her newly wedded life with Ted in ecstatic, glowing terms. Her life was now perfect and it had a purpose. She could not remember what her life had been like without Ted.

> I felt myself melting into the shadows like the negative of a person I'd never seen before in my life.[15]

Back in Cambridge in the fall, Plath went back to her studies while she and Ted continued writing and submitting poems and stories. They received many rejections, but also some acceptances. In February 1957, Ted's volume of poems entitled *Hawk in the Rain* won the Poetry Centre First Publication Award and was accepted for publication by Harper's in the US and Faber in England.

> I'm so happy *his* book is accepted *first*. It will make it so much easier for me when mine is accepted—if not by the Yale Series, then by some other place. I can rejoice then, much more, knowing Ted is ahead of me. There is no question of rivalry, but only mutual joy and a sense of us doubling our prize-winning and creative output.[16]

In the summer of 1957, she and Ted returned to the United States and rented an apartment in Northampton: Plath had a job teaching English at Smith. She soon discovered, however, that the amount of labour involved in teaching was 'death to writing'. She was frustrated and unhappy in the airless campus life. After the first year,

[11] Aurelia Schober Plath, *Letters Home.*

[12] Ibid.

[13] Ibid.

[14] Plath, *The Bell Jar.*

[15] Ibid.

[16] Aurelia Schober Plath, *Letters Home.*

she quit and they moved again, this time to an apartment on the 'slummy side' of Beacon Hill, and she worked part-time for Massachusetts General Hospital. During this period she met poet Anne Sexton in Robert Lowell's poetry course.

Anne Sexton:
Often, very often, Sylvia and I would talk at length about our first suicides, at length, in detail, in depth ... Suicide is, after all, the opposite of the poem.[17]

By October 1959, she was pregnant. She and Ted decided to return to London to live. They moved into a small, inexpensive flat in Chalcot Square. In February, Plath signed a contract with Heinemann to publish her first book of poems, *The Colossus*, some of which had been written during the previous fall at Yaddo, an artists' colony in Saratoga, New York. The dedication read: 'For Ted.' In March, a daughter, Frieda Rebecca, was born at home.

I also remembered Buddy Willard saying in a sinister, knowing way that after I had children I would feel differently, I wouldn't want to write poems any more. So I began to think maybe it was true that when you were married and had children it was like being brainwashed, and afterwards you went about numb as a slave in some private, totalitarian state.[18]

In January 1961, Plath became pregnant again; she miscarried a month later. The *New Yorker* offered her a 'first reading' contract in March which she accepted. In May, Alfred Knopf announced it would publish an American edition of her book of poetry entitled *The Colossus*. In September, pregnant once more, she moved into a cottage in Devon with Ted and Frieda. Nicholas, a son, was born in the new year.

I do not stir.
The frost makes a flower,
The dew makes a star,

The dead bell,
The dead bell.

Somebody's done for.[19]

The bubble burst: the world of the tall handsome 'writing Hugheses' with their two beautiful babies in their cottage in Devon ended when Ted Hughes became seriously involved with another woman. Plath was stunned, heartbroken, and finally outraged. By August 1962, Ted had departed. Plath tried to manage in the country but it was difficult, and, above all, isolated.

Everything is breaking—my dinner set cracking in half, the health inspector says the cottage should be demolished—there is no hope for it ... Even my beloved bees set upon me today when I numbly knocked aside their sugar feeder, and I am all over stings.[20]

Plath moved herself and the children back to London, to a flat in 'Yeats's house!' arriving just in time for one of the worst winters in the city's history. Severe bouts with flu for her and the babies, blackouts, frozen pipes, the inescapable cold, and no outside help

[17] Anne Sexton, *A Self-Portrait in Letters*, Boston: Houghton Mifflin, 1978.

[18] Plath, *The Bell Jar*.

[19] Plath, 'Death & Co.', *Ariel*.

[20] Aurelia Schober Plath, *Letters Home*.

contributed to her emotional and physical exhaustion. At first she managed to sustain herself, writing poem after poem each morning in the dawn hours before the children awoke and needed her.

> If I've killed one man, I've killed two—
> The vampire who said he was you
> And drank my blood for a year,
> Seven years, if you want to know.
> Daddy, you can lie back now.[21]

On a cold Monday morning, 11 February 1963, Sylvia Plath, her two children asleep, went downstairs to the kitchen, turned on the gas jets, and put her head in the oven. Her body was discovered several hours later by a nurse who had been sent over by her physician to help out with the children. Plath was thirty years old.

> The woman is perfected.
> Her dead
>
> Body wears the smile of accomplishment,
> The illusion of a Greek necessity
>
> Flows in the scrolls of her toga,
> Her bare
>
> Feet seem to be saying:
> We have come so far, it is over.[22]

[21] Plath, 'Daddy', *Ariel.*
[22] Plath, 'Edge', *Ariel.*

Sources

Aird, Eileen. *Sylvia Plath: Her Life and Work.* Edinburgh: Oliver & Boyd, 1973.
Butscher, Edward. *Sylvia Plath: Method and Madness.* New York: Pocket Books, 1977.
—. *Sylvia Plath: The Woman and the Work.* London: Faber & Faber, 1968.
Plath, Aurelia Schober, ed. *Letters Home by Sylvia Plath, 1950–63.* New York: Bantam, 1977.
Plath, Sylvia. *Ariel.* New York: Harper & Row, 1966.
—. *The Bell Jar.* London: Faber & Faber, 1963.
—. *The Colossus.* London: Faber & Faber, 1972.

A MEMORABLE TEACHER

Many people have a well-loved teacher in their past who opened their eyes to new possibilities in the world around them or who alerted them to new possibilities in themselves. Few teachers have been more fondly and amusingly depicted than Russell Baker's third-year English teacher, the prim Mr. Fleagle, "notorious among City students for dullness and inability to inspire." No wonder Baker anticipated "a listless unfruitful year." What a happy reversal, then, of expectations! We learn about it ("don't you see?" as Mr. Fleagle would put it) in the following essay which combines description and narration to produce a picture of the quintessentially good teacher lurking beneath the reputed "comic antique" the students laughed at.

The Prim Mr. Fleagle

Russell Baker

When our class was assigned to Mr. Fleagle for third-year English I anticipated another grim year in that dreariest of subjects. Mr. Fleagle was notorious among City students for dullness and inability to inspire. He was said to be stuffy, dull, and hopelessly out of date. To me he looked to be sixty or seventy and prim to a fault. He wore primly severe eyeglasses, his wavy hair was primly cut and primly combed. He wore prim vested suits with neckties blocked primly against the collar buttons of his primly starched white shirts. He had a primly pointed jaw, a primly straight nose, and a prim manner of speaking that was so correct, so gentlemanly, that he seemed a comic antique.

I anticipated a listless, unfruitful year with Mr. Fleagle and for a long time was not disappointed. We read *Macbeth*. Mr. Fleagle loved *Macbeth* and wanted us to love it too, but he lacked the gift of infecting others with his own passion. He tried to convey the murderous ferocity of Lady Macbeth one day by reading aloud the passage that concludes

... I have given suck, and know
How tender 'tis to love the babe that milks me.
I would, while it was smiling in my face,
Have plucked my nipple from his boneless gums....

The idea of prim Mr. Fleagle plucking his nipple from boneless gums was too much for the class. We burst into gasps of irrepressible snickering. Mr. Fleagle stopped.

"There is nothing funny, boys, about giving suck to a babe. It is the—the very essence of motherhood, don't you see."

He constantly sprinkled his sentences with "don't you see." It wasn't a question but an exclamation of mild surprise at our ignorance. "Your pronoun needs an antecedent, don't you see," he would say, very primly. "The purpose of the Porter's scene, boys, is to provide comic relief from the horror, don't you see."

Late in the year we tackled the informal essay. "The essay, don't you see, is the ..." My mind went numb. Of all forms of writing, none seemed so boring as the essay. Naturally we would have to write informal essays. Mr. Fleagle distributed a homework sheet offering us a choice of topics. None was quite so simpleminded as "What I Did on My Summer Vacation," but most seemed to be almost as dull. I took the list home and dawdled until the night before the essay was due. Sprawled on the sofa, I finally faced up to the grim task, took the list out of my notebook, and scanned it. The topic on which my eye stopped was "The Art of Eating Spaghetti."

This title produced an extraordinary sequence of mental images. Surging up out of the depths of memory came a vivid recollection of a night in Belleville when all of us were seated around the supper table—Uncle Allen, my mother, Uncle Charlie, Doris, Uncle Hal—and Aunt Pat served spaghetti for supper. Spaghetti was an exotic treat in those days. Neither Doris nor I had ever eaten spaghetti, and none of the adults had enough experience to be good at it. All the good humor of Uncle Allen's house reawoke in my mind as I recalled the laughing arguments we had that night about the socially respectable method for moving spaghetti from plate to mouth.

Suddenly I wanted to write about that, about the warmth and good feeling of it, but I wanted to put it down simply for my own joy, not for Mr. Fleagle. It was a moment I wanted to recapture and hold for myself. I wanted to relive the pleasure of an evening at New Street. To write it as I wanted, however, would violate all the rules of formal composition I'd learned in school, and Mr. Fleagle would surely give it a failing grade. Never mind. I would write something else for Mr. Fleagle after I had writtein this thing for myself.

When I finished it the night was half gone and there was no time left to compose a proper, respectable essay for Mr. Fleagle. There was no choice next morning but to turn in my private reminiscence of Belleville. Two days passed before Mr. Fleagle returned the graded papers, and he returned everyone's but mine. I was bracing myself for a command to report to Mr. Fleagle immediately after school for discipline when I saw him lift my paper from his desk and rap for the class's attention.

"Now, boys," he said, "I want to read you an essay. This is titled 'The Art of Eating Spaghetti.'"

And he started to read. My words! He was reading *my words* out loud to the entire class. What's more, the entire class with listening. Listening attentively. Then somebody laughed, then the entire class was laughing, and not in contempt and ridicule, but with openhearted enjoyment. Even Mr. Fleagle stopped two or three times to repress a small prim smile.

I did my best to avoid showing pleasure, but what I was feeling was pure ecstasy at this startling demonstration that my words had the power to make people laugh. In the eleventh grade, at the eleventh hour as it were, I had discovered a calling. It was the happiest moment of my entire school career. When Mr. Fleagle finished he put the final seal on my happiness by saying, "Now that, boys, is an essay, don't you see. It's—don't you see—it's of the very essence of the essay, don't you see. Congratulations, Mr. Baker."

For the first time, light shone on a possibility. It wasn't a very heartening possibility, to be sure. Writing couldn't lead to a job after high school, and it was hardly honest work, but Mr. Fleagle had opened a door for me. After that I ranked Mr. Fleagle among the finest teachers in the school.

DISCUSSION AND EXERCISES

1. Consider "Mary White."

   a. List the qualities attributed to Mary and indicate how White supports his attributions with "evidence" (for example, "... she loved books. On her table when she left her room were a book by Conrad, one by Galsworthy...").

   b. In what ways does Mary seem an "ordinary" sixteen-year-old? In what ways extraordinary?

   c. Comment on the following sentences in terms of their content and style:

      1. No angel was Mary White, but an easy girl to live with, for she never nursed a grouch five minutes in her life.
      2. Everybody rode with Mary White—white and black, old and young, rich and poor, men and women.
      3. But young people—great spring-breaking, varnish-cracking, fender-bending, door-sagging carloads of "kids"—gave her great pleasure.
      4. She was a Peter Pan, who refused to grow up.

   d. Describe the overall organization of the piece. Comment on the effectiveness of the opening and closing paragraphs and of the one-sentence paragraph, "That was all."

   e. Quote passages of description and narration in this character sketch. Which predominates?

   f. Using the information provided by her father, try—in your own words—to characterize Mary White. Now try to characterize the father, William Allen White. In what ways does his essay about his daughter reveal his own character? What is his tone throughout? What kind of father-daughter relationship do you think they had? Cite details from the piece to support your points.

g. What details in this piece suggest that it was written in 1921?

h. Consider the following sentence: "For her pallbearers, only her friends were chosen...." Why do you suppose this sentence is cast in the passive voice (not "I chose the pallbearers," but rather "pallbearers were chosen")? Speculate on the possible significance of this rhetorical decision.

i. White's original audience of this "editorial" (as he called it) were the readers of *The Emporia Gazette*, where he served as editor. What clues reveal that White envisioned a relatively small, local audience rather than the large national readership that the piece eventually won?

j. Why do you think the essay "Mary White" has become an American classic? What specific features might have appealed to generations of readers? Speculate.

2. Contemplate and comment upon Cummings's virtuoso one-sentence essay, noting in particular the striking selection of details, the parenthetic additions, and the final statement: "my father gave me Plato's metaphor of the cave with my mother's milk." What does this mean?

3. After doing some prewriting, write a one-sentence paragraph characterizing an unusual person you know.

4. Consider Yeats's "Grandfather."

a. What is formidable and what is helpless about the grandfather?

b. What does the "daring little girl" who asks for a doll contribute to the narration?

5. Try a freewriting exercise. Begin with the sentence "There is one person I have always been afraid of."

6. Consider "Uncle Bun" by Maxine Hong Kingston.

a. Describe what was likeable about Uncle Bun. What was not likeable?

b. What did he bring of value to the Hong family? What harm did he do?

c. Can you identify Kingston's feelings about her uncle from the tone of the piece? Explain.

d. Make a list of Uncle Bun's physical characteristics.

e. Make a list of his opinions.

f. How did the children's attitudes toward Uncle Bun differ from their parents? How were they the same?

g. In your opinion, is someone like Uncle Bun worth listening to? Why or why not?

h. How do you feel about Uncle Bun by the end of the piece? About the parents? Were they justified in rejecting him? Did they have cause for alarm? Explain.

i. "We never saw him or heard from him again," Kingston tells us. What might have happened to Uncle Bun in China?

j. In what way does the short epilogue between Kingston and her sister enhance the narrative which frames this portrait?

7. Consider the portrait, "Sylvia Plath: A Short Life."

a. How does Katinka Matson weave together the facts of Plath's life and Plath's emotional responses to the facts?

b. In what ways is this technique of allowing Plath essentially to "speak for herself" effective?

c. What contrasts do you note between Plath's outward appearance and her inner turmoil?

d. Why was she called "a category unto herself"?

e. Characterize her feelings about her father. Love and/or hate? What evidence that reveals her feelings do you find in her poems?
What was her attitude toward her mother? Do you note signs of affection? Resentment? What evidence does the author give us in the essay?

g. When did Plath begin to feel "something was wrong"? Discuss points of contrast between what she was doing and what she was feeling.

h. What metaphors does Plath use to describe happiness and unhappiness?

i. What evidence does Matson provide for Sylvia Plath's progression toward suicide? Documented facts? Poems? Letters? Other?

8. Consider Russell Baker's Mr. Fleagle.

a. How does the word "prim" work in describing him? Does the repetition of the word "pall" detract from or enhance the description? What is Baker's tone? Does it tend to make the reader dismiss Mr. Fleagle or become more interested in him? What expression does the teacher repeat?

b. What words convey Baker's boredom with English and the writing of essays? What words convey his excitement upon discovering a topic that stimulated him? For whom did he write his essay? Why was the writing of it so important to him? What feelings did it bring back? What memories? Why was he willing to take a chance on violating the rules of formal composition?

c. Compare Baker's feelings before and after the reading of his essay aloud in class. What had he expected from Fleagle when he turned in the paper? What were his feelings when his words were read? What was the class's response? What was Mr. Fleagle's response? What power did Baker find in the words he had written? What difference did it make in his life? What caused him to rank Mr. Fleagle among "the finest teachers in the school"?

d. List the subquestions you 'see "at work" in this portrait.

9. Look carefully at the portrait, noting such details as the posture of the woman, her quizzical (possibly mischievous) expression, the position of her hands, her wine glass, and other details. Who is she? What is she "up to"? Write a short character sketch.

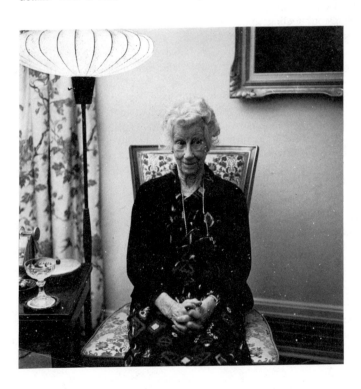

ESSAY SUGGESTIONS

1. Write an essay (500–1,000 words) in which you draw a portrait of a particular friend or relative. Try in prewriting to focus on one dominant quality that in your view characterizes the person (as "obsessiveness" characterizes Uncle Bun). Present your character in action, as Kingston does; in other words, set your character sketch within the frame of the narration.

2. Write an essay (500–750 words) about someone you both fear and admire, as Yeats did his grandfather.

3. Katinka Matson's anthology of "Short Lives: Portraits of Writers, Painters, Poets, Actors, Musicians, and Performers in Pursuit of Death" includes the following prominent people who died young:

F. Scott Fitzgerald	Billie Holiday	Edgar Allan Poe
Jack Kerouac	Montgomery Cliff	Elvis Presley
Marilyn Monroe	James Dean	Judy Garland
Vincent Van Gogh	Janis Joplin	Simone Weil
Anne Sexton		

Select one of the above (or a comparable character of your own choosing) and compose a "portrait" of 750–1,000 words, using documented facts and quotes drawn from outside sources. This is an opportunity to practice "Gathering Information" (pages 47–75) and to incorporate research notes into a finished piece.

4. Write an essay (500–750 words) about a teacher who influenced you in some positive way and possibly changed the direction of your life—or a teacher whose influence was memorable but *negative*.

5. Expand the character sketch (based on the photo on page 196) into a 500–750 word portrait.

4. What Is My Memory of X?

"*I*t is necessary to remember and necessary to forget, but it is better for a writer to remember." So said William Saroyan in a truism worth repeating, for it points to a large body of literature built upon "remembrance of things past."

THE QUALITY OF MEMORY

No writer had a more prodigious memory than Thomas Wolfe whose novels are distinguished by his genius for conjuring up sense impressions from the past: sounds, sights, odors, colors, shapes—the very texture of experience reexperienced in memory. In a remarkable and revealing account of his creative process. Wolfe described the compulsive memory which, with its shattering intensity, drove him "night and day."

The Quality of Memory

Thomas Wolfe

The quality of my memory is characterized, I believe, in a more than ordinary degree by the intensity of its sense impressions, its power to evoke and bring back the odors, sounds, colors, shapes, and feel of things with concrete vividness. Now [during a summer in Paris] my memory was at work night and day, in a way that I could at first neither check nor control and that swarmed unbidden in a stream of blazing pageantry across my mind, with the million forms and substances of the life that I had left, which was my own, America. I would be sitting, for example, on the terrace of a cafe watching the flash and play of life before me on the Avenue de l'Opéra and suddenly I would remember the iron railing that goes along the boardwalk at Atlantic City. I could see it instantly just the way it was, the heavy iron pipe; its raw galvanized look; the way the joints were fitted together. It was all so vivid and concrete that I could feel my hand upon it and know the exact dimensions, its size and weight and shape. And suddenly I would realize that I had never seen any railing that looked like this in Europe. And this utterly familiar, common thing would suddenly be revealed to me with all the wonder with which we discover a thing which we have seen all our life and yet have never known before. Or again, it would be a bridge, the look of an old iron bridge across an American river, the sound the train makes as it goes across it; the spoke-and-hollow rumble of the ties below; the look of the muddy banks; the slow, thick, yellow wash of an American river; an old flat-bottomed boat half filled with water stogged in the muddy bank; or it would be, most lonely and haunting of all the sounds I know, the sound of a milk wagon as it entered an American street just at the first gray of the morning, the slow and lonely clopping of the hoof upon the street, the jink of bottles, the sudden rattle of a battered old milk can, the swift and hurried footsteps of the milkman, and again the jink of bottles, a low word spoken to his horse, and then the great, slow, clopping hoof receding into silence, and then quietness and a bird song rising in the street again. Or it would be a little wooden shed out in the country two miles from my home town where people waited for the street car, and I could see and feel again the dull and rusty color of the old green paint and see and feel all of the initials that had been carved out with jackknives on the planks and benches within the shed, and smell the warm and sultry smell so resinous and so thrilling, so filled with a strange and nameless excitement of unknown joy, a coming prophecy, and hear the street car as it came to a stop, the moment of brooding, drowzing silence; a hot thrum and drowsy stitch at three o'clock; the smell of grass and hot sweet clover; and then the sudden sense of absence, loneliness and departure when the street car had gone and there was nothing but the hot and drowsy stitch at three o'clock again.

Or again, it would be an American street with all its jumble of a thousand ugly architectures. It would be Montague Street or Fulton Street in Brooklyn, or Eleventh Street in New York, or other streets where I had lived; and suddenly I would see the gaunt and savage webbing of the elevated structure along Fulton Street, and how the light swarmed through in dusty, broken bars, and I could remember the old, familiar rusty color, that incomparable rusty color that gets into so many things here in America.

Wolfe's memory was, of course, a phenomenon, a miracle. I quote him here simply to indicate the extent of an ability that all of us possess to some degree. Most of us can *remember*, in other words, but only vaguely and in snatches. Images do not ordinarily loom up on their own, "in a stream of blazing pageantry." If we ask ourselves the question "What is my memory of X?" we must make a conscious and sustained effort to recover the past. It is not waiting on the surface of the mind, ready to be recalled in all its original concreteness and intensity.

Even so, those of us with a less natural endowment than Wolfe's can, by probing and pondering and digging beneath the surface layers of consciousness, recapture scattered episodes and experiences from the past. For they are still *there*, fixed in the memory and capable of being conjured up through such prewriting strategies as freewriting, brainstorming, and clustering (See Part One, pages 26–35).

EARLIEST MEMORIES

In the following selection Penelope Mortimer goes back to her earliest memories, centering—as is natural—on home ("the first place I remember") and the immediate family: mother, father, brother. Note how judiciously she selects her details and how vividly she renders them (for example, Mrs. Jessup, "the doubled-up old witch no bigger than myself"). Even when the memory is blurry, Mortimer manages— paradoxically, it would seem—to depict the blur vividly: Her father, not recalled with continuity, "comes in fits and starts, like a poorly received spirit." In this image of "a poorly received spirit"—so descriptive and rich in connotation—Mortimer renders the poorly remembered *memorably*.

In the First Place

Penelope Mortimer

The first place I remember is the Vicarage, Chilton, near Thame, Oxon. ('an abbreviation of Oxfordshire which always perplexed me and still does). As far as I know, I never wrote a letter to this address, since I never left it without my parents. But letters must have arrived—from my brother, away at school, perhaps? ...

My brother had been born in Chilton, which, I always felt uneasily, gave him a prior claim to it. This was illogical, because he didn't seem to live there. For the four years before my birth, our mother lavished all her love and care on him; she wrote "The Future Prime Minister!" under a photograph of him standing unsteadily on a lawn; she had smocked his linen smocks and written down every move he made in a big freckled notebook. Then, when she was pregnant with me, she sent him away to boarding-school. He was four years old, and he never came back.

Oh, there was a moody figure, a kind of small, embodied tension around in the school holidays. There is an oval, sepia photograph of a small boy holding a teddy bear and smiling at a pretty nurse, who holds me. I remember a red tape tied round a child's grey flannel sleeve after a smallpox vaccination, and later I heard about academic brilliance and scholarships and shining hopes for his future. But the memories I have of him at Chilton are like the moments when a shadow suddenly seems to solidify and take some recognizable, usually threatening, shape. I didn't realize for years how much—whether he knew it or not—he must hate me, connecting my birth with his exile. I only remember the times when he tricked or tortured me, and that I felt my wails of indignation were righteous. I'm surprised, in fact, that he let me live at all....

The village of Chilton was—and still is—haphazard, mainly consisting of a thirteenth-century church on a hill, a vast Queen Anne manor, the exquisite dower house at its gate—where the schoolmaster, a Mr. Ambrose, lived—a couple of farms and the Vicarage. There was a blacksmith (the smell of singeing hooves is as powerfully nostalgic as the smell of paraffin) and a village shop, which was the front room of a small, dark cottage—a jumble of boot-laces, pencils and boiled sweets, in which Mrs. Jessup, a doubled-up old witch no taller than myself, crouched behind the counter, alert as a crab. Until my father built his Village Club, there was no pub for at least a mile. There were a few what my mother disparagingly referred to as "council houses" (which I suppose they were, but she made them sound almost immoral), in one of which lived a family called Hubbard. There were a great many young, friendly Hubbards, but I was seldom allowed to play with them, and then only in the Vicarage garden.

The Vicarage was—is—one of those serene, modestly beautiful houses that could never have been newly built (and yet think of the din there must have been in those parts through the Middle Ages and up to the eighteenth century—the hammering and sawing, cranking and hauling, half-built churches littering the hillsides, manors and mansions rising out of rubble, incessant industry where now there is only architecture). Some ruthless Victorian parson with twelve children had slapped a hideous gabled appendage on to the side of it and that, for a few of my first eight years, housed the dormitory and schoolroom for my mother's residential nursery, which she whimsically called "The Little People's Garden." Before this shrewd or willful venture, my father's bedroom was in the gabled wing; during it, he left home and lived in a restored Army hut in the orchard. As the orchard was on the other side of the road from the house and garden, I didn't so much see my father as visit him or meet him accidentally. Therefore, according to my convictions at the time—which were loosely based on Bishop Berkeley's doctrine that matter as an unperceived substance is both impossible and unreal—he seldom existed. . . . If I try to evoke him, he comes in fits and starts, like a poorly received spirit. . . .

He drove a Morris Oxford, and allowed me to ride astride the bonnet, which burned the insides of my thighs. Once, when he had gone to London for the day, I listened with my ear to the ground like a Red Indian to hear the car coming back from fifty miles away; but didn't hear it. He showed me a book of female anatomy, in which a flap opened over the womb, revealing a very small, ugly, upside-down foetus; but I thought it was rather a beautiful book. He played tennis in the summer, and golf in the right season, and was often in a bad temper, once throwing my brother out of the diningroom window, which was all of two feet above a bed of wall-flowers.

I remember even less about my mother in those early years. She was always busy cooking or gardening, hurrying about. Sometimes we may have played Up Jenkins or Hunt the Thimble. She sent me off to tea at the Squire's mansion, grizzling and reluctant, a clean handkerchief tucked into my knickers. She took me to church on Sunday mornings, though always let me go before the sermon. During the week, I sometimes went with her and pottered about while she arranged the altar flowers or changed the frontal or hung up a clean surplice for my father or checked the supplies of blood and body. She loved to decorate the church, and did it with no sense of religion at all: at Christmas only ("No Popery" was written on her heart) there were candles, at Easter every white and yellow flower or blossom she could lay hands on; at Harvest Festival her imagination ran riot with vegetables and fruit, Michaelmas daisies and wheat, so that altar, pulpit, choir stalls, lectern and font looked like exhibits at a county fair. Until the start of the Little People's Garden, I connect my mother only with rooms and with things, colours and furniture and food. She must have spoken; but my impression is that the sound of her voice didn't reach me.

The rooms she furnished were, like the church she decorated, made very much her own. My mother had collected furniture all her life, scrounging about in woodsheds and dairies, finding treasures. Most of it was made of fruit woods, though there was also oak and walnut and a few strictly simple pieces of mahogany. She had a weakness for chintz, but the designs were never fussy; basically she was a hessian woman, and indulged in linen—William Morris browns and plums and terracottas—on the rare occasions when she could afford it. Unlike all the other Vicarages I was to visit in my childhood, my homes had no religious pictures or emblems on their white—or, at their most flamboyant, pale primrose—walls, except, perhaps, for a Margaret Tarrant in the nursery, a Rossetti print on the back stairs; they were not lit by dismal forty-watt bulbs hanging from dingy ceilings, were never icy with poverty, never smelled of last Sunday's boiled cabbage. For the hardy, pioneering little woman my mother seemed to be, she had a great appreciation of comfort. The mattress on her bed was always of a make called Vi-spring; she had a rubber hot-water bottle when the rest of us had to make do with stone ones; there was always a mohair rug available to tuck round her knees in a draught. . . .

For eight years I waddled or trotted, scurried or scuffed round the garden, the orchard, the farmyard, sometimes in the company of the Little People, sometimes not. And then came the day when a Mr Ravenscroft, fat, red-faced, dressed in a black suit, black hat and sanctimonious smile, was introduced to me—in the orchard, for some reason—as the new vicar of Chilton. We were moving, it seemed immediately, to Thornton Heath, a suburb of London.

It was, I think, early September, the apples not yet ripe, the leaves rusting. "We are moving to London and this is Mr Ravenscroft, who will be coming to live here," they said, or something like that. And Mr Ravenscroft smiled and smiled, barely creasing his tight red skin, little black shoes stamped firmly in my grass, black hat set perfectly straight on his loathsome head. Nobody had asked my permission. Nobody explained why. I hated Mr Ravenscroft, new incumbent of my territory, invader of Bath hound, and I hate him still, in whatever prim Anglican heaven he now illegitimately resides.

REMEMBERING PLACES

Next to people, places generally fix themselves most firmly in the mind, especially in the child's mind. Is there anyone, for example, who does not have clear memories associated with that must impressionable period of life, that central experience of childhood—going to school?

Notice that in the essay that follows, Laurie Lee—like Penelope Mortimer—makes a judicious, *yet ample*, selection of details in order to evoke a picture of the village school he attended as a child in the west of England. The memory of that school is so vivid he can still hear the exact roll call of classmates, "the names resounding in the long-ago air...Walt Kerry, Bill Timbrell, Spadge Hopkins." By the use of such concrete sensory details (see Question 1, "How can X be described?") the writer evokes a past reality, the "lively reek of steaming life: boys' boots, girls' hair, stoves and sweat"—the *feel* of an experience. Only in this way can writers put us into the place they are describing, enabling us to experience it somewhat the same way they did.

The Village School

Laurie Lee

The village school [in Gloucestershire in the 1920s] provided all the instruction we were likely to ask for. It was a small stone barn divided by a wooden partition into two rooms—the Infants and the Big Ones. There was one dame teacher, and perhaps a young girl assistant.... Our village school was poor and crowded, but in the end I relished it. It had a lively reek of steaming life: boys' boots, girls' hair, stoves and sweat, blue ink, white chalk and shavings. We learnt nothing abstract or tenuous there—just simple patterns of facts and letters, portable tricks of calculation, no more than was needed to measure a shed, write out a bill, read a swine-disease warning. Through the dead hours of the morning, through the long afternoons, we chanted away at our tables. Passers-by could hear our rising voices in our bottled-up room on the bank: "Twelve-inches-one-foot. Three-feet-make-a-yard. Fourteen pounds-make-a-stone. Twelve-stone-a-hundred-weight." We absorbed these figures as primal truths declared by some ultimate power. Unhearing, unquestioning, we rocked to our chanting, hammering the gold nails home. "Twice-two-are-four. One-God-is-Love. One-Lord-is-King. One-King-is-George. One-George-is-Fifth..." So it was always, had been, would be for ever; we asked no questions; we didn't hear what we said; yet neither did we ever forget it.

So do I now, through the reiteration of those days, recall that school-room which I scarcely noticed—Miss Wardley in glory on her high desk throne, her long throat tinkling with glass. The bubbling stove with its chink of red fire, the old world map as dark as tea; dead field-flowers in jars on the windowsills; the cupboard yawning with dog-eared books. Then the boys and the girls, the dwarfs and the cripples; the slow fat ones and the quick bony ones; giants and louts, angels and squinters—Walt Kerry, Bill Timbrell,

Spadge Hopkins, Clergy Green, the Ballingers and Browns, Betty Gleed, Clarry Hogg, Sam and Sixpence, Rose and Jo—were ugly and beautiful, scrofulous, warted, ring-wormed and scabbed at the knees; we were noisy, crude, intolerant, cruel, stupid and superstitious. But we moved together out of the clutch of the fates, inhabitors of a world without doom; with a scratching, licking and chewing of pens, a whisper and passing of jokes, a titter of tickling, a grumble of labour, a vague stare at the wall in a dream.

REMEMBERING EVENTS

It is not surprising that a child raised in the New York ghetto of Harlem would have memories of violence, such as the following "The Day I Got Shot," narrated by Claude Brown with all the attendant terror intact. Note the plentiful dialogue, an authentic reproducing of the event as it occurred, with voices rendered in their still-remembered inflections.

Unlike Penelope Mortimer who tells us "In the First Place" that she can no longer hear her mother's voice, Brown can clearly hear the distraught cries of his "Mama screaming like a crazy woman"—for, indeed, it is Brown himself, her son, who is shot and perhaps dying. And he hears Mama's voice again the next day when he is beginning to recover; she is at his bedside assuring him that he will live: "the Lord had told her...."

The Day I Got Shot

Claude Brown

"Run!"

Where?

Oh, hell! Let's get out of here!

"Turk! Turk! I'm shot!"

I could hear Turk's voice calling from a far distance, telling me not to go into the fish-and-chips joint. I heard, but I didn't understand. The only thing I knew was that I was going to die.

I ran. There was a bullet in me trying to take my life, all thirteen years of it.

I climbed up on the bar yelling, "Walsh, I'm shot. I'm shot." I could feel the blood running down my leg. Walsh, the fellow who operated the fish-and-chips joint, pushed me off the bar and onto the floor. I couldn't move now, but I was still completely conscious.

Walsh was saying, "Git outta here, kid. I ain't got no time to play."

A woman was screaming, mumbling something about the Lord, and saying, "Somebody done shot that poor child."

Mama ran in. She jumped up and down, screaming like a crazy woman. I began to think about dying. The worst part of dying was thinking about the things and the people that I'd never see again. As I lay there trying to imagine what being dead was like, the policeman who had been trying to control Mama gave up and bent over me. He asked who had shot me. Before I could answer, he was asking me if I could hear him. I told him that I didn't know who had shot me and would he please tell Mama to stop jumping up and down. Every time Mama came down on that shabby floor, the bullet lodged in my stomach felt like a hot poker.

Another policeman had come in and was struggling to keep the crowd outside. I could see Turk in the front of the crowd. Before the cops came, he asked me if I was going to tell them that he was with me. I never answered. I looked at him and wondered if he saw who shot me. Then his question began to ring in my head: "Sonny, you gonna tell 'em I was with you?" I was bleeding on a dirty floor in a fish-and-chips joint, and Turk was standing there in the doorway hoping that I would die before I could tell the cops that he was with me. Not once did Turk ask me how I felt.

Hell, yeah, I thought, I'm gonna tell 'em.

It seemed like hours had passed before the ambulance finally arrived. Mama wanted to go to the hospital with me, but the ambulance attendant said she was too excited. On the way to Harlem Hospital, the cop who was riding with us asked Dad what he had to say. His answer was typical: "I told him about hanging out with those bad-ass boys." The cop was a little surprised. This must be a rookie, I thought.

The next day, Mama was at my bedside telling me that she had prayed and the Lord had told her that I was going to live. Mama said that many of my friends wanted to donate some blood for me, but the hospital would not accept it from narcotics users.

REMEMBERING PEOPLE

In the household of Virginia and Leonard Woolf, sixteen-year-old Richard Kennedy, who came to work at their Hogarth Press, had all the status of "a fly on the wall." And since he was of so little consequence, there was no need for the Woolfs to squander upon him their celebrated wit and charm or to be on their best behavior. They could not have known that this unworldly, seemingly naive young man was keeping a diary, later discovered and published under the title "A Boy at Hogarth Press." Although its editor says that "this book can be thought of, in no way unkindly, as a sort of literary 'Diary of a Nobody,'" it contains some sharp and revealing observations about the great lady of Bloomsbury. She's "rather cruel" says the young diarist, whose honest eye and knack for detail provides us with a lively, if somewhat unflattering account of an evening with the Woolfs.

A Social Evening with the Woolfs

Richard Kennedy

I went to supper with the Woolfs. We had strawberries and cream. Mrs W was in a very happy mood. She said she had been to a nightclub the night before and how marvellous it was inventing new foxtrot steps. I thought LW's back looked a bit disapproving as he was dishing out the strawberries. The other guest was George Rylands, a very good-looking young man who had worked for the Woolfs before going to university. We were publishing a book by him called *Words and Poetry* and McKnight Kauffer had done a design for the cover. George Rylands egged Mrs W on to talk about how much she enjoyed kicking up her heels. I couldn't help feeling a little shocked.

Some people came in with huge bundles of flowers to give her. They had been commissioned to write an article about dirt-track racing. As they were very hard up, they were very anxious to get the job, but the editor had turned down their manuscripts. Mrs W had come to their rescue and written a description of the sport, in which she had compared the roaring machines and the arc lights to a medieval tournament.

Some more people came in after supper. Mrs Woolf started rolling her shag cigarettes. She gave one to an American lady who nearly choked to death.

She started talking about the Hogarth Press in a way that I thought didn't please LW very much, saying it was like keeping a grocer's shop. I think she is rather cruel in spite of the kind rather dreamy way she looks at you. She described Mrs Cartwright as having the step of an elephant and the ferocity of a tiger, which gives a very false impression as Ma Cartwright has no ferocity at all, although she does charge about everywhere. She also described her sliding down the area steps on her bottom, during the frost.

I consider it bad form to laugh at your employees.

Kennedy's own sketch of the evening

DISCUSSION AND EXERCISES

1. Consider Thomas Wolfe's "The Quality of Memory."
   a. Identify and comment on the sense impressions Wolfe describes.
   b. Evaluate the choice of words (nouns, verbs, adjectives).
   c. What special rhetorical devices (alliteration, repetition) contribute to the rhythm and momentum of Wolfe's sentences?

2. Write a paragraph (150–250 words) describing a vivid memory of some past experience. Be sure to include concrete sensual detail (colors, shapes, sounds) so that you do not merely recount but evoke the experience. Be sure to begin prewriting with a cluster using "The Day I…." as your nucleus words.

3. Evaluate the use of the following rhetorical features in Laurie Lee's "The Village School":

selection of details	sensory images	rhythm
choice of adjectives	metaphors	inverted word order
repetition of words	parallelism	voice

4. Try to simulate a creativity workshop with three or four other people, either in class (if the instructor suggests) or outside of class. Work together to trigger memories and excite recollections; write your impressions in a cluster or list them, whichever is more comfortable. Your cluster should begin like the one below and continue to radiate outward.

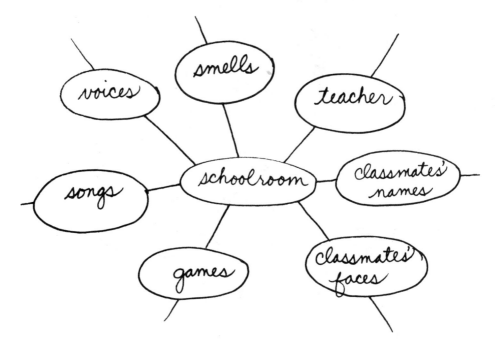

ESSAY SUGGESTIONS

1. Using a cluster based on "The first place I remember" write an essay (750–1,000 words) dealing with your earliest memories, as in Penelope Mortimer's essay "In the First Place."

2. Write an essay (750–1,000 words) based on your "schoolroom" cluster.

3. In an essay (750–1,000 words) describe a period in your life, during childhood or adolescence, that remains marked off from other times by specific events, experiences, or feelings you associate with it (like Brown's "The Day I Got Shot"). Begin by clustering around the event.

4. Read Dylan Thomas's "A Child's Christmas in Wales" and write an essay (750–1,000 words) describing any holiday as you remember your family celebrating it. Be sure to begin prewriting with a cluster which uses the holiday as the nucleus term.

5. In an essay (500–750 words) draw upon a social or formal occasion you recall during which people were behaving artificially, as in Richard Kennedy's "A Social Evening with the Woolfs." Begin prewriting with a cluster using the occasion as your nucleus word.

6. Consider Richard Kennedy's "A Social Evening with the Woolfs."

   a. Notice the abundant detail in this essay. List some of the precise and amusing observations Kennedy makes.

   b. What impression does the reader get of the Woolfs? Their relationship with each other? Their attitudes toward their friends? Their treatment of friends and employees?

   c. What judgment does Richard Kennedy make of the Woolfs? What does he consider "good form" and "poor form"? What does he find "shocking"?

   d. The publisher comments that "his naiveté is his greatest asset." In what sense do you think this true? How would his observations have been different if he had been older and more worldly?

   e. How do you view Kennedy's view of the Woolfs? Do you find him fair? Perceptive? Prudish? Moralistic? Compassionate? Characterize him as a person.

5. What Is My Personal Response to X?

THE PERSONAL ESSAY

*O*ne of the most common and popular types of writing is the personal essay, an informal, discursive piece in which you describe your response to some aspect of your surroundings: an object, situation, or event; a fleeting thought or observation; an emotional opinion or reaction. This type of essay is friendly, often intimate in tone, perhaps even confessional in nature. The writer, rather than the subject of the essay, is the main source of interest. Indeed, the success of your personal essays will depend largely on your personality and the quality of your imagination. Are you sensitive and perceptive? Do you see things with a fresh eye and clear spirit? Do you respond in a recognizably human way? Can readers feel for you—and with you?

A good personal essay requires the writer to use a composite of writing skills centered mainly on the ability to render experiences with feeling through vivid description and narration, believable characterization, and sharply evoked memory. The personal or "familiar" essay, as it was once called (for it places writer and reader on close or familiar terms) is not easy to write, but it is generally rewarding and may even be therapeutic. People need to "talk," to tell their secrets within the frame of a literary form. Here, then, is another human use of writing: through the personal essay people share experiences and thereby come to see the many ways in which they are both different and alike.

The personal essayist talks to us—as our friend, with no need to stand on ceremony. Loosely organized, flowing as smoothly as the mind and pen, the personal essay is a relaxed form, usually brief and tentative in tone, for it is searching for answers, not giving them. The writer is sharing his or her thoughts with us; they may not even be rational thoughts. The writer will freely admit this as Joan Didion does in the following personal essay.

A Reflection

Joan Didion's essay, "At the Dam," draws heavily on description and memory to produce a highly personal response to a feature of the landscape that is—as Didion herself acknowledges—hardly worth reflecting on: "Dams, after all, are commonplace: we have all seen one." But this particular dam—Hoover Dam—has such a haunting quality that "its image," Didion says, "has never been entirely absent from my inner eye."

What is it about this dam, we wonder, that sets off such an intense response? We must turn to the essayist herself to find out.

At the Dam

Joan Didion

Since the afternoon in 1967 when I first saw Hoover Dam, its image has never been entirely absent from my inner eye. I will be talking to someone in Los Angeles, say, or New York, and suddenly the dam will materialize, its pristine concave face gleaming white against the harsh rusts and taupes and mauves of that rock canyon hundreds or thousands of miles from where I am. I will be driving down Sunset Boulevard, or about to enter a freeway, and abruptly those power transmission towers will appear before me, canted vertiginously over the tailrace. Sometimes I am confronted by the intakes and sometimes by the shadow of the heavy cable that spans the canyon and sometimes by the ominous outlets to unused spillways, black in the lunar clarity of the desert light. Quite often I hear the turbines. Frequently I wonder what is happening at the dam this instant, at this precise intersection of time and space, how much water is being released to fill downstream orders and what lights are flashing and which generators are in full use and which just spinning free.

I used to wonder what it was about the dam that made me think of it at times and in places where I once thought of the Mindanao Trench, or of the stars wheeling in their courses, or of the words *As it was in the beginning, is now and ever shall be, world without end, amen.* Dams, after all, are commonplace: we have all seen one. This particular dam had existed as an idea in the world's mind for almost forty years before I saw it. Hoover Dam, showpiece of the Boulder Canyon project, the several million tons of concrete that made the Southwest plausible, the *fait accompli* that was to convey, in the innocent time of its construction, the notion that mankind's brightest promise lay in American engineering.

Of course the dam derives some of its emotional effect from precisely that aspect, that sense of being a monument to a faith since misplaced. "They died to make the desert bloom," reads a plaque dedicated to the 96 men who died building this first of the great high dams, and in context the worn phrase touches, suggests all of that trust in harnessing resources, in the meliorative power of the dynamo, so central to the early Thirties. Boulder City, built in 1931 as the construction town for the dam, retains the ambience of a model city, a new town, a toy triangular grid of green lawns and trim bungalows, all fanning out from the Reclamation building. The bronze sculptures at the dam itself evoke muscular citizens of a tomorrow that never came, sheaves of wheat clutched heavenward, thunderbolts defied. Winged Victories guard the flagpole. The flag whips in the canyon wind. An empty Pepsi-Cola can clatters across the terrazzo. The place is perfectly frozen in time.

But history does not explain it all, does not entirely suggest what makes that dam so affecting. Nor, even, does energy, the massive involvement with power and pressure and the transparent sexual overtones to that involvement. Once when I revisited the dam I walked through it with a man from the Bureau of Reclamation. For a while we trailed behind a guided tour, and then we went on, went into parts of the dam where visitors do not generally go. Once in a while he would explain something, usually in that recondite language having to do with "peaking power," with "outages" and "dewatering," but on the whole we spent the afternoon in a world so alien, so complete and so beautiful unto itself that it was scarcely necessary to speak at all. We saw almost no one. Cranes moved above us as if under their own volition. Generators roared. Transformers hummed. The gratings on which we stood vibrated. We watched a hundred-ton steel shaft plunging down to that place where the water was. And finally we got down to that place where the water was, where the water sucked out of Lake Mead roared through thirty-foot penstocks and then into thirteen-foot penstocks and finally into the turbines themselves. "Touch it," the Reclamation man said, and I did, and for a long time I just stood there with my hands on the turbine. It was a peculiar moment, but so explicit as to suggest nothing beyond itself.

There was something beyond all that, something beyond energy, beyond history, something I could not fix in my mind. When I came up from the dam that day the wind was blowing harder, through the canyon and all across the Mojave. Later, toward Henderson and Las Vegas, there would be dust blowing, blowing past the Country-Western Casino FRI & SAT NITES and blowing past the Shrine of Our Lady of Safe Journey STOP & PRAY, but out at the dam there was no dust, only the rock and the dam and a little greasewood and a few garbage cans, their tops chained, banging against a fence. I walked across the marble star map that traces a sidereal revolution of the equinox and fixes forever, the Reclamation man had told me, for all time and for all people who can read the stars, the date the dam was dedicated. The star map was, he had said, for when we were all gone and the dam was left. I had not thought much of it when he said it, but I thought of it then, with the wind whining and the sun dropping behind a mesa with the finality of a sunset in space. Of course that was the image I had seen always, seen it without quite realizing what I saw, a dynamo finally free of man, splendid at last in its absolute isolation, transmitting power and releasing water to a world where no one is.

For Didion, who makes a startling imaginative leap in this essay, the dam is nothing less than an image of eternity, that which "was in the beginning, is now, and ever shall be, world without end." Seen in this light—as she reveals it in her extended reflection—we are moved to return to the essay for another look—and possibly a shared glimpse of that astonishing dynamo standing, "where no one is."

AN APPRECIATION

"Children love snow but adults don't." That's the view of city people, says essayist Carol Bly whose personal response to "great weather"—great snows, in particular—follows. Born in Duluth, Minnesota (and referred to by one critic as the "Joan Didion of Duluth"), she has lived in rural Minnesota for twenty-five years. Most country and small-town Minnesotans—adults and children alike—"relish" all aspects of snow, she tells us: "the excesses of it ... the threat of it ... the endless work of it, the glamour of it."

Not that it's all glamour. Snowstorms are "inconvenient," even dangerous; more than that, they give us pause in the day's occupation, a chance to face the darker side not only of nature but of ourselves as well. Note how Bly cites New Hampshire poet Robert Frost to reinforce the negative and apprehensive side of her personal response, using a passage from Frost in the body of the essay. To reinforce the positive side of her response, she cites poet Robert Bly, using a passage from his "Silence in the Snowy Fields," as epigraph. Marshalling the energy and courage to survive snowstorms can help us view the world more serenely and plan our lives more creatively "instead of just following along."

Note how the essay ends with a hopeful image that refers back to the epigraph, tying the piece together by affirming the rewards of ambitious struggle: seeing "with such clear eyes the white flake of snow." Note, finally, in the margins of the essay, subquestions that, we may infer, shaped the organization of this deeply thoughtful personal statement about storms and stress and how we confront them.

Great Snows

Carol Bly

How strange to think of giving up all ambition!
Suddenly I see with such clear eyes
The white flake of snow
That has just fallen in the horse's mane.

—"Watering the Horse," by Robert Bly,
Silence in the Snowy Fields

Introduction
Thesis:
"Small-town
Minnesotans ...
relish snow in
large
inconvenient
storms"

What do
people do
before a storm?
(Note
descriptive
detail)

What do
people do after
a storm?

More
descriptive
detail

It is sometimes mistakenly thought by city people that grown-ups don't love snow. They think only children who haven't got to shovel it love snow, or only people like the von Fürstenburgs and their friends who get to go skiing in exotic places and will never backslope a roadside in all their lives: that is a mistake. The fact is that most country or small-town Minnesotans love snow. They relish snow in large inconvenient storms; they like the excesses of it, they like the threat of it, the endless work of it, the glamour of it.

Before a storm, Madison is full of people excitedly laying in food stocks for the three-day blow. People lay in rather celebratory food, too. Organic-food parents get chocolate for the children; weight watchers lay in macaroni and Sara Lee cakes; recently converted vegetarians backslide to T-bones. People hang around the large Super-Valu window and keep a tough squinty-eyed watch on the storm progress with a lot of gruff, sensible observations (just like Houston Control talking to the moon, very much on top of it all) like "Ja, we need this for spring moisture ..." or "Ja, it doesn't look like letting up at all ..." or "Ja, you can see where it's beginning to drift up behind the VFW." The plain pleasure of it is scarcely hidden.

That is before the storm. Then the town empties out as the farmers and their families take their stocks home before U.S. 75, Minnesota 40, and Lac Qui Parle 19 close up. During the storm itself heroism is the routine attitude. I remember once when the phone was out, before all the telephone lines went underground, and the power was off, our neighbor came lightly in his huge pack boots across the drift top, high up from our house level, like an upright black ant, delicately choosing his footing over the hard-slung and paralyzed snow waves. He looked as if he were walking across a frozen North Atlantic. He had come over to see if we were O.K. It was before snowmobiles, at −40 degrees a welcome gesture.

Then right after a storm we all go back uptown because we have to see how the town has filled. The streets are walled ten and eleven feet high. If they had had underground parking ramps in the pyramids this is what they'd have looked like, white-painted, and we crawl between the neatly carved clean walls. The horrible snow buildup is a point of pride. In 1969 a fine thing happened: the county of Lac Qui Parle imported a couple of gigantic snow-removal machines from Yellowstone Park. It cost several thousand dollars to get those monsters here; when they arrived our heavy, many-layered, crusted snow broke the machines—they couldn't handle it. With glittering eyes we sent them back to Yellowstone Park....

If one has any kind of luck one garners comfort from great weather, but if there is some anxious and unresolved part of one's inner life, snowfall and certainly snowboundness can make it worse. During the winter of 1968–69, the three doctors of our town prescribed between two and three times as much tranquilizing medicine as usual. And Robert Frost, despite being one of the best snow poets going, has an odd, recurring fretfulness about snow:

What happens to anxious, nervous people?

> The woods are lovely, dark and deep,
> But I have promises to keep

What does Robert Frost ("one of our best snow poets") say about this anxiety or "fretfulness"?

What promises? To whom? If we think about it it sounds moralistic and self-denying—a moral showing-off in some way. The nervousness is stronger, though, in "Desert Places":

> Snow falling and night falling fast, oh, fast
> In a field I looked into going past,
> And the ground almost covered smooth in snow,
> But a few weeds and stubble showing last.
>
> The woods around it have it—it is theirs.
> All animals are smothered in their lairs.
> I am too absent-spirited to count;
> The loneliness includes me unawares.

I am struck by the malaise of the word *absent-spirited*. It must mean—this joy in snow or fretfulness in snow—that whatever is providential and coming to each of us from within is sped the faster by snowfall.

Being out in a blizzard is not lovely. Nature then feels worse than inimical; it feels simply impersonal. It isn't that, like some goddess in Homer, she wants to grab and freeze your body in her drifts; it is that you can be taken and still the wind will keep up its regular blizzard whine and nothing has made a difference. In February of 1969 the fuel men couldn't get through for weeks; one midnight my husband and I had to transfer oil from a drum behind an old shed to our house tank. We did this in cans, load after load, crawling on all fours and rolling in the ravines between the drifts. It had some nice moments: every ten minutes or so we'd meet behind the old shed, when one returned an empty can and the other was coming away with a full one, and we'd crouch in the scoured place, leaning over the nasty, rusted, infuriatingly slow spigot of the oil tank there. Looking at each other, we saw we had that impersonal aspect of snow-covered people. It was peculiar to think that anyone behind those freezing, melting, refreezing eyebrows ever objected to an act of Congress or ever loved a summer woods or memorized the tenor to anything by Christopher Tye. Back inside, our job done, still cold and rough-spoken, still walking like bears, we studied the children in their beds....

How do people feel "being out in a blizzard"? (Personal narrative example of how the writer and her family responded to the blizzard of 1969 ...)

... Since we don't *use* blizzards in western Minnesota, the question lingers: why the pleasure in great weather? As with children in thunderstorms, I think we all have a secret affair of long standing with the other face of things. Children want the parents and the police and the other irritating powers to have their measure taken; they want a change of justice; but it goes further: they have a secret affection for bad weather.

Why do people take "pleasure in great weather"?

Conclusion:
Cyclical return
to thesis idea
suggested in
epigraph and in
paragraph one:
personal
strengths may
emerge by
responding
positively to
the stress of
"ambition" and
"inconvenient
storms"

Storms, what is more, force us to look at nature closely, and that is never boring. All meetings of the Business Improvement Association and the Countryside Council and the play rehearsal committees stop in a blizzard. It is a help. Two things make nature lovely to people, I think: enforced, extended leisure in a natural place—which storms give us out here; and second, planning our own lives instead of just following along. The moment, for example, that someone finally decides not to take the promising job offered by Reserve Mining, for example, or the moment someone decides not to pad a travel-expense account at the Ramada is a moment in which ice and snow and bare trunks look better, less happenstance, less pointless. C. S. Lewis goes very far: he claims that the fact that we all agree on what is meant by *good* or *holy* (that is, no one thinks robbery or despoiling the land or depriving the poor is good) indicates that goodness and holiness are actually a normal, planned part of our universe—perfectly natural to the species. He would not be surprised at all to see snow on a horse's mane all the better for having just worked out an ethical decision.

AN APPRECIATION AND DEFENSE

Like Carol Bly, George Orwell has written an appreciation, in this case a warm, affectionate personal response to a most unlikely creature, the common toad. Unlike the skylark or the primrose, the toad, Orwell admits, "has never had much of a boost from the poets." Nor anyone else, we might add. On that very ground, as anyone familiar with Orwell's work might predict, Orwell comes to their rescue, for Orwell's personal sympathies were habitually extended to the poor and powerless, the unheralded, the uncelebrated, the overlooked, the "common toads" of the earth. Orwell could respond to their virtues with all his being; he could see—specifically —that the toad has a character all its own: it salutes the coming spring; it has "a very spiritual look" and "the most beautiful eye of any living creature."

Such devotion to simple creatures and seasonal pleasures makes the politically conscious and committed Orwell feel momentarily guilty. Is it "politically reprehensible," he asks later in the essay, to respond pleasurably to "a blackbird's song, a yellow elm tree in October, or some other natural phenomenon which does not... have what the editors of the Left-wing newspapers call a class angle?" Orwell earnestly defends not only our *right* to respond pleasurably and appreciatively to nature but our political *responsibility* to do so: "By retaining one's childhood love of such things as trees, fishes, butterflies and ... toads, one makes a peaceful and decent future a little more probable...."

Some Thoughts on the Common Toad

George Orwell

Before the swallow, before the daffodil, and not much later than the snowdrop, the common toad salutes the coming of spring after his own fashion, which is to emerge from a hole in the ground, where he has lain buried since the previous autumn, and crawl as rapidly as possible towards the nearest suitable patch of water. Something—some kind of shudder in the earth, or perhaps merely a rise of a few degrees in the temperature—has told him that it is time to wake up: though a few toads appear to sleep the clock round and miss out a year from time to time—at any rate, I have more than once dug them up, alive and apparently well, in the middle of the summer.

At this period, after his long fast, the toad has a very spiritual look, like a strict Anglo-Catholic towards the end of Lent. His movements are languid but purposeful, his body is shrunken, and by contrast his eyes look abnormally large. This allows one to notice, what one might not at another time, that a toad has about the most beautiful eye of any living creature. It is like gold, or more exactly it is like the golden-colored semi-precious stone which one sometimes sees in signet rings, and which I think is called a chrysoberyl.

For a few days after getting into the water the toad concentrates on building up his strength by eating small insects. Presently he has swollen to his normal size again, and then he goes through a phase of intense sexiness. All he knows, at least if he is a male toad, is that he wants to get his arms around something, and if you offer him a stick, or even your finger, he will cling to it with surprising strength and take a long time to discover that it is not a female toad. Frequently one comes upon shapeless masses of ten or twenty toads rolling over and over in the water, one clinging to another without distinction of sex. By degrees, however, they sort themselves out into couples, with the male duly sitting on the female's back. You can now distinguish males from females, because the male is smaller, darker and sits on top, with his arms tightly clasped round the female's neck. After a day or two the spawn is laid in long strings which wind themselves in and out of the reeds and soon become invisible. A few more weeks, and the water is alive with masses of tiny tadpoles which rapidly grow larger, sprout hindlegs, then forelegs, then shed their tails: and finally, about the middle of the summer, the new generation of toads, smaller than one's thumb-nail but perfect in every particular, crawl out of the water to begin the game anew.

I mention the spawning of the toads because it is one of the phenomena of spring which most deeply appeal to me, and because the toad, unlike the skylark and the primrose, has never had much of a boost from the poets. But I am aware that many people do not like reptiles or amphibians, and I am not suggesting that in order to enjoy the spring you have to take an interest in toads. There are also the crocus, the missel thrush, the cuckoo, the blackthorn, etc. The point is that the pleasures of spring are available to everybody, and cost nothing. Even in the most sordid street the coming of spring will register itself by some sign or other, if it is only a brighter blue between the chimney pots or the vivid green of an elder sprouting on a blitzed site. Indeed it is remarkable how Nature goes on existing unofficially, as it were, in the very heart of London. I have seen a kestrel flying over the Deptford gasworks, and I have heard a first-rate performance by a blackbird in the Euston Road. There must be some hundreds of thousands, if not millions, of birds living inside the four-mile radius, and it is rather a pleasing thought that none of them pays a halfpenny of rent.

As for spring, not even the narrow and gloomy streets round the Bank of England are quite able to exclude it. It comes seeping in everywhere, like one of those new poison gases which pass through all filters. The spring is commonly referred to as "a miracle," and during the past five or six years this worn-out figure of speech has taken on a new lease of life. After the sort of winters we have had to endure recently, the spring does seem miraculous, because it has become gradually harder and harder to believe that it is actually going to happen. Every February since 1940 I have found myself thinking that this time winter is going to be permanent. But Persephone, like the toads, always rises from the dead at about the same moment. Suddenly, towards the end of March, the miracle happens and the decaying slum in which I live is transfigured. Down in the square the sooty privets have turned bright green, the leaves are thickening on the chestnut trees, the daffodils are out, the wallflowers are budding, the policeman's tunic looks positively a pleasant shade of blue, the fishmonger greets his customers with a smile, and even the sparrows are quite a different color, having felt the balminess of the air and nerved themselves to take a bath, their first since last September.

Is it wicked to take a pleasure in spring, and other seasonal changes? To put it more precisely, is it politically reprehensible, while we are all groaning, under the shackles of the capitalist system, to point out that life is frequently more worth living because of a blackbird's song, a yellow elm tree in October, or some other natural phenomenon which does not cost money and does not have what the editors of the Left-wing newspapers call a class angle? There is no doubt that many people think so. I know by experience that a favorable reference to "Nature" in one of my articles is liable to bring me abusive letters, and though the key-word in these letters is usually "sentimental," two ideas seem to be mixed up in them. One is that any pleasure in the actual process of life encourages a sort of political quietism. People, so the thought runs, ought to be discontented, and it is our job to multiply our wants and not simply to increase our enjoyment of the things we have already. The other idea is that this is the age of machines and that to dislike the machine, or even to want to limit its domination, is backward-looking, reactionary, and slightly ridiculous. This is often backed up by the statement that a love of Nature is a foible of urbanized people who have no notion what Nature is really like. Those who really have to deal with the soil, so it is argued, do not love the soil, and do not take the faintest interest in birds or flowers, except from a strictly utilitarian point of view. To love the country one must live in the town, merely taking an occasional week-end ramble at the warmer times of year.

This last idea is demonstrably false. Medieval literature, for instance, including the popular ballads, is full of an almost Georgian enthusiasm for Nature, and the art of agricultural peoples such as the Chinese and Japanese centres always round trees, birds, flowers, rivers, mountains. The other idea seems to me to be wrong in a subtler way. Certainly we ought to be discontented, we ought not simply to find out ways of making the best of a bad job, and yet if we kill all pleasure in the actual process of life, what sort of future are we preparing for ourselves? If a man cannot enjoy the return of spring, why should he be happy in a labor-saving Utopia? What will he do with the leisure that the machine will give him? I have always suspected that if our economic and political problems are ever really solved, life will become simpler instead of more complex, and that the sort of pleasure one gets from finding the first primrose will loom larger than the sort of pleasure one gets from eating an ice to the tune of a Wurlitzer. I think that by retaining one's childhood love of such things as trees, fishes, butterflies and—to return to my first instance—toads, one makes a peaceful and decent future a little more probable, and that by preaching the doctine that nothing is to be admired except steel and concrete, one merely makes it a little surer that human beings will have no outlet for their surplus energy except in hatred and leader-worship.

At any rate, spring is here, even in London, N.1, and they can't stop you enjoying it. This is a satisfying reflection. How many a time have I stood watching the toads mating, or a pair of hares having a boxing match in the young corn, and thought of all the important persons who would stop me enjoying this if they could. But luckily they can't. So long as you were not actually ill, hungry, frightened or immured in a prison or a holiday camp, spring is still spring. The atom bombs are piling up in the factories, the police are prowling through the cities, the lies are streaming from the loudspeakers, but the earth is still going round the sun, and neither the dictators nor the bureaucrats, deeply as they disapprove of the process, are able to prevent it.

A PROTEST

The personal essay may also be a protest—a "sounding off" at something one finds objectionable. The following essay, now a classic, appeared first in the introductory issue of *Ms.* magazine. The writer, contemplating the countless duties and responsibilities of the "ideal" wife, decides ironically that—of course—she too would like a wife. Who wouldn't? Where else can anyone get so many multi-purpose services performed? By framing her personal essay in the form of casual analysis—a deadpan listing of the reasons *why* she'd like a wife—the writer transforms a seeming explanation into a subtle attack.

Why I Want a Wife

Judy Syfers

I belong to that classification of people known as wives. I am A Wife. And, not altogether incidentally, I am a mother.

Not too long ago a male friend of mine appeared on the scene fresh from a recent divorce. He had one child, who is, of course, with his ex-wife. He is looking for another wife. As I thought about him while I was ironing one evening, it suddenly occurred to me that I, too, would like to have a wife. Why do I want a wife?

I would like to go back to school so that I can become economically independent, support myself, and, if need be, support those dependent upon me. I want a wife who will work and send me to school. And while I am going to school I want a wife to take care of my children. I want a wife to keep track of the children's doctor and dentist appointments. And to keep track of mine, too. I want a wife to make sure my children eat properly and are kept clean. I want a wife who will wash the children's clothes and keep them mended. I want a wife who is a good nurturant attendant to my children, who arranges for their schooling, makes sure that they have an adequate social life with their peers, takes them to the park, the zoo, etc. I want a wife who takes care of the children when they are sick, a wife who arranges to be around when the children need special care, because, of course, I cannot miss classes at school. My wife must arrange to lose time at work and not lose the job. It may mean a small cut in my wife's income from time to time, but I guess I can tolerate that. Needless to say, my wife will arrange and pay for the care of the children while my wife is working.

I want a wife who will take care of *my* physical needs. I want a wife who will keep my house clean. A wife who will pick up after my children, a wife who will pick up after me. I want a wife who will keep my clothes clean, ironed, mended, replaced when need be, and who will see to it that my personal things are kept in their proper place so that I can find what I need the minute I need it. I want a wife who cooks the meals, a wife who is a *good* cook. I want a wife who will plan the menus, do the necessary grocery shopping, prepare the meals, serve them pleasantly, and then do the cleaning up while I do my studying. I want a wife who will care for me when I am sick and sympathize with my pain and loss of time from school. I want a wife to go along when our family takes a vacation so that someone can continue to care for me and my children when I need a rest and change of scene.

I want a wife who will not bother me with rambling complaints about a wife's duties. But I want a wife who will listen to me when I feel the need to explain a rather difficult point I have come across in my course of studies. And I want a wife who will type my papers for me when I have written them.

I want a wife who will take care of details of my social life. When my wife and I are invited out by my friends, I want a wife who will take care of the babysitting arrangements. When I meet people at school that I like and want to entertain, I want a wife who will have the house clean, will prepare a special meal, serve it to me and my friends, and not interrupt when I talk about things that interest me and my friends. I want a wife who will have arranged that the children are fed and ready for bed before my guests arrive so that the children do not bother us. I want a wife who takes care of the needs of my guests so that they feel comfortable, who makes sure that they have an ashtray, that they are passed the hors d'oeuvres, that they are offered a second helping of the food, that their wine glasses are replenished when necessary, that their coffee is served to them as they like it. And I want a wife who knows that sometimes I need a night out by myself.

I want a wife who is sensitive to my sexual needs, a wife who makes love passionately and eagerly when I feel like it, a wife who makes sure that I am satisfied. And, of course, I want a wife who will not demand sexual attention when I am not in the mood for it. I want a wife who assumes the complete responsibility for birth control, because I do not want more children. I want a wife who will remain sexually faithful to me so that I do not have to clutter up my intellectual life with jealousies. And I want a wife who understands that *my* sexual needs may entail more than strict adherence to monogamy. I must, after all, be able to relate to people as fully as possible.

If, by chance, I find another person more suitable as a wife than the wife I already have, I want the liberty to replace my present wife with another one. Naturally, I will expect a fresh, new life; my wife will take the children and be solely responsible for them so that I am left free.

When I am through with school and have a job, I want my wife to quit working and remain at home so that my wife can more fully and completely take care of a wife's duties.

My God, who *wouldn't* want a wife?

DISCUSSION AND EXERCISES

1. The effectiveness of a personal essay depends on the authenticity of the writer's voice. Does that voice speak in a natural rhythm that you can hear? Is it distinctively and recognizably the writer's own? Is a suitable tone established and maintained throughout the essay? How do you derive from this tone a sense of how the writer feels about his or her subject and how he or she wants you to feel? These are the questions you address to the personal essay. Since the writer is the unifying thread running through the piece, it is important that he or she plays a clear and consistent role. Before attempting to write your own personal essays, it will be helpful to analyze those in this chapter so that you can see exactly how these writers have achieved their special effects and made their essays work.

a. In a sentence or two summarize the substance and what you believe to be the writer's purpose in each essay.
b. In a sentence tell why you think the writer has or has not succeeded in achieving his or her purpose.
c. In terms of the following rhetorical features, show how the writer establishes and maintains an attitude and tone of voice appropriate to his or her purpose.

  1. words

       precision of nouns, verbs, adjectives
       concreteness
       levels of usage
       connotation
       repetition
       sound

  2. sentences

       construction (word order, economy, emphasis, main and subordinate ideas)
       length
       variety
       rhythm and balance (use of parallelism, antithesis)
       texture
       opening and closing sentences

  3. choice of examples and illustrations
  4. citing of authorities
  5. use of images
  6. use of figurative language
  7. use of irony
  8. use of allusions
  9. smoothness of transitions

2. William Hazlitt (1778–1830), an early master of the familiar style, recorded and defined it as follows:

> It is not easy to write a familiar style. Many people mistake a familiar for a vulgar style, and suppose that to write without affectation is to write at random. On the contrary, there is nothing that requires more precision, and, if I may so say, purity of expression, than the style I am speaking of. It utterly rejects not only all unmeaning pomp, but all low, cant phrases, and loose, unconnected slipshod allusions. It is not to take the first word that offers, but the best word in common use; it is not to throw words together in any combinations we please, but to follow and avail ourselves of the true idiom of the language. To write a genuine familiar or truly English style, is to write as any one would speak in common conversation, who had a thorough command and choice of words, or who could discourse with ease, force and perspicuity, setting aside all pedantic and oratorical flourishes.

Comment on Hazlitt's description of the familiar style, explaining what is meant by the following terms:

a. familiar versus vulgar
b. unmeaning pomp
c. low, cant phrases
d. slipshod allusions
e. the true idiom of our language

    f. ease, force, and perspicuity

    g. pedantic and oratorical flourishes

3. Write a personal response (150–250 words) to a painting such as Edward Hopper's "Cape Cod Morning." Examine the details carefully: the way the woman is standing at the window, the quality of the light outdoors, the mass of trees in the background.

4. Think of a place that has affected you deeply—as the Hoover Dam affected Joan Didion and create a cluster using the name of the place as your nucleus word or phrase.

5. Consider Carol Bly's essay on "Great Snows."

    a. In what ways is the epigraph by Robert Bly appropriate to the piece?

    b. Who loves snow? Why?

    c. What mistakes are made regarding people's reactions to snow?

    d. How do most people react to a blizzard? Before? During? After? What attitudes do they tend to strike according to Bly?

    e. In what ways does an emergency situation cause some people to behave differently? What does Frost mean by "absent spirited"? In what sense is the word "malaise" appropriate? Comment on Frost's poem and its relevance to this essay.

    f. How does Bly describe the "personality" of a blizzard? How can a great snow be useful?

    g. What does Bly mean by our "long standing affair with the other face of things"?

    h. In what sense do children have a "secret affection" ... with the "other face of things"? What is Bly referring to here?

6. George Orwell's warm and delightful essay "Some Thoughts on the Common Toad" is divided into three distinct sections, the first devoted to describing the writer's response to the toad; the second to explaining why he responds to the toad; and the third to a defense of his response. Consider the following questions from section one of the essay:

    a. How does the toad "salute the coming of spring"?

    b. What does Orwell mean by the toad's "very spiritual look"?

    c. What other human characteristics does Orwell attribute to the toad?

    d. What evidence do we have that Orwell's interest in toads is not a new one?

    e. Orwell describes the toad's eye as "being like the golden-colored, semi-precious stones which one sometimes sees in signet rings." What other adjectives add to the music of this piece?

In section two, Orwell's tone changes somewhat.

    f. What explanation does he give for "boosting toads"?

    g. How does the sentence "... (spring) comes seeping in everywhere, like one of those new poison gases which pass through all filters" seem to change the tone of the piece?

    h. Why does Orwell consider spring a "miracle"?

In section three, Orwell feels he must defend his love and appreciation of nature.

    i. Why do you think Orwell raises the seemingly naive question: "Is it wicked to take a pleasure in spring ...?"

    j. Why is he so uneasy in his pleasure? From whom does he feel he must defend himself?

    k. What is Orwell suggesting in the following quotation: " ... a love of Nature is a foible of urbanized people who have no notion what Nature is really like."

    l. How does Orwell argue against this statement?

    m. What does Orwell mean when he writes "If man cannot enjoy the return of spring, why should he be happy in a labor-saving Utopia?"

    n. What dangers does he prophesy if man has no outlet for surplus energy?

    o. How does he reconcile nature and progress?

ESSAY SUGGESTIONS

1. Using a cluster as the basis for an essay of 750–1,000 words, describe your personal response to a place that "haunts" you—as Hoover Dam haunted Joan Didion.

2. Write an essay (750–1,000 words), in the manner of Carol Bly, describing your response to a severe weather situation: snow, flood, hurricane, tornado. Try to indicate not only how *you* responded but how most people responded, as you observed them. In what sense, if any, was the challenge a strengthening one?

3. a. Write an essay (500–750 words) giving your personal response to ("Some thoughts on …") a creature that interests you, using your own observations, experience, information. You might also check with a reference work that would provide background information. Some "creature suggestions" are the cow, clam, caterpillar, and cockatoo. Some titles might be: "The Hilarious Hyena," "The Haughty Peacock," or "The Malicious Mongoose." Characterize your creature as you see fit. Use the prewriting techniques you have learned.

   b. You may, like Orwell, have a nagging political conscience—or perhaps you can invent an impertinent reader muttering over your shoulder "So what?" "Who cares?" "What's the big deal?" Write a 150–250 word "defense" to append to your essay, in which you justify your "appreciation" and forgive yourself.

4. As Judy Syfer protests the traditional role of a wife, address yourself to some current social arrangements that you find irritating (500–750 words). If you prefer, describe instead your negative response to some innovation in our culture.

5. During his lifetime Hazlitt wrote essays on the subjects listed below, most of them collected in his *Table Talk: Opinions on Books, Men and Things*. Choose one topic as the basis for a personal essay of your own (500–750 words).

   > On Prejudice
   > On Disagreeable People
   > On the Want of Money
   > On Reading New Books
   > On Persons One Would Wish to Have Seen
   > On Going on a Journey
   > On the Pleasure of Painting
   > On the Ignorance of the Learned
   > On the Fear of Death
   > On Sitting for One's Picture
   > On Fashion
   > On Nicknames
   > On Public Opinion
   > On Personal Identity
   > Dreams
   > The Qualifications Necessary to Success in Life
   > Envy
   > Egotism
   > Hot and Cold
   > The Pleasure of Hating

6. What Are the Facts About X?

THE FACTUAL ESSAY

"*I* try to report facts as I see them," said the journalist John Gunther, whose massive compilations of fact resulted in such famous books as *Inside USA* and *Inside Europe*. Gunther was commenting on the difficulty of being completely objective in reporting facts, for it is almost impossible to separate our "view" of the facts from the actual "facts" themselves. As Gunther pointedly added: "A reporter with no bias at all would be a vegetable." And it is our "biases" that determine the facts we see and often the way in which we see them. The central question, then, in a piece of factual writing is: How do we know what *really* happened?

For a reporter, facts are the data that emerge from research, study, investigation, and corroboration by authority or reliable witnesses. Scientists, of course, apply an even more rigorous standard to matters of fact, regarding them merely as hypotheses until they have been verified by experiment or demonstration. Not as exacting as the scientist, nor as dogged as the reporter, conscientious student writers should begin early on to address themselves to the facts of a given subject or situation. In doing so, they will come to recognize that there are countless sources for a factual or informative essay, ranging from matters of historical significance, to the timely and newsworthy, to the seemingly trivial. The obvious prerequisite of good fact piece is knowing how to track down the facts (see "Gathering Information"). Equally important is getting the facts straight; accuracy is a prime virtue in this type of reportorial writing. So are genuine interest and enthusiasm, for as one wise observer remarked, "There are no boring subjects, only boring writers." Writers, then, must play to their own strengths, sticking to subject matter that they know something about or would like to know something about. An informed essay on bowling by someone who bowls and enjoys the sport has infinitely more merit than a listlessly written survey of a so-called important topic of presumed social significance.

RANGE OF PURPOSES

When writing factual essays writers must also know how to select facts judiciously. Since writers cannot tell everything, they include only those details that promote a particular purpose. The purpose determines what specific facts writers present and *how* they present them (seriously, satirically, calmly, angrily). Since the purpose of the fact essay gives it its distinctive shape and tone, we will review certain recurrent purposes that impel writers to approach a subject with this question in mind: "What are the facts about X?"

Providing Information

The purpose of a fact piece may be simply to provide interesting information and to satisfy what Aristotle called "natural curiosity." Certainly the following piece fulfills these conditions. *Everyone* is interested in the weather—especially its more violent moods. Here, then, are the facts about hurricanes, as set down in a brochure—a small, factual pamphlet designed to provide basic information on a given subject. This brochure has an appropriately simple format that we can outline as follows:

1. What hurricanes are
2. Dangers of the hurricane
3. Location and frequency of occurrence
4. How hurricanes form

In each of these sections the writer has included numerous details, which are easy to follow because of their logical arrangement and intrinsic interest.

Hurricanes

Hurricanes are tropical cyclones in which winds reach speeds of 74 miles per hour or more, and blow in a large spiral around a relatively calm center—the eye of the hurricane. Every year, these violent storms bring destruction to coastlines and islands in their erratic path. Tropical cyclones of the same type are called typhoons in the North Pacific, baguios in the Philippines, and cyclones in the Indian Ocean.

Stated very simply, hurricanes are giant whirlwinds in which air moves in a large, tightening spiral around a center of extreme low pressure, reaching maximum velocity in a circular band extending outward 20 or 30 miles from the rim of the eye. This circulation is counterclockwise in the Northern Hemisphere, and clockwise in the Southern Hemisphere. Near the eye, hurricane winds may gust to more than 200 miles per hour, and the entire storm dominates the ocean surface and lower atmosphere over tens of thousands of square miles.

The eye, like the spiral structure of the storm, is unique to hurricanes. Here, winds are light and skies are clear or partly cloudy. But this calm is deceptive, bordered as it is by hurricane-force winds and torrential rains. Many persons have been killed or injured when the calm eye lured them out of shelter, only to be caught in the hurricane winds at the far side of the eye, where the wind blows from a direction opposite to that in the leading half of the storm.

Hurricane winds do much damage, but drowning is the greatest cause of hurricane deaths. As the storm approaches and moves across the coastline, it brings huge waves, raising tides some 15 feet or more above normal. The rise may come rapidly, and produce flash floods in coastal lowlands, or may come in the form of giant waves—which are mistakenly called "tidal waves." Waves and currents erode beaches and barrier islands, undermine waterfront structures, and wash out highway and railway beds. The torrential rains produce sudden flooding; as the storm moves inland and its winds diminish, floods constitute the hurricane's greatest threat.

The hurricanes that strike the eastern United States are born in the tropical and subtropical North Atlantic Ocean, the Caribbean Sea, and the Gulf of Mexico. Most occur in August, September, and October, but the six-month period from June 1 to November 30 is considered the Atlantic hurricane season.

The principal regions of tropical cyclone origin vary during the season. Most early (May and June) storms originate in the Gulf of Mexico and western Caribbean. In July and August, the areas of most frequent origin shift eastward, and by September are located over the larger area from the Bahamas southeastward to the Lesser Antilles, and thence eastward to south of the Cape Verde Islands, near the west coast of Africa. After mid-September, the principal areas of origin shift back to the western Caribbean and Gulf of Mexico.

On average, six Atlantic hurricanes occur per year. However, there are significant deviations from this average. In 1916 and 1950, 11 hurricanes were observed, and no hurricanes were observed in 1907 and 1914. During 1893, 1950, and 1961 seasons, four hurricanes were observed in progress at the same time.

Hurricanes also form along the west coast of Mexico and Central America, but their effects are seldom felt as far north as California. These threaten shipping and aviation, however, and are watched as carefully as their Atlantic cousins.

Hurricanes begin as relatively small tropical cyclones which drift gradually to the west-northwest (in the Northern Hemisphere), imbedded in the westward-blowing tradewinds of the tropics. Under certain conditions these disturbances increase in size, speed, and intensity until they become full-fledged hurricanes.

The storms move forward very slowly in the tropics, and may sometimes hover for short periods of time. The initial forward speed is usually 15 miles per hour or less. Then, as the hurricane moves farther from the Equator, its forward speed tends to increase; at middle latitudes it may exceed 60 miles per hour in extreme cases.

The great storms are driven by the heat released by condensing water vapor, and by external mechanical forces. Once cut of from the warm ocean, the storm begins to die, starved for water and heat energy, and dragged apart by friction as it moves over the land.

Another basic fact of nature is that—given a certain fruit or vegetable—some soils produce better or more notable crops than others. Thus we have Florida oranges, Maine potatoes, California avocadoes, and so on. In the following article, a New Jersey writer presents us with the Jersey tomato, making it clear that it is both beautiful to behold and delicious to eat. What else would you like to know about this unique strain of a popular vegetable? The writer has provided a view of the subject from every possible angle including who grows it, how it grows, where and when it grows, why it is grown, and how it came into being. Note the first five subquestions indicated in the margin; see how many additional questions you can observe "at work" in the piece (almost thirty more).

Here Is the Jersey Tomato

Deborah A. Boerner

How would you characterize a Jersey tomato?

Who grows them?

How long is the growing season?

Anyone who has ever tasted a "Jersey tomato" does not need to be told of its unique flavor and quality. For those who haven't, it's impossible to describe. New Jersey tomato lovers suffer all winter long, tolerating expensive yet bland-tasting tomatoes sold in the supermarket. But when summer comes, farmers and backyard gardeners throughout the state, grow a tomato that knocks the "imports" right off the market produce counters.

In fact, the tomatoes grown during New Jersey's three-month growing season are enough to make this state the fourth-ranked producer of fresh

What is New
Jersey's rank
among tomato
producers?

Why is the
term "Jersey
tomato" a
misnomer?

market tomatoes in the nation. The three states which exceed New Jersey
—Florida. California, and South Carolina—are all states where the growing
season is much longer. If production was tabulated by the month, New Jersey
would undoubtably rank much higher in the production of tomatoes for the
fresh market.

"The term 'Jersey tomato' is really a misnomer," says W. Bradford
Johnson, Extension Specialist for Vegetable Crops at Rutgers University.
There's no particular variety the term refers to, but it's a term used for any
large-size tomato grown in New Jersey. Although it's not known what makes
the tomatoes grown in this state so special, an important factor is the soil.
Farmers who retire to Florida often send for seed but are disappointed when
they find the product is just not the same, Johnson said.

The latest figures (1980—from New Jersey Agricultural Statistics 1981)
indicate New Jersey farmers produce more than 500,000 cwt. (hundred-
weight) of fresh tomatoes each summer. Year after year, tomatoes rank first in
value over all other vegetable crops grown in the state. In 1980, tomatoes
accounted for 21 percent of the value of all major vegetables. Fresh market
varieties were valued close to $9.7 million while the value of processing
tomatoes was $4.6 million.

Even though production of tomatoes for processing is only half as valuable
as fresh-variety production in the state, tomato processing is an important
industry. It is especially important in the southern counties of Salem,
Gloucester, and Cumberland, where 85 percent of the processing crop is
grown. Unfortunately, five major processing plants have closed down in
recent years, resulting in hard economic times for some South Jersey
communities. However, six canneries are still operating in the state and New
Jersey has been able to retain its rank among the top five states in the country
producing processed tomatoes. Another indication tomato processing will not
become a dying industry here is the fact that much of the tomato research
being done in New Jersey today is geared towards the processing varieties.

The fact that tomato production is any kind of business at all in New Jersey
is somewhat ironic, considering how unpopular the vegetable was just a few
generations ago. The South Jersey community of Salem boasts of a legend
which explains how the tomato was finally accepted there. Colonel Robert
Gibbon Johnson, who later became the town's first mayor, is said to have
stood on the county courthouse steps in 1820 and eaten a tomato. A crowd
which had gathered to watch him gasped in disbelief. Quite a feat it was, for
tomatoes, or "love apples" as they were called then, were thought to be
poisonous. When the crowd saw that Johnson suffered no ill effects, others
tried eating them and so began the tomato's popularity.

It is not known why tomatoes were believed to be poisonous. Most likely, it
had something to do with the nightshade plant family, which is a group of
plants that includes some very toxic plants as well as the non-toxic tomato.
Whatever the reason, these mistaken fears persisted even into this century and
definitely stunted the tomato's improvement and its migration between
continents.

Because all parts of the tomato plants are perishable, it's difficult to trace its
origin through archeological records. The genus to which the tomato belongs
is native to South Africa. It is believed a wild, tiny, red-fruited tomato of
Peruvian origin was carried northward to Mexico by prehistoric Indians.

There it was domesticated in Pre-Columbia times. Introduction of the Mexican cultivars to the Mediterranean region probably did not occur until the 16th century. Even after the tomato reached Europe, migration to northern Europe was slow. It was first grown there as a curiosity or for decoration, possibly because of its poisonous mystique.

There is no evidence the American Indian knew of the tomato. It was reintroduced to the New World via the colonists in the 1700s. Here, too, it was initially grown in flower gardens. In 1781, Thomas Jefferson was one of the first in the country to grow the tomato for its food value. It was brought to the Philadelphia area in 1798 but was not sold in the market until 1829.

The first real attempts to breed improved varieties since the tomato's domestication in Mexico, occurred after the Civil War. Until the tomato gained popularity as a food which could be eaten, breeding was done mainly by selecting plants within European stocks. More recently, primitive cultivars and the native wild species have proven useful for breeding resistance to wilt diseases and nematodes, two major problems with tomatoes today.

New Jersey has played a dominant role in improving its most valued vegetable crop, the tomato. In 1934, L. G. Schermerhorn, working at Rutgers University, developed a tomato which was popular well into the 1950s, longer than any variety since then. Dubbed the "Rutgers" tomato, it was excellent for both processing and fresh sales; it was particularly noted for producing a flavorful, red-colored tomato juice. Grown flat or on stakes, the Rutgers tomato was widely adapted in the southern states, too.

When a tomato more resistant to wilt diseases was needed, Ramapo, another variety developed at Rutgers, replaced the Rutgers variety on the fresh market. Many varieties for canning and the fresh market have been developed since that time, as the research at Rutgers, the Agricultural Experiment Station, and research plots throughout the state continues. As mentioned before, much of the research today is geared not towards finding a bigger tomato but towards developing a smaller, more crack-resistant tomato that will ripen fast and withstand more punishment from mechanical harvesters when picked for processing.

For fresh market and home gardeners, however, the biggest is still the best. For the past five years, the New Jersey Championship Tomato Weigh-In has been held with that theme in mind. Last year, a 3.905-pound Super Steak tomato earned its grower, John Malyar, Sr., a $1000 check. Drawing local winners from all over the state, the idea of the contest is to "further popularize the already popular Jersey tomato," according to Joseph Heimbold, originator of the contest. Heimbold's goal is to have a tomato grown in New Jersey which will triumph over the current 6.5-pound World Champion from Wisconsin. He believes it will happen and predicts the "champ" will not be grown by a farmer; only one of the past five winning tomatoes was farm-grown.

The tomato has certainly come a long way to become a summer tradition and to affect so many facets of life in New Jersey. If the legend of Colonel Johnson eating a tomato at the Salem County Courthouse is true, there are many people who would gladly thank him. New Jersey farmers would thank him for bringing the most valued crop they grow out of the flower garden. The processing plants and people they employ would have him to thank for making possible a million-dollar industry in catsup, tomato juice, and spaghetti sauce. Backyard gardeners would thank him for giving them something to brag about, whether they win a contest for their tomatoes or just show them off to friends and neighbors. But best of all, tomato lovers have a summertime treat they'd find it difficult to live without.

Clearing Up Misconceptions

In recent years the public has grown increasingly concerned about the relationship of food to health and disease. Which foods that we eat are nutritionally sound? Which ones contribute to physical fitness and longevity? Which should be shunned as bad for our health and mental outlook? After all, "you are what you eat," as one nutritionist pointed out.

Sugar is one food that has had a consistently bad press in that it has been accused of "causing everything from obesity to learning disabilities." Does sugar deserve its bad reputation? Is it, *in fact* "one of the world's most fearsome scourges"? Not if you look at the facts as presented by two health authorities who have recently published a book with the tongue-twisting title *The One-Hundred Percent Natural, Purely Organic, Cholesterol-Free Megavitamin, Low Carbohydrate Nutrition Hoax*. According to these experts, many of the charges against sugar are "devoid of solid scientific support." The short article that follows presents the "facts" in condensed form:

Sweet Truths About Sugar

Elizabeth M. Whelan and Frederick J. Stare, M.D.

In recent years sugar has increasingly been pronounced one of the world's most fearsome scourges — right up there with the Black Plague. We are told that sugar causes everything from obesity to learning disabilities. No one, from infant to centenarian, seems immune to its deadly attack.

The U.S. government itself has stood ready to further this belief. Soon after the Senate Select Committee on Nutrition and Human Needs dubbed sugar an unnecessary evil in its 1977 report, the Federal Trade Commission proposed banning the advertising of sugary products from children's television shows. (The proposal was later dropped.) Even food processors jumped on the bandwagon: "Low in Sugar" scream their TV commercials. People brag that they no longer use the substance, as though that by itself was a virtue.

Much of this apprehension is based on two popular misconceptions: that Americans are consuming more table sugar than ever before; that sugar consumption contributes to poor health.

In fact, government statistics reveal that consumption of table sugar (sucrose) in the United States is now about the same as it was 70 years ago, while the use of other sweeteners — especially the corn syrups in processed foods — *has* greatly increased. But the figures for sweeteners include those in products such as ketchup and salad dressings, as well as those in soft drinks and desserts, and therefore estimates of the amount that people actually consume vary widely.

Just what *is* sugar? Chemically, there are many compounds called sugars, but only a few are found naturally in the foods we eat. Among sweeteners that are added the most common are sucrose — refined from cane or beet sugar — and corn syrups. Naturally occurring sugars include lactose, found in milk, and glucose and fructose, both common in fruits and vegetables. In order to be used by the body, all sugars must be converted to glucose—the sugar found in our blood. The human body cares little where its supplies originate.

Health faddists maintain that refined white sugar is dangerous, and that natural sweeteners are fine. But a molecule of sugar, refined or not, is a molecule of sugar. While it is true that table sugar contains no vitamins, minerals or protein, the amounts of nutrients in less-refined sugars such as raw or brown sugar or in honey, for example —are too small to be important. If you prefer the taste of brown sugar or honey to table sugar, use them. But don't think that you are swallowing anything nutritionally superior.

Of course, popular misconceptions about sugar extend far beyond a vague, "It's not good for you." Let's look at some of the specific charges laid at sugar's door:

Obesity. Excess calories, regardless of where they come from, are fattening. No one kind of calorie is more fattening than any other. Fat, however, contains more than twice as many calories per ounce as carbohydrates (including sugar) or proteins. Thus, a pat of butter on a slice of toast is more than twice as fattening as an equal weight of jelly. Clearly, then, it makes no sense to attempt a sugar-free reducing diet if you replace the sugar with gravies, french fries and other fatty foods.

Diabetes. Insulin, a hormone produced by the pancreas, is necessary for metabolizing glucose in the blood. In diabetes, the pancreas either fails to produce enough insulin or the insulin it does produce is unable to function properly. Diabetics, therefore, are subject to excessive blood-sugar levels, especially after ingesting sugar. Eating sugary foods, however, has *not* been shown to cause the disease.

Hypoglycemia. The opposite of diabetes occurs when the pancreas produces too much insulin, resulting in blood-sugar levels that are abnormally low. True hypo-glycemia is an extremely rare condition, with symptoms that display a remarkable parallel to those of anxiety neurosis. This condition is tailor-made for some hypochondriacs who insist that a vague collection of symptoms be tagged with a name.

Low blood-sugar levels in those few genuine hypoglycemics can be caused by pancreatic tumors. However, popular "wisdom" has decreed that too much sugar in the diet (particularly refined sugar) stimulates the pancreas to produce too much insulin, thus leading to lowered blood sugar. This is unadulterated hogwash.

Tooth decay. Although sugar can indeed contribute to cavities, don't think that dental problems can be avoided simply by replacing table sugar with good old "natural" honey or dried fruits. *Exposure time* is what we need to be concerned with. The stickier the sweet, the longer it will remain in contact with the tooth, the more damage will be done. The only way to cut down on exposure time is to eliminate sticky sweets between meals—and to clean your teeth more often. The bacteria in the mouth that cause cavities aren't the least bit particular about the type of sugar they feed on. In fact, some "health" foods, such as raisins, can nestle among the teeth all day, providing hours of tasty fare for bacteria.

Heart disease. In 1964 an English physician, John Yudkin, made the widely publicized charge that sugar is a causative factor in heart disease. Yudkin had arrived at his theory by comparing the sugar intake of 45 heart patients with 13 hospitalized accident victims and 12 men residing in the area. His study found that the heart patients consumed substantially more sugar. Thus he concluded, and the press duly reported, that sugar is bad for the heart.

When other scientists repeated his study in four hospitals—using as a control only people outside the hospital—they found that heart patients consumed the same amount of sugar as did their controls. But this attracted nowhere near the publicity of Yudkin's original statements.

A quick look at some simple statistics illustrates why the sugar-heart-disease theory makes so little sense. If the relationship were positive, countries with high sugar consumption should have a higher rate of heart disease. In fact, some—such as Venezuela, Cuba, Brazil and Costa Rica—have a rather low incidence.

Learning disabilities. In this case there aren't even any scientific studies to refute. We hear a great deal about sugar creating learning difficulties, but what is being circulated is a combination of uncontrolled studies, testimonials, opinion and conjecture. Also unsubstantiated is the contention that sugar and sugar products cause deviant behavior. After killing the mayor and a supervisor of San Francisco in 1978, former supervisor Dan White included as part of his legal defense testimony that he had eaten a lot of junk food shortly before the murder. (This was the so-called "Twinkie Defense.") One health-food advocate even claimed that the infamous Manson "family" who murdered Sharon Tate had subsisted mainly on candy bars. "Where the diet is good," she declared, "there is no crime." These and similar hypotheses are still devoid of solid scientific support.

"Empty" calories. The charge that sugar is full of "empty" calories is plain silly. All calories are full calories—i.e., full of energy. If sugar products are consumed in place of other needed nutrients, dietary deficiencies can occur. But as long as the Recommended Dietary Allowance is being met for all nutrients, there is no harm whatever in using snack foods to fulfill additional calorie requirements.

So, the evidence is clear: sugar is sweet. But that *doesn't* mean it's bad for you.

Making a Social Comment

Frequently, of course, informative essays do more than simply inform. Woven into the facts is a social commentary, an aside to the reader (only partly explicit), that asks, "Isn't this absurd?" In the following piece of reportage, Joan Didion uses the "new nonfiction" technique of piling fact upon fact, detail upon detail, and of combining these facts and details in such a way as to make a statement or social comment on what it is like to be married in the bizarre, commercial atmosphere of Las Vegas.

Marrying Absurd

Joan Didion

To be married in Las Vegas, Clark County, Nevada, a bride must swear that she is eighteen or has parental permission and a bridegroom that he is twenty-one or has parental permission. Someone must put up five dollars for the license. (On Sundays and holidays, fifteen dollars. The Clark County Courthouse issues marriage licenses at any time of the day or night except between noon and one in the afternoon, between eight and nine in the evening, and between four and five in the morning.) Nothing else is required. The State of Nevada, alone among these United States, demands neither a premarital blood test nor a waiting period before or after the issuance of a marriage license. Driving in across the Mojave from Los Angeles, one sees the signs way out on the desert, looming up from that moonscape of rattlesnakes and mesquite, even before the Las Vegas lights appear like a mirage on the horizon: "GETTING MARRIED? Free License Information First Strip Exit." Perhaps the Las Vegas wedding industry achieved its peak operational efficiency between 9:00 P.M. and midnight of August 26, 1965, an otherwise unremarkable Thursday which happened to be, by Presidential order, the last day on which anyone could improve his draft status merely by getting married. One hundred and seventy-one couples were pronounced man and wife in the name of Clark County and the State of Nevada that night, sixty-seven of them by a single justice of the peace, Mr. James A. Brennan. Mr. Brennan did one wedding at the Dunes and the other sixty-six in his office, and charged each couple eight dollars. One bride lent her veil to six others. "I got it down from five to three minutes," Mr. Brennan said later of this feat. "I could've married them *en masse*, but they're people, not cattle. People expect more when they get married."

What people who get married in Las Vegas actually do expect—what, in the largest sense, their "expectations" are—strikes one as a curious and self-contradictory business. Las Vegas is the most extreme and allegorical of American settlements, bizarre and beautiful in its venality and in its devotion to immediate gratification, a place the tone of which is set by mobsters and call girls and ladies' room attendants with amyl nitrite poppers in their uniform pockets. Almost everyone notes that there is no "time" in Las Vegas, no night and no day and no past and no future (no Las Vegas casino, however, has taken the obliteration of the ordinary time sense quite so far as Harold's Club in Reno, which for a while issued, at odd intervals in the day and night, mimeographed "bulletins" carrying news from the world outside); neither is there any logical sense of where one is. One is standing on a highway in the middle of a vast hostile desert looking at an eighty-foot sign which blinks "STARDUST" or "CAESAR'S PALACE." Yes, but what does that explain? This geographical implausibility reinforces the sense that what happens there has no connection with "real" life; Nevada cities like Reno and Carson are ranch towns, Western towns, places behind which there is some historical imperative. But Las Vegas seems to exist only in the eye of the beholder. All of which makes it an extraordinarily stimulating and interesting place, but an odd one in which to want to wear a candlelight satin Priscilla of Boston wedding dress with Chantilly lace insets, tapered sleeves and a detachable modified train.

And yet the Las Vegas wedding business seems to appeal to precisely that impulse. "Sincere and Dignified Since 1954," one wedding chapel advertises. There are nineteen such wedding chapels in Las Vegas, intensely competitive, each offering better, faster, and, by implication, more sincere services than the next: Our Photos Best Anywhere, Your Wedding on a Phonograph Record, Candlelight with Your Ceremony, Honeymoon Accommodations, Free Transportation from Your Motel to Courthouse to Chapel and Return to Motel, Religious or Civil Ceremonies, Dressing Rooms, Flowers, Rings, Announcements, Witnesses Available, and Ample Parking. All of these services, like most others in Las Vegas (sauna baths, payroll-check cashing, chinchilla coats for sale or rent) are offered twenty-four hours a day, seven days a week, presumably on the premise that marriage, like craps, is a game to be played when the table seems hot.

But what strikes one most about the Strip chapels, with their wishing wells and stained-glass paper windows and their artificial bouvardia, is that so much of their business is by no means a matter of simple convenience, of late-night liaisons between show girls and baby Crosbys. Of course there is some of that. (One night about eleven o'clock in Las Vegas I watched a bride in an orange minidress and masses of flamecolored hair stumble from a Strip chapel on the arm of her bridegroom, who looked the part of the expendable nephew in movies like *Miami Syndicate*. "I gotta get the kids," the bride whimpered. "I gotta pick up the sitter, I gotta get to the midnight show." "What you gotta get," the bridegroom said, opening the door of a Cadillac Coupe de Ville and watching her crumple on the seat, "is sober.") But Las Vegas seems to offer something other than "convenience"; it is merchandising "niceness," the facsimile of proper ritual, to children who do not know how else find it, how to make the arrangements, how to do it "right." All day and evening long on the Strip, one sees actual wedding parties, waiting under the harsh lights at a crosswalk, standing uneasily in the parking lot of the Frontier while the photographer hired by The Little Church of the West ("Wedding Place of the Stars") certifies the occasion, takes the picture: the bride in a veil and white satin pumps, the bridegroom usually in a white dinner jacket, and even an attendant or two, a sister or a best friend in hot-pink *peau de soie*, a flirtation veil, a carnation nosegay. "When I Fall in Love It Will Be Forever," the organist plays, and then a few bars of Lohengrin. The mother cries; the stepfather, awkward in his role, invites the chapel hostess to join them for a drink at the Sands. The hostess declines with a professional smile; she has already transferred her interest to the group waiting outside. One bride out, another in, and again the sign goes up on the chapel door: "One moment please—Wedding."

I sat next to one such wedding party in a Strip restaurant the last time I was in Las Vegas. The marriage had just taken place; the bride still wore her dress, the mother her corsage. A bored waiter poured out a few swallows of pink champagne ("on the house") for everyone but the bride, who was too young to be served. "You'll need something with more kick than that," the bride's father said with heavy jocularity to his new son-in-law; the ritual jokes about the wedding night had a certain Panglossian character, since the bride was clearly several months pregnant. Another round of pink champagne, this time not on the house, and the bride began to cry. "It was just as nice," she sobbed, "as I hoped and dreamed it would be."

DISCUSSION AND EXERCISES

1. "Anyone who has ever tasted a 'Jersey Tomato' does not need to be told of its unique flavor and quality," says Deborah A. Boerner in "Here's the Jersey Tomato." Many subquestions were noted as underlying the data gathered for this piece. In what sense does the voluminous data of this short article give you a sense of the unique character and quality of the Jersey tomato? Discuss. List additional subquestions (20–25 more than those cited in the margin).

2. Consider Elizabeth M. Whelan and Frederick J. Stare, M.D.'s article on "Sweet Truths About Sugar."

   a. What are some popular beliefs about the dangers of sugar?
   b. What sources of information do Whelan and Stare cite in their article?
   c. How do they define sugar?
   d. What are the "specific charges" laid at sugar's door?
   e. How do statistics debunk the sugar-heart disease theory?
   f. Upon concluding the article, are you convinced that sugar is acceptable? Why? Why not?

3. Consider Didion's essay, "Marrying Absurd."

   a. What does the simple declarative sentence early in the piece: "Nothing else is required" suggest?
   b. What is ironic about the statement by the justice of the peace: "I could've married them *en masse*, but they're people, not cattle. People expect more when they get married"?
   c. Why do you suppose the writer put quotation marks around the word "expectations" ("What people who get married in Las Vegas actually do expect—what, in the largest sense, their 'expectations' are...")?
   d. What is "curious and self-contradictory" about these expectations?

e. In what sense does the writer mean that what happens here has no connection with "'real' life"?

f. In what sense does Las Vegas exist "in the eye of the beholder"?

g. Explain the contradiction: it is "an extraordinarily stimulating and interesting place, but an odd one in which to want to wear a candlelight satin Priscilla of Boston wedding dress with Chantilly lace inserts, tapered sleeves and a detachable modified train."

h. Why do you think the writer describes the wedding dress in such detail? Do you know exactly what "a candlelight satin Priscilla of Boston" is? What "Chantilly lace" is? Does it matter whether you know or not? Do these details create a rhetorical effect independent of literal meaning? Comment on the following words:

candlelight	Chantilly
satin	lace
Priscilla of Boston	modified

i. Does the listing of chapel advertisements ("Our Photos Best Anywhere," "Your Wedding on a Phonograph Record," and so on) become tedious? Does it serve any purpose?

j. Evaluate the effectiveness of the simile "… marriage, like craps, is a game to be played when the table seems hot."

k. This essay has two illustrative incidents: comment on their rhetorical impact—that is, indicate how they develop and reinforce the point the writer is trying to make throughout her exposition.

l. Comment on the effectiveness of the phrases "merchandising 'niceness'" and "the facsimile of proper ritual."

m. Discuss irony as the prevailing tone and unifying principle of this essay.

4. Write a paragraph of 150–250 words in which you develop your answers to the above questions.

ESSAY SUGGESTIONS

1. Write a brochure (500–1,000 words) on one of the following subjects:

cosmic rays	digestion	fire
inertia	coral reefs	haunted houses
gravity	opera	tobacco
mirages	pigeons	hara-kiri
cyclotrons	drought	sea serpents
glaciers	buried treasure	falling stars
earthquakes	giants	clowns
Artic Ocean	lullabies	astrology
wind	gypsies	sundials
cavemen	magic	ice fishing
cavewomen	voodoo	
chromosomes	dwarfs and midgets	

2. In Boerner's article "Here's the Jersey Tomato," we are given the "facts" about this well-known item of produce. Consider other fruits and vegetables that are associated with specific states, use prewriting techniques, and write an essay (750–1,000 words) giving comparable facts about Hawaiian pineapples, Georgia peaches, or Michigan apples. You might want to compare and contrast such competing items as Idaho and Maine potatoes, or

California and Florida oranges. (See Question 16, "How does X compare to Y?") In gathering information on your subject, begin with your own experience and observations and move on to library research, consulting such reliable sources as the United States Department of Agriculture or local Chambers of Commerce.

3. Write a fact piece on one of the following (500–750 words) designed to entertain or inform:

cosmic rays	cavemen	magic
inertia	cavewomen	voodoo
gravity	chromosomes	fire
mirages	digestion	haunted houses
cyclotrons	buried treasure	tobacco
glaciers	giants	hara-kiri
earthquakes	lullabies	sea serpents
Arctic Ocean	gypsies	falling stars
wind	dwarfs and midgets	

4. Select one of the following controversial foods:

chocolate	coffee	herb tea
beef	fried foods	milk
frozen foods	canned foods	salt
MSG	bacon	eggs
cheeses		

Write an essay (750–1,000 words) entitled "The Truth About ..." Here again you should look into various government publications such as the U.S. Department of Agriculture, or the Food and Drug Administration. Pertinent articles in such reliable publications as *Science* and *Scientific American* will be listed in *Reader's Guide*, as will popular articles in *Newsweek* and *Time*. Many of these articles will give helpful leads and will cite medical and nutritional sources and authorities which can then be investigated as follow-up.

5. Write an essay (500–750 words) on one of the following widely misunderstood topics (see "Gathering Information").

hypnotism	conservation
group therapy	capital punishment
missionaries	abortion
conscientious objectors	chemical welfare
alcoholism	Daughters of the American Revolution
drug addiction	parochial schools
Zen	sex education
pollution	pesticides
homosexuality	smoking

6. In an essay (750–1,000 words) describe a place, procedure, situation, or event that you have observed or have participated in, characterizing it indirectly through your presentation of the objective, observable facts rather than through explicit comment (as in "Marrying Absurd"). The tone of your piece should be appropriate to the subject matter and to the conclusion you want the reader to draw.

7. How Can X Be Summarized?

SUMMARIZING IDEAS

*H*ow can I briefly and accurately restate the main points in a body of information? How can I see through to its essence? How can I strip it bare of details and implications? How can I condense and communicate its core meaning? These are the questions you ask about summarizing, an intellectual challenge and a skill that some people regard as mechanical and routine, not at all creative. The truth is, however, that no greater challenge to the intellect and no more accurate test of understanding exists than the ability to filter an idea through your mind and restate it briefly in your own words. Indeed, to read and study efficiently, to do research, to take satisfactory notes, to write papers, critiques, and examinations, to grasp an idea and hold it in the mind—all require the ability to "boil down" materials and see their basic intentions, their main points, and the relation of these points to one another. Writing a summary is a demanding exercise in analysis and interpretation (seeing the parts and judging which are more or less important).

The significant and recurrent question is, then: "How can X be summarized?" Most often you will need an answer to complete a summary for a *section* of an essay you are working on rather than a whole essay, although there are occasions when summary is the purpose of a piece of writing: in the "Week in Review" section of the Sunday *New York Times*, for example, and in *Time* and *Newsweek* magazines.

Reviewing the different situations and types of material that call for summary is useful. Observe at the outset that the basis of all summary is careful and repeated reading of the text you want to summarize and sustained critical thinking about what you have read. This process of probing to "the heart of the matter" will enable you to render the essence in a clear, concise, accurate restatement.

In trying to summarize more complex ideas—for example, a proposal that contains several parts and a rationale—you must again commit yourself to several readings. You must again carefully search for the main points and the key terms that embody them, noting also recurrent words and phrases and summing-up sentences that might profitably be quoted. In the following proposal, educator James B. Conant suggests a new approach to an introductory science course.

The Tactics and Strategy of Science

James B. Conant

Let me now be specific as to my proposal for the reform of the scientific education of the layman. What I propose is the establishment of one or more courses at the college level on the Tactics and Strategy of Science. The objective would be to give a greater degree of understanding of science by the close study of a relatively few historical examples of the development of science. I suggest courses at the college level, for I do not believe they could be introduced earlier in a student's education; but there is no reason why they could not become important parts of programs of adult education. Indeed, such courses might well prove particularly suitable for older groups of men and women.

The analogy with the teaching of strategy and tactics of war by examples from military history is obvious. And the success of that educational procedure is one reason why I venture to be hopeful about this new approach to understanding science. I also draw confidence from the knowledge of how the case method in law schools and a somewhat similar method in the Harvard Business School have demonstrated the value of this type of pedagogic device. The course would not aim to teach science—not even the basic principles or simplest facts—though as a byproduct considerable knowledge of certain sciences would be sure to follow. Of course, some elementary knowledge of physics would be a prerequisite, but with the improvement in the teaching of science in high schools which is sure to come, this should prove no serious obstacle.

The case histories would almost all be chosen from the early days in the evolution of the modern discipline. Certain aspects of physics in the seventeenth and eighteenth centuries; chemistry in the eighteenth and nineteenth; geology in the early nineteenth; certain phases of biology in the eighteenth; others in the nineteenth. The advantages of this method of approach are twofold: first, relatively little factual knowledge is required either as regards the science in question or other sciences, and relatively little mathematics; second, in the early days one sees in clearest light the necessary fumblings of even intellectual giants when they are also pioneers; one comes to understand what science is by seeing how difficult it is in fact to carry out glib scientific precepts.

A few words may be in order as to the principles which would guide me in selecting case histories for my course in the Tactics and Strategy of Science. I should wish to show the difficulties which attend each new push forward in the advance of science, and the importance of new techniques: how they arise, are improved, and often revolutionize a field of inquiry. I should hope to illustrate the intricate interplay between experiment, or observation, and the development of new concepts and new generalizations; in short, how new concepts evolve from experiments, how one conceptual scheme for a time is adequate and then is modified or displaced by another. I should want also to illustrate the interconnection between science and society about which so much has been said in recent years by our Marxist friends. I should have very little to say about the classification of facts, unless it were to use this phrase as a straw man. But I should hope that almost all examples chosen would show the hazards which nature puts in the way of those who would examine the facts impartially and classify them accurately. The "controlled experiment" and the planned or controlled observation would be in the forefront of every discussion. The difference in methods between the observational sciences of astronomy, geology, systematic biology on the one hand, and the experimental sciences of physics, chemistry, and experimental biology on the other should be emphasized.

To what extent a course in the Tactics and Strategy of Science should take cognizance of the existence of problems in metaphysics and epistemology would depend on the outlook of the instructor and the maturity and interest of the student. Obviously the course in question would not be one on the metaphysical foundations of modern science; yet the teacher can hardly ignore completely the influence of new scientific concepts on contemporary thinking about the structure of the universe or the nature and destiny of man. Nor can one fail in all honesty to identify at least vaguely those philosophic problems which have arisen when man has sought to examine critically the basis of his knowledge about "the external world." Perhaps in collaboration with a colleague from the department of philosophy the instructor would wish to suggest the reading of extracts from the writings of certain philosophers. If so, the existence of more than one school of thought should certainly be emphasized.

As I shall show in subsequent chapters, a discussion of the evolution of new conceptual schemes as a result of experimentation would occupy a central position in the exposition. This being so, there would be no escape from a consideration of the difficulties which historically have attended the development of new concepts. Is a vacuum really empty, if so, how can you see through it? Is action at a distance imaginable? These questions at one time in the forefront of scientific discussion are well worthy of careful review. The Newtonian theory of gravitation once disturbed "almost all investigators of nature because it was founded on an uncommon unintelligibility." It no longer disturbs us because "it has become a common unintelligibility." To what extent can the same statement be made about other concepts which have played a major part in the development of modern science? When we say that the chemists have "established" that chlorophyll is essential for photosynthesis and that they also have "established" the spatial arrangements of the carbon, hydrogen, and oxygen atoms in cane sugar, are we using the word "establish" in two different senses? These and similar questions should be explored in sufficient degree to make the students aware of some of the complexities which lie hidden behind our usual simplified exposition of the basic ideas of modern science in an elementary course.

However, I cannot emphasize too often that the course in question must *not* be concerned with the fruits of scientific inquiries, either as embodied in scientific laws or theories or cosmologies, or in the applications of science to industry or agriculture or medicine. Rather, the instructor would center his attention on the ways in which these fruits have been attained. One might call it a course in "scientific method" as illustrated by examples from history, except that I am reluctant to use this ambiguous phrase. I should prefer to speak of the methods by which science has been advanced, or perhaps we should say knowledge has been advanced, harking back to Francis Bacon's famous phrase, the advancement of learning.

Before attempting to summarize this essay, you should construct a hypothetical purpose for our labor. (You should never write in a vacuum but always with a definite occasion and audience in mind—a rhetorical stance.) Assume you are taking notes on Conant's projected science course for a paper you are preparing on the modern function and status of science education. You plan to use Conant's proposal as one of several illustrations of innovative suggestions offered by educators. The limited length of your paper requires boiling down this proposal to a short paragraph. How can you do this without distorting its essential features?

One way to begin is by isolating key terms and concepts. The title is a helpful clue, for it contains the words "tactics" and "strategy." Conant is proposing that the introductory science course concentrate on the tactics and strategy of science—its long and difficult struggle to break through to new areas of knowledge—rather than with the fruits of such struggles—scientific knowledge, neatly classified into systems and codified into laws. Conant is proposing further that instructors use a "case history" method (note how many times this term appears). By observing scientific discoveries "in process," says Conant, as if they were watching a drama unfold, students in introductory science will learn the true nature of the scientific enterprise, as they do *not* learn it in the conventional course.

The writer is not yet summarizing Conant's proposal, only exploring it to discover its main contours. Note, then, that the word "difficult" recurs frequently along with various synonyms that refer to the assembling of scientific percepts.

> The *necessary fumblings* of even intellectual giants when they are also pioneers...
> One comes to understand what science is by seeing how *difficult* it is in fact to carry out glib scientific precepts.

Note the juxtaposition here of "difficult" and "glib." In a sense this sums up the difference between the course Conant would institute (one that would demonstrate how *difficult* it is to arrive at scientific precepts) and the conventional course (which Conant sees as a *glib*, packaged presentation of scientific facts).

> I should wish to show the *difficulties* which attend each new push forward....
> I should hope to illustrate the *intricate* interplay between experiment, or observation, and the development of new concepts....
> I should... show the *hazards* which nature puts in the way of those who would examine the facts impartially....
> ... There would be no escape from a consideration of the *difficulties* which historically have attended the development of new concepts.
> ... make the students aware of some of the *complexities* which lie hidden behind our usual simplified exposition of the basic ideas of modern science in an elementary course.

Here again note the juxtaposition of the two approaches: Conant's emphasis on *complexities* (difficulty) as against the *simplified* (and therefore falsified) conventional presentation.

The last paragraph of Conant's essay, though not a formal recapitulation, nonetheless sums up his case. "I cannot emphasize too often that the course in question must *not* be concerned with the fruits of scientific inquiries.... Rather [with] the ways in which these fruits have been attained." Clearly this is the central theme of Conant's essay, the main point of his argument in favor of a new type of science course. Recognizing this, the writer must plan to organize the summary around this point, adding whatever further information the writer interprets as important. Thus the summary of Conant's proposal (as it appears in the hypothetical paper on "Science Education Today") might read as follows:

> Conant proposes a new type of introductory science course that would concentrate not on the "fruits" of scientific inquiry (a presentation of scientific fact, neatly formulated into theory and law), but rather on the *way* scientists have attained these fruits—on what Conant calls the "Tactics and Strategy of Science." Rejecting the "usual simplified exposition" of the usual introductory course, which makes science seem static and "glib," Conant calls for a "case history" approach: a close study of a few historical examples of scientific discovery that would give students a realistic picture of how the scientific method works in actual practice: the countless difficulties and "necessary fumblings" that accompany every scientific advance, as well as the ultimate triumphs. Conant's introductory course would emphasize the difficulties and complexities of the scientific enterprise, and its tentativeness and ongoing dialectic. For science is always advancing, says Conant: "One conceptual scheme for a time is adequate and then is modified or displaced by another."

SUMMARIZING PLOT (SYNOPSIS)

The ability to write a plot summary, or synopsis, underlies much writing about literature, for we cannot discuss a literary work such as a novel or play unless we are sure that the reader knows its story line—the sequence of events that constitutes its action. We may relate the events in chronological order, adding neither interpretive asides nor explanations of the work's structure or underlying logic. Thus in "outline" versions of major works of literature, the summary is a bare recital of unfolding events, as in the following one-paragraph summary of Chapter XXII in Book I of *Don Quixote* (Bass).

> Don Quixote saw trudging towards him in the road twelve convicts linked together by a chain, manacled, and accompanied by four armed guards. Because these men were obviously not going to their destination of their own free will, the Don believed that this was a situation which called for the services of a knight-errant. He rode up and asked each convict what crime he had committed, receiving honest answers in return. Despite these accounts of roguery, the Don, according to his duty as a knight-errant, requested the guards to free the men. When they refused, he attacked them. The convicts, seizing this opportune moment, broke their chain and proceeded to stone the guards who finally took to their heels. Sancho, fearing that a posse of the Holy Brotherhood would set upon himself and his master, advised the Don to get away as fast as possible. But Don Quixote gathered the criminals around him and commanded them to present themselves to his lady Dulcinea del Toboso. However, unwilling to risk apprehension and already suspicious of the sanity of a man who would free convicts, they began to pelt the Don with stones. When they had felled him, they stripped him and Sancho of a goodly portion of their clothing, then departed leaving the Don in a sullen mood and Sancho trembling for fear of the Holy Brotherhood.

Naturally, the author omits all narrative details such as dialogue, description, and reflection from this one-paragraph summary. What is left is a bare-bones account of the action—a helpful tool for charting one's way through a long and involved novel such as *Don Quixote*, which contains many more details and episodes than one could possibly keep track of without a chapter-by-chapter outline.

Such outlines are available in various series, such as the one cited above. Some of these publications are accurate and reliable; others are filled with errors and distortions of the original text.

In any case, it is far better to make your own outlines, for in outlining a work, as mentioned earlier, you come to see its shape and the progressive unfolding of its purpose on a far deeper and more intimate level than in reading the work alone or reading someone else's summary. Approached in this way, then, as a note form, the section-by-section plot summary is a helpful study aid.

Also useful is the overall plot summary, which sweeps across the terrain of an entire novel, reducing it to two pages, or even a single paragraph, as in the following:

> Don Quixote de la Mancha, the history of, a satirical romance by Miguel Cervantes, the first part of which appeared in 1605 and the second in 1615. A kindly and simple-minded country gentleman has read the romances of chivalry until they have turned his brain. Clad in a suit of old armor and mounted on a broken-down hack which

he christens Rozinante, he sets out on a career of knight-errantry, assuming the name of Don Quixote de la Mancha. For the object of his devotion he chooses a village girl, whom he names Dulcinea del Toboso and as squire he takes an ignorant but faithful peasant, Sancho Panza. The ordinary wayfarers of the Spanish roads of the seventeenth century are transformed by the knight's disordered imagination into warriors, distressed damsels, giants, and monsters. For instance, he tilts on one occasion, at the sails of a group of wind-mills, thinking them living creatures, and his attempts to right fictitious wrongs and win chivalric honor among them lead him and his squire into ludicrous and painful situations. Yet amidst their discomfitures Don Quixote retains a dignity, a certain nobility, and a pathetic idealism, and Sancho a natural shrewdness and popular humor which endear them to the reader. In the second part the interest is fully sustained, and variety is introduced by the sojourn of the pair with a duke and duchess and Sancho's appointment as governor of the imaginary island of Baratoria. At the end, Don Quixote, as the result of a dangerous illness, recovers his senses, renounces all books of chivalry, and dies penitent. The book was begun as an attack on the absurdities of the late chivalric romances, not on the essential chivalric ideals. As the work progresses it becomes a picture of human nature, its absurdities and its aspirations, its coarse materialism and lofty enthusiasm.

The length of a summary does not determine its excellence. A good summary is as long as it *needs* to be in order to fulfill your purpose. It may be objective and analytic or subjective and interpretive, again depending on your purpose. You may not want to intrude any judgments or comments on the work, but simply to tell it as it is—in brief space.

Generally weaving into the recital of bare facts an interpretive description of the work's underlying logic and theme is preferable. You will not usually summarize just to summarize, but rather to provide plot background for a literary review or literary analysis.

In such cases the length of the plot summary will vary according to how important plot is in the development of your main theme, how much space is available, and how much plot the work has. Some stories have weak, virtually nonexistent plots, as the writer of the following summary notes:

> *Adolphe*, a romance by Benjamin Constant. The story has very little incident or action. The whole plot may be summed up in a few words: Adolphe loves Eleonore, and can be happy neither with her nor without her. The beauty of the author's style and the keenness and delicacy with which he analyzes certain morbid moods of the soul have placed this work among the masterpieces of French literature. The romance is almost universally believed to be an autobiography, in which Constant narrates a portion of the adventures of his own youth.

A summary that provides a background for a literary paper should not merely recite happenings ("first this happened, then this, then this"). Rather, it should explain *why* things happen as they do, how events are significant, how they contribute to the pattern of the total work. The literary plot summary, in other words, should go beyond the superficial story line to analysis and interpretation. In such a summary you weave in your own view of the plot even as you recount the bare facts.

SUMMARIZING EVENTS

As mentioned earlier, the weekly news magazines and the "Week in Review" section of the Sunday *New York Times* are devoted specifically to summarizing events in time—a week, a month, or more. A presentation of highlights in relation to the broad sweep of events is fundamental to a good "capsule" summary of the news, a form that helps busy readers find out quickly what is happening or has happened in the world.

The following ambitious summary, for example, attempts to touch upon major historic events, "surprises," and trends during the first sixty years of this century. Note that the writer sums up the past decade in a single term: "paradox."

The Paradox of the Sixties

James Reston

This has been a century of stunning surprises, yet the resident seers and magicians here seem to think the seventies will be menacing but manageable. It is a puzzler. The mood of the capital about present problems is pessimistic, but the forecasts for the coming decade are fairly optimistic.

No major war, retreat from Vietnam, probably a controlled war in the Middle East with the big powers on the sidelines, endless local and tribal conflict in Africa and maybe even in Latin America, more spheres of influence or Monroe Doctrines for the Soviet Union in Eastern Europe and for China in Southeast Asia; more people, more inflation, more trouble—in short, more of the same—but nothing apocalyptic. This seems to be the forecast of many thoughtful people in the capital.

The Historical Record

There is very little in the history of these last sixty years to justify this assumption that the human race has run out of spectacular stupidities. These sixty years started with the decline of the British and French and ended with the triumph of the Mets—with two tragic wars and endless barbarities and futilities in between.

Herman Kahn and Anthony J. Wiener have kept the boxscore on the astounding surprises that took place in the first and second thirds of the century. It started, they note, with parliamentary democracy in pretty good shape, and Christianity on the rise. The Western world felt fairly optimistic and secure. Then in the first third of the century, the following:

The Russo-Japanese War; the First World War, which devastated Europe; the collapse of the five major dynasties (Hohenzollern, Habsburg, Manchu, Romanov and Ottoman); the rise of Communism and the Soviet Union and Fascism; the Great Depression; and the intellectual influence of Bohr, de Broglie, Einstein and Freud.

The Big Surprises

The second third of the century produced even more surprises: The Second World War; mass murders and evacuations beyond all previous dreams of human depravity; the collapse of the old empires; the reunification and centralization of China and its development of nuclear weapons; the emergence of two superpowers (the U.S. and the U.S.S.R.), five large powers (Japan, West Germany, France, China and Britain); the new confrontation of Washington and Moscow in the cold war; and the emergence of new techniques, new post-Keynesian and post-Marxian economic theories.

Why, then, after all these apocalyptic events—why now when Washington is depressed about its frustrations over Vietnam, inflation, the blacks, the rebellious university whites—should thoughtful men and women here be taking a comparatively calm and even optimistic view of the seventies?

The Major Trends

Maybe it is merely wishful thinking or lack of imagination, and maybe the optimists are wrong, for there are many others who think the country and the world are hopelessly lost and divided and headed for chaos. But this does not seem to be the view of most reflective and experienced minds in the capital.

In fact, the majority seems to be suggesting that the sixties, for all the violence, defiance and confusion, were just violent and defiant and confused enough to force a reappraisal of past assumptions, and make the major powers think about adopting new attitudes and policies in defense of their vital interests.

Within their own geographical spheres of influence, the great powers are still demanding control, and in contested areas like the Middle East, they are still competing for influence in the most dangerous way, but on the big questions, which could produce a world and nuclear war, they are finally talking with a little more common sense.

The major trends elsewhere are also a little more rational. Europe is talking seriously again about cooperation and even economic integration; the war in Vietnam is not escalating but de-escalating; the Soviet Union is just worried enough about China's belligerent tone to reduce tensions in the West and avoid trouble on both fronts at the same time.

Accordingly, at least some observers think they see a new balance of power developing at the turn of the decade. The Congress is challenging the President's right to make war as he chooses; the Communist parties of the world are challenging Moscow's use of power against Czechoslovakia; the militant blacks and militant students in the United States are finding that violence by the minority produced counterviolence by the white majority.

So while all these struggles still go on, there is a feeling here that maybe they can be contained in the seventies, mainly because we learned in the sixties that violence doesn't always pay off, either at home or abroad.

DISCUSSION AND EXERCISES

1. Summarizing Ideas

   1. In a paragraph of no more than 200 words sum up each of the following:

      a. Allen Gilbert's argument for abolishing college lectures (see "College Lectures Are Obsolete," pages 419–22).

      b. The "Sweet Truths About Sugar" (pages 231–33).

      c. One of the reviews in Question 19.

      d. One of the "functions" in Question 9.

   2. Summarizing Plot: In a paragraph of 100–150 words summarize Peter Cameron's short story, "Memorial Day," (see pages 395–98).

ESSAY SUGGESTIONS

1. Write an essay (500–750 words) in which you summarize the ideas presented in one of the essays in this book and comment on them (let half the essay be summary, the other half comment).

2. Write an essay (500–750 words) in which you summarize the plot of a short story, novel, play, film, or television drama; follow your summary with a two-paragraph evaluation (see Question 19, "What is the value of X?" pages 405–15).

3. Write an essay (500–750 words) summarizing events of the 1970s. As Reston characterizes the sixties (the decade is summed up in the term "paradox") try to find a word or phrase that will characterize the decade of the seventies. Was it, as some "seers" prophesized, "The Menacing but Manageable Decade"?

8. What Does X Mean?

EXPLORING A SUBJECT THROUGH DEFINITION

*C*icero said that every discourse should begin with a definition to make clear what the subject under consideration *is*. True enough: Whether the subject is a matter of dispute or of discussion, a definition helps to clarify the issues. Definition, then, is important when readers must understand the meaning of a term or terms, if the rest of the piece is to make sense, and if writer and readers are to stand on common ground. Thus many essays, articles, and books begin with statements of how authors intend to use a given word or words, *what they mean by them*.

In his introduction to a *History of Western Philosophy*, for example, Bertrand Russell states that since the term "philosophy" is used in many different ways, he will explain what *he* means by it:

A Definition of Philosophy

Bertrand Russell

"Philosophy" is a word which has been used in many ways, some wider, some narrower. I propose to use it in a very wide sense, which I will now try to explain.

Philosophy, as I shall understand the word, is something intermediate between theology and science. Like theology, it consists of speculations on matters as to which definite knowledge has, so far, been unascertainable; but like science, it appeals to human reason rather than to authority, whether that of tradition or that of revelation. All *definite* knowledge—so I should contend—belongs to science; all *dogma* as to what surpasses definite knowledge belongs to theology. But between theology and science there is a No Man's Land, exposed to attack from both sides; this No Man's Land is philosophy. Almost all the questions of most interest to speculative minds are such as science cannot answer, and the confident answers of theologians no longer seem too convincing as they did in former centuries. Is the world divided into mind and matter, and, if so, what is mind and what is matter? Is mind subject to matter, or is it possessed of independent powers? Has the universe any unity or purpose? Is it evolving towards some goal? Are there really laws of nature, or do we believe in them only because of our innate love of order? Is man what he seems to the astronomer, a tiny lump of impure carbon and water impotently crawling on a small and unimportant planet? Or is he what he appears to Hamlet? Is he perhaps both at once? Is there a way of living that is noble and another that is base, or are all ways of living merely futile? If there is a way of living that is noble, in what does it consist, and how shall we achieve it? Must the good be eternal in order to deserve to be valued, or is it worth seeking even if the universe is inexorably moving towards death? Is there such a thing as wisdom, or is what seems such merely the ultimate refinement of folly? To such questions no answer can be found in the laboratory. Theologies have professed to give answers, all too definite; but their very definiteness causes modern minds to view them with suspicion. The study of these questions, if not the answering of them, is the business of philosophy.

Russell has done more than look up the word "philosophy" in the dictionary (that repository of all accepted, conventional meanings of words) and sets forth the *one* meaning he likes best or finds most useful. In a sense, Russell has gone beyond conventional meaning in this definition; certainly he has particularized and elaborated on the conventional meaning in a way that is both inventive and illuminating. Thus, we do not receive from Russell any of the routine dictionary definitions:

1. Philosophy is the love or pursuit of wisdom.
2. Philosophy is the search for underlying causes.
3. Philosophy is a critical examination of fundamental beliefs.
4. Philosophy is the study of the principles of human nature and conduct.

Instead, Russell begins by locating the word with almost geographical precision: "Philosophy ... is something intermediate between theology and science." We can almost *see* it:

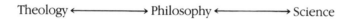

Theology ⟷ Philosophy ⟷ Science

This spatial placement of a word accords with the original meaning of "definition," for the term is derived from the Latin *definire:* to put boundaries around. Thus, when we define a term we set up boundaries or limits that separate it from other terms, just as a fence separates one piece of land from another. An agricultural metaphor lurks in the background here and is appropriate, since the definer does in fact stake out for his or her term a special territory of meaning. Under the "No Man's Land" of philosophy, for example, Russell has very skillfully included all the traditional concerns of the discipline: questions relating to the nature of reality ("Is the world divided into mind and matter?"); the problem of good and evil ("Is there a way of living that is noble and another that is base?"); and the possibility of knowledge ("Is there such a thing as wisdom?"). Russell concludes his definition by further restricting the domain of the discipline by indicating that it is the *studying* of these questions rather than the *answering* of them that is "the business of philosophy."

Like Russell's definition, many definitions are really introductory essays to larger units of discourse, ranging in length from one paragraph to several pages. At the same time, the definition can exist as an independent form—an essay in definition.

Whatever its form or length, however, definition offers vast possibilities to the student writer, for you can hit upon your topic simply by asking "What does it mean?" or "What *should* it mean?" about any term that seems uncertain, mystifying, curious, provocative, troublesome, or simply in need of refurbishing (you might strip away a hard crust of connotation, for example, to find a more fundamental meaning). As we shall see ("The Limits of Language"), many abstract and ambiguous words in our language mean different things to different people: a word like "excellence," for example, about which John Gardner said, "It is a little like those ink blots that psychologists use to interpret personality. As the individual contemplates the word 'excellence' he reads into it his own aspirations, his own conceptions of high standards, his hopes for a better world." (*Excellence*, xii–xiii) The same is true of words such as "honor," "loyalty," "liberty," "progress," "courage," "justice," "democracy," "capitalism," and "communism" (any -ism). They are all "ink blots" and as such create an opportunity for an essay which may establish common criteria of meaning or offer a personal meaning, as E. B. White does in his essay "Democracy" (page 261).

In addition to ambiguous terms, you may contemplate words that are, in your opinion, not well understood either because their meaning has changed or because they have acquired connotations. Linguists have shown that language grows organically, moved by its own inner forces. No external pressure—not even the most determined efforts of the strictest purists—can dictate its destiny. This does not imply, however, that the users of language may not concern themselves with the way specific words are faring. Since meanings often blur, it is appropriate that periodically someone reappraises a word by recognizing and redefining its boundaries. It may even happen, as in the case of the word "grammar," that in the course of its development a word will radiate so widely from its original sense that it will come to mean several different things and require several different definitions. The essay "Three Meanings of Grammar" by W. Nelson Francis illustrates this point.

"What does X mean?" You might address this question to a word you believe should have its original and potential fullness of meaning reviewed and restored. You could write an essay on the word "discipline," for example, in which you could replace the commonly used negative and restrictive notion of punishment by the wider meaning of training. In actual, etymological fact the derivation of "discipline" is the same as that of "disciple": "one who learns or voluntarily follows a leader." Seen in this light, the word "discipline" carries no stigma; it means "making a disciple." Similarly the words "welfare" (welfare state), "charity" (handout), "intellectual" (egghead), and "politician" (opportunist) have all taken on negative connotations that you might decide are objectionable. In answer to the question "What does it mean?" you might try to rescue a word from its progressive "degradation" by redefining it in a more affirmative context. A dictionary definition merely sums up and informs, but an essay in definition may agitate for reform.

METHODS OF DEVELOPING A DEFINITION

You can develop a definition in many ways. Bertrand Russell, as we have seen, lists the questions that in his view constitute the subject matter or "business" of philosophy. Allan Nevins (pages 254–55) develops his definition of "history" by contrasting it with what it is *not*. So these writers establish the boundaries of their subject. The essays that follow illustrate various methods writers may use to set boundaries and thereby answer the question "What does X mean?"

By Citing Different Meanings of X

Three Meanings of Grammar

W. Nelson Francis

Need for defini-
tion stated

A curious paradox exists in regard to grammar. On the one hand it is felt to be the dullest and driest of academic subjects, fit only for those in whose veins the red blood of life has long since turned to ink. On the other, it is a subject upon which people who would scorn to be professional grammarians hold very dogmatic opinions, which they will defend with considerable emotion. Much of this prejudice stems from the usual sources of prejudice—ignorance and confusion. Even highly educated people seldom have a clear idea of what grammarians do, and there is an unfortunate confusion about the meaning of the term "grammar" itself.

Current uses
are confusing

Hence it would be well to begin with definitions. What do people mean when they use the word "grammar"? Actually the word is used to refer to three different things, and much of the emotional thinking about matters grammatical arises from confusion among these different meanings.

Three
meanings
isolated

The first thing we mean by "grammar" is "the set of formal patterns in which the words of a language are arranged in order to convey larger meanings." It is not necessary that we be able to discuss these patterns self-consciously in order to be able to use them. In fact, all speakers of a language above the age of five or six know how to use its complex forms of organization with considerable skill; in this sense of the word—call it "Grammar 1"—they are thoroughly familiar with its grammar.

The second meaning of "grammar"—call it "Grammar 2"—is "the branch of linguistic science which is concerned with the description, analysis, and formularization of formal language patterns." Just as gravity was in full operation before Newton's apple fell, so grammar in the first sense was in full operation before anyone formulated the first rule that began the history of grammar as a study.

The third sense in which people use the word "grammar" is "linguistic etiquette." This we may call "Grammar 3." The word in this sense is often coupled with a derogatory adjective: we say that the expression "he ain't here" is "bad grammar." What we mean is that such an expression is bad linguistic manners in certain circles. From the point of view of "Grammar 1" it is faultless; it conforms just as completely to the structural patterns of English as does "he isn't here." The trouble with it is like the trouble with Prince Hal in Shakespeare's play—it is "bad," not in itself, but in the company it keeps.

Why the new
three-part
definition is
better (it
unravels
confusion)

As has already been suggested, much confusion arises from mixing these meanings. One hears a good deal of criticism of teachers of English couched in such terms as "they don't teach grammar any more." Criticism of this sort is based on the wholly unproved assumption that teaching Grammar 2 will increase the student's proficiency in Grammar 1 or improve his manners in Grammar 3. Actually the form of Grammar 2 which is usually taught is a very inaccurate and misleading analysis of the facts of Grammar 1; and it therefore is of highly questionable value in improving a person's ability to handle the structural patterns of his language. It is hardly reasonable to expect that teaching a person some inaccurate grammatical analysis will either improve the effectiveness of his assertions or teach him what expressions are acceptable to use in a given social context.

Summary

These, then, are the three meanings of "grammar": Grammar 1, a form of behavior; Grammar 2, a field of study, a science; and Grammar 3, a branch of etiquette.

By Contrasting X with What It Is Not

What Is History?

Allan Nevins

Need for definition

What history is not

Because history has been approached from many different points of view, it has received more amusingly varied definitions than even the novel. The cynic's definition of it as a *mensonge convenu*, a lie agreed upon, may harmonize with the statement attributed to Disraeli that he preferred romances to history because they told more truth; but it is a piece of baseless flippancy. It is precisely the fact that historians are always ready to disagree with each other which makes any persistence of lies in history—that is, true

Inadequate definitions

history—unlikely. Carlyle, approaching the subject from his special predilection, which emphasized the role of the individual, termed history the essence of innumerable biographies. But obviously it is a good deal more than that; it takes account of many forces which are not personal at all. John Cotter Morison defined it as "the prose narrative of past events, as probably true as the fallibility of human testimony will allow." Good so far as it goes, that definition is too pedestrian to be wholly satisfactory. Conversely, a familiar modern statement that history is the record of everything in the past which helps explain how the present came to be, is too philosophical and priggish. It emphasizes too much the utilitarian role of history, which we often wish to read without any reference whatever to the present—even to get entirely away from the present.

New definition

History is any integrated narrative or description of past events or facts written in a spirit of critical inquiry for the whole truth. A definition which attempts to be more precise than this is certain to be misleading. For above all, it is the historical point of view, the historical method of approach—*that is, the spirit of critical inquiry for the whole truth*—which, applied to the past, makes history. It will not do to lay down a more exclusive formula. There are as many different schools and theories of history as the schools of philosophy, of medicine, and of painting. But it will be agreed that a newspaper report of some current event, a debate in Congress, a diplomatic exchange between France and Germany, is not history, because it cannot be written as an inquiry into the *whole* truth. Only superficial sources of information, generally speaking, are open to newspapermen. It will also be agreed that a Democratic or Republican campaign-book reviewing events of the four years just preceding publication is not history; it is not written as a *critical* inquiry into the truth. A careful historical novel, like Charles Reace's *Cloister and the Hearth*, holds many historical values. But it will be agreed that it is not history, for it is not written primarily as an inquiry into past *truth* at all, but primarily to entertain and please by an artistic use of the imagination.

By Tracing the Historical Development of X

"Universe" and "University"

Isaac Asimov

Origin of word

A group of individuals acting, in combination, toward a single goal under a single direction, behaves as though it were one person. In the Middle Ages, such a group was called a "universitas," from the Latin "unum" (one) and "vertere" (to turn); a group, in other words, had "turned into one" person. In the most general sense, this came to mean the group of everything in existence considered as a unit; that is, the *universe*.

Historical context

It also came to be used in a more restricted sense. In the early Middle Ages, for instance, a school of higher learning was called a "studium," from the Latin "studere," meaning "to be zealous" or "to strive after." From this, come our words *study* and *student*. The Italian version of "studium" is *studio*, which has come into English as a place where the fine arts, particularly, are studied or practiced (a memorial to the fact that in Renaissance times, Italy was the center of the world of fine art).

New definition

A group of students at such a school would refer to themselves (with the usual good opinion of themselves that students always have) as "universitas magistrorum et scholarium"—a "group of masters and scholars." They were a "universitas," you see, because they were all pursuing the single goal of learning. And gradually the name of the group became, in shortened form, the name of the schools which, around 1300, began to be known as *universities*.

Origin of parallel term

Meanwhile, within the university, groups of students following a particular specialty, as, for instance, law, would band together for mutual aid. They were a group of *colleagues* (Latin, "collegae") from the Latin "com-" (together) and

New definition of parallel term

"ligare" (to bind). They were bound together for a common purpose. Such a group of colleagues formed a *college* (Latin, "collegium"), a word now used to denote a particular school within a university.

Continuity of original sense

The older meaning as simply "a group of colleagues" persists today in the College of Cardinals of the Roman Catholic Church, and in America's own electoral college which meets every four years to elect a president.

By Restoring the Original Meaning of X

The Security of Discipline

Franklin S. Du Bois, M.D.

General introduction

From time immemorial discipline has been recognized as an essential ingredient of man's life. Experience has demonstrated that objectives can be achieved and individuals can be happy only if human energies are directed in an orderly fashion. Since a person's desires often conflict with the desires of others, society has set up regulations for the common good, to which each member of the group must adhere or suffer a penalty. Fortunate is the individual who can so govern the expression of his instinctive drives as to experience the least conflict in adaptation. Attainment of such adequate self-direction leads to the inner security, the preservation of mental health, and the integrity of personality necessary for wise decisions and ethical conduct. The well-disciplined person is guided by certain principles in which he believes, and he follows those principles because he has been taught by example, by training, and by experience, that intelligent action based on practical ideals brings satisfaction to him and to others.

Need for definition

Background meanings

Restored definition

To arrive at helpful conclusions, one must first have an understanding of what is meant by discipline. The immediate and restrictive connotation is apt to be what is done *to* an individual when he is disturbing to others, but we shall deal with the broader concept that *discipline is a process of training and learning that fosters growth and development.* Its derivation is the same as that of disciple: "one who learns or voluntarily follows a leader" (Webster). Discipline is, therefore, primarily the process of "making a disciple." Parents attempt to help their children become disciples of a way of life that leads to usefulness and happiness. They teach by precept and example, and their children learn by imitation and practice; consequently, techniques of discipline are less significant than the spirit of the relationship between parents and children. And in this relationship it is the warmth and genuine affection of both the father and the mother that is most important because, as Rose has said, "learned parenthood" is ineffective as contrasted with spontaneous feeling states of parents that make children feel wanted and secure in their efforts to develop independence.

How restored definition applies

While discipline may carry with it an idea of punishment, this should be only the discomfort that logically follows the pursuance of a selected course of action and is voluntarily accepted as incidental to the attainment of a desired goal.

One speaks of the discipline of medicine, of art, of athletic training, when one refers to hardships foreseen and endured in an undertaking that leads to the chosen objective. Like the athlete, the child in training must learn to accept the restriction of many of his impulses. Discipline, in essence, means adherence to the rules of life; not a hardship to be endured intolerantly, but an educational opportunity to be welcomed enthusiastically, since it is only through discipline that lasting satisfactions can be obtained.

A child cannot be expected to see discipline in this light, but his parents must so view it. Parents must think in terms not only of the immediate behavior at two, six, or sixteen years—even though mismanagement of reactions in childhood can lead to fundamental character disturbances—but also of the ultimate results of discipline at twenty, forty, and sixty, when parental control is no longer in force. Then the individual must be constructively self-directed or else suffer remorse because of violation of his personal code, or be punished by society when his conduct is contrary to its laws. Hence, one should think of discipline as the educational process by which parents lead the child to independent self-discipline and the inner security of the wholesome, well-integrated personality that is characteristic of the emotionally mature adult.

You will agree that Du Bois's treatment of the term "discipline" is not altogether out of bounds; it does not strain either our credibility or the limits of language itself. This is a prerequisite, of course, of all definition: although it may depart from ordinary meaning, it must remain in the neighborhood of common usage. One cannot whimsically decide to use a word in a strictly personal or singular sense. Thus when Humpty Dumpty tells Alice in Wonderland that *for him* the word "glory" means "there's a knockdown argument for you!" Alice—quite naturally—cannot continue the conversation. Humpty Dumpty is violating the tacit agreement among users of the language—that they will accept the definitions of words as codified in our dictionaries.

In trying, then, to control or qualify the common meaning of a word, we may attempt to restore its original luster, or we may attempt to sharpen, deepen, enlarge, or enrich its current domain of denotation and connotation. But we may *not* try to rewrite the dictionary.

By Combining Methods of Development

The Meaning of "Negro"

Negro History Bulletin

History
    The word "Negro" has a long history. The Spanish and Portuguese with their Latin background began the African slave trade. They called black Africans "Negroes" because *negro* meant black in their languages. During most of the nineteenth century, black Americans preferred the terms African or Colored or African-American. Those who favor the latter point out that many Americans are called by the name of their ancestors' land, Italian-American, Polish-American, Jewish-American; and others prefer the word "black" and are using it widely, so that books and magazine articles carry it, as the opposite to "white." However, black is a misnomer, just as white is, for neither white nor black convey adequately the color or race of the people described; and certainly, there is genetically neither a white race nor a black race.

Sociological examples
    The word "Negro" is mainly a sociological word and has little relation to biology. Persons who by appearance are "white" have been designated as Negroes, because there were some ancestors who were Africans. Accordingly, the study of "the Negro" in the United States has to face first of all the difficulty of definition. It is difficult to give a fixed and definite meaning to this word. It has been used, in its narrow sense, to include the primitive group of darker African peoples. Characterized by darker skins, curly hair, broad facial features and dolichocephalic (long) heads; their colors varied from nearly black to light brown and yellow. Their original habitation was Africa, south of the Sahara and north of the line running southeast from the Gulf of Biafra to the Tana River, and they have never numbered more than a million persons. In its widest sense, it has been used in the United States especially, to embrace all of

the peoples—not only of dark skin, but also any person whose ancestors have been Negroes. In few cases of racial designations is the term more loosely used and in no case is it more difficult to fix an established meaning. The term "white" and "black" are equally as indefinite and are used loosely without scientific exactness.

Geographical contrasts and examples

In the United States, one may be called a Negro and be white in appearance. In Africa one may be called a Negro only if he is one of the definite Negroid types, who perhaps have never been in relatively large numbers as the continent goes. The brown, the yellow and some of the black peoples of Africa are excluded in the African use of the term. If we use the term "Negro" in its American use—for if one is a Negro for all negative purposes, certainly the positive purposes do not make one any less a Negro—we then find that the Negroes of Africa and the United States have been the creators of a valuable civilization, and have no need to hide themselves under the umbrella of a new name.

There has not been and there is not one unvarying Negro type. Persons of various colors and features have been found in Africa. Many of the Bantus, for instance, have been known to have "caucasian-like features." The pygmies have been described by some observers as coffee-brown, and at times, by others as red and light yellow. The Fellatahs and Nigritians vary in color from light brown to dark brown. The Fellatah girls were described by one traveller as having beautiful forms which with their complexions "of freshest bronze" gave him the impression that they could not be "excelled in symmetry by the women of any other country." Another seventeenth-century contemporary wrote, "The women of Nekans (in north) are handsome body'd and fair, with black and shining hair, which makes them take pride to frequent the Bathes." The Bahima people were a "tall and finely formed race of nutty brown color with almost European features." This variation of color has been so typical over the African continent that one student of the problem has been led to conclude that the mulatto is as typically African as the black man.

Further contrasts

The Negroes in America are essentially Americans and not Africans. There is little except color which shows their relationships to Africa and there are Negroes whose color does not show it, but who are proud of their African background. They have learned the language and social techniques of the United States, the country in which they lived. But they came to this country from a culture which had been developing in Africa through many centuries. There are few traces of African culture in Negro life in America, and the Negro-American seems not to be essentially different in this respect from the Irish-American, the German-American, the Jewish-American, the Scotch-American, or any other American types so far as the cultures of the lands of their ancestors are concerned. Millions of Europeans have come to America and millions of Africans have been brought from Africa to America. They have all become a part of the American population.

These Africans, designated as Negroes, have been marching forward in all lines of endeavors and achievement. They are proving that civilization and contributions to it are not based on race or color but upon the individual men or women of ability who seek to advance themselves, be they white or black. In these respects God is no respecter of persons, whatever their names and colors.

FORMAL DEFINITION

If you examine the above definitions carefully, you will note that a three-part *formal* or *logical* definition (so-called by rhetoricians) is at the core of most of them. According to this pattern, place a term to be defined in a larger category or class; then distinguish it from other members of the class by noting "differentiae." The following illustrates this process:

Term (to define)	*Class* (or genus)	*Differentiae* (distinguishing characteristics)
philosophy	is a field of study	that speculates on matters for which there is no definite knowledge and that appeals to reason rather than authority
grammar 1	is a set of formal patterns	whereby the words of a language are arranged to convey a larger meaning
grammar 2	is a branch of linguistic science	concerned with the description, analysis, and formularization of formal language patterns
grammar 3	is a branch of language study	concerned with etiquette
a symbol	is any "thing"	that stands for something else
history	is an integrated narrative of past events	written in a spirit of inquiry for the whole truth
universitas	is a group of individuals	acting, in combination, toward a single goal
discipline	is a process of training and learning	that helps children become "disciples" of a way of life that leads to usefulness and happiness
Negro	is a person	of African ancestry[1]

Unlike the logician, the writer is not obliged to follow the logical formula *exactly*. Yet most good expository definitions have the three-part formal pattern, even if it is implicit rather than explicit. And most rhetorical definitions satisfy the basic *logical* prerequisites of a good definition: that the differentiae be neither too broad nor too narrow and that the definition be the equivalent of the term defined.

In any case, both the writer and reader should search out and apply the basic logical pattern of a term to the rhetorical definition, for nothing marks off an area of meaning with greater precision than the formal one-sentence definition. It often provides a foundation and thesis for the entire piece that the writer may then extend by a number of methods, as we have seen in the preceding illustrations. Thus a general principle is that whenever possible the writer should answer the question "What does X mean?" by developing a formal logical definition.

---

[1] This definition is implicit in the article reprinted from *Negro History Bulletin*.

By Composing One's Own Definition

What Makes a "Jerk" a Jerk?

Sidney J. Harris

Background

I don't know whether history repeats itself, but biography certainly does. The other day, Michael came in and asked me what a "jerk" was—the same question Carolyn put to me a dozen years ago.

At that time, I fluffed her off with some inane answer, such as "A jerk isn't a very nice person," but both of us knew it was an unsatisfactory reply. When she went to bed, I began trying to work up a suitable definition.

Need for definition

It is a marvelously apt word, of course. Until it was coined, not more than twenty-five years ago, there was really no single word in English to describe the kind of person who is a jerk—"boob" and "simp" were too old hat, and besides they really didn't fit, for they could be lovable, and a jerk never is.

Preliminary definition

Thinking it over, I decided that a jerk is basically a person without insight. He is not necessarily a fool or a dope, because some extremely clever persons can be jerks. In fact, it has little to do with intelligence as we commonly think of it; it is, rather, a kind of subtle but pervasive aroma emanating from the inner part of the personality.

Example of use

I know a college president who can be described only as a jerk. He is not an unintelligent man, nor unlearned, nor even unschooled in the social amenities. Yet he is a jerk *cum laude*, because of a fatal flaw in his nature—he is totally incapable of looking into the mirror of his soul and shuddering at what he sees there.

Definition of word

A jerk, then, is a man (or woman) who is utterly unable to see himself as he appears to others. He has no grace, he is tactless without meaning to be, he is a bore even to his best friends, he is an egotist without charm. All of us are egotists to some extent, but most of us—unlike the jerk—are perfectly and horribly aware of it when we make asses of ourselves. The jerk never knows.

EXPERIENTIAL DEFINITION

Formal definition is not always possible. Some words are too inextricably tied to an individual vantage point: too subjective, too relative, too experimental. One such word, as Abraham Lincoln pointed out, is "liberty":

> The world has never had a good definition of the word liberty.... We all declare for liberty, but using the same word we do not mean the same thing. With some, the word liberty may mean for each man to do as he pleases with himself and the product of his labor; while with others the same word may mean for some men and the product of other men's labor....
>
> The shepherd drives the wolf from the sheep's throat, for which the sheep thanks the shepherd as his liberator, while the wolf denounces him for the same act.... Plainly the sheep and the wolf are not agreed upon a definition of liberty.
>
> —Abraham Lincoln, "Definition of Liberty"

What should writers do, then, with such subjective words? They can write essays containing *not* formal definitions, worked out against fixed, objective standards, but rather personal definitions worked out on the basis of their own beliefs, feelings, and experiences. Thus the eloquent judge Learned Hand had this to say about the spirit of liberty:

> What then is the spirit of liberty? I cannot define it; I can only tell you my own faith. The spirit of liberty is the spirit which is not too sure that it is right; the spirit of liberty is the spirit which seeks to understand the minds of other men and women; the spirit of liberty is the spirit which weighs their interests alongside its own without bias; the spirit of liberty remembers that not even a sparrow falls to earth unheeded; the spirit of liberty is the spirit of Him who, near two thousand years ago, taught mankind that lesson it has never learned, but has never quite forgotten: that there may be a kingdom where the least shall be heard and considered side by side with the greatest.
>
> —Learned Hand, "The Spirit of Liberty"

Similarly, E. B. White was moved, during the Second World War, to define "democracy" *not* by following formal procedures, but by exploring his own experiences and associations.

Democracy

E. B. White

We received a letter from the Writers' War Board the other day asking for a statement on "The Meaning of Democracy." It presumably is our duty to comply with such a request, and it is certainly our pleasure.

Surely the Board knows what democracy is. It is the line that forms on the right. It is the don't in don't shove. It is the hole in the stuffed shirt through which the sawdust slowly trickles; it is the dent in the high hat. Democracy is the recurrent suspicion that more than half of the people are right more than half of the time. It is the feeling of privacy in the voting booths, the feeling of communion in the libraries, the feeling of vitality everywhere. Democracy is a letter to the editor. Democracy is the score at the beginning of the ninth. It is an idea that hasn't been disproved yet, a song the words of which have not gone bad. It's the mustard on the hot dog and the cream in the rationed coffee. Democracy is a request from a War Board, in the middle of a morning in the middle of a war, wanting to know what democracy is.

According to political scientist Anatol Rapoport, the personal definition is no less valuable than the formal; in fact, it is sometimes the best, perhaps the *only* way to formulate certain definitions—by indicating the feelings, experiences, and ideas associated with the term in question. What *happens* in connection with it? What is done? What is thought, felt? In Rapoport's view the question "What do you mean?" is essentially a request to share the experiences associated with the words you are using.

In the following definition of "prejudice," for example, psychologist Gordon Allport achieves this form of "sharing" by citing four instances in which prejudice was "happening." Thus he establishes—as no formal definition alone could—the experiential common denominator of "prejudice":

The Nature of Prejudice

Gordon W. Allport

Before I attempt to define prejudice, let us have in mind four instances that I think we all would agree are prejudice.

The first is the case of the Cambridge University student, who said, "I despise all Americans. But," he added, a bit puzzled, "I've never met one that I didn't like."

The second is the case of another Englishman, who said to an American, "I think you're awfully unfair in your treatment of Negroes. How *do* Americans feel about Negroes?" The American replied, "Well, I suppose some Americans feel about Negroes just the way you feel about the Irish." The Englishman said, "Oh, come now! The Negroes are human beings!"

Then there's the incident that occasionally takes place in various parts of the world (in the West Indies, for example, I'm told). When an American walks down the street the natives conspicuously hold their noses till the American gets by. The case of odor is always interesting. Odor gets mixed up with prejudice because odor has great associative power. We know that some Chinese deplore the odor of Americans. Some white people think Negroes have a distinctive smell and vice versa. An intrepid psychologist recently did an experiment; it went as follows. He brought to a gymnasium an equal number of white and colored students and had them take shower baths. When they were nice and clean he had them exercise vigorously for fifteen minutes. Then he put them in different rooms, and he put a clean white sheet over each one. Then he brought his judges in, and each went to the sheeted figures and sniffed. They were to say, "white" or "black," guessing at the identity of the subject. The experiment seemed to prove that when we are sweaty we all smell bad in the same way. It's good to have experimental demonstration of the fact.

The fourth example I'd like to bring before you is a piece of writing that I quote. Please ask yourselves who, in your judgment, wrote it. It's a passage about the Jews.

> The synagogue is worse than a brothel. It's a den of scoundrels. It's a criminal assembly of Jews, a place of meeting for the assassins of Christ, a den of thieves, a house of ill fame, a dwelling of iniquity. Whatever name more horrible to be found, it could never be worse than the synagogue deserves.

> I would say the same things about their souls. Debauchery and drunkenness have brought them to the level of lusty goat and pig. They know only one thing; to satisfy their stomachs and get drunk, kill, and beat each other up. Why should we salute them? We should have not even the slightest converse with them. They are lustful, rapacious, greedy, perfidious robbers.

Now who wrote that? Perhaps you say Hitler, or Goebbels, or one of our local anti-Semites? No, it was written by Saint John Chrysostom, in the fourth century A. D. Saint John Chrysostom, as you know, gave us the first liturgy in the Christian church still used in the Orthodox churches today. From it all services of the Holy Communion derive. Episcopalians will recognize him also as the author of that exalted prayer that closes the offices of both matin and evensong in the *Book of Common Prayer*. I include this incident to show how complex the problem is. Religious people are by no means necessarily free from prejudice. In this regard be patient even with our saints.

What do these four instances have in common? You notice that all of them indicate that somebody is "down" on somebody else—a feeling of rejection, or hostility. But also, in all these four instances, there is indication that the person is not "up" on his subject—not really informed about Americans, Irish, Jews, or bodily odors.

So I would offer, first a slang definition of prejudice: *Prejudice is being down on somebody you're not up on*. If you dislike slang, let me offer the same thought in the style of St. Thomas Aquinas. Thomists have defined prejudice as *thinking ill of others without sufficient warrant.*

You notice that both definitions, as well as the examples I gave, specify two ingredients of prejudice. First there is some sort of faulty generalization in thinking about a group. I'll call this the process of *categorization*. Then there is the negative, rejective, or hostile ingredient, a *feeling* tone. "Being down on something" is the hostile ingredient; "that you're not up on" is the categorization ingredient. "Thinking ill of others" is the hostile ingredient; "without sufficient warrant" is the faulty categorization.

Parenthetically I should say that of course there is such a thing as *positive* prejudice. We can be just as prejudiced *in favor of* as we are *against*. We can be biased in favor of our children, our neighborhood or our college. Spinoza makes the distinction neatly. He says that *love prejudice* is "thinking well of others, through love, more than is right." *Hate prejudice*, he says, is "thinking ill of others, through hate, more than is right."

In summary, the way you answer the question "What does X mean?" depends on what X *is* and what your purpose is in defining it. If you are trying to communicate what "prejudice" means *experientially*, then of course illustrations will best serve your purpose, for they bridge the gap most directly between words and experience. If, however, your purpose is to evaluate an alleged violation of the Fair Employment Practices Act, you need a general working definition of "prejudice"; not the feeling or experience of prejudice, but the category of practice into which you may classify and further describe it in terms of its "differentiae" (those distinguishing characteristics that, added together, can fairly constitute "prejudicial treatment" of a job applicant). In this instance, you must set up formal, fixed, and objective criteria to indicate what constitutes prejudice toward a job applicant—formally, logically, and legally.

DISCUSSION AND EXERCISES

Reminder: A definition, as I have pointed out, never occurs in a vacuum but always within a specific rhetorical stance, within a given context established by the writer to meet the needs of a given occasion. Consequently, before you begin an assignment in definition you should visualize or (if the assignment is merely an exercise) *invent* the occasion that calls it forth. As a writer you should keep in mind a particular problem or situation, a specific audience, a fixed point of view, and follow the prewriting guidelines.

1. Read the following definition of an intellectual and evaluate its structure, stated purpose, and the degree of success with which it fulfills that purpose.

> In certain ways the word "intellectual" is not a happy choice in America, for it seems to set aside the individual falling within this category from the rest of society. But no substitute can be found for the term. We use "intellectual" here in a functional sense, as seems to be the common practice in this country. Thus Merle Curti uses it to include all who "are dedicated to the pursuit of truth in some special field or to the advancement of learning in general." This would include scholars, teachers, and perhaps others such as editorial writers, columnists, and serious journalists who are concerned with the

advancement of learning. More specifically, Peter Viereck tells us: "I define intellectuals as all who are full-time servants of the Word or of the word. This means educators in the broadest sense: philosophers, clergymen, artists, professors, poets, and also such undreamy and uncloudy professions as editors and the more serious interpreters of news." In an attempt to separate the true intellectual from his pseudo counterpart or the "egghead"—from the blind specialist, who knows nothing but his specialty, and from the dilettante, who purveys what he does not really understand—Professor Charles Frankel describes the intellectual thus: "He has, in fact, become increasingly rare. He is the man who has made himself master of some definite intellectual skill or field of learning, and who knows from his own first-hand experience what the difference is between solid thinking and empty vaporizing. But while he cultivates his own private garden, he is also a man who looks beyond its walls occasionally and comments on the public world as it looks from his angle of vision." This definition excludes many scholars who are obviously engaged in intellectual activity but do not possess the broadness of view that Frankel would like all those deserving the term "intellectual" to have.

Let us accept as a functional definition of the term "intellectual" one who is engaged professionally in the pursuit or the propagation of the truth. This includes those who may be mistaken in their view of the truth as long as they believe they are pursuing or propagating the truth in their professional capacity. Just as the incompetent or dishonest physician does not discredit medicine as a profession, nor can it be denied that he is a physician, neither does the incompetent or dishonest intellectual discredit intellectuals as a class or intellectual activity as a profession.

—Thomas P. Neill

2. Write a one-sentence formal or logical definition of each of the following terms. Compare your definitions with those of classmates, noting relative merits of each.

lawyer	idiot	navy	photosynthesis
doctor	imbecile	marines	fireplace
rhetoric	needle	psychotic	radar
biology	pencil	neurotic	book
botany	rock	jet	
archeology	rock music	star	

3. Expand one of your definitions into a paragraph of 100–150 words, using the definition as your topic sentence. Cite examples wherever possible.

4. Compare Bertrand Russell's definition of "philosophy" with Allan Nevins's definition of "history." How are they similar? Note their basic organization or structure. Examine each paragraph, noting its topic sentence, method of development, ordering principle, coordinate and subordinate sequences, transitional devices, tone, and point of view.

5. In a paragraph (150–250 words) trace recent changes in the meaning of one of the following words:

survey	affluent	computer
recession	retarded	beat
stoned	cool	tough
center	liquidate	loophole

6. About the spirit of liberty, Judge Learned Hand said "I cannot define it; I can only tell you my own faith." In a paragraph (150–300 words) tell your "own faith" in the spirit of one of the following words:

justice	honor	brotherhood
courage	sportsmanship	democracy
love	loyalty	idealism
freedom	charity	neighborliness

ESSAY SUGGESTIONS

1. In a form comparable to that of Russell's definition of "philosophy" or Nevins's definition of "history," write a definition essay (500–750 words) of one of the following disciplines:

literature	chemistry	sociology
music	physics	anthropology
history	geology	political science
economics		

2. Write a definition essay (500–750 words) of one of the following general terms, using the one-sentence, formal definition (explicitly stated or implicit) as a base or thesis:

patriotism	public opinion	mass media
plagiarism	libel	isolationist
atheism	heresy	internationalist
communism	reactionary	myth
(any) -ism	liberal	jazz
censorship	radical	temperance
poverty	religion	nature

3. In an essay (500–750 words) restore one of the following words to respectability by stripping it of negative connotations and redefining it in a more respectable light:

gang	exploit	censorship
politician	charity	slang
bookworm	cliché	militarist
shrewd	informer	welfare
manipulator	gossip	intellectual

4. In the manner of Isaac Asimov's essay "'Universe' and 'University'" write an essay (500–750 words) tracing the history of one of the following words:

romance	grammar	hussy	serious
tragedy	citizen	pride	undertaker
comedy	boor	science	scruple
epic	boycott	atomic	lynch
gossip	affair	bunk	corporation
logic	cad	scissors	rifle
rhetoric			

5. In an essay (500–750 words) written in the manner of Dr. Du Bois's essay on discipline suggest a revised definition of one of the following terms:

politician	bookworm	atheist
miser	cheat	agnostic
preacher	hero	religious person
soldier	coward	heretic
militarist	explorer	adventurer

6. Compose your own definition of a "Jerk" (500–750 words) by combining different methods of development (examples, contrast, and so forth).

7. In an essay (500–750 words) written in the manner of Gordon Allport's essay on prejudice, establish the common denominator for one of the following terms by citing three or four instances in which it clearly has application:

courage	wisdom	freedom
cowardice	intelligence	oppression
wit	genius	tyranny
love	patriotism	maturity
hate	discrimination	beauty
happiness	peace	violence

8. Choose a word that interests you and write an essay (500–750 words) defining that word. Remember that in defining a word you are in effect setting the boundaries for the legitimate use of that word. Use the following outline as a guide in writing your essay:

a. State the need for a definition.

b. Review past or current usage and show how or in what way it is inadequate, inappropriate, or confusing.

c. Offer your own definition (which can be a restatement of diversely held opinions of the word) and show how it can be applied to the situation that prompted the need for definition.

9. What Is the Essential Function of X?

*I*f definition of terms is an appropriate first step in discourse, a second step may well invoke the question of function. In each case the writer is attempting to reach the heart of a subject: What does the subject *mean*? What is it *for*? What is it *by its very nature* supposed to do? What is its central duty or obligation? Its special end or purpose? Its main business? Its province? How can it best meet and fulfill that function for which it is most suited? How can it best satisfy human needs?

Writers may, for example, generate essays by addressing these pointed questions to a member of a profession—to a teacher, a lawyer, a doctor, a philosopher, or a clergyman. Certain professions, of course, will be more difficult for writers to define than others. Many people, for example, may need a precise description of the functions of theater producers or directors. What are their special roles, their main business, and their responsibilities?

In defining in writing the functions of a person's profession, you actually carry over an interest you have if you call a police officer to make an arrest, a firefighter to put out a fire, a lawyer to protect your legal rights, a doctor to cure an illness. In each case you assign special and essential functions to appropriate specialists.

THE FUNCTION OF A CRITIC

Poet W. H. Auden addressed the question of function to the somewhat mystifying, frequently misunderstood profession of the critic, characterized as "not merely someone whose knowledge is extensive." How does the critic serve the rest of us? As tutor? Teacher? Guide?

Auden organizes his answer in the form of a simple listing, comparable to Updike's listing of what he saw in Central Park (pages 146–47). As Updike gives us a series of nouns: (he saw *rocks, a pigeon, a policeman*) so Auden, following the same grammatical pattern, gives us a series of verbs. The function of the critic, he tells us, is to *introduce...*, *convince...*, *show...*, *give...*, *throw light on....* Following the listing Auden goes on to offer two paragraphs of explanation: the first three services demand "scholarship," he tells us; the last three "demand...insight." In a final paragraph Auden specifies what function the critic should *not* serve: he should "not...lay down the law."

What Is the Function of a Critic?

W. H. Auden

What is the function of a critic? So far as I am concerned, he can do me one or more of the following services:

1. Introduce me to authors or works of which I was hitherto unaware.
2. Convince me that I have undervalued an author or a work because I had not read them carefully enough.
3. Show me relations between works of different ages and cultures which I could never have seen for myself because I do not know enough and never shall.
4. Give a "reading" of a work which increases my understanding of it.
5. Throw light upon the process of artistic "Making."
6. Throw light upon the relation of art to life, to science, economics, ethics, religion, etc.

The first three of these services demand scholarship. A scholar is not merely someone whose knowledge is extensive; the knowledge must be of value to others. One would not call a man who knew the Manhattan Telephone Directory by heart a scholar, because one cannot imagine circumstances in which he would acquire a pupil. Since scholarship implies a relation between one who knows more and one who knows less, it may be temporary; in relation to the public, every reviewer is, temporarily, a scholar, because he has read the book he is reviewing and the public has not. Though the knowledge a scholar possesses must be potentially valuable, it is not necessary that he recognize its value himself; it is always possible that the pupil to whom he imparts his knowledge has a better sense of its value than he. In general, when reading a scholarly critic, one profits more from his quotations than from his comments.

The last three services demand, not superior knowledge, but superior insight. A critic shows superior insight if the questions he raises are fresh and important, however much one may disagree with his answers to them. Few readers, probably, find themselves able to accept Tolstoi's conclusions in "What is Art?", but, once one has read the book, one can never again ignore the questions Tolstoi raises.

The one thing I most emphatically do not ask of a critic is that he tell me what I "ought" to approve of or condemn. I have no objection to his telling me what works and authors he likes and dislikes; indeed, it is useful to know this for, from his expressed preferences about works which I have read, I learn how likely I am to agree or disagree with his verdicts on works which I have not. But let him not dare to lay down the law to me. The responsibility for what I choose to read is mine, and nobody else on earth can do it for me.

THE FUNCTION OF EDUCATION

Let us take subject five on the checklist of subjects on page 17 of this book—Education—narrow this down to College Education, and ask: "What is its essential function?" In other words, what main purpose does—and should—a college serve, particularly a liberal arts college? Replying to the question, poet-educator John Ciardi develops his "enrichment of life" principle through a lively illustration, concluding with the conviction that . . . the business of the college is not only to train you, but to put you in touch with what the best human minds have thought.

In terms of audience: Ciardi originally wrote this essay for an incoming freshmen class at a large state university.

Another School Year—What For?

John Ciardi

Let me tell you one of the earliest disasters in my career as a teacher. It was January of 1940 and I was fresh out of graduate school starting my first semester at the University of Kansas City. Part of the reading for the freshmen English course was *Hamlet*. Part of the student body was a beanpole with hair on top who came into my class, sat down, folded his arms, and looked at me as if to say: "All right, damn you, teach me something." Two weeks later we started *Hamlet*. Three weeks later he came into my office with his hands on his hips. It is easy to put your hands on your hips if you are not carrying books, and this one was an unburdened soul. "Look," he said, "I came here to be a pharmacist. Why do I have to read this stuff?" And not having a book of his own to point to, he pointed at mine which was lying on the desk.

New as I was to the faculty, I could have told this specimen a number of things. I could have pointed out that he had enrolled, not in a drugstore-mechanics school, but in a college, and that at the end of his course he meant to reach for a scroll that read Bachelor of Science. It would not read: Qualified Pill-Grinding Technician. It would certify that he had specialized in pharmacy and had attained a certain minimum qualification, but it would further certify that he had been exposed to some of the ideas mankind has generated within its history. That is to say, he had not entered a technical training school but a university, and that in universities students enroll for both training and education.

I could have told him all this, but it was fairly obvious he wasn't going to be around long enough for it to matter: at the rate he was going, the first marking period might reasonably be expected to blow him toward the employment agency.

Nevertheless, I was young and I had a high sense of duty and I tried to put it this way: "For the rest of your life," I said, "your days are going to average out to about twenty-four hours. They will be a little shorter when you are in love, and a little longer when you are out of love, but the average will tend to hold. For eight of these hours, more or less, you will be asleep, and I assume you need neither education nor training to manage to get through that third of your life.

"Then for about eight hours of each working day you will, I hope, be usefully employed. Assume you have gone through pharmacy school—or engineering, or aggie, or law school, or whatever—during those eight hours you will be using your professional skills. You will see to it during this third of your life that the cyanide stays out of the aspirin, that the bull doesn't jump the fence, or that your client doesn't go to the electric chair as a result of your incompetence. These are all useful pursuits, they involve skills every man must respect, and they can all bring you good basic satisfactions. Along with everything else, they will probably be what sets your table, supports your wife, and rears your children. They will be your income, and may it always suffice.

"But having finished the day's work what do you do with those other eight hours—with the other third of your life? Let's say you go home to your family. What sort of family are you raising? Will the children ever be exposed to a reasonably penetrating idea at home? We all think of ourselves as citizens of a great democracy. Democracies can exist, however, only as long as they remain intellectually alive. Will you be presiding over a family that maintains some basic contact with the great continuity of democratic intellect? Or is your family life going to be strictly penny-ante and beer on ice? Will there be a book in the house? Will there be a painting a reasonably sensitive man can look at without shuddering? Will your family be able to speak English and to talk about an idea? Will the kids ever get to hear Bach?"

That is about what I said, but his particular pest was not interested. "Look," he said, "you professors raise your kids your way; I'll take care of my own. Me, I'm out to make money."

"I hope you make a lot of it," I told him, "because you're going to be badly stuck for something to do when you're not signing checks."

Fourteen years later, I am still teaching, and I am here to tell you that the business of the college is not only to train you, but to put you in touch with what the best human minds have thought. If you have no time for Shakespeare, for a basic look at philosophy, for the continuity of the fine arts, for that lesson of man's development we call history—then you have no business being in college. You are on your way to being that new species of mechanized savage, the Push-button Neanderthal. Our colleges inevitably graduate a number of such life-forms, but it cannot be said that they went to college; rather the college went through them—without making contact.

No one gets to be a human being unaided. There is not time enough in a single lifetime to invent for oneself everything one needs to know in order to be a civilized human.

Assume, for example, that you want to be a physicist. You pass the great stone halls of, say, M.I.T., and there cut into the stone are the names of the master scientists. The chances are that few if any of you will leave your names to be cut into those stones. Yet any one of you who managed to stay awake through part of a high school course in physics, knows more about physics than did many of those great makers of the past. You know more because they left you what they knew. The first course in any science is essentially a history course. You have to begin by learning what the past learned for you. Except as a man has entered the past of the race he has no function in civilization.

And as this is true of the techniques of mankind, so is it true of mankind's spiritual resources. Most of these resources, both technical and spiritual, are stored in books. Books, the arts, and the techniques of science, are man's peculiar accomplishment. When you have read a book, you have added to your human experience. Read Homer and your mind includes a piece of Homer's mind. Through books you can acquire at least fragments of the mind and experience of Virgil, Dante, Shakespeare—the list is endless. For a great book is necessarily a gift: it offers you a life you have not time to live yourself, and it takes you into a world you have not time to travel in literal time. A civilized human mind is, in essence, one that contains many such lives and many such worlds. If you are too much in a hurry, or too arrogantly proud of your own limitations, to accept as a gift to your humanity some pieces of the minds of Sophocles, of Aristotle, of Chaucer—and right down the scale and down the ages to Yeats, Einstein, E. B. White, and Ogden Nash—then you may be protected by the laws governing manslaughter, and you may be a voting entity, but you are neither a developed human being nor a useful citizen of a democracy.

I think it was La Rochefoucauld who said that most people would never fall in love if they hadn't read about it. He might have said that no one would ever manage to become human if he hadn't read about it.

I speak, I am sure, for the faculty of the liberal arts college and for the faculties of the specialized schools as well, when I say that a university has no real existence and no real purpose except as it succeeds in putting you in touch, both as specialists and as humans, with those human minds *your* human mind needs to include. The faculty, by its very existence, says implicity: "We have been aided by many people, and by many books, and by the arts, in our attempt to make ourselves some sort of storehouse of human experience. We are here to make available to you, as best we can, that experience."

THE FUNCTION OF SCIENCE

In the following essay, Lewis Thomas's "The Tucson Zoo," the question "What is the function of X?" is more subtly, although just as firmly, at work. Is it the proper function of science to be reductionist—"exploring the details, then the details of the details, until the smallest bits of the structure, or the smallest parts of the mechanism, are laid out for counting and scrutiny"?

Thomas suggests that this "endless, obsessive preoccupation with the parts" may not be the true or appropriate function of science. Perhaps science should provide us with a broader perspective. Thomas's personal experience at the zoo points to an answer that involves a view not only of the essential function of science but of mankind itself. "I am coded, somehow, for otters and beavers," Thomas concludes, feeling for them a sudden rush of "surprised affection." Perhaps this, then, is our essential and natural function as human beings: to *like* one another. There is a lovely hope-engendering thought pulsating through this essay: "Maybe altruism is our most primitive attribute."

The Tucson Zoo

Lewis Thomas

Science gets most of its information by the process of reductionism, exploring the details, then the details of the details, until all the smallest bits of the structure, or the smallest parts of the mechanism, are laid out for counting and scrutiny. Only when this is done can the investigation be extended to encompass the whole organism or the entire system. So we say.

Sometimes it seems that we take a loss, working this way. Much of today's public anxiety about science is the apprehension that we may forever be overlooking the whole by an endless, obsessive preoccupation with the parts. I had a brief, personal experience of this misgiving one afternoon in Tucson, where I had time on my hands and visited the zoo, just outside the city. The designers there have cut a deep pathway between two small artificial ponds, walled by clear glass, so when you stand in the center of the path you can look into the depths of each pool, and at the same time you can regard the surface. In one pool, on the right side of the path, is a family of otters; on the other side, a family of beavers. Within just a few feet from your face, on either side, beavers and otters are at play, underwater and on the surface, swimming toward your face and then away, more filled with life than any creatures I have ever seen before, in all my days. Except for the glass, you could reach across and touch them.

I was transfixed. As I now recall it, there was only one sensation in my head: pure elation mixed with amazement at such perfection. Swept off my feet, I floated from one side to the other, swiveling my brain, staring astounded at the beavers, then at the otters. I could hear shouts across my corpus callosum, from one hemisphere to the other. I remember thinking, with what was left in charge of my consciousness, that I wanted no part of the science of beavers and otters; I wanted never to know how they performed their marvels; I wished for no news about the physiology of their breathing, the coordination of their muscles, their vision, their endocrine systems, their digestive tracts. I hoped never to have to think of them as collections of cells. All I asked for was the full hairy complexity, then in front of my eyes, of whole, intact beavers and otters in motion.

It lasted, I regret to say, for only a few minutes, and then I was back in the late twentieth century, reductionist as ever, wondering about the details by force of habit, but, not, this time, the details of otters and beavers. Instead, me. Something worth remembering had happened in my mind. I was certain of that; I would have put it somewhere in the brain stem; maybe this was my limbic system at work. I became a behavioral scientist, an experimental psychologist, an ethologist, and in the instant I lost all the wonder and the sense of being overwhelmed. I was flattened.

But I came away from the zoo with something, a piece of news about myself: I am coded, somehow, for otters and beavers. I exhibit instinctive behavior in their presence, when they are displayed close at hand behind glass, simultaneously below water and at the surface. I have receptors for this display. Beaver and otters possess a "releaser" for me, in the terminology of ethology, and the releasing was my experience. What was released? Behavior. What behavior? Standing, swiveling flabbergasted, feeling exultation and a rush of friendship. I could not, as the result of the transaction, tell you anything more about beavers and otters than you already know. I learned nothing new about them. Only about me, and I suspect also about you, maybe our reaction to each other as well. We are stamped with stereotyped, unalterable patterns of response, ready to be released. And the behavior released in us, by such confrontations, is, essentially, a surprised affection. It is compulsory behavior and we can avoid it only by straining with the full power of our conscious minds, making up conscious excuses all the way. Left to ourselves, mechanistic and autonomic, we hanker for friends.

Everyone says, stay away from ants. They have no lessons for us; they are crazy little instruments, inhuman, incapable of controlling themselves, lacking manners, lacking souls. When they are massed together, all touching, exchanging bits of information held in their jaws like memoranda, they become a single animal. Look out for that. It is a debasement, a loss of individuality, a violation of human nature, an unnatural act.

Sometimes people argue this point of view seriously and with deep thought. Be individuals, solitary and selfish, is the message. Altruism, a jargon word for what used to be called love, is worse than weakness, it is sin, a violation of nature. Be separate. Do not be a social animal. But this is a hard argument to make convincingly when you have to depend on language to make it. You have to print up leaflets or publish books and get them bought and sent around, you have to turn up on television and catch the attention of millions of other human beings all at once, and then you have to say to all of them, all at once, all collected and paying attention: be solitary; do not depend on each other. You can't do this and keep a straight face.

Maybe altruism is our most primitive attribute, out of reach, beyond our control. Or perhaps it is immediately at hand, waiting to be released, disguised now, in our kind of civilization, as affection or friendship or attachment. I don't see why it should be unreasonable for all human beings to have strands of DNA coiled up in chromosomes, coding out instincts for usefulness and helpfulness. Usefulness may turn out to be the hardest test of fitness for survival, more important than aggression, more effective, in the long run, than grabbiness. If this is the sort of information biological science holds for the future, applying to us as well as to ants, then I am all for science.

One thing I'd like to know most of all: when those ants have made the Hill, and are all there, touching and exchanging, and the whole mass begins to behave like a single huge creature, and *thinks*, what on earth is that thought? And while you're at it, I'd like to know a second thing: when it happens, does any single ant know about it? Does his hair stand on end?

A SYMBOLIC FUNCTION

Glenn Collins applies the question of function to an unlikely subject—a child's teddy bear. According to his article, adults as well as children may feel strong attachments to "solacing objects": to stuffed animals when one is very young; to record or tape collections on reaching adolescence; to cars or paintings later on. One of our "most persistent human needs," a psychiatrist points out, "is for solace." Since the grown-up equivalents of the lovable old teddy bear can function as solacing objects, they serve a significant and a symbolic purpose in our lives, as the writer below reports:

The Teddy Bear—Solace for life

Glenn Collins

The urge to cuddle a teddy bear does not appear to be one of the more popular strategies that grown-ups use in coping with the stress of existence. Nevertheless, the mechanism that lies behind a child's quest for a "lovey" may be an important source of comfort throughout our lives.

"Whenever we're faced with a sense of loss, or of danger, we call upon some object or idea, an inner resource," said Dr. Paul C. Horton, a psychiatrist who practices in Meriden, Conn. "These are orienting objects—and by touching them, they allow people to get their emotional bearings, and enable them to face the challenges before them."

Dr. Horton's thesis is that this process continues from childhood to adulthood. He says that we keep trading objects like teddy bears for other, age-appropriate artifacts and concepts that serve to comfort us. And we do so in a way "that is not unhealthy or dependent," said Dr. Horton. "It is a mature and sophisticated process that fosters growth and change."

Dr. Horton has spent five years working on a book, *Solace*, which will be published next September by the University of Chicago Press. It is a compilation of research, clinical observation and analysis that systematically addresses the psychological mechanisms of comforting behavior. "The solacing process has been fairly well ignored in the literature," said Dr. Horton, who has been an associate clinical professor at Yale University and has taught at the University of Connecticut Medical School.

To many adults, thoughts about teddy bears conjure up childhood memories of Winnie the Pooh, or of young Linus clutching his blanket in the comic-strip universe of Charles Schulz. But Dr. Horton's work involves long-debated concepts such as the age at which children develop "object constancy" (the sustained recognition of objects apart from the self), and our relatedness to what the psychological literature terms "the transitional object"—things animate or inanimate that are experienced by people in a reliably soothing manner, and that connect us in some way with the comfort of the maternal presence.

For children, this "transitional object" can be a teddy bear, a security blanket, the fringe of a coverlet, or even a beloved diaper. For long the conventional wisdom has been that, as normal children mature, they outgrow such fixations. And the attachment to blankets and the like *after* 3 or so was, in the classic psychoanalytic framework, defined as disturbed or regressive behavior.

"The connotation has been negative, that it was a passive, dependent kind of attraction, but I believe the evidence is against that," said Dr. Horton. His work embodies a school of thought among those in psychiatry who hold that such attachments can continue normally: "The relationship that I'm talking about is vital, humane and essential to development throughout one's life," he said.

To Dr. Horton, the "transitional objects of choice" for older children can be things like baseball mitts or bottle-cap collections, and among adolescents they can be things like tape cassettes bearing treasured rock music that, when played, seems to serve as a safe port in the teen-age storm.

Among adults, solacing objects can be things—like cars or paintings—or they can be people, frequently mentors to whom one can relate transitionally: teachers, ministers, priests (or, stated Dr. Horton, psychiatrists).

The hunger for solace among adults can also foster the attachment to religious ideals, to works of art, to music or poetry. The "transitional object" can even be a whole country: "If you look closely at the language in Saul Bellow's 'To Jerusalem and Back,' the mother earth of Israel itself serves as his powerful object of solace and connection," said Dr. Horton.

Naturally, an adult who clutches a for-real teddy bear may not be wholly normal: the psychiatric literature is crowded with reports of patients suffering from psychosis, depression and schizophrenia who cling to security blankets or their equivalents.

But most adults who derive comfort from their grown-up teddy-bear equivalents are normal, Dr. Horton suggested. "One of the most persistent human needs is that for solace," he said. "Solace is a resource that soothes pain and great psychic stress, it gives us a neutral framework so we can cope with changing circumstances. Human suffering is ubiquitous, and we need to find tangible or intangible relief for it, as long as we live."

A HIDDEN FUNCTION

A second unlikely subject to which a writer may apply the question of function is the modest, mundane picture postcard. "What is its function?" asks humorist Russell Baker. To send a cheery "hello" to the folks back home? To let them know they're remembered and missed ("wish you were here!")? Such surface pleasantries conceal the deeper purpose and *essential function* of "dropping a line," says Baker. It's to gloat, to remind those who receive the card that while you (the sender) are "having a wonderful time," they (the receivers) are *not*. "Boy, what you're missing!" is the implied message.

The Postcard: Count Your Miseries

Russell Baker

Here is a postcard from Sheila and Dick. They are in Athens, having a wonderful time. They saw the moon over the Acropolis. It was fantastic. I should have seen it.

Of course I should have seen it, but I couldn't, could I? It's impossible to see the moon over the Acropolis if you're stuck in Manhattan with an air-conditioner blocking the only windows in the room. Sheila and Dick know that, so why did they bother to send a postcard?

Why does anybody bother to send a postcard?

Here's one from Belle and Ollie. Judging from the picture, they are renting the Rocky Mountains for the summer. It's really cool there. Have to wear sweaters every night. They bet I'm really suffering in fetid, steamy New York.

That's Belle and Ollie for you. They only bet on sure things. They know for an absolute fact that I'm really suffering in fetid, steamy New York. But do they care? Really care?

If you really care about somebody who is suffering, you don't send him a gloating postcard. You send him a letter to cheer him up. With people who send postcards, having a wonderful time isn't enough; they have to remind you that you are not having a wonderful time.

Here's a postcard from Sam, who goes around on yachts. Every summer he manages to ingratiate himself into becoming the yachting guest of somebody who has beaten the income tax. This summer he is guesting on the bracing water off Maine.

Sam warned me that he would send a postcard. "I'll send you a card," he said.

"I don't want a card," I said. "I want your tax-chiseler friend to send me an envelope stuffed with enough cash to get me to Athens. I want to see the moon over the Acropolis."

Sam sent the card anyhow. After four weeks on yachtboard, he hasn't been mugged once, he says. "Hah hah."

Anyone who didn't know Sam well might think his "Hah hah" was a subtle way of expressing satisfaction at the thought of his friends back in New York being mugged twice a night. This is not the case. Sam is just one of those people who develop writer's block when they see all that blank space to be filled on the back of postcards. So he writes "Hah hah" a lot to get his money's worth out of the stamp.

I once had a postcard from Sam in Jamaica. It was February. He was yachtguesting around the Caribbean and paused at Jamaica to read the papers reporting a blizzard in New York. His card said, "Don't get sunburned," followed by 14 "Hah hah's."

It's strange about postcards: People only feel the urge to send them from elegant surroundings. Take Sheila, for instance, who is in Athens seeing what I should have seen; to wit, the moon over the Acropolis. Sheila goes down to Trenton three or four times a year, but she never sends a postcard from Trenton.

The moon shines on the Amtrak station at Trenton just as it shines on the Acropolis, but I have yet to receive a card from Sheila announcing that she has seen the moon over the Trenton Amtrak station.

Another curiosity is that nobody ever sends a postcard to let you know when the vacation is a disaster. Two years ago Belle hauled Ollie out to India to see the moon over the Taj Mahal. Belle's aim was to lay the groundwork for a postcard from Agra stating that the moon over the Taj Mahal was fantastic and I should have seen it.

She failed to reckon with Ollie's terror of snakes. On arrival in Agra, their car was approached by a roving snake showman wearing some 20 feet of python around his waist and thrusting the other 8 feet proudly in front of him.

The man's only purpose was to cadge a rupee or two from Ollie by letting him admire and stroke the snake, but as he approached the car, obviously intending to thrust six feet of serpent through the open window for Ollie's admiration, Ollie screamed, "For God's sake, close the window!"

The snake man, thinking Belle and Ollie were being coy and wanted to be coaxed out of the sealed machine, spent what seemed to Ollie like years thrusting his pet against the glass and grinning proudly at its muscularity. Since the temperature that night was 120 degrees in the moonlight, Ollie and Sheila finally had to be removed by stretcher bearers. On leaving the hospital Ollie insisted on flying at once to Ireland, where, he had heard, St. Patrick had rid the landscape of reptiles.

Did Ollie or Belle send a card from Agra saying that they were having a miserable time and telling me I was lucky to be in fetid, steamy New York? "Hah hah," as Sam would write. The only card I had from them came from Ireland. They had seen the mist over Galway Bay. It was fantastic. I should have seen it.

DISCUSSION AND EXERCISES

1. Consider the Auden essay on the function of a critic.

   a. Do you agree with the six basic services of the critic as Auden states them? Explain.
   b. Comment on Auden's statement: "But let him [the critic] not dare to lay down the law to me."

2. Compose a paragraph (150–250 words) using the following topic sentence. "So far as I am concerned, _____ (Choose one: a doctor, lawyer, teacher or clergyman) can do me one or more of the following services." Be sure to follow Auden's listing pattern; also be sure your sentences are grammatically parallel (in Christensen's words, "like things in like ways"; see pages 120–23).

3. Evaluate Ciardi's essay in terms of the following:

   a. general readability, tone, style
   b. organization (do you like the story that introduces the piece?)
   c. paragraphs (locate topic sentences)
   d. sentence construction
   e. choice of words, level of usage (for example, how do you respond to the phrase "this particular pest"?)

4. Summarize Ciardi's description of the function of education in a one-paragraph coordinate sentence, using the following topic sentence: "Ciardi's essay describes the several ways that a liberal arts education enriches life." (See question seven, "How can X be summarized?") According to a Christensen schematization (see pages 120–23), your paragraph will look like this:

   > 1 (topic sentence)
   >   2—function one
   >   3—comment on function one
   >   2—function two
   >   3—comment on function two
   >   2—function three
   >   3—comment on function three

5. Consider the various audiences for which Ciardi might have prepared his statement on the function of education (children, faculty colleagues, college administrators, general public, senior citizens). In what ways would the address have needed changing to meet the special needs of each audience?

6. Consider the Thomas essay, "The Tucson Zoo."

   a. Describe the organization of the essay; is it effective?
   b. Describe the theme of the essay, as Thomas expresses it in the following sentence: "Maybe altruism is our most primitive attribute, out of reach, beyond our control."
   c. Comment on the effectiveness of the last sentence about the single ant who together with other ants "made the Hill": "Does his hair stand on end?"
   d. What audience do you think Thomas is addressing: general public? scientists?

7. Compose a paragraph (150–250 words) using the following topic sentence, drawn from Thomas's essay: "Left to ourselves . . . we hanker for friends." Again, write a coordinate sentence and then rewrite the paragraph as a subordinate sentence.

8. Contemplate the "Teddy Bear: Solace for Life."

   a. To what extent is the report factual? To what extent interpretive?

b. What does the writer mean by the following quotation: "... the mechanism that lies behind a child's quest for a 'lovey' may be an important source of comfort throughout our lives." Explain.

c. What sort of objects serve as "loveys" for children? For teenagers? For adults?

d. What does Dr. Horton mean by "transitional objects of choice"?

e. How do solacing objects function? When do people call on them?

f. According to Dr. Horton, "We keep trading objects like teddy bears for other age-appropriate artifacts and concepts that serve to comfort us." Is this a normal, natural and healthy function? Does it serve a mature purpose? Is it appropriate for an adult?

g. Give yourself ten minutes to compose a cluster around the nucleus word "lovey" (see pages 32–35).

ESSAY SUGGESTIONS

1. Using Auden's description of the function of the critic as a model, write an essay (500–750 words) in which you describe the function of one of the following professionals:

scientist	minister, rabbi, priest, or nun
artist	police officer
musician	lawyer
writer	doctor
teacher	philosopher
athlete	

Follow Auden's organization:

Introduction: A listing of five or six "services" or functions
    I. What special qualifications the first two or three services demand
    II. What special qualifications the rest of the services demand
    III. What services or functions should *not* be performed
Conclusion (optional)

2. In an essay (700–1,000 words) describe the main function of higher education as you view it, drawing on the essay reprinted here and on any other sources you wish to consult.

3. Using your cluster as a point of departure, write an essay of 500–750 words on some "orienting object" in your childhood, some teddy bear or its equivalent that once served as solace and perhaps does so even now.

4. Considering Russell Baker's essay on postcards, ask yourself what other "social niceties" can sometimes cover a darker intent. Write an essay (500–750 words) about one that you have observed or experienced.

5. Write an essay (750–1,000 words) in which you explain the essential function, as you view it, of any aspect of your life or environment: a hobby, sport, or recreation; a person or place; an object. If you are scientifically inclined, you might consider, in a less personal manner, the essential function of some element of nature, such as the moon or sun; or of some organ of the body, such as the heart or spleen; or of some social ritual, such as courtship or the cocktail party.

10. What Are the Component Parts of X?

THINKING ANALYTICALLY

*T*o analyze means to ask about the parts of whatever we are examining. We ask what the parts are and how they relate to each other. We analyze continually because the only way to understand a person, an object, an idea, an event, a process, or an organization is to take it apart in a systematic manner to see what makes it function as a whole, what made it happen, why it is as it is. Analysis is a natural function of the human mind. We analyze all the time as we explore the world around us in order to understand it better. Thinking itself is impossible without analysis; we necessarily analyze every subject we contemplate with any seriousness—whether we write or talk about it.

All the questions in this book, but especially the next ten, deal with analysis. They attempt to break down a total subject into its parts. Logicians call this process *division*; This first step is essential in problem-solving and in writing. Before we can deal with a subject we must see its internal divisions.

WRITING ANALYTICALLY

Analysis is a challenging and demanding form of writing: It requires systematic and rigorously logical thinking conducted in the light of clear and consistent principles. Three basic logical principles are fundamental to all analysis, whether performed by a logician or by a writer:

1. Analysis (or division) must take place according to the structure of the thing being observed. In logical terms, to smash a glass is not to divide it, because a glass is not composed of fragments of glass. A chemical analysis is necessary to determine the component parts of a glass.
2. The interest of the analyzer determines the kind of structure being analyzed. Thus, you can analyze English literature as a chronological structure into old, middle, modern, or you can analyze it by separating it into various genres—poetry, drama, essays, and so on. Whatever structure you choose to work with, you must be consistent to achieve the primary purpose of analysis: to keep component parts clear and distinct. Thus, you cannot analyze literature by separating it into old, middle, and poetry; such an analysis shifts its basis of division from chronology to genre.
3. Analysis should also be complete—that is, you should divide X into *all* its component parts, not just some of them. In scientific or technical analysis this is mandatory; in a general essay on a nonscientific subject, however, you need not be quite as strict. You may choose to deal with only the main part or selected aspects of your subject. In that case you should indicate that the analysis is partial and incomplete, letting the reader

know you have not inadvertently overlooked the elements you have not mentioned. One simple device for completing a division is to include the category "others" or "miscellaneous." In analyzing the body of an author's works, you might divide the works into novels, plays, short stories, and "miscellaneous writings." In this way you leave nothing out.

The following essays by Bishop and Millikan amply fulfill these prerequisites of logical analysis. In "The Composition of Blood," Bishop analyzes blood in terms of its natural components: He never shifts the basis of division (to "rich" or "poor" blood, color of blood, rate of flow). The analysis is also complete: Although the writer does not name every protein or enzyme found in plasma, he indicates that there are other substances ("other products," "also various gases") that fall into the explicitly stated main categories.

Similarly, in his essay on modern science, Millikan analyzes this vast and complex subject in terms of his special interest—its spirit. At no point does he shift his ground to contemplate the various types of sciences (biology, chemistry), their degree of "purity," their difficulty. And Millikan's analysis is complete: As he sees it, there are three and no more than three "basic elements" of the scientific spirit.

Analysis of a Physical Structure

Once the writer has answered the question "What are the parts of X?" the outline for the essay is in place: the parts of the subject become the parts of the piece. Therefore, the organization depends on answering the question. In the following essay the three kinds of blood cells plus the plasma constitute the four basic units of the discourse, which the author breaks down into subunits, as he analyzes each of the components of blood into *its* respective parts.

The Composition of Blood

Louis Faugeres Bishop

Introduction (states component elements)

Under the microscope we can see that [blood] is composed of a watery fluid called plasma, in which certain formed elements are suspended. The formed elements are different types of cells—red blood cells, white blood cells and platelets.

1. Red blood cells

The red blood cells are the most numerous of the formed elements. There are normally about 5,000,000 in each cubic millimeter of blood in men and about 4,500,000 in women during the child bearing years. Each cell is about $\frac{1}{3500}$ of an inch in diameter. Normally the cells are in the form of disks, both sides of which are concave.

Red blood cells are developed in the red marrow, found in the ends of the long bones and throughout the interior of flat bones, such as the vertebrae and ribs. The cells have definite nuclei in the early stages of their formation; in man and the other mammals the nuclei are lost by the time the cells have become mature and before they are released into the blood stream.

(Broken down into their elements)

Each mature red blood cell has a structural framework called the stroma, which is made up chiefly of proteins and fatty materials. It forms a mesh extending into the interior of the cell; it gives the cell its shape and flexibility. The most important chemical substance in the cell is hemoglobin, which causes blood to have a red color. Hemoglobin is composed of an iron-containing pigment called heme and a protein called globin; there are about four parts of heme to ninety-six parts of globin. In man the normal amount of hemoglobin is 14 to 15.6 grams per 100 cubic centimeters of blood; in woman it is 11 to 14 grams.

Hemoglobin combines with oxygen in the lungs after air has been inhaled; the resulting compound is called oxyhemoglobin. When the red blood cells later make their way to other parts of the body deficient in oxygen, the oxygen in the compound breaks its bonds and makes its way by diffusion to the tissues of the oxygen-poor areas. Thus the red blood cells draw oxygen from the lungs, transport it in the blood stream and release it to the tissues as needed.

2. White blood cells

The white blood cells are the body's military force, attacking disease organisms such as staphylococci, streptococci and meningococci. These cells are far less numerous than the red variety; the proportion of white to red under normal conditions is 1 to 400 or 500. The white cells are semi-transparent bodies. They differ from red cells in several important respects; among other things, they contain no hemoglobin and they always have nuclei.

(Indication of the varieties)

There are several easily distinguished varieties of white cells: neutrophils, lymphocytes, basophils, eosinophils and monocytes. Neutrophils, basophils and eosinophils are formed in the bone marrow. Lymphocytes are made in the lymphatic tissues; monocytes, in the reticulo-endothelial system.

The neutrophils are by far the most numerous of the white blood cells, making up from 65 to 70 per cent of the total. They derive their name from the fact that they readily take the color of a neutral dye. These cells are about half as large again as red blood cells.

3. Platelets

Platelets are tiny circular or oval disks, which are derived from certain giant cells in the bone marrow, called megakaryocytes. Their number ranges from 200,000 per cubic millimeter to 500,000 or more. The platelets, which are much smaller than the blood cells, serve several useful purposes. When they disintegrate, they liberate a substance called thrombokinase or thromboplastin, which is vital in the blood-clotting process. They also help to plug leaks in the tiny blood vessels called capillaries.

4. Analysis of plasma

The plasma is the watery part of the blood, making up from 50 to 60 per cent of the total. It is a clear yellow fluid, serving as a vehicle for the transportation of red blood cells, white blood cells, platelets and various substances necessary for the vital functioning of the body cells, for clotting and for the defense of the body against disease. After clotting occurs, a straw-colored fluid called serum is left; this retains its liquid form indefinitely.

About 90 per cent of plasma is water, in which a great variety of substances are held in suspension or in solution. These include proteins, such as fibrinogen, albumin and the globulins, and also sugar, fat and inorganic salts derived from food or from the storage depots of the body. Plasma contains urea, uric acid, creatine and other products of the breakdown of proteins. There are enzymes, such as adrenal hormones, thyroxine and insulin, derived from the glands of internal secretion. There are also various gases: oxygen and nitrogen, diffused into the blood from the lungs; and carbon dioxide, diffused into the blood from the tissues.

Analysis of an Intellectual Structure

Just as you may break down objects and substances into their physical parts, you may also divide ideas and concepts into their conceptual and psychological components: for example, the thoughts, attitudes, and feelings that make up the concept of "patriotism." Conceptual analysis is more common than physical analysis. Most people regularly try to "figure things out" in their heads, whereas relatively few want to know about "taking things apart" (like a television set or a clock).

Ultimately, if a writer is determined enough, no concept is too abstract for analysis. The renowned physicist Robert Andrew Millikan, for example, believed that most people do not understand the conceptual whole called the "scientific spirit," and he wrote the following essay to analyze what it is by describing its three basic elements. Though no longer scientifically acceptable, this essay remains a classic statement.

The Spirit of Modern Science

Robert Andrew Millikan

The spirit of modern science is something relatively new in the history of the world, and I want to give an analysis of what it is. I want to take you up in an aeroplane which flies in time rather than in space, and look down with you upon the high peaks that distinguish the centuries, and let you see what is the distinguishing characteristic of the century in which we live. I think there will be no question at all, if you get far enough out of it so that you can see the woods without having your vision clouded by the proximity of the trees, that the thing which is characteristic of our modern civilization is the spirit of scientific research,—a spirit which first grew up in the subject of physics, and which has spread from that to all other subjects of modern scientific inquiry.

That spirit has three elements. The first is a philosophy; the second is a method; and the third is a faith.

Look first at the philosophy. It is new for the reason that all primitive peoples, and many that are not primitive, have held a philosophy that is both animistic and fatalistic. Every phenomenon which is at all unusual, or for any reason not immediately intelligible, used to be attributed to the direct action of some invisible personal being. Witness the peopling of the woods and streams with spirits, by the Greeks; the miracles and possession by demons, of the Jews; the witchcraft manias of our own Puritan forefathers, only two or three hundred years ago.

That a supine fatalism results from such a philosophy is to be expected; for, according to it, everything that happens is the will of the gods, or the will of some more powerful beings than ourselves. And so, in all the ancient world, and in much of the modern, also, three blind fates sit down in dark and deep inferno and weave out the fates of men. Man himself is not a vital agent in the march of things; he is only a speck, an atom which is hurled hither and thither in the play of mysterious, titanic, uncontrollable forces.

Now, the philosophy of physics, a philosophy which was held at first timidly, always tentatively, always as a mere working hypothesis, but yet held with ever increasing conviction from the time of Galileo, when the experimental method may be said to have had its beginnings, is the exact antithesis of this. Stated in its most sweeping form, it holds that the universe is rationally intelligible, no matter how far from a complete comprehension of it we may now be, or indeed may ever come to be. It believes in the absolute uniformity of nature. It views the world as a mechanism, every part and every movement of which fits in some definite, invariable way into the other parts and the other movements; and it sets itself the inspiring task of studying every phenomenon in the confident hope that the connections between it and other phenomena can ultimately be found. It will have naught of caprice. Such is the spirit, the attitude, the working hypothesis of all modern science; and this philosophy is in no sense materialistic, because good, and mind, and soul, and moral values,—these things are all here just as truly as are any physical objects; they must simply be inside and not outside of this matchless mechanism.

Second, as to the method of science. It is a method practically unknown to the ancient world; for that world was essentially subjective in all its thinking, and built up its views of things largely by introspection. The scientific method, on the other hand, is a method which is ready for the discard the very minute that it fails to work. It is the method which believes in a minute, careful, wholly dispassionate analysis of a situation; and any physicist or engineer who allows the least trace of prejudice or preconception to enter into his study of a given problem violates the most sacred duty of his profession. This present cataclysm, which has set the world back a thousand years in so many ways, has shown us the pitiful spectacle of scientists who have forgotten completely the scientific method, and who have been controlled simply by prejudice and preconception. This fact is no reflection on the scientific method; it merely means that these men have not been able to carry over the methods they use in their science into all the departments of their thinking. The world has been controlled by prejudice and emotionalism so long that reversions still occur; but the fact that these reversions occur does not discredit the scientist, nor make him disbelieve in his method. Why? Simply because that method has worked; it is working to-day, and its promise of working to-morrow is larger than it has ever been before in the history of the world.

Do you realize that within the life of men now living, within a hundred years, or one hundred and thirty years at most, all the external conditions under which man lives his life on this earth have been more completely revolutionized than during all the ages of recorded history which preceded? My great-grandfather lived essentially the same kind of life, so far as external conditions were concerned, as did his Assyrian prototype six thousand years ago. He went as far as his own legs, or the legs of his horse, could carry him. He dug his ditch, he mowed his hay, with the power of his own two arms, or the power of his wife's two arms, with an occasional lift from his horse or his ox. He carried a dried potato in his pocket to keep off rheumatism, and he worshipped his God in almost the same superstitious way. It was not until the beginning of the nineteenth century that the great discovery of the ages began to be borne in upon the consciousness of mankind through the work of a few patient, indefatigable men who had caught the spirit which Galileo perhaps first notably embodied, and passed on to Newton, to Franklin, to Faraday, to Maxwell, and to the other great architects of the modern scientific world in which we live,—the discovery that man is not a pawn in a game played by higher powers, that his external as well as his internal destiny is in his own hands.

You may prefer to have me call that not a discovery but a faith. Very well! It is the faith of the scientist, and it is a faith which he will tell you has been justified by works. Take just this one illustration. In the mystical, fatalistic ages, electricity was simply the agent of an inscrutable Providence: it was Elijah's fire from Heaven sent down to consume the enemies of Jehovah, or it was Jove's thunderbolt hurled by an angry god; and it was just as impious to study so direct a manifestation of God's power in the world as it would be for a child to study the strap with which he is being punished, or the mental attributes of the father who wields the strap. It was only one hundred and fifty years ago that Franklin sent up his famous kite, and showed that thunderbolts are identical with the sparks which he could draw on a winter's night from his cat's back. Then, thirty years afterward Volta found that he could manufacture them artificially by dipping dissimilar metals into an acid. And, thirty years farther along, Oersted found that, when tamed and running noiselessly along a wire, they will deflect a magnet: and with that discovery the electric battery was born, and the erstwhile blustering thunderbolts were set the inglorious task of ringing house bells, primarily for the convenience of womankind. Ten years later Faraday found that all he had to do to obtain a current was to move a wire across the pole of a magnet, and in that discovery the dynamo was born, and our modern electrical age, with its electric transmission of power, its electric lighting, its electric telephoning, its electric toasting, its electric foot warming, and its electric milking. All that is an immediate and inevitable consequence of that discovery,—a discovery which grew out of the faith of a few physicists that the most mysterious, the most capricious, and the most terrible of natural phenomena is capable of a rational explanation, and ultimately amenable to human control.

At the [Pennsylvania state] Capitol in Harrisburg is a picture of Sir Edwin Abbey, which is entitled, "Wisdom, or the Spirit of Science." It consists of a veiled figure with the forked lightnings in one hand, and in the other, the owl and the serpent, the symbols of mystery; and beneath is the inscription:

> I am what is, what hath been, and what shall be.
> My veil has been disclosed by none.
> What I have brought forth is this: The sun is born.

It is to lighten man's understanding, to illuminate his path through life, and not merely to make it easy, that science exists.

Here again the essay, like most essays in simple analysis, takes on form and organization at the moment the writer indicates what the component parts of the subject are: the elements of the "spirit" are also the units of the piece. Thus we can outline Millikan's essay as follows:

INTRODUCTION:
> The spirit of modern science is relatively new; has three elements: philosophy, method, and faith.
>   I. Philosophy
>   II. Method
>   III. Faith

CONCLUSION:
> As the picture "Wisdom, or the Spirit of Science" illustrates, science exists to illuminate life, not merely to make it easy.

Analysis of an Art

Skillfully written analysis can reveal the essence of a seemingly difficult or esoteric subject. Take music, for example, which many people enjoy, but relatively few understand. Hoping to increase enjoyment by promoting understanding, musicologist David Randolph wrote the following analysis, in which he considers the totality of "music" from his chosen point of view: what the listener responds to. The analysis is strictly logical in that Randolph sticks scrupulously throughout to the special ground on which the analysis rests. He never shifts to types of music, individual instruments, and so on. He also leaves no question as to whether it is complete. There are five and only five important elements to respond to in music. Even "if we wanted to be rigid about definitions," Randolph assures us, "we could say that music consists of nothing but the manipulation of the five elements."

Five Basic Elements of Music

David Randolph

Let us see what it is that you respond to in music.

Do you find something appealing about the famous tune from Schubert's Unfinished Symphony? If so, then you are responding to one of the most important elements of music—*melody.*

Do you find that you feel like tapping your foot during the march movement of Tchaikovsky's Pathétique Symphony? If so, then you are responding to another extremely important element—*rhythm.*

Yet observe that rhythm is present in the melody of Schubert's Unfinished (just tap out the melody on a table with your finger, without singing, and you will isolate the rhythm), and that melody is present in even the most rhythmic portion of the Tchaikovsky march. Therefore, in the process of merely "liking" one of these works, you are actually appreciating two musical elements at once. While this example may not impress you by its profundity, the *principle*—being aware of what it is that you respond to—is at the root of all genuine music appreciation.

Now imagine how much less satisfying Schubert's melody would be if it were buzzed through a tissue-papered comb, instead of being played by the entire cello section of an orchestra. The melody and the rhythm would still be present as before; the difference would lie only in the quality of the sound that reached your ears. Therefore, when you enjoy the richness of the sound of the massed cellos playing the melody, you are responding to another of the basic elements—*tone color.* Your appreciation, then, really involves *three* elements.

Now, let us suppose that a pianist is playing one of your favorite songs—the melody in the right hand, the accompanying chords in the left. Suppose that his finger slips as he plays one of the chords, causing him to play a sour note. Your immediate awareness of that wrong note comes from your response to another of the basic elements—*harmony.*

Let us briefly consider the more positive implications of harmony. Whether you are attracted by barbershop-quartet singing, or by an atmospheric work by Debussy, or by the powerful, forthright ending of Beethoven's Fifth Symphony, *part* of your reaction stems from your response to the harmony, which may be defined as the simultaneous sounding of two or more notes (usually more than two, as in these three examples). Thus we have found a *fourth* element in your appreciation.

Do you have a sense of completeness at the conclusion of a performance of (we will use only one of countless possible examples) Beethoven's Ninth Symphony? Are you left with a feeling of satisfaction as well as of elation? If so, part of that sense of satisfaction—of completion—comes from your feeling for *form,* which is the last of the five basic elements of music. . . .

·If we wanted to be rigid about definitions, we could say that music consists of nothing but the manipulation of the five elements. The statement is correct in that there is no music in the world, regardless of the time or place of its origin, that can be based upon anything other than some combination of these five elements. Thus, to offer the most extreme contrast possible, what we may imagine as the ritual stamping on the ground by the savage appealing to his god partakes of some of the same basic elements as does Bach's *Passion According to St. Matthew*, notably rhythm and tone color, and certainly, to a degree, form.

ANALYSIS OF AN ESSAY

In Part One, The Prewriting Process, we examined aspects of a writer's "rhetorical stance"—a term used by rhetoricians to describe a writer's view of his or her (1) purpose, (2) audience, (3) occasion or context, and (4) reader-writer relationship (see "Visualizing Your Audience" and "Establishing a Reader-Writer Relationship," pages 40–46).

From the vantage point of rhetorical stance, we might analyze any essay in this text (or elsewhere), in order to see or infer how the writer envisioned it—such as its projected purpose and readers. We might look at how well the writer carried out his or her projections. Because such analyses can benefit those who wish to improve their writing, it will be helpful to do a sample analysis of the preceding essay.

The Rhetorical Stance of David Randolph in "Five Basic Elements of Music"

Assessing the rhetorical stance of David Randolph in his short, helpful essay describing the basic features that all of us respond to when we listen to music is not difficult, for we may infer whatever his words and style omit. Let us consider the four aspects of rhetorical stance, each in its turn:

Purpose:
: Clearly Randolph's purpose is to help readers understand what is "going on" when they listen to music, what they are *responding* to, whether in a pop tune or Bach's *Passion According to St. Matthew*. The title of the book—*This is Music: A Guide to the Pleasures of Listening*—from which this essay was excerpted provides a further clue to Randolph's purpose. The author is trying to help people increase their listening pleasure by increasing their information and deepening their sensitivity.

Audience:
: Is Randolph visualizing an audience of peers, his fellow musicologists? A special age, education, or interest group? Or is he addressing the general public? Clearly Randolph is addressing people interested in music who are not musicians (if they were professionals, they would already know what Randolph is telling them). Seeking to know more about music, then, presumably so that they can enjoy it more, they are implicitly asking Randolph, "Can you help me?"

Occasion or Context:
: His readers have bought his book or borrowed it from the public library. Randolph is "meeting" with them, although not in a lecture hall where he can "talk" to them, face to face. On this occasion, however, at this moment of reading (the moment when readers open the book, eager to find answers to their questions), Randolph will try to answer them—as if he were face to face with them "telling" them what they need to know.

Reader-Writer
Relationship:

"Let us see what it is that you respond to in music." With these words of direct address Randolph opens his "conversation." "Let *us*," he says—meaning *you* (in the library or in your easy chair at home) and *I* (here at my typewriter) "take a look together at how *you* respond." The writer asks the reader questions: "Do you find...? Do you have a sense that...?" In this "simulated" personal encounter, the reader silently replies, nodding in agreement or shaking the head in disagreement. "Observe this...," Randolph suggests (note low-key imperative verb); "Now imagine..." (another imperative). The reader-writer relationship here is clearly like that of teacher and student, lecturer and audience, specialist and nonspecialist. The elements, tone, diction, level of usage, and voice indicate that this was the relationship Randolph envisioned and, as we can judge, the one he successfully established.

DISCUSSION AND EXERCISES

1. Using the above analysis of Randolph's "Five Basic Elements of Music" as a guide, explain the rhetorical stance assumed by the writers of the following essays:
   Bishop: "The Compositions of the Blood"
   Millikan: "The Spirit of Modern Science"
   Ciardi: "Another School Year—What For?"
   (see Question 9, pages 267–78).
2. In the same essays, evaluate paragraph structure according to where "breaks" occur. Indicate how they do or do not coincide with steps in the unfolding and development of the ideas in each essay. Are the paragraphs themselves unified? Are they internally consistent? Reconstruct what you perceive to have been the writer's "working outline" (see the sample outline of Millikan's essay on page 283).
3. Write a paragraph (100–250 words) in which you break down the "spirit" of one of the following into three or more component parts. Be prepared to describe your rhetorical stance.

> The spirit of modern art
> The spirit of the new morality
> The spirit of dissent
> The spirit of revolution
> The spirit of liberal education

Instead of devoting a paragraph or two to each part (as Millikan does in his full-length essay), devote only two sentences, the first naming the part and the second adding specific details or examples. In Christensen's terms (see pages 120–23) this paragraph will be a three-level, coordinate sequence.

> 1 Topic sentence
>   2 Naming of first part
>   3 Specific detail of first part
>   2 Naming of second part
>   3 Specific detail of second part
>   2 Naming of third part
>   3 Specific detail of third part

ESSAY SUGGESTIONS

1. Expand the preceding paragraph into a full-length essay (750–1,000 words).
2. Write an essay (500–750 words) in which you analyze the component parts of a physical or physiological structure (as in "The Composition of the Blood").
3. Assuming a rhetorical stance similar to Randolph's and using the informal direct "you" address to the reader, write an essay (500–750 words) in which you isolate the elements of one of the following:

Arts	*Sports*
ballet	baseball
painting	football
architecture	soccer
photography	tennis
opera	golf
literature	skiing

4. Write an essay (500–750 words) in which you compare Robert Andrew Millikan's historically dated concepts to modern views in the philosophy of science. (See questions 16 and 17 for examples of essays in comparison).

11. How Is X Made or Done?

*I*f you were to ask how to make or do something, you would be entering into a special form of analysis that rhetoricians call *process analysis*. Here, instead of dividing a given subject into its component parts, you divide an ongoing process into its successive stages.

An essay of this kind presents an orderly, step-by-step, chronologically arranged description of how a process of some kind takes place: how a poet writes a poem (a *creative* process); how we think (an *intellectual* process); how a clock keeps time (a *mechanical* process); how plants make chlorophyll (a *natural* process); how a baker makes bread (a *manufacturing* process); how women won the franchise (a *social* process); how the Russian Revolution began (a *historical* process). An essay in process analysis is likely to be readable and lively, for by its very nature it keeps moving from stage one, to stage two, to stage three, and so on.

CREATIVE PROCESS

Suppose, for example, you address the question "How is X made or done?" to one aspect of creativity (subject four in the checklist on page 17): the creative art of choreography. In this case you might write an essay like the following vividly descriptive analysis by choreographer Agnes DeMille of how she composes a ballet.

Composing a Ballet

Agnes DeMille

To make up a dance, I still need . . . a pot of tea, walking space, privacy and an idea. . . .

When I first visualize the dance, I see the characters moving in color and costume. Before I go into rehearsal, I know what costumes the people wear and generally what color and texture. I also, to a large extent, hear the orchestral effects. Since I can have ideas only under the stress of emotion, I must create artificially an atmosphere which will induce this excitement. I shut myself in a studio and play gramophone music, Bach, Mozart, Smetana, or almost any folk music in interesting arrangements. At this point I avoid using the score because it could easily become threadbare.

I start sitting with my feet up and drinking pots of strong tea, but as I am taken into the subject I begin to move and before I know it I am walking the length of the studio and acting full out the gestures and scenes. The key dramatic scenes come this way. I never forget a single nuance of them afterwards; I do usually forget dance sequences.

The next step is to find the style of gesture. This is done standing and moving, again behind locked doors and again with a gramophone. Before I find how a character dances, I must know how he walks and stands. If I can discover the basic rhythms of his natural gesture, I will know how to expand them into dance movements.

It takes hours daily of blind instinctive moving and fumbling to find the revealing gesture, and the process goes on for weeks before I am ready to start composing. Nor can I think any of this out sitting down. My body does it for me. It happens. That is why the choreographic process is exhausting. It happens on one's feet after hours of work, and the energy required is roughly the equivalent of writing a novel and winning a tennis match simultaneously. This is the kernel, the nucleus of the dance. All the design develops from this.

Having established a scenario and discovered the style and key steps, I then sit down at my desk and work out the pattern of the dances. If the score is already composed, the dance pattern is naturally suggested by and derived from the pattern of the music. If it remains to be composed as it does in all musical comedies, the choreographer goes it alone. This, of course, is harder. Music has an enormous suggestive power and the design of the composer offers a helpful blueprint....

Through practice I have learned to project a whole composition in rough outline mentally and to know exactly how the dancers will look at any given moment moving in counterpoint in as many as five groups. As an aid in concentration, I make detailed diagrams and notes of my own arbitrary invention, intelligible only to me and only for about a week, but they are not comparable in exactness to music notation.

At this point, I am ready, God help me, to enter the rehearsal hall.

Obviously, organizing an essay in process analysis is not difficult, because it generally organizes itself in a time sequence. What *is* difficult is dividing the process into logical sequential stages, and making certain that you describe each stage accurately, for if the chain has one weak link the entire explanation can collapse, leaving the reader in confusion.

Notice how carefully DeMille has divided the choreographic act into its stages— the six successive steps through which it is carried out:

Step one: getting the ideas (and the conditions for developing them; a pot of tea, walking space)

Step two: visualizing the dancers "moving" in color and costume and "hearing" the music

Step three: establishing key dramatic scenes

Step four: discovering the basic gestures, rhythms, and style of character ("My body does it for me.")

Step five: writing down the pattern of the dances (detailed diagrams and notes)

Step six: entering the rehearsal hall (with God's help!)

Notice also that the six steps *flow* into one another. At no point do you wonder what stage you are at, for "time" words (plus "place" words, pronouns that refer to earlier nouns, repetition of key words) keep you oriented and moving steadily *ahead:*

When I first visualize the dance...
Before I go into rehearsal...
At this point I avoid using the score...
I *begin* to move and *before* I know it...
I never forget a single nuance... *afterwards*...
The *next* step is to find the style...
... *again* behind locked doors and *again* with a gramophone...

Before I find how a character dances...
...the process *goes on for weeks*...
...*after* hours of work...
I *then* sit down at my desk...
At this point, I am ready...

HISTORICAL-SOCIAL PROCESS

As mentioned above, process analysis is relatively easy to organize because it falls naturally into a chronological progression. What happens, however, when the process you are analyzing is so complex (as in many historical events or complicated scientific processes) that dozens, maybe hundreds, of stages are involved? In such a case, analyzing each stage would be unwieldy if not impossible. One solution is to "block out" the process into three or four key units around which you can arrange a multitude of events.

In historical analysis, then, your main challenge is to find an appropriate way of grouping the stages of a given event, for the limitless day-by-day, minute-by-minute details involved in any historical occurrence could easily swamp you. Certainly you cannot include everything. You must group your facts around particular "centers"; you must also be scrupulously clear about chronology. Notice how the writer of the following historical process sweeps through centuries of history in a single paragraph by clustering all the events of the prehistoric period around three main groups of migrants who arrived in Britain in three waves (note also the time transitions: *"first,"* *"next,"* and *"later"*).

Migrating to England

Edward P. Cheyney

First wave

First were the paleolithic men, or men of the rough-stone age, who used rude weapons, ornaments, and implements of stone and bone. They probably lived in caves and depended for their subsistence on the wild beasts they captured and the vegetable products they found growing wild. *Next* were the neolithic men, or men of the polished-stone age, who used the well-shaped stone, bone, and horn implements that are frequently found, and probably lived in some kind of artificial buildings, raised crops, kept domestic animals, knew how to weave cloth and to make pottery, and perhaps traded with other peoples. They built and deposited their dead in long burial mounds such as those whose remains still exist. They were small men, perhaps of the same race as is now represented by the Basques of Spain. *Later* than these came a race who knew the use of bronze, who buried their dead in small, round burial mounds, and who were probably the builders of Stonehenge, Kit's Coty House, and the other mysterious groups of standing stones which are found scattered through England. These are known as men of the bronze age, and may have been the earliest immigrants of the race dominant in Britain when our written knowledge of it begins.

Second wave

Third wave

TECHNICAL-NATURAL PROCESS

Another common type of process analysis involves description of natural or technical operations. Here again transitional devices are especially important, for they link the stages of a process that might otherwise seem fragmented or discontinuous. What keeps the stages clearly sequential are "time" words, "place" words (such as "here"), pronouns that refer to nouns in preceding sentences, and repetition of key words. Observe how these several factors work in the following paragraph, a brief but clear and precise analysis of a physiological process: how blood circulates. (Key transitions and repetitions are italicized.)

> Part of the *blood* in the heart [receives] a fresh store of *oxygen* from the *lungs*. This *blood* is pumped into a large *artery*—the *aorta*—and from the *aorta* it is carried into a branched system of smaller *arteries*. From the *arteries* it passes into the capillaries. *Here oxygen* and food materials (which have been absorbed from the small intestine and liver) are given up to the tissues. Waste materials, including the gas carbon dioxide, are received. The *blood then* passes to the *veins*. It is returned to the heart by way of two large *veins*.
>
> *Next*, the *blood* is pumped from the heart through the large *pulmonary artery* to the *lungs*. (*Pulmonary* comes from the Latin *pulmo*: "lung.") In the *lungs* carbon dioxide is discharged and *oxygen* is received. The *blood* is *then* returned to the heart through the *pulmonary veins*, and another cycle begins.

The analysis that follows, "The Process of Riveting," is also technical, but it is lively and readable as well because the process in this case is *humanized*; that is, written from the point of view of the riveters themselves. Thus their collective effort at each step—their skillful and risky manipulation of the rivet—introduces an element of drama and suspense to an otherwise mechanical procedure.

The Process of Riveting

The actual process of riveting is simple—in description. Rivets are carried to the job by the rivet boy, a riveter's apprentice whose ambition it is to replace one of the members of the gang—which one, he leaves to luck. The rivets are dumped into a keg beside a small coke furnace. The furnace stands on a platform of loose boards roped to steel girders which may or may not have been riveted. If they have not been riveted there will be a certain amount of play in the temporary bolts. The furnace is tended by the heater or passer. He wears heavy clothes and gloves to protect him from the flying sparks and intense heat of his work, and he holds a pair of tongs about a foot and a half long in his right hand. When a rivet is needed, he whirls the furnace blower until the coke is white-hot, picks up a rivet with his tongs, and drives it into the coals. His skill as a heater appears in his knowledge of the exact time necessary to heat the steel. If he overheats it, it will flake, and the flakes will permit the rivet to turn in its hole. And a rivet which gives in its hole is condemned by the inspectors.

When the heater judges that his rivet is right, he turns to face the catcher, who may be above or below him or fifty or sixty or eighty feet away on the same floor level with the naked girders between. There is no means of handing the rivet over. It must be thrown. And it must be accurately thrown. And if the floor beams of the floor above have been laid so that a flat trajectory is essential, it must be thrown with considerable force. The catcher is therefore armed with a smallish, battered tin can, called a cup, with which to catch the red-hot steel. Various patented cups have been put upon the market from time to time but they have made little headway. Catchers prefer the ancient can.

The catcher's position is not exactly one which a sportsman catching rivets for pleasure would choose. He stands upon a narrow platform of loose planks laid over needle beams and roped to a girder near the connection upon which the gang is at work. There are live coils of pneumatic tubing for the rivet gun around his feet. If he moves more than a step or two in any direction, he is gone, and if he loses his balance backward he is apt to end up at street level without time to walk. And the object is to catch a red-hot iron rivet weighing anywhere from a quarter of a pound to a pound and a half and capable, if he lets it pass, of drilling an automobile radiator or a man's skull 500 feet below as neatly as a shank of shrapnel. Why more rivets do not fall is the great mystery of skyscraper construction. The only reasonable explanation offered to date is the reply of an erector's foreman who was asked what would happen if a catcher on the Forty Wall Street job let a rivet go by him around lunch hour. "Well," said the foreman, "he's not supposed to."

There is practically no exchange of words among riveters. Not only are they averse to conversation, which would be reasonable enough in view of the effect they have on the conversation of others, but they are averse to speech in any form. The catcher faces the heater. He holds his tin can up. The heater swings his tongs, releasing one handle. The red iron arcs through the air in one of those parabolas so much admired by the stenographers in the neighboring windows. And the tin can clanks.

Meantime the gun-man and the bucker-up have prepared the connection—aligning the two holes, if necessary, with a drift pin driven by a pneumatic hammer—and removed the temporary bolts. They, too, stand on loose-roped boards with the column or the beam between them. When the rivet strikes the catcher's can, he picks it out with a pair of tongs held in his right hand, knocks it sharply against the steel to shake off the glowing flakes, and rams it into the hole, an operation which is responsible for his alternative title of sticker. Once the rivet is in place, the bucker-up braces himself with his dolly bar, a short heavy bar of steel, against the capped end of the rivet. On outside wall work he is sometimes obliged to hold on by one elbow with his weight out over the street and the jar of the riveting shaking his precarious balance. And the gun-man lifts his pneumatic hammer to the rivet's other end.

The gun-man's work is the hardest work, physically, done by the gang. The hammers in use for steel construction work are supposed to weigh around thirty pounds and actually weigh about thirty-five. They must not only be held against the rivet end, but held there with the gun-man's entire strength, and for a period of forty to sixty seconds. (A rivet driven too long will develop a collar inside the new head.) And the concussion to the ears and to the arms during that period is very great. The whole platform shakes and the vibration can be felt down the column thirty stories below. It is common practice for the catcher to push with the gun-man and for the gun-man and the bucker-up to pass the gun back and forth between them when the angle is difficult. Also on a heavy rivet job the catcher and the bucker-up may relieve the gun-man at the gun.

The weight of the gun is one cause, though indirect, of accidents. The rivet set, which is the actual hammer at the point of the gun, is held in place, when the gun leaves the factory, by clips. Since the clips increase the weight of the hammer, it is good riveting practice to knock them off against the nearest column and replace them with a hank of wire. But wire has a way of breaking, and when it breaks there is nothing to keep the rivet set and the pneumatic piston itself from taking the bucker-up or the catcher on the belt and knocking him into the next block.

INTELLECTUAL PROCESS

When you try to present a "train of thought" or a line of reasoning—in order to explain your views, or to argue a case for or against something—you are attempting to describe an intellectual or logical process based on the laws of reasoning. No one has written a finer essay in this category than Thomas Huxley. He has created an eminently readable analysis of the act of thinking itself: how we use the inductive and deductive modes in our everyday lives.

Thinking Scientifically

Thomas Henry Huxley

There is a well-known incident in one of Molière's plays, where the author makes the hero express unbounded delight on being told that he had been talking prose during the whole of his life. In the same way, I trust, that you will take comfort, and be delighted with yourselves, on the discovery that you have been acting on the principles of inductive and deductive philosophy during the same period. Probably there is not one here who has not in the course of the day had occasion to set in motion a complex train of reasoning, of the very same kind, though differing of course in degree, as that which a scientific man goes through in tracing the causes of natural phenomena.

A very trivial circumstance will serve to exemplify this. Suppose you go into a fruiterer's shop, wanting an apple,—you take up one, and, on biting it, you find it sour; you look at it, and see that it is hard and green. You take up another one, and that too is hard, green, and sour. The shopman offers you a third; but, before biting it, you examine it, and find that it is hard and green, and you immediately say that you will not have it, as it must be sour, like those that you have already tried.

Nothing can be more simple than that, you think; but if you will take the trouble to analyse and trace out into its logical elements what has been done by the mind, you will be greatly surprised. In the first place you have performed the operation of induction. You found that, in two experiences, hardness and greenness in apples went together with sourness. It was so in the first case, and it was confirmed by the second. True, it is a very small basis, but still it is enough to make an induction from; you generalise the facts, and you expect to find sourness in apples where you get hardness and greenness. You found upon that a general law, that all hard and green apples are sour; and that, so far as it goes, is a perfect induction. Well, having got your natural law in this way, when you are offered another apple which you find is hard and green, you say, "All hard and green apples are sour; this apple is hard and green, therefore this apple is sour." That train of reasoning is what logicians call a syllogism, and has all its various parts and terms,—its major premiss, its minor premiss, and its conclusion. And, by the help of further reasoning, which if drawn out, would have to be exhibited in two or three other syllogisms, you arrive at your final determination, "I will not have that apple." So that, you see, you have, in the first place, established a law by induction, and upon that you have founded a deduction, and reasoned out the special conclusion of the particular case. Well now, suppose, having got your law, that at some time afterwards, you are discussing the qualities of apples with a friend: you will say to him, "It is a very curious thing,—but I find that all hard and green apples are sour!" Your friend says to you, "But how do you know that?" You at once reply, "Oh, because I have tried them over and over again, and have always found them to be so." Well, if we were talking science instead of common sense, we should call that an experimental verification. And if still opposed, you go further, and say, "I have heard from the people in Somersetshire and Devonshire, where a large number of apples are grown, that they have observed the same thing. It is also found to be the case in Normandy, and in North America. In short, I find it to be the universal experience of mankind wherever attention has been directed to the subject." Whereupon, your friend, unless he is a very unreasonable man, agrees with you, and is convinced that you are quite right in the conclusion you have drawn. He believes, although perhaps he does not know he believes it, that the more extensive verifications are,—that the more frequently experiments have been made, and results of the same kind arrived at,—that the more varied the conditions under which the same results are attained, the more certain is the ultimate conclusion, and he disputes the question no further. He sees that the experiment has been tried under all sorts of conditions, as to time, place and people, with the same result; and he says with you, therefore, that the law you have laid down must be a good one, and he must believe it.

In science we do the same thing;—the philosopher exercises precisely the same faculties, though in a much more delicate manner. In scientific inquiry it becomes a matter of duty to expose a supposed law to every possible kind of verification, and to take care, moreover, that this is done intentionally, and not left to a mere accident, as in the case of the apples. And in science, as in common life, our confidence in a law is in exact proportion to the absence of variation in the result of our experimental verifications. For instance, if you let go your grasp of an article you may have in your hand, it will immediately fall to the ground. That is a very common verification of one of the best established laws of nature—that of gravitation. The method by which men of science establish the existence of that law is exactly the same as that by which we have established the trivial proposition about the sourness of hard and green apples. But we believe it in such an extensive, thorough, and unhesitating manner because the universal experience of mankind verifies it, and we can verify it ourselves at any time; and that is the strongest possible foundation on which any natural law can rest.

DISCUSSION AND EXERCISES

1. Answer the following questions based on the essay "The Process of Riveting."
   a. Outline the main stages involved in riveting steel.
   b. How does the writer move us through the stages? (Note his point of view.)
   c. What additional information (that is, additional to the "outline of stages") does the writer include in this analysis: biographical data, descriptive details, suggestion of attitudes, anecdotes, description of people? Why does he include them?
   d. Comment on the writer's style: length of paragraphs and unity; choice of words (technical? plain?); length and difficulty of sentences; transitional devices; general flow and readability; appropriateness of tone.
   e. Comment specifically on the following sentences. In what way do they contribute to the overall tone of the piece?
      1. "It must be thrown. And it must be accurately thrown."
      2. "Catchers prefer the ancient can."
      3. "The catcher's position is not exactly one which a sportsman catching rivets for pleasure would choose."
      4. "Well, he's not supposed to."
      5. "And the tin clanks."

2. In a paragraph (150–250 words) support or challenge the rhetorician who called "The Process of Riveting" "a justly admired example of description of a process."

3. Consider Huxley's examples of scientific thinking in everyday life.

   a. Write a paragraph (150–250 words) called "Thinking Scientifically," in which you illustrate your own everyday use of inductive and deductive reasoning.
   b. Write another paragraph of equal length supporting Dr. Samuel Johnson's counterobservation that "most men think indistinctly." Cite examples of the illogical, the irrational, the impulsive, the half-thought-through. Suggested title: "Thinking Unscientifically."

ESSAY SUGGESTIONS

1. Creative Process

   The creative process, as it has been described by many scientists and artists, falls roughly into four stages: *preparation*—the stage of deliberate and conscious planning, training, and effort; *incubation*—the stage in which you are not *consciously* dwelling on a problem but are nonetheless "mulling it over" on a subconscious level; *illumination*—the "flash" wherein you see the solution to the problem; and finally *verification*—the stage in which you test your newly discovered hypothesis, reviewing and possibly revising it. Knowing these stages of the creative process may help you to organize an essay around one of the following: (Notice how similar these stages are to the prewriting techniques you are using.)

   a. Write an essay (500–750 words) describing, as Agnes DeMille does, a creative experience you have had—the composition of a poem, story, or piece of music; the painting of a picture; the design of a room or a piece of furniture.

      or

   b. Describe in an essay (500–750 words) the process of learning how to do something. Any accomplishment will provide a suitable topic: how you learned to swim, ski, speak French, play bridge—maybe even how you learned "to think," that is, to think *rigorously*.

2. Historical-Social Process

   Write an essay (500–750 words) on one of the following topics, chosen from one of the following groups: (Be sure to use prewriting techniques after you have done your preliminary research.)

   a. Discoveries and Inventions

      How Schliemann discovered Troy
      How Columbus discovered America
      How Salk discovered the polio vaccine
      How Pasteur discovered the pasteurization process
      How the Curies discovered radium
      How Bell invented the telephone
      How Edison invented the electric light

   b. General Historical Events
      Beginnings:
      How Alaska became a state
      How the Great Wall of China was built
      How the Third Reich rose

   Endings:

      How Belgium lost the Belgian Congo
      How the French Revolution ended
      How the Roman Empire fell

   c. Social and Political Processes

> How Congress conducts investigations
> How a U.S. president is elected
> How women won the vote
> How Prohibition was repealed

  d. General Enterprises

> How a newspaper or magazine is "put to bed"
> How the paper is delivered (from press to doorstep)
> How a class is conducted
> →How a party is organized   *conduct a meeting*
> How a paper is written
> How a trip is planned
> How traffic is regulated
> How a university (or any part thereof) is run

3. Technical-Natural Processes

  a. Write an essay (500–750 words) on one of the following complex processes, *humanizing* it in the manner of "The Process of Riveting":

> How explosives are manufactured
> How glass is blown
> How skyscraper windows are washed
> How paintings are restored
> How tobacco is cured

  b. Write an essay (500–750 words) explaining one of the following natural processes:

   1. Physiology (how X is done)

> How we see
> How we hear
> How we maintain balance
> How we breathe
> How we digest food
> How we think
> How we remember
> How we fall asleep

   2. Botany (how X is made)

> How plants manufacture chlorophyll
> How plants manufacture oxygen
> How plants manufacture food
> How plants reproduce
> How plants evolve
> How trees develop "rings"

4. Intellectual Process

   Using Huxley's discussion of induction, write an essay (500–750 words) in which you show how you use the inductive mode of thinking in your daily life.

12. How Should X Be Made or Done?

QUALITIES OF GOOD "HOW-TO" WRITING

*W*ith this question we come to the most practical type of writing: the "how-to" piece, a form of process analysis that tells readers not only how a particular process *is* made or done, but how it *should be* made or done. This analysis becomes a set of directions from you to your readers, telling them precisely how to move through a series of steps toward a given goal. All recipes are instances of the "how-to" form, as are all inside-the-package instructions. We conduct much of the business of the world by means of this kind of writing.

"How-to" or directional writing automatically puts you in the authoritative position of instructor, telling your "less informed" readers-students exactly what to do and how to do it. With the sense of self-importance that inevitably accompanies the use of imperative voice, you should feel an equal sense of responsibility, for in assuming the role of teacher and counselor, you must make certain you are teaching well and counseling wisely.

Your first responsibility, of course, is to be accurate and clear. If, for example, you are instructing readers in "the art of winning at bridge," you should be absolutely certain first that you have your facts right, and second that you explain them clearly, not leaving out a single step or important detail, taking nothing for granted, and allowing for no uncertainties or ambiguities as to what you mean. The cardinal virtues of directional writing are accuracy, clarity, and conciseness. No extra words should clog the free flow of information. You should write instructions in a systematic, lucid, and readable manner.

"How-to" pieces present no serious organizational problems since directions must follow a strict chronological order (first do this, then do that, and so on), and the mode of address, as we have seen, is invariably imperative. The "how-to" form clearly lends itself to an extraordinarily wide range of readers and of subject matter, plus an equally wide variety of tones. In general, the writer and reader come together in close contact (direct address from *me* to *you*), thereby establishing a situation in which the deeper humanistic purposes of writing can be fulfilled: increasing understanding among people, sharing knowledge and skills, and helping one another.

Obviously the first step must be to win the reader's trust. This requires that the reader hear a trustworthy voice, a writer's voice that demonstrates knowledge, honesty, and directness.

In the following piece, for example, a former candidate for political office shows us "the ropes" of campaigning; her purpose is to take the reader behind the scenes and reveal the comic, sometimes absurd side of campaigning. By preparing the reader for the realities of the elective process she is also pointing out the pitfalls. Candidates must maintain a delicate balance and plan their strategy carefully. For example, they must wage appropriately aggressive campaigns, but at the same time avoid alienating their opponents.

How to Run For Office in a Very Small Town

Shirley Weissenborn

If you feel stirred to serve your community or to revamp the system, or perhaps—simply to "be in charge," you may someday decide to run for political office. If you do, and you live in a very small town (10,000 or less) here are some basic rules to follow.

Find out who is on your side. To enter a political race, you must present a petition signed by a designated number of registered voters composed of your family, friends, neighbors and people who owe you money. Your petition may or may not be greeted with hurrahs, depending upon whether the party leaders have you labeled as a winner or loser. Next, call on your supporters to serve as Campaign Manager, Activities Chairman, Publicity Chairman, Treasurer and Ego Chairman. Ego Chairman's job is to call you every morning during the campaign to tell you that you are a shoo-in and the whole town reveres you.

Define your issues. Deciding what you stand for in a small town is a difficult task, for the basic issues have probably remained static for the past 20 years. You may get lucky with a public frenzy over the possible grand opening of a massage parlor in the center of town. Failing that, you may find a safe issue in a heated denouncement of rising taxes. Because incumbents find high taxes difficult to defend, they are frequently placed on the defensive. You, on the other hand, as a non-incumbent, have a simpler time. You are free to attack, sneer, and point with scorn at the many mistakes of those already in office.

Present a news release each week to your local newspaper. Each release must contain a different issue or a new version of an old one. Finding new issues is very difficult. The subject matter must be innocuous enough to offend no one and yet present you as a dedicated, innovative public servant and a wonderful human being. Accompany your article with a photograph of yourself staring with tight-lipped disapproval at some object of public concern, such as a pot hole in the middle of Main Street.

Learn to give speeches with confidence and flair. You will be called upon during your months of campaigning to speak to many groups. The most terrifying of these is the League of Women Voters. They have done their homework and will challenge a candidate fearlessly. Be ready to back up your statements. Know what you are talking about. Salt the audience with friends and provide them with questions that you can answer effectively. Panic is a speaker's greatest hazard. It causes one's mouth to become dry and the upper lip to stick to one's teeth, making speech unintelligible. Fortunately, if one cannot be understood, one cannot be disagreed with.

Ring every doorbell in town. Get to know the people. They are more likely to give you their vote if they have had some personal contact. And don't worry about snubs: most people are friendly and pleased to meet you; it is their dogs that have a bad attitude. You are advised to wear high stout boots to protect your legs from painful bites and "anointing" as surrogate fire hydrants.

Attend everything. Your Activities Chairman will arrange coffees, teas, sherry parties, desserts, and brunches in order for you to meet and talk to as many people as possible.

Try to attend all the public meetings the town provides. Make every effort to stand and contribute to the proceedings. Be sure your comments are intelligent and pertinent. A public statement might get your name in the paper or at least bring you to the attention of others attending the meeting. Of course, your opponents will be making themselves heard too. Often the clamor of candidates drowns out the business at hand.

Avoid dirty tricks. In a small town, your opponents are almost always people you know well and you will still be neighbors after the election is over. Beware the snide tracts slipped under doors at the dawning of Election Day, accusing opponents of unspeakable closet activities. Do not resort to spreading rumors through the town gossip that your opponent has been transferred and will be moving to Indianapolis shortly after the election. If you are the victim of dirty tricks, rise above it. Pray for a backlash of public opinion that will turn the voters against your worthy opponents and make them look like the bums they are.

Embarking on a political campaign is like a ride on the roller coaster. There are peaks and valleys, thrills and frights, and no way off until you roll to a complete stop. That stop is called Election Day. If you win, you have the privilege of serving your community. If you lose, you will have gained experience and self-knowledge. But win or lose, the chances are you will be back in line someday, ticket in hand, ready to take another ride.

VISUALIZING THE "HOW-TO" AUDIENCE

No "how-to" today wins a larger audience than how to lose weight. Thus we see this "how-to" everywhere: in newspapers and magazines throughout the country, in best-selling books as well: how not to ruin your body, endanger your health, jeopardize your love life, or die young. Most of these "how-to-lose-weight" guides are geared to a huge audience ranging from chubby children to obese elders, from the marginally literate to the lofty intellectual (even geniuses get fat and—young or old—must seek advice).

The writer of the following article has the most impressive credentials, a medical degree certifying that he understands the processes of the human body as well as the essentials of nutrition. His credentials give his readers reason to trust him. Note how he adjusts his rhetorical stance to this central fact: He is talking to plain people, not medical colleagues, and he gets directly to the point, avoiding technical terms or explanations. He speaks in a calm, reassuring voice, gently but firmly describing how we can "win at the losing game" (as one Diet Center advertises). Confidently and authoritatively he issues simple imperatives: "Eat three meals a day"; "Go slow"; "Set sensible goals."

Although he cites ample supporting facts and figures, he is careful not to inundate or overwhelm his audience: One good statistic can stun readers into awareness: "$10 billion a year spent on weight losing methods." And finally, note the topography of the piece. Each paragraph is numbered, representing a separate step of the process. Following instructions is much easier when the writer presents them in this graphic 1-2-3 fashion.

How to Lose Weight Sensibly and Successfully and Permanently

Norman Kaplan, M. D.

For most persons wanting to lose weight, the problem of both calorie intake and calorie expenditure must be attacked....Here are some sensible guidelines for successful weight loss:

1. Set sensible short-term goals for yourself. If you're 75 pounds overweight, the idea of shedding all of that in a short period of time is so overwhelming that most people give up in desperation. Go after 5 or 10 pounds at a time and feel good when you've managed that.

2. Recognize that the tendency to be overweight is an incurable but controllable condition, in many ways like hypertension. You've got to establish a new set of eating habits.

3. Go slow and be thankful for small blessings. It doesn't seem you're accomplishing much if you lose 1 pound a week, but remember, that's 52 pounds in a year! Since it took you 5 or maybe 10 years to gain that much, try to accept a gradual but steady weight loss as a reasonable goal.

4. Weigh in only once a week so as not to become frustrated by a slow weight loss. If you accomplish your short-term goal, reward yourself with a nonfattening treat. You may want to go on a "maintenance" diet for a few weeks before taking on another 5 to 10 pounds, or you may be so flushed by victory as to want to go right on.

5. Use various techniques to modify your eating behavior: Prepare only enough food for the meal; put the food on the plate (a small one) without having extra portions at the table: eat without distractions, never in front of the TV set; eat slowly; realize that it is not a sin to leave food on your plate—the starving Armenians will not find out.

6. If your willpower fails and you give in to temptation, try to be satisfied with the first few bites of "forbidden" foods. And when you do give in, recognize that you're only human. Falling off the wagon temporarily needn't mean that you have to lose the whole wagon and the horse as well.

7. Eat three meals a day and always have low-calorie snacks available. You never know when the urge will strike, and you must be ready with carrots, cauliflower or other ammunition.

8. Don't look for magic from pills or spas. They may provide temporary help, but it still gets down to cutting calories—roughly 500 a day less than what you burn in order to lose a pound a week, since there are 3,500 calories in a pound of fat.

9. Exercise as much as you can, starting slowly and gradually building up your capacity. Be sensible about the form of exercise you perform. Few people will stick with jogging a mile every day. But everyone can walk an extra mile a day, particularly if it's six blocks to the office or shopping center. Make this part of your regular routine and not a time-consuming extra effort that quickly becomes such a burden that you quit. A mile of brisk walking a day burns about 90 calories, enough to shed 7 pounds in a year.

10. Remember that both beer and booze have several calories each. Lower-calorie beer and wine are available. Nevertheless, a six-pack of lite beer is still almost 600 calories.

You need to reduce your caloric intake below your caloric expenditure by 500 calories per day to lose 3,500 calories or one pound of fat a week. To lose two pounds of weight per week, a daily deficit of 1,000 calories is needed. That should be accomplished by a combination of decreased intake by a diet and, to a lesser degree, increased expenditure by exercise.

There are many sources of complete diet programs, but you really may not need to do much more than cut out some high-calorie sweets, desserts, breads and dressings and substitute lower-calorie foods for very caloric ones.

Obesity is common, and we've not been very successful up to this point in overcoming it. Despite spending more than $10 billion a year on weight-losing methods and ideas, millions of Americans continue on their seemingly hopeless quest for a size-six figure or a 34-inch waist.

Much more likely to succeed is a program of prevention. Infant feeding habits can be altered to provide adequate nutrition without increasing the child's risk for later obesity or hypertensions. The renewed interest in breast-feeding is a good sign. In Stanford, California, children in the fourth and fifth grades of school were given an effective instructional program and altered their own eating behavior, increased their level of physical activity and influenced their family's eating patterns as well. If we can reach parents and children early enough, healthy eating habits should be easy to adopt and easier to maintain.

For humorists as well as serious advice-givers, the "how-to" piece opens up vast possibilities, as you can see in the following delightfully zany parody. Notice the amusing topography of this analysis. Thomas uses the weighty formality of Roman numerals to separate the steps as though he expects the reader to take note and carefully dismount from an elephant precisely as he suggests:

How to Dismount from an Elephant

Richard L. Thomas

Anyone can manage to get down from an elephant, in the sense of scrambling around without the least regard for appearances or proper form. Indeed, falling off is one surefire method. But people of poise and breeding do not feel the end justifies the means—they insist on dismounting in style. They are the natural aristocrats who have so mismanaged their lives that now they're marooned atop an elephant and not at all sure what to do about it.

I

The first thing you do in dismounting from an elephant is to compose yourself.

II

In step II, we begin to familiarize ourselves with the beast. I know this sounds remote from your current needs and aspirations, and perhaps even a trifle academic. Nonetheless, I must ask you to have confidence in me and place yourself completely in my hands.

Very well then. Now, there are many ways you can go about familiarizing yourself with your host. I'll merely advise you to try to obtain this personal information about him without his knowledge. Many elephants chafe under close scrutiny, and others become sullen and withdrawn, so it's best to employ an extremely tactful, circuitous approach.

III

Our next step will be to learn the nomenclature of the elephant. This kind of careful preparation will help you avoid getting rattled and losing your composure in the hectic hours ahead. ...

Now, the elephant is an animal of many parts, but we will confine ourselves to those portions which directly concern us here. This should not lead you to think there is nothing more to it. In fact, *the elephant is a very complex animal, mentally and emotionally, and should never be dismissed lightly.*

Notice how I have not bothered to mention the elephant's eye. This was a precautionary measure, not an oversight. You see, it is important to avoid, at all costs, *any* contact with the eye. The reasons for this are fascinating:

(a) An elephant does not see very well to begin with.

(b) But he is *not* blind, for heaven's sake, and if you were suddenly to appear before him on your way down, it could startle him, especially if he hasn't been aware that you were on him.

(c) Elephants do not like people sneaking on and off them.

IV

Try to decide in advance from which side you want to dismount, and then *stick to your decision!* If you put off making up your mind until the last possible minute or keep changing your plans, you may find yourself unable to decide at all and end up running around in a flurry of indecision. It is surprising how quickly any panic you feel can communicate itself to the elephant, who in turn may decide to go berserk.[1] But that's nothing compared with how quickly *his* panic can communicate itself to you.

Once you've settled on a point of debarkation, walk quietly and casually to the site you have chosen. By now the elephant will surely know something is up, even if he is not sure it is you. But if you have been following these rules diligently, the news should not rankle him.

V

Generally speaking, it's best to select one of the orthodox ways of dismounting—the Right Side Descent, the Prefrontal Slide, the Posterial Crawl, etc. Do *not* attempt anything fancy your first time down, such as swinging grandly from the elephant's ear ... and alighting with a springly little leap onto the ground. Even the experts can't carry off this sort of thing with much success. Running starts and other grandstand plays should similarly be eschewed.

VI

Miscellaneous Hints and Caveats

1. Wait until the elephant stops before dismounting. This is *not* a boxcar or a trolley you are dealing with, but a flesh-and-blood animal with hopes, fears, and ambitions not so very different from your own.

If the elephant happens to be sprinting at the time you decide to make your move, you'll especially want to wait for him to stop. For those of you to whom this would be an intolerable delay, at least wait until he slows down to a canter. This is no time to become impatient or hotheaded, even if you *have* whipped yourself into a frenzy of courage to prepare for the moment of truth. Besides, he won't run forever, so it won't be a long wait anyway. He's probably just remembered something he meant to do earlier.

2. Better yet, wait until he is asleep if you can hold out that long, the better to avoid any acrimonious confrontations. It's always politic to avoid showdowns of *any* kind with an elephant, but most particularly when the time and place are not of your own choosing.

---

[1] The elephant is very high-strung, a condition normally attributed to his deep-seated (but probably mistaken) feeling of inadequacy.

If you wait until dusk or later before starting your descent, the elephant isn't so likely to see you and take umbrage at your effrontery. However, you increase your chances of running into things and tipping him off that you're up to something. If you've never groped around at night on the back of an elephant, perhaps you shouldn't start now.

3. Do not leave anything behind, such as camera equipment, clothing, or magazines. These give the elephant a cluttered appearance, which he is likely to resent, and may also give him a clue to your present whereabouts, a fact you'll of course want to keep from him.

4. If he's one of those elephants who wear a lot of expensive jewelry and trappings, leave it all alone. It means the animal belongs to somebody, and you'll have enough trouble as it is trying to explain what you were doing up there, without being caught red-handed like a common second-story man.

5. Don't kick the elephant after you're down, or use similar crude techniques to vent your ill feelings on him. On the other hand, don't stop and chat with him in a fit of camaraderie, or chuck him affectionately under the tusks, or make a fuss about how glad you are to be down. Some elephants have very thin skins and are quick to detect a slur in the most harmless remarks. A waspish elephant is no laughing matter. If you *must* communicate with him, be sure to choose your words carefully, using pleasing gestures, and try to keep your tone of voice civil and well modulated. Above all, don't be condescending.

If you can manage all right now, I must be on my way.

CARRYING THE "HOW-TO" TOO FAR

Some people feel that writers have extended how-to articles to ridiculous extremes, that they threaten to run our lives, for writers seem to have provided us with instructions for every conceivable activity.

> How to eat, talk, breathe, sleep, cook with sour cream, play canasta, give a church supper, raise parakeets, and bet on the horses. How to be healthy, wealthy, wise, and happily married. How to become popular, articulate, refined, charming, virile, cultured, and couth. How to cope with children, sex, religion, old age, Christmas, in-laws, and other common problems of life. (Macdonald 361)

More disturbing how-to essays often distort difficult processes by depicting them in a rosy glow of simplicity ("there's nothing to it!"). Three actual titles establish this point clearly enough: "You Can Make a Stradivarius Violin," "The Art of Becoming an Original Writer in Three Days," and most grandiose, "How to Get Whatever You Want Out of Life." Most of us have read similar pieces that simplify the intricacies of real life. Take, for example, the following:

How to Stop Worrying

Dale Carnegie

Rule 1: Get the facts. Remember that Dean Hawks of Columbia University said that "half the worry in the world is caused by people trying to make decisions before they have sufficient knowledge on which to base a decision."

Rule 2: After carefully weighing all the facts, come to a decision.

Rule 3: Once a decision is carefully reached, act! Get busy carrying out your decision—and dismiss all anxiety about the outcome.

Rule 4: When you, or any of your associates, are tempted to worry about a problem, write out and answer the following questions:

  a. What is the problem?
  b. What is the cause of the problem?
  c. What are all possible solutions?
  d. What is the best solution?

There is probably nothing wrong with these suggestions as thumbnail guides for the average "worrywart." But in the face of the complexities of human nature and human predicaments, such guides are pathetically pat and superficial. Indeed, anyone who sincerely believes that he or she can solve the problem of worrying simply by following Dale Carnegie's four basic rules has in fact something to worry about!

DISCUSSION AND EXERCISES

1. To what extent do each of the "how-to" essays in this section fulfill the following principles of writing:

   a. accuracy (Are the facts correct? Indicate in what ways the writer may have oversimplified or overcomplicated a process.)
   b. clarity (Are the steps clearly presented?)
   c. economy (Are there any unnecessary words? Any irrelevant information?)
   d. rhetorical stance (To whom is the piece addressed? What is the writer's point of view? Tone? Purpose in writing the piece?)
   e. What special aspects of style such as the use of imperative voice and short sentences are especially useful in how-to's?

2. Consider Weissenborn's "How to Run for Office in a Very Small Town":

   a. How does the writer convey the impression of having first-hand knowledge of her subject?
   b. What is the effect of short sentences and the use of imperatives in the piece?
   c. Indicate touches of humor. What effect do they have?
   d. To what audience does the author direct this piece? What is the tone?
   e. Using a comparable tone, write a short set of instructions (200–250 words) for some simple process like how to iron a shirt, whittle a stick, apply mascara, serve a volleyball. Remember: each step should be cast in parallel imperatives (as in Weissenborn's progression: *find out, define, present, learn.*)

3. Read the following paragraph written by Benjamin Franklin in a letter to David Hume describing a technical process for which he was famous:

   > Secure to the big end of the rod a strong eye or a ring half an inch in diameter. Fix the rod upright to the chimney or the highest part of a house. It should be fixed with some sort of staples or special nails to keep it steady. The pointed end should extend upward, and should rise three or four feet above the chimney or building to which the rod is fixed. Drive into the ground an iron rod about one inch in diameter, and ten or twelve feet long. This rod should also have an eye or ring fixed to its upper end. It is best to place the iron rod some distance from the foundation of the house. Ten feet away is a good

distance, if the size of the property permits. Then take as much length of iron rod of a smaller diameter as will be necessary to reach from the eye on the rod above to the eye of the rod below. Fasten this securely to the fixed rods by passing it through the eyes and bending the ends to form rings too. Then close all the joints with lead. This is easily done by making a small bag of strong paper around the joints, tying it tight below, and then pouring in the molten lead. It is useful to have these joints treated in this way so that there will be a considerable area of contact between each piece. To prevent the wind from shaking this long rod, it may be fastened to the building by several staples. If the building is especially large or long, extending more than one hundred feet for example, it is wise to erect a rod at each end. If there is a well sufficiently near to the building to permit placing the iron rod in the water, this is even better than the use of the iron rod in the ground. It may also be wise to paint the iron to prevent it from rusting. A building so protected will not be damaged by lightning.

a. In what ways has Franklin made each step clear and distinct?
b. Comment on Franklin's choice of verbs, transitional devices, qualifications, and explanations.
c. Write a paragraph (150–250 words) comparable to Franklin's in which you explain to a friend how to make something. Suggestions:

a loudspeaker	a ceramic bowl
a bookcase	a decal
a tray	a blanket
a wax figure	a basket
a lamp	a bracelet
pickles (or any other food)	a string of beads
a sweater	a leather belt
a slipcover	a dress (or any other article of clothing)
a potholder	

4. Write a short self-help piece (150–250 words) in which you:

a. Offer concrete suggestions on how to treat the following physical ills:

high fever	hangover
cold	first-degree burn
frostbite	bee sting
poison ivy	dog bite
acne	muscle strain
athlete's foot	

b. Offer concrete, sensible, and restrained suggestions on how to deal with the following psychological problems:

attempts to stop smoking	anxiety
insomnia	fatigue
hysteria	guilt
shock	drug abuse
depression	

c. Offer sweepingly oversimplified advice on the problems listed above.
d. Give yourself ten minutes to "cluster" around the nucleus phrase "Let me tell you how to _____" (see pages 32–35).

5. Visualizing your "how-to" audience (see Part One, "Visualizing Your Audience," pages 40–44), write three paragraphs (250 words each) on a subject in which you have some level of expertise such as how to design a computer program, write a poem, prepare a quiche, restore a vintage Ford, or win at tennis (Be sure to use prewriting techniques):

   a. Address your first paragraph to your "peers"—people who "speak your language," or share your enthusiasm. Since you are "one with your audience," feel free to use terms and jokes outsiders would not understand.

   b. Address a second paragraph to a general audience of readers who may know little or nothing about your subject. Your purpose here is to get them interested and involved if possible. In this paragraph avoid technical terms and "in-jokes." Take nothing for granted. The cautionary approach to your audience bears repeating here: Never underestimate the intelligence of your readers, but never overestimate their intelligence either.

   c. Finally, in a third paragraph, speak to an audience of preschoolers, instructing them in language they can readily understand—in simple, basic terms, free of jargon, technicalities, embellishment. Avoid being patronizing or simplistic, however. As critic Northrop Frye (among others) has pointed out, the ability to explain your subject to a four- or five-year-old child is a test of your own grasp of the subject.

ESSAY SUGGESTIONS

1. Following the example of Weissenborn's "How to Run for Office" or Kaplan's "How to Lose Weight," write an essay (750–1,000 words) in which you present basic instructions for one of the following:

bird-watching	diving
folk dancing	hiking
tightrope walking	pitching horseshoes
hunting an alligator	mountain climbing
bicycle riding	kite flying
serving a tennisball	fishing
playing billiards	planning a picnic
planning a political rally	
planning a campus campaign	

   Where you think it will be helpful, clarify the process by using an appropriate topography. Use separate paragraphs for each step; first lines of each paragraph indented five spaces and numbered. Remember that topographical devices do not take the place of careful analysis —they merely clarify it; further clarification is achieved by maintaining parallel structures at each stage in the series: *fix, drive, fasten,* and *close* as Franklin tells us in his directions on making lightning rods. Use prewriting techniques to prepare for actual writing.

2. Write a set of instructions (500–750 words) for improving any skill, craft, art, or sport in which you are proficient.

3. Write a "how-to" essay (500–750 words) on a topic as compelling and instructive as "How to Dismount from an Elephant."

13. What Are the Causes of X?

THE PERENNIAL "WHY?"

*S*urely there is no more provocative question than the simple "Why?" Why is the sky dark at night? Why are we more or less intelligent? Why do we choose one way of life over another?

When asking "Why?" the writer is preparing to write a *causal analysis*—that is, seeking to locate and explain the causes for a given act, idea, feeling, condition, or event. As Aristotle pointed out, human beings are naturally curious; almost as soon as we begin to think, we begin to wonder "Why?" As early as the fifth century B.C. the Greek philosopher Leucippus said: "Nothing happens without a ground but everything through a cause and of necessity." Here, then, is the "principle of universal causation," believed to run through all things, confirming us in our impulse to ask "Why?"

THE FIRST PRINCIPLE OF CAUSATION: UNIFORMITY

Why, for instance, do natural events occur as they do—why the tides of the sea, why the movement of the planets, why the cycle of seasons? There will be little guesswork or speculation in answering these questions, for the course of nature is regarded as *uniform*: natural events proceed by natural, uniform law. Thus, under the same circumstances the same things will always happen in the same way. The leaves fall from the trees every autumn, and the first leaf and the last fall for the same reasons as all the billions of leaves in between.

We refer, then, to the "law of causation," which establishes that two events (X and Y) are so closely and unconditionally connected that one *cannot* occur without the other. That is, Y can take place only if X has previously occurred; if X occurs, then Y necessarily and inevitably follows. In such an instance we say that X is the cause of Y.

In writing about natural events, your first responsibility is to familiarize yourself fully with the uniform laws that govern the event in question. Firmly in command of this information, you can then explain the event clearly and engagingly so that the reader can understand and enjoy the explanation, even if it is necessarily complicated—as many scientific explanations are. Certainly the writer of the following essay (not a scientist but a journalist) has managed to render an extraordinarily vivid account of a complicated natural process. Because the material is inherently complicated, however, you may find that you need to read it more than once, moving slowly from point to point. Note that the writer himself encourages this kind of reading by dividing his paragraphs into relatively short, easy-to-encompass units.

Why Is the Sky Dark at Night?

Bruce Bliven

Since the childhood of our race, mankind has accepted the darkness of the nighttime sky as an unquestioned commonplace fact of life on earth. The sun rises each morning, bringing with it daylight. When the sun sets, the one major source of light is gone. Hence the sky can no longer be bright. So have reasoned generation upon generation of men—but their reasoning overlooked something.

The first man who seems to have thought deeply about this phenomenon was a German physician, Heinrich W. M. Olbers, who lived in Bremen and who, in 1826, set out to produce a scientific and mathematical answer to the question: *Why is the world dark at night?*

Dr. Olbers had a lifelong passion for astronomy. Even during the years when he was practicing medicine he spent the greater part of each night in his homemade observatory on top of his house, studying the heavens. He located the comet of 1815, which was named for him; he took part in the rediscovery of Ceres and discovered Pallas and Vesta—three tiny planets that circle the sun. But his greatest achievement was to ask this seemingly obvious question.

The sun, Olbers figured, provides only about half the light we on earth should theoretically be receiving; the other half should come from the billions of stars in the heavens. With all that starlight, why is midnight not as bright as day?

Dr. Olbers would have been even more puzzled had he had today's knowledge of the incredible vastness of the universe, the uncounted billions of light-giving stars in the depths of space. Our sun and its planets are only a microscopic part of the Milky Way, an average-size galaxy containing 100 billion stars—which are on the average as bright as our sun. And the Milky Way itself is only one of a seemingly limitless number of galaxies. Radio telescopes can now "hear" several billion light-years out into space; and however far they penetrate, in every direction, the galaxies continue to appear.

The number of the stars is, in fact, far beyond the power of the mind to grasp; yet so great is space that it is sparsely populated.

Though he was aware of only a small part of the stellar universe, the total number of stars known to Dr. Olbers was yet huge indeed. Taking into account their numbers, brightness and distance, making painstaking calculations, he came to an amazing conclusion: with light streaming from so many stars, the sky should *not* be dark at night. The earth even at midnight should be blazing with light and heat. It should, in fact, be frying.

How did he figure this? Suppose, said Dr. Olbers, you think of the universe as a vast hollow ball studded with stars and trillions of miles in diameter, with the earth at its center. Light will reach the earth from a multitude of stars; and while the rays from those far away will be very faint, this will be offset because the farther out you go, the greater the number of stars. In fact, the number of stars increases much faster than the distance (just as the volume of a sphere increases in proportion to its radius). Thus the weakening of the light at greater distances is *more than offset* by the greater number of stars there are when such distances are taken into account. No matter how weak the effect of any one star, therefore, if the number is large enough and the elapsed time long enough, the planet at the center should be ablaze with light and heat.

Why is this not so? Why then *is* the sky dark at night? The good doctor thought that interstellar fog must absorb almost all the starlight. But other astronomers were not satisfied that this was a sufficient explanation, and the question became famous as "Olbers' paradox."

For 100 years astronomers tried to solve the paradox. A clue came only 16 years after Olbers had raised the question, but nobody at the time recognized its relevance.

In 1842, an Austrian professor of mathematics, Christian Doppler, discovered what has ever after been known as the Doppler effect. Stand by a railroad track; as a train comes toward you the pitch of its whistle sounds high, but after it has passed, the whistle sounds lower. Doppler found the clue. As the train approaches, the sound waves it sends toward you seem, to you, shortened or "crowded"—and since short-wave sounds are higher pitched, the whistle sounds higher. Conversely, when the train speeds *away* from you, the sound waves must travel a greater distance; so they seem to you to be farther apart and therefore sound lower.

The Doppler effect applies to light waves, too. Light waves appear to the eye as longer when they come from an object moving away from us; they seem shorter and "crowded" if the object is approaching us.

With light the effect shows up in color. Light waves are longer (and weaker) at the red end of the color spectrum, shorter at the violet end. So light waves from a source that is moving away tend to be shifted down the spectrum toward the red end, a phenomenon called the "Red Shift." Thus astronomers came to realize that a slight redness in the light coming from a celestial body means that it is moving away from the observer.

Among those in this century who pondered Olbers' paradox, knowing there *must* be an answer to it, was Dr. Edwin P. Hubble of California's Mount Wilson Observatory. In 1924, with the superior instruments available, Dr. Hubble found that light from distant sources, from distant galaxies outside the Milky Way, showed the Red Shift. This, he reasoned, could only mean that their light waves were being stretched out—hence these stars, these whole galaxies of stars, must be traveling away from us at tremendous speed.

Could it be? Hubble continued to watch the sky, and the evidence mounted that this was so. He found that the farther out he looked, the redder was the light that his telescope picked up. In fact, he saw, the galaxies were escaping from us with speeds that increased in a mathematically precise manner with their distance.

Hubble concluded that the whole universe is expanding—everything in it is moving farther and farther apart from everything else. Other observers confirmed his theory, and "the expanding universe" became the fundamental, though almost unbelievable, discovery of modern astronomy.

With this discovery Dr. Olbers' question at last was answered. *The sky is dark at night because the universe expands*! The galaxies are moving away from us so fast as to weaken the radiation we receive from them. This is what gives us our restful nocturnal darkness, and also saves us from being vaporized in the never-ending shower of hot starlight. Were it not for this fact, life on earth would not be possible.

Note that in this essay the author explains the phenomenon of the dark sky as the necessary result of the Doppler effect, the Red Shift, and, underlying both, the expanding universe. It is possible, of course, to extend the principle of uniformity beyond scientific causal analysis. Thus, even in everyday reasoning, we tend to search for a principle of uniformity: "Why did Johnny break his truck?" "Because he was tired." Generalization (principle of uniformity): "Tired children tend to break their toys."

THE SECOND PRINCIPLE OF CAUSATION: SUFFICIENCY

Cause-and-effect sequences are of several types.

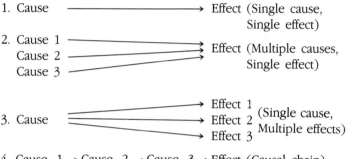

1. Cause ⟶ Effect (Single cause, Single effect)

2. Cause 1 ⟶ Cause 2 ⟶ Effect (Multiple causes, Cause 3 ⟶ Single effect)

3. Cause ⟶ Effect 1 (Single cause, ⟶ Effect 2 Multiple effects) ⟶ Effect 3

4. Cause 1 → Cause 2 → Cause 3 → Effect (Causal chain)

The following essay, drawn from an award-winning study by two university psychologists, explains the several reasons why bystanders often ignore a crime victim's cries for help. We read horrifying accounts, such as the classic story of Kitty Genovese, murdered in her apartment while thirty-eight of her neighbors heard her cries but failed to do anything, not even call the police. "How could they have been so indifferent, so heartless, so inhuman?" we wonder, condemning them as monsters, not at all like the rest of us.

The authors of this study show that such a view is not supportable. First they pose the question: What factors cause us to reach out a helping hand and what factors cause us to turn the other way? Their answers are based not on theory or speculation but rather on systematic and scientifically controlled experiments. People who witness a crime, they discovered, will intervene only under three specific conditions; if these conditions are not met, they will not intervene. No one condition or cause is sufficient in and of itself to account for the refusal to intervene, the investigators concluded. The situation is more complex than it seems on the surface. In any case, the stereotype of the unconcerned, depersonalized *homo urbanus* (urban man) blandly watching the misfortunes of others is demonstrably inaccurate; an unjustified, unsupported slur on human nature.

Unresponsive Bystanders: Why Don't They Help?

John M. Darley and Bibb Latané

Introduction   Kitty Genovese is set upon by a maniac as she returns home from work at 3:00 a.m. Thirty-eight of her neighbors in Kew Gardens come to their windows when she cries out in terror; none come to her assistance even though her stalker takes over half an hour to murder her. No one even as much as calls the police. She dies.

Short illustrations of indifferent bystanders

Andrew Mormille is stabbed in the stomach as he rides the A train home to Manhattan. Eleven other riders watch the 17-year-old boy as he bleeds to death; none come to his assistance even though his attackers have left the car. He dies....

Eleanor Bradley trips and breaks her leg while shopping on Fifth Avenue. Dazed and in shock, she calls for help, but the hurrying stream of executives and shoppers simply parts and flows past. After 40 minutes a taxi driver helps her to a doctor.

Question— Why don't bystanders help?—in statement form

The shocking thing about these cases is that so many people failed to respond....Although it seems obvious that the more people who watch a victim in distress, the more likely someone will help, what really happens is exactly the opposite. If each member of a group of bystanders is aware that other people are also present, he will be less likely to notice the emergency, less likely to decide that it is an emergency, and less likely to act even if he thinks there is an emergency....

Background: earlier causal explanations unsatisfactory

Since we started research on bystander responses to emergencies, we have heard many explanations for the lack of intervention. "I would assign this to the effect of the megapolis in which we live, which makes closeness very difficult and leads to the alienation of the individual from the group," contributed a psychoanalyst. "A disaster syndrome," explained a sociologist, "that shook the sense of safety and sureness of the individuals involved and caused psychological withdrawal from the event by ignoring it." "Apathy," claimed others. "Indifference...."

Why they are unsatisfactory

All of these analyses of the person who fails to help share one characteristic: they set the indifferent witness apart from the rest of us as a different kind of person. Certainly not one of us who reads about these incidents in horror is apathetic, alienated or depersonalized. Certainly not one of us enjoys gratifying his sadistic impulses by watching others suffer. These terrifying cases in which people fail to help others certainly have no personal implications for us. That is, we might decide not to ride subways any more, or that New York isn't even "a nice place to visit," or "there ought to be a law" against apathy, but we needn't feel guilty, or re-examine ourselves, or anything like that.

Looking more closely at published descriptions of the behavior of witnesses to these incidents, the people involved begin to look a little less inhuman and a lot more like the rest of us. Although it is unquestionably true that the witnesses in the incidents above did nothing to save the victims, apathy, indifference and unconcern are not entirely accurate descriptions of their reactions. The 38 witnesses of Kitty Genovese's murder did not merely look at the scene once and then ignore it. They continued to stare out of their windows at what was going on. Caught, fascinated, distressed, unwilling to act but unable to turn away, their behavior was neither helpful nor heroic; but it was not indifferent or apathetic.

The problem stated in a question

Actually, it was like crowd behavior in many other emergency situations. Car accidents, drownings, fires and attempted suicides all attract substantial numbers of people who watch the drama in helpless fascination without getting directly involved in the action. Are these people alienated and indifferent? Are the rest of us? Obviously not. Why, then, don't we act?

Thesis: Three
conditions:
What bystander
must do if he is
to intervene

The bystander to an emergency has to make a series of decisions about
what is happening and what he will do about it. The consequences of these
decisions will determine his actions. There are three things he must do if he is
to intervene: *notice* that something is happening, *interpret* that event as an
emergency, and decide that he has *personal responsibility* for intervention. If
he fails to notice the event, if he decides that it is not an emergency, or if he
concludes that he is not personally responsible for acting, he will leave the
victim unhelped. This state of affairs is shown graphically as a "decision tree."
Only one path through this decision tree leads to intervention; all others lead
to a failure to help. As we shall show, at each fork of the path in the decision
tree, the presence of other bystanders may lead a person down the branch of
not helping.

First condition:
bystander
must notice
something is
happening

Suppose that an emergency is actually taking place; a middle-aged man has
a heart attack. He stops short, clutches his chest, and staggers to the nearest
building wall, where he slowly slumps to the sidewalk in a sitting position.
What is the likelihood that a passerby will come to his assistance? First, the
bystander has to *notice* that something is happening. The external event has to
break into his thinking and intrude itself on his conscious mind. He must tear
himself away from his private thoughts and pay attention to this unusual event.

But Americans consider it bad manners to look too closely at other people
in public. We are taught to respect the privacy of others, and when among
strangers, we do this by closing our ears and avoiding staring at others—we
are embarrassed if caught doing otherwise. In a crowd, then, each person is
less likely to notice the first sign of a potential emergency than when alone.

Experimental evidence corroborates this everyday observation. Darley and
Latané asked college students to an interview about their reactions to urban
living. As the students waited to see the interviewer, either by themselves or
with two other students, they filled out a preliminary questionnaire. Solitary
students often glanced idly about the room while filling out their question-
naires; those in groups, to avoid seeming rudely inquisitive, kept their eyes on
their own papers.

As part of the study, we staged an emergency: smoke was released into the
waiting room through a vent. Two-thirds of the subjects who were alone when
the smoke appeared noticed it immediately, but only a quarter of the subjects
waiting in groups saw it as quickly. Even after the room had completely filled
with smoke one subject from a group of three finally looked up and
exclaimed, "God! I must be smoking too much!" Although eventually all the
subjects did become aware of the smoke, this study indicates that the more
people present, the slower an individual may be to perceive that an
emergency does exist and the more likely he is not to see it at all.

Second condi-
tion: bystander
must see an
event as an
emergency

Once an event is noticed, an onlooker must decide whether or not it is
truly an emergency. Emergencies are not always clearly labeled as such;
smoke pouring from a building or into a waiting room may be caused by a
fire, or it may merely indicate a leak in a steam pipe. Screams in the street may
signal an assault or a family quarrel. A man lying in a doorway may not be
having a coronary or be suffering from diabetic coma—he may simply
be sleeping off a drunk. And in any unusual situation, Candid Camera may be
watching.

A person trying to decide whether or not a given situation is an emergency
often refers to the reactions of those around him; he looks at them to see how

he should react himself. If everyone else is calm and indifferent, he will tend to remain calm and indifferent; if everyone else is reacting strongly, he will become aroused. This tendency is not merely slavish conformity; ordinarily we derive much valuable information about new situations from how others around us behave....

In a potentially dangerous situation, then, everyone present will appear more unconcerned than they are in fact. Looking at the *apparent* impassivity and lack of reaction of the others, each person is led to believe that nothing really is wrong. Meanwhile the danger may be mounting, to the point where a single person, uninfluenced by the seeming calm of others, would react.

A crowd can thus force inaction on its members by implying, through its passivity and apparent indifference, that an event is not an emergency. Any individual in such a crowd is uncomfortably aware that he'll look like a fool if he behaves as though it were—and in these circumstances, until someone acts, no one acts.

In the smoke-filled room study, the smoke trickling from the wall constituted an ambiguous but potentially dangerous situation. How did the presence of other people affect a person's response to the situation? Typically, those who were in the waiting room by themselves noticed the smoke at once, gave a slight startled reaction, hesitated, got up and went over to investigate the smoke, hesitated again, and then left the room to find somebody to tell about the smoke. No one showed any signs of panic, but over three-quarters of these people were concerned enough to report the smoke.

Others went through an identical experience but in groups of three strangers. Their behavior was radically different. Typically, once someone noticed the smoke, he would look at the other people, see them doing nothing, shrug his shoulders, and then go back to his questionnaire, casting covert glances first at the smoke and then at the others. From these three-person groups, only three out of 24 people reported the smoke. The inhibiting effect of the group was so strong that the other 21 were willing to sit in a room filled with smoke rather than make themselves conspicuous by reacting with alarm and concern—this despite the fact that after three or four minutes the atmosphere in the waiting room grew most unpleasant. Even though they coughed, rubbed their eyes, tried to wave the smoke away, and opened the window, they apparently were unable to bring themselves to leave.

These dramatic differences between the behavior of people alone and those in a group indicate that the group imposed a definition of the situation upon its members which inhibited action....

Third condition: bystander must decide he has personal responsibility

Even if a person has noticed an event and defined it as an emergency, the fact that he knows that other bystanders also witnessed it may still make him less likely to intervene....

If your car breaks down on a busy highway, hundreds of drivers whiz by without anyone's stopping to help; if you are stuck on a nearly deserted country road, whoever passes you first is apt to stop. The personal responsibility that a passerby feels makes the difference. A driver on a lonely road knows that if he doesn't stop to help, the person will not get help; the same individual on the crowded highway feels he personally is no more responsible than any of a hundred other drivers. So even though an event clearly is an emergency, any person in a group who sees an emergency may feel less responsible, simply because any other bystander is equally responsible for helping.

This diffusion of responsibility might have occurred in the famous Kitty Genovese case, in which the observers were walled off from each other in separate apartments. From the silhouettes against windows, all that could be told was that others were also watching.

To test this line of thought, Darley and Latané simulated an emergency in a setting designed to resemble Kitty Genovese's murder. People overheard a victim calling for help. Some knew they were the only one to hear the victim's cries, the rest believed other people were aware of the victim's distress. As with the Genovese witnesses, subjects could not see each other or know what others were doing. The kind of direct group inhibition found in the smoke and fallen-woman studies could not operate.

For the simulation, we recruited male and female students at New York University to participate in a group discussion. Each student was put in an individual room equipped with a set of headphones and a microphone and told to listen for instructions over the headphones. The instructions informed the participant that the discussion was to consider personal problems of the normal college student in a high-pressure urban university. It was explained that, because participants might feel embarrassed about discussing personal problems publicly, several precautions had been taken to insure their anonymity: they would not meet the other people face to face, and the experimenter would not listen to the initial discussion but would only ask for their reactions later. Each person was to talk in turn. The first to talk reported that he found it difficult to adjust to New York and his studies. Then, very hesitantly and with obvious embarrassment, he mentioned that he was prone to nervous seizures, similar to but not really the same as epilepsy. These occurred particularly when he was under the stresses of studying and being graded.

Other people then discussed their own problems in turn. The number of other people in the discussion varied. But whatever the perceived size of the group—two, three or six people—only the subject was actually present; the others, as well as the instructions and the speeches of the victim-to-be, were present only on a pre-recorded tape.

When it again was the first person's turn to talk, after a few comments he launched into the following performance, getting increasingly louder with increasing speech difficulties:

"I can see a lot of er of er how other people's problems are similar to mine because er er I mean er it's er I mean some of the er same er kinds of things that I have and an er I'm sure that every everbody has and er er I mean er they're not er e-easy to handle sometimes and er I er er be upsetting like er er and er I er um I think I I need er if if could er er somebody er er er er er give me give me a little er give me a little help here because er I er I'm er h-h-having a a a a a real problem er right now and I er if somebody could help me out it would it would er er s-s-sure be sure be good be ... because er there er er a cause I er *uh* I've got a a one of the er seiz—er er things coming *on* and and and I c-could really er use er some h-help s-so if somebody would er give me a little h-help uh er-er-er-er-er c-could somebody er er help er uh uh uh (choking sounds)... I'm gonna die er er I'm... gonna...die er help er er seizure er er..." (chokes, then quiet).

While this was going on, the experimenter waited outside the student's door to see how soon he would emerge to cope with the emergency. Rather to our surprise, some people sat through the entire fit without helping; a disproportionately large percentage of these nonresponders were from the largest-size group. Eighty-five per cent of the people who believed themselves to be alone with the victim came out of their rooms to help, while 62 per cent of the people who believed there was one other bystander did so. Of those who believed there were four other bystanders, only 31 per cent reported the fit before the tape ended. The responsibility-diluting effect of other people was so strong that single individuals were more than twice as likely to report the emergency as those who thought other people also knew about it.

People who failed to report the emergency showed few signs of apathy and indifference thought to characterize "unresponsive bystanders." When the experimenter entered the room to end the situation, the subject often asked if the victim was "all right." Many of these people showed physical signs of nervousness; they often had trembling hands and sweating palms....

Why, then, didn't they respond? It is our impression that nonintervening subjects had not decided *not* to respond. Rather, they were still in a state of indecision and conflict concerning whether to respond or not. The emotional behavior of these nonresponding subjects was a sign of their continuing conflict; a conflict that other people resolved by responding. The distinction seems an academic one for the victim, since he gets no help in either case, but it is an extremely important one for arriving at an understanding of why bystanders fail to help....

Thus, the stereotype of the unconcerned depersonalized *homo urbanis*, blandly watching the misfortunes of others, proves inaccurate. Instead, we find a bystander to an emergency is an anguished individual in genuine doubt, concerned to do the right thing but compelled to make complex decisions under pressure of stress and fear. His reactions are shaped by the actions of others—and all too frequently by their inaction.

And we are that bystander. Caught up by the apparent indifference of others, we may pass by an emergency without helping or even realizing that help is needed. Aware of the influence of those around us, however, we can resist it. We can choose to see distress and step forward to relieve it.

*Side notes (left margin):*

Conclusion: Bystanders do not show apathy and indifference

The stereotype of indifferent bystander is inaccurate; bystander is actually "an anguished individual in genuine doubt"

In establishing causal connections, the writer must think carefully and rigorously, recognizing that it is easy to fall into such common fallacies as *post hoc ergo propter hoc* (after this, therefore because of this). Only to the simple mind (or the mind intent on deceiving) is any event that follows another necessarily the *result* of it. Thus, as Mark Twain once pointed out in a humorous *post hoc* application: "I joined the Confederacy for two weeks. Then I deserted. The Confederacy fell."

Most superstitions grow out of this fallacy: "A black cat crossed my path. Later that day I twisted my ankle. The black cat *caused* my twisted ankle. Black cats are therefore unlucky." And: "John eats a lot of fish. John is smart. Eating fish is good for the brain."

The writer who wishes to be taken seriously must guard against superstitious, oversimplified cause-and-effect connections. The first question a critical mind addresses to an assertion of causal relationship should be: "Was the supposed cause *sufficient* to produce the given effect?" Obviously a black cat cannot be sufficient cause for a twisted ankle, fish cannot stimulate the brain, and a four-leaf clover cannot bring luck. In each case the stated cause, however colorful, is *insufficient* to produce the given effect.

CAUSE AND CONDITION

Thus, as a careful thinker and writer, you must make certain that you consider *all* possible causes for any given event. You must recognize not only that there *can* be more than one cause behind any given situation (war, recession, racial unrest), but that there usually *is*, that the world of events is rarely characterized by

$$\text{Single Cause} \rightarrow \text{Single Effect.}$$

More than that, you must be aware that for every individual effect, you must also take into account countless conditions if your causal explanation is to be reasonably accurate and complete. Let us say that the direct cause of my answering the telephone is that it rings:

$$\underset{\text{(telephone ringing)}}{\text{Cause}} \xrightarrow{\hspace{3cm}} \underset{\text{(I answer the telephone)}}{\text{Effect}}$$

You could view this event in this linear manner; It is accurate, but only roughly. In actual fact, countless conditions enter into this situation that enable it to occur: The telephone is in good repair (each small part is working); my ears are "attuned" (here again, each small part is working); I am within hearing distance (I might have stepped outside for a moment). And so on. If any one of these numerous small conditions had not held to its exact course at the precise moment the telephone rang, I would not have answered it: The given effect would *not* have followed the supposed cause.

With this in mind, we can look back to Bliven's essay on nighttime darkness and note that many conditions had to remain equal and constant in order for the law of causation to operate in its ordinary manner. Of course the sun rises each morning, as he states—but only if no untoward occurrences take place in the solar system that throw the entire causal chain out of gear.

The careful thinker and writer, then, will take into account not only the basic *causes* of a given effect, but the surrounding *conditions* as well.

EXPLAINING REASONS

The writer of the following article was a junior at Brown University when he wrote this "causal explanation" of why students "stop out" (rather than "drop out") for a year or two during their college careers. Although he himself did not take a sabbatical, he did investigate thoroughly the reasons why many of his classmates chose to do so: to travel, to work, to think, to—in effect—restore their souls.

The organization of this article rests on categories of evidence the writer obtained from such sources as personal interviews with students, deans of colleges, administrators, and "job banks." He has succeeded in weaving many strands of information and explanation into a clear, coherent whole, an article with an obvious purpose: to explain a "common practice" on the contemporary college scene.

Why College Students Take a 'Sabbatical'

Hilary Stout

Salil Mehta, an undergraduate at Brown University, doesn't know whether he wants to be a doctor or a lawyer, so for the last two years he has sampled courses in political science and biology. This fall he is in Washington, interning for a Congressman and doing volunteer work for a public defender; next spring he plans to be somewhere else, working in a hospital, after which he expects to be sitting in Brown classrooms again—this time with a major and a goal.

Kevin White, a junior at the University of Pennsylvania's Wharton School, is having a hard time meeting Penn's $12,000 yearly cost. Next January, while continuing to live in his fraternity at school, he will stop taking classes for a semester and get a job. And because of advanced credits awarded when he entered college, he will still graduate with his class next June.

One day last September, Stuart Handlesman was sitting in the University of Vermont's Bailey-Howe Library feeling restless, confused and bored. "This is ridiculous," he said to himself and withdrew from school to travel and work for a year. This September he was back in the library with a new sense of purpose, he said, studying political science and art history.

According to administrators and students throughout the country, taking a leave from college to work, think and pursue something other than academics has become a common practice. The students have even coined a name for it—"stopping out"—to distinguish it from dropping out.

Half of all Stanford undergraduates "stop out" during their college careers, making the average period for degree completion five years. The assistant director of career services at Wesleyan University, Suzanne Kiar-Tuttle, said that 30 to 40 percent of the student body took a leave at some point, and Haverford's president of student services and administration, David Potter, estimated that a quarter to a third of all Haverford students did so.

"The nature of the times makes stopping out more likely," said George Clever, a dean and student adviser at Stanford.

Had Mr. Mehta, Mr. White and Mr. Handlesman been students 15 to 20 years ago, they probably would have plodded through college in four years like the rest of their classmates. Fear of the draft kept young men in school; lower tuition and abundant Government grants minimized financial hardship; a stable job market made career concerns less pressing, and when students left college it was generally assumed they wouldn't come back.

"Today's leave-takers are very different students," said Katherine Hall, associate dean of the college at Brown. "They don't drop out." According to a report prepared by deans at Brown, only 70 percent of recent classes graduated in four years. An average of 95 percent of all stop-outs return to school.

"I knew there was no way I was going to walk out of this place without a degree," said Dean Rapoza, who is now completing his senior year at Brown after having spent a year working at several part-time hospital jobs.

Uncertainty about a major or a career, academic exhaustion and general malaise are the reasons most often cited by students for stopping out. "I experienced senior panic a year early," said Jacquelyn Clymore, a student at Vassar who spent last semester as a writer for a New York City advertising agency. "It wasn't academic burnout. I just wasn't sure where I was going to go and what I was going to do after college."

And Peggy Willens, a senior at Wesleyan who worked for six weeks in a health-food store last winter, then spent the rest of her semester off teaching fifth-graders about nature and the environment, explained, "It was the big old question: 'What am I doing here?'"

Stanford's Dean Clever said that sometimes athletes and musicians took a leave from school to develop their talents. Others, he said, take time off to pursue cultural interests, such as returning to the country of their origin.

Few of today's leave-takers, however, seem to be wandering aimlessly in the manner of the 1960's. "The leave to surf is almost nonexistent," said Stanford's Dean Clever. "Most students who decide to stop out have thought about it very thoroughly." In fact, the advice most often given by former stop-outs seems to be: "Know what you want to do with your time."

What most are doing is working—at jobs, in internships or in volunteer positions. A stack of "Re-admit Surveys" of 1981–82 stop-outs at Brown shows students working as anything from waitresses, mother's helpers and department-store clerks to surgeon's technicians, staff members in political campaigns and counselors for emotionally disturbed children.

"The majority do go out and work—to earn money, and gain practical experience," said Jeff Ashby, adviser in the division of undergraduate studies at Pennsylvania State University.

Dean Clever believes the opportunities for undergraduates stopping out are growing. "The number of internships available is expanding," he said. "A lot of people are seriously working to provide undergraduates with opportunities for experience."

Both Miss Clymore and Miss Willens found their jobs through the College Venture Program, founded in 1974 for the purpose of placing students on leave in jobs or internships. About 200 students at the 10 colleges that make up the College Venture consortium—Bates, Brown, Colby, the University of Chicago, Oberlin, Skidmore, Wesleyan, Northwestern, William and Mary and Vassar—obtain employment through the organization each year, according to Susan Stroud, the director.

More than 400 annually consult Venture's "job bank," which lists a vast array of temporary jobs including teaching posts in Zimbabwe, apprenticeships to graphic designers and positions with the National Coalition to Ban Handguns. "We will work with students with any interest at trying to develop any job," Miss Stroud said.

In general, colleges are supportive of stop-outs these days. Several departments at Penn State strongly encourage students to take a break from studies to gain related experience. Brown holds a party at the start of each academic year to welcome returning stop-outs. Nearly every college offers a period, usually between one and three years, during which a student can leave school and be accepted back automatically.

Stopping out "is a perfectly normal and reasonable part of some students' development," said Haverford's Dean Potter. And Mrs. Hall of Brown added: "It is a very positive experience. I have never seen a person harmed by a year away."

According to Mrs. Hall, parents are also more accepting than they used to be to proposals by their son or daughter that he or she leave school for a time. "The more it is done, the less anxiety you see from parents," she said.

Students' verdicts on stopping out are overwhelmingly positive. Preliminary findings of a survey of stop-outs from the schools in the Venture consortium show that 29 percent think their leaves exceeded their highest hopes, and 62 percent say their time off was fully justified.

"It was a phenomenal year," said one student who worked for Ralph Nader. "Now I'm definitely a lot calmer about going out into the world."

Miss Clymore, who wrote copy for the advertising agency, said that as a result, "I'm hoping to go into advertising." And Miss Willens, who worked in the health-food store and taught children about nature, declared: "I have a better idea now of why I'm at Wesleyan."

Some students and administrators fear that the hard financial times and uncertain job market will begin to have the opposite effect on students considering leaves. "The pressure to get through and get a job may be increasing," said Miss Stroud. And with tuition rising 10 to 15 percent each year, Mrs. Hall predicts, "Students will feel they can't afford to stop out." But for now, students still seem to be following the advice so often given by former stop-outs in Brown's Re-admit Survey: "Do it!"

PRESENTING PERSONAL REASONS

In a still more subjective type of causal analysis the writer tries to explain why he or she has felt or acted a certain way. In this case the causes are *personal* and therefore cannot be evaluated objectively as accurate or inaccurate but rather as sincere or insincere, convincing or unconvincing, logically consistent or inconsistent, and reasonable or unreasonable in terms of themselves. Thus Simone de Beauvoir explains her reasons for becoming a writer.

Why I Decided to Be a Writer

Simone de Beauvoir

Why did I decide to be a writer? As a child, I had never taken my scribblings very seriously; my real aim had been to acquire knowledge; I enjoyed doing French compositions, but my teachers objected to my stilted style; I did not feel I was a "born" writer. Yet at the age of fifteen when I wrote in a friend's album the plans and preferences which were supposed to give a picture of my personality, I answered without hesitation the question "What do you want to do later in life?" with "To be a famous author." As far as my favorite composer and my favorite flower were concerned I had invented more or less factitious preferences. But on that one point I had no doubts at all: I had set my heart on that profession, to the exclusion of everything else.

The main reason for this was the admiration I felt for writers: my father rated them far higher than scholars, philosophers, and professors. I, too, was convinced of their supremacy: even if his name was well-known, a specialist's monograph would be accessible to only a small number of people; but everyone reads novels: they touched the imagination and the heart; they brought their authors universal and intimate fame. As a woman, these dizzy summits seemed to me much more accessible than the lowlier slopes; the most celebrated women had distinguished themselves in literature.

I had always had a longing to communicate with others. In my friend's album I cited as my favorite hobbies reading and conversation. I was a great talker. I would recount, or try to, everything that had struck me in the course of the day. I dreaded night and oblivion; it was agony to condemn to silence all that I had seen, felt, and liked. Moved by the moonlight, I longed for pen and paper and the ability to describe my feelings. When I was fifteen I loved volumes of letters, intimate journals—for example, the diary of Eugénie de Guérin—books that attempted to make time stand still. I had also realized that novels, short stories, and tales were not divorced from life but that they are, in their own way, expressions of it.

If at one time I had dreamed of being a teacher it was because I wanted to be a law unto myself; I now thought that literature would allow me to realize this dream. It would guarantee me an immortality that would compensate for the loss of heaven and eternity; there no longer was a God to love me, but I would burn as a beacon in millions of hearts. By writing a work based on my own experience I would re-create myself and justify my existence. At the same time I would be serving humanity: what finer offering could I make to it than books? I was concerned at the same time with myself and with others; I accepted the individuality of my "incarnation," but I did not wish to surrender membership in the universal. This writing project reconciled everything; it gratified all the aspirations which had been unfolding in me during the past fifteen years.

DISCUSSION AND EXERCISES

1. Answer the following questions based on Darley and Latane's essay "The Unresponsive Bystander: Why Doesn't He Help?"

   a. What reasons do psychologists and others offer to explain the apparent apathy of those witnessing others in distress?

   b. What are the three things bystanders must do if they are to intervene in an emergency?

   c. How does the presence of other people affect a person's interpretation of an emergency?

   d. Why is a person who is alone (rather than in a crowd) more likely to help someone?

   e. What have studies proved about the apathy of so-called "unresponsive bystanders"?

   f. Under what circumstances can you imagine yourself willing or unwilling to help in an emergency? Explain.

   g. Has it ever been your experience that being in a crowd defuses your sense of responsibility? Explain.

   h. Give yourself ten minutes to cluster around the nucleus term "Help!" (see pages 32–35).

2. Consider Hilary Stout's article, "Why College Students Take a Sabbatical"; then answer the following questions:

   a. If you were to "stop out" at some future date, how would you spend your time away from school?

   b. Do you feel that "stopping out" is a valuable practice? Why or why not? How does it differ from "dropping out"?

   c. Why was "stopping out" virtually unheard of fifteen to twenty years ago?

d. What reasons do students give for stopping out today?

e. How does your college regard stop-outs?

3. Examine each of the paragraphs in de Beauvoir's essay, "Why I Decided to Be a Writer." Note topic sentence, method of development, ordering principle, coordinate and subordinate sequences (see pages 121–26), transitional devices, tone, and point of view. Also note sentence construction: subordination and coordination, use of semicolons and commas.

4. Study Edvard Munch's *The Cry*, and try to imagine or infer the causes of the "cry." Write a one-paragraph explanation (150–200 words) in coordinate sequence (see pages 121–23).

Edvard Munch, *The Cry* (1895).
National Gallery of Art, Washington, D.C.
Rosenwald collection.

5. Study the following picture, noting the man, the placards, the setting (a New York street corner), and speculate on the causes of his present state (150–250 words.)

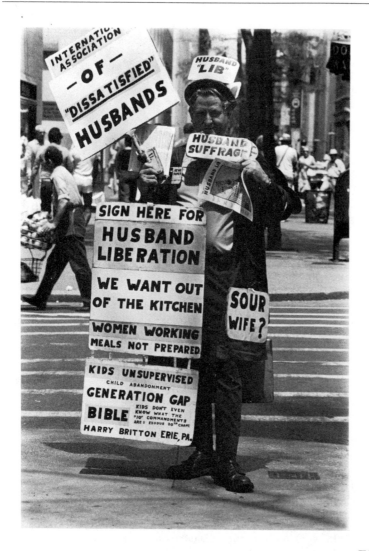

ESSAY SUGGESTIONS

1. Write an essay (750–1,000 words) indicating the main causes for any one of the following:
   (Be sure to use the prewriting techniques you have learned.)

   a. Natural phenomena

   > green grass
   > rain
   > blue sky
   > white clouds
   > appearance of stars at night
   > revolution of the earth around the sun
   > sunrise
   > sunset
   > movement of the tides

b. Biological-psychological conditions

Disorders

headaches	hay fever
arteriosclerosis	stuttering
high blood pressure	schizophrenia
diabetes	suicide
cirrhosis	aphasia
epilepsy	amnesia
hiccoughing	

Accidents

automobile accidents
home accidents
fires
airplane crashes
mining accidents

c. Architecture

the construction of one of the Seven Wonders of the World
the construction of cathedrals (or one particular cathedral) in the Middle Ages
the popularity of prefabricated houses
the evolution of the skyscraper in the United States
the belief that Frank Lloyd Wright was a great architect

2. Write an essay (500–750 words) correcting the causal fallacies at the root of the medical superstitions listed below; in other words, cite the *facts* behind the superstition:

Night air is unhealthy.
Fish is brain food.
Insanity is inherited.
Green apples cause a stomach ache.
Children born of cousins will be defective or deformed.
Frogs and toads cause warts.
Feed a cold, starve a fever.

3. Write an essay (500–750 words) in which you explain the causal implications in arguing for or against one of the following:

a. Law

the death penalty
legal abortion
civil rights legislation
present divorce laws
alimony
the jury system
immigration quotas
the presumption of innocence until guilt is proven
diplomatic immunity
present income tax laws
inheritance tax
Executive privilege

treating prostitution as a crime
treating drug abuse as a crime
conscientious objectors

b. Religion

religion *per se*	missionaries
God as "giver"	papal infallibility
going to church	the Trinity
the Bible as revelation	salvation
the Bible as literature	Day of Judgment
the Immaculate Conception	original sin
immortality	free will
heaven and hell	doctrine of the elect

4. Write an essay (750–1,000 words) comparable in form to "Why TV Stars Don't 'Make it' in the Movies." Take the opposite position: "Why TV Stars Do 'Make it' in the Movies." Be sure to cite specific TV stars and specific movies.

5. Write an essay (500–750 words) based on Stout's essay "Why College Students Take a Sabbatical," focusing on a student or group of students on campus who have either stopped-out or are considering it. Interview as many students as you can, using quotes, facts, and statistics.

6. Write an essay (500–750 words) in which you offer your personal reasons for making an important decision in your life, as Simone de Beauvoir does in "Why I Decided to Be a Writer."

14. What Are the Consequences of X?

PREDICTING CONSEQUENCES

Computers and the New Literacy,
Benjamin Compaine

REPORTING CONSEQUENCES

My Wood, E. M. Forster

IGNORING AND DEPLORING CONSEQUENCES

Our Strange Indifference to Nuclear Peril,
Jonathan Schell

PREDICTING CONSEQUENCES

*J*ust as we are naturally curious about the causes of various ideas, acts, or events, so are we naturally curious about consequences—what follows from various ideas, acts, or events. Thus while the previous question, "What are the causes of X?" started with effects and traced them *back* to causes ("I failed the exam. I wonder why."), the present question, "What are the consequences of X?" reverses the direction. It starts with a given or hypothetical condition and projects *ahead* to what naturally or necessarily follows. ("If I don't study, I will—as a consequence—fail the exam.")

In predicting consequences, as in tracing causes, it is essential that you be rigorously logical. (See pages 314–23.)

You may also need to draw on the past to establish a casual explanation envisioning consequences. In the following article, for example, "Computers and the New Literacy," Benjamin Compaine, executive director of the Harvard Information Bureau Resource Policy program, gives us a glimpse of the future, basing his prediction of what *will happen* upon his observation of what *has happened* in the past. Combining his historical analysis with facts and figures drawn from present studies and statistical data, he takes a leap into the future: The fast-approaching "computer age" will surely revolutionize and redefine our patterns of literacy, he tells us, pointing to a long list of "trends."

Note that this article is a model of clear, logical organization. (Marginal notes indicate the main structural units.) Note also how skillfully the writer has generated supporting materials by addressing multiple questions to his topic:

> Question 6, "What are the facts about X?" (produces data and hard evidence)
> Question 8, "What does X mean?" (produces a definition of "literacy")
> Question 11, "How is X made or done" (produces an historical account of how concepts of literacy have changed through the ages)
> Question 17, "What is the present status of X?" (produces the observation that today we seem to be entering the stage at which the masses can use [the computer] without having to understand how it works)

As for the specific question we are concerned with here, we can see that the question that represents the main thrust of this piece—*What are the consequences of X?*—has shaped the article as a whole: the consequences of our present entrance into the computer age should "be neither saluted nor feared." Compaine ends the article with a reassuring prediction about the essentially orderly character of evolution in society.

Computers and the New Literacy
Benjamin Compaine

Introduction: Youngsters today are "fluent in the language of the future"; their elders are not

Thesis: The new literacy of the future will require familiarity with computers

Note development here in terms of historic process: how concepts of literacy changed through the ages

After last year's World Future Society assembly on telecommunications, a 16-year-old suggested that youngsters already fluent in the language of the future are amused by their elders' tentative, tortured attempts to make contact: "I think the message was clear that it's really our world. I was kind of laughing at the people here. This technology, all they talked about, they really couldn't grasp. This belongs to us."

Some people are going to have trouble grasping the fact that we are on the verge of an era in which the ability to read and write may not be sufficient to define what it is to be literate. Literacy may soon mean being able to access, manipulate and store information in a computer.

Each generation tends to assume its definition of literacy is the ultimate; literacy is, however, a dynamic construct, a bundle of culturally relevant skills that change over time. Before the written word was widely used, the oral tradition predominated. In twelfth-century England, for example, literacy meant the ability to compose and recite in Latin. To "make a record" of something meant to bear oral witness, not produce a document for others to read. Eventually, English replaced Latin as the language for discourse. But even then, because of the difficulty of using a quill on parchment or a stylus on wax, writing in the Middle Ages was considered a special skill that was not automatically coupled with the ability to read. The most common way of committing words to writing was by dictating to a scribe, not himself necessarily able to compose. Thus, reading and dictating, rather than reading and writing, were typically paired.

With the development of the printing press in the fifteenth century, the basic skills of modern literacy—reading and writing—became relatively widespread. Still, the definition of literacy did not remain static. By the mid-nineteenth century, the English literati stiffened the requirements for admission to their ranks. Not merely the ability to read, they said, but the reading of the "right" materials separated the truly literate from the great unwashed. "How, if at all, they asked, did the spread of the printed word contribute to the spiritual enrichment and intellectual enlightenment of the nation?" wrote Altick in *The English Common Reader*.

Even an institution as sacrosanct as the library has not always been held in high regard by the literary elite. Free libraries for the English common man were viciously criticized by those who felt that, instead of encouraging study and self-improvement, they inflamed the popular passion for the wanton reading of fiction. Indeed, one librarian told a meeting in 1879 that "schoolboys or students who took to novel reading to any great extent never made much progress in after life." The irony of attitudes such as this may be instructive to critics of video games, who decry them as a corrupting influence on today's schoolchildren.

Historically, literacy developed in a series of identifiable stages. It starts in the hands of specialists, then begins to have a wider impact on institutions as it becomes the preferred medium of business, culture and politics. Finally, it becomes so pervasive that even the masses are considered handicapped without it. We can trace modern notions of literacy from their beginnings in twelfth-century England—with its movement away from reliance on the spoken word and toward written records—to their first plateau, which appeared with the introduction of the printing press. The development culminated in newspapers and mass-market books, along with popular education, in the nineteenth century.

History also suggests that one does not have to be fully literate to participate in literacy. One measure of changing literacy in thirteenth-century England was the possession of a seal. Earlier, only the king possessed a seal; it was used to authenticate documents. In the reign of Edward I, however, the Statute of Exeter required even unlettered serfs to have one.

Looking back over the 35 or so years since the development of modern computers, we can spot trends similar to the much slower advance of traditional literacy. At first, computers were strictly for a "priestly" class that could read and write the *lingua electronica*. All computer users were dependent upon this group of plugged-in clergy. As computers became more widespread and their application more pervasive, however, they began to have a greater impact on business and social institutions. The languages (COBOL, FORTRAN, BASIC, etc.) evolved into something closer to the vernacular, and more people were able to use them.

Today, we seem to be entering the stage at which the computer is becoming so simple and inexpensive that the masses can use it without having to understand how it works. They can thus participate in computer literacy without necessarily being part of the electronic elite themselves. It may be no more necessary for the mass of people to understand how a computer works than it is to understand the mechanics of the internal combustion engine in order to drive a car.

Last year, about $2 billion was spent, worldwide, on cartridges for home video games. And well over 22 billion quarters were dropped into arcade video games. Meanwhile, about 7 million people—from stockbrokers to travel agents—use VDTs, video display terminals, as part of their everyday work. In ever greater numbers, secretaries are writing the boss's letters and memos on word processors. And the executives themselves are likely to be getting information for their decisions via a desktop computer.

The kids playing video games and the adults working with VDTs have one thing in common. To an increasing degree, they are using a computer for storing and manipulating data. They are using computers directly and they are using them in place of older information and entertainment processes, most notably ink and paper. By the time today's 10-year-olds graduate from college, they may be using computers as readily as an older generation uses books.

The video game craze, even if it turns out to be a passing fad, may hold considerable cultural significance. For the first time, the video tube is something more than a medium for passive masses. Without becoming computer experts, the kids and others who play the games may be intuitively learning the strengths and limitations of computer logic. They are certainly learning how to manipulate a computer (whether with a keyboard, joy stick or some other mechanism). The U.S. Army, which must train large numbers of youngsters just removed from the video game parlors, is experimenting with training exercises that use video-game-like lessons played on micro-computers. The schools are not far behind. Microcomputers are showing up

Looking into
the future
in classrooms all over the country; surprisingly, it's the kids and their parents, not the educational establishment, who are pushing for the change. PTAs are holding bake sales to raise money not for library books but for desktop computers. According to Mary Alice White, chief of the Electronic Learning Laboratory at Columbia University's Teachers College, today's youth spend more time using electronic devices (like television and video games) to learn with than they spend with print.

Some of these changes are already showing up on the job market. A study shows that jobs in the help wanted ads in the *New York Times* that required some form of computer literacy doubled between 1977 and 1982. None of the listings for travel agents in 1977 mentioned the need for any computer-related skills, for example, but five years later, 71 percent required the ability to operate computer-based reservations systems. Secretary-typist jobs that demanded word-processing skills went from zero to 15 percent.

To speculate on the long-term societal impacts that may grow out of the trends identified here would be foolish. Indeed, most of the predictions being made today about the new information technologies are reminiscent of Victorian warnings. There was once speculation that the pneumatic tire would lead to the demise of books because the family out riding bicycles would forever shun the tradition of fireside reading.

While the evidence points to another step in the evolution of literacy, it is unlikely that the older skills will die. Neither the printing press nor the telephone resulted in the elimination of handwriting or postal services. The electronic calculator has not replaced the need to *understand* mathematics. The new literacy is likely to involve a greater emphasis on graphics and the spoken word, continuing a trend that reflects improvements in photography, printing, recordings and television. Above all, the new literacy need be neither saluted nor feared. Whatever evolves will take place in stages, giving society a chance to adjust.

REPORTING CONSEQUENCES

Writers need not speculate on consequences; they may simply report them. E. M. Forster, for example, builds an entire essay around the effects or consequences of owning property. What happens, he asks, when you "own things"? Forster cites an example from his own life. He bought himself "a wood" with a check he received for writing a book about the difficulties of the English in India. Although it was not "a large wood," the consequences of owning it—as he vividly describes them—were considerable.

My Wood

E. M. Forster

A few years ago I wrote a book which dealt in part with the difficulties of the English in India. Feeling that they would have had no difficulties in India themselves, the Americans read the book freely. The more they read it the better it made them feel, and a check to the author was the result. I bought a wood with the check. It is not a large wood—it contains scarcely any trees, and it is intersected, blast it, by a public footpath. Still, it is the first property that I have owned, so it is right that other people should participate in my shame, and should ask themselves, in accents that will vary in horror, this very important question: What is the effect of property upon the character? Don't let's touch economics; the effect of private ownership upon the community as a whole is another question—a more important question, perhaps, but another one. Let's keep to psychology. If you own things, what's their effect on you? What's the effect on me of my wood?

In the first place, it makes me feel heavy. Property does have this effect. Property produces men of weight, and it was a man of weight who failed to get into the Kingdom of Heaven. He was not wicked, that unfortunate millionaire in the parable, he was only stout; he stuck out in front, not to mention behind, and as he wedged himself this way and that in the crystalline entrance and bruised his well-fed flanks, he saw beneath him a comparatively slim camel passing through the eye of a needle and being woven into the robe of God. The Gospels all through couple stoutness and slowness. They point out what is perfectly obvious, yet seldom realized: that if you have a lot of things you cannot move about a lot, that furniture requires dusting, dusters require servants, servants require insurance stamps, and the whole tangle of them makes you think twice before you accept an invitation to dinner or go for a bathe in the Jordan. Sometimes the Gospels proceed further and say with Tolstoy that property is sinful; they approach the difficult ground of asceticism here, where I cannot follow them. But as to the immediate effects of property on people, they just show straightforward logic. It produces men of weight. Men of weight cannot, by definition, move like the lightning from the East unto the West, and the ascent of a fourteen-stone bishop into a pulpit is thus the exact antithesis of the coming of the Son of Man. My wood makes me feel heavy.

In the second place, it makes me feel it ought to be larger.

The other day I heard a twig snap in it. I was annoyed at first, for I thought that someone was blackberrying, and depreciating the value of the undergrowth. On coming nearer, I saw it was not a man who had trodden on the twig and snapped it, but a bird, and I felt pleased. My bird. The bird was not equally pleased. Ignoring the relation between us, it took fright as soon as it saw the shape of my face, and flew straight over the boundary hedge into a field, the property of Mrs. Henessy, where it sat down with a loud squawk. It had become Mrs. Henessy's bird. Something seemed grossly amiss here, something that would not have occurred had the wood been larger. I could not afford to buy Mrs. Henessy out, I dared not murder her, and limitations of this sort beset me on every side. Ahab did not want that vineyard—he only needed it to round off his property, preparatory to plotting a new curve—and all the land around my wood has become necessary to me in order to round off the wood. A boundary protects. But—poor little thing—the boundary ought in its turn to be protected. Noises on the edge of it. Children throw stones. A little more, and then a little more, until we reach the sea. Happy Canute! Happier Alexander! And after all, why should even the world be the limit of possession? A rocket containing a Union Jack, will, it is hoped, be shortly fired at the moon. Mars. Sirius. Beyond which ... But these immensities ended by saddening me. I could not suppose that my wood was the destined nucleus of universal dominion—it is so small and contains no mineral wealth beyond the blackberries. Nor was I comforted when Mrs. Henessy's bird took alarm for the second time and flew clean away from us all, under the belief that it belonged to itself.

In the third place, property makes its owner feel that he ought to do something to it. Yet he isn't sure what. A restlessness comes over him, a vague sense that he has a personality to express—the same sense which, without any vagueness, leads the artist to an act of creation. Sometimes I think I will cut down such trees as remain in the wood, at other times I want to fill up the gaps between them with new trees. Both impulses are pretentious and empty. They are not honest movements towards moneymaking or beauty. They spring from a foolish desire to express myself and from an inability to enjoy what I have got. Creation, property, enjoyment form a sinister trinity in the human mind. Creation and enjoyment are both very very good, yet they are often unattainable without a material basis, and at such moments property pushes itself in as a substitute, saying, "Accept me instead—I'm good enough for all three." It is not enough. It is, as Shakespeare said of lust, "The expense of spirit in a waste of shame": it is "Before, a joy proposed; behind, a dream." Yet we don't know how to shun it. It is forced on us by our economic system as the alternative to starvation. It is also forced on us by an internal defect in the soul, by the feeling that in property may lie the germs of self-development and of exquisite or heroic deeds. Our life on earth is, and ought to be, material and carnal. But we have not yet learned to manage our materialism and carnality properly; they are still entangled with the desire for ownership, where (in the words of Dante) "Possession is one with loss."

And this brings us to our fourth and final point: the blackberries.

Blackberries are not plentiful in this meagre grove, but they are easily seen from the public footpath which traverses it, and all too easily gathered. Foxgloves, too—people will pull up the foxgloves, and ladies of an educational tendency even grub for toadstools to show them on the Monday in class. Other ladies, less educated, roll down the bracken in the arms of their gentlemen friends. There is paper, there are tins. Pray, does my wood belong to me or doesn't it? And, if it does, should I not own it best by allowing no one else to walk there? There is a wood near Lyme Regis, also cursed by a public footpath, where the owner has not hesitated on this point. He has built high stone walls each side of the path, and has spanned it by bridges, so that the public circulate like termites while he gorges on the blackberries unseen. He really does own his wood, this able chap. Dives in Hell did pretty well, but the gulf dividing him from Lazarus could be traversed by vision, and nothing traverses it here. And perhaps I shall come to this in time. I shall wall in and fence out until I really taste the sweets of property. Enormously stout, endlessly avaricious, pseudo-creative, intensely selfish, I shall weave upon my forehead the quadruple crown of possession until those nasty Bolshies come and take it off again and thrust me aside into the outer darkness.

IGNORING AND DEPLORING CONSEQUENCES

The following essay is drawn from Jonathan Schell's grimly prophetic treatise, *The Fate of the Earth*. Reflecting on the nuclear situation and contemplating the consequences of our refusal to face the horrifying realities, he warns us that "we are not only threatening our own lives; we are threatening to bring about the extinction of the species."

In the following excerpt Schell examines the possible consequences of what he calls our "failure of response." What has this failure "been doing to our world"?

Our Strange Indifference to Nuclear Peril

Jonathan Schell

It is a matter of record that in our thirty-six years of life in a nuclear-armed world we have been largely dead to the nuclear peril, and I would like to consider more closely what this failure of response seems to have been doing to our world. Pascal, taking note of the cerebral character of the condition of mortality, once observed that "it is easier to endure death without thinking about it than to endure the thought of death without dying." His observation perfectly describes our response so far to the peril of extinction: we have found it much easier to dig our own grave than to think about the fact that we are doing so. Almost everyone has acknowledged on some level that the peril exists, but the knowledge has been without consequences in our feelings and our actions, and the superpowers have proceeded with their nuclear buildups, in the recent words of George Kennan, "like the victims of some sort of hypnotism, like men in a dream, like lemmings heading for the sea."

For a very short while before and after the first bomb was produced, a few men at and near the top of the American government seemed prepared to deal with the nuclear predicament at its proper depth. One of them was Secretary of War Henry Stimson, who knew of the Manhattan Project and, in March of 1945—four months before the Trinity test, at Alamogordo—confided to his diary an account of a discussion he had had about the new weapon with Harvey Bundy, his closest personal assistant. "Our thoughts," he wrote, "went right down to the bottom facts of human nature, morals, and governments, and it is by far the most searching and important thing that I have had to do since I have been here in the Office of the Secretary of War because it touches matters which are deeper even than the principles of present government." Yet those deep thoughts somehow did not take root firmly enough in the hearts of the American leaders or of the world at large, and the old ways of thinking returned, in the teeth of the new facts. The true dimensions of the nuclear peril, and of its significance for mankind, had been glimpsed, but then the awareness faded and the usual exigencies of international political life—including, shortly, the Cold War between the United States and the Soviet Union—laid claim to people's passions and energies. The nuclear buildup that has continued to this day began, and the nuclear question, having emerged abruptly from the twofold obscurity of scientific theory and governmental secrecy, was almost immediately thrust into the new obscurity of the arcane, abstract, denatured world of the theorists in the think tanks, who were, in effect, deputized to think the "unthinkable" thoughts that the rest of us lacked the will to think.

Thus began the strange double life of the world which has continued up to the present. On the one hand, we returned to business as usual, as though everything remained as it always had been. On the other hand, we began to assemble the stockpiles that could blow this supposedly unaltered existence sky-high at any second. When the scientists working on the Manhattan Project wanted to send word to President Truman, who was at the Potsdam Conference, that the detonation near Alamogordo had been successful, they chose the horrible but apt code phrase "Babies satisfactorily born." Since then, these "babies"—which are indeed like the offspring of a new species, except that it is a species not of life but of anti-life, threatening to end life—have "proliferated" steadily under our faithful care, bringing forth "generation" after "generation" of weapons, each more numerous and more robust than the last, until they now threaten to do away with their creators altogether. Yet while we did all this we somehow kept the left hand from knowing—or from dwelling on—what the right hand was doing; and the separation of our lives from awareness of the doom that was being prepared under us and around us was largely preserved.

It is probably crucial psychologically in maintaining this divorce that, once Hiroshima and Nagasaki had been pushed out of mind, the nuclear peril grew in such a way that while it relentlessly came to threaten the existence of everything it physically touched nothing, and thus left people free not to think about it if they so chose. Like a kindhearted executioner, the bomb permitted its prospective victims to go on living seemingly ordinary lives up to the day that the execution should suddenly and without warning be carried out. (If one nuclear bomb had gone off each year in one of the world's cities, we can well imagine that public attitudes toward the nuclear peril would now be quite different.) The continuity, however illusory, between the pre-nuclear world and the nuclear world which was made possible by these years of not using nuclear weapons was important in preserving the world's denial of the peril because it permitted a spurious normality to be maintained—although "normality" was at times embraced with a fervor that betrayed an edge of hysterical insecurity. The spectacle of life going on as usual carried with it a strong presumption that nothing much was wrong. When we observed that no one seemed to be worried, that no one was showing any signs of alarm or doing anything to save himself, it was hard to resist the conclusion that everything was all right. After all, if we were reasonable people and we were doing nothing how could there be anything the matter? The totality of the peril, in particular, helped to disguise it, for, with everyone and everything in the world similarly imperilled, there was no flight from imperilled things to safe things—no flow of capital from country to country, or migration of people from one place to another. Thoughts of the nuclear peril were largely banned from waking life, and relegated to dreams or to certain fringes of society, and open, active concern about it was restricted to certain "far-out" people, whose ideas were on the whole not so much rejected by the supposedly sober, "realistic" people in the mainstream as simply ignored. In this atmosphere, discussion of the nuclear peril even took on a faintly embarrassing aura, as though dwelling on it were somehow melo-dramatic, or were a sophomoric excess that serious people outgrew with maturity.

It was not unless one lifted one's gaze from all the allegedly normal events occurring before one's eyes and looked at the executioner's sword hanging over everyone's head that the normality was revealed as a sort of mass insanity. This was an insanity that consisted not in screaming and making a commotion but precisely in *not* doing these things in the face of overwhelming danger, as though everyone had been sedated. Passengers on a ship who are eating, sunning themselves, playing shuffleboard, and engaging in all the usual shipboard activities appear perfectly normal as long as their ship is sailing safely in quiet seas, but these same passengers doing these same things appear deranged if in full view of them all their ship is caught in a vortex that may shortly drag it and them to destruction. Then their placidity has the appearance of an unnatural loss of normal human responses—of a pathetic and sickening acquiescence in their own slaughter. T. S. Eliot's well-known lines "This is the way the world ends/Not with a bang but a whimper" may not be literally correct—there will decidedly be a very big bang—but in a deeper sense it is certainly right; if we do end the world, the sequence is likely to be not a burst of strong-willed activity leading to a final explosion but enervation, dulled senses, enfeebled will, stupor, and paralysis. Then death....

DISCUSSION AND EXERCISES

1. Read the following poem, which explores the consequences of postponing the fulfillment of a dream.

Dream Deferred

Langston Hughes

What happens to a dream deferred?

Does it dry up
like a raisin in the sun?

Or fester like a sore—
And then run?

Does it stink like rotten meat?
Or crust and sugar over—
like a syrupy sweet?

Maybe it just sags
like a heavy load.

Or does it explode?

a. List the various similes used by Hughes and indicate in what ways they are effective.
b. Why, do you suppose, are all but one of the possible consequences framed as questions?
c. What is gained by italicizing the last line?
d. Does the poet provide an answer to his original question?

2. Write a paragraph (150–250 words) in which you contemplate the possible consequences of repressing any strong feeling or desire; base your speculations on your own experience or that of someone you know; shape your topic sentence in the form of a question, use the prewriting techniques you have learned, and develop the paragraph in terms of specific possibilities.

3. The woman in the photograph below has just been crowned a beauty queen. Where does she go from here? Write a paragraph (150–200 words) in which you describe the consequences of winning the contest.

4. Consider Benjamin Compaine's "Computers and the New Literacy."

   a. To whom will the Computer Age belong? Why?
   b. Some people consider the computer a possible corrupting influence for school children. What presently respectable practices were considered similarly "corrupting" in the past? Do you feel that computers can corrupt? Why or why not?
   c. How has computer use grown over the past ten years?
   d. What part do computers play in your life, if any?
   e. Do you foresee that the computer will replace present literary skills such as reading and writing, or will it improve them? Explain.

5. Answer the following questions based on the essay "My Wood."

   a. What is the purpose of this essay?
   b. To whom is it addressed?
   c. What is the tone?
   d. What is the writer's relationship to the subject matter?
   e. How does he want his reader to relate to the subject matter? Is he successful? (See Analysis of an Essay, pages 287–88.)
   f. In what ways does the organization of this essay resemble Christensen's coordinate sequence paragraph (pages 121–23)? What other essays in this text are similarly organized? Comment on the effectiveness of this organization.
   g. Comment on the following quotations. In what ways do they develop and illuminate the central meaning and purpose of the essay?

      1. "It is not a large wood ... and it is intersected, blast it, by a public footpath."
      2. "It was a man of weight who failed to get into the Kingdom of Heaven."
      3. "I could not afford to buy Mrs. Henessy out."
      4. "Sometimes I think I will cut down such trees as remain in the wood, at other times I want to fill up the gaps between them with new trees."
      5. "Possession is one with loss."
      6. "I shall wall in and fence out until I really taste the sweets of property."

6. One critic wrote about Jonathan Schell's "The Strange Indifference to the Nuclear Peril," "It compels us—and compel *is* the right word—to confront head on the nuclear peril in which we all find ourselves." Answer the following questions based on this essay.

   a. What specific information does the writer offer to build his thesis: descriptive details, suggestion of attitudes, historical data, possible consequences? What effect do they have?
   b. Comment on the writer's style: length of paragraphs and unity; choice of words (technical or plain); length and difficulty of sentences; transitional devices; and general flow and readability.
   c. Evaluate the point of view.
   d. What specific phrases in the piece contribute to the overall tone, mood, and atmosphere?
   e. Speculate on the audience Schell was addressing: address such things as their eductional levels and their political and ethical stances.
   f. In what ways is the allusion to T. S. Eliot's famous lines appropriate and effective at the end of Schell's essay? Comment on Schell's last line.

ESSAY SUGGESTIONS

1. Write an essay (500–750 words) indicating what you think were, are, or will be the major effects or consequences of any one of the following (on the individual, the family, or society at large). (Be sure to use prewriting techniques before you actually begin to write.)

a. Inventions

> the automobile
> telephone
> television
> the airplane
> electric light

b. Social changes

> space travel
> human organ transplants
> war on poverty
> fight against pollution
> increased drug usage
> increased divorce rate

> increased mixed marriages
> increased urbanization
> increased automation
> increased income tax
> increased leisure
> the new morality

2. In an essay (500–750 words) describe the effect on your mind or sensibilities of one of the following:

> the moon
> the sun
> long hair and beards
> hot weather
> cold weather
> noise
> silence

> prejudice
> current fashions
> nightmares
> fatigue
> religion
> advertising

3. Considering Compaine's article on "Computers and the New Literacy," write an essay (500–750 words) predicting how a college student's education will be different in five or ten years as a consequence of the Computer Age.

4. Write an essay (500–750 words) describing the effect on you of some possession you have acquired (such as a word processor) or the consequences of some action ("breaking up"). Like Forster, you might try to suggest not only the personal but wider social consequences as well.

5. Write an essay (500–750 words) in which you answer the question "What would happen if...?" Base your answer on Schell's essay and predict what would happen if there were a nuclear war.

15. What Are the Types of X?

CREATING A CLASSIFICATION

   Jung's Psychological Types, Frieda Fordham

CLASSIFICATION ACCORDING TO PURPOSE

   Three Types of Resistance to Oppression, Martin Luther King, Jr.

COMPLETE CLASSIFICATION

   Three Kinds of Discipline, John Holt

CREATING A CLASSIFICATION

*C*lassification is a highly methodical form of analysis and an indispensable condition of systematic thought, for it involves a sorting process that groups elements into categories based on similar characteristics. We see this process at work in the story of Adam who brought order out of chaos when he named the creatures around him. We can reconstruct the procedure in our imagination: as the multitude of creatures was paraded before him, Adam began a sorting process in his own mind. Noting at the outset that some creatures were of the field, he called them "beasts"; noting that others were of the air, he called them "fowl" or "birds." We can imagine that within these two large categories, Adam classified further. Some of the beasts—or animals—were large and lumbering, with extraordinarily long noses: these he named "elephants." Others with long sleek bodies and stripes he called "tigers"; still others with spots, "leopards"; and so on. Adam continued the classification and naming procedure until all the birds and beasts had been grouped together into appropriate identifying categories.

Since earliest times, then, human beings have been classifying things, arranging them in order to see their similarities and differences more clearly, and in that way to learn more about them.

We frequently use classification in our daily living; for example, we may sort our daily mail into three categories: bills, junk mail, and personal letters (an incomplete but still useful system of classification). We put the bills to one side, throw away the junk mail unopened, and give our time to the letters. Or a friend may say to us: "I have just met your neighbor Joe Smith. What kind of person is he?" The friend is asking us to classify Joe Smith. We may reply: "Oh, Joe is the aggressive junior-executive-on-the-way-up type, but very friendly." If our friend knows other such junior executives, he will have some idea of Joe Smith's characteristics.

In using classification we can either start with an individual member and put it into a class (as we did with Joe Smith) or (as in the piece below) start with a class (human beings) and divide it into its constituent members.

You can see that an essay concerned with "the types of X" presents no serious problem in organization, because the organization is more or less given: the three or four (or however many) designated types generally make up the three or four sections of the piece.

This organization underlies Carl Jung's classic division of people into two personality types (extravert and introvert). Note that in this essay the author does not regard the types as mutually exclusive, with discernibly fixed personalities (an imperative of the scientific or technical classification), but rather as poles on the scale of personality (people are predominantly one or the other; no one is purely extravert or introvert). Thus in this essay, as in all rhetorical rather than strictly logical classifications, the categories may overlap to some extent.

Jung's Psychological Types

Frieda Fordham

Introduction

Jung's contribution to the psychology of the conscious mind is largely embodied in his work on psychological types. The attempt to classify human beings according to type has a long history; it is nearly two thousand years since the Greek physician, Galen, tried to distinguish four fundamental temperamental differences in men, and his descriptive terms (though psychologically naive)—the sanguine, the phlegmatic, the choleric, and the melancholic—have passed into common speech. There have been various attempts which, taking modern knowledge into account, aim at a more precise formulation—for instance, Kretschmer's—and [Carl] Jung's division of people into extraverts and introverts has already come to be widely known, if not fully understood. Jung distinguishes two differing attitudes to life, two modes of reacting to circumstances which he finds sufficiently marked and widespread to describe as typical.

> There is a whole class of men [he says] who at the moment of reaction to a given situation at first draw back a little as if with an unvoiced "No," and only after that are able to react; and there is another class who, in the same situation, come forward with an immediate reaction, apparently confident that their behavior is obviously right. The former class would therefore be characterized by a certain negative relation to the object, and the latter by a positive one . . . the former class corresponds to the introverted and the second to the extraverted attitude.

Type one

The extraverted attitude is characterized by an outward flowing of libido, an interest in events, in people and things, a relationship with them, and a dependence on them; when this attitude is habitual to anyone Jung describes him or her as an *extraverted type*. This type is motivated by outside factors and greatly influenced by the environment. The extraverted type is sociable and confident in unfamiliar surroundings. He or she is generally on good terms with the world, and even when disagreeing with it can still be described as related to it, for instead of withdrawing (as the opposite type tends to do) they prefer to argue and quarrel, or try to reshape it according to their own pattern.

Type two

The introverted attitude, in contrast, is one of withdrawal; the libido flows inward and is concentrated upon subjective factors, and the predominating influence is "inner necessity." When this attitude is habitual Jung speaks of an "introverted type." This type lacks confidence in relation to people and things, tends to be unsociable, and prefers reflection to activity. Each type undervalues the other, seeing the negative rather than the positive qualities of the opposite attitude, a fact which has led to endless misunderstanding and even in the course of time to the formulation of antagonistic philosophies.

Conclusion   In the West we prefer the extraverted attitude, describing it in such
favourable terms as outgoing, well-adjusted, &c., while on the other hand, in
the East, at least until recent times, the introverted attitude has been the
prevailing one. On this basis one may explain the material and technical
development of the Western Hemisphere as contrasted with the material
poverty but greater spiritual development of the East.

CLASSIFICATION ACCORDING TO PURPOSE

What characteristics you use as the basis of a classification depend on your own
interests and purpose. You can classify people politically, socially, economically, or
even by the color of their eyes, depending on what special point you want to make.

You are, of course, free to choose whatever basis of classification best suits your
purpose, but once you have chosen you must not switch midway to a different ground.
If you do, you will be committing the logical error of cross-ranking, that is, producing
overlapping rather than mutually exclusive categories. Someone who classifies the
types of houses in a town as Victorian, colonial, ranch, and two-story is guilty of
cross-ranking because Victorian and colonial style houses can have an upstairs and a
downstairs.

When properly envisioned, classification is an extraordinarily useful method of
inventing an essay, for there is always a "story" in the designation of types—as you
choose to depict them. And the choice will depend on *why* you are making the
classification in the first place, and on what new insights or refinements of
understanding you hope to provide by analyzing your subject in terms of a given set of
categories.

It is clear that, in the essay below, Martin Luther King, Jr., is presenting three ways
of resisting oppression in order to demonstrate to his followers the futility of two of
the ways; only the third way—nonviolence—should be pursued.

Three Types of Resistance to Oppression

Martin Luther King, Jr.

Oppressed people deal with their oppression in three characteristic ways. One way is
acquiescence: the oppressed resign themselves to their doom. They tacitly adjust
themselves to oppression, and thereby become conditioned to it. In every movement
toward freedom some of the oppressed prefer to remain oppressed. Almost 2800 years
ago Moses set out to lead the children of Israel from the slavery of Egypt to the freedom
of the promised land. He soon discovered that slaves do not always welcome their
deliverers. They become accustomed to being slaves. They would rather bear those ills
they have, as Shakespeare pointed out, than flee to others that they know not of. They
prefer the "fleshpots of Egypt" to the ordeals of emancipation.

There is such a thing as the freedom of exhaustion. Some people are so worn down by
the yoke of oppression that they give up. A few years ago in the slum areas of Atlanta, a
Negro guitarist used to sing almost daily: "Ben down so long that down don't bother me."

This is the type of negative freedom and resignation that often engulfs the life of the oppressed.

But this is not the way out. To accept passively an unjust system is to cooperate with that system; thereby the oppressed become as evil as the oppressor. Noncooperation with evil is as much a moral obligation as is cooperation with good. The oppressed must never allow the conscience of the oppressor to slumber. Religion reminds every man that he is his brother's keeper. To accept injustice or segregation passively is to say to the oppressor that his actions are morally right. It is a way of allowing his conscience to fall asleep. At this moment the oppressed fails to be his brother's keeper. So acquiescence—while often the easier way—is not the moral way. It is the way of the coward. The Negro cannot win the respect of his oppressor by acquiescing; he merely increases the oppressor's arrogance and contempt. Acquiescence is interpreted as proof of the Negro's inferiority. The Negro cannot win the respect of the white people of the South or the peoples of the world if he is willing to sell the future of his children for his personal and immediate comfort and safety.

A second way that oppressed people sometimes deal with oppression is to resort to physical violence and corroding hatred. Violence often brings about momentary results. Nations have frequently won their independence in battle. But in spite of temporary victories, violence never brings permanent peace. It solves no social problem; it merely creates new and more complicated ones.

Violence as a way of achieving racial justice is both impractical and immoral. It is impractical because it is a descending spiral ending in destruction for all. The old law of an eye for an eye leaves everybody blind. It is immoral because it seeks to humiliate the opponent rather than win his understanding; it seeks to annihilate rather than to convert. Violence is immoral because it thrives on hatred rather than love. It destroys community and makes brotherhood impossible. It leaves society in monologue rather than dialogue. Violence ends by defeating itself. It creates bitterness in the survivors and brutality in the destroyers. A voice echoes through time saying to every potential Peter, "Put up your sword." History is cluttered with the wreckage of nations that failed to follow this command.

If the American Negro and other victims of oppression succumb to the temptation of using violence in the struggle for freedom, future generations will be the recipients of a desolate night of bitterness, and our chief legacy to them will be an endless reign of meaningless chaos. Violence is not the way.

The third way open to oppressed people in their quest for freedom is the way of nonviolent resistance. Like the synthesis in Hegelian philosophy, the principle of nonviolent resistance seeks to reconcile the truths of two opposites—acquiescence and violence—while avoiding the extremes and immoralities of both. The nonviolent resister agrees with the person who acquiesces that one should not be physically aggressive toward his opponent; but he balances the equation by agreeing with the person of violence that evil must be resisted. He avoids the nonresistance of the former and the violent resistance of the latter. With nonviolent resistance, no individual or group need submit to any wrong, nor need anyone resort to violence in order to right a wrong.

It seems to me that this is the method that must guide the actions of the Negro in the present crisis in race relations. Through nonviolent resistance the Negro will be able to rise to the noble height of opposing the unjust system while loving the perpetrators of the system. The Negro must work passionately and unrelentingly for full stature as a citizen, but he must not use inferior methods to gain it. He must never come to terms with falsehood, malice, hate, or destruction.

Nonviolent resistance makes it possible for the Negro to remain in the South and struggle for his rights. The Negro's problem will not be solved by running away. He cannot listen to the glib suggestion of those who would urge him to migrate en masse to other sections of the country. By grasping his great opportunity in the South he can make a lasting contribution to the moral strength of the nation and set a sublime example of courage for generations yet unborn.

By nonviolent resistance, the Negro can also enlist all men of good will in his struggle for equality. The problem is not a purely racial one, with Negroes set against whites. In the end, it is not a struggle between people at all, but a tension between justice and injustice. Nonviolent resistance is not aimed against oppressors but against oppression. Under its banner consciences, not racial groups, are enlisted.

If the Negro is to achieve the goal of integration, he must organize himself into a militant and nonviolent mass movement. All three elements are indispensable. The movement for equality and justice can only be a success if it has both a mass and militant character; the barriers to be overcome require both. Nonviolence is an imperative in order to bring about ultimate community.

A mass movement of militant quality that is not at the same time committed to nonviolence tends to generate conflict, which in turn breeds anarchy. The support of the participants and the sympathy of the uncommitted are both inhibited by the threat that bloodshed will engulf the community. This reaction in turn encourages the opposition to threaten and resort to force. When, however, the mass movement repudiates violence while moving resolutely toward its goal, its opponents are revealed as the instigators and practitioners of violence if it occurs. Then public support is magnetically attracted to the advocates of nonviolence, while those who employ violence are literally disarmed by overwhelming sentiment against their stand.

COMPLETE CLASSIFICATION

In the following paragraph, Joseph Addison divides physical labor into two kinds; he makes a dichotomous (two-part) classification. All labor is either of one kind or the other.

> Bodily labor is of two kinds, either that which a man submits to for his livelihood, or that which he undergoes for his pleasure. The latter of them generally changes the name of labor for that of exercise, but differs only from ordinary labor as it rises from another motive.
>
> A country life abounds in both these kinds of labor, and for that reason gives a man a greater stock of health, and consequently a more perfect enjoyment of himself, than any other way of life. ("Recreation")

A dichotomous classification is necessarily complete because it divides everything into either A or B (X or not X). However, completeness is more difficult to achieve in a complex classification such as a scientific classification or the Dewey decimal system for classifying books in a library.

A scientific classification—like a simple analysis—must be complete, that is, each separate item must fall into its designated group with no loose ends. Thus a zoologist finds a place in his classification for *all* forms of animal life; a botanist does the same for plant life. Similarly, under the Dewey decimal system a library assigns every one of its holdings a general "number" heading: 900 if it is a history book, 700 if it deals with the arts, and so on. These numbers are then broken down further: 930 for ancient history; 940 for medieval and modern European history; and so on. A good classification embodies the dictum "a place for everything and everything in its place." Thus in the Dewey system, small items that are too specialized to have individual headings are grouped into categories such as "General Works," "Miscellaneous," and "Literature of Other Languages." (The "other" includes all languages that have not been specifically named, so that no language spoken or written anywhere is overlooked; each has a theoretical "place" into which it "fits" within the library's classification system.)

In using classification for rhetorical reasons—as the formal basis of an essay—writers have more latitude than the scientist will permit. Even so, note that in the following nonscientific classification of "Three Kinds of Discipline," the author covers the subject without any cross-ranking. A whole paragraph is devoted to "places where all three disciplines overlap."

Three Kinds of Discipline

John Holt

A child, in growing up, may meet and learn from three different kinds of disciplines. The first and most important is what we might call the Discipline of Nature or of Reality. When he is trying to do something real, if he does the wrong thing or doesn't do the right one, he doesn't get the result he wants. If he doesn't pile one block right on top of another, or tries to build on a slanting surface, his tower falls down. If he hits the wrong key, he hears the wrong note. If he doesn't hit the nail squarely on the head, it bends, and he has to pull it out and start with another. If he doesn't measure properly what he is trying to build, it won't open, close, fit, stand up, fly, float, whistle, or do whatever he wants it to do. If he closes his eyes when he swings, he doesn't hit the ball. A child meets this kind of discipline every time he tries to *do* something, which is why it is so important in school to give children more chances to do things, instead of just reading or listening to someone talk (or pretending to). This discipline is a great teacher. The learner never has to wait long for his answer; it usually comes quickly, often instantly. Also it is clear, and very often points toward the needed correction; from what happened he can not only see that what he did was wrong, but also why, and what he needs to do instead. Finally, and most important, the giver of the answer, call it Nature, is impersonal, impartial, and indifferent. She does not give opinions, or make judgments; she cannot be wheedled, bullied, or fooled; she does not get angry or disappointed; she does not praise or blame; she does not remember past failures or hold grudges; with her one always gets a fresh start, this time is the one that counts.

The next discipline we might call the Discipline of Culture, of Society, of What People Really Do. Man is a social, a cultural animal. Children sense around them this culture, this network of agreements, customs, habits, and rules binding the adults together. They want to understand it and be a part of it. They watch very carefully what people around them are doing and want to do the same. They want to do right, unless they become convinced they can't do right. Thus children rarely misbehave seriously in church, but sit as quietly as they can. The example of all those grownups is contagious. Some mysterious ritual is going on, and children, who like rituals, want to be part of it. In the same way, the little children that I see at concerts or operas, though they may fidget a little, or perhaps take a nap now and then, rarely make any disturbance. With all those grownups sitting there, neither moving nor talking, it is the most natural thing in the world to imitate them. Children who live among adults who are habitually courteous to each other, and to them, will soon learn to be courteous. Children who live surrounded by people who speak a certain way will speak that way, however much we may try to tell them that speaking that way is bad or wrong.

The third discipline is the one most people mean when they speak of discipline—the Discipline of Superior Force, of sergeant to private, of "you do what I tell you or I'll make you wish you had." There is bound to be some of this in a child's life. Living as we do surrounded by things that can hurt children, or that children can hurt, we cannot avoid it. We can't afford to let a small child find out from experience the danger of playing in a busy street, or of fooling with the pots on the top of a stove, or of eating up the pills in the medicine cabinet. So, along with other precautions, we say to him, "Don't play in the street, or touch things on the stove, or go into the medicine cabinet, or I'll punish you." Between him and the danger too great for him to imagine we put a lesser danger, but one he can imagine and maybe therefore want to avoid. He can have no idea of what it would be like to be hit by a car, but he can imagine being shouted at, or spanked, or sent to his room. He avoids these substitutes for the greater danger until he can understand it and avoid it for its own sake. But we ought to use this discipline only when it is necessary to protect the life, health, safety, or well-being of people or other living creatures, or to prevent destruction of things that people care about. We ought not to assume too long, as we usually do, that a child cannot understand the real nature of the danger from which we want to protect him. The sooner he avoids the danger, not to escape our punishment, but as a matter of good sense, the better. He can learn that faster than we think. In Mexico, for example, where people drive their cars with a good deal of spirit, I saw many children no older than five or four walking unattended on the streets. They understood about cars, they knew what to do. A child whose life is full of the threat and fear of punishment is locked into babyhood. There is no way for him to grow up, to learn to take responsibility for his life and acts. Most important of all, we should not assume that having to yield to the threat of our superior force is good for the child's character. It is never good for *anyone's* character. To bow to superior force makes us feel impotent and cowardly for not having had the strength or courage to resist. Worse, it makes us resentful and vengeful. We can hardly wait to make someone pay for our humiliation, yield to us as we were once made to yield. No, if we cannot always avoid using the Discipline of Superior Force, we should at least use it as seldom as we can.

There are places where all three disciplines overlap. Any very demanding human activity combines in it the disciplines of Superior Force, of Culture, and of Nature. The novice will be told, "Do it this way, never mind asking why, just do it that way, that is the way we always do it." But it probably *is* just the way they always do it, and usually for the very good reason that it is a way that has been found to work. Think, for example, of ballet training. The student in a class is told to do this exercise, or that; to stand so; to do this or that with his head, arms, shoulders, abdomen, hips, legs, feet. He is constantly corrected. There is no argument. But behind these seemingly autocratic demands by the teacher lie many decades of custom and tradition, and behind that, the necessities of dancing itself. You cannot make the moves of classical ballet unless over many years you have acquired, and renewed every day, the needed strength and suppleness in scores of muscles and joints. Nor can you do the difficult motions, making them look easy, unless you have learned hundreds of easier ones first. Dance teachers may not always agree on all the details of teaching these strengths and skills. But no novice could learn them all by himself. You could not go for a night or two to watch the ballet and then, without any other knowledge at all, teach yourself how to do it. In the same way, you would be unlikely to learn any complicated and difficult human activity without drawing heavily on the experience of those who know it better. But the point is that the authority of these experts or teachers stems from, grows out of their greater competence and experience, the fact that what they do *works*, not the fact that they happen to be the teacher and as such have the power to kick a student out of the class. And the further point is that children are always and everywhere attracted to that competence, and ready and eager to submit themselves to a discipline that grows out of it. We hear constantly that children will never do anything unless compelled to by bribes or threats. But in their private lives, or in extracurricular activities in school, in sports, music, drama, art, running a newspaper, and so on, they often submit themselves willingly and wholeheartedly to very intense disciplines, simply because they want to learn to do a given thing well. Our Little-Napoleon football coaches, of whom we have too many and hear far too much, blind us to the fact that millions of children work hard every year getting better at sports and games without coaches barking and yelling at them.

DISCUSSION AND EXERCISES

1. Write a paragraph (150–250 words), opening with the topic sentence "I can see three different types of students in this room." Instead of devoting a paragraph to each type (as in the full-length Holt essay), devote only two sentences—the first naming the type, the second adding specific details or examples of the type. In Francis Christensen's terms (see pages 121–23), this will be a three-level, coordinate sequence paragraph—one that moves from general to specific:

   1 Topic Sentence (general)
      2 First type (specific)
         3 Details or examples (more specific)
      2 Second type (specific)
         3 Details or examples (more specific)
      2 Third type (specific)
         3 Details or examples (more specific)

2. Evaluate King's classification of the types of resistance to oppression: Is it logically sound? Is the argument in favor of the third kind of resistance convincing? Use prewriting techniques to prepare to write a paragraph of your own in which you agree or disagree with King's position.

3. Consider Holt's classification of discipline into three kinds.

   a. What is the purpose of this classification?
   b. Is it complete? Explain.
   c. Is there any cross-ranking? Any overlapping? Discuss the writer's explanation of overlapping: Is it vital?
   d. Examine paragraph divisions. Locate topic sentences. Describe paragraph sequences by numbering them according to Christensen's levels of generality (pages 121–31).
   e. Consider the restored definition of discipline (page 351). How does that definition fit into Holt's classification?

f. Write a paragraph in which you classify discipline into two kinds, using as the basis for your classification that kind of discipline which you think is good and that which you consider bad.

ESSAY SUGGESTIONS

1. In an essay (500–750 words) classify people you know or know of into Jung's extravert and introvert types. You may wish to add a third category, the ambivert (one who balances or oscillates between extraversion and introversion). Use the prewriting techniques you have learned.
2. Write an essay (500–750 words) in which you warn against oversimplification by describing the many types of one of the following (as you have observed or experienced it):

intelligence	love	loyalty
freedom	beauty	charity
truth	goodness	courage
happiness		

3. In an essay (750–1,000 words) indicate the "common types" of any one of the following:

a. Psychology/Sociology

dreams	class conflict	fads
memories	talent or aptitude	pressure groups
mental disturbances	ambition	communities
propaganda	success	status seekers
conformity	prejudice	

b. Anthropology (customs in a given group)

marriage	courtship	hospitality
mourning	suicide	taboos
burials	drinking	

c. Travel

railroad
road
motor vehicle

d. Law

law courts	prisons	evidence
law specialties	crime prevention	misdemeanors
crimes	assaults	

e. zoology

whales	elephants	snakes
goats	reptiles	ants
crabs	monkeys	

f. Botany

plants	trees
vegetables	shrubs

4. An Aaron Copland essay opens with the following sentence: "I can see three different types of composers in musical history, each of whom conceives music in a somewhat different fashion." Substitute for "composers in musical history" one of the following and write an essay (750–1,000 words). You may have to vary the number of types. Use the prewriting techniques you have learned before you begin to write.

painters	novelists	students
dancers	architects	teachers
poets	photographers	doctors
playwrights	artists	

16. How Does X Compare to Y?

PRINCIPLES OF COMPARISON

*T*ake any two people, objects, events, ideas, books, disciplines, countries, continents, planets; take any two periods of time, works of art, artists; take two of *anything* (provided there is a logical basis of comparison), and ask these questions: How does one compare with the other? How are they similar? How are they different? With these questions you "invent" a study in comparative analysis.

Before making a comparison, you should be aware of the way this word is often used. Strictly speaking, the word "comparison" refers to the act or process of examining *similarities*, while the word "contrast" refers to the examination of *dissimilarities* or differences. Traditional rhetoricians usually call the study you are about to undertake "comparison and contrast," but in popular usage the term "comparison" generally covers both activities and means "setting things side by side to show how they are alike or different," while the word "contrast" retains its sense of "emphasizing differences." Also strictly speaking, a comparison may involve more than two subjects: you could theoretically set X alongside not only Y but also S, T, U, and V; or you could compare X with Y in the light of Z, and so on. I will concentrate on popular usage, since most of what should be said about comparison and contrast fits under this heading.

Read the following example, a short comparison of two presidents that shows how they were alike:

> Kennedy has been compared to Franklin Delano Roosevelt and he liked to pose in front of an F.D.R. portrait. In fact, some of his qualities more nearly recall Theodore Roosevelt, the apostle of the big stick, the strenuous life and the bully pulpit. Like T.R., for instance, Kennedy had a perhaps undue regard for Harvard and a craving for its approval. The only election he ever lost was one of the ones he wanted most to win—his first try for a seat on the Harvard Board of Overseers. He grimly ran again and his election to the Board was a cherished triumph. Like T.R., too, Kennedy fancied himself in the role of national taste maker—Roosevelt picked up Edwin Arlington Robinson and Kennedy adopted Robert Frost. Roosevelt let his rather rigid literary ideas get about and the Kennedys thought they ought to provide White House examples—Casals, Shakespeare and opera in the East Room—for the cultural uplift of the nation.... (Wicker, *Kennedy*)

Note that in this paragraph the two men are compared not merely *in general* but on the basis of *two specific qualities*. This is the basis of all good comparison. You should not simply say X is like Y; instead you should say X is like Y on the basis of the following specific points: 1, 2, 3, and so on—which is to say, in this case:

Kennedy was like Theodore Roosevelt in that both

1. regarded Harvard highly.
2. regarded themselves as taste makers.

Now note another comparison, this one showing—through an analogy—how two presidents were *different:*

> Lyndon Johnson's father once told him that he did not belong in politics unless he could walk into a roomful of men and tell immediately who was for him and who was against him. In fact, even the shrewd LBJ has not quite such occult power, but his liking for the story tells us something useful about him: he sets much store by instinct. No wonder, then, that it would be to his instincts—honed in the Texas hill country, sharpened in a life of politics, confirmed in his successful Congressional career—that he would often turn in the White House.
>
> This reliance on instinct enabled Johnson to put on the Presidency like a suit of comfortable old clothes. John Kennedy, on the other hand, came to it with a historical, nearly theoretical view of what was required of a strong President; he knew exactly what Woodrow Wilson had said about the office and he had read Corwin and Neustadt and he was unabashedly willing to quote Lincoln: "I see the storm coming and I know His hand is in it. If He has a place and work for me, I believe that I am ready."
>
> And Kennedy would add: "Today I say to you that if the people of this nation select me to be their President, I believe that I am ready." With eager confidence, Kennedy acquired a Presidential suit off the rack and put on a little weight to make himself fit it. (Wicker, *JFK and LBJ*)

As a form of analysis, comparison is not merely a rhetorical technique; it is a natural, instinctive process that goes on constantly in everyone's mind. We think and learn by comparing the unfamiliar with the familiar; we come to terms with a new situation by comparing it with an old one; we get our bearings by comparing the past with the present. Whether we are more impressed by the *similarities* between two situations or the *differences* depends, of course, on the situations themselves. The ability to see through the differences to the underlying similarities—or through the similarities to underlying differences—is the mark not only of critical intelligence but of the creative mind at work. Psychologist William James wrote, "Some people are far more sensitive to resemblances and far more ready to point out wherein they consist, than others are. They are the wits, the poets, the inventors, the scientific men, the practical geniuses." Speaking specifically of Newton and Darwin, James said, "The flash of similarity between an apple and the moon, between the rivalry for food in nature and the rivalry for man's selection, was too recondite to have occurred to any but exceptional minds."

But even the unexceptional mind naturally makes comparisons: Comparative situations are common in everyday life (before and after, then and now, loss and gain, here and there, promise and fulfillment). Because nothing indicates more clearly how well a person has grasped a subject than his or her ability to detect similarities and differences among its parts (hence the popularity of "How does X compare to Y? as an essay-type examination question), you should make an extra effort to master this form of discourse. It is not a difficult form if you approach it systematically; more than that, you can rely on it to produce interesting and engaging essays.

ORGANIZING A COMPARISON

You may organize comparative analysis in several forms. Each form also has many variations; the forms are flexible and give you ample freedom to shape your essay as you wish. What is important is that the essay always *have a shape*—a definite plan or pattern of development—so that it does not shift haphazardly back and forth: from X to Y; back to *part* of X; then more about Y; back to *another* part of X; and so on. Whatever shifting takes place must follow an orderly procedure.

Comparison of Wholes

The following essay by Civil War historian Bruce Catton compares two military leaders, Ulysses S. Grant and Robert E. Lee. These two men, Catton tells us, represented "two conflicting currents" in the nation which came together ultimately into a "final collision." The main part of this essay is organized according to *comparison of wholes* wherein Catton compares one whole subject (Lee) with another whole subject (Grant), so that the reader may regard the two men side by side; the writer places two portraits, as it were, next to one another on the same wall.

    I. Robert E. Lee
        A. Background
        B. Personality
        C. Underlying aspiration

   II. Ulysses S. Grant
        A. Background
        B. Personality
        C. Underlying aspiration

Interestingly, in the final section of the essay, Catton shifts both his thesis and his principle of organization to show that underneath their striking differences, the two soldiers had "much in common." The author links this final section so well to the rest of the essay ("Yet it was not all contrast, after all") that the shift to likenesses, to reconciliation of apparent opposites, serves to deepen rather than dilute the study in contrast. We recognize that life is like that: Under two "conflicting currents" may run a common current.

Grant and Lee: A Study in Contrasts

Bruce Catton

Introduction   When Ulysses S. Grant and Robert E. Lee met in the parlor of a modest house at Appomattox Court House, Virginia, on April 9, 1865, to work out the terms for the surrender of Lee's Army of Northern Virginia, a great chapter in American life came to a close, and a great new chapter began.

       These men were bringing the Civil War to its virtual finish. To be sure, other armies had yet to surrender, and for a few days the fugitive Confederate government would struggle desperately and vainly, trying to find some way to go on living now that its chief support was gone. But in effect it was all over when Grant and Lee signed the papers. And the little room where they wrote out the terms was the scene of one of the poignant, dramatic contrasts in American history.

Thesis: The two men were "oddly different."

They were two strong men, these oddly different generals, and they represented the strengths of two conflicting currents that, through them, had come into final collision.

Back of Robert E. Lee was the notion that the old aristocratic concept might somehow survive and be dominant in American life.

Lee

Lee was tidewater Virginia, and in his background were family, culture, and tradition . . . the age of chivalry transplanted to a New World which was making its own legends and its own myths. He embodied a way of life that had come down through the age of knighthood and the English country squire. America was a land that was beginning all over again, dedicated to nothing much more complicated than the rather hazy belief that all men had equal rights and should have an equal chance in the world. In such a land Lee stood for the feeling that it was somehow of advantage to human society to have a pronounced inequality in the social structure. There should be a leisure class, backed by ownership of land; in turn, society itself should be keyed to the land as the chief source of wealth and influence. It would bring forth (according to this ideal) a class of men with a strong sense of obligation to the community; men who lived not to gain advantage for themselves, but to meet the solemn obligations which had been laid on them by the very fact that they were privileged. From them the country would get its leadership; to them it could look for the higher values—of thought, of conduct, of personal deportment—to give it strength and virtue.

Lee embodied the noblest elements of this aristocratic ideal. Through him, the landed nobility justified itself. For four years, the Southern states had fought a desperate war to uphold the ideals for which Lee stood. In the end, it almost seemed as if the Confederacy fought for Lee; as if he himself was the Confederacy . . . the best thing that the way of life for which the Confederacy stood could ever have to offer. He had passed into legend before Appomattox. Thousands of tired, underfed, poorly clothed Confederate soldiers, long past the simple enthusiasm of the early days of the struggle, somehow considered Lee the symbol of everything for which they had been willing to die. But they could not quite put this feeling into words. If the Lost Cause, sanctified by so much heroism and so many deaths, had a living justification, its justification was General Lee.

Grant

Grant, the son of a tanner on the Western frontier, was everything Lee was not. He had come up the hard way and embodied nothing in particular except the eternal toughness and sinewy fiber of the men who grew up beyond the mountains. He was one of a body of men who owed reverence and obeisance to no one, who were self-reliant to a fault, who cared hardly anything for the past but who had a sharp eye for the future.

These frontier men were the precise opposites of the tidewater aristocrats. Back of them, in the great surge that had taken people over the Alleghenies and into the opening Western country, there was a deep, implicit dissatisfaction with a past that had settled into grooves. They stood for democracy, not from any reasoned conclusion about the proper ordering of human society, but simply because they had grown up in the middle of democracy and knew how it worked. Their society might have privileges, but they would be privileges each man had won for himself. Forms and patterns meant nothing. No man was born to anything, except perhaps to a chance to show how far he could rise. Life was competition.

Yet along with this feeling had come a deep sense of belonging to a national community. The Westerner who developed a farm, opened a shop, or set up in business as a trader, could hope to prosper only as his own community prospered—and his community ran from the Atlantic to the Pacific and from Canada down to Mexico. If the land was settled, with towns and highways and accessible markets, he could better himself. He saw his fate in terms of the nation's own destiny. As its horizons expanded, so did his. He had, in other words, an acute dollars-and-cents stake in the continued growth and development of his country.

Comment on the "most striking" contrast

And that, perhaps, is where the contrast between Grant and Lee becomes most striking. The Virginia aristocrat, inevitably, saw himself in relation to his own region. He lived in a static society which could endure almost anything except change. Instinctively, his first loyalty would go to the locality in which that society existed. He would fight to the limit of endurance to defend it, because in defending it he was defending everything that gave his own life its deepest meaning.

The Westerner, on the other hand, would fight with an equal tenacity for the broader concept of society. He fought so because everything he lived by was tied to growth, expansion, and a constantly widening horizon. What he lived by would survive or fall with the nation itself. He could not possibly stand by unmoved in the face of an attempt to destroy the Union. He would combat it with everything he had, because he could only see it as an effort to cut the ground out from under his feet.

So Grant and Lee were in complete contrast, representing two diametrically opposed elements in American life. Grant was the modern man emerging; beyond him, ready to come on the stage, was the great age of steel and machinery, of crowded cities and a restless, burgeoning vitality. Lee might have ridden down from the old age of chivalry, lance in hand, silken banner fluttering over his head. Each man was the perfect champion of his cause, drawing both his strengths and his weaknesses from the people he led.

Underlying similarities

Yet it was not all contrast, after all. Different as they were—in background, in personality, in underlying aspiration—these two great soldiers had much in common. Under everything else, they were marvelous fighters. Furthermore, their fighting qualities were really very much alike.

Each man had, to begin with, the great virtue of utter tenacity and fidelity. Grant fought his way down the Mississippi Valley in spite of acute personal discouragement and profound military handicaps. Lee hung on in the trenches at Petersburg after hope itself had died. In each man there was an indomitable quality...the born fighter's refusal to give up as long as he can still remain on his feet and lift his two fists.

Daring and resourcefulness they had, too; the ability to think faster and move faster than the enemy. These were the qualities which gave Lee the dazzling campaigns of Second Manassas and Chancellorsville and won Vicksburg for Grant.

Lastly, and perhaps greatest of all, there was the ability, at the end, to turn quickly from war to peace once the fighting was over. Out of the way these two men behaved at Appomattox came the possibility of a peace of reconciliation. It was a possibility not wholly realized, in the years to come, but which did, in the end, help the two sections to become one nation again ... after a war whose bitterness might have seemed to make such a reunion wholly impossible. No part of either man's life became him more than the part he played in their brief meeting in the McLean house at Appomattox. Their behavior there put all succeeding generations of Americans in their debt. Two great Americans, Grant and Lee—very different, yet under everything very much alike. Their encounter at Appomattox was one of the great moments of American history.

Comparison of Parts

If your purpose is to show how *parts* of one subject "play off" against parts of the other, then you will structure your piece according to those specific parts, or points of interest. Had Catton wanted to organize his essay in terms of parts, he would have done so as follows:

    I. Background
      A. Lee
      B. Grant

   II. Personality
      A. Lee
      B. Grant

  III. Underlying aspiration
      A. Lee
      B. Grant

A comparison may involve many parts, one following another in rapid succession with intricate (though always orderly) weaving back and forth between X and Y, sometimes within a single sentence. We see this process at work in the following essay which examines the comparative virtues of "fat" and "thin." Fat people are better, the author concludes, taking a highly provocative position by maintaining that "they're a hell of a lot *nicer* than the wizened and shriveled." Note how paragraphs alternate between how fat people and thin people relate to various *parts* of the total topic: "Thin people believe in logic," is the topic sentence of one paragraph, followed in the next paragraph with the topic sentence, "Fat people realize that life is illogical and unfair."

That Lean and Hungry Look

Suzanne Britt Jordan

Caesar was right. Thin people need watching. I've been watching them for most of my adult life, and I don't like what I see. When these narrow fellows spring at me, I quiver to my toes. Thin people come in all personalities, most of them menacing. You've got your "together" thin person, your mechanical thin person, your condescending thin person, your tsk-tsk thin person, your efficiency-expert thin person. All of them are dangerous.

In the first place, thin people aren't fun. They don't know how to goof off, at least in the best, fat sense of the word. They've always got to be adoing. Give them a coffee break, and they'll jog around the block. Supply them with a quiet evening at home, and they'll fix the screen door and lick S&H green stamps. They say things like "there aren't enough hours in the day." Fat people never say that. Fat people think the day is too damn long already.

Thin people make me tired. They've got speedy little metabolisms that cause them to bustle briskly. They're forever rubbing their bony hands together and eying new problems to "tackle." I like to surround myself with sluggish, inert, easygoing fat people, the kind who believe that if you clean it up today, it'll just get dirty again tomorrow.

Some people say the business about the jolly fat person is a myth, that all of us chubbies are neurotic, sick, sad people. I disagree. Fat people may not be chortling all day long, but they're a hell of a lot *nicer* than the wizened and shriveled. Thin people turn surly, mean and hard at a young age because they never learn the value of a hot-fudge sundae for easing tension. Thin people don't like gooey soft things because they themselves are neither gooey nor soft. They are crunchy and dull, like carrots. They go straight to the heart of the matter while fat people let things stay all blurry and hazy and vague, the way things actually are. Thin people want to face the truth. Fat people know there is no truth. One of my thin friends is always staring at complex, unsolvable problems and saying, "The key thing is..." Fat people never say that. They know there isn't any such thing as the key thing about anything.

Thin people believe in logic. Fat people see all sides. The sides fat people see are rounded blobs, usually gray, always nebulous and truly not worth worrying about. But the thin person persists. "If you consume more calories than you burn," says one of my thin friends, "you will gain weight. It's that simple." Fat people always grin when they hear statements like that. They know better.

Fat people realize that life is illogical and unfair. They know very well that God is not in his heaven and all is not right with the world. If God was up there, fat people could have two doughnuts and a big orange drink anytime they wanted it.

Thin people have a long list of logical things they are always spouting off to me. They hold up one finger at a time as they reel off these things, so I won't lose track. They speak slowly as if to a young child. The list is long and full of holes. It contains tidbits like "get a grip on yourself," "cigarettes kill," "cholesterol clogs," "fit as a fiddle," "ducks in a row," "organize" and "sound fiscal management." Phrases like that.

They think these 2,000-point plans lead to happiness. Fat people know happiness is elusive at best and even if they could get the kind thin people talk about, they wouldn't want it. Wisely, fat people see that such programs are too dull, too hard, too off the mark. They are never better than a whole cheesecake.

Fat people know all about the mystery of life. They are the ones acquainted with the night, with luck, with fate, with playing it by ear. One thin person I know once suggested that we arrange all the parts of a jigsaw puzzle into groups according to size, shape and color. He figured this would cut the time needed to complete the puzzle by at least 50 per cent. I said I wouldn't do it. One, I like to muddle through. Two, what good would it do to finish early? Three, the jigsaw puzzle isn't the important thing. The important thing is the fun of four people (one thin person included) sitting around a card table, working a jigsaw puzzle. My thin friend had no use for my list. Instead of joining us, he went outside and mulched the boxwoods. The three remaining fat people finished the puzzle and made chocolate, double-fudged brownies to celebrate.

The main problem with thin people is they oppress. Their good intentions, bony torsos, tight ships, neat corners, cerebral machinations and pat solutions loom like dark clouds over the loose, comfortable, spread-out, soft world of the fat. Long after fat people have removed their coats and shoes and put their feet up on the coffee table, thin people are still sitting on the edge of the sofa, looking neat as a pin, discussing rutabagas. Fat people are heavily into fits of laughter, slapping their thighs and whooping it up, while thin people are still politely waiting for the punch line.

Thin people are downers. They like math and morality and reasoned evaluation of the limitations of human beings. They have their skinny little acts together. They expound, prognose, probe and prick.

Fat people are convivial. They will like you even if you're irregular and have acne. They will come up with a good reason why you never wrote the great American novel. They will cry in your beer with you. They will put your name in the pot. They will let you off the hook. Fat people will gab, giggle, guffaw, gallumph, gyrate and gossip. They are generous, giving and gallant. They are gluttonous and goodly and great. What you want when you're down is soft and jiggly, not muscled and stable. Fat people know this. Fat people have plenty of room. Fat people will take you in.

Similarities and Differences

Still a third organizational pattern, in some ways the most straightforward, involves a simple grouping of *similarities and differences*. Had Catton chosen this pattern, he would have followed the procedure outlined as follows:

I. Differences between Lee and Grant

    A. Background
        1. Lee: tidewater Virginia
        2. Grant: Western frontier

    B. Personality
        1. Lee: an "English country squire" type
        2. Grant: a rugged individualist of the New World

    C. Underlying aspiration
        1. Lee: aristocratic
        2. Grant: democratic

II. Similarities between Lee and Grant

    A. Tenacity and fidelity to cause
        1. Lee
        2. Grant

    B. Daring and resourcefulness
        1. Lee
        2. Grant

    C. Ability to turn from war to peace
        1. Lee
        2. Grant

In most cases writers will present the position they want to stress in the later, more emphatic part of the essay. In the Catton piece, of course, contrast was the basic theme of the essay; similarities underlying the contrast were added thoughts. Where a writer wants to stress one or the other, however, it is generally wise to place the most important section in the final or "climactic" position. This principle of emphasis applies at every level of discourse, ranging from sentence to paragraph to whole essay: that which comes last is the most important, most dramatic, most surprising, most forcibly fixed in the reader's mind. Observing this psychological truth, Northrop Frye, in the essay below, moves from the obvious similarities between myth and folk tale to the not-so-obvious differences.

Myth and Folk Tale

Northrop Frye

Similarities
noted

By a myth . . . I mean primarily a certain type of story . . . in which some of the chief characters are gods or other beings larger in power than humanity. Very seldom is it located in history: its action takes place in a world above or prior to ordinary time. . . . Hence, like the folk tale, it is an *abstract story-pattern*. The characters can do what they like, which means what the story-teller likes: there is no need to be plausible or logical in motivation. The things that happen in myth are things that happen only in stories; they are in a self-contained literary world. Hence myth would naturally have the same kind of appeal for the fiction writer that folk tales have. It presents him with a ready-made framework, hoary with antiquity, and allows him to devote all his energies to elaborating its design. Thus the use of myth in Joyce or Cocteau, like the use of folk tale in Mann, is parallel to the use of abstraction and other means of emphasizing design in contemporary painting; and a modern writer's interest in primitive fertility rites is parallel to a modern sculptor's interest in primitive woodcarving.

Differences
noted

The differences between myth and folk tale, however, also have their importance. Myths, as compared with folk tales, are usually in a special category of seriousness: they are believed to have "really happened," or to have some exceptional significance in explaining certain features of life, such as ritual. Again, whereas folk tales simply interchange motifs and develop variants, myths show an odd tendency to stick together and build up bigger structures. We have creation myths, fall and flood myths, metamorphosis and dying-god myths, divine-marriage and hero-ancestry myths, etiological myths, apocalyptic myths; and writers of sacred scriptures or collectors of myth like Ovid tend to arrange these in a series. And while myths themselves are seldom historical, they seem to provide a kind of containing form of tradition, one result of which is the obliterating of boundaries separating legend, historical reminiscence, and actual history that we find in Homer and the Old Testament.

As a type of story, myth is a form of verbal art, and belongs to the world of art. Like art, and unlike science, it deals, not with the world that man contemplates, but with the world that man creates. The total form of art, so to speak, is a world whose content is nature but whose form is human; hence when it "imitates" nature it assimilates nature to human forms. The world of art is human in perspective, a world in which the sun continues to rise and set long after science has explained that its rising and setting are illusions. And myth, too, makes a systematic attempt to see nature in human shape: it does not simply roam at large in nature like the folk tale.

Note that in contrasting the two types of stories, myth and folk tale, Frye accentuates the qualities of each. This is one of the important rhetorical advantages of the comparative approach: each side of the comparison more clearly delineates the other; each *highlights* the other by bringing out distinctive points of similarity or difference.

Comparing Poems

The following poems deal with the same theme—death. Beyond this basic similarity, there are many differences. Read the poems carefully and see how many points of likeness and difference you can detect.

Death Be Not Proud

John Donne

Death, be not proud, though some have called thee
Mighty and dreadful, for thou art not so;
For those whom thou think'st thou dost overthrow
Die not, poor Death, nor yet canst thou kill me.
From rest and sleep, which but thy pictures be,
Much pleasure; then from thee much more must flow,
And soonest our best men with thee do go,
Rest of their bones, and soul's delivery.
Thou art slave to fate, chance, kings, and desperate men,
And dost with poison, war, and sickness dwell,
And poppy or charms can make us sleep as well
And better than thy stroke; why swell'st thou then?
One short sleep past, we wake eternally
And death shall be no more; Death, thou shalt die.

Do Not Go Gentle into That Good Night

Dylan Thomas

Do not go gentle into that good night,
Old age should burn and rave at close of day;
Rage, rage against the dying of the light.

Though wise men at their end know dark is right,
Because their words had forked no lightning they
Do not go gentle into that good night.

Good men, the last wave by, crying how bright
Their frail deeds might have danced in a green bay,
Rage, rage against the dying of the light.

Wild men who caught and sang the sun in flight,
And learn, too late, they grieved it on its way,
Do not go gentle into that good night.

Grave men, near death, who see with blinding sight
Blind eyes could blaze like meteors and be gay,
Rage, rage against the dying of the light.

And you, my father, there on the sad height,
Curse, bless, me now with your fierce tears, I pray.
Do not go gentle into that good night.
Rage, rage against the dying of the light.

Timor Mortis Conturbat Me

(The Fear of Death Disturbs Me)

R. L. Chapman

My Lord Death, hear this petition:
You are (Thou art?) a goodly lord,
I know cerebrally;
Handsomer than that grinning clanky clown
We show you as;
Goodly, opulently velvety dark
And somberly lovely.

Pray, Lord, when you extinguish me,
Do it micro-fast and from behind,
So he did not know what hit him.
And wait, if you can manage
In your cleansing economy,
Until I am old enough to be the elegant
Rarefied abstraction of a man,
A paper person so fined by abrasive years
As to be more symbolic than real.

Then strike, and hear him rustle as he falls.

DISCUSSION AND EXERCISES

1. After noting specific points of similarity and difference in the preceding poems, write a one- or two-paragraph report of your findings. Be prepared to describe and explain your choice of organizational pattern—for example, comparison of parts or of wholes.
2. In "Grant and Lee: A Study in Contrasts" the two generals are shown to be different and alike. Cite the specific points of difference and likeness, indicating whether they are organized methodically and logically.
3. Write a one-paragraph essay (150–250 words) showing that X is not like Y, on the basis of specific points. Choose one pair of topics from one of the following categories. (Note: The

specific points of difference need not be factual details in every case; a "point" may be an example, an analogy, an attitude, as in the comparison of Kennedy and Johnson. The "points" may also be the ramifications of one main point.) Use the prewriting techniques you have learned.

a. Warfare

> conventional/guerrilla
> Korea/Vietnam
> atomic weapons/conventional weapons
> atomic warfare/germ warfare
> offensive/defensive

b. Astronomy

> astronomy/astrology
> dawn/dusk
> sun/moon
> planet/star
> Earth/Mars

c. Eating

> appetite/hunger
> home cooking/college cafeteria
> eating to live/living to eat
> eating in the tropics/eating in the Arctic
> eating/dining

d. Fact and Fiction

> detectives/detectives in movies and television
> American Indians/Indians in movies and television
> family life/family life on a television series
> Marine Corps/movie marines
> courtroom/courtroom on television

4. Analyze the organization of parts in "That Lean and Hungry Look." Do you think the alternation of paragraphs addressed to "fat" and "thin" is the most effective mode of presentation? Explain. Would "comparison of wholes" or "similarities and differences" have worked as well? Explain. Comment on the tone of the piece.
5. Write a one- or two-paragraph comparison of the pair of pictures on page 370.
6. The following paired terms are close in meaning and therefore have to be distinguished from each other (either denotatively or connotatively—see page 515). Write one or two paragraphs in which you cite the essential difference or differences between the terms in one of the following pairs:

talent/genius	induction/deduction
aptitude/talent	libel/slander
conscience/guilt	liberty/license
knowledge/wisdom	class/caste
intelligence/knowledge	dissent/rebellion
cooperate/collaborate	wit/humor

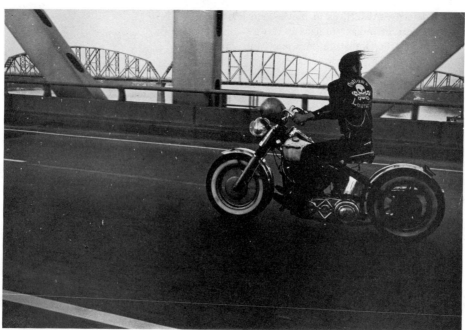

ESSAY SUGGESTIONS

1. Write an essay (500–1,000 words) in which you compare two men or two women, using as your organizational plan either comparison of wholes or comparison of parts. Use the prewriting techniques you have learned.

2. Drawing on your own experience, write an essay (500–1,000 words) on one of the following topics:

   a. Two things mistakenly believed to be alike

   b. A similarity (or difference) between two authors or two literary works (or two of anything) that no one, to your knowledge, has observed before.

3. Expand one of the paragraph exercises above into an essay of 500–750 words.

4. Write a defense (500–1,000 words) of "that lean and hungry look" in which you proclaim the superiority of thin people over fat people. Try to reply to points raised in Jordan's essay. Use the organization that best suits your purpose (comparison of wholes, comparison of parts, or similarities and differences).

17. What Is the Present Status of X?

CONCERNING A HISTORIC MONUMENT
No News from Auschwitz, A. M. Rosenthal
CONCERNING BASEBALL—AND WOMEN
The First Girl at Second Base, Susan Jacoby
CONCERNING TRAVEL
The Latest Fashion in Travel, Jan Morris

*A*lthough an aspect of comparison, the question of *present status* is important enough to merit a chapter of its own. You have only to consider the variety of timely, thought-provoking "then and now" essays to know why writers use present status so often. Indeed, in every professional field or discipline, as well as in every area of ordinary life, we must periodically bring things up to date, by asking "What is the present status of X?" or, in words we are more likely to use, "What is new about X?" or "What is happening with X?" or "How do people feel about X at the present moment?" or "How do *I* feel at the present time?" Whatever form it takes, the question leads to a special kind of comparison in which "now" is compared to "then."

We may properly ask the question, "What is its present status?" of almost any idea, habit, custom, condition, or belief. Is it "in" or "out"? Timely or obsolete? How is it different from or similar to what is was—and why? As Heraclitus pointed out more than two thousand years ago, the world is in a constant state of flux; nothing stands still; one never steps into the same stream twice. Thus there is always a story in an assessment of the present status of something.

CONCERNING A HISTORIC MONUMENT

Not surprisingly, then, in the summer of 1958—thirteen years after the defeat of Nazi Germany—an American correspondent went to Auschwitz, the most hideous of the Nazi concentration camps (where four million prisoners, mostly Jews, were murdered during the Second World War), to describe its present status. What is it like *now?* This was the question that he answered in the following news story, whose impact rests on the contrast between the ghastly activity of the past and the peaceful stillness of the present.

No News from Auschwitz

A. M. Rosenthal

The most terrible thing of all, somehow, was that at Brzezinka the sun was bright and warm, the rows of graceful poplars were lovely to look upon and on the grass near the gates children played.

It all seemed frighteningly wrong, as in a nightmare, that at Brzezinka the sun should ever shine or that there should be light and greenness and the sound of young laughter. It would be fitting if at Brzezinka the sun never shone and the grass withered because this is a place of unutterable terror.

And yet, every day, from all over the world, people come to Brzezinka, quite possibly the most grisly tourist center on earth. They come for a variety of reasons—to see if it could really have been true, to remind themselves not to forget, to pay homage to the dead by the simple act of looking upon their place of suffering.

Brzezinka is a couple of miles from the better-known southern Polish town of Oswiecim. Oswiecim has about 12,000 inhabitants, is situated about 171 miles from Warsaw and lies in a damp, marshy area at the eastern end of the pass called the Moravian Gate. Brzezinka and Oswiecim together formed part of that minutely organized factory of torture and death that the Nazis called Konzentrationslager Auschwitz.

By now, fourteen years after the last batch of prisoners was herded naked into the gas chambers by dogs and guards, the story of Auschwitz has been told a great many times. Some of the inmates have written of those events of which sane men cannot conceive. Rudolf Franz Ferdinand Hoess, the superintendent of the camp, before he was executed wrote his detailed memoirs of mass exterminations and the experiments on living bodies. Four million people died here, the Poles say.

And so there is no news to report about Auschwitz. There is merely the compulsion to write something about it, a compulsion that grows out of a restless feeling that to have visited Auschwitz and then turned away without having said or written anything would be a most grievous act of discourtesy to those who died here.

Brzezinka and Oswiecim are very quiet places now; the screams can no longer be heard. The tourist walks silently, quickly at first to get it over with and then, as his mind peoples the barracks and the chambers and the dungeons and flogging posts, he walks draggingly. The guide does not say much either, because there is nothing much for him to say after he has pointed.

For every visitor, there is one particular bit of horror that he knows he will never forget. For some it is seeing the rebuilt gas chamber at Oswiecim and being told that this is the "small one." For others it is the fact that at Brzezinka, in the ruins of the gas chambers and the crematoria the Germans blew up when they retreated, there are daisies growing. There are visitors who gaze blankly at the gas chambers and the furnaces because their minds simply cannot encompass them, but stand shivering before the great mounds of human hair behind the plate glass window or the piles of babies' shoes or the brick cells where men sentenced to death by suffocation were walled up.

One visitor opened his mouth in a silent scream simply at the sight of boxes—great stretches of three-tiered boxes in the women's barracks. They were about six feet wide, about three feet high, and into them from five to ten prisoners were shoved for the night. The guide walks quickly through the barracks. Nothing more to see here.

A brick building where sterilization experiments were carried out on women prisoners. The guide tries the door—it's locked. The visitor is grateful that he does not have to go in, and then flushes with shame.

A long corridor where rows of faces stare from the walls. Thousands of pictures, the photographs of prisoners. They are all dead now, the men and women who stood before the cameras, and they all knew they were to die.

They all stare blank-faced, but one picture, in the middle of a row, seizes the eye and wrenches the mind. A girl, 22 years old, plumply pretty, blonde. She is smiling gently, as at a sweet, treasured thought. What was the thought that passed through her young mind and is now her memorial on the wall of the dead at Auschwitz?

Into the suffocation dungeons the visitor is taken for a moment and feels himself strangling. Another visitor goes in, stumbles out and crosses herself. There is no place to pray at Auschwitz.

The visitors look pleadingly at each other and say to the guide, "Enough."

There is nothing new to report about Auschwitz. It was a sunny day and the trees were green and at the gates the children played.

CONCERNING BASEBALL—AND WOMEN

Things *ought* to have changed by now—but they haven't, laments feminist writer Susan Jacoby in the essay below. She is talking about the sports world and the dearth of women heroes with whom an athletically inclined young girl might identify. Notice the disappointment which surfaces at the end of the essay when Jacoby discovers that despite the feminist movement ten-year-old girls *still* have male rather than female sports idols.

The First Girl at Second Base

Susan Jacoby

Between the ages of seven and ten, I spent a good deal of time dreaming of the day I would follow in the footsteps of my hero, Jacob Nelson (Nellie) Fox, and play second base for the Chicago White Sox. The crowd would roar as I stepped up to the plate in the bottom of the ninth with two out, runners on second and third, and the Sox trailing by one run. The roar would turn to whoops of joy as I, like the ever-reliable Nellie, punched a game-winning hit through the infield.

In endless conversations between innings at Comiskey Park, I badgered my grandfather about my desire to break the sex barrier in major league baseball. Nellie was small for a ballplayer—the sportscasters called him "Little Nell"—and it was quite possible that I might grow up to be as tall as he was. If Jackie Robinson (another of my heroes) could become the first Negro in the big leagues, there was no reason why Susan Jacoby could not become the first girl on the diamond. No reason at all, my grandfather agreed. He was too softhearted to point out the facts of life to a granddaughter he had helped turn into a baseball nut.

Not all of my childhood heroes were sports figures, but they all had one thing in common: They were men. The most important nonsportsman in my pantheon was Franklin D. Roosevelt, who captured my imagination not because of anything he had done as President but because he had overcome polio. I associated heroism not only with courage but with the sort of courage that is expressed in a visible, physical way. I had never heard of any woman who embodied my notions of what a hero did and was.

When I questioned my women friends about their childhood heroes, an extraordinary number insisted they never had any. Of those who did remember, all but one acknowledged that their heroes had been men. It turned out that the exception—a woman who said Margaret Sanger had been her hero—was speaking from a newly acquired feminist consciousness rather than from any true memory of childhood.

When I asked men the same question, nearly all of them immediately produced long lists of heroes. All-male lists. Not a single man grew up with a woman for a hero. In fact, it seems that Eleanor Roosevelt was the only public woman (apart from movie stars) whose achievements impinged upon the consciousness of boys who were growing up in the 1930's, 40's, and 50's.

Growing up in a culture with male criteria for heroism undoubtedly exerts its influence on a boy's image of women. For a girl, though, the matter is more personal and more crucial: Her image of herself is at stake. Hero worship confined to the opposite sex—a phenomenon that seems to have been almost universal among women of my generation and almost nonexistent among men—poses a psychological problem on at least two levels.

On the surface level—the rational one—the problem is obvious and solvable. Reggie Jackson, who brought on a bad relapse of my baseball hero worship by hitting three home runs in the final game of this year's World Series, is just my age. I was not at all surprised to read in the sports pages that Jackie Robinson had been Reggie's hero as well as mine. The difference between us, of course, is that Reggie Jackson could grow up to play his hero's game.

The feminist movement has a sensible answer to the predicament of a girl who, having been born the wrong sex, can never grow up to be like her hero. Feminists say: "Give us our rightful place in the history books, establish equal opportunity for women now, and soon we'll have our share of heroes." Fair enough. A girl who dreams of achievement in sports or politics or law or medicine certainly has more women to emulate today than girls did when I was growing up.

The sensible feminist solution would be enough if a hero were only an object of emulation. The true function of the hero, however, lies in the realm of imagination. Most boys, after all, are no more likely to grow up to be Jackie Robinson than I was. Heroes give a child access to what the novelist Cynthia Ozick calls "the grand as if." When a young girl dreams of heroes, she dreams as if she were free: Limitations of height or weight or sex or race become irrelevant. A hero represents not so much a specific achievement as a whole range of human possibilities, an awe-inspiring glimpse of perfection.

On this level of awe and myth, it is difficult to develop a feminist alternative to the cultural values that have made both men and women regard heroism as a male characteristic. Heroism has almost always been linked with physical prowess and strength: Moral and physical courage are inseparable in most heroic sagas. This ideal of the hero places women at a disadvantage, because most societies have imposed severe restraints on public displays of female strength. Even today, when many of those restraints have crumbled, women are still at a disadvantage if the traditional concept of the hero is upheld. There is no getting around the fact that most men are stronger than most women.

Many adults talk about the need to smash traditional notions of heroism by stressing the moral rather than the physical aspects of courage. It sounds like a good idea, but I suspect these adults haven't been talking to many kids. In a sampling of my favorite ten-to-twelve-year-old girls, I elicited the name of just one woman hero: Billie Jean King. One of the girls expressed regret that her hero had trounced the aging Bobby Riggs rather than a man her own age. Two girls said their hero was the great Brazilian soccer player Pele, and two others, to my delight, mentioned Reggie Jackson. (I admit I spoke to the girls just a few days after the dramatic ending of the World Series.) One eleven-year-old said her ambition was to become a pilot and she was sorry America had never sent up a woman astronaut. So much for adult notions of dispensing with physical daring and achievement as standards of heroism.

There are people who think the end of the traditional hero would produce more realistic men and women. I doubt it. I still remember the pure joy I took in my baseball-playing fantasies. Doing well under extreme pressure was an important element in my fantasies, and that ideal is certainly suitable for any "realistic" adult. To dream as if you were free is a moving and beautiful experience—so beautiful that many adults feel obliged to forget it. I wish some of those dreams had come to me in the form of my own as well as of the opposite sex. Things ought to have changed by now, but it seems that barriers to women are more formidable in the world of heroes than in union hiring halls or executive suites.

CONCERNING TRAVEL

The following essay provides a witty description of the changing fashion in travel. While our grandfathers took the Grand Tour and ocean cruises, today's dedicated traveler heads for the Galápagos Islands and booby birds ("a place that almost nobody has been to, and a bird that practically no one has ever heard of"). Explaining that "class in holiday travel comes in cycles," Jan Morris points out with wry humor that the popular vacation place today is grubby, not glamorous. If you want to be a trendy traveler, she advises that you simply tell your travel agent "whether you prefer to freeze at the poles or boil in Equatoria, wade through swamps in search of amphibious reptiles or crouch in treetop blinds waiting for fruit bats." That's the "in" thing in travel today.

The Latest Fashion in Travel

Jan Morris

Not long ago a dear friend of mine who owns a travel agency invited me to join, as his guest, a group tour which was proving particularly popular, he said, among his more sophisticated clients. What could be more enjoyable? I asked myself. A week in Florence perhaps? A long meander through Japan? Wine tasting on the Côte d'Or? Unfortunately not. A short sharp trip to the Galápagos Islands was what he was offering, providing unrivaled opportunities, he assured me, for observation of the booby birds.

The *booby birds!* A world of great art, noble architecture, magnificent food, and lovely lazy beaches awaits the traveler out there, but what my friend's more urbane clients especially liked was ten days among the boobies of the Galápagos! "There's a nice little local boat," he said, "out of Guayaquil—not one of your luxury ships, of course, but with any luck you'll get a cabin to yourself."

It was a generous gift that he was offering me, for not only was the excursion extremely expensive, but it really was immensely popular. It exactly suited, it seems, the ethos of contemporary travel. It combined in just the right proportions a moderate degree of discomfort, at least the suggestion of adventure, a place that almost nobody has ever been to, and a bird that practically nobody has ever heard of. It was the very epitome of a classy traveling vacation, 1980s style.

For class in holiday travel comes in cycles. In our great-grandfathers' day the Grand Tour was the thing, and the vacationist boarded some grandiosely titled liner, *Leviathan* or *Majestic*, loaded with traveling trunks, patent medicines, and sketching materials, to potter amply around the trade routes in the process anomalously known as globe-trotting. Our grandparents, on the other hand, much preferred the frivolity of the Ocean Cruise—cocktails in Naples Bay, badinage at the captain's table, fox-trot rendezvous beneath the starboard lifeboats, and all that Noël Coward stuff.

After World War II, individual travel was the only socially acceptable kind (picking up a rented Mercedes at Frankfurt, revisiting the old squadron airfield at Chipping-in-the-Marsh) until the pauper-plutocrats of the hippie generation made the communal journey to Katmandu an absolute *sine qua non* of chic fulfillment. Today it is perfectly O.K. to go somewhere by train, preferably the Orient Express to Venice, or take a gastronomic barge tour through the French canals, but unquestionably the *really* smooth thing to do is to go and watch the booby birds.

They need not actually be boobies, of course, or even for that matter birds, and the Galápagos Islands are not a compulsory venue. Anywhere sufficiently remote, uncomfortable, and unfamiliar will do, and today there is almost no journey to be made on earth, almost no adventure to be undertaken, that cannot be arranged for you by a competent professional travel agent. Confide in him. Tell him whether you prefer to freeze at the poles or boil in Equatoria, wade through swamps in search of amphibious reptiles or crouch in treetop blinds waiting for fruit bats.

He will soon find the tour to suit you, for at any moment of the year these days there are ships full of tourists plowing through ice floes, planes full of tourists landing on jungle airstrips, jeeps full of tourists pursuing the yak tents of Mongolian nomads, pony caravans of tourists slogging through the Andes, trucks full of tourists being pushed out of flooded Bhutanese rivers.

The fashionable cycle has come full circle. The Grand Tourists, setting out so pompously to the blast of the farewell siren, were traveling partly for pleasure, of course, and partly for show, but partly for self-improvement. They wanted to see for themselves the marvels of art and architecture they had only read about, to learn more about the less fortunate peoples of the world, and to come home culturally and mentally richer for the trip. Travel in those days was, as they used to say in the brochures, a Truly Educational Experience. It Broadened the Mind.

Today rather the same emotions govern our generation of sophisticated travelers, for in many ways ours is an earnest age too. Even the hippies claimed to be traveling for enlightenment, and today your truly worldly pleasure traveler would not dream of traveling just for pleasure's sake. Holidaying is no longer just getting away from it all; it is more like jogging, and if you are into marathons, you are almost certainly into booby birds.

Of course there is a degree of exhibitionism still. Few of us are altogether immune to the temptations of self-display, and it really must be rather gratifying to be able to say that at this time last week you were in the Antarctic, or sharing a camel chop with an Uzbek chieftain. (Twenty years ago I used to like to claim that I was the thirtieth European ever to set foot in Namche Bazar, in the Sherpa country; now that there is an excellent small Japanese tourist hotel a little way up the Khumbu Valley, on the glacial track to Everest, I talk about the experience rather less often.) But there is also, I think, something a little wistful to the trend. It is as though history has gone rather too far for purely frivolous travel, time is shorter than we used to think, and we should treat the world in a spirit of adventurous but respectful inquiry, while we still have it. They may seem a little comical, those stalwarts of the PTA gnawing at their stew in the outback, those associate professors buckling on their Lapland snowshoes, those company presidents bumping sandgrimed across the Kalahari, but there is a certain grandeur to their folly, all the same.

Doubtless the fashion will shift again anyway, one of these days, and we shall enter another phase of holiday travel. What will it be next? I wonder. Shall we sophisticates of the group tour all be looking at disused coal mines or superannuated steam pumps on Industrial Archaeology Projects? Shall we all be going to Bath or Baden-Baden, taking the waters once again? Shall we be cycling through the Low Countries, or mucking out the shearing sheds on Farm Participation Holidays?

Anything is possible, in the ceaseless rotation of traveling fashion, but in the meantime there are always the boobies.

"Right, then," my friend said. "See you at Guayaquil, Tuesday week. Mind you bring strong shoes."

But no, I was nowhere near Guayaquil Tuesday week. Grateful though I was for the invitation, I had boobied out.

DISCUSSION AND EXERCISES

1. Answer the following questions about "No News from Auschwitz."
   a. In A. M. Rosenthal's grimly moving essay what is the basic and ironic contrast that makes everything seem "frighteningly wrong"?
   b. Point to other contrasting elements in this piece and show how they function as an organizing principle.
   c. Evaluate the function and effectiveness of the opening and closing paragraphs.
   d. In what way is the tone of this essay subdued?
   e. Discuss "restraint" as the fundamental rhetorical device of this essay. Cite specific examples of understatement, and speculate on what the piece might be like if the writer had not exercised restraint. Explain why the story would have been more or less effective.
   f. Discuss the simplicity of diction and the structure of the following sentences. Explain why you do or do not find them powerful.
      1. And so there is no news to report about Auschwitz.
      2. The guide does not say much either, because there is nothing much for him to say after he has pointed.
      3. Nothing more to see here.
   g. Explain the grammatical structure of the following sentences and indicate what rhetorical function they serve.
      1. A brick building where sterilization experiments were carried out on women prisoners.
      2. A long corridor where rows of faces stare from the walls.
      3. Thousands of pictures, the photographs of prisoners.
   h. Why does the writer single out and ponder the photograph of one prisoner—the "plumply pretty" blonde?
   i. What is the significance of the visitor who "crosses herself"? What extra dimension of meaning is introduced by this detail?
2. Write a one-paragraph (150–250 words) response to Rosenthal's essay. Consider the advantages and disadvantages of using a topic sentence at either the beginning (movement from general to specific) or the end of the paragraph (movement from specific to general). Be prepared to explain your decision.
3. Rhetorical Stance: Jan Morris, "The Latest Fashion in Travel"
   a. *Purpose:* What do you think to be the writer's purpose in this piece? What do you think she hopes to accomplish or communicate about "the ethos of contemporary travel"?
   b. *Occasion:* Appearing in the "Going to Extremes" travel department of *Vanity Fair* magazine, this column is one of a monthly series. Does the April issue sound appropriate for a piece of this kind? Characterize Morris's tone and point of view. Cite specific passages to support your answers.
   c. *Audience:* What sort of audience do you think Morris is addressing? How do you envision the readers of *Vanity Fair*?
   d. *Reader-Writer Relationship:* How does Morris see herself in relation to her audience? Is she "at a distance" or "one of them"? Is she critical? Approving? Discuss.

ESSAY SUGGESTIONS

1. In an essay (500–1,000 words) describe the present status of a place that has changed drastically—for better or worse—since you first knew or heard about it. Use the prewriting techniques you have learned before you begin to write.

2. Contemplate Susan Jacoby's lament. Write an essay (500–1,000 words) in which you support or challenge her observation that "barriers to women ... in the world of heroes" are still as formidable as ever.

OR

Write an essay (500–1,000 words) in which you cite another area in which "Things ought to have changed..." but have not.

3. In an essay (500–1,000 words) compare travelers of the past (THEN) with travelers of today (NOW) as you view them. Assume whatever rhetorical stance you feel is appropriate.

4. In an essay entitled "On the Status of the Soul," Bertrand Russell once pointed out that we are losing such "fine old simplicities" as the belief in an immortal soul. In an essay (500–1,000 words) describe the present status, as you view it, of one of the following established "simplicities":

> Be it ever so humble, there's no place like home.
> Honor thy father and thy mother.
> Love conquers all.
> You can't keep a good man down.
> There's always room at the top.
> Cleanliness is next to godliness.
> The good go to heaven and the bad go to hell.

18. How Should X Be Interpreted?

*B*eyond definition, description, and analysis—and to a large extent dependent on these basic processes—is the more subtle business of interpretation, of explaining what is not immediately apparent; of taking facts and going beyond them to discover the deeper meaning or significance of a subject, the relationship of particulars to a general principle, the truth that lies beneath the surface.

INTERPRETING AN ACTIVITY

Take the subject of football, for example. On the face of it, football is simply a popular spectator sport, a national pastime, a "he-man" game filled with action and excitement. On a deeper level, however—as the writer of the following essay points out—football is more than a game. It is an acting-out of basic and primitive human aggression, of a compulsion to gain and hold on to property. Note how the writer supports his interpretation by explaining explicit facts about the game on the basis of an implicit general principle.

Football—the Game of Aggression

George Stade

There are many ways in which professional football is unique among sports, and as many others in which it is the fullest expression of what is at the heart of all sports. There is no other major sport so dependent upon raw force, nor any so dependent on a complex and delicate strategy; none so wide in the range of specialized functions demanded from its players; none so dependent upon the undifferentiated athletic *sine qua non*, a quickwitted body; none so primitive; none so futuristic; none so American.

Football is first of all a form of play, something one engages in instinctively and only for the sake of performing the activity in question. Among forms of play, football is a game, which means that it is built on communal needs, rather than on private evasions, like mountain climbing. Among games it is a sport; it requires athletic ability, unlike croquet. And among sports, it is one whose mode is violence and whose violence is its special glory.

In some sports—basketball, baseball, soccer—violence is occasional (and usually illegal); in others, like hockey, it is incidental; in others still, car racing, for example, it is accidental. Definitive violence football shares alone with boxing and bullfighting, among major sports. But in bullfighting a man is pitted not against another man, but against an animal, and boxing is a competition between individuals, not teams, and that makes a great difference. If shame is the proper and usual penalty for failures in sporting competitions between individuals, guilt is the consequence of failing not only oneself and one's fans, but also one's teammates. Failure in football, moreover, seems more related to a failure of courage, seems more unmanning than in any other sport outside of bullfighting. In other sports one loses a knack, is outsmarted, or is merely inferior in ability, but in football, on top of these, a player fails because he "lacks desire," or "can't take it anymore," or "hears footsteps," as his teammates will put it.

Many sports, especially those in which there is a goal to be defended, seem enactments of the games animals play under the stimulus of what ethologists, students of animal behavior, call *territory*—"the drive to gain, maintain, and defend the exclusive right to a piece of property," as Robert Ardrey puts it. The most striking symptom of this drive is aggressiveness; but among social animals, such as primates, it leads to "amity for the social partner, hostility for the territorial neighbor." The territorial instinct is closely related to whatever makes animals establish pecking orders: the tangible sign of one's status within the orders is the size and value of the territory one is able to command. Individuals fight over status, groups over *lebensraum* and a bit more. These instincts, some ethologists have claimed, are behind patriotism and private property, and also, I would add, codes of honor, as among ancient Greeks, modern Sicilians, primitive hunters, teen-age gangs, soldiers, aristocrats, and athletes, especially football players.

The territorial basis of certain kinds of sports is closest to the surface in football, whose plays are all attempts to gain and defend property through aggression. Does this not make football *par excellence* the game of instinctual satisfactions, especially among Americans, who are notorious as violent patriots and instinctive defenders of private property? (At the same time, in football this drive is more elaborated than in other sports by whatever turns instinct into art; football is more richly patterned, more formal, more complex in the functions of its parts, which makes football *par excellence* the game of esthetic satisfactions.) Even the unusual amity, if that is the word, that exists among football players has been remarked upon, notably by Norman Mailer. And what is it that corresponds in football to the various feathers, furs, fins, gorgeous colors by means of which animals puff themselves into exaggerated gestures of masculine potency? The football player's equipment, of course. His cleats raise him an inch off the ground. Knee and thigh pads thrust the force lines of his legs forward. His pants are tight against his rump and the back of his thighs, portions of his body which the requirements of the game stuff with muscle. Even the tubby guard looks slim of waist by comparison with his shoulders, extended half a foot on each side by padding. Finally the helmet, which from the esthetic point of view most clearly expresses the genius of the sport. Not only does the helmet make the player inches taller and give his head a size proportionate to the rest of him; it makes him anonymous, inscrutable, more serviceable as a symbol. The football player in uniform strikes the eye in a succession of gestalt shifts: first a hooded phantom out of the paleolithic past of the species; then a premonition of a future of spacemen.

In sum, and I am almost serious about this, football players are to America what tragic actors were to ancient Athens and gladiators to Rome: models of perennially heroic, aggressive, violent humanity, but adapted to the social realities of the times and places that formed them.

INTERPRETING HUMAN BEHAVIOR

Just as George Stade probes beneath the surface activity of a national sport, so G. K. Chesterton, popular turn-of-the-century essayist, probes beneath the surface behavior of people coping with everyday inconveniences. Chesterton insists that inconveniences should not be interpreted as such, and he supports his position by ingeniously reinterpreting them as "of the mind." Is there a fly in your milk? A piece of cork floating in your glass of wine? Not to worry, Chesterton tells us, it's quite all right. One's "sense of wrong" is "really subjective and relative."

Chesterton's prose style has a touch of nineteenth century grandeur. One runs after a hat, for instance, "with the manliest ardor and the most sacred joy." On the other hand, there is an equal touch of the plain, uncluttered prose style characteristic of modern times. "A man running after a hat is not half so ridiculous as a man running after a wife," he observes with amusing directness. Most important, Chesterton's way of viewing the world and interpreting one's lot in life is timelessly lively, good-humored, and upbeat.

On Running After One's Hat

G. K. Chesterton

Most of the inconveniences that make men swear or women cry are really sentimental or imaginative inconveniences—things altogether of the mind. For instance, we often hear grown-up people complaining of having to hang about a railway station and wait for a train? No; for to him to be inside a railway station is to be inside a cavern of wonder and a palace of poetical pleasures. Because to him the red light and the green light on the signal are like a new sun and new moon. Because to him when the wooden arm of the signal falls down suddenly, it is as if a great king had thrown down his staff as a signal and started a shrieking tournament of trains. I myself am of little boys' habit in this matter. They also serve who only stand and wait for the two-fifteen. Their meditations may be full of rich and fruitful things. Many of the most purple hours of my life have been passed at Clapham Junction, which is now, I suppose, under water. I have been there in many moods so fixed and mystical that the water might well have come up to my waist before I noticed it particularly. But, in the case of all such annoyances, as I have said, everything depends upon the emotional point of view. You can safely apply the test to almost every one of the things that are currently talked of as the typical nuisances of daily life.

For instance, there is a current impression that it is unpleasant to have to run after one's hat. Why should it be unpleasant to the well-ordered and pious mind? Not merely because it is running, and running exhausts one. The same people run much faster in games and sports. The same people run much more eagerly after an uninteresting little leather ball than they will after a nice silk hat. There is an idea that it is humiliating to run after one's hat, and when people say it is humiliating they mean that it is comic. It certainly is comic; but man is a very comic creature, and most of the things he does are comic—eating, for instance. And the most comic things of all are exactly the things that are most worth doing—such as making love. A man running after a hat is not half so ridiculous as a man running after a wife.

Now a man could, if he felt rightly in the matter, run after his hat with the manliest ardor and the most sacred joy. He might regard himself as a jolly huntsman pursuing a wild animal, for certainly no animal could be wilder. In fact, I am inclined to believe that hat-hunting on windy days will be the sport of the upper classes in the future. There will be a meet of ladies and gentlemen on some high ground on a gusty morning. They will be told that the professional attendants have started a hat in such-and-such a thicket, or whatever be the technical term. Notice that this employment will in the fullest degree combine sport with humanitarianism. The hunters would feel that they were not inflicting pain. Nay, they would feel that they were inflicting pleasure, rich, almost riotous pleasure, upon the people who were looking on. When last I saw an old gentleman running after his hat in Hyde Park, I told him that a heart so benevolent as his ought to be filled with peace and thanks at the thought of how much unaffected pleasure his every gesture and bodily attitude were at that moment giving to the crowd.

The same principle can be applied to every other typical domestic worry. A gentleman trying to get a fly out of the milk or a piece of cork out of his glass of wine often imagines himself to be irritated. Let him think for a moment of the patience of anglers sitting by dark pools, and let his soul be immediately irradiated with gratification and repose. Again, I have known some people of very modern views driven by their distress to the use of theological terms to which they attached no doctrinal significance, merely because a drawer was jammed tight and they could not pull it out. A friend of mine was particularly afflicted in this way. Every day his drawer was jammed, and every day in consequence it was something else that rhymes to it. But I pointed out to him that this sense of wrong was really subjective and relative; it rested entirely upon the assumption that the drawer could, should, and would come out easily. "But if," I said, "you picture to yourself that you are pulling against some powerful and oppressive enemy, the struggle will become merely exciting and not exasperating. Imagine that you are roping up a fellow creature out of an Alpine crevasse. Imagine even that you are a boy again and engaged in a tug-of-war between French and English." Shortly after saying this I left him; but I have no doubt at all that my words bore the best possible fruit. I have no doubt that every day of his life he hangs on to the handle of that drawer with a flushed face and eyes bright with battle, uttering encouraging shouts to himself, and seeming to hear all round him that roar of an applauding ring.

So I do not think it altogether fanciful or incredible to suppose that even the floods in London may be accepted and enjoyed poetically. Nothing beyond inconvenience seems really to have been caused by them; and inconvenience, as I have said, in only one aspect, and that the most unimaginative and accidental aspect of a really romantic situation. An adventure is only an inconvenience rightly considered. An inconvenience is only an adventure wrongly considered. . . .

INTERPRETING A STORY

Whereas analysis breaks down a subject, interpretation synthesizes or puts it together. To formulate a convincing interpretation, then, the writer must see the scattered parts of a subject as contributing on a deeper level to a unified whole. Seen in this light, all of literary criticism involves interpretation, a probing into the individual elements of a poem or story to see how they are related to one another and to the whole. What is the writer trying to tell us beyond the surface details? What larger statement is he or she making? How do the single details contribute to the statement? All of literature, like most other human activities, lends itself to interpretation. Take a relatively simple, seemingly pointless short story such as the following, and then judge one critic's interpretation of what the surface details add up to.

Clay

James Joyce

The matron had given her leave to go out as soon as the women's tea was over and Maria looked forward to her evening out. The kitchen was spick and span: the cook said you could see yourself in the big copper boilers. The fire was nice and bright and on one of the side-tables were four very big barmbracks. These barmbracks seemed uncut; but if you went closer you would see that they had been cut into long thick even slices and were ready to be handed round at tea. Maria had cut them herself.

Maria was a very, very small person indeed but she had a very long nose and a very long chin. She talked a little through her nose, always soothingly: *"Yes, my dear,"* and *"No, my dear."* She was always sent for when the women quarrelled over their tubs and always succeeded in making peace. One day the matron had said to her:

"Maria, you are a veritable peace-maker!"

And the sub-matron and two of the Board ladies had heard the compliment. And Ginger Mooney was always saying what she wouldn't do to the dummy who had charge of the irons if it wasn't for Maria. Everyone was so fond of Maria.

The women would have their tea at six o'clock and she would be able to get away before seven. From Ballsbridge to the Pillar, twenty minutes; from the Pillar to Drumcondra, twenty minutes; and twenty minutes to buy the things. She would be there before eight. She took out her purse with the silver clasps and read again the words *A Present from Belfast.* She was very fond of the purse because Joe had brought it to her five years before when he and Alphy had gone to Belfast on a Whit-Monday trip. In the purse were two half-crowns and some coppers. She would have five shillings clear after paying tram fare. What a nice evening they would have, all the children singing! Only she hoped that Joe wouldn't come in drunk. He was so different when he took any drink.

Often he had wanted her to go and live with them; but she would have felt herself in the way (though Joe's wife was ever so nice with her), and she had become accustomed to the life of the laundry. Joe was a good fellow. She had nursed him and Alphy too; and Joe used often say:

"Mamma is mamma but Maria is my proper mother."

After the break-up at home the boys had got her that position in the *Dublin by Lamplight* laundry, and she liked it. She used to have such a bad opinion of Protestants but now she thought they were very nice people, a little quiet and serious, but still very nice people to live with. Then she had her plants in the conservatory and she liked looking after them. She had lovely ferns and wax-plants and, whenever anyone came to visit her, she always gave the visitor one or two slips from her conservatory. There was one thing she didn't like and that was the tracts on the walks; but the matron was such a nice person to deal with, so genteel.

When the cook told her everything was ready she went into the women's room and began to pull the big bell. In a few minutes the women began to come in by twos and threes, wiping their steaming hands in their petticoats and pulling down the sleeves of their blouses over their red steaming arms. They settled down before their huge mugs which the cook and the dummy filled up with hot tea, already mixed with milk and sugar in huge tin cans. Maria superintended the distribution of the barmbrack and saw that every woman got her four slices. There was a great deal of laughing and joking during the meal. Lizzie Fleming said Maria was sure to get the ring and, though Fleming had said that for so many Hallow Eves, Maria had to laugh and say she didn't want any ring or man either; and when she laughed her grey-green eyes sparkled with disappointed shyness and the tip of her nose nearly met the tip of her chin. Then Ginger Mooney lifted up her mug of tea and proposed Maria's health while all the other women clattered with their mugs on the table, and said she was sorry she hadn't a sup of porter to drink it in. And Maria laughed again till the tip of her nose nearly met the tip of her chin and till her minute body nearly shook itself asunder because she knew that Mooney meant well though, of course, she had the notions of a common woman.

But wasn't Maria glad when the women had finished their tea and the cook and the dummy had begun to clear away the tea-things! She went into her little bedroom and, remembering that the next morning was a mass morning, changed the hand of the alarm from seven to six. Then she took off her working skirt and her house-boots and laid her best skirt out on the bed and her tiny dress-boots beside the foot of the bed. She changed her blouse too and, as she stood before the mirror, she thought of how she used to dress for mass on Sunday morning when she was a young girl; and she looked with quaint affection at the diminutive body which she had so often adorned. In spite of its years she found it a nice tidy little body.

When she got outside the streets were shining with rain and she was glad of her old brown waterproof. The tram was full and she had to sit on the little stool at the end of the car, facing all the people, with her toes barely touching the floor. She arranged in her mind all she was going to do and thought how much better it was to be independent and to have your own money in your pocket. She hoped they would have a nice evening. She was sure they would but she could not help thinking what a pity it was Alphy and Joe were not speaking. They were always falling out now but when they were boys together they used to be the best of friends: but such was life.

She got out of her tram at the Pillar and ferreted her way quickly among the crowds. She went into Downes's cake-shop but the shop was so full of people that it was a long time before she could get herself attended to. She bought a dozen of mixed penny cakes, and at last came out of the shop laden with a big bag. Then she thought what else would she buy: she wanted to buy something really nice. They would be sure to have plenty of apples and nuts. It was hard to know what to buy and all she could think of was cake. She decided to buy some plumcake but Downes's plumcake had not enough almond icing on top of it so she went over to a shop in Henry Street. Here she was a long time in suiting herself and the stylish young lady behind the counter, who was evidently a little annoyed by her, asked her was it wedding-cake she wanted to buy. That made Maria blush and smile at the young lady; but the young lady took it all very seriously and finally cut a thick slice of plumcake, parcelled it up and said:

"Two-and-four, please."

She thought she would have to stand in the Drumcondra tram because none of the young men seemed to notice her but an elderly gentleman made room for her. He was a stout gentleman and he wore a brown hard hat; he had a square red face and a greyish moustache. Maria thought he was a colonel-looking gentleman and she reflected how much more polite he was than the young men who simply stared straight before them. The gentleman began to chat with her about Hallow Eve and the rainy weather. He supposed the bag was full of good things for the little ones and said it was only right that the youngsters should enjoy themselves while they were young. Maria agreed with him and favoured him with demure nods and hems. He was very nice with her, and when she was getting out at the Canal Bridge she thanked him and bowed, and he bowed to her and raised his hat and smiled agreeably; and while she was going up along the terrace, bending her tiny head under the rain, she thought how easy it was to know a gentleman even when he has a drop taken.

Everybody said: *"O, here's Maria!"* when she came to Joe's house. Joe was there, having come home from business, and all the children had their Sunday dresses on.

There were two big girls in from next door and games were going on. Maria gave the bag of cakes to the eldest boy, Alphy, to divide and Mrs. Donnelly said it was too good of her to bring such a big bag of cakes and made all the children say:

"Thanks, Maria."

But Maria said she had brought something special for papa and mamma, something they would be sure to like, and she began to look for her plumcake. She tried in Downes's bag and then in the pockets of her waterproof and then on the hallstand but nowhere could she find it. Then she asked all the children had any of them eaten it—by mistake, of course—but the children all said no and looked as if they did not like to eat cakes if they were to be accused of stealing. Everybody had a solution for the mystery and Mrs. Donnelly said it was plain that Maria had left it behind her in the tram. Maria, remembering how confused the gentleman with the greyish moustache had made her, coloured with shame and vexation and disappointment. At the thought of the failure of her little surprise and of the two and fourpence she had thrown away for nothing she nearly cried outright.

But Joe said it didn't matter and made her sit down by the fire. He was very nice with her. He told her all that went on in his office, repeating for her a smart answer which he had made to the manager. Maria did not understand why Joe laughed so much over the answer he had made but she said that the manager must have been a very overbearing person to deal with. Joe said he wasn't so bad when you knew how to take him, that he was a decent sort so long as you didn't rub him the wrong way. Mrs. Donnelly played the piano for the children and they danced and sang. Then the two next-door girls handed round the nuts. Nobody could find the nutcrackers and Joe was nearly getting cross over it and asked how did they expect Maria to crack nuts without a nutcracker. But Maria said she didn't like nuts and that they weren't to bother about her. Then Joe asked would she take a bottle of stout and Mrs. Donnelly said there was port wine too in the house if she would prefer that. Maria said she would rather they didn't ask her to take anything: but Joe insisted.

So Maria let him have his way and they sat by the fire talking over old times and Maria thought she would put in a good word for Alphy. But Joe cried that God might strike him stone dead if ever he spoke a word to his brother again and Maria said she was sorry she had mentioned the matter. Mrs. Donnelly told her husband it was a great shame for him to speak that way of his own flesh and blood but Joe said that Alphy was no brother of his and there was nearly being a row on the head of it. But Joe said he would not lose his temper on account of the night it was and asked his wife to open some more stout. The two next-door girls had arranged some Hallow Eve games and soon everything was merry again. Maria was delighted to see the children so merry and Joe and his wife in such good spirits. The next-door girls put some saucers on the table and then led the children up to the table, blindfold. One got the prayer-book and the other three got the water; and when one of the next-door girls got the ring Mrs. Donnelly shook her finger at the blushing girl as much as to say: *O, I know all about it!* They insisted then on blindfolding Maria and leading her up to the table to see what she would get; and, while they were putting on the bandage, Maria laughed and laughed again till the tip of her nose nearly met the tip of her chin.

They led her up to the table amid laughing and joking and she put her hand out in the air as she was told to do. She moved her hand about here and there in the air and descended on one of the saucers. She felt a soft wet substance with her fingers and was surprised that nobody spoke or took off her bandage. There was a pause for a few seconds; and then a great deal of scuffling and whispering. Somebody said something about the garden, and at last Mrs. Donnelly said something very cross to one of the next-door girls and told her to throw it out at once: that was no play. Maria understood that it was wrong that time and so she had to do it over again: and this time she got the prayer-book.

After that Mrs. Donnelly played Miss McCloud's Reel for the children and Joe made Maria take a glass of wine. Soon they were all quite merry again and Mrs. Donnelly said Maria would enter a convent before the year was out because she had got the prayer-book. Maria had never seen Joe so nice to her as he was that night, so full of pleasant talk and reminiscences. She said they were all very good to her.

At last the children grew tired and sleepy and Joe asked Maria would she not sing some little song before she went, one of the old songs. Mrs. Donnelly said *"Do, please, Maria!"* and so Maria had to get up and stand beside the piano. Mrs. Donnelly bade the children be quiet and listen to Maria's song. Then she played the prelude and said *"Now, Maria!"* and Maria, blushing very much, began to sing in a tiny quavering voice. She sang *I Dreamt that I Dwelt*, and when she came to the second verse she sang again:

> *I dreamt that I dwelt in marble halls*
> *With vassals and serfs at my side,*
> *And of all who assembled within those walls*
> *That I was the hope and the pride.*
>
> *I had riches too great to count; could boast*
> *Of a high ancestral name,*
> *But I also dreamt, which pleased me most,*
> *That you loved me still the same.*

But no one tried to show her her mistake; and when she had ended her song Joe was very much moved. He said that there was no time like the long ago and no music for him like poor old Balfe, whatever other people might say; and his eyes filled up so much with tears that he could not find what he was looking for and in the end he had to ask his wife to tell him where the corkscrew was.

Interpretation of Joyce's "Clay"

Florence L. Walzl

Conflicting elements in Maria, the heroine of James Joyce's "Clay" in *Dubliners*, have led to contradictory interpretations of the character: as saint (William T. Noon, "Joyce's 'Clay': An Interpretation," *College English*, XVII, 1955, 93–95); as thematically disunified combination of laundress, witch, and Virgin Mary figure (Marvin Magalaner and Richard M. Kain, *Joyce: The Man, The Work, The Reputation*, New York, 1956, 84–91); and as unconsciously selfish troublemaker (Richard Carpenter and Daniel Leary, "The Witch Maria," *James Joyce Review*, III, 1959, 3–7). I believe "Clay" is a thematic whole based on a set of contrasts relating to the two church holidays which provide the setting and to the two fortunes the heroine receives in a fortune-telling game.

The setting is Halloween, the night in folk tradition when the dead walk, and (by the anticipation of the heroine) All Saints' Day, a feast honoring all the blessed, both those proclaimed publicly in canonization and those completely unknown to the world. The fact that it celebrates, especially, the unheralded saints of ordinary life has a thematic relationship to the story, as does the walking abroad of spirits on All Hallows' Eve.

The plot of "Clay" is simple. A middle-aged spinster named Maria, a humble kitchen worker in a laundry, spends Halloween with a family, perhaps relatives, for whom she has been nursemaid. While blindfolded in a game of fortunes, she chooses the clay portending death. Her friends quickly hide this choice from her and substitute a prayerbook prophetic of a future convent life. The pathos is deepened by the contrast between the emptiness and futility of her life as it is and as it might have been. For this little laundress has the potential qualities of ideal woman and mother but their development has been stunted by the circumstances of her life.

In a sense, there are two Marias in this story: the Maria of the laundry and the Maria of the Halloween excursion. Within the confines of the laundry, several of Maria's qualities, her goodness, peaceableness, and loving motherliness, are greatly stressed. Both as a worker and a person her goodness is evident. She labors to make the scullery of the laundry a pleasant happy place: the kitchen is "spic and span," the fire "nice and bright," the barmbracks perfectly cut, the plants well-kept. She sees that each laundress is well served at teatime. She spends her hard-earned money buying cakes for the children of the family and plumcake for their elders. Much also is made of her peaceableness. "She was always sent for when the women quarreled over their tubs and always succeeded in making peace." She always thinks the best of people. The matron of the laundry calls her a veritable peace-maker." Finally, she is loving and motherly. She evokes the affection of the rough washerwomen who all are "so fond of Maria." She likes to recall the children she formerly nursed who called her their "proper mother." She looks forward happily to the family evening with "all the children singing." Even her name suggests the Church's prototype of the ideal maid and mother in the Virgin Mary. This Maria with her alarm clock set for the early morning mass of All Saints' Day suggests the very kind of saint this feast was inaugurated to honor.

But Maria on her Halloween visitation seems quite different. Though her goodness and generosity within the rounds of the laundry are effective, outside it they are not. In her timidity and lack of experience she loses the plumcake that was to have been her gift to the family and irritates the children over its loss. Moreover, her very presence upsets the adults because they feel the pathos of her life. At one point, Joe's eyes so fill with tears that he cannot find the corkscrew for the family toast. Her peaceableness, which is so marked within the laundry, is also ineffective without. She annoys the salesgirl in the bakeshop, is unable to heal the breach between the two brothers, and unwittingly provokes three near-quarrels: over Alphy, over some nuts, and over her choice of the clay. Also the emotional frustration of her life and its lack of human love are emphasized. Through a series of incidents suggesting romance, Joyce indicates that romantic and maternal love remain undeveloped in Maria. The laundresses' teasing about the ring, the shop girl's suggestion that the plumcake is for a wedding, the gallantry of the gentleman in the tram, and, above all, the verse from "I Dreamt That I Dwelt in Marble Halls" Maria forgets, a verse dealing with marriage proposals—all remind us of the sterility of her life. Finally, her appearance is that of "a very, very small person" with a "very long nose and a very long chin" which nearly meet. This Maria, ineffectual and trouble-making, suggests a Halloween witch.

What is Joyce's intent in this contrast which suggests saint and witch, life and death? I believe the answer is suggested in part by the two fortunes Maria receives at the party, the prayerbook and the clay—the first thematically associated with the saints' day, the second with the Halloween spirits. Both represent her future; both are death symbols.

The prayerbook, the fortune contrived by the family and forced upon her, is her immediate future, the life Irish society has molded for Maria. (In fact, her laundry job had been arranged for her by the family.) Her life in the laundry is a convent-like existence of narrow piety and goodness but without spiritual elevation, a life of small endeavors spent among women of a low class. Yet Maria had the potentialities for being the kind of heroic woman of full experience sainthood implies. Celibacy for a person ideally suited for marriage is a deprivation of life. The prayerbook for Maria is a sterility-death symbol.

Her hidden fortune, the clay, prophetic of death, suggests all that the ultimate future holds for her. In combination with Joyce's description of her as a Halloween wraith, it probably suggests also that she is not fully alive. Prevented by circumstances from full development of self, she represents virtue in an arrested state. Maria is one of the living dead of *Dubliners* who like Eliot's Hollow Men are "Shape without form, shade without colour,/Paralyzed force, gesture without motion."

INTERPRETING A POEM

Since poetry is the most compressed and cryptic of all literary forms, it requires careful interpretation in order to be experienced in its deepest and fullest sense. The E. E. Cummings poem reprinted below, for example, may appear on the surface to be mere nonsense, yet as critic R. W. Stallman points out, it is actually "rich in meanings." At the literal level it is a miniature short story: at the thematic level it makes a profound observation about how we live and how we love.

anyone lived in a pretty how town

E. E. Cummings

anyone lived in a pretty how town
(with up so floating many bells down)
spring summer autumn winter
he sang his didn't he danced his did.   4

Women and men(both little and small)
cared for anyone not at all
they sowed their isn't they reaped their same
sun moon stars rain   8

children guessed(but only a few
and down they forgot as up they grew
autumn winter spring summer)
that noone loved him more by more   12

when by now and tree by leaf
she laughed his joy she cried his grief
bird by snow and stir by still
anyone's any was all to her   16

someones married their everyones
laughed their cryings and did their dance
(sleep wake hope and then)they
said their nevers they slept their dream   20

stars rain sun moon
(and only the snow can begin to explain
how children are apt to forget to remember
with up so floating many bells down)   24

one day anyone died i guess
(and noone stooped to kiss his face)
busy folk buried them side by side
little by little and was by was   28

all by all and deep by deep
and more by more they dream their sleep
noone and anyone earth by april
wish by spirit and if by yes.   32

Women and men(both dong and ding)
summer autumn winter spring
reaped their sowing and went their came
sun moon stars rain   36

An Interpretation of E. E. Cummings's "anyone lived in a pretty how town"

R. W. Stallman

This poem, apparently obscure nonsense, is rich in meanings; and though it may appear difficult at first glance, it is actually very simple to understand. Cummings uses language "reflexively," every word being counterpointed against another. At the literal level of the language there is a narrative plot, a miniature short story. What makes the poem seem so strange or seemingly incomprehensible is its uncommon arrangement of common words, its wrenched syntax, and its coining of new words from old ones by reconverting their dictionary meaning and usage.

Cummings's case study is a certain anonymous fellow, a citizen of How[1] Town. The town disowns him. Why? Well, for one thing their conventions are shocked by his unconventional way of life. He simply does not conform. Of course they don't care for Mr. Anyone because they "cared for anyone not at all" (line 6); they care only selfishly for themselves alone. These people "both little [i.e., children] and small" (5) are small spiritually; which is why "*noone* loved him more by more" (12). And socially he didn't count because "anyone" married "noone." As for Miss "noone," she "loved him more by more." The non-lovers are the Someones who "married their everyones" (17). They play the social game, which is why they are Someones, but in conforming like "everyones" they have lost out in living, in loving life for its own sake. These Someones and Everyones do the conventional things in the conventional ways, and their life is a deadness and a monotony—"sleep wake hope and then"—because they live not at all spontaneously. And that is what sets them apart from Mr. Anyone. They "did their dance" (18), whereas he "*danced* his did" (4). they "*said* their nevers" (20), said their neverthelesses, talked about what they didn't do and made excuses; whereas he "*sang* his didn't" (4). In short, "anyone *lived.*" For him How Town was "pretty how town," beautiful, beautiful "with up so floating many bells down"—life in both its up's and down's, it was all singsong to him.

---

[1] The dictionary lists eight variant meanings for the word *how,* and all eight reverberate throughout the poem. Cummings uses the word as a noun. In the noun-sense the word means manner or method. But the meanings of *how* as adverb equally apply:— 1. In what manner or way; 2. to what number or degree; 3. in what state or condition; 4. for what reason; 5. with what meaning, to what effect; 6. at what price, how dear; and 7. *how* meaning "what," as how about it? How Town is the conventional town of conformity to convention, where what counts is social manner or method, social degree, state or condition. In How Town what counts is how you do it, and the price is dear. In the sense of *how* as "why," the question asked by the person is what meaning has this way of life?

Anyone and Noone lived happily forever in the point-present now—not in How Town so much as in Now Town. She loved him "by now and tree by leaf" (13), all of him by every part of him; "anyone's any [thing] was all to her" (16). She "laughed his joy she cried his grief" (14); whereas the Someones married to their Everyones "laughed [at] their cryings" (18); their marriage is no marriage, merely an empty form. Even in death the lovers "dream their sleep" (30), belong to eternity and are reborn ("earth by april"); whereas the non-lovers even while living seem dead—"they slept their dream" (20). Caring "for anyone not at all/they sowed their isn't they reaped their same" (6-7). Their routine, clocked existence repeats itself through the cycles of time—"autumn winter spring summer"—with one season the same as another and later generations repeating the same old stenciled way of life (stanza 9). Time passes, mechanical time clocked by "sun moon stars rain" (lines 8 and 36), with the variant—stars rain sun moon (21)—to indicate the passing of time. The life of Someones and Everyones is never punctuated by memorable moments. No comma halts these "busy folk." And their children repeat the same blurred, indiscriminate, humdrum existence; they too "went their came" (35), wasting their coming by their busy going. Thus the bells, symbolizing Time, sound to them only as "dong and ding" (33), which is as dead men hear it, hollow, whereas to Mr. Anyone the bells sang, and he danced his life in lilt with them. Himself childlike in spontaneity, "children guessed" *how to live,* by his example—"but only a few/and down they forgot as up they grew" (9-10). Living is by loving, and loving is by losing oneself in another:

> little by little and was by was
> all by all and deep by deep
> and more by more they dream their sleep
> noone and anyone

But like Someones and Everyones, children become time-busy and "forget to remember" how to live, how to love. And that is how it goes in How to Live Town. The day Anyone died (stanza 7) "noone stooped to kiss his face."

ADDITIONAL STORIES AND POEMS

Memorial Day

Peter Cameron

I am eating my grapefruit with a grapefruit spoon my mother bought last summer from a door-to-door salesman on a large three-wheeled bike. My mother and I were sitting on the front steps that day and we watched him glide down the street, into our driveway, and up our front walk. He opened his case on the handlebars, and it was full of fruit appliances: pineapple corers, melon ballers, watermelon seeders, orange-juice squeezers, and grapefruit spoons. My mother bought four of the spoons, and the man pedalled himself out of our lives.

That was about a year ago. Since then, a lot has changed, I think as I pry the grapefruit pulp away from the skin with the serrated edge of the spoon. Since then, my mother has remarried, my father has moved to California, and I have stopped talking. Actually, I talk quite a lot at school, but never at home. I have nothing to say to anyone here.

Across the table from me, drinking Postum, is my new stepfather. He wasn't here last year. I don't think he was anywhere last year. His name is Lonnie, and my mother met him at a Seth Speaks seminar. Seth is this guy without a body who speaks out of the mouth of this lady and tells you how to fix your life. Both Lonnie and my mother have fixed their lives. "One day at a time," my mother says every morning, smiling at Lonnie and then, less happily, at me.

Lonnie is only thirteen years older than I am; he is twenty-nine but looks about fourteen. When the three of us go out together, he is mistaken for my brother.

"Listen to this," Lonnie says. Both Lonnie and my mother continue to talk to me, consult with me, and read things to me, in the hope that I will forget and speak. "'If gypsy moths continue to destroy trees at their present rate, North America will become a desert incapable of supporting any life by the year 4000.'" Lonnie has a morbid sense of humor and delights in macabre newspaper fillers. Because he knows I won't answer, he doesn't glance up at me. He continues to stare at his paper and says, "Wow. Think of that."

I look out the window. My mother is sitting in an inflated rubber boat in the swimming pool, scrubbing the fibre glass walls with a stiff brush and Mr. Clean. They get stained during the winter. She does this every Memorial Day. We always open the pool this weekend, and she always blows up the yellow boat, puts on her Yankees hat so her hair won't turn orange, and paddles around the edge of the pool, leaving a trail of suds.

Last year, as she scrubbed, the diamond from her old engagement ring fell out and sank to the bottom of the pool. She was still married to my father, although they were planning to separate after a last "family vacation" in July. My mother shook the suds off her hand and raised it in front of her face, her fingers flat as if she were admiring a new ring. "Oh, Stephen!" she said. "I think I've lost my diamond!"

"What?" I said. I still talked then.

"The diamond fell out of my ring. Look."

I got up from the chair I was sitting on and kneeled beside the pool. She held out her hand, the way women do in old movies when they expect it to be kissed. I looked down at her ring and she was right: the diamond was gone. The setting looked like an empty hand tightly grabbing nothing.

"Do you see it?" she asked, looking down into the pool. Because we had just taken the cover off, the water was murky. "It must be down there," she said. "Maybe if you dove in?" She looked at me with a nice, pleading look on her face. I took off my shirt. I felt her looking at my chest. There is no hair on my chest, and every time my mother sees it I know she checks to see if any has grown.

I dove into the pool. The water was so cold my head ached. I opened my eyes and swam quickly around the bottom of the pool. I felt like one of those Japanese pearl fishers. But I didn't see the diamond.

I surfaced and swam to the side. "I don't see it," I said. "I can't see anything. Where's the mask?"

"Oh dear," my mother said. "Didn't we throw it away last year?"

"I forget," I said. I got out of the pool and stood shivering in the sun. Suddenly I got the idea that if I found the diamond, maybe my parents wouldn't separate. I know it sounds ridiculous, but at that moment, standing with my arms crossed over my thin chest, watching my mother begin to cry in her inflatable boat—at that moment, the diamond sitting on the bottom of the pool took on a larger meaning, and I thought that if it were replaced in the tiny clutching hand of my mother's ring, we might live happily ever after.

So I had my father drive me downtown, and I bought another diving mask at the five-and-ten, and when we got home I put it on—first spitting on the glass so it wouldn't fog—and dove into the water, and dove again and again, until I actually found the diamond, glittering in a mess of leaves and bloated inchworms at the bottom of the pool.

I throw my grapefruit rind away, and go outside and sit on the edge of the diving board with my feet in the water. My mother watches me for a second, probably deciding if it's worthwhile to say anything. Then she goes back to her scrubbing.

Later, I am sitting by the mailbox. Since I've stopped talking, I've written a lot of letters. I write to men in prison, and I answer personal ads, claiming to be whatever it is the placer desires: "an elegant educated young lady for afternoon pleasure," or a "GBM." The mail from prison is the best: long, long letters about nothing, since it seems nothing is done in prison. A lot of remembering. A lot of bizarre requests: Send me a shoehorn. Send me an empty egg carton (arts and crafts?). Send me an electric toothbrush. I like writing letters to people I've never met.

Lonnie is planting geraniums he bought this morning in front of the A. & P. when he did the grocery shopping. Lonnie is very good about "doing his share." I am not about mine. Every night I wait with delicious anticipation for my mother to tell me to take out the garbage: "How many times do I have to tell you? Can't you just do it?"

Lonnie gets up and walks over to me, trowel in hand. He has on plaid Bermuda shorts and a Disney World T-shirt. If I talked, I'd ask him when he went to Disney World. But I can live without the information.

Lonnie flips the trowel at me and it slips like a knife into the ground a few inches from my leg. "Bingo!" Lonnie says. "Scare you?"

I think when a person stops talking people forget that he can still hear. Lonnie is always saying dumb things to me—things you'd only say to a deaf person or a baby.

"What a day," Lonnie says, as if to illustrate this point. He stretches out beside me, and I look at his long white legs. He has sneakers and white socks on. He never goes barefoot. He is too uptight to go barefoot. He would step on a piece of glass immediately. That is the kind of person Lonnie is.

The Captain Ice Cream truck rolls lazily down our street. Lonnie stands up and reaches in his pocket. "Would you like an ice pop?" he asks me, looking at his change.

I shake my head no. An ice pop? Where did he grow up—Kentucky?

Lonnie walks into the street and flags down the ice-cream man as if it isn't obvious what he's standing there for.

The truck slows down and the ice-cream man jumps out. It is a woman. "What can I get you?" she says, opening the freezer on the side of the truck. It's the old-fashioned kind of truck, with the ice cream hidden in its frozen depths. I always thought you needed to have incredibly long arms to be a good Captain Ice Cream person.

"Well, I'd like a nice ice pop," Lonnie says.

"A Twin Bullet?" suggests the woman. "What flavor?"

"Do you have cherry?" Lonnie asks.

"Sure," the woman says. "Cherry, grape, orange, lemon, cola, and tutti-frutti."

For a second I have a horrible feeling that Lonnie will want a tutti-frutti. "I'll have a cherry," he says.

Lonnie comes back, peeling the sticky paper from his cherry Bullet. It's a bright pink color. The truck drives away. "Guess how much this cost," Lonnie says, sitting beside me on the grass. "Sixty cents. It's a good thing you didn't want one." He licks his fingers and then the ice stick. "Do you want a bite?" He holds it out toward me.

Lonnie is so patient and so sweet. It's just too bad he's such a nerd. I take a bite of his cherry Bullet.

"Good, huh?" Lonnie says. He watches me eat for a second, then takes a bite himself. He breaks the Bullet in half and eats it in a couple of huge bites. A little pink juice runs down his chin.

"What are you waiting for?" he asks. I nod toward the mailbox.

"It's Memorial Day," Lonnie says. "The mail doesn't come." He stands up and pulls the trowel out of the ground. I think of King Arthur. "There is no mail for anyone today," Lonnie says. "No matter how long you wait." He hands me his two Bullet sticks and returns to his geraniums.

I have this feeling, holding the stained wooden sticks, that I will keep them for a long, long time, and come across them one day, and remember this moment, incorrectly.

After the coals in the barbecue have melted into powder, the fireflies come out. They hesitate in the air, as if stunned by dusk.

Lonnie and my mother are sitting beside the now clean pool, and I am sitting on the other side of the "natural forsythia fence" that is planted around it, watching the bats swoop from tree to tree, feeling the darkness clot all around me. I can hear Lonnie and my mother talking, but I can't make out what they are saying.

I love this time of day—early evening, early summer. It makes me want to cry. We always had a barbecue on Memorial Day with my father, and my mother cooked this year's hamburgers on her new barbecue, which Lonnie bought her for Mother's Day (she's old enough to be his mother, but she isn't, I would have said, if I talked), in the same dumb cheerful way she cooked last year's. She has no sense of sanctity, or ritual. She would give Lonnie my father's clothes if my father had left any behind to give.

My mother walks toward me with the hose, then past me toward her garden, to spray the pea plants. "O.K.," she yells to Lonnie, who stands by the spigot. He turns the knob and then goes inside. The light in the kitchen snaps on.

My mother stands with one hand on her hip, the other raising and lowering the hose, throwing large fans of water over the garden. She used to bathe me every night, and I think of the peas hanging in their green skins, dripping. I lie with one ear on the cool grass, and I can hear the water drumming into the garden. It makes me sleepy.

Then I hear it stop, and I look up to see my mother walking toward me, the skin on her bare legs and arms glowing. She sits down beside me, and for a while she says nothing. I pretend I am asleep on the ground, although I know she knows I am awake.

Then she starts to talk, as I knew she would. My mother says, "You are breaking my heart." She says it as if it were literally true, as if her heart were actually breaking. "I just want you to know that," she says. "You're old enough to know that you are breaking my heart."

I sit up. I look at my mother's chest, as if I could see her heart breaking. She has on a polo shirt with a little blue whale on her left breast. I am afraid to look at her face.

We sit like that for a while, and darkness grows around us. When I open my mouth to speak, my mother uncoils her arm from her side and covers my mouth with her hand.

I look at her.

"Wait," she says. "Don't say anything yet."

I can feel her flesh against my lips. Her wrist smells of chlorine. The fireflies, lighting all around us, make me dizzy.

Winter Trees

Sylvia Plath

The wet dawn inks are doing their blue dissolve.
On their blotter of fog the trees
Seem a botanical drawing—
Memories growing, ring on ring,
A series of weddings.

Knowing neither abortions nor bitchery,
Truer than women,
They seed so effortlessly!

Tasting the winds, that are footless,
Waist-deep in history—

Full of wings, otherworldliness.
In this, they are Ledas.
O mother of leaves and sweetness
Who are these pietas?
The shadows of ringdoves chanting, but easing nothing.

Your Departure Versus the Hindenburg

Richard Brautigan

Everytime we say good-bye
I see it as an extension of
the Hindenburg:
that great 1937 airship exploding
in medieval flames like a burning castle
above New Jersey.
When you leave the house, the
shadow of the Hindenburg enters
to take your place.

INTERPRETING A FAVORITE BOOK

We all have childhood favorites, characters and stories that become part of our lives, sometimes serving as reference points later on (remember how Tom Sawyer got help painting the fence? Remember how Heidi won over stern old Grandfather?)

In the essay below, William Golding, Pulitzer-prize winning author of *Lord of the Flies*, looks back at *The Swiss Family Robinson*. "Can anyone think of it as just another book?" he asks. To him it is so much more. What others may criticize or find lacking in the book—"absence of story," for example—Golding interprets as a strength. "The charm of the book—lies precisely in the absence of story. The days are endless and time has no morning."

What makes this classic tale of shipwreck and rescue so meaningful? It is—very simply—as Golding interprets it "that family sense," that period when a family can look in on itself and be a whole world.

Swiss Family Robinson

William Golding

Has anyone ever resisted the charm of the Swiss Family? Indeed, can anyone think of it as just another book? Someone once likened Chaucer's stories to an English river, slow, quietly beautiful, and winding all the way. In the same terms, *The Swiss Family Robinson* is like a mountain lake. It is contained and motionless. It does not go anywhere. It has no story. Details, and detached incidents, are looked at separately without regard to what is coming next. This is how children live when they are happy, and this is why children will read *The Swiss Family Robinson* backwards and forwards and not bother about the end. To the adult eye, very little seems intended for out-and-out realism. When father Robinson puts together his boat of tubs with the ease and speed of a Popeye who has just eaten spinach, we, and children too, accept a literary convention. Nor are the vague people at all convincing. For Johann Wyss began, not by writing for a wide public but for his children who knew him and his wife and themselves too well to bother about characterization, even if he had been capable of it. Having isolated his characters, Wyss used the book from then onwards as a sort of holdall for conveying moral instruction and scientific information. He did not foresee the outcome of the book. One feels that the lively and capable Miss Montrose was brought in at the end because Wyss's eldest son had got engaged and Wyss wanted to bring his fiancée into the family. The charm of the book, then, lies precisely in the absence of story. The days are endless and time has no meaning. We sink completely into the milieu of these people who are not going anywhere and do not mind. Time is bright and uncomplicated as holidays spent by the sea in childhood.

At the back of the book stands the determination of Wyss to make and keep his family secure. How safe the Swiss Family Robinson is! That omniscient and omnipotent father, God's representative on earth to his family; that mild, womanly and devoted mother who is nevertheless so competent in her defined sphere—there is no hint that they can be anything but perfect. There is no flaw in their parental authority. This makes it disconcerting, in the new illustrated edition, to find father Robinson red-headed, and a fit hero for a Western, while Mother is a slim and beautiful girl, only a year or two older than her eldest child. I can't help feeling, if the illustrations are anything to go by, that *this time* family life may not be so uncomplicated and placid.

In the text, as ever, the children take a child's place. There is simply no possibility of juvenile delinquency. The guiding hand is gentle but adamant. The children are not allowed to overshadow their parents and save the day, perhaps because these are not the sort of days that have to be saved. It may be that the convention of children knowing more than their parents, being heroic and returning to a saved and admiring father, was a reaction against that gentle but adamantine hand. You can have too much of a good thing after all; and sometimes even a child's eye detects the absurdities in that godlike father-figure.

But no one, either child or adult, laughs at Johann Wyss without affection. He achieved more than he hoped or imagined possible. He gave his own family, and a good slice of European youth, total security between the covers of a book. For the great strength of *The Swiss Family Robinson* is not the brilliantly evoked spirit of place (the crystal cavern, the lobster pools, the grove of trees); it is not even the details held up to the eye and exactly observed (the tools and weapons, the plants and rocks, the good, earned meals). What Wyss captured effortlessly because it was so familiar to him was that family sense—the period when children are no longer babies and not yet young men: the period when a family, if it is lucky and emotionally stable, can look in on itself and be a whole world.

DISCUSSION AND EXERCISES

1. Sigmund Freud said that all behavior is a gesture—an "acting out" of deep-seated feelings and needs. Thus what we see on the surface is often (if not always) an expression of underlying "deeper meaning"; for example, football may be an expression of aggression.

Speculate on what larger human purposes are being "acted out"—and satisfied—in five of the following activities:

stealing	baseball	wrestling
suicide	knitting	ventriloquism
alcoholism	dancing	bingo
stuttering	sailing	bullfighting
lying	skiing	fishing
swearing	gambling	playing pool
dreaming	hunting	mountain climbing
smoking	boxing	singing
promiscuity	hiking	working a crossword
ice skating	kite flying	puzzle
playing a musical instrument	automobile racing	

2. Write a paragraph (150–250 words) in which you interpret one of the above activities. Open with a general topic sentence; develop it into a coordinate sequence paragraph, a subordinate sequence, or a mixed construction (See examples pages 120–29). Be prepared to explain your choice.

3. Consider G. K. Chesterton's "On Running After One's Hat." Comment on the following sentences in terms of their content and style:

   1. "No; for him to be inside a railway station is to be inside a cavern of wonder and a palace of poetical pleasure."
   2. "They also serve who stand and wait for the two-fifteen."
   3. "Let him think for a moment of the patience of anglers sitting by dark pools, and let his soul be immediately irradiated with gratification and repose."
   4. "An adventure is only an inconvenience rightly considered."

4. Answer the following questions based on Joyce's "Clay."

   a. How did her fellow workers in the laundry regard Maria?
   b. What sort of things disturbed Maria?
   c. What sort of things gave her joy?
   d. Did Maria's responses to situations seem sincere or hypocritical? Explain.
   e. How did Maria feel about herself?
   f. How did strangers treat her?
   g. Why did Joe and his family include Maria in the Hallow Eve festivities?
   h. Did she enhance or detract from the party?
   i. What was the significance of the clay in the dish?
   j. What is the significance of Hallow Eve in the story?
   k. Is Maria "a veritible peacemaker"? Why or why not?
   l. Are things as they seem to be in this story? Explain.

5. Write a paragraph (200–250 words) in coordinate sequence (see pages 121–23) using one of your answers to the above questions as your topic sentence. Write another paragraph in subordinate sequence.

6. Read "Winter Trees" and "Your Departure Versus the Hindenburg" (pages 398–99) at least three times; read them aloud; note their images line by line.

7. Write a two-paragraph interpretation (300–500 words) of one of the above poems, citing words, images, and lines to support your view (as Stallman does in his interpretation of the Cummings poem).

8. "Memorial Day" by Peter Cameron should be read several times, for multiple readings are an essential preparation for interpreting a story, or seeing it in the light of its deepest meaning and significance. Examine and comment on the importance of the following details:

1. a. the door-to-door salesman
   b. Stephen's silence
   c. mother's diamond ring
   d. Stephen's letters to prisoners
   e. Stephen's relationship with Lonnie
   f. Stephen's attitude toward Lonnie
   g. the wooden ice cream sticks
   h. Stephen's feelings about his mother
   i. the effect of water on Stephen
   j. the final refusal of Stephen's mother to let him speak

2. Examine and comment on the character of the narrator in the story, the stepfather, and the mother.

3. What do you think is the central issue in this story?

   a. A child's unhappiness at his parent's divorce?
   b. An Oedipal struggle within Stephen at his mother's marriage to a young man?
   c. A complicated adolescent rebellion?
   d. A combination of the above? Other interpretations?

4. How do you interpret the ending? Focus particularly on the following:

   a. The mother's accusation: "You are breaking my heart."
   b. The son's response: "I am afraid to look at her face."
   c. The setting: "We sit...and darkness grows around us."
   d. The mother's final words: "Don't say anything yet."
   e. The final image: "Fireflies, lighting all around us made me dizzy."

ESSAY SUGGESTIONS

1. Expand the paragraph you wrote in the first exercise into a full-length essay (500–1,000 words) interpreting "the deeper meaning" of a particular activity. Use the prewriting techniques you have learned.
2. Write an interpretation (500–1,000 words) of a poem of your own choosing.
3. Write an interpretation of "Clay" (500–1,000 words) in which you agree essentially with Walzl's interpretation, indicating and developing your reasons for agreeing; OR take issue with Walzl and follow one of the several "contradictory interpretations of the character" which she cites:

   a. Maria as saint
   b. Maria as "disunified combination of laundress, witch, and Virgin Mary figure"
   c. Maria as "unconsciously selfish troublemaker"

   OR

   Formulate your own interpretation.
4. Write your own interpretation (500–1,000 words) of a well-known myth (for example, the story of the Minotaur, the Tower of Babel, the Golden Fleece, Noah's Ark).
5. Write your own interpretation (500–1,000 words) of a well-known fairy tale such as "Beauty and the Beast" or "Hansel and Gretel." See Bruno Bettleheim's *The Uses of Enchantment: The*

Meaning and Importance of Fairy Tales (New York: Vintage Books, 1977) for provocative interpretations. You may wish to use one of these as a point of departure for your own interpretation.

6. Write an essay (500–750 words) in which you agree with G. K. Chesterton that "an adventure is only an inconvenience rightly considered." Or rebut Chesterton's interpretation as being itself sentimental and forced.

7. Write an essay (500–1,000 words) in which you interpret and celebrate (as William Golding does) a book read and loved in childhood.

19. What Is the Value of X?

When we ask about the "value" of something, we are moving still further beyond basic explanation into the greater complexities of judgment. Here we ask not merely "What does X do?" but "What does X do that is worth doing?" and "How well does X do it?" The purpose is not merely to inform but to appraise the worth, utility, excellence, distinction, truth, beauty, or goodness of something. To what extent does X meet or fail to meet specific standards? In an evaluative essay you, the writer, always set the standards. Even if they are standards you have adopted from someone else, you have made them your own. Thus, the moment you address yourself to the question "What is the value of X?" you become a critic. Whether the subject is books, movies, art, or society at large, you evaluate it in the light of your own notion of what it is and *should* be. As you can see, then, writing a critique is a special challenge, for your evaluation will have significance only if you are open-minded, well informed, and fair—ready to back up your opinions, but not opinionated.

Obviously, "What is the value of X?" is the guiding question behind most examples of critical writing and review. Whether you are concerned with books, movies, theater, music, or dance, you are expected to tell the readers of your review whether the offering in question is any good. Naturally, your opinion is, for the most part, exactly that—your *opinion*. This does not mean, however, that a good review cannot be objective. "I personally do not like courtroom drama," you might state, adding—if you want to be fair and to inform your audience of a truth larger and more important than your own likes and dislikes—that the courtroom scenes in one particular play are extraordinarily well done. To be a good reviewer, you must get outside yourself so that you see not only through your own eyes but also through the eyes of others. (See W. H. Auden on the function of a critic, pages 268–69.)

EVALUATING A BOOK

A good book review is informative, interpretive, and evaluative.

1. *It indicates the content and presumed purpose of the book.* The ability to write a good summary is important. More than that, if your review is to be fair, you must infer from the *fact* of the book what the author's intentions were—that is, *what* the author wanted to say and *how* he or she wanted it to be received. If, for example, a book is about poverty in Appalachia, you should not fault the author for lack of humor: clearly the book is not supposed to be funny. (One is reminded here of Mark Twain's spoofing criticism of the dictionary for its weak plot.)

2. *It assesses how successfully the author has achieved his or her purpose.* By examining rhetorical techniques, you can determine how well or how poorly the author has handled the material and how fully his or her purpose has been achieved.

3. *It judges the value of the book.* Is it any good? Do we have reason to be glad that

it was written? Was its purpose worth achieving? What contribution, if any, does it make to our store of knowledge or aesthetic pleasure?

Only the first two considerations require a measure of objectivity, while the third depends on your own judgment, on your opinion of what is valuable and worthy. However you deal with these necessarily subjective aspects of reviewing, one thing is certain: you should not use the review as a showcase for your personal tastes and preferences, featuring these at the expense of the book itself. Your main function is to describe the book in such a way that your readers, who presumably have not read the book, can decide whether or not they want to read it. In addition, you can help to illumine the work so that readers can understand and appreciate it more deeply.

Most reviews follow a basic but flexible pattern:

> Introduction
> I. Description of the work
>   A. what it is formally (novel, biography)
>   B. what it is about (plot, character, theme)
>
> II. Evaluation: to what extent it fulfills or fails to fulfill its purpose
>   A. strengths   [this order may
>   B. weaknesses   be reversed]
> Conclusion

In the review cited below, for example, John Leonard of the *New York Times* adapts this organization to reflect his unqualified approval of E. M. Broner's novel, *A Weave of Women*. Enthusiasm and description blend in his opening wrap-up evaluation of the novel as "an astonishment." Leonard then characterizes the novel—provocatively—as "a kind of epic poem, a recapitulation of the rhythms of female consciousness." Those not interested in epic poems or female consciousness need read no further; the reviewer's function is to inform, not force: Leonard has so far done his duty.

In succeeding paragraphs he supports his favorable judgment by interpreting the novel in terms of selected details. Note that he does not give the kind of point-by-point plot summary which is not only dull but also damaging to the book: It destroys all suspense for the prospective reader. Note also that throughout the review Leonard compares the novel under consideration to other novels, thereby placing it within a familiar framework while at the same time indicating how it is different, indeed unique.

Review of *A Weave of Women* by E. M. Broner

John Leonard

Even from the author of such a fine first novel as *Her Mothers, A Weave of Women* is an astonishment. E. M. Broner seeks nothing less than to achieve, in a kind of epic poem, a recapitulation of the rhythms of female consciousness. It is circular and sinuous and ceremonial. I know of nothing else quite like it, although certain other recent examples of what might be called "apocalyptic communalism" come occasionally to mind—such books as Marge Piercy's *Dance the Eagle to Sleep*, Monique Wittig's *Les Guerilleres* and

Doris Lessing's *The Four-Gated City.* Miss Broner, however, is interested in health; she proposes a myth of nurture.

Her 15 women do their weaving in a stone house in the Old City in Jerusalem in 1972. Simha, the only mother among them, is more or less the spiritual leader of the commune, but we are told that "each of the 15 women is saddled to a different horse, reined to another life: Terry to action; Gerda to molecules and numbers, exactness and abstraction; Gloria to self-glorification; Deedee to deaths and resurrections; Antoinette and Joan to the word; Dahlia to the note; Mickey to passion and regret; Hepzibah to the soul; Vered to responsibility; Tova to performance; among the wayward girls, Rina and Shula to respectability and Robin to confusion." They are "Temple Priestesses, renewing themselves and saving lives."

From England, Ireland and the United States, from Poland and Germany, and, of course, from Israel, variously wounded and searching, they have come or been brought to the stone house, where they make ceremonies. They dream up new ways of ridding their house of demons, of marrying their men and burying their dead. They invent "counterholidays" and the "hymenotomy," an equivalent of circumcision. They march and agitate and exact revenge. They are enemies of the state and the rabbinate, for what official politics and what official religion have done to women. They are creating new songs, a new therapy, a new religion, a healing cycle, out of scraps of Shakespeare and the Psalms. One betrays the circle and is excommunicated. One is murdered and mourned. One crosses the desert to the sea with a one-legged stork, and gives herself to a Bedouin prince. One, at the Wailing Wall, in a passage that seems to combine Isaac Bashevis Singer with Marc Chagall, turns into a pigeon.

We meet the women as a group before we are introduced to them as individuals, with their private stories. But even at the beginning, each voice is distinct, so that when it is finally matched with its story the effect is of intensification, proof, exegesis, a circle within the circle, almost a series of jazz riffs. The men, necessarily, are less distinct; they are peripheral to the circle, and often storyless. But they are particularized; the Arab student, the kibbutznik, the silk salesman, the despairing brother and the orthodox fanatic. They belong to the geography of the novel, not to its ideology.

And what a geography it is. One thinks: Of course, everything would have to start all over again in Jerusalem, with ideas of God and Africa and pure light. "Something about The Land," Miss Broner says, "makes this possible. In the Judean Hills one walks on stilts. Prophets come to the city to preach or people, after a sojourn in the city, decide they are prophets." Not the least of the many accomplishments is this sense of place, of fact and grit, on which her mysticism drapes itself. There is the shadow, the curse, of the mountain, but there is also the mountain. There are demons in the house, but there is also the house. There are Psalms, but also the law. When such a sense of place, a way with detail, joins with a sneaky sense of humor, we are no longer in the countries of Marge Piercy, Monique Wittig and Doris Lessing. War and madness yield to healing and music. Humor is subversive, just as beauty is beyond discussion. This circle is very large indeed, and all-encompassing. Its rhythm, its heartbeat, is renewal.

Any novel as ambitious as "A Weave of Women" is equally vulnerable. As the women sit around inventing their ceremonies, it is possible for the reader to nod off or to scoff, to resent the programmatic ringing of the thematic bells, to demand progression and to miss the point. Miss Broner, I think, insists on being watched and listened to, like the seasons and Bach. Repetition is indispensable to weaving; we are not involved in a narrative sprint and a gold medal. These women, we are told "intend a large deed." That deed will prove to be another exodus, a crossing of borders. The borders this time are of consciousness.

I hope there are many readers with the requisite patience, to hear "A Weave of Women" through to its affirmations. What seems new and distressing—the communal fiction, the abolition of the individual artist, the rejection of the authority of a point of view is actually at least as old as "The Canterbury Tales," and probably much older, before we invented Canterbury, going all the way back to the caves where the shadows were explained and, perhaps, we bought the explanations of storytellers of the wrong sex.

In reviewing a nonfiction book you must answer the same three questions: What is the content and purpose of the book? How skillfully does the author execute his or her purpose? Was the purpose worth achieving? The order in which you answer these questions is not important so long as they are all covered in a systematic fashion. For example, if you have strong feelings about a book, you may announce them in your first sentence, as critic Elizabeth Hardwick did in her review of a new Ernest Hemingway biography, which she dismissed in her first sentence as "bad news."

Some reviewers follow a convenient fixed form, thereby simplifying the enterprise. Note how the coordinate sequence (see pages 121–23) gives shape to the body of the following review, "The Nazi Question."

Clearly the reviewer had this structural principle in mind when he organized his review. Similarly the reviewer of the comparative study (that also follows) of two great "men of peace," Tolstoy and Gandhi, followed an appropriately fixed form. Just as the book under consideration puts each phase of the subject's lives side by side, so the reviewer organized the review according to a "comparison of parts" (see Question 16, "How does X compare to Y?" pages 357–71).

Review of *The Nazi Question* by Pierre Ayçoberry

E. J. Dionne

Introduction

Pierre Aycoberry's book is not a history of the Nazis, still less an exposition of any single theory about how German National Socialism came to power. It is rather an extremely useful accounting of how academics, journalists and political activists have tried to explain the rise of Hitler.

Mr. Ayçoberry's focus is primarily academic, and the book is essentially a history of ideas about Nazism, stressing the development of all sorts of theories—Marxist, liberal, psychological—regarding what happened in Germany between 1922 and 1945. One reads with wonder his description of The Rise and Fall of Theories of the Third Reich.

Three questions dominate text... First question is...

Three questions dominate the text, though Mr. Ayçoberry does not pretend to answer any of them. The first is: To what extent was Hitler genuinely in control of the events around him? In contrast to our view of Hitler as the preeminent totalitarian leader, one school of scholarship suggests that the Nazi Party was often a decentralized mess—that local officials wielded substantial power on their own, and different sectors of the business community often fought with one another for position.

Second question is...

A second question is: Who put the Nazis in power? Mr. Ayçoberry is blistering in his critique of simplistic Marxist formulations that attempt to prove that Hitler was simply a creation of big business. But he is sympathetic to more complex theories along these lines, and the result of almost any analysis of the rise of the Nazis is hardly likely to reassure those who see elites as the natural protectors of democratic values. They clearly were not in Germany, and the middle-classes, who generally supported Hitler, did not have much to be proud of either.

Finally...

Finally, Mr. Ayçoberry covers the lengthy debate over whether Hitlerism was a peculiarly German phenomenon, with roots going back hundreds of years, or something better explained by the specific social circumstances of the early 20th century.

All these matters, of course, are much more complex than they appear in this brief summary. The main difficulty with the book is that while Mr. Ayçoberry provides some chatty and occasionally devastating commentary, "The Nazi Question" is primarily a collation of other people's arguments.

Conclusion or "wrap-up"

Of course, since these debates concern one of the most important and tragic phenomena of this century, a collation is still valuable. Unfortunately missing, however, is a discussion of the vast scholarship that has developed around the holocaust, the most horrifying mystery of the Nazi regime.

Still, Mr. Ayçoberry's emphasis on the political roots of many of the explanations of Nazism is useful. If you wonder about the occasionally strange debate going on these days over "totalitarianism" and "authoritarianism," his chapter on the origins of theories of totalitarianism deserves a look.

Review of *Tolstoy and Gandhi, Men of Peace*

Malcolm Muggeridge

Introduction

It required considerable courage, if not audacity, on Martin Green's part to try to demonstrate the parallels between the lives and temperaments of a Russian nobleman who was a great writer and an Indian guru who was also a lawyer and an indefatigable *swarajist*—that is, nationalist—agitator. In "Tolstoy and Gandhi, Men of Peace," the final installment in the trilogy "The Lust for Power," which also includes "The Challenge of the Mahatmas" and "Dreams of Adventure, Deeds of Empire," Mr. Green puts each phase of his subjects' lives side by side, and this method works well.

Part I: "their common ground was peace"

Their common ground was peace, and both of them were in principle strongly in favor of beating swords into plowshares and spears into pruning hooks. Mohandas K. Gandhi endeavored most earnestly to make the *swaraj* movement nonviolent, and Count Leo Tolstoy advocated the end of Russian imperialism and total disarmament. As things turned out, however, the victory of the *swarajists*, resulting in the windup of the British raj and Indian independence, brought about one of the most appalling blood baths of the 20th century, while Lenin rejoiced over Tolstoy's denunciation of czarist expansionism and armament, since it prepared the way for the Bolshevik Revolution and the coming of the most authoritarian regime Russia has ever known.

Tolstoy and Gandhi

Mr. Green understandably leaves his readers to work out for themselves the pros and cons of peace movements like those Tolstoy and Gandhi promoted. I recall very vividly how easily violence resulted from nonviolence in India. For instance, a crowd of Gandhi's disciples would block a road in Delhi, whereupon the police, to clear a way, would knock them on the head with their lathis. Other disciples would then move in and get knocked on the head, and so *ad infinitum*. For spectators, it was a scene of violence, practiced by the police in carrying out their duty to maintain law and order but engineered by the nonviolent demonstrators. Who, then, if anyone, was to blame?

Part II: Transition: "Another characteristic of [the] two heroes... is their *sensual disposition*"

Another characteristic of Mr. Green's two heroes that he covers with considerable detail is their sensual dispositions. Gandhi has much to say about this in his autobiography, aptly subtitled "The Story of My Experiments With Truth." His wife, Kasturba, whom he married when they were 12, had to cope with his ardent and sometimes highly inconvenient sexual demands. Then, when he decided to practice total chastity—in Indian terms, *brahmacharya* —she had to make do with nothing of the kind. Mr. Green provides a considerate account of her. When she became ill and her doctor prescribed beef tea to keep her going, Gandhi refused to authorize this infringement of his dietary principles. Kasturba followed his wishes and as it turned out never recovered, but this can scarcely be attributed to her being deprived of beef tea. Later, when Gandhi set up his ashram, he got into the habit of taking young women to bed with him to demonstrate how completely he had extinguished his carnality. He also, it seems, sometimes obliged them by giving them enemas. How the young women reacted to this bizarre experience is not recorded, but the practice can scarcely be regarded as compatible with *brahmacharya*.

Gandhi

Tolstoy

Tolstoy's womanizing, as a young army officer, was of a more normal character, but when he married Sonya Bers, scarcely out of school, he made the fatal error of showing her his diaries, which recorded his debauches, including one homosexual relationship. This was to be a cause of much strife. The Tolstoy family were much given to writing diaries and to reading one another's when they could lay hands on them. At Yasnaya Polyana, the family home, there was much wandering about after dark diary-questing. After fathering a number of children, like Gandhi, Tolstoy opted for chastity, to Sonya's considerable indignation. Even so, when he went out riding he liked to have someone with him; alone, he feared, he might succumb to the temptation of chasing after one of his peasant girls. Mr. Green characterizes Tolstoy, when he was a young man about town, as a "dandy." He seems to like the word, for in his "Children of the Sun" he described me as "a national figurehead of the dandy movement." Alas, I fear my wardrobe would never have run to it.

Part III "... lives of both men *ended in tragedy*"

The lives of both men ended in tragedy. Gandhi was assassinated in 1948 by a fanatical Hindu after witnessing the achievement of Indian independence in terms of a fatal partition of India, the slaughter of millions of Indians and a mere transfer of power from white sahibs to brown ones. Tolstoy, as an old, disheartened man, left Sonya and Yasnaya Polyana with a view to living somewhere or other as a peasant or a monk. In 1910 he fell ill in a train and died in the stationmaster's house at Astapovo.

Gandhi and Tolstoy

Both Gandhi and Tolstoy tried assiduously to make their own lives virtuous and the world a better place, but the world defeated them on both counts. Both are honored in their own countries—Gandhi by, among other things, a museum display of his personal effects, including his dentures, and Tolstoy by the continued enjoyment of his books, especially "War and Peace" and "Anna Karenina," and the careful preservation of Yasnaya Polyana, a truly beautiful home. . . .

EVALUATING A FILM

Like a book reviewer, a film reviewer serves as intermediary between the film and the prospective viewer. This is what the film is about, you tell your readers, indicating not only basic plot line, character, and action but also what you take to be the intention of the director. You should also discuss technique (camera work, lighting, and so on) and quality of the performances (who plays what major roles and how well or how poorly they are performed). Finally, you should tell readers whether or not you think the film is worth going to see.

Review of Federico Fellini's *8½*

Penelope Gilliatt

INTRODUC-
TION

It would be a waste of time to wonder how precisely autobiographical Fellini was being when he made *8½*, his famous film about a famous film director. As he said once himself, there is a sense in which he would be autobiographical even if he were telling the life story of a sole.

(comparison)

What is certain is that this film is constructed so as to *seem* autobiographical, no matter what the facts are: it uses a scarcely veiled first-person as a deliberate artistic device. People are forever talking about subjective films, but the surprising thing is that nothing like *8½* has ever been done before in the cinema. The only work I can think of that has the same grim comic capacity for self-exposure in Evelyn Waugh's *The Ordeal of Gilbert Pinfold*.

DESCRIPTION

8½ is a rueful account of a peculiarly contemporary kind of man, imaginative, openly greedy, riddled with the bullet holes of his self-accusations, and almost dying of neurotic sloth. It has been made by a poet whose genius for film-making spills out of his ears, and I hope its courage isn't going to be dismissed because it is flamboyant and comic. Intellectuals here are hard on Fellini, especially since the words *la dolce vita* passed into the gossip-columnists' language. Sometimes they seem to feel his humor is something he should try to get over, something diminishing and vulgar: and my impression is that he would be much more respected if he would stop implying that sex can be cheerful and start concentrating on the misery of it, like Antonioni....

The film director-hero of *8½*, played by Marcello Mastroianni, has hit an immovable creative block. Living in the bedlam of preparing for a big picture, he hasn't an idea in his head. Sets are already being built, rival actresses are acting their heads off to each other in the pretense that they have parts, but no one has seen a page of his script. His imagination keeps submerging into the past, remembering the huge hips of a woman he once saw doing a rhumba when he was a small boy, and the punishment he got afterward from the priests at school.

Coming up gasping from this daydream and shaking the drops off himself, he thinks perhaps he may at last have rescued something off the ocean bed. But when he timidly describes his trophies to a critic-figure who seems to be working on the film, the critic-figure sternly replies that there's no point in thinking of using this kind of childhood memory to say something about the

Catholic conscience in Italy because there's nothing for reviewers to get their teeth into. You think again of Gilbert Pinfold, who is made dogged in his illness by awful critical utterances like this and has hallucinations of wet, snarling boobies carving him up on the BBC. The man in *8½* is the real arch nitpicker, the enemy of art whom all artists would like to murder, the one so glutted that he thinks anyone in danger of producing second-rate art should control himself and produce no art at all.

ANALYSIS

Like all creative people who are stuck, the director in *8½* finds himself feeling too many things at once. He is lonely for his wife, but as soon as she has arrived on the set they start to have bleak quarrels. He has also sent for his mistress, a plump, amiable girl with a mole on her chest that disconcertingly matches a spot on her eye veil, but though he feels tenderly toward her he can't help seeing her as absurd. He hates hurting his wife with his affairs, but he can't truthfully say that it stops him enjoying them: what he dreams of is

Example (one
funny scene)

not being able to give them up but of seeing his wife and dozens of mistresses sweetly getting on in a harem. This is a very, very funny sequence, and funny because it is aghast: he doesn't approve of himself at all for thinking what paradise it would be if his wife accepted polygamy and his actresses were longing to be whipped.

Example ("at
one point")

At one point, in despair, he arrives at the particularly modern notion that perfect happiness would lie in being able to tell the total truth without hurting anyone. But at other times—after he has talked to an aging cardinal in the

Example ("at
other times")

steam room of a health spa, for instance—his dozing Catholic conscience is booted into life and he believes that happiness shouldn't be a goal anyway. Nor perhaps truth-telling, he begins to think. In the best scene in the film he is

Example ("the
best scene")

watching some screen tests with his wife, whose misery about his lying he has transcribed as justly as he can in a film character who speaks with his wife's words. But when she hears her own lines coming back at her from the screen it doesn't seem to her an offering to the truth; it strikes her as the most terrible of all her husband's betrayals.

EVALUATION

Anouk Aimée as the wife, gray-faced and biting her nails, gives a scrupulous performance. So does Mastroianni. Apart from him none of the actors was allowed to see a full script, which sounds like a despotic piece of director's trickery, but I see now why Fellini did it. *8½* is about the way the world looks to a humorous man on the edge of a breakdown, a world full of extravagantly self-absorbed people who seem to him more like gargoyles than human beings. By putting the actors into a vacuum, Fellini has forced them to give performances that are almost uncannily narcissistic, which is the distortion he wanted. The camera work by Gianni di Venanzo is enthralling: so is the editing, and the whole organization of the film.

EVALUATING A TELEVISION SHOW

In reviewing a television show, a writer follows the same basic principles and overall organization that guide the book or film reviewer, as this review of still another Johnny Carson talk-show competitor demonstrates. Here again comparison provides the basic organizational principle.

Review: Thicke of the Night

Robert MacKenzie

"Move over, Johnny," said the ad for this 90-minute late-night show starring Alan Thicke. Well, so far there's no urgency for Johnny Carson to sign up for vocational guidance. *Thicke of the Night* has been pretty thin.

Thicke is a tall, loosely constructed Canadian, good-looking and mellow, funny sometimes, and as good a candidate as any to inherit Carson's *Tonight* spot someday. But Thicke isn't doing *Tonight.* He is presiding over a repertory group of indifferently talented young comedians, in a show that strains for a younger and groovier audience, with a format that's supposed to be loosely spontaneous but most often is just formless.

I think I am going to like Thicke if I ever get to know him, and he's probably not to blame for the ad campaign. In fact, he tried to defuse the "supposed competition" on his opening show, saying how much he admires Carson, how "there's room for all of us," and so forth. Thicke is appealing in his own way and isn't copying anything Carson does. But who can resist comparing the two shows?

Whatever happens on *The Tonight Show,* good or bad, we experience it *with* Carson. He's seldom out of view, and even when he's off-camera we know he is sitting there watching the guest performer with the rest of us. If there's a comedy sketch, Carson is in it, for better or worse. When Alan Thicke is off-screen, which is often, we have the feeling he is backstage having a cup of coffee while the repertory comics take over the show. If there is a comedy sketch, he usually *isn't* in it.

He does sing pop songs with the house band, coat sleeves rolled up in what a young woman friend of mine calls "a pretty good Rick Springfield imitation." He can be easy with an interview. He put Lana Turner at ease while she told a cute story about getting her chewing gum stuck on Clark Gable's teeth during a screen kiss, and he drew some funny lines from Ted Knight.

The interviews are brief, which often leaves Thicke sitting around with a few of his house comics, trying funny lines on each other and talking about how the show is going so far. After a little of this, you start wishing Dr. Joyce Brothers would drop in and talk about menopause or something.

I'd like the sketches better if they were written; I've always had an aversion to "improv." Apparently the studio audience doesn't mind watching the troupe grope their way through a sketch, trying to make up funny lines as they go along. Of course it isn't easy to do original comedy routines every night, but who said anyone had to?

When Thicke gets away from all this backup and wings his way through a real situation, he's charming. In his debut he dropped in backstage at a Barry Manilow concert, cracking that a roomful of trunks was where Barry kept his sweaters, and stuffing a genuine "Barry Manilow napkin" in his pocket for possible resale to a fan. But then he'll fall back on setup gags, as when he visited Erik Estrada's house and Estrada's "housekeeper" threw a fit because the cameraman was supposedly having a fling with her sister.

I'd like to see Thicke go it alone for a night. Then we'll see if Johnny has to move over.

DISCUSSION AND EXERCISES

Analyze and evaluate the reviews in this chapter by answering the following questions:

1. Do they provide readers with sufficient information to make a sound judgment of their own?
2. In what ways do the reviewers support their own evaluations (evidence, logical reasoning)?

3. Describe the tone of each review and indicate whether it is appropriate. Does it win readers' "good will"?
4. Comment on each reviewer's style and the overall readability of each review.
5. How effective are the opening and closing sentences of each review?
6. Comment on rhetorical stance.

ESSAY SUGGESTIONS

1. Write a review (500–1,000 words) of a book, a film, or a television show that interests you. Remember that writing a review requires many composite skills; be prepared, then, to draw not only on the models cited in the text here but on the following as well:

   a. *your ability to describe* and to assemble details (see question 1, "How can X be described?")

   b. *your ability to assemble facts* (see question 6, "What are the facts about X?")

   c. *your ability to summarize* (see question 7, "How can X be summarized?")

   d. *your ability to interpret* (see question 18, "How should X be interpreted?")

2. Write a review of a new television show, following the tone and organization of Robert MacKenzie's "Thicke of the Night."

20. What Case Can Be Made For or Against X?

THE NATURE OF ARGUMENT

*A*ristotle said: "If it is a disgrace to a man when he cannot defend himself in a bodily way, it would be odd not to think him disgraced when he cannot defend himself with reason." It is reason—and *mainly* reason—that you must marshal when you answer the question "What case can I make for or against X?" In trying to build a case, you move beyond plain exposition into the more active and aggressive realm of argumentation. You use an ancient and honored form of discourse: You try not merely to explain but also to defend or refute what logicians call a "proposition." This statement usually includes conflict and controversy. Unlike a plain statement of fact ("John Smith is the mayor of Squedunk"), readers cannot look up, verify, and establish a proposition once and for all. Instead, a proposition is debatable: It may or may not be true ("The mayor of Squedunk is corrupt and should be thrown out of office"). In making such a judgment about what *ought* to be done, you assume the burden of proof. You must therefore marshal evidence and exert rigorous reasoning in support of your proposed course of action; you must persuade your readers or listeners that the proposition is necessary and just; and you must win them over to your side by making them see that your side is their side—that you have common cause with them. You must recognize that all reform requires collective action, that you alone, for example, cannot sweep the corrupt mayor of Squedunk out of office: you will need help.

Obviously, of all forms of discourse, argumentation is the most morally compelling and significant. In addition, it is far more demanding and comprehensive than the other forms not only because it requires rigorous reasoning and persuasive tactics, but also because it frequently embraces other forms: definition, description, comparison, analysis, narration, characterization, interpretation, and evaluation. All these forms may enter into argumentation. Indeed, in answering "What case can I make for or against X?" you may include all these forms—and some others.

In making a case, then, you should try to raise as many pertinent points as possible, for the content of the argument—the evidence that substantiates your position—as well as the rigor of your reasoning—will establish and prove your case.

Also remember that in no form of writing is using the strengths of language to the best possible effect more important. Stylistic failings such as undefined terms that create ambiguity, confusing grammatical constructions, vague allusions, and pompous, overlong sentences will alienate those you might otherwise convince. Bad writing, in other words, can kill a case as surely as lack of evidence or fallacious reasoning.

Is and *Ought* Propositions

Basically, you use two different kinds of propositions in argument: the *is* proposition (an assertion of opinion or value) and the *ought* proposition (a proposal for action). Most of the illustrative essays in this chapter combine the two types of arguments, establishing the fundamental causal relationship that underlies most argumentation:

> Because A *is* the case, B *ought* to be done.

Woodrow Wilson's historic address to Congress in 1917 asking for a declaration of war against Germany provides an example of this logical formulation.

> Because Germany's aggressive submarine action against American commerce *is* an act of warfare against both the United States and mankind [an assertion of opinion or value], America *ought* to enter World War I [a proposal for action], which action would make the world "safe for democracy" [the projected conclusion].

President Wilson's aim in this classic example of making a case for a specific action was to win the assent of members of Congress, to convince them that what he asserted was true and just, worthy of wholehearted and unconditional support.

Similarly in the following essay Allan H. Gilbert combines *is* and *ought* propositions to make a spirited case against a hallowed academic tradition, the college lecture.

College Lectures Are Obsolete

Allan H. Gilbert

The advertising pamphlet of a well-known American university recently showed a picture of a professor presenting chemistry to some hundreds of students. Except for the costumes and the ugly angularity of the room, it might have been an academic scene in 1450, before the invention of printing. In 1766 Dr. Johnson remarked:

> I cannot see that lectures can do as much good as reading the books from which the lectures are taken.

And in 1781 he still thought:

> Lectures were once useful, but now, when all can read, and books are so numerous, lectures are unnecessary.

Yet after two hundred years, the modern professor has not overtaken Dr. Johnson. He has not discovered that printing has been invented—not to mention Xerox,® etc. The old-time methods are good enough for him. Academic photographers are especially amusing in that they delight in showing the most blatantly up-to-date subjects, such as physics, presented as in Abelard's Paris. Obviously this applies not to the occasional public lecture, but to the twice-a-week throughout the term.

What Is Wrong About Lectures?

1. Even a good speaker will not always be correctly heard by his audience. Horns toot, students cough. And sometimes professors mumble. Even in the notes of graduate

students the well-known Professor Fredson Bowers has appeared as Fritz and Brower, and Nike of Samothrace as the Decay of Sammy's Face.

2. What is written on a blackboard—often in professorial scribble—cannot be perfectly copied. Time presses; even modern lighting is not all-revealing; perfect vision is not universal.

3. A student trying to take excellent notes cannot think about their content; he must not lag. He is like the telegrapher of whom Edison tells. The man received, in dots and dashes, the news of Lincoln's assassination; when he went out on the street, he learned that such news had been reported. In the days of monotype composition for newspapers, I knew the man who set the gossip column for the local paper. When the paper appeared, he read it as something new to him. Such must be the mind of the student who takes notes so good that he can attain the ideal of giving back in his blue book what the lecturer has said. The Welsh professor of mediaeval literature, Dr. Ker, is said to have remarked: "How can I give less than 90 for my own words?"

4. Lectures prepared long since and read from yellowed paper cease to call on the professor's brain. His class in the morning need not call him from the idiot box in the evening. The chairman of a department in which I served once read the same lecture to a class for the third successive time.... It is reported of a Harvard professor that he moved to the door and put his hand on the knob for his last sentence. No student could catch him. Revision would disarrange the schedule and desecrate the sentences which, through many repetitions, the professor has come to regard as truth. He is a human tape recorder. The students are tape-receivers....

5. The college lecturer seldom has a prepared audience. How often can a lecturer on Shakespeare, for example, be sure that his hearers have read the play on which he speaks? If he can read aloud, he may read to his class with profit, but then he ceases to be a lecturer. The unprepared audience (or the audience not eager to learn the subject, and not impatient of failure to help them do so) affects the lecturer. He wishes to break through their boredom. So he tends to become an entertainer, giving a show. There is much in the story that the faculty of a well-known college for men opposes the admission of women because—evidently being old fogies—they imagine they would be deprived of the bawdy jokes supposed to amuse their captive audiences. But how often do professorial jokes illustrate the subject in hand? Or the popular lecturer turns to oratory. Newspaper pictures of some popular teachers who recently have gathered publicity by dismissal, show them making gestures suited to the soap box or the pulpit. An academic Savonarola or Billy Sunday or Graham may rouse in a few hearers an emotional desire to learn. Such a desire, when it lasts, prepares a youth to study and to seek aid from a teacher, but it is not teaching. Colleges, like the rest of life, need their share of emotion, but their primary business is intellectual. A man given over to his own convictions and beliefs is not a teacher because he cannot see both sides of a subject.

6. Especially for commuting students, attendance at lectures is a serious burden. If the teacher has lectures prepared, let them be mimeographed. Then the student can study them at home. Or let the professor require the student to read the books from which the lectures are drawn. They can be bought for less money than commuting requires; and the student is not wasting his time in a bus or automobile.

7. In the lecturer's audience, the student tends to become a mere numbered unit, deprived of power to question, much less to object. He is trained to accept the dicta of the professor—a habit worse than that of going to the library to find "a book"—author unobserved—from which to copy. At least the library offers more than one book, and even the most facile pedagogue is likely to take more pains with dicta to be printed than with those merely to be pronounced in the uncritical isolation of the lecture hall, before students who—if they wish good marks—will not murmur publicly against what they

are told. The lecture inculcates passivity of mind. The student is a spectator, with no part in the game, except that he selects the lecture course because it is called a crib.

8. The book, even when mimeographed, is better than any student's notes. There are no hiatuses for sickness, empty pens, noise. As Dr. Johnson said: "If your attention fails and you miss part of a lecture, you are lost; you cannot go back as you can upon a book."

Furthermore, the best lectures are most likely to attain printing. If a professor has lectures better than any printed book or even group of printed books, can he be defended for restricting them to his own university, instead of giving them to mankind? Are we to suppose that there are in America a hundred sets of lecture notes superior to anything in print? Is not the student better off with A. C. Bradley's own vindication of Falstaff—however absurd it is—than with the Shakespeare professor's diluted version of it? If the professor cannot do better than the authors on his reading list, why not omit the lectures and attend to the reading list?

9. Something can be said for the living presence of the lecturer. But this is again revivalistic; the college lecturer is supposed to be teaching a subject. There is, too, a presence behind the written word, usually stronger, though less immediate, than that on the platform. Does the student come to college for the personality of Professor X, or to learn? Indeed the professor who gives a course in himself is handicapped by the insignificance of his subject. "A good book is the precious life blood of a master spirit." How often are lecture-writers such spirits?

10. The important poets have been so richly annotated that even the most expert scholars can now add little detailed comment. Fortunate is the lecturer on Milton who can improve on Professor Hughes' notes. The lesser authors have been carefully worked. How many teachers of Herrick can correct any of Professor Patrick's notes, or explain difficulties he has not elucidated? As to more general comment, a lecturer may indeed warn his pupils against much that has been written on great authors, but how many lecturers are capable of anything else than riding with the tide? Poetry exists to be read; the lecture pushes it into the class of something to be talked about rather than experienced. (Non-lecture teaching is somewhat less subject to this danger.)

The Remedy

Perfect teaching will appear when we have teachers who have entered into their subjects and students eager to learn. With these, we would not need to bother about systems. Without them, not much can be done. We have always had, and always shall have, lawyers not aware of the nature of law, generals unaware of the nature of war, professors of physics who have not found out what their subject is, teachers of Chaucer and Dante who do not, as Benedetto Croce has said, sympathize with their authors. Yet something external can be done against lecturitis.

Let a teacher who sufficiently believes in his own greatness put his lectures in print to be revised frequently as he grows wiser. Then he can abandon his robes of glory, and the student will have more accurate statements and clearer diagrams, which he can copy at his leisure, if that will implant them in his memory.

In a normal lecture course, let us suppose thirty lectures per term, and 150 students. At that rate, each student gets of the professor's public time $\frac{1}{150}$ of thirty hours, or $\frac{1}{5}$ of an hour. If the professor abandons his rostrum, he has time to meet each student individually for ten minutes a term. The student is warned to prepare. The assistants who gather about such courses are consulted on what the student may profitably ask. Some students would treasure throughout life the memory of ten minutes' serious talk with an eminent professor.

I know students at some of our large places who have gone through their four years without ever speaking on their studies with a man of professorial rank. Such undergraduates deal with junior teachers, graduate students, some of them brilliant, but many of them destined to be mediocrities or failures. Yet from the class of a thousand, the hundred and fifty with the best records can still meet the eminent professor. Such a teacher, relieved from the strain of the large lecture—not entirely removed by the loud speaker—would usually be willing to go beyond the hundred and fifty. If freed from the ceremonial lecture, the pupil has two hours a week free for studying books, mimeographed or printed, and scientific specimens. He does not—in the computer age—spend thirty hours a term writing by hand. Nothing good in the present system need be abolished. The students in the big class can still be divided into small sections, presided over by the best junior teachers the college will pay for.

The survival of the lecture, for nearly five hundred years after the invention of printing, exhibits the unimaginative, unobserving professorial mind. Hidebound professors still read lectures to three or four students, even to one. This seems more ludicrous in nuclear physics than in the humanities, but does not reveal a more imperceptive mind. John Philip Holland, the father of the submarine, said that naval officers (who yield little to professors in holding to what has been) disliked the submarine because it provided no quarter deck to strut on. Do professors cling to lectures because they offer a rostrum to strut on and a lectern to sprawl over?

Lively and provocative as this argument is, are there not logical grounds on which readers could challenge its indictment of the lecture system? Are all lectures *necessarily* read "from yellowed paper"? Are all lecturers *necessarily* "human tape recorders"? Are all students *necessarily* "human tape-receivers"? Are mimeographed copies of a lecture read by students privately in the library *necessarily* more profitable than personal delivery in a lecture? (May not students fall asleep in the library as well as the lecture hall?) What about the creative lecturer who communicates fresh insights so compellingly that students "catch fire"—as they could not from the printed page? Cannot more be said about the possibilities and value of person-to-person classroom encounter? Must the lecture be an extended monologue? Is Gilbert talking about *some* kinds of lectures and lecturers of *all* kinds? (See page 427 on generalization.)

THE STRUCTURE OF ARGUMENT

It is interesting to note that although Gilbert wrote his essay in the twentieth century, its organization follows the classic three-part structure which provided the ground plan for Greek and Roman orators—and which is still useful today.

   I.   Introduction

       The introduction, consisting of single sentence or of several paragraphs, includes one or more of the following:

       A. *Exordium:* The beginning or opening words, designed to win attention and good will by introducing the case in an interesting and favorable light (a quotation, personal reference, story)

       B. *Exposition or narration:* An account of the history of the case (what gave rise to the present problem; how the issues developed)

C. *Direct statement of the case* (the *proposition* to be proved or defended)

D. *Division of proofs:* An *outline* of how the writer will present the evidence ("first I will explain...and then I will demonstrate...")

II. Body

A. *Confirmation* of one's case by presenting evidence in its favor:
1. facts
2. reasons
3. statistics
4. testimony of experts
5. opinions
6. reports
7. examples
8. logical reasoning (deductive and inductive)
9. analogy

B. *Refutation* of opposing views by demonstrating that they are:
1. untrue
2. illogical
3. self-contradictory
4. ambiguous (terms are not clearly defined)
5. dishonest (a deliberate attempt to deceive)
6. absurd

C. *Concession* of points to the opposition that the writer must in fairness concede; reply to them and offer alternate positions

III. Conclusion

A. *Recapitulation* and *summary* of argument: To repeat is to reinforce points, and to make certain readers have not misunderstood them

B. *Peroration:* A final, heightened appeal for support

FUNDAMENTALS OF LOGIC

Deduction and Induction

Making a case for or against something always entails choices. The most appropriate way depends on the particular subject and situation, the particular readers, and the particular purpose in the writer's mind. These factors are relative. What are constant and predictable are the two basic lines of reasoning along which argument inevitably proceeds. They are *deduction*—inferring a particular fact from a general truth (for example, since deciduous plants are known to shed their leaves in winter, I can expect the deciduous dogwood that I planted in my yard last spring to shed its leaves this winter) and *induction*—moving from particular facts to generalizations (for example, since I have tasted thirty green apples and each one was sour, I conclude that all green apples are sour). In actual experience the two modes run into one another, as Thomas Huxley demonstrated in his essay "Thinking Scientifically" (pages 297–98). Thus:

               1. You examine thirty green apples.

               2. Each one is sour.

(induction) 3. You generalize: green apples are sour.

               4. You pick up apple thirty-one, which is also green.

(deduction) 5. You infer that this apple—which you have not yet tasted—will also be sour.

Interdependent as they are, since each mode of reasoning has distinctive features, you should examine each individually.

DEDUCTION

In deductive reasoning we lay down *premises*, certain statements we know or strongly believe are true; from these premises we then derive a *conclusion*. Deduction, then, involves a closely linked *chain of reasoning*:

                  A   B

Major Premise: All human beings are mortal.

                  C   A

Minor Premise: Socrates is a human being.

                  C   B

Conclusion: Socrates is mortal.

The line of reasoning in this *syllogism* (as we call a three-part statement of this kind) is logically valid because given the two premises, the conclusion necessarily follows. In fact, the conclusion merely states *explicitly* what is already stated *implicitly* in the premises. The conclusion then derives logically and formally from the premises; in this case it points to the axiomatic truth that "things equal to the same thing are equal to each other." Thus in the example above, A equals B; C equals A; therefore ($\therefore$) C equals B.

Although formal rules for syllogisms exist, we need not go into them. Our interest is in compositional logic, not in logic per se. Furthermore, common sense—that inborn quality of mind that enables us to follow a logical line of reasoning even if we have never heard the word "logic" before—often alerts us to logical errors. We can tell, for example, that thinking is askew when the premises state that *some* of X is undesirable, and the inference drawn is that *all* of X is undesirable:

      Some people are cruel.

      John is a person.

    $\therefore$ John is cruel.

Obviously, John might not belong in the group of "cruel people." The conclusion changes "some" to "all."

This leap from "some" to "all" is an especially common logical error, or *fallacy;* most people will not specify "some" even when they mean it. Instead they will say,

"People are cruel." Such a statement is patently unfair. It can create ill feeling toward whole groups, when in truth only some members are blameworthy: because some students cheat on examinations, we should not conclude—as a sensational magazine story might maintain—that "college kids are dishonest."

Similarly, common sense tells us that another gross error has been committed in the following statement:

> All human beings are mammals.
> All monkeys are mammals.
> ∴ All monkeys are human beings.

Logicians call this "the fallacy of the undistributed middle";[1] but here again we need not name the logical flaw to see that it has been committed: we know that things belonging to the same general class are not necessarily identical. In this case, the fact that humans are mammals and monkeys are also mammals simply means that they, along with many other animals, share a larger biological category, as the logician's circular diagram shows:

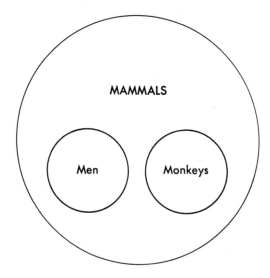

No one would fail to spot the fallacy of the undistributed middle in this example (we *know* monkeys are not people!); but the fallacy is not usually so easy to detect. Indeed it may be (and frequently is) used in a subtle and insidious way to create spurious arguments, such as that of guilt by association:

> All communists support the ABC Plan.
> Jack Smith supports the ABC Plan
> ∴ Jack Smith is a communist.

---

[1] In logic "distributed" means that a term refers to *all* members of the designated class. Thus, in the fallacy of the undistributed middle, the middle term of our syllogism ("human beings") does not refer to *all* members of the class. A syllogism consists of three terms: the predicate, subject, and middle term. The predicate appears in the major premise and conclusion, the subject in the minor premise and conclusion, and the middle term, which links the subject and predicate, appears *only* in the two premises.

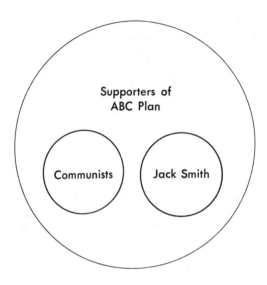

Syllogism is a logician's term, but the process of thought that it describes is hardly specialized; whenever you infer one idea from another, you are using a syllogism. If the reasoning is correct, the syllogism is valid—that is, the conclusion follows logically from the premises. But is it true? That is quite another question, since it is possible for a syllogism to be *valid* (correct in its formal reasoning) but factually *false*.

Thus the following two syllogisms are valid (given the premises, the conclusions may logically be inferred); yet the first one is nonsense and the second is patently false because the premises are false:

> All unicorns are girls.
> All boys are unicorns.
> ∴ All boys are girls.

> All weaklings are fools.
> All people are weaklings.
> ∴ All people are fools.

Clearly, it is important to examine the premises of an argument before making a judgment. If someone accuses a member of Congress of accepting graft, for example, by arguing that "it is a widely known fact that members of Congress take graft, so why should this member of Congress be any different? It should be obvious immediately that the basic premise is open to question. *Is* it widely known and is it a *fact* that all members of Congress accept graft? The attack conceals a faulty syllogism:

> All members of Congress take graft.
> Mr. X is a member of Congress.
> ∴ Mr. X takes graft.

Yes, the reasoning is valid; but the major premise is questionable, thereby dictating that the conclusion will be false.

INDUCTION

As noted above, when we reason inductively we follow the method of moving from particular facts that are objectively verifiable (what we can test, observe, or experience) to a broad generalization. We see the sun rise in the east and set in the west... once... twice... three times... four... five... six... seven. Finally we take the "inductive leap," the assertion of the general truth that the sun rises in the east and sets in the west and in all likelihood can be counted on to do so tomorrow, the next day, the day after that.

You can make a good inductive leap only when you have observed a sufficient number of particular instances. This number varies from situation to situation. The perfect induction is one in which the observer has taken every member of the class of things to which the proposition refers into consideration. This is clearly impossible in many cases and unnecessary in most cases; a fair sampling of typical instances chosen at random usually leads to a reliable enough generalization. For example, fifteen sour green apples certainly provide a reasonable basis for the generalization "green apples are sour." Yet if all the apples tasted came out of one orchard, or even one group of orchards located in one section of the country, we have to wonder, "Is it just *these* green apples that are sour? Perhaps green apples in other sections of the country are as sweet as red ones." A fair sampling of apples, then, should include apples from different parts of the country, thereby eliminating the possibility that special geographical or climatic conditions produce sour green apples.

Scientific investigators require a relatively large sampling—perhaps hundreds, thousands, or in some cases tens of thousands of subjects (especially in medical research)—before they can safely draw any generalizations.

In any induction, observers must guard against hasty generalizations made without a sufficient number of examples. This is perhaps the most widespread fallacy in popular thinking. Like the error in deductive reasoning that takes us from "some" to "all," this error in inductive reasoning can produce or reinforce prejudice. A person who is already prejudiced against a minority group (blacks, Jews, Chicanos) is predisposed to conclude after noting even a few "offenses" in the group that "that's the way they *all* are."

Interestingly, Lionel Ruby has observed that the tendency to wild generalization is a form of exhibitionism:

> The exhibitionist desires to attract attention to himself. No one pays much attention to such undramatic statements as "Some women are fickle," or that some are liars, or "Some politicians are no better than they ought to be." But when one says that "all women are liars" this immediately attracts notice.
>
> —Lionel Ruby, *The Art of Making Sense*

ARGUMENT BY ANALOGY

In argument by analogy, often regarded as a form of induction, you draw a crucial comparison in one inductive leap. Urging the United States to join the Allied cause in the First World War, Woodrow Wilson pointed to the fact that Russia had done so. In comparing his proposed action for the United States with Russia's earlier action, Wilson was making an analogy, telling Congress that just as Russia wisely joined the Allied cause, so should we. The reasoning here proceeds from one specific instance to a similar specific instance.

There is no doubt that analogical reasoning serves an important function in argumentation. It makes a point simply and economically (if Russia found it impossible to deal with Germany, why should the United States find it any easier?) Analogy is also vivid and may strike a strongly persuasive note when all direct reasoning fails. The story is told, for example, of the union organizer in the early days of the labor movement who, after reciting all rational reasons for joining the movement, finally won a prospective member by drawing a vivid and amusing analogy: "The top crowd's pressin' down! The bottom crowd's pressin' up. Whaddayou wanna be, a hamburger?"

Aside from its dramatic impact, you can only determine the value of inductive analogy by closely examining the two things being compared. Are they in fact similar in the essential characteristics relating to the conclusion? *Does the generalization underlying the analogy stand up to logical analysis?* In his book *Thinking Straight*, Monroe Beardsley points to what he calls a "simple and crude example" of how analogy may mislead.

> One old gambit of the temperance orator was to say: "The delicate membranes of the stomach are like the delicate membranes of the eye; if you want to see what alcohol does to your stomach, just pour some gin in your eye." Now we may grant that there are *some* resemblances between eye tissue and stomach tissue: the question is whether these are *relevant* resemblances. In other words, the question is whether there is some true generalization like "Everything that hurts the eye will hurt the stomach" that will allow us to infer that if gin hurts the eye it will also hurt the stomach.
>
> So we might reply to him, "So you mean that *everything* that hurts the eye will also hurt the stomach?" He may wish to narrow the suggested generalization from "everything" to "every liquid," or in some other way. But unless he is willing to subscribe to *some* relevant generalization, he simply hasn't got what it takes to draw the conclusion he wants. We are therefore justified in saying to him, "If your argument proved anything, it would prove just as well that lemonade, vinegar, and hot coffee are bad for the stomach because they will hurt the eye. Doesn't that show that there must be important *differences* between the eye and stomach, so that what is true of one is not necessarily true of the other?"
>
> —Monroe Beardsley, *Thinking Straight*

The important thing to remember about analogy, then, is this: the fact that two things are alike in some respect does not necessarily mean they are alike in others. Mental processes and bodily processes, for example, are comparable but not identical; therefore the following analogy represents a deceptive argument in favor of censorship: "We don't allow poisonous substances to be put into our foods, so why should we permit books to be published that will poison the minds of our citizens?" Do you see the dangerously authoritarian generalization that underlies this argument? It is just as unsound as the old defense of monarchy that maintained that since the earth revolved around the sun, circular motion was "natural"; consequently, by analogy, monarchy was a "natural" form of government because the subjects revolved around their monarch (Huppé and Kiminsky, *Logic* 204).

We cannot trust analogy alone to prove a point. It is useful only as a supplement to factual evidence mounted in support of a proposition. In the following essay, for example, note how effectively the writer uses analogies to illuminate and reinforce his contention that in its own terms and within the context of its own premises, Marxist theory does not stand up to analysis. Instead, it denies itself.

Marxism

W. T. Jones

We have criticized Marxism as a theory of social causation because, of course, it was put forward as a definitive account of social change. Just as in physics a "law" is supposed to describe a necessary pattern of behavior that makes prediction and control possible, so the formula of dialectical materialism was supposed to reveal a necessary sequence of social relations. Marx the social scientist believed that what men do is not the product of "free will" but merely the expression of economic forces over which they have no control and which develop according to a purely deterministic sequence.

But Marx was not only a social scientist; he was a reformer. Now suppose for the sake of argument that dialectical materialism is the "scientifically correct" formula describing the social process. Since the overthrow of bourgeois capitalism is inevitable, what is the point of agitating for its overthrow? If we take Marx seriously as a social scientist, Marx the reformer looks about as silly in writing his *Manifesto* urging the workers of the world to unite as we would look inviting a falling stone to fall a little faster. Of course, Marx could reply that the economic forces at work in the society of which he was a part determined that he would fight for the revolution, just as they determined that somebody else with a different economic background would fight against it. But this plunges Marxism—the theory—into the struggle about which it theorizes. It is not just a question of whether or not it is silly to try to further an inevitable end (e.g., induce the stone to fall faster), but whether, if the course of events is inevitable, "end" has anything more than a purely subjective meaning.

On the other hand, when Marx the reformer spoke, Marx the social scientist took a back seat, and we get a wholly different conception of the function of the theory and of its claim to truth. Marx the reformer was aware that the objective truth of a theory is no measure of its utility as a rallying point for aspiration and endeavor. (The Arian and orthodox theories of the Trinity are cases in point.) For Marx the reformer, Marxism was not a theory of social causation; it only pretended to be for propagandistic purposes. It was actually a call to the working class to rise and overthrow their masters, and it should be judged on the basis of its effectiveness in producing a class war from which the proletariat emerge victorious.

But why, then, did Marxism pretend to be a theory of social causation? Because, given the time, the place, and the circumstances (e.g., the "vogue" of science), men want to be assured that what they are fighting and dying for has been "scientifically" proved to be true—just as purchasers of soap or cigarettes like to be assured that "science" shows the product they use to be superior. In another age, in another country, revolutionists would not formulate their program in terms of dialectical materialism, but in terms, say, of a crusade to free the Holy Places from the infidel. It just happens that in the present age the former type of formula appeals and so provides the oppressed classes with a rationale for the revolutionary acts which one wants them to perform.

This presents a totally different picture of the social process. Far from being rigorously determined, it now appears that free will and indeterminism are predominant factors.

Action, it would seem, can always alter the course of events. This would appear to rule out a science of social causation, but Marx the reformer would not be distressed: *qua* reformer, he had no interest in theory as theory. Thus, in his *Theses against Feuerbach*, Marx stated quite explicitly, "The question whether human thought can achieve objective truth is not a question of theory but a *practical* question. In practice man must prove the truth, i.e., the reality, power, and this-sidedness of his thought. The dispute over the reality or unreality of thought which is isolated from practice is a purely *scholastic* question." From this point of view, a theory proves itself true by its success in bringing about the state of affairs it describes—dialectical materialism would be a "true" theory if it incited the workers to rise and make an end of bourgeois capitalism.

It will be seen, then, that Marxism falls apart. It is impossible to ignore, as some have done, these pragmatic aspects of Marxism, but it is ridiculous to maintain, as others have, that this is the only "true" Marx. From a purely pragmatic point of view, dialectical materialism is encumbered with all sorts of impedimenta which can hardly have appealed to the working class but which Marx and Engels took very seriously—and took seriously not because they held them to be good propaganda but because they held them to be "true." This duality of point of view has persisted in Marxism to this day. On the one hand, we find a rigid and authoritarian dogmatism masquerading as a science of social causation; on the other, an extremely flexible and Machiavellian *Realpolitik*, designed to bring events which refuse to be determined by dialectic into conformity with the "fore-ordained" pattern. But it is only fair to say that Marxism is not unique in this respect; it is not the first philosophy that has combined doctrinaire self-assurance about ends with a cynical attitude toward means.

Common Logical Fallacies

Before looking at further examples of argumentation, we should consider some common logical fallacies. You should recognize that logical flaws are not necessarily *rhetorical* flaws. In fact, logical flaws may be extremely effective in their impact on readers. Lies, if they are bold enough, generate drama and excitement; emotional appeals often touch readers' hearts so deeply that they don't even try to understand. But these, of course, are tricks designed to fool and blind readers. Since I consider the ethics of rhetoric later on (in "The Limits of Language"), I shall not go into these matters here. But you should know that the good argument is based on reason and uses emotion only to reinforce reason; the good argument not only makes a case for or against its subject, it also illuminates it so that readers—whether they agree or disagree with the argument—will at least learn more about the issues.

CIRCULAR REASONING

To assume in the premise what you are supposedly trying to *prove* in the course of your argument is to argue in a circle—or beg the question. It has been observed that "the function of logic is to demonstrate that because one thing or group of things is true, another must be true as consequence." (See Davis, "Logic") But in a circular argument there is no progression; the same thing is said in different words: "We shall always be ruled by the will of the people because we have a democratic form of government." This statement establishes nothing because the people's will is already assumed in the word "democratic."

EQUIVOCATION

To equivocate is to change the meaning of a word in the course of an argument or to use an ambiguous word in two different senses (whether deliberately or unintentionally)—as in the following:

> Science has discovered many laws of nature. This is proof that there is a God, for a law implies the existence of a lawgiver, and God is the great Lawgiver of the universe.

Observe the confused and careless use of the word "law": it is first used with the scientific meaning of uniform behavior in nature; it is then used prescriptively to refer to regulations enforcible by a higher authority (Ruby, *Making Sense* 32–33).

EVADING THE ISSUE

This fallacy takes several forms:

Distraction

Raising extraneous considerations, such as emotions or sentiments can turn the course of an argument away from the main issues. Thus in making a case for the democratic form of government, the arguer may eulogize George Washington and the other founding fathers, extolling their personal courage and foresight. Such distractions may divert readers' attention and make them forget the real issues.

Ad hominem

Another way to evade the issue is by directing the argument against the character of the person making the case rather than the case itself. This fallacy is common and sinister ("You cannot trust Smith's reform bill because he has had questionable leftist leanings ... and there is his divorce ... and that suspicious suicide attempt ...").

Name-Calling

Still another evasive smear tactic (and verbal trick) is calling an opposing view by a "bad name," thereby suggesting that it is in reality bad. Thus an attempt to improve welfare legislation may be labeled "starry-eyed idealism" or "sheer romanticism," that will turn our government into a "welfare state." (See also pages 515–16.)

Appeal to Pity

When General Douglas MacArthur, pleading his case before the American people, cited the old refrain "Old soldiers never die, they just fade away," he was resorting to the popular and often successful ruse of making himself pitiful in order to win sympathy. Obviously, this focusing on "poor old me" is another way of evading substantive issues.

FALLACIOUS APPEAL TO AUTHORITY

To cite a Nobel Prize-winning chemist as an authority on civil rights legislation is to misunderstand the meaning of the word "authority." An authority's opinion is meaningful only when it concerns his or her special field of competence; otherwise the so-called authority is simply an ordinary citizen like the rest of us—neither wiser nor more foolish.

FALLACY OF THE UNDISTRIBUTED MIDDLE

(See "Deduction," pages 424–25.)

FALSE ANALOGY

(See "Argument by Analogy," page 427.)

HASTY GENERALIZATION

(See "Induction," page 427.)

NON SEQUITUR

When a conclusion does not follow from its premises, there has obviously been a serious slip in the deductive reasoning process.

> All artists are creative.
> Jackson is an artist.
> ∴ Jackson should be subsidized.

We can make this broken line of reasoning conform to a logical pattern by thinking it through carefully. We should say, if the conclusion we want to render valid is as follows, this:

> All creative artists deserve to be subsidized.
> Jackson is a creative artist.
> ∴ Jackson should be subsidized.

Both syllogisms contain the same conclusion; but in one case it does not follow from the premises, and in the other it does. To correct a non sequitur, we must remember that a conclusion is valid not in and of itself, but within the context of its own terms, within the body of the syllogism.

OVERSIMPLIFICATION

This is a root fallacy in which the arguer ignores the complexities of a problem so that he or she may solve it more easily.

Either...Or

This is a device in which the arguer states that there are two and only two alternatives in a given situation: *Either* you vote for the mayor's tax reform bill *or* you permit the city to become bankrupt. This allows for no intermediate choices although in fact there may be other possibilities.

Post Hoc, Ergo Propter Hoc ("After this, therefore because of this")
This error in cause-and-effect analysis was described earlier (see page 322).

PERSONIFYING ABSTRACTIONS

This fallacy involves both oversimplification and verbal distortion. It suggests that "Science tell us..." or "History teaches..." or "Poets believe..." as if each of these were a single person speaking with one voice instead of a complex abstraction representing many different points of view (see "The Limits of Language").

MODERN ARGUMENT: THE EDITORIAL

The newspaper or magazine editorial is the modern counterpart of the classical oration. For the editorial is basically a form of argument presented by the editors of a publication, a case drawn for or against an issue of timely, often pressing significance. Both *is* and *ought* propositions are at the heart of the editorial, plus a clear, cogent, and systematic review of the controversial issues involved. Ultimately the editorial writer asks the reader to think or act in a given way—as in the following editorial which asks readers to "save the trains" by spending more money on improvements.

Give the Trains a Chance

The alternative to blacktopping the entire nation with highways and airports, as more and more people are coming to realize, is a revival of passenger trains. To rescue some of the remaining intercity trains, Congress last year created a new corporation called Amtrak to take over and upgrade a basic network of routes. Thanks to Amtrak, you can still see the Rocky Mountains from a dome car. More important, the new corporation is expanding service in medium-length "corridor" runs, including the New York-Washington route, thus relieving the congestion of airline and auto traffic. Such corridor passenger loads are rising, and there is no inherent reason why Amtrak should not ultimately pay its way.

But it takes time and capital to reverse decades of neglect, and right now Amtrak is losing roughly a dollar for each dollar it takes in from passengers. Its pitifully small appropriation of $40 million already gone. Amtrak has asked Congress for another $170 million to keep the trains running through mid-1973. If the money isn't forthcoming, the infant corporation warns, it will have to use borrowed funds that had been earmarked for new rolling stock, improved stations and a nationwide reservation system.

It would be disastrous to kill off this promising venture before a true "market test" of modern trains can be carried out. The sum involved is but half the cost of one moon shot. More to the point, it's only 1/30th of what the federal government spends annually on highway construction.

Congress should not only grant the funds but should amend the law to improve Amtrak's chances of becoming profitable. In particular, it should require Amtrak to operate its own trains with its own crews. At present, the railroads run the trains and Amtrak reimburses their losses, an arrangement that gives the railroads no more incentive than in the past to keep their trains clean and punctual. Furthermore, if present crews became Amtrak employees, the corporation could negotiate directly with the unions on wages and work rules. Under work rules that go back to World War I, trains have more employees per 100 passengers than airplanes or buses. Overmanning has always been one of the railroads' economic burdens. Easing that is also part of giving Amtrak a fighting chance.

Note that, brief as it is, this editorial follows the three-part structure of classical argument:

I. Introduction

    A. Direct statement of the case: a call for the revival of passenger trains.

    B. Exposition: an account of how Congress created Amtrak to upgrade basic routes.

II. Body

    A. Evidence supporting additional federal funding for Amtrak:
      1. Facts
      2. Statistics
      3. Reasons and reasoning
      4. Analogy

III. Conclusion

    A. Peroration: a wrap-up of ways to improve Amtrak's chances of becoming profitable.

Note also how the title, framed as an imperative—"Give the Trains a Chance"— orients the reader instantly to both the issue and its proposed resolution. Note also how the absurd possibility presented in the first sentence (blacktopping the entire nation) startles the reader into attention and how the last sentence builds to a convincing final plea for a "fighting chance."

In addition to being brief and forceful, a good editorial will generate a sense of urgency, for almost by definition the issues involved in editorials are urgent.

Thus the following editorial urges that a program providing prisoners with "real work for real money" receive "quick approval by the full Senate and House." Time is generally a pressing factor in editorial issues: "Most prisoners eventually get out of prison," this editorial reminds us; we should see that it is "in everyone's interest" to help these convicts make a successful "re-entry" into society...."

Real Work for Real Money in Prison

Chief Justice Warren Burger has been insisting lately that the nation's prisons put more of their inmates to work in productive jobs. It's a sound idea that raises a question: How come real work isn't already common in prison?

"Prison industry" has a long history. In the 19th century, prisons commonly rented out convicts for work on farms and in factories and mines. The practice ended in scandals over exploitation and brutality. More recently, organized labor has resented the competition from inmates paid 30 cents an hour. Today a Federal prohibition against interstate traffic in goods made by inmates inhibits interest in the use of convicts as a labor pool.

Some inmates make products like license plates that aren't sold in interstate commerce. But such projects flourish only in a few states, notably Texas, and in the Federal prison system. Elsewhere, work with road gangs or crews that move rocks around the prison yard has been seen primarily as another form of punishment.

The case for truly productive prison work is stronger than ever. Overcrowding and the failure of rehabilitation have left prisoners with little to do except get into trouble. Revenues from prison-made products could help recoup prison costs and finance compensatory payments to crime victims. In 1980, Congress authorized an experimental program that encourages private businesses to establish small operations in seven prisons.

It remains a tiny effort, involving only 400 inmates in data processing and producing television antennas and brooms. The programs are voluntary, pay the prevailing wage, and have so far averted union objections. The Federal law permits deductions from the inmate's earnings for room and board, support for his family and restitution payments to victims.

Since 1981, these programs have paid out $900,000 in wages to the 400 participants. With a thousand times as many prisoners behind bars, the potential is immense. The Senate Judiciary Committee recently approved a measure extending the concept to another 13 prisons.

Is it right to help convicts obtain paying jobs when unemployment is so high among law-abiding workers? The answer has to be yes, for the simple reason that most prisoners eventually get out of prison. It is clearly in everyone's interest to help convicts prepare for re-entry into society with skills, self-esteem and some honest money in the bank.

A program affecting a total of 20 prisons is certainly desirable, but that hardly taps the enormous possibilities. The current measure deserves quick approval by the full Senate and House. And all levels of government should pay attention to the results.

HUMANIZING ARGUMENT: ROGERIAN STRATEGY

Even Aristotle, who defined man as a rational animal, recognized that man is not *always* rational. Sometimes—indeed frequently—he is exactly the opposite: he is emotional, irrational, existentially adrift; he feels lonely, frustrated, helpless, isolated, threatened on all sides. Recognizing this deeper and darker dimension of human nature—that it is pervasive in all people however mighty their accomplishments and lofty their positions—psychotherapist Carl R. Rogers has proposed that we incorporate the recognition into our rhetoric. He asks that we modify our traditionally aggressive and intellectually derived principles of persuasion to accommodate newer and more profound psychological insights into the way people really feel and think.

One set of rhetoricians (See Young, Becker, and Pike, *Rhetoric*), acting on Rogers's advice, describes "Rogerian strategy" as an approach to argument which reduces threat and subsequent defensiveness, thereby encouraging both parties in an argument to try to "encounter" one another, to enter "reciprocally and empathetically" into the other's position. Compared to the strictly "win" tactics of traditional argumentation, Rogerian strategy

> . . . is based on quite different assumptions about men and . . . has quite different goals. It rests on the assumption that a man holds to his beliefs about who he is and what the world is like because other beliefs threaten his identity and integrity. Hence, the first

requirement for changing beliefs is the elimination of this sense of threat. If this assumption is true, then the weaknesses of the other strategies are apparent. A strong sense of threat may render a person immune to even the most carefully reasoned and well developed argument. Likewise, attempts to condition him or to explain away his beliefs become very threatening once he discovers what is happening to him. From the Rogerian point of view, man has free will, but his ability to consider alternative positions is limited if he feels threatened. The primary goal of this rhetorical strategy is to reduce the reader's sense of threat so that he is *able* to consider alternatives to his own beliefs. The goal is thus not to work one's will on others but to establish and maintain communication *as an end in itself (Rhetoric).*

By shifting the primary emphasis of argument from working one's will on others to establishing and maintaining lines of communication and exchanging views, Rogerian rhetoricians make possible new goals, particularly the goal of working toward consensus rather than a one-sided win. The significance of this strategy is obvious to anyone surveying the national and international scene.

Profound changes are taking place in the system of Western values that has for centuries guided conduct and provided social stability and continuity between generations. Thus it becomes more and more difficult to reason from ethical assumptions that are generally accepted. Truth has become increasingly elusive and man are driven to embrace conflicting ideologies. Ours is an age of isms. As a result of rapid and mass means of communication and transportation, our world is becoming smaller, and all of us are learning to become citizens of the world, confronting people whose beliefs are radically different from our own and with whom we must learn to live (*Rhetoric*).

No wonder, then, that Rogerian rhetoricians remind us that "it has become imperative to develop a rhetoric that has as its goal not skillful verbal coercion but discussion and exchange of ideas" (*Rhetoric*).

Although Rogerian rhetoricians are making a systematic attempt to codify strategies to achieve this goal, the idea of reaching out sympathetically and empathetically to one's so-called opponent has its own tradition. In his *Autobiography*, for instance, Benjamin Franklin vividly describes his method for reducing defensiveness by reassuring adversaries that at the very least they are *understood.*

A Rule to Forbear All Direct Contradictions

Benjamin Franklin

I made it a rule to forbear all direct contradictions to the sentiments of others, and all positive assertion of my own. I even forbade myself ... the use of every word or expression in the language that imported a fix'd opinion, such as *certainly, undoubtedly,* etc., and I adopted, instead of them, *I conceive, I apprehend,* or *I imagine* a thing to be so or so; or it *so appears to me at present.* When another asserted something that I thought an error, I deny'd myself the pleasure of contradicting him abruptly, and of showing immediately some absurdity in his proposition: and in answering I began by observing that in certain cases or circumstances his opinion would be right, but in the present case there *appear'd* or *seem'd* to me some difference, etc. I soon found the advantage of this change in my manner; the conversations I engag'd in went on more pleasantly. The modest way in which I propos'd my opinions procur'd them a readier reception and less contradiction; I had less mortification when I was found to be in the wrong, and I more easily prevail'd with others to give up their mistakes and join with me when I happened to be in the right.

And this mode, which I at first put on with some violence to natural inclination, became at length so easy, and so habitual to me, that perhaps for these fifty years past no one has ever heard a dogmatical expression escape me. And to this habit (after my character of integrity) I think it principally owing that I had early so much weight with my fellow-citizens when I proposed new institutions, or alterations in the old, and so much influence in public councils when I became a member; for I was but a bad speaker, never eloquent, subject to much hesitation in my choice of words, hardly correct in language, and yet I generally carried my points.

Benjamin Franklin's intuitive perception that a modest way of setting forth one's ideas promotes "a readier reception" appears to be at the heart of the following argument in favor of raising safety standards in U.S. coal mines. It is a compelling argument because the writer cites facts and figures as well as personal opinion and experience. He clearly knows what he is talking about: he checked his information with the International Labor Office; he obtained production figures and accident rates for U.S. and foreign mines. He moves through his subject with assurance because he is thoroughly familiar with it; he does not lapse into vague generalities, nor does he simply play on emotion. Instead he combines objective data with first-hand accounts of what working in a coal mine is like. It is grim, and we are made to see how and why it is grim. We are also made to feel, with the writer, a deep compassion for the miner, whose fears are rooted in the realities of an inherently hazardous situation, but whose pride (the writer himself projects this attitude) persists in the face of all dangers. By the time we have finished reading this piece we have a deeper understanding of the coal miner's situation.

We do not have an oversimplified or one-sided explanation of the problem, however, nor have we a malefactor who has been singled-out for blame. What is Rogerian about the strategy of this writer is that he does not polarize interest groups, setting one solidly and stubbornly against the other. Instead he recognizes the complexity of the situation—at one point even making a concession to "apologists for the industry." More than that, he cites a British mining official whose superior safety record might well provide a basis for boasting. But wouldn't boasting intensify the defensive stance of the other side? The writer appears to incorporate this Rogerian insight into his argument, for he has the British official disclaim harsh criticism: "It sounds as if I'm being beastly and critical of your mining people and I would hate to be so, because we have a lot to learn from them in some matters...." According to Rogerian rhetoricians, making this admission not only decreases the sense of threat inherent in this situation but also increases the possibility of establishing an ongoing and fruitful future exchange between mining representatives of the two countries.

Life, and Death, in the Coal Mines

Duane Lockard

INTRO-
DUCTION

Nearly thirty years ago, 350 feet beneath a West Virginia mountain, I stood paralyzed with fear when a greasy haulage motor caught fire. Having heard endless mine lore from my father and grandfather, I knew that fire in a mine

Narration

was death, especially when the mine was not rockdusted to reduce the explosiveness of coal dust. I knew many miles of volatile coal dust lay in the tunnels of that mine, since I was at that moment preparing to spray the walls with tons of an incombustible matter.

We worked 24 hours that Saturday and Sunday rockdusting because the boss said the state mine inspector was coming Monday and the mine had to be · prepared for him. The fire burned itself out, but not before it impressed me as deeply as any fright I ever experienced, including wartime air combat.

BODY

This memory returns as I observe the current maneuvers to prevent the raising of U.S. coal mine safety standards.

Citing vital statistics as evidence

Mining is dangerous and always will be; no other industry levies a higher toll in lives and disabling accidents. To produce half a billion tons of bituminous coal last year cost the lives of 307 miners; 88 of them died in explosions and an equal number were crushed in roof falls. Besides these fatalities another 9,500 men suffered serious injuries. And an undetermined number breathed the decisive quantity of coal dust that assured their lingering death of asphyxiation from pneumoconiosis or "black lung."

Conceding an opposing point... and modifying it

Apologists for the industry point to the reduction in the number of accidents in recent decades, and it is true that since 1930 the number of accidents has declined from 100,000 to about 10,000. Not all the reduction is due to safety advances, however, for 135,000 miners now produce as much coal as did half a million during World War II.

Citing comparative statistics as evidence

Does the production of coal necessitate such a cost in lives? Coal can be and long has been mined in other countries with lower accident rates. On the average Western European nations have mining fatality rates that are a third to a half of those for the United States.

Citing authority

The International Labor Office reports that American mining fatality rates are matched only by those for Canada, Taiwan, Korea and Turkey among the 22 nations for which it has data. Morocco and Southern Rhodesia have rates only half as high as ours, while India, Czechoslovakia, Poland, Great Britain and Yugoslavia have rates that are lower still.

Quoting authority

Is this because American mines are more dangerous than others? I posed this question to a British mining official. He replied that on the contrary, "British mines are inherently more dangerous than yours and therefore our safety standards have to be all the higher.... Our rockdusting standards are very high and rigidly enforced. I believe our standards of electrical safety are higher than in the U.S. Indeed, most American machinery—if not all—that has been installed over here has had to be redesigned on the electrical side."

He concluded, "It sounds as if I'm being beastly and critical of your mining people and I would hate to be so, because we have a lot to learn from them in some matters while still trying to retain our safety standards. We have learned by experience, much of which has been bitter, and I am quite sure that it is the inherently greater danger in our mines that makes us the more careful and creates our higher standards."

Citing personal experience

Mining has changed greatly since I left it, but that dreaded top still hangs overhead always ready to avenge its loss. I recall once that my father asked me to stop shoveling while he sounded the roof with his pick-handle, listening carefully. Coal began to snap and fly just as he shouted a warning and we ran from the coal face. Within seconds the half-filled coal car, the tracks, some tools (but not the lunch buckets—I saw to their safety) disappeared in a roar

CONCLUSION

Peroration

of rubble and a cloud of dust. A thick layer of slate had given way, splintering huge safety posts like twigs as it came down.

Every miner is aware of this risk, as he is of explosions, and his body bears blue scars to mark each injury by a hank of coal. I never knew a miner lacking in fear of the mine nor one without a certain compensating pride.

Too many of these brave men will be killed even with the best of safety rules, but in this technologically advanced nation need we have so much blood on our coal?

TESTING YOUR ARGUMENT: A CHECKLIST

Whatever case you may make for or against any subject, you should test your argument against the following questions:

1. Have you defined the terms? (see "What Does X Mean?" and "The Limits of Language")
2. Have you established exactly what the argument is about? That is, have you stated the proposition clearly and indicated precisely what issues are to be defended and refuted?
3. Are you certain that the facts and assumptions are correct?
4. Have you offered sufficient evidence—facts, statistics, illustrations, testimony—that will further illuminate and substantiate each point as well as the overall position? (see "Gathering Information")
5. Are generalizations fair and reliable?
6. Do conclusions follow logically from the premises?
7. Have you cited reliable authorities?
8. Is the presentation rhetorically effective, that is, clear, cogent, well-organized?
9. Have you examined *every* important aspect of the case? Aristotle maintained that we should be able to argue on either side of a question—not because we are without personal conviction or commitment but because only then can we feel certain that no aspect of the case has escaped us.
10. Is the tone appropriate to the subject, the occasion, and the purpose you are trying to achieve? Have you taken Rogerian strategy into consideration; in other words, have you tried to reduce threat and defensiveness by entering empathetically into your opponent's position? Is your overall approach flexible, reasonable, and sympathetic, rather than rigid, dogmatic, unnecessarily and irritatingly disputatious?

DISCUSSION

1. Discuss Allan H. Gilbert's essay "College Lectures Are Obsolete." Consider arguments in favor of the lecture system.
2. Read the letter below and answer the questions that follow.

A Letter to the Editor

(1) With a great show of moral indignation, it was recently revealed that 47 percent of Monroe College students "cheated" on quizzes, prelims, and examinations. Since then, readers of *The Bulletin* have been deluged with pious commentaries. Isn't it about time someone asked whether our modern Puritans aren't being overly righteous in this matter? A little giving or taking of information on an examination, or the use of a few crib notes, is not such a bad thing as some prudish minds would have us think. The very fact that so many loyal Monroe students indulge in this is evidence that it can't be very wrong.

(2) On the contrary, copying or the use of crib notes seems quite pardonable in many courses. In a course which requires remembering a lot of facts, why not use crib notes? It's only a difference of degree between using them and using some elaborate system for memorizing facts. Both are artificial means to help you remember.

(3) If we view the problem from another angle, we can see that what is so smugly denounced as "dishonesty" may actually reveal foresight—which is certainly a praise-worthy trait. If you were going into an unknown wilderness, you would take along the things you knew were needed for survival, wouldn't you? Taking crib notes into the unknown territory of an examination shows the same foresight. Now suppose also that one of your companions on this expedition desperately needed water or food or help of some sort. You'd do what you could for him, wouldn't you? Helping someone on an examination isn't any different.

(4) To put the question another way, suppose we define charity as "giving to a person in need." Isn't one, therefore, performing an act of charity during an examination when one gives some "needy" person the desired information? The fact that one isn't giving money or food doesn't make the act any less charitable.

(5) If we inquire *who* is stirring up this fuss over alleged "cheating," we find it's the faculty—in other words, the persons who have selfish interests to protect. Obviously, they flunk students to make them repeat the course and thus to keep it filled.

(6) Finally, to take a long-range view, why should colleges get all excited over what they choose to call "cheating" when there are much more urgent things for them to worry about? When the very existence of our democracy is being threatened by Communism, why fret about the source of Johnny X's information on an exam in ancient history?

—Name Withheld

a. What is the writer's main point? State the reasons given in support of it.
b. What is the writer's implied definition of cheating? Comment on its adequacy as a definition?
c. What is the writer's view of people who denounce cheating? What purpose does this view serve in the argument?
d. What is the implied premise or underlying assumption of: "The very fact that so many loyal Monroe students indulge in this is evidence that it can't be very wrong"?
e. Identify and briefly describe the fallacy in paragraph 2.
f. What kind of argument does the writer use in paragraph 3? Appraise its soundness.
g. Comment on the argument used in paragraph 4 and again in paragraph 6.

3. Discuss the advantages and possible disadvantages of Benjamin Franklin's advice. Do his rules preclude the kind of confident assertion necessary to win the reader's agreement and assent? Explain the psychological value of Franklin's approach.
4. Analyze and evaluate the editorial below in terms of the following:

Title
Opening sentence/closing sentence
Organization
Soundness of argument
Use of Rogerian strategy

Time to Start Saving the Soil

We are accustomed to think of soil destruction as a problem confronting other lands and other times: the inexorable spread of the Sahara Desert, the parching of lands in India, the American Dust Bowl of the 1930's. But as a United Nations conference in Nairobi, Kenya, begins to assess the global problem of the loss of arable lands, it is sobering to note that even in this country, the reputed world leader in modern agricultural practices, the land is eroding away.

Over the past two centuries, erosion has ruined some 200 million arable acres, more than half as much land as we currently have under cultivation. Today an estimated one-third of our croplands are losing topsoil at a rate too great to be sustained without eventually reducing productivity. Crop yields continue high only because of the use of fertilizers and modern technology and management methods. Water alone carried off nine tons of soil per average acre of American cropland in 1975; five tons are generally considered the upper limit tolerable over a sustained period in even deep soils. Wind has added to the destruction, and some observers fear conditions are ripe for another dust bowl.

How can this be—some four decades after Franklin D. Roosevelt launched the nation on the path toward soil conservation? The answers lie in economics. Farmers seek to maximize their immediate crop yields by planting continuous single crops and eliminating protective cover crops. They are often reluctant to adopt costly conservation practices.

The Agriculture Department and key Congressional committees have begun a major reassessment of the nation's soil conservation programs. The House and Senate have already approved bills designed to help stem the loss of land. The approaches so far have been essentially voluntary; they seek to persuade the farmer to adopt conservation practices through education, technical assistance and cost-sharing incentives.

That may not be enough. Compulsion may be needed. The farm bloc would of course oppose mandatory regulations, but the time has probably come to insist that farmers follow good soil conservation practices as a condition of receiving farm loans, crop insurance, price supports and other Federal aid. Conserving the nation's land is too important to be left to the individual farmer.

5. Analyze the analogies in W. T. Jones's essay "Marxism." Indicate in what ways they enhance the argument.
6. Select an editorial from your local or college newspaper and analyze as in question 4 above.
7. Read the following "Letter to the Editor" and evaluate the quality of the argument. Use the checklist on page 439.

A Case for Senior Theatergoers

To the Editor:
I am writing on behalf of many senior citizens—especially the 1,200 members of the Hudson Guild Fulton Senior Center in Manhattan, of which I am a member.

Since I was 16 years old, I have been going to ballet, theater, classical concerts and to many and various recitals. I worked in the garment factories in New York City and my wages were very low. But that did not deter me from spending my last penny for books and concerts. If I could not afford a seat, I would buy a ticket to stand. I went to Carnegie Hall so often in my youth, my mother would tell me I ought to pay rent there. I am now 79 years old, and in my lifetime I think I have heard and seen every great artist and dancer in the world, including Paderewski, Rachmaninoff, Caruso, Anna Pavlova, Isadora Duncan and hundreds of others. In fact, I was present at the debut recitals of Yehudi Menuhin and Jascha Heifetz—two of the world's greatest violinists. Also, I have heard the greatest orchestras in the world, and I was an original subscriber to the American Opera Society and the Little Orchestra Society, and I retained these subscriptions about 20 years or more until these wonderful musical organizations went out of existence.

Since I retired in 1971, I have not had the means to attend many concerts, theaters, dance recitals, etc. There are thousands of retirees with fixed low incomes who love music and the arts as much as I do, but cannot afford the extremely high prices for tickets. It is a pity that we have to be deprived of the pleasure and joy of hearing a great orchestra or seeing a great ballet just because we are older and poor.

Not so long ago, senior centers and neighborhood organizations would get free tickets from Hospital Audiences, Inc. (H.A.I.), but that too is no more. H.A.I. says there are no funds available for such purposes. The senior centers occasionally do get some free tickets from Carnegie Hall, but they are very few and far between. Even when we did get free tickets from H.A.I., they were no big deal. First, there were never more than for a small number of people; and second, many tickets were either side or obstructed view or in the very top balconies. If any of your readers are at all acquainted with Carnegie Hall or the City Center balconies, they will know what I mean when I say that by the time we climb up the six or seven flights of stairs to the very top where our free seats are located we have no breath or energy left to enjoy whatever we came to see or hear. It is especially hard on most of us who have high blood pressure or arthritis or both; and I happen to be one of them. The City Center has no elevator at all; Carnegie Hall does have an elevator, but it goes only to the dress circle. So, you have to climb two flights of stairs when you get off the elevator to get to the balcony. The only place that has no obstructed view is Alice Tully Hall. But the Metropolitan Opera House, the New York State Theater and the newly renovated Avery Fisher Hall have very bad side seats where you have to crane your neck out of position to get a good view of the stage. And these are the seats we generally get when we do get them.

A friend of mine who is 81 years of age got a "free" ticket for a ballet from the senior center for the City Center Theater. When she looked at the seating map in the lobby, she saw that the seat was in the very last row of the top balcony. She went to the box office and asked to have the ticket exchanged because she could not climb up all those flights of stairs, and besides she could not see too well from so far away. And do you know what the cashier told her? "What do you expect for nothing?" She got very angry and replied that she had paid for that ticket many times over with taxes she had been paying for years and she deserves and demanded a better seat. And she got it!

I think it is a disgrace that in New York City, which is considered to be the cultural center of the world in the richest country in the world, the poor and the elderly are treated with such contempt. Because of my activities and my interest in music and the arts for so many years, my name is on many mailing lists. Very often I get letters and invitations to theaters and concerts asking me to buy tickets at special prices for senior citizens. And these so-called special prices range from $25 to $7.50; and very often from $5 to $6. How in the world can a person like me pay such prices when with my very low income I could live two or three days on $5? And there are literally hundreds of elderly people like me who, because they have so little, spend their days in loneliness watching mostly trash on television or listening to the radio for hours at a time. Why can't our government provide special funds from the general revenue to brighten the lives of our elderly citizens after many years of work and paying taxes?

Why can't we transfer funds from the swollen military budget of $140 billion that would only be used for MX missiles and nuclear weapons for death and destruction and use those funds for the humane, recreational and cultural needs of the people who have worked hard all of their lives and deserve something better than to live out their days in poverty and loneliness? We could use our half-fare cards for identification to be admitted to concerts, theaters and other cultural activities for a general admission of 25 or 50 cents. Many young people are admitted on their school I.D. cards. Why can't we elderly be granted the same privileges? We do not want any patronizing favors from *anyone*. We have earned our right to some of the good and better things of life.

Mary Gale, New York City

8. Read the following news item carefully, noting the many complications in the situation. Indicate how a Rogerian rhetorician might analyze the explosive problems described—and how they might have been avoided.

Having written about his lacerating experience in a forthcoming Anchor/Doubleday book, *Academic Turmoil*, due next month, Theodore L. Gross, former dean of humanities at City College and now provost at the Capitol Campus of Penn State outside of Harrisburg, can be a little more objective about it all, though both his voice and manner suggest that it has been rough going for the last two years.

It all started with an article that appeared in the Feb. 4, 1978, issue of the *Saturday Review* with the startling headline, "How to Kill a College" and an illustration of a bloody dagger plunged into the heart of academe. The article was a sober assessment of the open admissions program at City College, which the then-dean had advocated but which he felt had been less than successful. But the trappings of the piece, the headline and illustration, neither of which he was responsible for, evidently sensationalized the entire issue. The result, among other things, brought confrontations with organized student groups on campus and severe criticism from the president of the college, Robert E. Marshak, with whom Dean Gross had had cordial relations.

Mr. Gross was removed as dean and though he could have returned to an earlier position of professor of English, he accepted the offer made to him by Penn State to take the Capitol Campus post.

"I did not realize that the president would take the piece so personally," Mr. Gross said. "It was a piece about open admissions. It was not a personal matter. Had I known what would develop, I would have written the essay but held off from publishing it until it was a book."

The book is now in, and it tells not only what Mr. Gross wanted to say about open admissions and higher education and its relation to pre-college schooling, but it includes also a blow-by-blow account of the events that followed publication of the article.

He is still for open admissions. "We don't have any choice in regard to the program," the educator said. "It is pragmatic and it is education as practiced in America. It can be sloppy, it can be messy, but there is about it a sense of promise, of openness that is marvelous and tremendously exciting." He sees his book as a 1970's case history and hopes it will offer guidance to inner-city educators.

Taking a long look back now, would he say that these recent events constitute a triumph or failure?

"Neither," said the former dean, "A circumstance of life." (Lask, "Publishing").

ESSAY SUGGESTIONS

1. In an essay (750–1,000 words) reply to Allan H. Gilbert's essay "College Lectures Are Obsolete." Support the position or assert a contrary position in favor of the lecture system. Prepare to write this essay by using the prewriting techniques you have learned.

2. Write an essay (750–1,000 words) arguing against another aspect or procedure of our educational system that you consider obsolete or otherwise inadequate (the grading system, required courses, awarding of degrees, formal class meetings). Be sure to locate specific issues and to include in the body of your argument not only evidence in behalf of your case, but evidence refuting points of opposition. Attempt to weave in a Rogerian strategy, if possible.

3. In an essay (500–750 words) make a case against any -ism of your choice (atheism, romanticism, racism) by showing that it is either self-contradictory (a logical flaw) or self-defeating (a moral flaw). Use analogies to develop your argument.

4. Fill in the space(s) of one of the headlines below and write an editorial for your college or local newspaper (500–750 words).

   Give the _____ a Chance

   Time to Start _____

   Hold That _____ at _____

5. Write an editorial (500–750 words) on any subject of timely or urgent concern.

6. Write a "Letter to the Editor" entitled "A Case for _____." Use as your first sentence your own variation of "I am writing on behalf of many _____" (see "A Case for Senior Theatergoers," pages 441–43). (750–1,000 words).

7. Read the essay below, originally a paper presented by Carl Rogers at Northwestern University's Conference on Communications (October 11, 1951). Evaluate the arguments in behalf of the main thesis: "That the major barrier to mutual interpersonal communication is our very natural tendency to judge, to evaluate, to approve or disapprove, the statement of the other person, or the other group." Test out Rogerian strategy by setting up with a classmate an experimental argument in which you try, as Rogers suggests, "creating a situation in which each of the different parties come to understand the other from the *other's* point of view."

   Using the results of your experiment, plus Rogers's argument in support of his thesis (you might also draw upon Benjamin Franklin's advice), write an argument of your own (750–1,000 words) entitled "The Case For Rogerian Strategy," or "The Case Against Rogerian Strategy."

Communication: Its Blocking and Its Facilitation

Carl R. Rogers

It may seem curious that a person whose whole professional effort is devoted to psychotherapy should be interested in problems of communication. What relationship is there between providing therapeutic help to individuals with emotional maladjustments and the concern of this conference with obstacles to communication? Actually the relationship is very close indeed. The whole task of psychotherapy is the task of dealing with a failure in communication. The emotionally maladjusted person, the "neurotic," is in difficulty first because communication within himself has broken down, and second because as a result of this his communication with others has been damaged. If this sounds somewhat strange, then let me put it in other terms. In the "neurotic" individual, parts of himself which have been termed unconscious, or repressed, or denied to awareness, become blocked off so that they no longer communicate themselves to the conscious or managing part of himself. As long as this is true, there are distortions in the way he communicates himself to others, and so he suffers both within himself, and in his interpersonal relations. The task of psychotherapy is to help the person achieve, through a special relationship with a therapist, good communication within himself. Once this is achieved he can communicate more freely and more effectively with others. We may say then that psychotherapy is good communication, within and between men. We may also turn that statement around and it will still be true. Good communication, free communication, within or between men, is always therapeutic.

It is, then, from a background of experience with communication in counseling and psychotherapy that I want to present here two ideas. I wish to state what I believe is one of the major factors in blocking or impeding communication, and then I wish to present what in our experience has proven to be a very important way of improving or facilitating communication.

I would like to propose, as an hypothesis for consideration, that the major barrier to mutual interpersonal communication is our very natural tendency to judge, to evaluate, to approve or disapprove, the statement of the other person, or the other group. Let me illustrate my meaning with some very simple examples. As you leave the meeting tonight, one of the statements you are likely to hear is, "I didn't like that man's talk." Now what do you respond? Almost invariably your reply will be either approval or disapproval of the attitude expressed. Either you respond, "I didn't either. I thought it was terrible," or else you tend to reply, "Oh, I thought it was really good." In other words, your primary reaction is to evaluate what has just been said to you, to evaluate it from *your* point of view, your own frame of reference.

Or take another example. Suppose I say with some feeling, "I think the Republicans are behaving in ways that show a lot of good sound sense these days," what is the response that arises in your mind as you listen? The overwhelming likelihood is that it will be evaluative. You will find yourself agreeing, or disagreeing, or making some judgment about me such as "He must be a conservative," or "He seems solid in his thinking." Or let us take an illustration from the international scene. Russia says vehemently, "The treaty with Japan is a war plot on the part of the United States." We rise as one person to say "That's a lie!"

This last illustration brings in another element connected with hypothesis. Although the tendency to make evaluations is common in almost all interchange of language, it is very much heightened in those situations where feelings and emotions are deeply involved. So the stronger our feelings, the more likely it is that there will be no mutual element in the communication. There will be just two ideas, two feelings, two judgments, missing each other in psychological space. I'm sure you recognize this from your own experience. When you have not been emotionally involved yourself, and have listened to a heated discussion, you often go away thinking, "Well, they actually weren't talking about the same thing." And they were not. Each was making a judgment, an evaluation, from his own frame of reference. There was really nothing which could be called communication in any genuine sense. This tendency to react to any emotionally meaningful statement by forming an evaluation of it from our own point of view is, I repeat, the major barrier to interpersonal communication.

But is there any way of solving this problem, of avoiding this barrier? I feel that we are making exciting progress toward this goal and I would like to present it as simply as I can. Real communication occurs, and this evaluative tendency is avoided, when we listen with understanding. What does that mean? It means to *see the expressed idea and attitude from the other person's point of view, to sense how it feels to him, to achieve his frame of reference in regard to the thing he is talking about.*

Stated so briefly, this may sound absurdly simple, but it is not. It is an approach which we have found extremely potent in the field of psychotherapy. It is the most effective agent we know for altering the basic personality structure of an individual, and improving his relationships and his communications with others. If I can listen to what he can tell me, if I can understand how it seems to him, if I can see its personal meaning for him, if I can sense the emotional flavor which it has for him, then I will be releasing potent forces of change in him. If I can really understand how he hates his father, or hates the university, or hates communists—if I can catch the flavor of his fear of insanity, or his fear of atom bombs, or of Russia—it will be of the greatest help to him in altering those very hatreds and fears, and in establishing realistic and harmonious relationships with the very people and situations toward which he has felt hatred and fear. We know from our research that such empathic understanding—understanding *with* a person, not *about him*—is such an effective approach that it can bring about major changes in personality.

Some of you may be feeling that you listen well to people, and that you have never seen such results. The chances are very great indeed that your listening has not been of the type I have described. Fortunately I can suggest a little laboratory experiment which you can try to test the quality of your understanding. The next time you get into an argument with your wife, or your friend, or with a small group of friends, just stop the discussion for a moment and for an experiment, institute this rule. "Each person can speak up for himself only *after* he has first restated the ideas and feelings of the previous speaker accurately, and to the speaker's satisfaction." You see what this would mean. It would simply mean that before presenting your own point of view, it would be necessary for you to really achieve the other speaker's frame of reference—to understand his thoughts and feelings so well that you could summarize them for him. Sounds simple doesn't it? But if you try it you will discover it is one of the most difficult things you have ever tried to do. However, once you have been able to see the other's point of view, your own comments will have to be drastically revised. You will also find the emotion going out of the discussion, the differences being reduced, and those differences which remain being of a rational and understandable sort.

Can you imagine what this kind of an approach would mean if it were projected into larger areas? What would happen to a labor-management dispute if it was conducted in such a way that labor, without necessarily agreeing, could accurately state management's point of view in a way that management could accept; and management, without approving labor's stand, could state labor's case in a way that labor agreed was accurate? It would mean that real communication was established, and one could practically guarantee that some reasonable solution would be reached.

If then this way of approach is an effective avenue to good communication and good relationships, as I am quite sure you will agree if you try the experiment I have mentioned, why is it not more widely tried and used? I will try to list the difficulties which keep it from being widely utilized.

In the first place it takes courage, a quality which is not too widespread. I am indebted to Dr. S. I. Hayakawa, the semanticist, for pointing out that to carry on psychotherapy in this fashion is to take a very real risk, and that courage is required. If you really understand another person in this way, if you are willing to enter his private world and see the way life appears to him, without any attempt to make evaluative judgments, you run the risk of being changed yourself. You might see it his way, you might find yourself influenced in your attitudes or your personality. This risk of being changed is one of the most frightening prospects most of us can face. If I enter, as fully as I am able, into the private world of a neurotic or psychotic individual, isn't there a risk that I might become lost in that world? Most of us are afraid to take that risk. Or if we had a Russian communist speaker here tonight, or Senator Joe McCarthy, how many of us would dare to try to see the world from each of these points of view? The great majority of us could not *listen*; we would find ourselves compelled to *evaluate*, because listening would seem too dangerous. So the first requirement is courage, and we do not always have it.

But there is a second obstacle. It is just when emotions are strongest that it is most difficult to achieve the frame of reference of the other person or group. Yet it is the time the attitude is most needed, if communication is to be established. We have not found this to be an insuperable obstacle in our experience in psychotherapy. A third party, who is able to lay aside his own feelings and evaluations, can assist greatly by listening with understanding to each person or group and clarifying the views and attitudes each holds. We have found this very effective in small groups in which contradictory or antagonistic attitudes exist. When the parties to a dispute realize that they are being understood, that someone sees how the situation seems to them, the statements grow less exaggerated and less defensive, and it is no longer necessary to maintain the attitude, "I am 100% right and you are 100% wrong." The influence of such an understanding catalyst in the group permits the members to come closer and closer to the objective truth involved in the relationship. In this way mutual communication is established and some type of agreement becomes much more possible. So we may say that though heightened emotions make it much more difficult to understand *with* an opponent, our experience makes it clear that a neutral, understanding, catalyst type of leader or therapist can overcome this obstacle in a small group.

This last phrase, however, suggests another obstacle to utilizing the approach I have described. Thus far all our experience has been with small face-to-face groups—groups exhibiting industrial tensions, religious tensions, racial tensions, and therapy groups in which many personal tensions are present. In these small groups our experience, confirmed by a limited amount of research, shows that this basic approach leads to improved communication, to greater acceptance of others and by others, and to attitudes which are more positive and more problem-solving in nature. There is a decrease in defensiveness, in exaggerated statements, in evaluative and critical behavior. But these findings are from small groups. What about trying to achieve understanding between larger groups that are geographically remote? Or between face-to-face groups who are not speaking for themselves, but simply as representatives of others, like the delegates at Kaesong? Frankly we do not know the answers to these questions. I believe the situation might be put this way. As social scientists we have a tentative test-tube solution of the problem of breakdown in communication. But to confirm the validity of this test-tube solution, and to adapt it to the enormous problems of communication-breakdown between classes, groups, and nations, would involve additional funds, much more research, and creative thinking of a high order.

Even with our present limited knowledge we can see some steps which might be taken, even in large groups, to increase the amount of listening *with,* and to decrease the amount of evaluation *about.* To be imaginative for a moment, let us suppose that a therapeutically oriented international group went to the Russian leaders and said, "We want to achieve a genuine understanding of your views and even more important, of your attitudes and feelings, toward the United States. We will summarize and resummarize these views and feelings if necessary, until you agree that our description represents the situation as it seems to you." Then suppose they did the same thing with the leaders in our own country. If they then gave the widest possible distribution to these two views, with the feelings clearly described but not expressed in name-calling, might not the effect be very great? It would not guarantee the type of understanding I have been describing, but it would make it much more possible. We can understand the feelings of a person who hates us much more readily when his attitudes are accurately described to us by a neutral third party, than we can when he is shaking his fist at us.

But even to describe such a first step is to suggest another obstacle to this approach of understanding. Our civilization does not yet have enough faith in the social sciences to utilize their findings. The opposite is true of the physical sciences. During the war when a test-tube solution was found to the problem of synthetic rubber, millions of dollars and an army of talent was turned loose on the problem of using that finding. If synthetic rubber could be made in milligrams, it could and would be made in the thousands of tons. And it was. But in the social science realm, if a way is found of facilitating communication and mutual understanding in small groups, there is no guarantee that the finding will be utilized. It may be a generation or more before the money and the brains will be turned loose to exploit that finding.

In closing, I would like to summarize this small-scale solution to the problem of barriers in communication, and to point out certain of its characteristics.

I have said that our research and experience to date would make it appear that breakdowns in communication, and the evaluative tendency which is the major barrier to communication, can be avoided. The solution is provided by creating a situation in which each of the different parties come to understand the other from the *other's* point of view. This has been achieved, in practice, even when feelings run high, by the influence of a person who is willing to understand each point of view emphatically, and who thus acts as a catalyst to precipitate further understanding.

This procedure has important characteristics. It can be initiated by one party, without waiting for the other to be ready. It can even be initiated by a neutral third person, providing he can gain a minimum of cooperation from one of the parties.

This procedure can deal with the insincerities, the defensive exaggerations, the lies, the "false fronts" which characterize almost every failure in communication. These defensive distortions drop away with astonishing speed as people find that the only intent is to understand, not judge.

This approach leads steadily and rapidly toward the discovery of the truth, toward a realistic appraisal of the objective barriers to communication. The dropping of some defensiveness by one party leads to further dropping of defensiveness by the other party, and truth is thus approached.

This procedure gradually achieves mutual communication. Mutual communication tends to be pointed toward solving a problem rather than toward attacking a person or group. It leads to a situation in which I see how the problem appears to you, as well as to me, and you see how it appears to me, as well as to you. Thus accurately and realistically defined, the problem is almost certain to yield to intelligent attack, or if it is in part insoluble, it will be comfortably accepted as such.

This then appears to be a test-tube solution to the breakdown of communication as it occurs in small groups. Can we take this small-scale answer, investigate it further, refine it, develop it and apply it to the tragic and well-nigh fatal failures of communication which threaten the very existence of our modern world? It seems to me that this is a possibility and a challenge which we should explore.

Part Four

WRITING A LONG PAPER: ANSWERING THE TWENTY QUESTIONS

The Long Paper

Scholarly Documentation

The Long Paper

ANSWERING MANY QUESTIONS

*I*n the context of this book, the writer of the short paper (500–1,000 words) takes the impulse for the paper from a single question and concentrates most energy on answering that question. Even the subquestions enhance the treatment of the main question and support its point of view.

This section examines longer and more complex forms of writing: The writer combines questions to expand the main thrust of the piece, specifically:

1. To explore an issue beyond its most obvious features—presenting not only the facts but *how* they got to be facts, why and with what consequences;

2. To describe not only the basic steps of a process but also to explain the deeper meanings of a process and its ultimate value;

3. To describe a character, not only in broad brush strokes as in the sketch, but also to describe the nuances of detail which fill out the portrait; and

4. To examine systematically the many facets of an explanation, an interpretation, or an argument.

In the "'long paper" that follows, for example, the inspired writer, Martin Luther King, Jr., amplified his defense of black civil disobedience by calling upon most of the 20 questions and also asked a variety of subquestions he needed to answer to complete his defense.

Widely recognized as one of the great human documents of our time, a brilliant argument in behalf of the nonviolent struggle for freedom and brotherhood, King's long "Letter" is worth our closest study. Calmly convincing in tone, rigorously and patiently reasoned throughout, King wrote the letter in reply to eight fellow clergymen who had jointly published a statement denouncing his nonviolent protest marches, demonstrations, voter registrations, and sit-ins, as "unwise and untimely."

As an ordained minister with a doctorate in theology, King was addressing an audience of his peers, appealing to them as spiritual brothers, in language they could understand, replete with biblical allusions. No wonder, then, that sympathizers would liken his letter to St. Paul's letters to the Corinthians. That King, like St. Paul, was writing from prison (in King's case for organizing luncheon counter sit-ins) heightens this plea for racial equality for which King dedicated his life and for which he ultimately lost it.

King set down the first draft of this letter—in his own understated description—"under somewhat constricting circumstances." Specifically, he began it, as he would later report, "…on the margins of the newspaper in which the [clergymen's] statement appeared while I was in jail,...continued on scraps of writing paper supplied by a friendly Negro trustee, and concluded on a pad my attorneys were eventually permitted to leave me." Before presenting it to a wider audience, King "indulged in the author's prerogative of polishing it for publication."

The final version, as one commentator has aptly observed, "is a model of careful and reasonable analysis of a very complex situation. It succeeds largely because it remains concrete." King also systematically treats one issue after another, "refusing to be caught up in passion or posturing. King remains grounded in logic. He is convinced that his statement of his view will convince his audience" (Jacobus, *Ideas*).

King's confidence was more than confirmed in 1964 when he was awarded the Nobel Peace Prize.

As you read "Letter from Birmingham Jail," note the succession of questions that King addresses to his subject, returning to them time and time again as new occasions and contexts arise. For example, he asks "What are the causes of X?" at five separate points. In repeatedly providing reasons for his position and (it would seem) in intuitively following Rogerian strategy (pages 435–36), he humanizes his argument by recognizing that his readers are apt to feel threatened and defensive. By reaching out to them in the patiently reasoning tone that characterizes the entire letter, he deflects any defensiveness by anticipating it, transcending the need for defense. "I will tell you," King says, "how these grievances came into being ("How is X made or done?"); and I will further show you their consequences." King calls upon one dimension of explanation after another: These are the facts and these are the types; this is the purpose and here is my summary. This long, richly textured "position" on black civil rights obviously grew out of a creative combination of pointed questions addressed to the subject at hand and leading—inevitably—to a moving and climactic conclusion.

Letter from Birmingham Jail

Martin Luther King, Jr.

April 16, 1963

My Dear Fellow Clergymen:

(1) While confined here in the Birmingham city jail, I came across your recent statement calling my present activities "unwise and untimely." Seldom do I pause to answer criticism of my work and ideas. If I sought to answer all the criticisms that cross my desk, my secretaries would have little time for anything other than such correspondence in the course of the day, and I would have no time for constructive work. But since I feel that you are men of genuine good will and that your criticisms are sincerely set forth, I want to try to answer your statement in what I hope will be patient and reasonable terms.

Question 13: What are the causes of X?

(2) I think I should indicate why I am here in Birmingham, since you have been influenced by the view which argues against "outsiders coming in." I have the honor of serving as president of the Southern Christian Leadership Conference, an organization operating in every southern state, with headquarters in Atlanta, Georgia. We have some eighty-five affiliated organizations across the South, and one of them is the Alabama Christian Movement for Human Rights. Frequently we share staff, educational and financial resources

with our affiliates. Several months ago the affiliate here in Birmingham asked us to be on call to engage in a nonviolent direct-action program if such were deemed necessary. We readily consented, and when the hour came we lived up to our promise. So I, along with several members of my staff, am here because I was invited here. I am here because I have organizational ties here.

(3) But more basically, I am in Birmingham because injustice is here. Just as the prophets of the eighth century B.C left their villages and carried their "thus saith the Lord" far beyond the boundaries of their home towns, and just as the Apostle Paul left his village of Tarsus and carried the gospel of Jesus Christ to the far corners of the Greco-Roman world, so am I compelled to carry the gospel of freedom beyond my own home town. Like Paul, I must constantly respond to the Macedonian call for aid.

Question 7:
What is the
present status
of X?

(4) Moreover, I am cognizant of the interrelatedness of all communities and states. I cannot sit idly by in Atlanta and not be concerned about what happens in Birmingham. Injustice anywhere is a threat to justice everywhere. We are caught in an inescapable network of mutuality, tied in a single garment of destiny. Whatever affects one directly, affects all indirectly. Never again can we afford to live with the narrow, provincial "outside agitator'" idea. Anyone who lives inside the United States can never be considered an outsider anywhere within its bounds.

(5) You deplore the demonstrations taking place in Birmingham. But your statement, I am sorry to say, fails to express a similar concern for the conditions that brought about the demonstrations. I am sure that none of you would want to rest content with the superficial kind of social analysis that deals merely with effects and does not grapple with underlying causes. It is unfortunate that demonstrations are taking place in Birmingham, but it is even more unfortunate that the city's white power structure left the Negro community with no alternative.

Question 10:
What are the
component
parts of X?

(6) In any nonviolent campaign there are four basic steps: collection of the facts to determine whether injustices exist; negotiation; self-purification; and direct action. We have gone through all these steps in Birmingham. There can be no gainsaying the fact that racial injustice engulfs this community. Birmingham is probably the most thoroughly segregated city in the United States. Its ugly record of brutality is widely known. Negroes have experienced grossly unjust treatment in the courts. There have been more unsolved bombings of Negro homes and churches in Birmingham than in any other city in the nation. These are the hard brutal facts of the case. On the basis of these conditions, Negro leaders sought to negotiate with the city fathers. But the latter consistently refused to engage in good-faith negotiation.

Question 6:
What are the
facts about X?

(7) Then, last September, came the opportunity to talk with leaders of Birmingham's economic community. In the course of the negotiations, certain promises were made by the merchants—for example, to remove the stores' humiliating racial signs. On the basis of these promises, the Reverend Fred Shuttlesworth and the leaders of the Alabama Christian Movement for Human Rights agreed to a moratorium on all demonstrations. As the weeks and months went by, we realized that we were the victims of a broken promise. A few signs, briefly removed, returned; the others remained.

(8) As in so many past experiences, our hopes had been blasted, and the shadow of deep disappointment settled upon us. We had no alternative except to prepare for direct action, whereby we would present our very bodies as a

means of laying our case before the conscience of the local and the national community. Mindful of the difficulties involved, we decided to undertake a process of self-purification. We began a series of workshops on nonviolence, and we repeatedly asked ourselves: "Are you able to accept blows without retaliating?" "Are you able to endure the ordeal of jail?" We decided to schedule our direct-action program for the Easter season, realizing that except for Christmas, this is the main shopping period of the year. Knowing that a strong economic-withdrawal program would be the by-product of direct action, we felt that this would be the best time to bring pressure to bear on the merchants for the needed change.

Question 11:
How is X made
or done?

(9) Then it occurred to us that Birmingham's mayoralty election was coming up in March, and we speedily decided to postpone action until after election day. When we discovered that the Commissioner of Public Safety, Eugene "Bull" Connor, had piled up enough votes to be in the run-off, we decided again to postpone action until the day after the run-off so that the demonstrations could not be used to cloud the issues. Like many others, we waited to see Mr. Connor defeated, and to this end we endured postponement after postponement. Having aided in this community need, we felt that our direct-action program could be delayed no longer.

Question 13:
What are the
causes of X?

(10) You may well ask: "Why direct action? Why sit-ins, marches and so forth? Isn't negotiation a better path?" You are quite right in calling for negotiation. Indeed, this is the very purpose of direct action. Nonviolent direct action seeks to create such a crisis and foster such a tension that a community which has constantly refused to negotiate is forced to confront the issue. It seeks so to dramatize the issue that it can no longer be ignored. My citing the creation of tension as part of the work of the nonviolent-resister may sound rather shocking. But I must confess that I am not afraid of the word "tension." I have earnestly opposed violent tension, but there is a type of constructive nonviolent tension which is necessary for growth. Just as Socrates felt that it was necessary to create a tension in the mind so that individuals could rise from the bondage of myths and half-truths to the unfettered realm of creative analysis and objective appraisal, so must we see the need for nonviolent gadflies to create the kind of tension in society that will help men rise from the dark depths of prejudice and racism to the majestic heights of understanding and brotherhood.

Question 9:
What is the
essential
function of X?

(11) The purpose of our direct-action program is to create a situation so crisis-packed that it will inevitably open the door to negotiation. I therefore concur with you in your call for negotiation. Too long has our beloved Southland been bogged down in a tragic effort to live in monologue rather than dialogue.

Question 3:
What kind of
person is X?

(12) One of the basic points in your statement is that the action that I and my associates have taken in Birmingham is untimely. Some have asked: "Why didn't you give the new city administration time to act?" The only answer that I can give to this query is that the new Birmingham administration must be prodded about as much as the outgoing one, before it will act. We are sadly mistaken if we feel that the election of Albert Boutwell as mayor will bring the millennium to Birmingham. While Mr. Boutwell is a much more gentle person than Mr. Connor, they are both segregationists, dedicated to maintenance of the status quo. I have hope that Mr. Boutwell will be reasonable enough to see the futility of massive resistance to desegregation. But he will not see this

without pressure from devotees of civil rights. My friends, I must say to you that we have not made a single gain in civil rights without determined legal and nonviolent pressure. Lamentably, it is an historical fact that privileged groups seldom give up their privileges voluntarily. Individuals may see the moral light and voluntarily give up their unjust posture; but, as Reinhold Niebuhr has reminded us, groups tend to be more immoral than individuals.

Question 17: What is the present status of X?

(13) We know through painful experience that freedom is never voluntarily given by the oppressor; it must be demanded by the oppressed. Frankly, I have yet to engage in a direct-action campaign that was "well timed" in the view of those who have not suffered unduly from the disease of segregation. For years now I have heard the word "Wait!" It rings in the ear of every Negro with piercing familiarity. This "Wait" has almost always meant "Never." We must come to see, with one of our distinguished jurists, that "justice too long delayed is justice denied."[1]

(14) We have waited for more than 340 years for our constitutional and Godgiven rights. The nations of Asia and Africa are moving with jetlike speed toward gaining political independence, but we still creep at horse-and-buggy pace toward gaining a cup of coffee at a lunch counter. Perhaps it is easy for those who have never felt the stinging darts of segregation to say, "Wait." But when you have seen vicious mobs lynch your mothers and fathers at will and drown your sisters and brothers at whim; when you have seen hate-filled policemen curse, kick and even kill your black brothers and sisters; when you see the vast majority of your twenty million Negro brothers smothering in an airtight cage of poverty in the midst of an affluent society; when you suddenly find your tongue twisted and your speech stammering as you seek to explain to your six-year-old daughter why she can't go to the public amusement park that has just been advertised on television, and see tears welling up in her eyes when she is told that Funtown is closed to colored children, and see ominous clouds of inferiority beginning to form in her little mental sky, and see her beginning to distort her personality by developing an unconscious bitterness toward white people; when you have to concoct an answer for a five-year-old son who is asking: "Daddy, why do white people treat colored people so mean?"; when you take a cross-country drive and find it necessary to sleep night after night in the uncomfortable corners of your automobile because no motel will accept you; when you are humiliated day in and day out by nagging signs reading "white" and "colored"; when your first name becomes "nigger," your middle name becomes "boy" (however old you are) and your last name becomes "John," and your wife and mother are never given the respected title "Mrs."; when you are harried by day and haunted by night by the fact that you are a Negro, living constantly at tiptoe stance, never quite knowing what to expect next, and are plagued with inner fears and outer resentments; when you are forever fighting a degenerating sense of "nobodiness"—then you will understand why we find it difficult to wait. There comes a time when the cup of endurance runs over, and men are no longer willing to be plunged into the abyss of despair. I hope, sirs, you can understand our legitimate and unavoidable impatience.

[1] The jurist referred to here is Earl Warren who adapted the line from the English writer, Walter Savage Landor, who had written: "Justice delayed is justice denied."

Question 15:
What are the
types of X?

(15) You express a great deal of anxiety over our willingness to break laws. This is certainly a legitimate concern. Since we so diligently urge people to obey the Supreme Court's decision of 1954 outlawing segregation in the public schools, at first glance it may seem rather paradoxical for us consciously to break laws. One may well ask: "How can you advocate breaking some laws and obeying others?" The answer lies in the fact that there are two types of laws: just and unjust. I would be the first to advocate obeying just laws. One has not only a legal but a moral responsibility to obey just laws. Conversely, one has a moral responsibility to disobey unjust laws. I would agree with St. Augustine that "an unjust law is no law at all."

Question 16:
How does X
compare to Y?

(16) Now, what is the difference between the two? How does one determine whether a law is just or unjust? A just law is a man-made code that squares with the moral law or the law of God. An unjust law is a code that is out of harmony with the moral law. To put it in the terms of St. Thomas Aquinas: An unjust law is a human law that is not rooted in eternal law and natural law. Any law that uplifts human personality is just. Any law that degrades human personality is unjust. All segregation statutes are unjust because segregation distorts the soul and damages the personality. It gives the segregator a false sense of superiority and the segregated a false sense of inferiority. Segregation, to use the terminology of the Jewish philosopher Martin Buber, substitutes an "I-it" relationship for an "I-thou" relationship and ends up relegating persons to the status of things. Hence segregation is not only politically, economically and sociologically unsound, it is morally wrong and sinful. Paul Tillich has said that sin is separation. Is not segregation an existential expression of man's tragic separation, his awful estrangement, his terrible sinfulness. Thus it is that I can urge men to obey the 1954 decision of the Supreme Court, for it is morally right; and I can urge them to disobey segregation ordinances, for they are morally wrong.

(17) Let us consider a more concrete example of just and unjust laws. An unjust law is a code that a numerical or power majority group compels a minority group to obey but does not make binding on itself. This is *difference* made legal. By the same token, a just law is a code that a majority compels a minority to follow and that it is willing to follow itself. This is *sameness* made legal.

(18) Let me give another explanation. A law is unjust if it is inflicted on a minority that, as a result of being denied the right to vote, had no part in enacting or devising the law. Who can say that the legislature of Alabama which set up that state's segregation laws was democratically elected? Throughout Alabama all sorts of devious methods are used to prevent Negroes from becoming registered voters, and there are some counties in which even though Negroes constitute a majority of the population, not a single Negro is registered. Can any law enacted under such circumstances be considered democratically structured?

(19) Sometimes a law is just on its face and unjust in its application. For instance, I have been arrested on a charge of parading without a permit. Now, there is nothing wrong in having an ordinance which requires a permit for a parade. But such an ordinance becomes unjust when it is used to maintain segregation and to deny citizens the First-Amendment privilege of peaceful assembly and protest.

(20) I hope you are able to see the distinction I am trying to point out. In no sense do I advocate evading or defying the law, as would the rabid segregationist. That would lead to anarchy. One who breaks an unjust law must do so openly, lovingly, and with a willingness to accept the penalty. I submit that an individual who breaks a law that conscience tells him is unjust, and who willingly accepts the penalty of imprisonment in order to arouse the conscience of the community over its injustice, is in reality expressing the highest respect for law.

(21) Of course, there is nothing new about this kind of civil disobedience. It was evidenced sublimely in the refusal of Shadrach, Meshach and Abednego to obey the laws of Nebuchadnezzar, on the ground that a higher moral law was at stake. It was practiced superbly by the early Christians, who were willing to face hungry lions and the excruciating pain of chopping blocks rather than submit to certain unjust laws of the Roman Empire. To a degree, academic freedom is a reality today because Socrates practiced civil disobedience. In our own nation, the Boston Tea Party represented a massive act of civil disobedience.

Question 8: What does X mean?

(22) We should never forget that everything Adolf Hitler did in Germany was "legal" and everything the Hungarian freedom fighters did in Hungary was "illegal." It was "illegal" to aid and comfort a Jew in Hitler's Germany. Even so, I am sure that, had I lived in Germany at the time, I would have aided and comforted my Jewish brothers. If today I lived in a Communist country where certain principles dear to the Christian faith are suppressed, I would openly advocate disobeying that country's anti-religious laws.

Question 5: What is my personal response to X?

(23) I must make two honest confessions to you, my Christian and Jewish brothers. First, I must confess that over the past few years I have been gravely disappointed with the white moderate. I have almost reached the regrettable conclusion that the Negro's great stumbling block in his stride toward freedom is not the White Citizen's Counciler or the Ku Klux Klanner, but the white moderate, who is more devoted to "order" than to justice; who prefers a negative peace which is the absence of tension to a positive peace which is the presence of justice; who constantly says: "I agree with you in the goal you seek, but I cannot agree with your methods of direct action"; who paternalistically believes he can set the timetable for another man's freedom; who lives by a mythical concept of time and who constantly advises the Negro to wait for a "more convenient season." Shallow understanding from people of good will is more frustrating than absolute misunderstanding from people of ill will. Lukewarm acceptance is much more bewildering than outright rejection.

(24) I had hoped that the white moderate would understand that law and order exist for the purpose of establishing justice and that when they fail in this purpose they become the dangerously structured dams that block the flow of social progress. I had hoped that the white moderate would understand that the present tension in the South is a necessary phase of the transition from an obnoxious negative peace, in which the Negro passively accepted his unjust plight, to a substantive and positive peace, in which all men will respect the dignity and worth of human personality. Actually, we who engage in nonviolent direct action are not the creators of tension. We merely bring to the surface the hidden tension that is already alive. We bring it out in the open, where it can be seen and dealt with. Like a boil that can never be cured so long as it is covered up but must be opened with all its ugliness to

the natural medicines of air and light, injustice must be exposed, with all the tension its exposure creates, to the light of human conscience and the air of national opinion before it can be cured.

Question 20:
What case can
be made for or
against X?

(25) In your statement you assert that our actions, even though peaceful, must be condemned because they precipitate violence. But is this a logical assertion? Isn't this like condemning a robbed man because his possession of money precipitated the evil act of robbery? Isn't this like condemning Socrates because his unswerving commitment to truth and his philosophical inquiries precipitated the act by the misguided populace in which they made him drink hemlock? Isn't this like condemning Jesus because his unique God-conscious-ness and never-ceasing devotion to God's will precipitated the evil act of crucifixion? We must come to see that, as the federal courts have consistently affirmed, it is wrong to urge an individual to cease his efforts to gain his basic constitutional rights because the quest may precipitate violence. Society must protect the robbed and punish the robber.

Question 18:
How should X
be interpreted?

(26) I had also hoped that the white moderate would reject the myth concerning time in relation to the struggle for freedom. I have just received a letter from a white brother in Texas. He writes: "All Christians know that the colored people will receive equal rights eventually, but it is possible that you are in too great a religious hurry. It has taken Christianity almost two thousand years to accomplish what it has. The teachings of Christ take time to come to earth." Such an attitude stems from a tragic misconception of time, from the strangely irrational notion that there is something in the very flow of time that will inevitably cure all ills. Actually, time itself is neutral; it can be used either destructively or constructively. More and more I feel that the people of ill will have used time much more effectively than have the people of good will. We will have to repent in this generation not merely for the hateful words and actions of the bad people but for the appalling silence of the good people. Human progress never rolls in on wheels of inevitability; it comes through the tireless efforts of men willing to be co-workers with God, and without this hard work, time itself becomes an ally of the forces of social stagnation. We must use time creatively, in the knowledge that the time is always ripe to do right. Now is the time to make real the promise of democracy and transform our pending national elegy into a creative psalm of brotherhood. Now is the time to lift our national policy from the quicksand of racial injustice to the solid rock of human dignity.

Question 10:
What are the
component
parts of X?

Question 16:
How does X
compare to Y?

(27) You speak of our activity in Birmingham as extreme. At first I was rather disappointed that fellow clergymen would see my nonviolent efforts as those of an extremist. I began thinking about the fact that I stand in the middle of two opposing forces in the Negro community. One is a force of compla-cency, made up in part of Negroes who, as a result of long years of oppression, are so drained of self-respect and a sense of "somebodiness" that they have adjusted to segregation; and in part of a few middle-class Negroes who, because of a degree of academic and economic security and because in some ways they profit by segregation, have become insensitive to the problems of the masses. The other force is one of bitterness and hatred, and it comes perilously close to advocating violence. It is expressed in the various black nationalist groups that are springing up across the nation, the largest and best-known being Elijah Muhammad's Muslim movement. Nourished by the Negro's frustration over the continued existence of racial discrimination, this

movement is made up of people who have lost faith in America, who have absolutely repudiated Christianity, and who have concluded that the white man is an incorrigible "devil."

(28) I have tried to stand between these two forces, saying that we need emulate neither the "do-nothingism" of the complacent nor the hatred and despair of the black nationalist. For there is the more excellent way of love and nonviolent protest. I am grateful to God that, through the influence of the Negro church, the way of nonviolence became an integral part of our struggle.

(29) If this philosophy had not emerged, by now many streets of the South would, I am convinced, be flowing with blood. And I am further convinced that if our white brothers dismiss as "rabble-rousers" and "outside agitators" those of us who employ nonviolent direct action, and if they refuse to support our nonviolent efforts, millions of Negroes will, out of frustration and despair, seek solace and security in black-nationalist ideologies—a development that would inevitably lead to a frightening racial nightmare.

Question 13:
What are the causes of X?

(30) Oppressed people cannot remain oppressed forever. The yearning for freedom eventually manifests itself, and that is what has happened to the American Negro. Something within has reminded him of his birthright of freedom, and something without has reminded him that it can be gained. Consciously or unconsciously, he has been caught up by the *Zeitgeist*, and with his black brothers of Africa and his brown and yellow brothers of Asia, South America and the Caribbean, the United States Negro is moving with a sense of great urgency toward the promised land of racial justice. If one recognizes this vital urge that has engulfed the Negro community, one should readily understand why public demonstrations are taking place. The Negro has many pent-up resentments and latent frustrations, and he must release them. So let him march; let him make prayer pilgrimages to the city hall; let him go on freedom rides—and try to understand why he must do so. If his repressed emotions are not released in nonviolent ways, they will seek expression through violence; this is not a threat but a fact of history. So I have not said to my people: "Get rid of your discontent." Rather, I have tried to say that this normal and healthy discontent can be channeled into the creative outlet of nonviolent direct action. And now this approach is being termed extremist.

Question 8:
What does X mean?

(31) But though I was initially disappointed at being categorized as an extremist, as I continued to think about the matter I gradually gained a measure of satisfaction from the label. Was not Jesus an extremist for love: "Love your enemies, bless them that curse you, do good to them that hate you, and pray for them which despitefully use you, and persecute you." Was not Amos an extremist for justice: "Let justice roll down like waters and righteousness like an ever-flowing stream." Was not Paul an extremist for the Christian gospel: "I bear in my body the marks of the Lord Jesus." Was not Martin Luther an extremist: "Here I stand; I cannot do otherwise, so help me God." And John Bunyan: "I will stay in jail to the end of my days before I make a butchery of my conscience." And Abraham Lincoln: "This nation cannot survive half slave and half free." And Thomas Jefferson: "We hold these truths to be self-evident, that all men are created equal. . . . " So the question is not whether we will be extremists, but what kind of extremists we will be. Will we be extremists for hate or for love? Will we be extremists for the preservation of injustice or for the extension of justice? In that dramatic scene on Calvary's hill three men were crucified. We must never forget that all three were crucified for the same crime—the crime of extremism. Two were extremists

for immorality, and thus fell below their environment. The other, Jesus Christ, was an extremist for love, truth and goodness, and thereby rose above his environment. Perhaps the South, the nation and the world are in dire need of creative extremists.

(32) I had hoped that the white moderate would see this need. Perhaps I was too optimistic; perhaps I expected too much. I suppose I should have realized that few members of the oppressor race can understand the deep groans and passionate yearnings of the oppressed race, and still fewer have the vision to see that injustice must be rooted out by strong, persistent and determined action. I am thankful, however, that some of our white brothers in the South have grasped the meaning of this social revolution and committed themselves to it. They are still all too few in quantity, but they are big in quality. Some—such as Ralph McGill, Lillian Smith, Harry Golden, James McBride Dabbs, Ann Braden and Sarah Patton Boyle—have written about our struggle in eloquent and prophetic terms. Others have marched with us down nameless streets of the South. They have languished in filthy, roach-infested jails, suffering the abuse and brutality of policemen who view them as "dirty nigger-lovers." Unlike so many of their moderate brothers and sisters, they have recognized the urgency of the moment and sensed the need for powerful "action" antidotes to combat the disease of segregation.

(33) Let me take note of my other major disappointment. I have been so greatly disappointed with the white church and its leadership. Of course, there are some notable exceptions. I am not unmindful of the fact that each of you has taken some significant stands on this issue. I commend you, Reverend Stallings, for your Christian stand on this past Sunday, in welcoming Negroes to your worship service on a nonsegregated basis. I commend the Catholic leaders of this state for integrating Spring Hill College several years ago.

Question 5:
What is my
personal
response to X?

(34) But despite these notable exceptions, I must honestly reiterate that I have been disappointed with the church. I do not say this as one of those negative critics who can always find something wrong with the church. I say this as a minister of the gospel, who loves the church; who was nurtured in its bosom; who has been sustained by its spiritual blessings and who will remain true to it as long as the cord of life shall lengthen.

(35) When I was suddenly catapulted into the leadership of the bus protest in Montgomery, Alabama, a few years ago, I felt we would be supported by the white church. I felt that the white ministers, priests and rabbis of the South would be among our strongest allies. Instead, some have been outright opponents, refusing to understand the freedom movement and misrepresenting its leaders; all too many others have been more cautious than courageous and have remained silent behind the anesthetizing security of stained-glass windows.

(36) In spite of my shattered dreams, I came to Birmingham with the hope that the white religious leadership of this community would see the justice of our cause and, with deep moral concern, would serve as the channel through which our just grievances could reach the power structure. I had hoped that each of you would understand. But again I have been disappointed.

Question 4:
What is my
memory of X?

(37) I have heard numerous southern religious leaders admonish their worshipers to comply with a desegregation decision because it is the law, but I have longed to hear white ministers declare: "Follow this decree because integration is morally right and because the Negro is your brother." In the midst of blatant injustices inflicted upon the Negro, I have watched white

churchmen stand on the sideline and mouth pious irrelevancies and sanctimonious trivialities. In the midst of a mighty struggle to rid our nation of racial and economic injustice, I have heard many ministers say: "Those are social issues, with which the gospel has no real concern." And I have watched many churches commit themselves to a completely other-worldly religion which makes a strange, un-Biblical distinction between body and soul, between the sacred and the secular.

Question 1:
How can X be
described?

(38) I have traveled the length and breadth of Alabama, Mississippi and all the other southern states. On sweltering summer days and crisp autumn mornings I have looked at the South's beautiful churches with their lofty spires pointing heavenward. I have beheld the impressive outlines of her massive religious-education buildings. Over and over I have found myself asking: "What kind of people worship here? Who is their God? Where were their voices when the lips of Governor Barnett dripped with words of interposition and nullification? Where were they when Governor Wallace gave a clarion call for defiance and hatred? Where were their voices of support when bruised and weary Negro men and women decided to rise from the dark dungeons of complacency to the bright hills of creative protest?"

Question 5:
What is my
personal
response to X?

(39) Yes, these questions are still in my mind. In deep disappointment I have wept over the laxity of the church. But be assured that my tears have been tears of love. There can be no deep disappointment where there is not deep love. Yes, I love the church. How could I do otherwise? I am in the rather unique position of being the son, the grandson and the great-grandson of preachers. Yes, I see the church as the body of Christ. But, oh! How we have blemished and scarred that body through social neglect and through fear of being nonconformists.

(40) There was a time when the church was very powerful—in the time when the early Christians rejoiced at being deemed worthy to suffer for what they believed. In those days the church was not merely a thermometer that recorded the ideas and principles of popular opinion; it was a thermostat that transformed the mores of society. Whenever the early Christians entered a town, the people in power became disturbed and immediately sought to convict the Christians for being "disturbers of the peace" and "outside agitators." But the Christians pressed on, in the conviction that they were "a colony of heaven," called to obey God rather than man. Small in number, they were big in commitment. They were too God-intoxicated to be "astronomically intimidated." By their effort and example they brought an end to such ancient evils as infanticide and gladiatorial contests.

Question 17:
What is the
present status
of X?

(41) Things are different now. So often the contemporary church is a weak, ineffectual voice with an uncertain sound. So often it is an archdefender of the status quo. Far from being disturbed by the presence of the church, the power structure of the average community is consoled by the church's silent—and often even vocal—sanction of things as they are.

Question 14:
What are the
consequences
of X?

(42) But the judgment of God is upon the church as never before. If today's church does not recapture the sacrificial spirit of the early church, it will lose its authenticity, forfeit the loyalty of millions, and be dismissed as an irrelevant social club with no meaning for the twentieth century. Every day I meet young people whose disappointment with the church has turned into outright disgust.

(43) Perhaps I have once again been too optimistic. Is organized religion too inextricably bound to the status quo to save our nation and the world?

Perhaps I must turn my faith to the inner spiritual church, the church within the church, as the true *ekklesia* and the hope of the world. But again I am thankful to God that some noble souls from the ranks of organized religion have broken loose from the paralyzing chains of conformity and joined us as active partners in the struggle for freedom. They have left their secure congregations and walked the streets of Albany, Georgia, with us. They have gone down the highways of the South on tortuous rides for freedom. Yes, they have gone to jail with us. Some have been dismissed from their churches, have lost the support of their bishops and fellow ministers. But they have acted in the faith that right defeated is stronger that evil triumphant. Their witness has been the spiritual salt that has preserved the true meaning of the gospel in these troubled times. They have carved a tunnel of hope through the dark mountain of disappointment.

Question 5:
What is my
personal
response to X?

(44) I hope the church as a whole will meet the challenge of this decisive hour. But even if the church does not come to the aid of justice, I have no despair about the future. I have no fear about the outcome of our struggle in Birmingham, even if our motives are at present misunderstood. We will reach the goal of freedom in Birmingham and all over the nation, because the goal of America is freedom. Abused and scorned though we may be, our destiny is tied up with America's destiny. Before the pilgrims landed at Plymouth, we were here. Before the pen of Jefferson etched the majestic words of the Declaration of Independence across the pages of history, we were here. For more than two centuries our forebears labored in this country without wages; they made cotton king; they built the homes of their masters while suffering gross injustice and shameful humiliation—and yet out of a bottomless vitality they continued to thrive and develop. If the inexpressible cruelties of slavery could not stop us, the opposition we now face will surely fail. We will win our freedom because the sacred heritage of our nation and the eternal will of God are embodied in our echoing demands.

Question 13:
What are the
causes of X?

Question 12:
How is X made
or done?

Question 7:
How can X be
summarized?

Question 13:
What are the
causes of X?

(45) Before closing I feel impelled to mention one other point in your statement that has troubled me profoundly. You warmly commended the Birmingham police force for keeping "order" and "preventing violence." I doubt that you would have so warmly commended the police force if you had seen its dogs sinking their teeth into unarmed, nonviolent Negroes. I doubt that you would so quickly commend the policemen if you were to observe their ugly and inhumane treatment of Negroes here in the city jail; if you were to watch them push and curse old Negro women and young Negro girls; if you were to see them slap and kick old Negro men and young boys; if you were to observe them as they did on two occasions, refuse to give us food because we wanted to sing our grace together. I cannot join you in your praise of the Birmingham police department.

Question 19:
What is the
value of X?

(46) It is true that the police have exercised a degree of discipline in handling the demonstrators. In this sense they have conducted themselves rather "nonviolently" in public. But for what purpose? To preserve the evil system of segregation. Over the past few years I have consistently preached that nonviolence demands that the means we use must be as pure as the ends we seek. I have tried to make clear that it is wrong to use immoral means to attain moral ends. But now I must affirm that it is just as wrong, or perhaps even more so, to use moral means to preserve immoral ends. Perhaps Mr. Connor and his policemen have been rather nonviolent in public, as was Chief Pritchett in Albany, Georgia, but they have used the moral means of

nonviolence to maintain the immoral end of racial injustice. As T. S. Eliot has said: "The last temptation is the greatest treason: To do the right deed for the wrong reason."

(47) I wish you had commended the Negro sit-inners and demonstrators of Birmingham for their sublime courage, their willingness to suffer and their amazing discipline in the midst of great provocation. One day the South will recognize its real heroes. They will be the James Merediths, with the noble sense of purpose that enables them to face jeering and hostile mobs, and with the agonizing loneliness that characterizes the life of the pioneer. They will be old, oppressed, battered Negro women, symbolized in a seventy-two-year-old woman in Montgomery, Alabama, who rose up with a sense of dignity and with her people decided not to ride segregated buses, and who responded with ungrammatical profundity to one who inquired about her weariness: "My feet is tired, but my soul is at rest." They will be the young high school and college students, the young ministers of the gospel and a host of their elders, courageously and nonviolently sitting in at lunch counters and willingly going to jail for conscience' sake. One day the South will know that when these disinherited children of God sat down at lunch counters, they were in reality standing up for what is best in the American dream and for the most sacred values in our Judaeo-Christian heritage, thereby bringing our nation back to those great wells of democracy which were dug deep by the founding fathers in their formulation of the Constitution and the Declaration of Independence.

Question 13: What are the causes of X?

(48) Never before have I written so long a letter. I'm afraid it is much too long to take your precious time. I can assure you that it would have been much shorter if I had been writing from a comfortable desk, but what else can one do when he is alone in a narrow jail cell, other than write long letters, think long thoughts and pray long prayers?

(49) If I have said anything in this letter that overstates the truth and indicates an unreasonable impatience, I beg you to forgive me. If I have said anything that understates the truth and indicates my having a patience that allows me to settle for anything less than brotherhood, I beg God to forgive me.

(50) I hope this letter finds you strong in the faith. I also hope that circumstances will soon make it possible for me to meet each of you, not as an integrationist or a civil-rights leader but as a fellow clergyman and a Christian brother. Let us all hope that the dark clouds of racial prejudice will soon pass away and the deep fog of misunderstanding will be lifted from our fear-drenched communities, and in some not too distant tomorrow the radiant stars of love and brotherhood will shine over our great nation with all their scintillating beauty.

Yours for the cause of Peace and Brotherhood,
Martin Luther King, Jr.

DISCUSSION AND EXERCISES

Consider Dr. King's "Letter from Birmingham Jail" and answer the following questions:
1. Notice that King answers all but one of the twenty questions. Which one is that? Has King implied this question anywhere? Had King written a longer letter might he have woven in

this question and answer? Discuss the places where two questions work together. Can you find additional instances where a pair of questions might have worked together? Cite other questions King asks. In paragraph 21, for example, he is clearly asking "What other examples can you cite of civil disobedience?".

2. What is King's purpose in writing this letter? Why is he so careful to begin by defining his audience? In the beginning he refers to his audience as "men of good will." What does he say later that indicates to the reader that King does not really trust their "good will"? What indicates that King may actually have intended this letter for a larger audience?

3. Locate key "is" and "ought" prepositions in King's letter. Discuss.

4. Show how King's letter follows the three-part structure used by Greek and Roman orators (as described in "What case can be made for or against X?"—see pages 422–23). Note the equivalents of exordium, exposition; direct statement of case, and division of proofs; locate confirmation (facts, reasons, statistics, logical reasoning, analogy), refutation, concession, recapitulation and peroration. Discuss.

5. What evidence of deductive and inductive reasoning do you find? Discuss.

6. In many places King uses the device of analogy: "the drawing, in one inductive leap, of a crucial comparison." Locate these places and indicate whether he uses analogy in place of direct reasoning or as a supplement. Do you find any examples of false analogy? Explain.

7. According to Rogerian strategy (see pages 435–36), you can understand another position only if you see it from "the other's point of view." Describe King's point of view and indicate in what ways he tries to see the situation from "the other's point of view" (the eight clergymen, the Birmingham police, the townspeople). Apply Rogerian strategy by putting yourself in the place of King, the demonstrators, the police, Southerners, and the clergy.

8. What are the topic sentences in paragraphs 25, 27 and 31? In what sense are they typical and successful coordinate sequences, as Christensen describes them (see pages 121–23)? What other paragraphs in this letter are basically in coordinate sequence? Which paragraphs are primarily subordinate sequences?

9. Characterize the description in paragraph 38. What does King achieve by using questions for half the sentences? How does this paragraph "set up" the next three paragraphs? Characterize one of these paragraphs.

10. How does paragraph 41 provide a distinct "turn" from the previous paragraphs?

11. Evaluate the effectiveness of the image which closes paragraph 43: "They have carved a tunnel of hope through the dark mountain of disappointment."

12. Indicate how King achieves strong emphasis in the following sentence from paragraph 44: "Abused and scorned though we may be, our destiny is tied up with America's destiny."

13. How does King use word repetitions to unify paragraph 45?

14. Discuss the effectiveness of King's "conclusion," viewing paragraphs 45 through 48 as a first concluding block, and paragraphs 48 through 50 as the final block.

Analysis of Style

1. Comment upon the straightforwardness and simplicity of the introduction. How does this first paragraph set the tone for the rest of the letter?

2. Characterize paragraph organization: paragraph division, paragraph length (is there appropriate variety between long, short, intermediate paragraphs?)

3. Note paragraph 6. How does it relate to paragraphs 7, 8, and 9?

4. Evaluate the transitional sentence leading into paragraph 10. Identify other transitional words and phrases that connect different parts of the argument.

5. Evaluate the virtuoso "suspended sentence" in paragraph 14 (see pages 582–84) for definition and further illustration of suspended sentences). What binds this sentence into a unified whole? In what sense does this compare to Christensen's description of sentences in coordinate sequence ("like things in like ways": see pages 121–23)?
6. Discuss King's exploration of the meaning of words in paragraph 22.
7. Consider paragraphs 23 to 33 as a unit. What binds them together? Characterize the tone of the opening sentence of paragraph 23.
8. Were your opinions changed in any way by King's letter? Discuss. What arguments do you consider most effective or ineffective? Explain.
9. Is King's tone optimistic or pessimistic? Cite specific passages to support your answer.
10. In your opinion, what is the most moving passage in Dr. King's letter? Explain.
11. In what ways does King promote what Benjamin Franklin (page 436) calls "a reader's reception to one's ideas"?
12. This letter, addressed originally to eight clergymen, has since become one of the most widely anthologized works of our time. Why do you think this letter has such an appreciative audience? What special audience would be particularly responsive?
13. Identify the following terms and explain why King obviously felt no need to provide footnotes for his original letter. Why is it necessary to make adjustments for different audiences?

Tarsus	The Millenium
Hungarian Freedom Fighters	The Muslim Movement
Elijah Muhammad	Nebuchadnezzar

Also identify the following people:

Socrates	Reinhold Niebuhr	St. Augustine
St. Thomas Aquinas	Martin Buber	Paul Tillich
Amos	Martin Luther	John Bunyan
Abraham Lincoln	Thomas Jefferson	Paul
Thomas Stearns Eliot	James Meredith	

ESSAY SUGGESTIONS

1. Write a letter—an extended argument (2,500–3,500 words)—in which you protest an injustice—a deeply held belief of your own. Develop your argument in terms of what "ought" to be done. Let King's argument serve as your model for organization, tone, logical development, and rhetorical effectiveness. Assume that your audience, like King's, is not openly hostile to your position.
2. Write an extended argument on what you support or take issue with in King's position on civil disobedience. Pay close attention to King's distinction between laws that are morally right and those that are morally wrong (do you agree with this distinction?). Would you be moved to defend or protest any laws now in effect or proposed (Equal Rights Amendment, Gun Control, or Affirmative Action)? Build your argument carefully and logically: provide as much supporting material (such as facts and statistics) as possible.
3. Take the stance of a black militant writing a letter to King. Argue that he does not go far enough, that he settles for too little. Address potential objections to your position. Research magazine and newspaper articles from the 1960s.

THE ARTICLE AS A TERM PAPER

A so-called term paper is a strictly academic form, named for the period of time in which the student must complete the paper. It is essentially a long paper—what the journalist calls an "article"; that is, a relatively thorough study of an aspect of a given subject that averages (in an introductory course) 2,500 to 3,000 words. It usually requires some research. Instructors in every discipline may assign term papers, on the justifiable assumption that term papers require more independent, intensive, and creative effort than any other single unit of work.

When you prepare a term paper, you generally select your own topic. You then locate appropriate reference materials and abstract what information you need. Finally, you reassemble data to conform to the new statement you wish to make, expressed in your own style. No other piece of work, then, requires more imagination and patience, more sustained intellectual effort, more persistence and rhetorical skill than this full-term research and writing project; nor does any single piece of work give the instructor a better measure of your ability to relate meaningfully and verbally to some aspect of the discipline in question.

You will note that two of the four longer pieces that follow are in the journalistic rather than the academic tradition. They were written as articles and published as such in magazines; similarly King's original "letter" has repeatedly been treated as an article and reprinted as such in many magazines and anthologies. Only one example, the extended analysis ("The Mollie Maguire Movement"), is a traditional term paper, complete with scholarly documentation: footnotes and bibliography. Your instructor may require you to make an appropriately academic adaptation of the article form by using the formal and systematic procedures of the scholar. For example, instead of weaving the source of a quotation into the sentence (and perhaps not citing the *exact* page reference or date)—which is the way of the journalist—you may have to provide scrupulously detailed documentation. Be assured that scholarly adaptation of the journalistic form will present no problems; on the contrary, it can enhance your paper by encouraging you to draw upon the best of both traditions: the readability of the journalist and the reliability of the scholar.

EXTENDED "FACTS ABOUT..." AND "PRESENT STATUS OF X": AN UPDATE

The subject of the following article, originally published in *The Atlantic Monthly*, is dwarfs, people whose growth has been stunted but who are normal in other respects. When Aristotle said "people are naturally curious" he was probably referring to subjects of this kind—people and events that are slightly offbeat, perhaps askew in some way. How can they be explained? Why do they occur? With what consequences?

To provide an update on the subject, *the latest facts* about the estimated 100,000 Americans who fall into the category of "dwarfs" have been systematically gathered and shaped into an account of their *present status*. Two questions in combination then—"What are the facts about?" and "What is the present status of X?"—provide the main thrust of this piece. Additional questions help to develop it: What kind of person is X? How can X be described? (The first paragraph introduces us to forty-year-old Charles Bedou who "stands four and a half feet tall".) How can a writer summarize the facts about dwarfs? How do dwarfs compare to people of normal height? What are the types of dwarfs? The causes and consequences? And so on.

Observe the introductory "headnote," a feature of most magazine articles: its function is to provide readers with a quick overview of the article as a whole, pinpointing not only its content but the particular point of view the author takes in writing it.

Dwarfs

Sonny Kleinfield

Roughly 100,000 Americans are dwarfs. They have trouble finding mates, buying shoes, using elevators or public telephones—and admitting to themselves that they are, in fact, different.

Question 1:
"How can a dwarf be described?"

Question 3:
"What kind of person is a dwarf?"
(Charles Bedou is presented)

(1) Charles Bedou, at the age of forty, stands four and a half feet tall. When the tow-headed Bedou was born, he weighed nearly nine pounds and was the size of any normal baby. Five years later, however, he was less than two feet tall; at ten, he was three feet; when he celebrated his eighteenth birthday, he was four-foot-six; and in the ensuing twenty-two years, he did not grow another inch. His body is all out of whack. His head and torso are the size of a much taller person's; his arms and legs are much too small. He is what is known as a dwarf.

(2) Bedou's parents split up when he was six, and since neither wanted custody, he was shuffled from relative to relative, "like a plate of spaghetti," until, at last, when he was eighteen he ran away. "I had no dates in school, and I didn't have many friends," he says. "When you're the only dwarf in sixteen counties, whom do you date? It took me more than six months to find a job. I applied to more places then you have fingers and toes, and everyone felt my brain must be as stunted as my body. When I finally got work at an insurance company in Minnesota, there were still things my boss didn't want me to do. Life hasn't been exactly marvelous."

Question 6:
What are the facts about X?

(weaving in of historical facts)

(3) Dwarfs receive mention in the Bible, and during ancient times household dwarfs were extremely popular: they were kept by the early pharaohs and abounded at the courts of the Ptolemies. They flourished once again in imperial Rome, where slave children were occasionally stunted to increase the fetching price. Kings in medieval Europe and during the Renaissance kept them at hand, and some dwarfs became such favorites that they themselves were given servants. Isabella d'Este designed part of her palace for dwarfs, and remembered two of them in her will. They appear in a number of Velasquez's paintings. During the eighteenth and nineteenth centuries, the czars and noblemen of Russia kept innumerable dwarfs, and elaborate dwarf weddings and funerals were not uncommon. However, while especially personable dwarfs earned responsible positions, most of them functioned as lowly entertainers and as household fools. In Western Europe, household dwarfs were still heard of in the eighteenth century, but their visibility had declined.

Question 9: "What is the essential function of Little People of America?"

(4) In the United States today, dwarfs have formed a national organization called The Little People of America, which has its headquarters in Owatonna, Minnesota. The association was founded in 1957 by a group of twenty dwarfs who convened in Reno, Nevada. The idea for the meeting, as it happens, came from Spike Jones, of zany music fame, who urged his friend, dwarf actor Billy Barty, to start an outfit that would speak for little people. Barty served as the first president, and by 1960 the association had a hundred members. Now, more than 2200 little people have joined the association. Anyone four-foot-ten or smaller (the height arbitrarily fixed by the medical profession as distinguishing dwarfs from normal-sized people) can join. The organization's motto is "Think Big," and its basic message is that dwarfs suffer mainly because of society's attitude toward them.

Question 10: "What are the component parts of X?" (What are the various problems in the lives of dwarfs?)

(5) Among other things, the association maintains an adoption referral service, which finds homes for dwarf children abandoned by parents. "A lot of dwarfs used to be committed to mental institutions by parents who didn't want them," an LPA man says. In 1968, the LPA established a foundation to raise funds for scholarships and for the ordinary expenses of needy dwarfs. A special division is devoted to problems faced by teen-aged dwarfs. "At one time, the world thought the only thing to do with little people was to put them in sideshows and laugh at them," says Gerald Rasa, a Pennsylvania public relations man who is the LPA's president. "They were labeled 'heaven's curse.' We're trying to show the world that we are useful, that we're not society's black sheep."

Question 4: "What is Bedou's memory?"

(6) "Dwarfs have a lot of architectural problems that we're trying to learn to deal with," says Bedou, a former president of the LPA. "Ever since I can remember, my feet have dangled over the edge of chairs. I would literally slide off the seat. To stay on, I have to wrap my legs around the chair, like I'm riding a bucking bronco. It's not very dignified. Get on your knees and try to make a phone call from a public telephone. Get on your knees and try to negotiate the first step on a bus. Get into an elevator and try to push the button for the seventy-eighth floor. I have to have clothing custom-made, and it costs me just as much as it does Wilt Chamberlain. Imagine going into a shoe store and asking for a nice loafer in a size one."

Question 5: "What is his personal response?"

(7) Bedou, however, makes the most of his four feet and six inches. "If I have to make a phone call," he says, "I holler at someone, 'Put the damn dime in for me.' I have a very good set of lungs, and I don't hesitate to use them. I can't use a urinal in a men's room. It's outrageous that I should have to pay a dime, so I crawl under a stall, and I usually go down the line and open them all up. You plan a little better when you're short. I use pedal extensions to drive a car. Other dwarfs I know fly their own planes with similar devices. Our homes aren't much different, except we favor modern furniture, because it's usually low-slung. I have lots of stools around the house. Some of us, you know, are not much more than two feet tall."

(8) Largely under the auspices of the LPA, dwarfs have brought to the attention of legislators and architectural problems they face. They have joined other minority groups, such as the National Association of the Physically Handicapped, to push for legislation requiring lower pay phones, curbside ramps, railings in public toilets, and similar conveniences.

Question 7: "How can problems be summarized?

(9) Short-statured persons share a fierce pride in their heritage, and they take pleasure in pointing out the movers and shakers of their kind who have played important roles in history. Attila the Hun, for instance, is believed to

have been a dwarf, an unusually bloodthirsty one. Both Charles III, king of Sicily and Naples in the fourteenth century, and his contemporary, Ladislas I of Poland, were midgets. Ladislas won the nickname of the Warrior Midget King, and the history books credit (or discredit) him with having trimmed a substantial number of taller men down to his size in battle. The twenty-three-inch midget Richebourg of Paris played no small part in the French Revolution. Along with hidden dispatches, he was thumbed through enemy lines as a babe in arms; he would nurse a bottle until safety was reached and then, after fumbling in his clothes, would produce and light up a tremendous cigar. Sir Jeffrey Hudson, a midget courtier during the reign of Charles I in seventeenth-century England, polished off his share of men in his country's wars, only to wind up a captive of Turkish pirates.

(10) A number of noncombatant midgets and dwarfs also made the history books — Coppernin, who served the mother of George II; Nicholas Ferry, a counselor-attendant to King Stanislas of Poland. Even so, dwarf history owes most of its notoriety to Phineas T. Barnum, whose midget showpiece, General Tom Thumb, became one of the most popular men of his era. Thumb was not a career soldier. Originally, his name was Charles Sherwood Stratton; the alias derived from the ballad containing the line, "In Arthur's court, Tom Thumb did live," and Barnum threw on the "General" in the interest of public relations.

(11) Thumb stood thirty-one inches tall, and weighed almost seventy pounds. Barnum presented him as the tiniest man in the annals of civilization, a bit of mendacity willfully indulged by the General. Barnum found Thumb a pint-sized bride named Lavinia Warren, who, he claimed, was the smallest woman to walk the earth, though she would have needed several inches of cropping to warrant that distinction. With customary hoopla, Barnum arranged a wedding in New York's Grace Episcopal Church in 1863, a tribute to bad taste that afforded possibly the worst start ever made by newlyweds, whatever their height. The honeymoon junket included a pause for dinner at the White House with President Lincoln, whose waist was higher than either Thumb or his new bride. In the end, Thumb and his wife proved of heartier substance than their theatrical mentor. While Barnum's financial condition took a nose dive, General and Mrs. Thumb gradually left the stage and went into the real estate business in Connecticut. They made a fortune.

(12) The vast majority of dwarfs stand between forty and fifty-four inches tall. (Pygmies, who aren't classified as dwarfs, average around fifty-six inches, and, without exception, inherit their stunted stature.) If one is to believe Ripley's *Believe It or Not* anthology, the smallest dwarf was Pauline Musters of Holland, all of nineteen inches. Fully erect, she could walk under the dining-room table and not even muss her hair. Juan de la Cruz of the Philippines billed himself the world's smallest father; he measured two feet tall. Forty-eight-inch John Louis Roventini gained worldwide fame by serving for forty-one years as a living trademark for Philip Morris Inc.'s cigarettes. His shrill voice was insured for $50,000, and, for his own protection, his contract forbade that he ride the subway during rush hour. A former New York bellboy, "Johnny" retired last year after millions of calls for "Phil-lip Mor-rees!"

A number of dwarfs, for unknown reasons, start to grow again and, usually in their late twenties or early thirties, attain normal height. Austria's Adam Rainer zoomed from three-foot-ten at the age of twenty-one to seven-foot-two

Question 12: "How is X made or done?" (a brief historical account of dwarfs "who have played important roles in history")

Summary of facts; additional historical analysis

Question 3: "What kind of people are dwarfs?" (a series of illustrations)

at thirty-two, the most dramatic growth spurt known. Some dwarfs, despite their initial grief over being tiny, are haunted by the prospect of a late spurt. Once they have become oriented to their special adulthood, they are understandably wary of realigning themselves to a new and puzzling scale. Dwarf legend has it that small people lead short lives, and though medical research disproves the idea, life insurance companies tend to believe it; dwarfs complain they have trouble purchasing policies. Le Petit M. Richebourg of Paris lived to the ripe old age of ninety.

Question 16: "How does X compare to Y?" (jobs that are harder for dwarfs)

For many years dwarfs had few job opportunities outside the field of entertainment. The outbreak of World War II did a lot to change that. For the first time, they were able to enter aircraft factories, defense plants, shipyards, and government offices, and much to the surprise of employers, they proved capable and dependable workers. Many still work as sales promotional representatives. Meat-packer Oscar Meyer & Co. uses five midgets as "Little Oscars" to peddle its wieners, mostly to taller customers.

"But it would be like an ostrich putting his head in the sand to say job discrimination doesn't persist," says Charles Bedou. "I know of a dwarf rejected for a teaching job because the school board thought she couldn't discipline a class. Another dwarf was turned down for a research job by several drug firms because, they said, he couldn't reach laboratory instruments, which is pretty ridiculous. But people now realize we can do a lot more than was thought. Some jobs are hard for us. Nursing would be difficult, because it involves moving people around. Ditch-digging wouldn't be any good, because a dwarf would have to throw the dirt a lot farther from the bottom of a six-foot hole. But dwarfs are doctors, lawyers, truck drivers, elevator operators, some even work in light construction."

Question 18: "How should X be interpreted?" (facts plus interpretation and illustration of facts—provided by research authority)

Since among disabilities dwarfism seems one of the hardest to face, many parents of sufferers tend to react quite strongly to it. "When a dwarf is born into a family, the typical reaction is one of shock, almost a reaction of mourning for the perfect child who didn't come," says Joan Weiss, a social worker for the Moore Clinic, the nation's leading dwarfism research center and a unit of Johns Hopkins Medical Center. "The parents, especially the mother, tend to treat a dwarf as a living family skeleton. If the dwarfed child's father and mother are inhibited in their parental roles by their disappointment and sense of failure, the child will not be able to develop into an emotionally secure adult, and will regard himself as inadequate and insufficient in measurements other than height." What frequently happens, Mrs. Weiss goes on, is that parents become overly protective of their child, thus deflating his ego. Lee Kitchens, for instance, a Texas engineer, was helped across streets by his mother until he was sixteen. Another dwarf remembers being refused use of the family car while in high school. When he got to college, he holed away enough money to buy a car of his own, and taught himself to drive with help from pedal extensions.

Question 16: "How does X compare to Y"? (The "love life" of dwarfs compared to that of the average person)

One of the most consuming, and frustrating, interests a dwarf has is finding a mate. Mrs. Weiss says, "Social problems for dwarfs begin about the time they enter the second grade, mostly in the form of physical and verbal teasing. This foments insecurity. Then the second crucial period is in the teens, once puberty is reached, when dwarfs suffer four or five times the dating problems of other teens." A small proportion of dwarfs date, and sometimes marry, people of normal height, though the LPA reports that the mortality rate of mixed-height marriages is exceedingly high.

Painfully aware of the persistent romantic woes of its members, the LPA sponsors weekend regional conferences (social get-togethers), furnishes members with names of eligible partners, and otherwise intrigues to throw together potential spouses. Three quarters of the married couples in the organization met as a result of this planning. Perhaps the most anticipated event on a dwarf's social calendar is the LPA annual convention, where no one in attendance is more than five feet tall. At the convention, rotated around the country, organizers offer a wide-ranging set of activities—dances, boat rides, shows.

Quite a number of dwarfs, however, refuse to join the LPA; mainly, say LPA people, because they refuse to accept the reality of their abnormal stature. Professor Martin Weinberg of Rutgers, in a study he conducted on dwarfs in 1968, found that many dwarfs believe they are normal in every way, a belief they reinforce by refraining from virtually all social contact with other dwarfs. "Dwarfs who join the LPA have already come to grips with the fact that they have a big problem," Rasa says, "I know one dwarf, immensely talented as a musician, who has closeted herself off from society. It's very sad."

Question 15: "What are the types of X?" ("undersized persons fall into two categories …")

Abnormally undersized persons fall into two general categories, and although as many as seventy-five possible causes of dwarfism have been isolated—hormonal failure, defective genes, bone diseases, inadequate nutrition, to name a few—the common malfunction with both varieties is glandular. In the type known loosely as dwarfs and identified medically as achondroplastic dwarfs, a bone disorder at birth results in a stumpiness of the extremities, a large, globular head, and the powerful torso of a person much taller. Growth plods along at a quarter of an inch a year, rather than the customary two-inch speed. Doctors estimate that more than three quarters of dwarfs are of this type (including the dwarf of Norse mythology). Pituitary dwarfs, commonly known as midgets, are unremarkable at birth, but they cease growing in early childhood, and, though very small, are perfectly proportioned. Midgets rarely grow taller than forty inches.

Many dwarfs marry among themselves, and have children (usually by Cesarean section) who almost always grow to full adult height. A prolific English couple sired fourteen normal children. Some midgets, however, fail to reach puberty, and therefore remain sexually immature. Male voices retain a high pitch. While carnivals often tout midget wrestlers, midgets are almost invariably ineffective grapplers. They are, on the whole, extremely feeble.

Update to present status: Question 7: "How can recent statistics and other research findings be summarized?"

One in every few thousand births is a dwarf baby, and doctors reckon that roughly 100,000 Americans are dwarfs. They appear in especially great numbers in cultures which marry only among themselves. The Amish, for example, who prohibit wedlock outside their own bloodlines, have a population that is nearly one percent abnormally undersized. This data comes from Dr. Victor McKuisick, head of the Department of Medicine at Johns Hopkins Medical Center, who has studied the Amish and dwarfism at great length. "An island called Krk, off the coast of Yugoslavia, has a high incidence of pituitary dwarfs for the same reason," McKuisick says, "and the same is true of a few other places around the world."

Owing partly to The Little People of America, partly to greater interest in clinical genetics, and partly to gratifying results attained in tissue culture work, medical practitioners have recently intensified their examination of the roots of dwarfism. Progress has been painfully slow, and the prognosis is guardedly hopeful, but researchers soldier on.

Some important encouragement has already been offered the slender percentage (less than one percent) of dwarfs plagued by deficiencies of human growth hormone (HGH). HGH is one of eight hormones manufactured by the pituitary gland, an organ no bigger than a pea that sits beneath the brain at the base of the skull. Released into the bloodstream, HGH assists in the complex chemical process of growth. Among other things, it helps the body lasso amino acids needed to build proteins and it raises the level of blood sugar needed for energy. Nothing whatsoever could be done about hypopituitary dwarfs until 1956, when Dr. Maurice Rabin of Tufts University School of Medicine first extracted purified HGH from the pituitaries of cadavers. Since then, HGH injections have stimulated the growth of some 2000 midget children. Some of them have grown as tall as five-foot-five. Mature hypopituitary dwarfs can't be restored in this manner, since their bone cells have already fused and resist stimulation.

Question 14: "What are the consequences of recent research findings?"

Though HGH treatment of dwarfism is a distinguished medical achievement, only HGH from human or monkey pituitaries works, and the supply from these sources is all too limited. Doctors reckon that thousands more midget children would be taller today if the hormone had been more plentiful in the last decade. To get more HGH, a National Pituitary Agency was formed in 1963 by the U.S. Institute of Arthritis and Metabolic Diseases and the College of American Pathologists. It has been overseeing an educational campaign to persuade pathologists to save human pituitaries after performing autopsies, and to urge the public to will their pituitaries in the same way they will their eyes and other organs. Human Growth Inc., an educational foundation formed in 1965, largely by parents and relatives of hypopituitary dwarfs, has been carrying on the same campaign. The real answer, doctors think, probably lies in synthetic HGH. Biochemist C. H. Li of the University of California at Berkeley has done the spadework here. In 1966, he first identified the structure of the HGH molecule—a baffling sequence of 188 amino acids. In 1971, he synthesized the hormone. His product, however, proved only 10 percent as effective as the natural hormone. Dr. Li says that 25 to 50 percent effectiveness can be achieved, and that large-scale treatment would essentially eradicate hypopituitary dwarfism.

Question 19: "What is the value of recent findings?"

(value of recent findings)

"Dwarfism, generally, I think of as rather like running a business," says Dr. Edmund Murphy, the Moore Clinic's director. "You need management, materials, and labor. You can think of an absence of pituitary growth hormone as being deficient management, so to speak. You can think of lack of materials as being undernutrition. Then you have shortage of labor. There are people who have abnormal bone structure or cartilage cells, which make them unable to make use of the labor. All we have so far is a cure for deficient management, which, as a cause of dwarfism, is hardly a big problem at all. So if you've got a shoe factory and you're plumb out of leather, it does little good to have a great many cobblers at hand."

Question 5: "What is Bedou's personal response to present status of medical research and future outlook?"

Some disproportionate dwarfs plagued by bone disorders have been administered a modified sex hormone called oxandrolone, which is far more abundant than HGH. It is also far less effective. Continuing to frustrate medical science is the considerable task of identifying the cause in a specific case of dwarfism, a process which in many instances requires years. In fact, in certain extremely rare cases, the origin can be entirely psychological. This disorder is known as the emotional deprivation syndrome, in which children cease growing because of a home environment stripped of love. Such children are brought to hospitals, where loving nurses stimulate growth. When they return home, growth stops.

On the whole, dwarfs have refrained from placing all their hopes on medicine. "We are willing to accept our deficiencies, and to make the best of them," says Charles Bedou. "When people stare at me—and they invariably do—I make out that it's more curiosity than anything else. Let them look."

DISCUSSION AND EXERCISES

1. "Updating" ("What are the latest facts and findings . . . ?") is a recurring form of article. People always want up-to-date information on such topics as sleep, dreams, and the common cold. In what sense does this article fall into that category? In what sense is it different?
2. Note how skillfully the author weaves the facts (data, statistics, and quotations) into the piece. Indicate blocks of facts. What kinds of facts does the author group together? How are they positioned in the piece?
3. Discuss popular misconceptions regarding dwarfs. List a few that you may have had. How has Kleinfield's article changed your misconception?
4. In addition to "What are the facts about X?" and "What is the current status of X?", a third question appears again and again in this piece in various guises: "What are the component parts of X?"—that is, what are the constituent problems that make up the larger "challenge" in the lives of dwarfs? See paragraph 5 for one application of this question. Where else does it appear?
5. How has humor been introduced into the piece? Do you find it appropriate? Explain.
6. Do you still have unanswered questions about dwarfs? How would you go about getting more information?

Analysis of Style

1. How does the topic sentence of paragraph 4 provide a transition to the present status of dwarfs? What key word alerts the reader?
2. Journalist John Gunther once remarked that "a reporter with no bias at all would be a vegetable." Define the bias in this piece. What would you use as evidence of bias?'
3. How do the following brief and "flat" statements help to create emotional impact?
   a. His body is all out of whack.
   b. He is what is known as a dwarf.
   c. "Life hasn't been exactly marvelous."
   d. "Put the damn dime in for me."
   e. When they return home, growth stops.
   f. "Let them look."
4. What makes this piece more than just a compilation of fact upon fact? What devices does the writer use to bring his account to life? To make it entertaining?
5. What is the writer's tone (disinterested, warm, concerned, flat, ironic, or enthusiastic.) Is his tone consistent throughout the piece?
6. In what ways has the writer taken into account the special reader of *The Atlantic Monthly*? How might the article have been changed if the reading audience had been changed to: *The National Enquirer*, *People Magazine*, *Rolling Stone*, *Vogue*? Cite other publications and speculate.

ESSAY SUGGESTIONS

1. Suggested writing topic: The Latest Facts About Twins (2,500–3,500 words)

   An anomaly of nature, twins are a subject of perpetual curiosity and constant study. What are the physiological causes? The psychological effects? What is the difference between identical and fraternal twins? How are twins viewed by others? How do they view themselves? What are the advantages and disadvantages of being a twin? What differences does it make in one's life? A presentation of the facts, accompanied by first-hand reports (based on interviews with twins) is certain to produce a lively and absorbing factual article.

   For a discussion of research procedure and library sources, read the section on "Gathering Information." For a list of possible sources for this topic, see page 68.

2. For additional topics for extended "facts about" articles (2,500–3,500 words), see Essay Suggestions following Question 6, "What are the facts about X?"

3. If you are interested in other anomalies of nature, see Leslie Fiedler's *Freaks* (New York: Simon and Schuster, 1978) for information and bibliography on such special groups—or "phenomena"—as giants, wild men, feral children, and so on. See also Diane Arbus, *An Aperture Monograph* (Millerton, N.Y.: Aperture, 1972), a collection of photographs.

CHARACTERIZATION-INTERPRETATION

Like the short character sketch, the extended characterization focuses on a single individual, posing the questions, "What kind of person is this? What makes him or her tick?" The extra length of the extended study enables you to probe more deeply into the complexities of your subject and to compose a fuller portrait, richer in descriptive detail, illustrative episode, and possible interpretations. Even so, like the 500-word sketch, the 2,500-word character study should have a unifying thread; it should point to the quality or qualities that define the person and provide a key to his or her character (Question 3, "What kind of person is X?").

The following article on the great seventeenth century scientist, Isaac Newton, provides a straightforward, chronologically organized account (see Outline, pages 83–85) of this "strange solitary figure" whose inner life and motivations were "hidden even from his contemporaries." In this article, as in the previous two long papers, you will observe that the writer has drawn upon a variety of questions to round out his subject—a character analysis and interpretation of a mysterious loner whose "voyagings through strange seas of thought" changed the face of science and our vision of the universe.

Isaac Newton

I. Bernard Cohen

(1) The mind and personality of Isaac Newton challenge any historian. Newton was a strange, solitary figure, and the wellsprings of his behavior were hidden even from his contemporaries. A biographer of his time compared Newton to the River Nile, whose great powers were known but whose source had not been discovered. Nevertheless, the few facts we have about his early life do allow some speculation about Newton's character and development.

(2) He was born prematurely, a physical weakling. It is said that he had to wear a "bolster" to support his neck during his first few months, that no one expected him to live. Newton later was fond of saying that his mother had said he was so tiny at birth that he could have been put into a quart mug.

(3) Newton's father died three months before he was born. When the boy was less than two years old, his mother remarried, and he was turned over to his aged grandmother. He lived on an isolated farm, deprived of parental care and love, without the friendly companionship and rivalry of brothers and sisters. The late Louis T. More, author of the best-known modern biography of the man, held that much of Newton's "inwardness" could be attributed to his lonely and unhappy childhood.

(4) Born in 1642, Newton grew up in an era when England was still tasting the "terrors of a protracted and bitter civil war." Raiding and plundering parties were common. His grandmother was "suspected of sympathy to the royal forces." In the face of these real terrors and "the frights of his imagination," he could not have received much comfort from his grandmother or the hired laborers on the farm. Naturally enough, as More observed, the boy turned to "the solace of lonely meditation" and developed a strong habit of self-absorption. A girl who knew him in his youth described him as a "sober, silent, thinking lad" who "was never known scarce to play with the boys abroad, at their silly amusements."

(5) He evidently overcame his physical weakness by the time he reached school age, for a schoolmate reported that Newton challenged a bully who had kicked him in the belly to a fight and "beat him till he would fight no more"—winning out because he had "more spirit and resolution." The bully stood high in the class, and Newton was so determined "to beat him also at his books" that "by hard work he finally succeeded, and then gradually rose to be the first in the school."

(6) When Newton was 14, his mother took the boy back into her home, her second husband having died. She conceived the idea of making him a farmer, but the experiment proved an unqualified failure. Newton found farming totally distasteful. Instead of attending properly to his chores, he would read, make wooden models with his knife, or dream. Fortunately for science, his mother gave up the attempt and allowed him to prepare for Cambridge University.

(7) At the age of 18, Newton entered Trinity College. In his early years at the University he was not outstanding in any way. The he came under the influence of Isaac Barrow, a professor of mathematics and an extraordinary man. He was an able mathematician, a classicist, an astronomer and an authority in the field of optics. Barrow was one of the first to recognize Newton's genius. Soon after his student had taken a degree, Barrow resigned his professorship so that Newton might have it. Thus at 26 Newton was established in an academic post of distinction and was free to pursue his epoch-making studies.

(8) He had already sown the seeds of his revolutionary contributions to three distinct fields of scientific inquiry: mathematics, celestial mechanics and physical optics. After his graduation from the University he had returned to his home at Woolsthorpe for 18 months of work which can fairly be described as the most fruitful 18 months in all the history of the creative imagination. Newton's subsequent life in science consisted to a large degree in the elaboration of the great discoveries made during those "golden" months. What Newton did at Woolsthorpe is best stated in his words:

(9) "In the beginning of the year 1665 I found the method for approximating series and the rule for reducing any dignity [power] of any binomial to such a series [i.e., the binomial theorem]. The same year in May I found the method of tangents of Gregory and Slusius, and in November [discovered] the direct method of Fluxions [i.e., the elements of

the differential calculus], and the next year in January had the Theory of Colours, and in May following I had entrance into the inverse method of Fluxions [i.e., integral calculus], and in the same year I began to think of gravity extending to the orb of the Moon ... and having thereby compared the force requisite to keep the Moon in her orb with the force of gravity at the surface of the earth, and found them to answer pretty nearly...."

(10) As a by-product of his analysis of light and colors, which he had shyly kept to himself, Newton invented a reflecting telescope, to free telescopes from the chromatic aberration of refracting lenses. He made a small version of his new telescope for the Royal Society of London, and was shortly elected, at the age of 30, as a Fellow of the Royal Society, the highest scientific honor in England.

Newton was understandably overwhelmed by his sudden public recognition. He had been loath to announce his discoveries, but within a week after his election to the Society he asked permission to communicate an account of the "philosophical discovery" which had induced him "to the making of the said telescope." With a disarming lack of false modesty, he said that in his judgment he had made "the oddest, if not the most considerable detection, which hath hitherto been made in the operations of nature."

(11) Newton's letter to the Royal Society, "containing his new theory of light and colours," was sent to London on February 6, 1672. This paper can claim a number of "firsts." It was Newton's initial publication; it founded the science of spectroscopy, and it marked the beginning of a sound analysis of color phenomena. Briefly, what Newton showed is that a prism separates white light into its component colors, associated with specific indices of refraction, and that a second prism can recombine the dispersed light and render it white again. These magnificent experiments provided a new departure for the formulation of theories about the nature of color. Yet the paper did not win for Newton the universal applause that he had sought. The Royal Society was bombarded with letters disputing Newton's conclusions. Some of the objectors were unimportant, but others were men of stature: Christian Huygens, Robert Hooke. With astonishing patience, Newton wrote careful letters answering each objection. But he won over only one of his opponents—the French Jesuit Father Pardies.

(12) The controversy had an acid effect on Newton's personality. He vowed that he would publish no further discoveries. As he wrote later to Leibnitz: "I was so persecuted with discussions arising from the publication of my theory of light, that I blamed my own imprudence for parting with so substantial a blessing as my quiet to run after a shadow." And yet he did later continue to publish; he wanted the applause of the scientific world. This ambivalence was not overlooked by Newton's enemies. The astronomer John Flamsteed, who broke with Newton, described him as "insidious, ambitious, and excessively covetous of praise, and impatient of contradiction. ... I believe him to be a good man at the bottom; but, through his nature, suspicious."

(13) At Cambridge Newton was the very model of an absent-minded professor. His amanuensis, Humphrey Newton (no relative), wrote that he never knew Newton "to take any recreation or pastime either in riding out to take the air, walking, bowling, or any other exercise whatever, thinking all hours lost that were not spent in his studies." He often worked until two or three o'clock in the morning, ate sparingly and sometimes forgot to eat altogether. When reminded that he had not eaten, he would go to the table and "eat a bite or two standing." Newton rarely dined in the college hall; when he did, he was apt to appear "with shoes down at heels, stockings untied, surplice on, and his head scarcely combed." It was said that he often delivered his lectures to an empty hall, apparently with as much satisfaction as if the room had been full of students.

(14) After the controversy, Newton withdrew from the public eye as a scientist. He served the University as its representative in Parliament and worked away in private at

chemistry and alchemy, theology, physics and mathematics. He became acquainted with Leibnitz, but refused to give his great contemporary any exact information about his discoveries in mathematics. Today it is generally agreed that the calculus was discovered more or less independently by both Newton and Leibnitz, but the two men and their partisans quarreled acrimoniously over priority, and Newton accused Leibnitz of plagiarism. Newton conceived a jealous proprietary interest in every subject he studied, and almost every achievement of his creative life was accompanied by some quarrel.

(15) In 1684 came the famous visit to Newton by the astronomer Edmund Halley. He had a problem concerning the gravitational attraction between the sun and the planets. Halley and Hooke had concluded from Johannes Kepler's accounting of planetary motions that the force of attraction must vary inversely with the square of the distance between a planet and the sun. But they had been unable to prove their idea. "What," Halley asked Newton, "would be the curve described by the planets on the supposition that gravity diminished as the square of the distance?" Newton answered without hesitation: "An ellipse." How did he know that? "Why," replied Newton, "I have calculated it." These four words informed Halley that Newton had worked out one of the most fundamental laws of the universe—the law of gravity. Halley wanted to see the calculations at once, but Newton could not find his notes. He promised to write out the theorems and proofs. Under Halley's insistent urging he completed a manuscript for the Royal Society. Thus was born the *Philosophiae Naturalis Principia Mathematica,* known ever since simply as the *Principia.*

(16) Just before its publication a crisis arose when Hooke laid claim to the inverse-square law. Newton threatened to withdraw the climactic chapters of his work, but Halley mollified him and the great classic went to press intact. Halley's credit in this enterprise is enormous. He not only got Newton to write the work but also saw it through the press and paid the costs of publication, although he was not a wealthy man.

(17) The *Principia* is divided into three "books." In the first Newton laid down his three laws of motion and explored the consequences of various laws of force. In the second he explored motion in various types of fluids; here he was somewhat less successful, and much of his work had to be revised in the succeeding decades. In the third he discussed universal gravitation and showed how a single law of force explains at once the falling of bodies on the earth, the motion of our moon or of Jupiter's satellites, the motions of planets and the phenomenon of tides.

(18) One of the most vexing problems for Newton was to find a rigorous proof that a sphere acts gravitationally as if all its mass were concentrated at its center. Without this theorem, the whole theory of gravitation would rest on intuition rather than precise calculation. For instance, in the simple case of an apple falling to the ground—the occasion of the central idea of gravitation according to Newton's own account—what is the "distance between" the earth and the apple? Here the calculus came into play. Newton considered the earth as a collection of tiny volumes of matter, each attracting the apple according to the inverse-square law of gravitation. Then he summed up the individual forces and showed that the result was the same as if the earth were a point mass, as if all the matter of the earth were shrunk into a tiny region at its center.

(19) Newton suffered some kind of "nervous breakdown" after the completion of the *Principia.* He complained that he could not sleep, and said that he lacked the "former consistency of his mind." He wrote angry letters to friends and then apologized; he protested bitterly to John Locke, for example, that the philosopher had attempted to "embroil him with women."

(20) In 1696 Newton abandoned the academic life for the position of Warden, later Master, of the Mint. Honors for his scientific achievements continued to come to him: he

was knighted in 1705 and served many years as president of the Royal Society. But the last quarter century of his life produced no major contributions to science. Some say that his creative genius had simply burned out. Others argue that after having founded the science of physical optics, invented the calculus and shown the mechanism of the universe, there just wasn't anything left for him to do in the realm of science.

(21) Although he made no important discoveries, Newton's last years were not barren of ideas. Now famous and honored, he felt secure enough to offer many public speculations on scientific problems. He suggested various possible hypotheses as to the "cause" of gravitation and speculated on the nature of the "ether," the size of the constituent units of matter, the forces of electricity and magnetism, the cause of muscular response to the "commands of the will," the origins of sensation, the creation of the world, the ultimate destiny of man. In the century after Newton, physical experimenters followed up many of his bold speculations.

(22) Newton is often described as the inaugurator of the "Age of Reason." Alexander Pope expressed the sentiment of his time in the famous lines:

> Nature and Nature's laws lay hid in night:
> God said, Let Newton be! and all was light.

DISCUSSION AND EXERCISES

1. What picture does the reader get of the 17th century? What was the political situation, and how did it affect Newton's life?
2. What conditions of Newton's birth might have contributed to his meditative genius?
3. If born today, how different would Newton's life and work have been? What advantages and disadvantages would he have encountered? Might he achieve more or less than he did in the seventeenth century? Explain.
4. Some have said that in the last quarter of his life, Newton's creative genius burned out. Others have said that there "just wasn't anything left for him to do in the realm of science." Which statement do you find the most credible? Discuss.
5. Is there anyone in this century comparable to Newton? Discuss.

Analysis of Style

1. List some of the general sources from which Cohen drew his facts about Newton. What effect does the reference to such sources have on the piece? Speculate on the effect of formal footnotes: Would they enhance or detract from overall readability and credibility?
2. How do the small details about Newton enhance the portrait (for example, "He was so tiny he could have been put into a quart mug"; "He would go to the table and eat a bite or two standing")?
3. What adjectives reveal Cohen's attitude toward Newton? How would you describe that attitude? What is your attitude toward Newton?
4. How effective are the lines by Pope at the end of the article? Do they serve as appropriate summary and conclusion? Explain.
5. Analyze the paragraph sequences in the essay, noting the patterns of the paragraphs and their movement from beginning to end.

ESSAY SUGGESTIONS

1. Write an extended characterization-interpretation (2,500–3,500 words) centered around one of the following:

    a. Any major scientist, such as Albert Einstein, Copernicus, Galileo, Charles Darwin, or Leonardo da Vinci.

    b. Any major artist, such as Rembrandt, El Greco, Edvard Munch, or Hieronymus Bosch.

Scholarly Documentation: A Student's Term Paper

EXTENDED HISTORICAL PROCESS ANALYSIS

The Mollie Maguire Movement, Melody Rammel

EXTENDED HISTORICAL PROCESS ANALYSIS

*I*n tracing the development of the nineteenth-century labor movement, named for a widowed Irish tenant farmer, Molly Maguire, the student who wrote the term paper below followed the lines of process analysis—an orderly, chronologically organized account of an historical event. Note how judiciously the writer separates fact from speculation, documenting her materials by citing authorities, historians, and published reports to support opposing views. Note how she maintains distance and objectivity throughout. The subject remains controversial, she concludes, indicating that even today we cannot be certain "whether the Mollies were actually a terrorist group" or simply a secret society. What is incontrovertible is that the Mollie Maguires exerted a powerful and memorable influence on the labor movement in the United States. (Note the use of the new Modern Language Association documentation style. For more information see pages 73–74.)

The Mollie Maguire Movement

Melody Rammel

(1) In nineteenth-century Ireland, tenant farmers worked on estates owned by absentee landlords living in England and managed by on-site agents. Tenant farmers, kept at a level of near-poverty, were regarded by the agents as the dregs of society and treated as such. These farmers were so impoverished that they were frequently evicted for nonpayment of rent.

(2) By the middle 1800s, the farmers' animosity toward the landlords and agents reached the boiling point. The most popular explanation of the movement's origin is that Molly Maguire, a widowed tenant farmer, organized a movement to resist the rent system and to run the English ruling party out of Ireland. Her followers, adopting the name "Mollie Maguires," formed a secret society. Dressing up as women, they would launch surprise attacks on land agents which often escalated into violent beatings and even murders (Adamic 12; Roy 93; "Molly Maguires" 678).

(3) Eventually, the Mollie Maguires had control of entire counties. The landlords used their political connections to force the authorities into action. Alleged Mollie Maguire members were rounded up, tried, convicted and sentenced to harsh punishment. Suffering under these pressures and hoping to escape their poverty, many Irish farmers emigrated to America in the middle and late 1800s.

(4) The new settlers concentrated in the mining areas of Pennsylvania where work was plentiful and there were enough of their countrymen to carry on Irish traditions. Here they established a benevolent secret society, the Ancient Order of Hibernians, which was officially chartered in Pennsylvania in 1871 as a group to promote friendship, unity and Christian charity among members (Rayback 132). The primary focus of the

organization was to maintain a charity fund to support the aged, sick, and infirm. In order to become a member, a person had to be Irish or of Irish descent, a good Roman Catholic, and of good moral character. The Hibernians' constitution read in part, "The Supreme Being has implanted in our natures tender sympathies and most humane feelings toward our fellow-creatures in distress; and all the happiness that human nature is capable of enjoying must flow from and terminate in the love of God and our fellows" (Adamic 13).

(5) The miners, most of whom were Irish, soon found that their economic and societal status was not changed by their migration. For the most part, they were Roman Catholic, while the mine bosses were almost all English or Welsh Protestants. In America, as in their homeland, they were considered the lowest of social classes.

(6) As the miners' disillusionment increased, a small terrorist faction broke off from the Hibernians. Adopting the violent methods and the name of the Mollie Maguires, its intent was to run the Welsh and English miners, mine bosses, and police out of the district ("Molly Maguires" 678). Thomas Brooks, a labor historian, thinks the terrorist faction formed when attempts to unionize the Irish miners failed. With the defeat of unionism, Brooks writes, "the young Irish hotheads in the Mollies turned to derailing mine cars and burning breakers. Then they took to the hills to snipe at mine supers and unpopular foremen" (Brooks 48). Years after the Mollie movement ended, on the eve of a trial of I.W.W. members, President Theodore Roosevelt said, "I think that the Western Federation of Miners is a body just like the Molly Maguires of Pennsylvania. That there are a number of good, honest and stupid men in the ranks I have no doubt, just as I have no doubt that this was true of the Molly Maguires; but the moving spirit is to be described as representing 'a revolt against economic and social injustice' only in the sense that we thus describe a band of road agents who rob a coach" (Foner 11). Labor historian Sidney Lens wrote of the faction, "Without a union to absorb their pain and relieve their fury, a few zealots took to terror" (Lens 17).

(7) The Mollies numbered about 450 at the height of their power in the 1870s. They regarded themselves as superior to other foreigners in the district and demanded the easiest jobs in the mines. According to Louis Adamic's account of class violence in America, if a foreman refused their demands, he would probably die a violent death. Mine bosses who would not hire Irishmen were also murdered (14).

(8) Adamic also reports that a Mollie member could order death for a mine boss by filing a complaint with the proper committee, which would then vote on the proposed assassination. Once approved, the committee would assign two or more Mollie members from another area to carry it out. If a member refused to carry out a death order, he himself would be killed by fellow members (16).

(9) Thus the name "Mollie Maguires" become a synonym for terror. People in the mining districts would not leave their homes after dark and they would go forth during the daylight hours only if armed. In January 1877, the *American Law Review* observed in an article about the coal regions of Pennsylvania: "From their dark and mysterious regions there came forth to the outside world an appalling series of tales of murder, arson, and violent crime of every description" (Adamic 14). The *Miners' Journal* reported 63 unsolved murders in the Eastern Pennsylvania coal region between January 1860 and April 1867 (Lens 16).

Several Mollie leaders also headed the Miners' and Laborers' Benevolent Association, a group which organized the Long Strike of 1875. Pent-up bitter feelings turned the strike into a bloody labor war with the Mollie members and strikebreakers hired by the railroad and mine owners on the front lines. Miners who tried to return to work were threatened with murder by Mollie members. Such threats were not new to strikers. A laborer in 1853 had written in the *London Times* about his fear of being a "marked man" if he crossed the picket line (Ford 283). Strikebreakers who dared to cross the Mollie picket lines were beaten to death (Adamic 13; Lens 24).

(10) Franklin Benjamin Gowen, an ambitious young Irish attorney, was the head of the Legal Department of the Reading Railroad, the largest transporter of coal in the area, and therefore the main target of the Mollies' vandalism. Gowen, an antiunion ex-district attorney, became president of the railroad just before the start of the Long Strike. Gowen later admitted to spending four million dollars of the railroad's money to break the Long Strike. According to his reasoning, he had to keep the railroad "from the arbitrary control of an irresponsible trades union" (Lens 23). Even so, during one seven-month period, Gowen recorded 92 incidents of arson, derailed trains, assaults, threats, and murders (Lens 25).

(11) Some observers, like Sidney Lens, believed that "many if not most of these illegal acts were instigated by the operators and perpetrated by their agents" (25). During the Long Strike, Edward Coyle, a union head and Hibernian leader, was found murdered on Reading Railroad property. A mine boss killed another Hibernian member. A mine foreman shot at random into a crowd of strikers. None of these people were ever convicted (Lens 24). Lens is not the only historian who feels that Gowen himself had much to do with the violence during the Long Strike. "Gowen appeared to realize that violence connected with the strike could be meshed with the violence long attributed to the Molly Maguires," Wayne G. Broehl, Jr., writes, "and the two tied up into a neat package for clubbing all union activities under the guise of preserving law and order" (Lens 24).

(12) The Long Strike actually lasted only five to seven months, after which the miners were forced to give in because their families were dying (Lens 24). Former miner Andrew Roy described the Mollie families:

> Hundreds of families rose in the morning to breakfast on a crust of bread and a glass of water, who did not know where a bite of dinner was to come from. Day after day, men, women and children went to adjoining woods to dig roots and pick up herbs to keep body and soul together, and still the strike went on. The end came in the unconditional surrender of the miners. The force of nature could no further go (93).

(13) Even after the strike ended the violence went on. Riots broke out and the murders, assaults, robberies and arson continued. According to the newspapers, the victims of these crimes were usually foremen and officials, and only mine owners' property was destroyed (Rayback 132).

(14) During the strike, Frank Gowen had contacted the Pinkerton Detective Agency for help in destroying the Mollie organization. Allan Pinkerton sent a young detective named James McParlan to do the job. McParlan, a young Irish-Catholic immigrant, was a gregarious, red-headed tenor who could dance a jig and hold his own in a drinking contest or barroom brawl. His work-background included stints as a factory laborer, teamster, wood-chopper, coachman and policeman. McParlan was probably America's first labor spy (Brooks 48–49). Using the alias "James McKenna" he went into the mine district disguised as a tramp, a recent immigrant from Ireland, and a member of the Irish Mollies. Establishing his new identity in a hotel in Pottsville that was owned by a reputed Mollie member, "McKenna" made his appearance memorable by hard drinking, dancing and singing a Mollie ballad well-known in the homeland. The Mollies accepted him as one of their own group and he distinguished himself as a leader in many of their violent acts. In fact "McKenna" was soon elected secretary of his district, primarily on his reputation as a proponent of violence and terrorism. After three years of Mollie membership,

McParlan's true identity was discovered and he had to leave the coal fields on the run. His almost daily letter reports to the Pinkerton headquarters proved to be enough to undermine the entire Mollie organization (Roy 94; Lens 11).

(15) In late 1875 and early 1876 the Mollie members arrested during the Long Strike were brought to trial. McParlan and other Pinkerton operatives gave most of the testimony leading to conviction. It was corroborated by Mollie Maguire members (also on the Pinkerton/Gowen payroll) who turned state's evidence in exchange for immunity from prosecution (Adamic 19). McParlan's "evidence" led to the arrest of 70 Mollie members, 12 convictions of first degree murder, four of second degree murder, four of accessory murder and six of perjury (Roy 94). Gowen, a former district attorney, took an active role in the trials as a prosecutor.

(16) The Mollie members who had received immunity testified that the purpose of the group was to get members elected to public offices that handled money. They also said that there were 6,000 Mollie lodges in the United States and that the organization was "criminal in character." Historian Joseph Rayback commented, "The 'members' who testified as to the purposes of the order were either Pinkerton detectives or criminals who had joined the order after 1875" (132). The rest of the testimony was also faulty and contradictory. At one point, a witness testified that he saw a union head (and Mollie member) kill a mine boss. When the accused man stood up, however, the witness testified that it was not the person he saw commit the murder. Incredibly, the falsely accused man was convicted and executed (Lens 28).

(17) Some historians have characterized the Mollie Maguire trials as witch hunts which served the purpose of the mine owners. On June 21, 1877, Pennsylvania had a "Day With a Rope." Two thousand people watched the hanging of six men on a double gallows near Pottsville. All of the men were members of the Ancient Order of Hibernians. Four other Hibernian members were hanged at Mauck Chunk on the same date. During the rest of the year, seven more Mollies were executed at scattered sites in the state. Even as late as January 1879, two men were hanged for their alleged roles as Mollies during the Long Strike (Lens 9–10).

(18) The Mollie trials and executions changed the nation's image of the labor union movement. As the organization came to an end, the country had a picture of miners as murderers, arsonists, and rioters (Rayback 37; Foner 41). The nation's newspapers celebrated the end of the movement. On May 9, 1876, the "Pittsburgh Gazette" wrote, "The Mollie Maguires represented the spirit of French Communism and enforced their views by secret murders. The principle involved was simply that of permitting them to dictate the operations of labor. Their men were to be employed, their prices admitted and their directions obeyed. . . ." Lens comments, "Plainly and simply, the miners were guilty of wanting a union" (25).

(19) The day following the "Day With a Rope," news media applauded the executions:

> *The Chicago Tribune:* "A Triumph of Law and Justice"
> *The Philadelphia Times:* "Justice at Last"
> *The Miners' Journal* (published by mine owners): "What did they do? Whenever prices of labor did not suit them they organized and proclaimed a strike" (Lens 10).
> *The New York Commercial and Financial Chronicle:* "Labor is under control for the first time since the war." (The war referred to was the Long Strike.) (Rayback 133)

(20) Labor authorities and historians have never agreed on whether the Mollies were actually a terrorist group. Andrew Roy, mining geologist and ex-chief mine inspector in

Ohio, wrote of the Mollies in 1907, "The anthracite region had been infested for several years by a desperate class of men, banded together in secret, oath-bound association, known as the Mollie Maguires. Murder inspired these wicked men. They met in secret places and, under the influence of intoxicating liquor, planned incendiarism and murder" (12). Many others hold the opposing view. On June 30, 1877, the *Irish World*, a nationalist paper, claimed that the trials and executions were a set-up. The paper said the coal mine owners had invented and popularized the myth of the Mollies because they "found it necessary to frighten the country with a bugbear" (Lens 11). Labor historian Joseph Rayback agrees with this opinion and writes that, except for the trial testimony, there was no evidence of a large, widespread number of Mollie lodges or of Mollie political involvement. He also writes that the violence in the mine fields did not begin until after the railroad brought the Pinkerton detectives into the fields. According to Rayback, many of the victims were union leaders and ordinary miners. Rayback concludes that "the Mollies were a figment of Pinkerton's and coal operators' imagination": they were invented to destroy unionism (132–33). Another historian, Herbert Harris, believes that the Mollies and Hibernians were a harmless secret fraternal order (Lens 12).

(21) Sidney Lens thinks the Mollies were set up by the coal mine owners. "All that is certain," he maintains, "is that the men referred to as Molly Maguires were Irish, were members of the Ancient Order of Hibernians, were miners or sympathizers, and were participants in the strikes. Doubtless they engaged in violence, but they were as frequently the victims as the victimizers" (12). Philip Foner, author of a multivolume history of the American labor movement, writes that the Pennsylvania miners were "railroaded to the gallows, trade unionism in the anthracite regions set back for many years, and the cause of organized labor throughout the country injured" (41).

(22) The passage of time has not settled the argument or lessened the Mollies' fame in labor circles. Whether they were terrorists or family men desperately trying to secure a decent wage and better working conditions, the Mollies changed the course of labor history by their very existence. Years after the movement, Eugene V. Debs, the radical labor leader, wrote of the Mollies, "… they were the neglected children of poverty, the product of a wretched environment. The men who perished upon the scaffold as felons were labor leaders, the first martyrs to the class struggle in the United States" (Adamic 20).

Works Cited

Adamic, Louis. *Dynamite: The Story of Class Violence in America*. Gloucester: Peter Smith, 1963.

Broehl, Wayne G., Jr. *The Molly Maguires*. Cambridge: Harvard University Press, 1964.

Brooks, Thomas R. *Toil and Trouble: A History of American Labor*. New York: Delacorte Press, 1964.

Dewees, F. P. *The Molly Maguires*. Philadelphia: Lippincott, 1877.

Foner, Philip S. *History of the Labor Movement in the United States*. Vol. 4. New York: International Publishers, 1965.

Ford, George, and Sylvere Monod, eds. *Hard Times*. New York: Norton, 1966.

Lens, Sidney. *The Labor Wars*. New York: Doubleday, 1973.

"Molly Maguires." *Encyclopaedia Britannica*, 1951.

Pinkerton, Allan. *The Mollie Maguires and the Detectives*. New York: The G. W. Dillingham, 1877.

Rayback, Joseph G. *A History of American Labor*. New York: Macmillan, 1959.

Roy, Andrew. *A History of the Coal Miners of the United States*. Columbus: J. L. Trauger Printing Co., 1907.

Works Consulted

Broehl, Wayne G., Jr. *The Molly Maguires*. Cambridge: Harvard University Press, 1964.

Dewees, F. P. *The Molly Maguires*. Philadelphia: Lippincott, 1877.

Pinkerton, Allan. *The Molly Maguires and the Detectives*. New York: The G. W. Dillingham, 1877.

DISCUSSION AND EXERCISES

1. Indicate how many of the twenty questions the writer has called upon to develop her "process analysis."
2. How did the Mollie Maguire movement originate? When were the insurgents at the height of their power? Characterize the movement at that point.
3. How did the name "Mollie Maguire" come to stand for terror?
4. Describe The Long Strike. How does the writer depict its impact on the miners and their families in day-to-day living? What was the outcome of the strike?
5. How do historians characterize the Mollie Maguire trials? What was the impact on the Labor Movement? What was the attitude of the nation's newspapers?
6. In what sense is the nature and impact of the Mollie Maguire movement still inconclusive and controversial?

Analysis of Style

1. Characterize tone and point of view. Does the writer take sides? Do you get the impression that she is for or against the Mollie Maguire Movement?
2. Is there any evidence that the author indulged in speculation regarding the Maguires?
3. The writer of this term paper draws heavily on factual data such as statistics and dates. How does she keep the piece from being dry or dull and lifeless?
4. Notice the topic sentences. How do they keep the article moving forward?
5. How do the first and final paragraphs work together? Characterize the concluding quotation in terms of its tone, meaning, and effectiveness as a final statement and unifying device.

ESSAY SUGGESTIONS

1. Suggested writing topic: The Women's Suffrage Movement in the United States (1848–1920) (2,500–3,500 words).

   Trace the development of this early wave of the contemporary women's liberation movement. Begin with the first women's suffrage convention held in Seneca Falls, New York, in 1848, citing proponents and opponents of the movement, prominent crusaders, and early successes (in 1869 the territory of Wyoming was the first in the nation's history to grant women the right to vote). Develop your historical analysis further by showing how other states followed suit and how World War I contributed to the ultimate passage in 1920 of the Nineteenth Amendment to the Constitution. Bring the analysis up to date by assessing the impact of this movement on our own time.

For a discussion of research procedures and library resources, read the section on "Gathering Information."

2. Additional topics for an extended historical analysis (2,500–3,500 words) include the following:

a. The Women's Liberation Movement of our time (1960s to the present)

b. The Abolitionist Movement of the 1800s (to abolish slavery)

c. Prohibition (from the organization of the Prohibition Party in 1869 to the repeal of the Eighteenth Amendment in 1932)

d. The Civil Rights Movement of the 1960s

e. Any other self-contained educational, social, or political movement in American history or in the history of a foreign nation with which you are familiar (for example, the rise of the Nazi party in Germany in the 1930s)

f. See also suggested topics following Question 11, "How is X made or done?"

Part Five

THE REWRITING PROCESS: REVISING AND EDITING

Writing and Rewriting

WRITING AND REWRITING

*T*he rewriting process includes revising, editing, and proofreading. In one sense writers may view rewriting as the final stage in the preparation of a paper, but in another sense they recognize that they rewrite as they go along. They compose a sentence, for example, in longhand or at the typewriter. They look at it, and perhaps they read it aloud so that they can *hear* it. One word might sound funny, so they substitute another. That may sound better and so may the repositioning of a modifier closer to the noun being modified. They may arrow in the change immediately. And then they may compose a closing sentence for the paragraph. Somehow the paragraph may sound "up in the air" without it.

Writers revise their work—writing and rewriting at the same time. The process is not strictly linear. Many novelists testify, for example, that they start each writing session with a *pre*writing warm-up. Then they *re*write a passage of the previous day's work. Only then do they begin writing *per se*, by moving ahead to new pages. To some extent, then, the three stages of prewriting, writing, and rewriting may be seen as running concurrently, circling back on one another even as they leap ahead from one draft to another and yet another.

Different writers work differently, of course. Some linger over separate sentences, fussing with problems as they arise; others forge ahead, confident that however rough their first draft may be, they can fix it later on. Student writers should follow the procedure that feels most comfortable for them and that proves most productive.

VISION AND REVISION

In learning how to revise, student writers would do best to follow the lead of professionals who, in turn, follow the lead of editors—people outside the manuscript who read it with a cool, critical eye, maintaining at the same time a concerned and sympathetic attitude. Indisputably, they are on the side of the manuscript, committed to making it better by reinforcing its strengths and reducing, if not eliminating, its weaknesses. They regard revision as just that—a *re*vision, a second look, perhaps a third and fourth as well. Indeed, revision means not only "to look *at*" but also "to look *over*," to note every mechanical and rhetorical detail, every choice of word, every turn of phrase, every sentence construction, paragraph division, and transition from paragraph to paragraph. Do the elements work? Could they work better? If so, how? The good editor is endlessly painstaking in the effort to improve the manuscript: to clarify, simplify, and unify; to sharpen the focus, enliven the style, reduce the verbiage.

Once you have committed the first draft of a piece of writing to paper, you are, of course, entitled to a sense of satisfaction, accomplishment. You have assembled random thoughts and feelings and shaped them into a new whole; you have wrenched words from your mind—from your heart—and organized them into an orderly sequence of sentences; this, in turn, you have organized into a series of paragraphs and finally a series of sections that make up a whole. The worst is over when your first draft is done. BUT, you should remember that *the best still lies ahead*. Every student writer must recognize this basic, irrefutable truth, for as one observer has noted, "There is no such thing as good writing, only good re-writing."

Earlier we saw (pages 87–95) how a medical student moved through four successive revisions of a statement describing his reasons for wanting to be a doctor. The first draft was a carefree, careless, off-the-top-of-his-head approximation of what he thought and felt (also of what he *thought* he felt). Only on closer examination did he discover that he needed to probe more deeply; he needed to return to his original statement, to reconsider it, and finally to revise it according to what he *really* meant to say. And he had to indicate precisely what that was, leaving no room for doubt or misunderstanding.

BECOMING YOUR OWN EDITOR

Students who are serious about improving their writing must learn to become their own painstaking editors. It is, admittedly, a difficult role to assume because at given points, writer and editor have different points of view, different emphases. On producing a first draft, for example, the writer will feel not only satisfaction but blessed relief as well. "There it is—at long last—down on paper! It looks so good—*just as it is*."

"*Not quite good enough*," must be the editorial reply. Most professional writers have internalized some such insistent voice, however tiresome and unreasonable it may initially sound, however grating and irritating. For it is at this crucial point—on completion of a first draft—that the writer must shift his or her perspective in order to see the finished product not simply *as it is* (a hard won triumph over chaos) but also as it *could* be and *should* be when it has fulfilled its potential. Estimating and fulfilling that potential is the job of revision.

Students often ask "Aren't there any forms of writing exempt from such rigorous restraints and constraints?" Students are generally referring here to deeply personal writing in which they have tried to capture and distill some special inner quality of their experience. What they are aspiring to is total honesty, sincerity, spontaneity—an admirable goal. But personal writing is not only not exempt from the rigors of revision but is perhaps even more in need of it than any other form of writing. As countless professionals have testified, emotional honesty is itself maddeningly elusive. No one hides the truth more zealously from ourselves than we ourselves.

Spontaneous writing—and this would include freewriting and prewriting of all kinds—"is a good way to start to learn to write," as poet Donald Hall has pointed out. It is "a good way to uncover material you didn't know was in you." We saw this process at work in clustering and other such "spontaneous" procedures (see pages 32–34). But, Hall adds, "we need to revise because spontaneity is never adequate.

> Writing that is merely emotional release for the writer becomes emotional chaos for the reader. Even when we write as quickly as our hand can move, we slide into emotional

falsity, into cliché, or other static. And we make leaps by private association that leave our prose unclear. And we often omit steps in thinking, or use a step that we later recognize as bad logic. Sometimes we over-explain something obvious. Or we include irrelevant material. (6)

Hall very sensibly concludes that "First drafts remain first drafts. They are the material that we must shape, a marble block that the critical brain chisels into form."

THREE STEPS IN SUCCESSFUL REVISION

Briefly, we may think of the revision process as consisting of three distinct steps, the last one involving five specific strategies. Given a "fair chance," the revision process cannot help but improve your writing.

Step One—as suggested above, ASSUME A NEW IDENTITY—THAT OF READER-EDITOR. If possible put a day or two between completion of the first draft and your first rereading. In that span of time you may be able to achieve some degree of distance and detachment. Poet John Ciardi once suggested that bad writers are incapable of being editors because they never see what is on paper but only what is in their heads. (They see what they wanted to say rather than what they actually said.) Unfortunately, this is often true of beginning writers as well. They are often passionately subjective, attached to some unworthy feature of their piece—an introductory paragraph, perhaps, that does not effectively introduce the subject (many first paragraphs are mere warm-ups and should be deleted in revision).

Thus as an imperative first step, the writer must make a determined effort to stand outside the role of writer, to become—first of all—a reader reading the piece for the first time; and—secondly—an editor who is also a reader but more than that, a person committed to making the piece better than it is.

Step two: ASSESS THE STRENGTHS AND PROBLEMS OF THE PAPER. Read it through carefully, pencil in hand, making observations, notations, and scribblings in the margin: "good!" where it's good; "no! no!" where you spot such problems as an inaccuracy, a possible contradiction, or a shift in tone; an exclamation mark where you are surprised (favorably or unfavorably); a question mark where you are confused.

Expect to be confused. You may be only one day away from what you've written but now that you are approaching it with fresh eyes and a rigorously critical standard of judgment, you will find that some lines already seem unclear, mystifying, as though someone else had written them.

Hold on to this feeling of detachment; you should cultivate it at this stage. Also, remember the counsel of E. B. White who told writers to make sure at the outset that they said what they intended to say because the chances of their having said it was "only fair." You are now putting your entire paper to the test: Does it accomplish its main purpose and observe its commitments, both stated and implied? Equally important: Is the pervasive tone of the piece appropriate to the projected audience, and do you maintain it consistently throughout? Where you see lapses, you should note them in the margin.

Let us assume that you now have a reasonable assessment of the paper's strengths and weaknesses. You've done a fair job. Your argument against capital punishment (let's say) has in fact been convincing. Certainly it has not turned out to *support* capital punishment. This reversal of impact can occur in papers if students lose control because they do not realize—until too late—the full implications of their position or how they *really* feel about an issue.

However, in the hypothetical paper we are envisioning here we shall assume that you have written a competent argument. But the paper does have some typical problems. Individual points overlap somewhat; one or two need additional supporting data; others are not in the preferred order of climax. Also, the conclusion needs strengthening so that readers can see unmistakably that it follows *logically* and *inevitably* from the premises of the argument and the facts as presented. The writing itself seems clear for the most part but "needs tightening."

Having taken two preliminary steps—adopted an objective point of view and assessed the strengths and weaknessess—you are now ready to move ahead to the next important step.

Step three: MAKE A REVISION AGENDA. Before you make up a formal agenda, survey those "problem islands" which need attention, beginning—of course—with the most fundamental and urgent. If your light, supposedly humorous essay is not especially humorous, you had better improve that sagging aspect of the piece first; otherwise you may not have a piece to improve. The logical place to start is with content. Ask yourself whether you have said enough about your subject to satisfy the reader. Remember, you are now the reader; remind yourself to respond as such. If you've encountered disorienting gaps in thought, inadequate development of ideas, or insufficient examples, then clearly your first revision strategy will be *to add*. Beyond that you may well be required to *reorganize, delete, alter,* and *correct*. These are the five basic revision strategies.

FIVE REVISION STRATEGIES

Let's consider these strategies one at a time since that is precisely how the revision process must proceed: problem by problem, conveniently grouped together under five main headings. In all cases the "Style Guide" of *Twenty Questions* willl provide guidance on such specific questions as how to revise unwieldy sentences; develop paragraphs; check mechanics. (Use the Index and Table of Contents to find the appropriate sections.)

Addition

Addition is obviously a basic aspect of revision. It includes all insertions into the first draft. They may range from the addition of a one word image-making modifier (a *gray* sky) to the enrichment of an enlivening one-sentence example ("The grandfather clock, for instance, was worth at least $5,000—and that was only one item of her inheritance") to the addition of a full paragraph of causal explanation. The writer should read through every first draft very carefully with this question in mind: "Have I said enough on the subject? What added details, facts, statistics—research data, reasons, examples, illustrations, quotations, or allusions would add substance and further credibility and authority?" Professional writers testify to the value of writing from abundance. Although the first draft will necessarily represent a screening process (since far more information is generally assembled than the writer can incorporate into the finished piece), every writer should make sure that nothing that *belongs* in the piece—that will enhance it—has been left out.

Since gaps in thought are a recurring problem in student writing (in all writing, actually), you should "fill them in" with needed matter or with suitable transitional devices (see pages 113–16). Sometimes, in order to make necessary connections, you may have to generate new materials; you may have to think more deeply, or return to the library for a missing link of information. The medical student cited earlier (pages 87–95) needed to locate and render explicit a missing link of awareness, for in his first draft he had not realized that his second reason for wanting to be a doctor appeared to contradict his first reason, making him sound either hypocritical or foolishly naive. By adding an explanation, this student was able to convey more accurately and sympathetically what he had in mind. Only then was the intended idea in *his mind* capable of being transmitted to the *mind of the reader*. His purpose, after all, was not merely to express his ideas but to communicate them.

Reorganization

Reorganization is closely related to addition as a revising strategy. Just as one entire first reading of the first draft should test its content—what the paper is all about—so another reading should test its organization and possible reorganization. Perhaps you should move up page eight (otherwise the reader will have to wait too long for important information); or reverse pages three and four; perhaps an early fore-shadowing paragraph tells too much too soon; perhaps the overall organization does not "hold up" and you need to reorganize the whole paper.

You are now reviewing (re-viewing) the outer shape of your paper, studying it closely to determine whether it is a logical, efficient structure. You need to ask such questions as: Is the outer structure compatible with the inner parts? Are the inner parts compatible with one another?

A good place to begin such considerations is with the introduction and conclusion which frame the piece and serve as anchors. Ask yourself the following questions:

1. Is the introduction interesting? Provocative? An accurate and appropriate preparation for what follows?
2. Does the conclusion serve as an effective "wrap up"? Does it project a sense of closure and completeness?
3. Have I arranged the materials of the paper in a logical and readable order?
4. Do the parts flow smoothly and coherently into one another—*without* jarring breaks or unexplained turns of thought? *With* graceful transitions?
5. Does each paragraph contain material that clearly belongs to that paragraph? Or should I move some passages elsewhere?
6. Does the paragraph sequence accurately reflect the relationship of the paragraphs to one another? Should I combine any paragraphs? Or break them up? Or reposition them to an earlier or later place?

7. Have I organized the paragraphs coherently within themselves? Do they have clearly stated topic sentences, followed by sentences arranged in logical order? (see Christensen on coordinate and subordinate sequence, pages 121–26.)

Deletion

Once you feel that your organization—or reorganization—is satisfactory, begin to "tighten" at all levels by deleting what you do not need. Whenever possible cut out a solid block of material that does not develop or directly relate to the main thrust of your piece; similarly, cut back on all materials and sentence elements that slow the main action, blur the main point, impede the smooth flow. The importance of economy has been stressed throughout this text. Begin, then, by reviewing those sections that deal specifically with the war on wordiness. Note, at the outset (page 5) E. B. White's rousing "call to arms"; it is worth repeating here:

> A sentence should contain no unnecessary words, a paragraph no unnecessary sentences, for the same reason that a drawing should have no unnecessary lines and a machine no unnecessary parts. This requires not that the writer make all his sentences short or that he avoid all detail…but that every word tell.

In short, as E. B. White exhorts: *let every word tell.*

As a warm-up to this cycle of revision, review the principles of sentence economy. They will sensitize you to clutter, a blight on all prose writing, fiction and nonfiction (pages 568–72):

> unnecessary words
> useless repetition
> ineffective intensifiers (*rather, somewhat*)
> anticipatory phrases (*there is, it was*)
> redundancy
> deadwood ("fatty deposits")

Alteration

Closely related to deletion as a way of tightening your prose is *alteration*—revising to brighten as well as tighten; to strengthen, clarify, enliven; to render more rhythmic, more graceful, more cogent. On the sentence level (see pages 576–84) you should make up your mind to accomplish the following:

> To condense long sentence elements and reduce piled-up prepositional phrases.
> To convert negative to positive phrasing.
> To establish proper emphasis.
> To vary word order, sentence length and pattern.
> To use active rather than passive voice wherever possible.
> To invigorate verbs: Avoid weak forms of "to be."

To put the action of the sentence into the verb.
To subordinate whenever possible.

Beyond this, you should check to make certain you have not violated sentence integrity through one of the following:

careless sentence fragments
comma splice
fused sentences

Equally distracting are the "seven deadly sins of rhetoric," so-called because they are so pervasive, so easy to "fall into":

unnecessary splits
dangling and otherwise misplaced modifiers
failure in subject-verb agreement
faulty parallelism
unnecessary shifts in subject
faulty or ambiguous pronoun reference
mixed constructions

Moving into a consideration of individual words (see pages 523–34) you should test yourself by asking the following questions:

Have I chosen words aptly and accurately, with a sensitivity to connotation?
Have I used suitable synonyms to avoid needless repetition?
Have I avoided long and pretentious words, preferring the more direct and natural?
Have I avoided jargon and clichés?

Correction

It will be convenient for us to review matters of correctness under two main headings: the factual and the grammatical.

Factual: You should check your notes to make certain that you have properly transcribed your facts, accurately reproduced your statistics, and presented in your quotations a fair rendering of what actually was said. You should also check bibliographical items whenever you have a question as to date of publication, page number, and authorship.

Grammatical: To make certain your sentences are grammatically correct, review the section dealing with rules and guidelines (pages 536–55.) Take the grammar quiz (pages 585–86) as a test of your competence. Most important, read your sentences aloud—once again—so that your ear can respond to possible lapses. Most students can hear a grammatical error more readily than they can see it.

Beyond these categories of the factual and the grammatical, we find ourselves entering the realm of copyediting.

Copyediting:
A Guide

CHECKING AND PROOFREADING

CASE STUDY OF REVISION

   Inaugural Address, John F. Kennedy

   Writing and Rewriting the Inaugural Address,
     Theodore Sorensen

CHECKING AND PROOFREADING

*W*hen we address ourselves to mechanical concerns—when we turn our attention to such issues as punctuation, capitalization, abbreviation and contractions, spelling—we are concerned with the copyediting process. Although you have undoubtedly spotted errors all along—during your first rereading of the first draft and even earlier as you read completed sections of the paper—you should now plan on a special run-through devoted solely to checking and standardizing mechanical details.

Move through your paper slowly, line by line, word by word, comma by comma, to make certain that you detect and correct not merely the most blatant errors but *all* errors. Where you are uncertain about a usage (colon or semi-colon? capital letter or small case?) consult with the punctuation and general mechanics sections presented on (pages 589–606).

As a last step, when the paper is in the final draft, be sure to proofread carefully. Read the paper with one single purpose: to make certain everything has been set down as you intended, with no accidental omissions, misspellings, typographical errors, and so on. If possible, get a classmate, roommate, friend, or relative to do another proofreading. It is always helpful to get a second set of eyes looking at your paper. By now you are so familiar with what you have written that in your mind you may unconsciously correct errors—adjust misspelling, even fill in a missing line.

CASE STUDY OF REVISION

On January 20, 1961 when John F. Kennedy was sworn in as the 35th president of the United States, he gave an Inaugural Address that has since become a classic, comparable in its impact, its economy, and simple but soaring eloquence to Lincoln's Inaugural Address, delivered a century before. According to Kennedy aide and speechwriter, Theodore Sorensen, Kennedy planned this speech with meticulous care, calling upon many of his aides for advice and suggestions, even though he himself knew what he wanted to say and the general tone he wanted to establish. As Sorensen tells us:

> He wanted it short. He wanted it focused on foreign policy. He did not want it to sound partisan, pessimistic or critical of his predecessor. He wanted neither the customary cold war rhetoric about the Communist menace nor any weasel words that Krushchev might misinterpret. And he wanted it to set a tone for the era about to begin.

That Kennedy achieved his goals has since become a matter of historical record; *how* he achieved them is not as well known: namely, through endlessly painstaking effort. "The easily flowing connection of sentence with sentence and paragraph with paragraph has always been won by the sweat of the brow," said nineteenth-century British historian G. M. Trevelyan. "What is easy to read has been difficult to write," he concluded. This brief, simply stated observation is certainly borne out by the case study reported below: an account of the revision process at work in the preparation of John F. Kennedy's famous inaugural address.

Inaugural Address

John F. Kennedy

Vice-President Johnson, Mr. Speaker, Mr. Chief Justice, President Eisenhower, Vice-President Nixon, President Truman, Reverend Clergy, Fellow Citizens:

We observe today not a victory of party but a celebration of freedom—symbolizing an end as well as a beginning—signifying renewal as well as change. For I have sworn before you and Almighty God the same solemn oath our forebears prescribed nearly a century and three-quarters ago.

The world is very different now. For man holds in his mortal hands the power to abolish all forms of human poverty and all forms of human life. And yet the same revolutionary beliefs for which our forebears fought are still at issue around the globe—the belief that the rights of man come not from the generosity of the state but from the hand of God.

We dare not forget today that we are the heirs of that first revolution. Let the word go forth from this time and place, to friend and foe alike, that the torch has been passed to a new generation of Americans—born in this century, tempered by war, disciplined by a hard and bitter peace, proud of our ancient heritage—and unwilling to witness or permit the slow undoing of those human rights to which this nation has always been committed, and to which we are committed today at home and around the world.

Let every nation know, whether it wishes us well or ill, that we shall pay any price, bear any burden, meet any hardship, support any friend, oppose any foe to assure the survival and the success of liberty.

This much we pledge—and more.

To those old allies whose cultural and spiritual origins we share, we pledge the loyalty of faithful friends. United, there is little we cannot do in a host of co-operative ventures. Divided, there is little we can do—for we dare not meet a powerful challenge at odds and split asunder.

To those new states whom we welcome to the ranks of the free, we pledge our word that one form of colonial control shall not have passed away merely to be replaced by a far more iron tyranny. We shall not always expect to find them supporting our view. But we shall always hope to find them strongly supporting their own freedom—and to remember that, in the past, those who foolishly sought power by riding the back of the tiger ended up inside.

To those people in the huts and villages of half the globe struggling to break the bonds of mass misery, we pledge our best efforts to help them help themselves, for whatever period is required—not because the Communists may be doing it, not because we seek their votes, but because it is right. If a free society cannot help the many who are poor, it cannot save the few who are rich.

To our sister republics south of our border, we offer a special pledge—to convert our good words into good deeds—in a new alliance for progress—to assist free men and free governments in casting off the chains of poverty. But this peaceful revolution of hope cannot become the prey of hostile powers. Let all our neighbors know that we shall join with them to oppose aggression or subversion anywhere in the Americas. And let every other power know that this hemisphere intends to remain the master of its own house.

To that world assembly of sovereign states, the United Nations, our last best hope in an age where the instruments of war have far outpaced the instruments of peace, we renew our pledge of support—to prevent it from becoming merely a forum for invective—to strengthen its shield of the new and the weak—and to enlarge the area in which its writ may run.

Finally, to those nations who would make themselves our adversary, we offer not a pledge but a request: that both sides begin anew the quest for peace, before the dark powers of destruction unleashed by science engulf all humanity in planned or accidental self-destruction.

We dare not tempt them with weakness. For only when our arms are sufficient beyond doubt can we be certain beyond doubt that they will never be employed.

But neither can two great and powerful groups of nations take comfort from our present course—both sides overburdened by the cost of modern weapons, both rightly alarmed by the steady spread of the deadly atom, yet both racing to alter that uncertain balance of terror that stays the hand of mankind's final war.

So let us begin anew—remembering on both sides that civility is not a sign of weakness, and sincerity is always subject to proof. Let us never negotiate out of fear. But let us never fear to negotiate.

Let both sides explore what problems unite us instead of belaboring those problems which divide us.

Let both sides, for the first time, formulate serious and precise proposals for the inspection and control of arms—and bring the absolute power to destroy other nations under the absolute control of all nations.

Let both sides seek to invoke the wonders of science instead of its terrors. Together let us explore the stars, conquer the deserts, eradicate disease, tap the ocean depths, and encourage the arts and commerce.

Let both sides unite to heed in all corners of the earth the command of Isaiah—to "undo the heavy burdens ... [and] let the oppressed go free."

And if a beachhead of co-operation may push back the jungle of suspicion, let both sides join in creating a new endeavor, not a new balance of power, but a new world of law, where the strong are just and the weak secure and the peace preserved.

All this will not be finished in the first one hundred days. Nor will it be finished in the first one thousand days, nor in the life of this administration, nor even perhaps in our lifetime on this planet. But let us begin.

In your hands, my fellow citizens, more than mine, will rest the final success or failure of our course. Since this country was founded, each generation of Americans has been summoned to give testimony to its national loyalty. The graves of young Americans who answered the call to service surround the globe.

Now the trumpet summons us again—not as a call to bear arms, though arms we need—not as a call to battle, though embattled we are—but a call to bear the burden of a long twilight struggle, year in and year out, "rejoicing in hope, patient in tribulation" —a struggle against the common enemies of man: tyranny, poverty, disease, and war itself.

Can we forge against these enemies a grand and global alliance, North and South, East and West, that can assure a more fruitful life for all mankind? Will you join in that historic effort?

In the long history of the world, only a few generations have been granted the role of defending freedom in its hour of maximum danger. I do not shrink from this responsibility—I welcome it. I do not believe that any of us would exchange places with any other people or any other generation. The energy, the faith, the devotion which we bring to this endeavor will light our country and all who serve it—and the glow from that fire can truly light the world.

And so, my fellow Americans: ask not what your country can do for you—ask what you can do for your country.

My fellow citizens of the world: ask not what America will do for you, but what together we can do for the freedom of man.

Finally, whether you are citizens of America or citizens of the world, ask of us here the same high standards of strength and sacrifice which we ask of you. With a good conscience our only sure reward, with history the final judge of our deeds, let us go forth to lead the land we love, asking His blessing and His help, but knowing that here on earth God's work must truly be our own.

Writing and Rewriting the Inaugural Address

A Report on the Process

Theodore Sorensen

Early in January, with work on his program well under way and his principal nominees named, the President-elect's thoughts turned more and more to his inauguration. He took a lively interest in plans for the Inaugural Concert and five simultaneous Inaugural Balls (all of which he would attend), in plans for the four-hour-long Inaugural Parade (all of which he would watch in twenty-degree temperature), the million-dollar Democratic fund-raising Inaugural Gala (which he greatly enjoyed, despite a two-hour delay due to blizzards) and in all the other festivities. He asked Robert Frost to deliver a poem at the inauguration ceremony. He wanted Marian Anderson to sing "The Star-Spangled Banner." He sought a family Bible on which he could take the oath of office without arousing the POAU. He indicated that top hats instead of Homburgs would be in order for the official party. And, finally and most importantly, he began to work on his Inaugural Address.

He had first mentioned it to me in November. He wanted suggestions from everyone. He wanted it short. He wanted it focused on foreign policy. He did not want it to sound partisan, pessimistic or critical of his predecessor. He wanted neither the customary cold war rhetoric about the Communist menace nor any weasel words that Khrushchev might misinterpret. And he wanted it to set a tone for the era about to begin.

He asked me to read all the past Inaugural Addresses (which I discovered to be a largely undistinguished lot, with some of the best eloquence emanating from some of our worst Presidents). He asked me to study the secret of Lincoln's Gettysburg Address (my conclusion, which his Inaugural applied, was that Lincoln never used a two- or three-syllable word where a one-syllable word would do, and never used two or three words where one word would do).

Actual drafting did not get under way until the week before it was due. As had been true of his acceptance speech at Los Angeles, pages, paragraphs and complete drafts had poured in, solicited from Kraft, Galbraith, Stevenson, Bowles and others, unsolicited from newsmen, friends and total strangers. From Billy Graham he obtained a list of possible Biblical quotations, and I secured a similar list from the director of Washington's Jewish Community Council, Isaac Franck.

The final text included several phrases, sentences and themes suggested by these sources, as did his address to the Massachusetts legislature. He was, in fact, concerned that the Massachusetts speech had preempted some of his best material and had set a mark that would be hard to top. Credit should also go to other Kennedy advisers who reviewed the early drafts and offered suggestions or encouragement.

But however numerous the assistant artisans, the principal architect of the Inaugural Address was John Fitzgerald Kennedy. Many of its most memorable passages can be traced to earlier Kennedy speeches and writings. For example:

Inaugural Address	*Other Addresses*
For man holds in his mortal hands the power to abolish all forms of human poverty and all forms of human life.	...man...has taken into his mortal hands the power to exterminate the entire species some seven times over. *Acceptance speech at Los Angeles*
...the torch has been passed to a new generation of Americans....	It is time, in short, for a new generation of Americans. *Acceptance speech and several campaign speeches*
And so, my fellow Americans, ask not what your country can do for you; ask what you can do for your country.	We do not campaign stressing what our country is going to do for us as a people. We stress what we can do for the country, all of us. *Televised campaign address from Washington, Sept. 20, 1960*

No Kennedy speech ever underwent so many drafts. Each paragraph was reworded, reworked and reduced. The following table illustrates the attention paid to detailed changes:

First Draft	*Next-to-Last Draft*	*Final Text*
We celebrate today not a victory of party but the sacrament of democracy.	We celebrate today not a victory of party but a convention of freedom.	We observe today not a victory of party but a celebration of freedom.
Each of us, whether we hold office or not, shares the responsibility for guiding this most difficult of all societies along the path of self-discipline and self-government.	In your hands, my fellow citizens, more than in mine, will be determined the success or failure of our course.	In your hands, my fellow citizens, more than mine, will rest the final success or failure of our course.

First Draft	*Next-to-Last Draft*	*Final Text*

First Draft

Nor can two great and powerful nations forever continue on this reckless course, both overburdened by the staggering cost of modern weapons...

And if the fruits of cooperation prove sweeter than the dregs of suspicion, let both sides join ultimately in creating a true world order—neither a Pax Americana, nor a Pax Russiana, nor even a balance of power—but a community of power.

Next-to-Last Draft

...neither can two great and powerful nations long endure their present reckless course, both overburdened by the staggering cost of modern weapons...

And if a beachhead of cooperation can be made in the jungles of suspicion, let both sides join some day in creating, not a new balance of power but a new world of law...

Final Text

...neither can two great and powerful groups of nations take comfort from our present course—both sides overburdened by the cost of modern weapons...

And if a beachhead of cooperation can push back the jungle of suspicion, let both sides join in creating a new endeavor, not a new balance of power, but a new world of law...

Initially, while he worked on his thoughts at Palm Beach, I worked at my home in a Washington suburb with telephoned instructions from the President-elect and the material collected from other sources. Then I flew down, was driven to his father's oceanside home, and gave him my notes for the actual drafting and assembling. We worked through the morning seated on the patio overlooking the Atlantic.

He was dissatisfied with each attempt to outline domestic goals. It sounded partisan, he said, divisive, too much like the campaign. Finally he said, "Let's drop out the domestic stuff altogther. It's too long anyway." He wanted it to be the shortest in the twentieth century, he said. "It's more effective that way and I don't want people to think I'm a windbag." He couldn't beat FDR's abbreviated wartime remarks in 1944, I said—and he settled for the shortest (less than nineteen hundred words) since 1905.

"I'm sick of reading how we're planning another 'hundred days' of miracles," he said, "and I'd like to know who on the staff is talking that up. Let's put in that this won't all be finished in a hundred days or a thousand."

That afternoon, as he was busy with other meetings at the house, I put his notes, changes and additions into a clean draft, working beside the Palm Beach Towers Hotel swimming pool.

The next morning, on the patio in sport clothes, he reworked it further. "Let's eliminate all the "I's," he said. "Just say what 'we' will do. You'll have to leave it in about the oath and the responsibility, but let's cut it everywhere else." The ending, he said, "sounds an awful lot like the ending of the Massachusetts legislature speech, but I guess it's OK." He worked and reworked the "ask not" sentence, with the three campaign speeches containing a similar phrase (Anchorage, Detroit, Washington) spread out on a low glass coffee table beside him.

Later that day—January 17—as we flew back to Washington from Palm Beach, working in his cabin on the *Caroline*, the final phrasing was emerging. A Biblical quotation that was later used in his American University speech was deleted. The opening paragraphs were redictated by the President-elect to Evelyn Lincoln en route, and he similingly placed in the plane's desk drawer his handwritten notes from which he had dictated, saying, "An early draft of Roosevelt's Inaugural was discovered the other day—and brought $200,000 at an auction."

Arriving back in Washington, the work went on at his house and in our Senate offices. Kenneth Galbraith suggested "cooperative ventures" with our allies in place of "joint ventures," which sounded like a mining partnership. Dean Rusk suggested that the other peoples of the world be challenged to ask "what together we can do for freedom" instead of "what you can do for freedom." Walter Lippmann suggested that references to the Communist bloc be changed from "enemy" to "adversary." The President-elect inserted a phrase he had used in a campaign speech on Latin America—"a new alliance for progress." At the last moment, concerned that his emphasis on foreign affairs would be interpreted as an evasion on civil rights, he added to his commitment on human rights the words "at home and around the world."

On January 19, one day before inauguration, it was finished.

DISCUSSION AND EXERCISES

1. Consider Kennedy's Inaugural Address and Sorensen's analysis of the prewriting, writing, and rewriting process—as Kennedy moved through the various stages:

   a. What single sentence in the speech is still widely cited both as a memorable summation of what the speech was all about (its "thesis") and as an exhortation worth repeating to later generations? Is it still timely? Discuss.

   b. If delivered today, would this address be as appropriate to world conditions as it was twenty years ago? In what way? What problems still exist? Are specific problems and programs the main feature and "thrust" of this address? If not, what does seem to you to be the essential purpose Kennedy was trying to fulfill?

   c. Discuss the several audiences Kennedy addresses in the course of the speech—over and beyond the specific audience he formally addresses—the public officials and "Fellow Citizens" cited at the outset. Discuss Kennedy's tone: does it change as he moves from one audience to another? What underlying feature of tone remains consistent? Why was tone especially important in this address?

   d. Why did Kennedy want his address "to be the shortest in the twentieth century"? Do you agree with his reasons? Explain. What kind of considerations did he eliminate from the address in order to keep it short? Was he justified, in your opinion?

   e. Sorensen tells us that Kennedy "wanted suggestions from everyone" before he began composing his speech. Comment on this and any other features of "prewriting" that Sorensen describes.

   f. What is Sorensen referring to when he says that "the principal architect of the Inaugural Address was John Fitzgerald Kennedy"? Why does Sorensen bother making this point?

   g. Comment on the three passages Kennedy incorporated from earlier addresses. What made them worth drawing on a second time? How did he change them? What did he achieve by the changes? Are they improvements, in your opinion?

   h. Trace the successive versions of the four passages drawn from Kennedy's first, next-to-last, and final drafts. How do the various word changes, additions, and deletions strengthen the passages?

   i. Proceed through the speech paragraph by paragraph, noting the rhetorical features that have made it a "classic." How do they function? Concentrate especially on the following:

      1. opening and closing sections
      2. parallel constructions

3. balanced antithesis
4. paragraph length
5. one-sentence paragraphs
6. variety in sentence length and type (note questions, and imperatives, as well as declarative statements)
7. long and short sentences
8. sentence rhythm
9. transitions
10. word repetitions
11. precision in the choice of words
12. alliteration

j. How does the fact that the Inaugural Address was written primarily to be read aloud influence the writing? What specific rhetorical features reflect its form and purpose as a *speech* rather than an article or position paper?

PRINCIPLES OF STYLE: A GUIDE

The Limits
of Language

LANGUAGE IS REMOVED FROM REALITY

*I*n his Second Meditation, the French philosopher René Descartes complained that "words often impede me." It is difficult to imagine what unutterable insights, what wordless thoughts (if such is possible) this most original of thinkers was contemplating when he made this paradoxical complaint. T. S. Eliot echoed this complaint three hundred years later in a great comic-tragic line: "I gotta use words when I talk to you."

Yes, we all "gotta use words." Philosophers and scientists have demonstrated that without the ordering convention of words, we would be overwhelmed by what William James called the "booming, buzzing confusion" of real life. In the world "out there" nothing stands still long enough to be named; "Stately Nature" is in actual, measurable fact a dynamic, ongoing process; "objects" are really "events" flowing into one another by insensible gradations. Our words are still-cameras that artificially freeze reality, making us believe that it conforms to the linear, cause-and-effect structure of our language. But language is removed from reality and, in fact, imposes a pattern on reality that is essentially a distortion. Semanticist Alfred Korzybski vividly illustrates this point:

> If we take something, anything, let us say the object ... called "pencil" and enquire what it represents ... we find that the "scientific object" represents an "event," a mad dance of "electrons," which is different every instant, which never repeats itself, which is known to consist of extremely complex dynamic processes of very fine structure, acted upon by and reacting upon the rest of the universe, inextricably connected with everything else and dependent on everything else. If we enquire *how many characteristics* we should ascribe to such an event, the only possible answer ... is that we should ascribe to an event infinite numbers of characteristics (387).

Clearly ascribing to an event an infinite number of characteristics is impossible: Time is too short; words are too few. In order, then, to cope with the world "out there" (and the world within as well, for there is a "mad dance of 'electrons'" going on within as well as outside us), we must change it; we must somehow stop the world long enough to make contact with it and with one another. So we select and simplify, with the help, first of all, of our senses, which compress time, mass, motion, light, and sound to cut us off from much of what is going on. What is, in reality, an incessant process, we simply see as an object. And we call that object by a name, thereby simplifying still further. These dancing atoms we designate "rock"; that vast mass of gases spinning in space we designate "star." We name these things as if they were fixed entities, unchanging from one moment to the next.

But obviously *the word is not the thing*. The thing itself is beyond our grasp to know or talk about. In addition to scientists, philosophers, and semanticists, poets and writers emphasize this point; for they too sense that in talking about the world—as opposed to directly experiencing it—we somehow shape it into something different:

> In the way you speak
> You arrange, the thing is posed
> What in nature merely grows.
> —Wallace Stevens, "The Idea of Order at Key West"

WORDS ARE GENERALIZATIONS

Language both helps and hinders us in our attempt to know the world. It helps by freezing the infinite, ongoing process of reality into fixed, finite objects. It also helps by enabling us to generalize about these objects, for, again, we could not have a name for every separate object in the world; every idea, every thought that passes through the mind of every person; every feeling, every sensation, every emotion. To make our world intelligible, we must group things together into categories so that every work (with the exception of proper nouns) is a class word or generalization, representing not one particular idea, object, person, or action, but a whole class of ideas, objects, persons, or actions.

Thus verbs are class words; each one points to a class of actions characterized by certain features: "to jump" is to engage in an action marked by a propulsive leap from the ground, repeated in bobbing, bouncing up-and-down movements of the legs and entire body. All actions sharing these particular features are thereby classified, categorized, abstracted, and generalized in the verb "jump." Likewise, nouns name a cluster of qualities that "sum up" an object; for example, a "dog": a furry, barking, four-legged, carnivorous, domesticated mammal. Every noun represents a list of qualities that, according to the abstracting process of our own minds, a group of objects have in common. Even function words like "and" and "to" perform a class function in that "and" joins together like grammatical elements and "to" indicates a relationship.

Words, then, are simply "convenient capsules of thought" that tell us what the members of a class have in common ("house"), but do not tell us anything about the differences (how my house differs from yours and a dozen other houses on the street). As T. S. Eliot observed, "The particular has no language."

Here is a curious predicament indeed. The most frustrating of limitations characterizes our most important means of communication: its generalizing tendency is always drawing us away from the particular thing we want to say. To achieve particularity, we must actively and constantly counteract this inherent resistance of language; we must use all the devices against it that we can command, so that we do not end up in realms of abstraction where no one knows exactly what anyone else is talking about. This happens all too often when we deal with abstract words such as the word "nature." One observer noticed that Western philosophers were using "nature" in no less than thirty-nine different senses and that some authors used it two or three different ways on the same page. What, then, does "nature" mean? Anyone using words at this level of abstraction should follow Cicero's counsel that every rational discourse begin with a definition.

This generalizing tendency of language has played into the hands of the prejudiced by enabling them to make sweeping statements and judgments about whole groups of people, treating them as if they were a single entity rather than an aggregate of individuals ("All conservatives are reactionary"). A group may be identified on the basis of race, religion, political affiliation, geographical location, nationality—whatever. The fallacy lies in not seeing that each member of a group—*any* group—is different from every other member, is indeed unique. Semanticist Alfred Korzybski has suggested that as an exercise we remind ourselves of this fact by adding index numbers to our general nouns. Then we would see, he says, that cow_1 is not cow_2; $Italian_1$ is not $Italian_2$; Jew_1 is not Jew_2; $politician_1$ is not $politician_2$. Apart from such obvious and harmless generalizations as "Cows give milk" or "Jews are a minority group," we should then avoid sweeping pronouncements.

LANGUAGE IS SUBJECTIVE

Another limit of language is that it is one of the most intensely subjective of media. No one can speak with total objectivity; there is no such thing as neutral language. The first person singular, whether or not it appears explicitly as "I," is implicit in every statement we make. Thus physicist P. W. Bridgeman observed:

> When I make a statement, even as cold and impersonal a statement as a proposition of Euclid, it is I that am making the statement, and the fact that it is I that am making the statement is part of the picture which is not to be discarded. And when I quote you it is I that am doing the quoting (42).

"We never get away from ourselves," concludes Bridgeman. "The brain that tries to understand is itself part of the world that it is trying to understand." No wonder then that we never "transcend the human reference point." We always filter words through our minds and emotions, so that we alone endow them with their special meaning for that situation; we have something "in mind." when we use words.

In their classic study of semantics, *The Meaning of Meaning*, C. K. Ogden and I. A. Richards constructed a "triangle of meaning" to illustrate the subjectivity of language. Semanticist Bess Sondel later "animated" and commented upon the diagram on page 515.

> At the peak of the "triangle" is a human being. Here is either the user of words—the person who has selected the words—or the recipient of the words who must, from his perspective, entertain those words.
> There is no base in this "triangle."
> There is no direct relation between words and things.
> Consider yourself at the peak of that "triangle." As you use the word "chair," if your thoughts and mine are directed to the same object out there in the world, then you and I come together—we communicate through the use of the word "chair." We "understand" each other (48–49).

But let us say that your thoughts and mine are *not* directed toward the same object. As we have seen, words are so general that they cannot automatically conjure up identical "referents" in different minds. Before they are referred outward to the real thing, words make a trip through the nervous system of a human being. Thus, as the triangle of meaning makes clear, the circuit of meaning is not completed until words

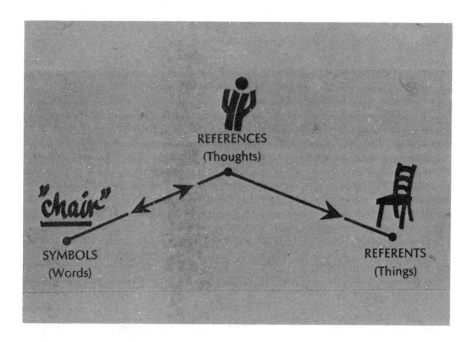

filter through the mind of an individual. The thought, then, stands between the word and the thing, even as the cartoon person at the peak of the triangle stands between the Words and the Things they refer to "out there" in the external world.

The nature of language, then, and the nature of the human constitution prevent us from ever achieving *total* communication. We can only do the best we can with what we have, and what we have, as we have seen, is flawed. Words distort reality, and we distort words by being inescapably subjective. We are also inescapably emotional—words never come to us as pure thought, but always as thought encased in sensation, attitude, mood, memory.

DENOTATION AND CONNOTATION

These associated overtones of meaning are called the *connotations* of a word, as opposed to the agreed-upon, more or less formal dictionary definition or *denotation*. All words, no matter how bloodless they seem on the surface—words such as "circular" or "flat"—are nonetheless capable of evoking emotional responses. Some words, of course, are richer in connotation than others. Take the word "house," for example, a relatively straightforward term referring to a dwelling place, a physical structure. Now take the word "home"; it too refers to a dwelling place, but the connotations of this word suggest the special place it is: the place where the family lives, where, as Robert Frost wrote, "when you have to go there they have to take you in." On Christmas and Easter vacations, you do not go to a house; you go home.

Many words change in connotation over time. The word "discrimination," for example, was once an admiring reference to a person's taste. Today, however, it may suggest bigotry. Similarly, the word "propaganda" once suggested a reliable and trustworthy source of information; now it implies thought manipulation and deception. Semantic games result from juggling with the connotations of words, as in Bertrand Russell's famous "I am firm; you are stubborn; he is pig-headed." All three terms have more or less the same *core* meaning (denotation); by cleverly manipulating the *overtone* of meaning (connotation), users can shade their statements into a commendation or a criticism. Consider the following pairs of words, which have essentially the same denotation. Do they mean the same thing, though?

debate	dispute	antique	old-fashioned
relax	loaf	slender	skinny
reflect	daydream	voluptuous	fat
carefree	unconcerned	restrained	repressed
statesman	politician	chatting	yakking
sweet	saccharine	intellectual	egghead
childlike	childish		

In most contexts the connotations of the words in the left columns would be favorable, whereas those in the right would be less favorable. You can see how useful and dangerous a tool connotation can be in the hands of those who would like to misinform without really lying. For example, during the late 1940s a news magazine, openly Republican in policy, would refer repeatedly to Democratic President Truman's friends as "cronies" (suggesting backroom, poker-playing types). Later, when Republican President Eisenhower was in office, however, the magazine spoke solemnly and respectfully of the president's "long-time associates" (suggesting dignified colleagues in high political office).

One of the strangest, most tragic accounts of mistaken connotation comes out of the Second World War. It involves a reply reportedly received through the official news agency of Japan in response to the surrender ultimatum issued by the Allies at Potsdam. The reply contained the Japanese word *mokusatsu*, which the Domei agency translated into the English word "ignore," thereby implying that the Emperor's regime would not consider surrender under any circumstances. In truth, however, the word *mokusatsu* suggests that one is not flatly dismissing or *ignoring* but only "reserving an answer until a decision is reached." If this careless translation of *mokusatsu*, which failed to incorporate the special connotations of this word, did in fact "confirm America's resolve to drop the atomic bomb, the error may well have been the most costly linguistic blunder in human history" (Girsdansky, 88).

EXTENDING THE LIMITS

By recognizing the limits of language we can begin extending them as well; we can begin making effective compensations. Aldous Huxley once noted that although no complete solution is possible for the problems language poses, the alternative need not be despair (the either-or fallacy). We can approach a language problem, the ambiguity of words, for example, "armed with suitable equipment to deal with it." In this way ambiguous words may be "considerably clarified"; a more modest goal than absolute clarity, to be sure, but with this advantage: It is obtainable.

Aristotle said, "It is the mark of an educated man to look for precision in each class of things just so far as the nature of the subject admits." The writer could adopt no better counsel, for without precision there is no possibility of communication. Sometimes we *think* we are communicating because words are going back and forth. But this is no test of communication; people can and often do talk at cross-purposes, answering questions that have not been asked, attacking arguments that have not been proposed. In other words, people can and often do talk *at* each other, without realizing that they are not talking about the same thing, without even knowing precisely what they *are* talking about:

> "The heart sees farther than the head," says Debater A.
> "Oh no," protests Debater B. "That's a blatantly romantic notion."
> "I don't think it's at all romantic. It's an experiential truth that's been demonstrated time and time again."
> "I regard it as immature and dangerous. All thought and action should be controlled by the head."

Is there a real argument going on here? Who can tell? Who can even know what the debaters are talking about until they specify what they mean by such abstractions as "Romantic" (one of the most protean terms in all of literature, criticism, history, art, and popular usage). And what is an "Experiential Truth" in this context? In what sense is it "Dangerous"?

In "A Note on Methods of Analysis," Professor Herbert J. Muller warns against discussions of this kind:

> The assertion that the Heart sees farther than the Head gets us nowhere, until we specify what kind of thing it sees better, under what circumstances, for what purposes—always remembering that heart and head see in conjunction, and are not engaged in a seeing contest.

The crucial test of communication, then, is not whether words are going back and forth, but whether ideas are being exchanged. Is there a crossing-over between one mind and another? A giving and receiving, not just a giving of information? After all, communication is a circular and not a linear process. Since I must make the case for precision emphatically, I include it here as one means of extending that most serious of all limits of language: its tendency to raise us to realms of abstraction where no one knows precisely what anyone else is talking about.

In *The Meaning of Meaning*, Ogden and Richards set up a "new science of symbolism" in which they rejected all general words that have no "concrete referent"—no object, situation, or event that could be pointed to as the external "thing" for which the word stands. Such words ("faith," "loyalty," "beauty") are not real symbols, said Ogden and Richards, but only expressions of emotion, not appropriate in a "language of fact."

> This distinction between symbolic and emotive language is not intended by these authors to depreciate emotive language. Emotive language is conceded by Ogden and Richards to have its usefulness in the communication process. It may be used, they say, to evoke desired attitudes in others or to incite others to action of one kind or another. But emotive language has no place in the new science of symbolism.

> Ogden and Richards are interested only in the correspondence of words and thoughts and things, and the language of science is set up as the exemplar of their theories. In the language of science, the words refer specifically and definitely and accurately to things, and this without the intrusion of the reporter's attitudes. A reporter doesn't say *It's hot today.* He says *The temperature is ninety degrees according to that thermometer.* The language of science is symbolic language at its best. (Sondel, 44)

Obviously Ogden and Richards set standards for a "language of fact" that the nonscientist may find overly rigid and restrictive (and that some scientists, like Bridgeman, quoted on page 514, do not agree with). Even so, when you are writing an expository essay, the primary purpose of which is to inform and explain, you should observe rigorous standards of fact to help sharpen your prose. You should also develop the important habit of distrusting the lofty abstractions and sweeping generalizations that give the *sound* of meaning but not the substance.

To review briefly: The nature of language and our own human nature are such that communication can never be more than approximate; we never deliver an idea directly (mind-to-mind) without contamination. Under the best of circumstances and with the best of intentions our words can constrain, constrict, and even distort meaning. Imagine, then, what happens when circumstances are *not* of the best and when intentions are *not* honest, when someone makes a deliberate attempt to deceive.

This is the problem to which professional semanticists address themselves, for they recognize that we use language not only to formulate our highest ideals and aspirations but also to justify our basest motives and our meanest behavior. Thus semanticists like Stuart Chase warn against "the tyranny of word": linguistic manipulations by advertisers, propagandists, demagogues, who try to control our behavior by stirring emotion rather than thought, thereby eliciting an uncritical conditioned response. Such manipulators use language for directive rather than communicative purposes. For words that convey absolutely no information may direct us, as if by hypnosis, to vote for candidate A rather than B ("He's the one!"), or to buy a car that will make us "feel like a million."

DEVELOPING SEMANTIC SOPHISTICATION

Our only protection against manipulations of this kind is our own semantic sophistication. We must be able to see through verbal tricks; we must recognize that language lends itself to subtle misrepresentation and sinister manipulation. If we are not aware of this, we will surely be victimized by it. Note how the dictator in the following story misuses language to promote his own dark purposes:

> A dictator rules a land. In the morning he orders that the able-bodied men of three villages be required to crush rock and construct roads of it. They are to work indefinitely and without pay. All other villagers, old men, all women and children, are lined up and machine-gunned. All of the villagers' goods are confiscated.
>
> In the evening the dictator speaks over the radio, telling of his morning's work. He says, "I have readjusted the population proportion in the north. I have arranged for the

more rapid and efficient improvement of our country's transportation system. I have arranged to have available a greater per capita supply of the basic necessities of life." The populace cheers. (Lord, 61)

Obviously, the populace does not know what it is cheering *for*. People think the dictator has given them the facts, but in truth he has grievously misled them. They are both uninformed and misinformed.

In our reading and listening, then—as in our writing—we must develop semantic sophistication; we must test words against the rigorous standards of fact (referents). Unless we do this, we become symbol worshippers. It is easy to become a symbol worshipper because most of the time many of us do not and cannot adhere to the strict language of fact that scientists and semanticists recommend. Instead we may get so caught up in the connotations of a word that we refuse to accept a fact that does not concur with our feelings. Thus a young woman was heard to protest a news story about a woman who had murdered her child, maintaining that it was "impossible for a *Mother* to do such a thing!"

We can extend the semantic limits of language only by extending the limits of our own critical intelligence. We must not allow words to mesmerize us. Only if we understand how others may use language against us can we hold our own against those who would deceive and mislead. Only if we understand how language can help solve rather than perpetuate problems, promote rather than impede understanding, can we aspire to "mutual communication and possible consensus."

WRITING VERSUS SPEECH

The last aspect of language I want to touch on is the special limits of writing (words on paper) as opposed to speech (words in the air). Both are language, of course, and both are therefore subject to the limits inherent in the medium itself and in ourselves. But writing deserves special attention. Writing is a special way of using language that has its own obvious strengths (it endures, for one thing, while speech drifts off into empty space), and its own not-so-obvious, very serious limitations.

Writing is flat, one-dimensional. Try raising your voice on paper. Well, maybe you can manage that with capital letters: LOOK, I'M RAISING MY VOICE! Very good. Now try raising your eyebrows on paper. Ah, you are stuck! But surely you are familiar with this gesture; it is so expressive that it has become part of our language: To raise one's eyebrows is to be disapproving, skeptical—or something like that. Translating into words the unstudied eloquence of that gesture—or others like it—lowering your eyes, closing them, lifting, narrowing, fluttering, rolling, winking—is impossible. You can carry on an extended conversation with someone with your eyes.

This is true of all the expressive features that supplement the spoken word: facial expressions (pursing the lips in stubborn defiance); body movements (a shrug of the shoulders); and most important, variations in the voice ("Is he *crazy*?" versus "Is *he* crazy?"). Loudness, stress, pitch, pause: all these expressive features, and many more, enter into every spoken sentence and impart to it a distinctive tone and point of view—all of which are absent on the written page where words stand alone, bearing the full burden of meaning.

Thus written English, an "artificial dialect of speech," as linguist Harold Whitehall called it, "must be so managed that it compensates for what it lacks." To begin with, we must organize written language more carefully than talk, for in discussing a subject orally, we may shift back and forth, digress, repeat ourselves, and even fall into contradiction. The other person is there to issue a direct challenge ("But you said earlier it was an ethical question, and now you're saying it's basically psychological"); or to ask a question ("I don't understand what you mean by 'diminishing returns.' Would you explain that term?"); or to pick up cues ("That half-smile on your face suggests that you are not completely serious...."). The reader, sitting alone with an article or book, has no such opportunity to observe signs or to ask for further information; nor does the writer have a second chance to clarify a point or to safeguard a meaning.

Thus the writer must be more painstaking than the speaker. As Quintilian said centuries ago, the writer must aim not merely "at being possible to understand, but at being impossible to misunderstand." And this the writer must do in the absence of personality and without the assistance of gestures, tone of voice, or timing. In truth, the writer can never make up for the many deficiencies of writing as compared to speaking; he or she can only make amends.

Specifically, the writer can try to anticipate the reader's questions and possible points of confusion; the writer can also organize the material carefully so that point follows point in reasonable, understandable, logical sequence.

Still a third consideration: the writer must be more concise and compressed than the speaker. A group of people can enjoy two or three hours of conversation, exchanging tens of thousands of words; but few people would be willing to spend an equal number of hours reading an equivalent number of words on a subject, if their book did not provide substantially more information than their conversation. For the writer, then, economy is an imperative: *every word must tell.*

Of course, writing has its advantages as well as its shortcomings. For the reader there is the opportunity to proceed slowly or rapidly and to reread what he or she does not understand or would like to understand better. Reading is a private and in some ways more thoughtful activity than listening; certainly it provides an opportunity for greater concentration.

Writing has obvious advantages for the writer, too. What the writer does not say well in the first rough draft, he or she can improve in a later polishing, and the reader will never see the earlier, less successful effort. In conversation or impromptu speech, people—including the writer—think as they talk, talk as they think—at the rate of about 200 to 300 words a minute. The writer can adjust the pace of writing to his or her needs. The writer can think, brood, rearrange, reclassify, rephrase, and delete as the writing goes along—a stuttering and stammering process that would be totally unacceptable in speech.

DISCUSSION AND EXERCISES

1. Language and Reality

   a. Nothing ever happens "again"; the word "again" is a verbal fiction. In a paragraph (150–200 words), explain why this is so, citing other verbal fictions in our language and indicating why most words distort reality.

b. Novelist Virginia Woolf distrusted language because, as she wrote, it draws "neat designs of life ... upon half sheets of notepaper." In a short essay (150–250 words), explain what you think she means by this, comment on her metaphor, and indicate your own sense of how well or poorly language represents ("re-represents") life.

2. The Generalizing Tendency of Language

   a. You can make language more precise in various ways: by quantifying (for example, instead of saying "a large crowd," saying "about 2,000 people"), exemplifying, illustrating, explaining, defining, describing. Using one of the opening sentences suggested below (all generalizations), write a paragraph (150–250 words) in which you provide specific referents for the general term or suggest specific applications to specific situations:

      1. Lincoln claimed that all *progress* may be laid to *discontent.*
      2. "A hungry man," said Montaigne, "would be very foolish to seek to provide himself with a fine garment, rather than a good meal: we must speed to what is *most urgent.*"
      3. Balthasar Gracián once wrote that women are *realists* and men are *romanticists.*
      4. The show was *wonderful.*
      5. Everyone should *work.*
      6. "*Pleasure*" is the main motive for human *action.*

   b. Write two versions of a paragraph based on an activity (such as *eating, dancing, writing poetry*) or a concept (*loyalty, beauty, justice*). In version one, use as many general and emotive words as you wish; in version two, confine yourself exclusively to "the language of fact."

3. The Subjectiveness of Language

   To what extent are we "prisoners of our own experience"? Write a one-paragraph "response" to one or more of the following terms and compare your response with that of another student who has written on the same subject.

auto racing	reading poetry	fighting a lost cause
divorce	a second chance	wounded vanity
falling in love	a salesman	lying
death	a dog	apologizing
writing a paper	hearing a sermon	parting
ballet	making a mistake	dissent

4. Connotations

   Consider the following words, all with good connotations. Cite for each a bad counterpart: a word that means approximately the same thing denotatively but *not* connotatively.

cautious	satisfied	leader
courageous	passion	cooperation
retaliation	discuss	independent
compromise	individualist	patriotism
liberty	clever	reformer
subtle	dissent	nonconformist

The Limits of Language

Choosing Words

THE WRITER'S TOOL

*D*espite the limitations of language, words are the writer's only tool. It is not surprising then that words preoccupy and even obsess the professional writer. Not simply their meaning but their sound, shape, texture, rhythm. Like strains of melody presenting themselves unbidden to the composer, words whirl about in the writer's mind, resound in the inner ear, impinge on the consciousness—as if they were palpable beings with lives of their own. Indeed, some writers even personify words, as the Mexican poet Octovio Paz has done in his observation that

> the easiest thing in the world is to break a word in two. At times the pieces continue to live with a frantic life, ferocious, monosyllabic. It's wonderful to throw that handful of newborns into the circus: they jump, they dance, they bound and rebound, they scream tirelessly, they raise their colored banners.

Ordinary people do not have this almost mystical affinity for words; they do not see them as "colored banners," but rather as conveyors of meaning, and properly so, for it is here that our concern should begin: with words that convey meaning most simply, clearly, and forcefully. Thus, as Lincoln said in his second Inaugural Address:

> With malice toward none, with charity for all, with firmness in the right as God gives us to see the right, let us strive on to finish the work we are in, to bind up the nation's wounds, to care for him who shall have borne the battle and for his widow and his orphan, to do all which may achieve and cherish a just and lasting peace among ourselves and with all nations.

Note the simplicity of the diction here; each word is *right* because it is appropriate not only to the speaker, but also to his subject and to the occasion for the address. There are no long, pretentious adjectives, no vague terms, no clichés, no fiery declamations. The inspired eloquence of the utterance can best be appreciated when we read George Orwell's parody of pretentious language:

> We want to terminate this conflict and have an equitable peace. We do not desire a vindictive peace but one that will restore the country to unity. We believe that we are right and are determined to gain the victory and have a fair peace. After the cessation of hostilities we must not forget to take care of the veterans and the dependents of those killed or wounded in the struggle.

You cannot—on order or even on exhortation—increase your sensitivity to words or enlarge your word-stock. Only as you read and pay attention to words, as words assume a prominent place in your thinking, will the right word be available when you need it; only then will the struggle for that word seem worthwhile. In the meantime, however, you can improve your writing by committing yourself to certain broad categories of words: to the natural word as opposed to the pretentious or trite; to the concrete word as opposed to the vague; to the exact word as opposed to the approximate. We shall consider each of these in turn.

THE NATURAL WORD

Bertrand Russell once advised the young writer never to use a long word if a short one will do. This somewhat sweeping dictum ignores those notable exceptions where a long word has a better sound or helps to establish a better rhythm in the sentence. Even so, the general principle has merit. Certainly we should avoid such pomposities as that reported of Samuel Johnson, who remarked casually and naturally of a comedy he had just seen that "It has not wit enough to keep it sweet." Disturbed by the simplicity of this statement, Dr. Johnson hastily amended it to "It has not vitality enough to preserve it from putrefaction."

We can forgive Dr. Johnson the lapse he viewed as a correction, for the sonorous, elevated style he used was accepted, and generally preferred, in his time. Today, however, it is absurd. Modern prose style is generally straightforward and relaxed, designed to capture the rhythms of everyday speech, to serve readers rather than to impress them, to talk to them rather than to pontificate. The modern prose stylist, as Bonamy Dobrée points out in *Modern Prose Style*, "is trying to be more honest with himself," is aiming at a style "that will faithfully reflect [the] mind as it utters itself naturally."

In this sense, the unknown author of Ecclesiastes was writing in a modern vein when composing the following verse:

> I returned, and saw under the sun, that the race is not to the swift, nor the battle to the strong, neither yet bread to the wise, nor yet riches to men of understanding, nor yet favour to men of skill; but time and chance happeneth to them all.

In his essay "Politics and the English Language" George Orwell praises this passage as an example of "good English"—simple, direct, concrete, smoothly flowing, harmonious, *natural*. By way of contrast Orwell offers a stiff, jargon-ridden variation, written by an imaginary but "typical" bad writer, a stylist of "the worst sort":

> Objective considerations of contemporary phenomena compel the conclusion that success or failure in competitive activities exhibits no tendency to be commensurate with innate capacity, but that a considerable element of the unpredictable must invariably be taken into account.

"This is a parody," Orwell admits, "but not a very gross one." He goes on to explain why Ecclesiastes is preferable:

> It will be seen that I have not made a full translation. The beginning and ending of the sentence follow the original meaning fairly closely, but in the middle the concrete illustrations—race, battle, bread—dissolve into the vague phrase "success or failure in competitive activities." This had to be so, because no modern writer of the kind I am discussing—no one capable of using phrases like "objective consideration of contemporary phenomena"—would ever tabulate his thoughts in that precise and detailed

way.... Now analyse these two sentences a little more closely. The first contains forty-nine words but only sixty syllables, and all its words are those of everyday life. The second contains thirty-eight words of ninety syllables: eighteen of its words are from Latin roots, and one from Greek. The first sentence contains six vivid images, and only one phrase ("time and chance") that could be called vague. The second contains nòt a single fresh, arresting phrase, and in spite of its ninety syllables it gives only a shortened version of the meaning contained in the first. (*Shooting*, 84–85)

In an attempt to be "formal" and to seem properly "authoritative," many students write stiff, dehumanized prose such as that which Orwell parodies. They must repress any impulse to use a word such as "transpire," for example, when they mean "take place." They must also repress the tendency to write phrases like "objective consideration of contemporary phenomena" or "commensurate with innate capacity" or "considerable element of the unpredictable." They only need to read these passages aloud and *listen* to them to know that they are hardly faithful reflections of "the mind as it utters itself naturally."

THE CONCRETE WORD

We have already discussed the generalizing tendency of language (see pages 513–14) which leads us away from clear, unambiguous statement. We saw that one word like "nature," for example, may have as many as thirty-nine specific referents. In addition to raising semantic problems and even dangers, general and abstract terms cause rhetorical problems, for they create dense, lifeless prose lacking in precision and energy. We cannot avoid such prose altogether, for a certain amount of classifying of ideas and experiences is necessary to all discourse. Nonetheless, every time we choose a word we can make a determined effort to be as specific and concrete as the subject will allow. In his *Philosophy of Style*, Herbert Spencer suggested that we avoid sentences like: "In proportion as the manners, customs, and amusements of a nation are cruel and barbarous, the regulations of their penal code will be severe." Instead, said Spencer, we should write a sentence like: "In proportion as men delight in battles, bull-fights, and combats of gladiators, will they punish by hanging, burning, and the rack."

The point to keep in mind is that most people do not think in general or abstract terms but in concrete particulars. Thus when readers encounter generalizations or abstractions, they tend to translate them into specific images of their own choosing. Conscientious writers, who do not want readers filling in their prose for them, will therefore write in concrete images. It is no accident that in Antony's speech over Caesar's body, Shakespeare—who wanted to excite in his audience the utmost horror—has Antony talk in the most highly particularized language: "those honorable men [not who merely *killed* Caesar, but] whose *daggers* have *stabbed* Caesar" (Whately, 322).

The following examples illustrate another way in which the general may be rendered more specific, the abstract more concrete, by adding details:

Example: My father and I argue about everything.

Improvement: My father and I argue about everything from politics and civil rights to the relationship between parents and children.

Example: She looked sensational.

Improvement: She looked sensational in her new purple knit suit, long dangling earrings, and brown leather sandals.

THE ACCURATE WORD

Choosing Words

To use words with any exactness, you must be painstaking. The first word that comes to mind is not always the best one. To try to clarify your meaning by rephrasing what you have just written—prefacing it with "in other words" or "that is to say"—does not help much. The precisely right word used in precisely the right place will say once and for all what you need to say.

Discussing "right" words in the abstract is difficult, for they depend on specific writing situations. Some general principles, however, may be set down.

1. **Make certain that the word you choose is literally correct and used in the customary way.** In the following examples the writers have made nearly right but ultimately wrong choices:

Example: Her selfishness is prevalent throughout the story.

Improvement: Her selfishness is *evident.* . . .

Example: There is a sadness that emits from the character's every action.

Improvement: There is a sadness that *issues.* . . .

Example: I banged my fist on the table, thereby instilling pain throughout my arm.

Improvement: I banged my fist on the table, thereby *inflicting.* . . .

Example: They are utterly ignorant to her fears.

Improvement: They are utterly ignorant *of* her fears.

Example: I found his poems unmeaningful.

Improvement: I found his poems *meaningless.*

Example: He became bitter when the job he was promised never happened.

Improvement: . . . never *came through.*

Example: The fishing trip had a remedial effect on their spirits.

Improvement: The fishing trip had a *restorative effect.* . . .

2. **Choose a word that is appropriate in tone and level of usage (formal, informal, colloquial, slang).** Although modern prose style tends to be informal and relaxed, you

should not introduce words that are clearly out of place in the context of your piece. Certainly anyone with the slightest sensitivity to words will recognize that the verb in the following sentence is ill-chosen.

> Plato's dialogues stuff the student's mind with new ideas.

The verb "stuff" in this sentence clearly has the wrong tone and the wrong connotation for any discourse that is not deliberately ironic. One may *stuff* one's mouth with food or *stuff* a bag with equipment, but readers of Plato do not have their minds *stuffed.*

Similarly, in the following sentence there is an awkward combination of three different levels of usage: formal, informal, and slangy:

> Students remember that despite the multitudinous tasks that confront them, they must somehow get their work done; they cannot permit themselves to goof off, even for a day.

[Today there are no fixed rules governing correctness; slang expressions and colloquialisms are often included in so-called formal writing.] As the National Council of Teachers of English announced in 1952, "All usage is relative." The correct or best expression always depends on many factors: What the writer is saying (a description of a soccer scrimmage or stoic philosophy); how the writer says it (written or spoken); to whom and on what occasion the writer says it (a bull session with a roommate or a presentation of a paper before an honors committee). Ultimately, [the writer must exercise his or her own taste and judgment and a sense of what is appropriate, acceptable, and comfortable in a given context.]

You may consult two recent reference works if you cannot make up your mind about a specific usage:

> Margaret Nicholsen, *A Dictionary of American-English Usage* (New York: Oxford University Press, 1957).

This American adaptation of H. W. Fowler's *Modern English Usage* strikes a sensible balance between purism and permissiveness.

> Margaret M. Bryant, *Current American Usage* (New York: Funk & Wagnalls, 1962).

A survey of 240 disputed points of usage, this book is readable and extremely helpful because it is based on how words are *in fact* being used today, rather than on how the author feels they *should* be used.

3. Choose a word that has suitable connotations. Your own sensitivity to words must be your guide here.

> *Example:* In their simple-mindedness, children are free of racial and religious prejudice.
>
> *Problem:* "Simple-mindedness" suggests that children are foolish, that they simply do not understand the complexities of the situation—and that if they did, they too would be prejudiced.
>
> *Improvement:* In their *innocence*, children are free of racial and religious prejudice. ("Innocence" is preferable here because it suggests—as the writer wanted to suggest—purity rather than ignorance.)

Example:	In his novels Faulkner lashes out at racial prejudice.
Problem:	"Lashes out" implies violence and lack of control.
Improvement:	In his novels Faulkner *attacks* racial prejudice. ("Attack" does not carry the connotation of uncontrollable fury but rather of a more measured and thoughtful action against an opposing evil.)

4. **In an official or formal context, choose the *single, exact* word in place of a series of words.**

Example:	He was introducing considerations that had nothing to do with the case.
Improvement:	He was introducing *extraneous* considerations.

Example:	They cut themselves off from the main group.
Improvement:	They *detached* themselves from the main group.

Example:	There are many factors contributing to the deficiencies in my writing, the most outstanding one being my unwillingness to work.
Improvement:	Many factors contribute to my writing deficiencies, most notably my *laziness.*

5. **Avoid ill-sounding combinations of words.** Although good readers read silently, they "hear" the sounds of the words. You should avoid inadvertent rhymes and words that have the same sound but different meanings (homonyms) because they are distracting.

Example:	Another explanation of his motivation can be found in his observation that . . .
Problem:	Too many *-tion* endings.

Example:	Those who lean toward leniency . . .
Problem:	Awkward repetition of *lean* sound.

Example:	The sole purpose of his soul-searching address was . . .
Problem:	Homonyms.

Example:	It must be clear that the fear of the atmosphere . . .
Problem:	Inadvertent rhyme.

6. **Avoid awkward variations.** "Repetition is bad," said Mark Twain, "but inexactness is worse." Guard against using an inexact or awkward variation of a word simply to avoid repetition.

Example:	Having considered Faulkner's vision, let us now go on to a consideration of the characters who exemplify the theory.
Improvement:	Repeat the word "vision" in place of "theory."

7. **Avoid quaint and archaic terms.**

Example:	We should treat the medium of writing with respect, nay with reverence.
Improvement:	We should treat the medium of writing with respect, *even* (or "as well as" or "indeed") with reverence.

8. Avoid clichés. Note the following conglomerate:

It was a deep dark secret that I would not for the life of me have revealed to a soul; certainly not to any Tom, Dick, or Harry that happened by, like a ship passing in the night.

CLICHÉS

A cliché is an expression that was once original and apt, a new and vivid metaphor, perhaps, that later acquires "an unfortunate popularity." The *Oxford English Dictionary* calls the cliché "a stereotyped expression, a commonplace phrase." We can add to this definition the adjectives "trite," hackneyed," "overworked," "worn out"—"a coin so battered by use as to be defaced" (cited in Partridge, 2).

Some are foreign phrases (*coup de grâce; et tu, Brute*). Some are homely sayings or are based on proverbs ("You can't make an omelet without breaking eggs," *blissful ignorance*). Some are quotations ("To be or not to be, etc."; "Unwept, unhonored, and unsung"). Some are allusions to myth or history (*Gordian knot, Achilles' heel*). Some are alliterative or rhyming phrases (*first and foremost, high and dry*). Some are paradoxes (*in less than no time, conspicuous by its absence*). Some are legalisms (*null and void, each and every*). Some are playful euphemisms (*a fate worse than death, better half*). Some are figurative phrases (*leave no stone unturned, hit the nail on the head*). And some are almost meaningless small change (*in the last analysis, by the same token*). (Bernstein, 104)

You cannot banish clichés altogether from your speech and writing; but **you should weed clichés out of your writing with patience and diligence before they destroy all possibility of meaningful discourse.** Stock phrases are the enemy of thought: people will repeat them mechanically without thinking about what they are saying. Thus the cliché can lead to a kind of mass No-Think.

Because the reader or listener participating in the No-Think of the cliché expects the language to proceed according to a set pattern, humorists twist or reverse the pattern and thwart the expectation. Thus wits have come up with: "She's as pure as the driven slush"; "It is better to have loved and lost then never to have lost at all"; "None but the brave desert the fair"; "Bachelors never make the same mistake once"; "Work is the curse of the drinking class." Bergen Evans has said that these anticlichés are "golden transmutations of some of the world's dullest lead."

FIGURES OF SPEECH

As I discussed earlier (see "The Limits of Language"), language is an abridgment of reality. No language has enough words to express the infinite variety of human ideas, feelings, and experiences. Because people instinctively recognize this, they try to expand and strengthen their power of expression by creating new ways of saying what they mean, specifically by using figures of speech—nonliteral expressions of meaning in which they say one thing in terms of something else.

> I think a poet is just a tree—
> it stands still and rustles its
> leaves; it doesn't expect to lead
> anyone anywhere.
> —Boris Pasternak

When I say, for instance, "That a good man enjoys comfort in the midst of adversity"; I just express my thought in the simplest manner possible. But when I say, "To the upright there ariseth light in darkness"; the same sentiment is expressed in a figurative style; a new circumstance is introduced; light is put in the place of comfort, and darkness is used to suggest the idea of adversity. In the same manner, to say, "It is impossible, by any search we can make, to explore the divine nature fully," is to make a simple proposition. But when we say, "Canst thou, by searching, find out God? Canst thou find out the Almighty to perfection? It is high as heaven, what canst thou do? deeper than hell, what canst thou know?" This introduces a figure into style; the proposition being not only expressed, but admiration and astonishment being expressed together with it.

> —Hugh Blair, *Lectures on Rhetoric and Belles Lettres*

Because figures of speech issue from the deepest recesses of the imagination, they cannot be learned. You can simply note the figures of other writers and hope that in sensitizing yourself and giving free play to your own imagination, you too will be inspired to create word-pictures. Let us examine, then, some of the more common forms of figurative language.

Metaphor
(identification of one thing with another)

To an imaginative person, what is a map? The silhouette of a chimera or a spot of colour? Trivial comparisons are futile, so be careful. What is South America? A pear upside down.

> —Adolfo Costa Du Rels, *Bewitched Lands*

In his financial operations, Monsieur Grandet was part tiger and part boa constrictor. He would crouch in ambush watching his prey until it was time to spring with open jaws; then, having swallowed the gold, he would slowly digest it, like a snake, impassive, methodical, cold to any human touch.

> —Honoré de Balzac, *Eugénie Grandet*

(Note also the simile here: "*like* a snake"; see "simile," below.)

Living was a field of grain blowing in the wind on the side of a hill. Living was a hawk in the sky. Living was an earthen jar of water in the dust of the threshing with the grain flailed out and the chaff blowing. Living was a horse between your legs and a carbine under one leg and a hill and valley and a stream with trees along it and the far side of the valley and hills beyond.

> —Ernest Hemingway, *For Whom the Bell Tolls*

No man is an island, entire of itself; every man is a piece of the continent, a part of the main.

> —John Donne, *Meditation XVII*

Choosing Words

Rhetorical
question

Be not righteous over much, neither make thyself over wise:
Why shouldest thou destroy thyself?
Be not over much wicked, neither be thou foolish:
Why shouldest thou die before thy time?

—Ecclesiastes 7:16–17

Implicit or
submerged
metaphor

Youth is the time to go flashing from one end of the world to the other
both in mind and body; to try the manners of different nations; to hear the
chimes at midnight.

—Robert Louis Stevenson

Outside the weather was winter, the trees medieval presences arching gray
through gray.

—John Updike, "Museums and Women"

About the middle of the nineteenth century, in the quiet sunshine of
provincial prosperity, New England had an Indian summer of the mind; and
an agreeable reflective literature showed how brilliant that russet and yellow
season could be.

—George Santayana, *Character and Opinion*
in the United States

A kind of splendid carelessness goes with surpassing power. The labor of
the file was not for Aeschylus as it was not for Shakespeare.

—Edith Hamilton, *The Greek Way to Western Civilization*

Simile
(comparison of
one thing with
another joined
by "like" or
"as")

Their prose—Tolstoy's sentences, heavy as blocks of granite; Chekhov's
rhythms, soft as autumn leaves; Dostoievsky's moaning and quivering like
telegraph wires at night—revealed itself to me in all its beauty of language
and depth and richness of meaning.

—Yevgeny Yevtushenko, *A Precocious Autobiography*

Human potentialities, so poignant and literally crucial in adolescence really
are trapped and vitiated in a mass society. But American society, just because it
is so very mass is attached to mass institutions like a factory to its parking lot,
or a church to its graveyard.

—Edgar Z. Friedenberg, *Coming of Age in America*

Personification
(attribution of
human
characteristics
to inanimate
objects or
ideas)

Wit is a lean creature with a sharp inquiring nose, whereas humor has a
kindly eye and comfortable girth.

—Charles Brooks, "Wit and Humor"

Falseness withered in her presence, hypocrisy left the room.

—Adlai Stevenson, eulogizing Eleanor Roosevelt

Death came for her, ashamed of itself.

—Bertolt Brecht, *Brecht on Brecht*, arr. and tr. George Tabori

EXERCISES

1. Rewrite the following sentences in concrete or specific terms to create a more vivid
impression in the reader's mind.

a. He seemed happy.

b. She seemed lovely.
c. She seemed intelligent.
d. He seemed rebellious.
e. He seemed tired.
f. She seemed angry.
g. He seemed restless.
h. They seemed frightened.
i. They seemed nervous.
j. The countryside was beautiful.
k. The city was awful.
l. The campus was in a turmoil.
m. The dormitory was noisy.
n. The room was crowded.
o. He had the patience of Job.

2. Improve the following sentences by changing one or more words.
   a. The park is rather circular, with momentous oak trees.
   b. The reversal of Robert Jordan in *For Whom the Bell Tolls* is Frederic Henry in *A Farewell to Arms*.
   c. Thomas Wolfe was abhorred by what he saw in society.
   d. One notices the author's occupation with this theme.
   e. He carries out his life in accordance with Faulkner's vision of fate and moral responsibility.
   f. The memory of Ben's death was so vivid that Wolfe was able to duplicate it in his novel with all its poignancy.
   g. The most beneficial source was *The International Index*.
   h. The room seemed to him to have too much in it.
   i. Many writers are too flowery and superfluous, so that the point they are trying to convey is lost in the garbage of irrelevant material.
   j. For a complete terminology of a word, see an unabridged dictionary.
   k. Oftentimes I yearn for the good old days.
   l. The speaker of the poem relates how he felt the loss of the pleasures he had once enjoyed.
   m. Hemingway looked very deeply into the nature of courage.
   n. He was admired for his stubborn principles.
   o. Mrs. Compson's last speech in *The Sound and the Fury* reiterates our assumptions about her.
   p. Most high school students are all the same.
   q. Words are one of the most essential sophistications humanity has devised.

3. Try to revitalize the following clichés by creating a "play" or "twist" on the words.
   a. Home is where the heart is.
   b. It never rains but it pours.
   c. The more the merrier.
   d. As ye sow, so shall ye reap.
   e. Hell hath no fury like a woman scorned.
   f. All work and no play makes Jack a dull boy.
   g. A fool and his money are soon parted.
   h. Spare the rod and spoil the child.
   i. People who live in glass houses shouldn't throw stones.
   j. Beggars can't be choosers.

Composing Sentences

SENTENCES: AN OVERVIEW

*I*mproving sentences is a formidable job, but you can do it if you take the trouble to contemplate them critically—that is, to see how they actually work on paper and what options you have for effective change and revision. Only in this way can you improve your writing style, for the rhetorical strengths that contribute to what we call "readability" operate principally on the level of the sentence. No matter how apt and interesting a subject is, no matter how carefully you visualize it and organize it, no matter how soundly you develop it, any subject cannot turn into a good essay unless you embody each element of thought in a smooth-flowing series of clear, forceful sentences.

Logically, writers may think in paragraphs or units of thought, but concretely they spin out their ideas sentence by sentence—subject/verb/object by subject/verb/object. This is the typical English prose sentence, which writers vary instinctively as they feel a need for change in rhythm and pace. The writer provides the reader with ideas sentence by sentence, from subject to predicate and adds various modifications and qualifications along the way. Every sentence advanced beyond the primer stage of "See John run!" contains more than a bald subject committed to a particular action. The writer always weaves conditions and descriptions into the assertion that deepen and enrich its core meaning.

Dr. Samuel Johnson said that "most men think indistinctly and therefore cannot speak with exactness." To some extent this is true, but it is also true that your special function as a writer is to overcome this human deficiency. Before setting down your thoughts on paper, you have a special obligation to probe your mind until you see your ideas clearly as a distinct and unified whole. Then your special obligation is to try out different forms for each sentence to see which one most exactly reproduces the idea as it exists in your mind. Only after you have made clear thinking *visible on paper* are you justified in claiming the time and attention of a reader.

Grammar: "'Twas brillig and the slithy toves..."

We learn in school how to compose paragraphs and essays, but we master the grammar of the sentence in early childhood, long before we are even conscious of the learning process. Whether it issues from our tongue or pen, the sentence appears as a spontaneous creation of the individual consciousness, a result of a lifetime's experience with language, not just the needs of the moment. Indeed, although many people feel uneasy about grammar, the fact is that all native speakers have a deep awareness of the basic structure of English. If you doubt this, consider Lewis Carroll's famous "Jabberwocky" from *Through the Looking-Glass*, which begins:

> 'Twas brillig and the slithy toves
> Did gyre and gimble in the wabe:
> All mimsy were the borogoves,
> And the mome raths outgrabe.

When Alice hears these lines she says: "Somehow it seems to fill my head with ideas—only I don't know exactly what they are!" Actually, the ideas are *patterns*—the structural or grammatical meanings that stand out unmistakably because the lexical meanings have been obliterated. That is, the words themselves do not mean anything, but the *forms* of the words and their arrangement within the line stir the mind to vague recognition. Let us see how this works. First of all, there are certain real words that frame the nonsense words. The verse starts with "it was" ("'Twas"). Ask yourself, what kind of word could follow "'Twas" in this particular line? Certainly not a verb. "'Twas *walked*"? Nobody would ever combine such words in English. Our intuition leads us to such expressions as "the night before Christmas," or "it was an evening in May." Which is to say that "brillig" is probably a time expression and "slithy" is probably an adjective followed by the noun "toves."

> 'Twas an evening in May and the happy girls
> Did dance and frolic in the snow:

Some such statement is being made here. We know it; we feel it; it could not be otherwise. Whatever particular words you might choose to fill in here, they would all have the same *form*: they would be time expression, adjective, noun/verb, verb, noun. The same principles apply to the next two lines:

> All mimsy were the borogoves,
> And the mome raths outgrabe.

> All (adjective) were the (noun),
> And the (adjective) (noun) (verb).

> All happy were the carolers,
> And the young boys rejoiced.

How do we know and why do we feel that these kinds of words fit into these particular places? As modern linguists point out (see Francis), we are responding here to the structural or grammatical meanings that we learned as children, long before we could read or write. We heard words in certain positions within an utterance: the subject came first, followed by an action, then by an object or adjective. We learned to identify the territories where we could expect to encounter one or another form. **In other words, we learned the basic grammatical process of the English language: word order.**

We also learned that certain kinds of words changed in set ways; some might have an *s* sound attached to the end, and when they did certain other words would change their form to be in *agreement* with them. Thus we feel that "borogoves" is plural; it has an *s* ending, and the verb that precedes it is a verb that goes with a plural noun. If "borogoves" were singular, the verb preceding it would be "was," not "were."

It does not matter what the individual word denotes here: "borogoves" could mean "cars" or "handkerchiefs." In either case—in *any* case—the structural or grammatical meaning (the terms are interchangeable) remains constant: an *s* ending signals plurality, and an alteration in verb form signals a particular relationship between the verb and the noun. Collectively these changes in form are known as *inflection*. Inflection is the second most important structural device in the English language.

There is a third formal device. Function words such as "the," "and," "by" have no concrete meaning when they stand alone but serve an important function within the context of a sentence. There they help to indicate how substantive words—that is, words with a full referential meaning—such as "water" and "sink" are related: "The water is *in* the sink"; "The shoes are *under* the bed." Function words are *determiners*, or *formal markers*, that help us to identify other words in the sentence and indicate how other words are functioning: as verbs? nouns? adjectives? After all, what a word *is* depends on how it functions in the sentence: one may *jump* across a puddle (verb); one may take a big *jump* (noun); or one may watch a referee at a basketball game toss up a *jump* ball (adjective).

When we find a "the" or "a" preceding words such as "toves" or "wabe," we know that they are words to which an *s* can be added, words that we, using traditional terminology, call "nouns." Thus when we substitute for "borogoves" we automatically do so with another noun. Similarly, by using the function word "and" at the beginning of the fourth line—"and the mome raths outgrabe"—the writer is telling us that the fourth line conveys a parallel assertion to the assertion in line three, "All mimsy were the borogoves." The past tense "were" (rather than "are") in line three is therefore carried over, by virtue of the connective "and" (a conjunction), to line four. The "borogoves *were*," and the "mome raths" also appear to have completed some action in the past.

I shall approach the subject of the sentence first by reviewing its basic grammar and then by considering rhetorical features of the sentence that provide a foundation for clarity and readability: unity, coherence, emphasis, economy, vigor, and rhythm. Upon this foundation each writer can build those subtler qualities of prose tone and style that best suit the needs and purposes of the individual piece and person. Every writer, student as well as professional, is entitled to his or her own style, just as everyone is entitled to his or her own personality (of which writing style is a reflection). The only imperative is that style begin with the minimum rhetorical proficiency without which a piece of writing, no matter how modest in purpose or limited in scope, is doomed to failure. Suggestions and illustrations from the eighteenth-century rhetorician Hugh Blair, whose observations on writing and style, although published in 1783 (*Lectures*), are still valid, will support this discussion.

Basic Grammar of the Sentence

Grammar, very simply, is the structure of a language or the study of how a language works. The review of the basic grammar of the sentence moves from a consideration of the various kinds of words to a discussion of the ways in which words are combined to form phrases, clauses, and sentences. The section concludes with a review of the principles of sentence correctness.

TYPES OF WORDS

Words are conventionally divided into eight categories, the so-called parts of speech: nouns, pronouns, verbs, adjectives and adverbs (modifiers), prepositions and conjuctions (connectives), and interjections. We will look at each of these in turn, except for the interjection, a word that is grammatically unrelated to the rest of the sentence, merely expressing an attitude or emotion ("*Oh*, I'm going to be late!" "*Ah*, what a relief!")

Nouns

A noun is conventionally defined as the name of a person, place, or thing (object, animal, idea, or quality). Thus:

> The *woman* is busy.
> Her *brother-in-law* was helpful. [compound noun]
> The *city* is beautiful.
> The *cat* is purring.
> The *thought* is well expressed.
> Her *beauty* is dazzling.

Pronouns

A pronoun is conventionally defined as a word that takes the place of, or refers to, a noun.

> *She* is busy.
> *It* is beautiful.
> *They* are quarreling.
> *Anyone* can learn to swim.

There are eight types of pronouns:

> Personal: *You* and *I* are going.
> Interrogative: *Who* is going? Give it to *whomever* you wish.
> Relative: The book, *which* was just published, is in the library.
> Demonstrative: *This* is preferable to *that*.
> Indefinite: *Each* of us should ask *someone*.
> Reciprocal: Speak to *each other*. Call *one another*.
> Reflexive: She helped *herself*. They helped *themselves*.
> Intensive: I *myself* need help. They *themselves* are lost

Relative pronouns—*who*, *which*, *that*—sometimes give trouble. The general rule for their usage is simple.

> *Who* refers to people: The girl *who* just spoke is a student.
> *Which* refers to things and animals: The notebooks, *which* are on the desk, will be returned.
> *That* refers to people or things and animals: The paintings *that* are on the wall are prize-winners. The dogs *that* are barking should be taken out.

Verbs

Verbs are conventionally defined as words that assert action or state of being. A more precise definition would incorporate the fact that verbs *predicate* some action of the subject; that is, they make a statement ("She worked hard"), ask a question ("Are you coming?"), or issue a command or direction ("Fold the batter into a cakepan"). A verb, then, is a word that functions in the sentence as the predicate or as part of the predicate.

Transitive and Intransitive

Verbs are two kinds: transitive and intransitive. A *transitive verb requires an object to complete its meaning.*

> The speaker *announced* his subject.

An *intransitive* verb does not require an object to complete its meaning.

> They *moaned* and *cried.*

Linking verbs (sometimes called "state of being" verbs)—for example, *feel, seem, be, appear, become, smell, taste*—are considered intransitive because they serve merely to connect or "link" a subject with its subject complement.

> She *felt* happier than ever.
> He was *becoming* anxious.
> It *smelled* terrible.

The same verb may sometimes be used transitively or intransitively.

> Mary *paints* pictures. [transitive]
> Mary *paints* beautifully. [intransitive]

Tense

Verbs are inflected to indicate tense, or time. Basically there are six tenses.

> Present: She *asks* no questions.
> Past: She *asked* no questions.
> Future: She *will ask* no questions.
> Present Perfect: She *has asked* no questions.
> Past Perfect: She *had asked* no questions.
> Future Perfect: She *will have asked* no questions.

A present tense verb is often used to express universal truth ("All people are mortal") or habitual action ("He longs for final answers").

Voice

Verbs may be cast in active or passive voice. A verb in the *active* voice has a direct object.

> The police officer *put* a parking ticket on the car.

A verb is in the *passive* voice when the object is converted to the subject by casting the verb into a phrase consisting of a form of the verb *to be,* followed by a past participle.

> A parking ticket *was put* on the car.
> The car *was given* a parking ticket.

Note that the subject of a verb cast in the active voice performs an action, while the subject of a verb cast in the passive voice receives an action.

Mood

Verbs are also inflected to indicate the manner or mode—the mood—in which an action or state of being is conceived. The English language has four basic moods:

> *Indicative:* makes a statement or assertion (The car needs repair.)
> *Interrogative:* asks a question (Does the car need repair?)
> *Imperative:* issues a command, request, or directive (Repair the car.)
> *Subjunctive:* suggests actions that are probable, possible, or contrary to fact or desire. Once used in a variety of constructions, the subjunctive mood is now used in a limited number of forms:
>
> in the present and past tense of the verb *to be* (If I *were* you, I would repair the car.)
>
> in *that* clauses pertaining to parliamentary motions, or in recommendation, resolution, demand, or command:
>
> > I move that the car *be* repaired.
> > She recommended that he *repair* the car.
> > Resolved that this car *be* repaired.

Modifiers

Variety and nuance in sentences are achieved primarily by adding modifying words, phrases, and clauses. **Basically, there are two types of modifiers: adjectival and adverbial.**

Adjectives

Adjectives are words that modify (qualify, quantify, describe, or limit) nouns and pronouns.

> The *four* women waved their *red* scarves.

Frequently, a word that ordinarily functions as another part of speech may be converted to adjectival use.

> In order to lose weight, she went to a *milk* farm.

Here the word *milk*, normally a noun and sometimes a verb ("She *milked* the cow"), is being used as an adjective. Similarly, nouns in the possessive case ("*Gloria's* room," "the *boy's* trousers") and such pronouns as *this, that, her, our, your* may serve an adjectival function ("*Our* clothes are wet"); so may certain phrases and clauses, as we shall see.

Adverbs

Adverbs are words that modify (qualify, quantify, describe, or limit) verbs, adjectives, or other adverbs.

> He drank his milk *slowly.*
> The milk was *terribly* sour.
> He drank his milk *very* slowly.

In addition, adverbs may modify gerunds, participles, and infinitives.

Adverbs generally indicate place (*nowhere, here*), definite time (*now, yesterday*), indefinite time (*often, always, seldom, never*), degree (*very, exactly, quite, almost*), and manner (*quietly, softly, stealthily*).

Sometimes a so-called adverb of modality may qualify an entire sentence:

> *Clearly,* that man is incompetent.
> *Surely* you don't mean that.
> I *certainly* do mean it.

Many adverbs are formed simply by adding *-ly* to an adjective: *rapid* (adjective), *rapidly* (adverb). However, there are many adverbs that do not have a final *-ly,* as is shown above in the list of adverbs signifying place, time, and manner. Still other adverbs have the same form as their corresponding adjectives. The word *slow,* for instance, may be used as either adjective or adverb. Contrary to what many people think, the road sign "Go Slow" is grammatically correct. (*Slowly* is used as an adverb but not as an adjective.)

Connectives

As the term suggests, connectives serve mainly to connect other words in the sentence and to show their relationship. Having no lexical meaning of their own apart from their function in the sentence, the two major kinds of connectives, prepositions and conjunctions, are often called "function words."

Prepositions

Prepositions connect nouns or noun equivalents to show how they are related to some other part of the sentence or to the whole sentence.

> She walked *into* the room two minutes *before* class ended.
> *Up* the street a man was watering his lawn.

The preposition and the noun (which may have its own modifiers) constitute a modifying unit, the noun serving as the so-called object of the preposition.

There are many prepositions in the English language (such as *out, in, to, toward, under, over, between, in front of, in back of*), and their use is generally established by idiom and usage. Sometimes usage is so lax and regionally determined that one may communicate the same idea by using different prepositions ("I got *up* from the bed," "I got *down* from the bed," "I got *out* of bed"). Those who are curious and would like to know more about prepositions may consult an entire book on the subject: Frederick T. Wood, *English Prepositional Idioms* (New York: St. Martin's Press, 1967).

One rule, however, has no exceptions: a pronoun following a preposition must be in the objective case (see page 552). Many people violate this rule by using the expression "between you and *I*" in the belief that *I* is somehow more elegant than plain *me*. To avoid such overcompensation, it may be helpful to think of the analogous expression "between *us*," for which "between *we*" would never be used.

There is an old prohibition against ending a sentence with a preposition, which grew out of a mistaken belief that English grammar must imitate Latin grammar. Winston Churchill is said to have dismissed this "rule" as "the sort of English up with which I will not put" (cited in Gowers, 131). As a general guideline, use a final preposition if the sentence sounds more natural and idiomatic and retains proper emphasis.

Conjunctions

Acting as function words, conjunctions connect words, phrases, or clauses. There are two kinds of conjunctions: coordinating and subordinating.

Coordinating conjunctions (*and, but, or, nor, for, yet*) connect words or word groups of equal grammatical rank.

> The girl *and* the boy were skating.
> It is a warm *but* cloudy day.
> Did you open the front door *or* the living room window?

In using a coordinating conjunction, make certain that the elements on both sides of the conjunction are of equal rank: If the conjunction joins two single words they should be the same part of speech; if two word groups are joined, both should be either phrases or clauses (see the discussion of parallelism on pages 578–80).

Subordinating conjunctions (*if, since, because, when, although,* and so on) connect sentence elements that are of unequal rank—specifically, main and subordinate clauses—and show their relationship. The following list presents the most commonly used subordinating conjunctions, grouped according to the specific relationships they establish.

Comparison: *than, as . . . as*

> She has no more feeling than a stone.

Condition: *if, unless, whether, as long as, provided that*

> If the rain continues, the picnic will be postponed until Saturday.

Concession or contrast: *though, although, even though*

> Although the archeologists dug steadily for six months, they failed to find any artifacts.

Degree or comparison: *as, just as, as much as, as . . . as, than*

They carried as much food and water to the survivors as they could.
John ranked higher on the College Boards than Jim ranked last year.

Manner: *as, as if, as though*

She studied for the exam as she had been instructed.

Place: *where, wherever*

Wherever you go in California, you are certain to see spectacular scenery.
I found my gloves where I had left them.

Purpose: *so that, in order that*

I have written full instructions on the board so that the exam can begin on time.

Reason or cause: *because, since, as*

They laughed because they were enjoying themselves.

Time: *when, until, before, while, since, as*

While they were attending the lecture, fire broke out in the basement.

Conjunctive adverbs simultaneously connect main clauses and provide an adverbial modifier. The chief conjunctive adverbs include single words (*however, furthermore, thus, therefore, indeed, consequently, nonetheless, moreover*) and transitional phrases (*for example, in addition, in fact, on the other hand, on the contrary, at the same time, that is*). In contrast to subordinating conjunctions, conjunctive adverbs generally relate two main clauses and are preceded by a semicolon rather than a comma:

The weather bureau was issuing storm warnings hourly;
nevertheless the crew decided to set sail and hope for the best.

RELATIONSHIPS OF WORDS

Phrases

A phrase is a group of words that functions as a unit but does not contain a subject and predicate. A phrase may be classified according to its own construction and according to the part of speech for which it performs a function.

Prepositional Phrase

A preposition introduces a prepositional phrase; it functions as an adjective or adverb.

Adjectival: modifies a noun or pronoun

The girl *in the bright green dress* entered the room.
Her yellow hat, *with its purple feathers*, attracted our attention.

Adverbial: modifies a verb, adverb, or adjective

The man walked *through a long, dark tunnel*.
Drive carefully *on icy streets*.
The bread was still hot *from the oven*.

Verbal Phrase

A verbal phrase consists of a verb form plus other words; it functions as a noun or an adjective.
Gerundive: often called a "verbal noun"; always ends in *-ing*; functions as a noun, taking objects, complements, or modifiers.

> *Stealing someone else's lines* is plagiarism.
> *Stealing with a grand flourish* is still stealing.
> *Dancing the polka* is my favorite exercise.

Participial: often called a "verbal adjective"; modifies a noun or pronoun.

> The woman *banging on the door* was obviously terrified.
> *Having been rejected*, he plunged into a depression.

Infinitival: functions as a noun, an adjective, or an adverb.

> To see is *to believe*. (noun)
> Jan is an artist *to be admired*. (adjective)
> The meat was marinated *to make it tastier*. (adverb)

Absolutes

An absolute is a group of words that is almost but not quite a complete sentence. Its basic pattern is often *noun plus participle*:

> We'll go on a picnic today, *weather permitting*.

Because it may modify a whole clause or entire sentence, absolutes are also called "sentence modifiers" or "parenthetical phrases."

> *The sun having come out*, we prepared for our picnic.
> Joan wandered in, *eyes bleary, hair disheveled, clothes rumpled*—a total wreck.

Clauses

A clause is a group of related words containing both a subject and a predicate and forming a sentence or part of a sentence.

Subordinate Clauses

Like a phrase, a subordinate clause is a group of related words which functions as a unit but cannot stand alone. The most helpful way to identify a subordinate (or dependent) clause is to distinguish it from a main (or independent) clause. Like a sentence, a main clause contains a subject and predicate and can stand alone:

> Sixteen-year-olds can get a permit when a parent accompanies them.

Composing Sentences

In the above sentence only the first clause, the main clause, can stand alone:

Sixteen-year-olds can get a permit.

The second clause *cannot* stand alone:

... when a parent accompanies them.

The sense of this statement depends on the rest of the sentence; therefore it is clearly a subordinate (dependent) clause.

Subordinate clauses may be used as adjectives, adverbs, or nouns.

An *adjective clause* modifies a noun or a pronoun and is generally introduced by a relative pronoun (*who, whom, which, that*) (see page 539) or by a relative adverb (*where, when, why*):

This pen, *which I found in the library*, belongs to Lee.
The store *where I bought the dress* is closed for the afternoon.
She is a girl *I cannot understand*. [relative pronoun *whom* omitted]

An *adverbial clause* is introduced by a subordinating conjunction, which indicates the exact relationship between the subordinate idea and the main idea:

His friends gave a party *when he returned.*
She agreed to go *although she had grave reservations.*

A *noun clause* functions like a noun and—like an adjective clause—is generally introduced by *who, whom, which, that*; also by *whichever, whoever, whomever, where, when, why.*

Whoever telephoned for an appointment this morning has just called back.
He said *that he would arrive at noon.*
   or
He said *he would arrive at noon.* [conjunction *that* may sometimes be omitted]

Using subordinate clauses effectively will enhance your writing greatly, enabling you to combine facts in varied sentence patterns which show more exact relationships than the mere stringing together, in a coordinate sequence, of one idea after another.

Coordination: I went downtown and it rained.
Subordination: When I went downtown, it rained.

Main Clauses

Main (for independent) clauses can stand alone as simple, separate sentences.

The man called my name, and I called his name in return.
They have made sensible plans; furthermore, they know how to implement them.
No higher praise can be given than this: he was a man who lived by principle.

SIX SENTENCE PATTERNS

A sentence is a group of words containing a subject and a predicate. The subject names the person, thing, or concept spoken about. The subject of a sentence can be

identified by asking, "Who or what is doing the action?" The predicate—a verb plus its object and complement, if any—makes an assertion about that person, thing, or concept. The verb can be identified by asking, "What is the action?" The object can be identified by asking, "Who or what receives the action?"

The three most important patterns of the English sentence are:

1. Subject and Verb (SV)

Subject	Verb
The girl	laughed.
Lions	roar.
The boy	is shouting.

2. Subject, Action Verb, and One or Two Objects (SVO or SVOO)

Subject	Verb	Object	Object
Cats	drink		milk.
The boy	called	her	a heroine.
Duane	bought	her	a necklace.

3. Subject, Linking Verb, and Complement (SLVC)

(A linking verb is one which does not indicate action but merely links the subject with descriptive words that complete its meaning, hence the words that follow such verbs are called *complements*.)

Subject	Verb	Complement
Einstein	was	a genius.
The boy	will become	a scientist.
The lion	seems	hungry.
The coat	felt	heavy.

To the above patterns three more may be added. These are not as frequently used, but they are equally important in that they represent variations on the usual order and relation of subject and predicate.

4. Passive Pattern (OVS)

The object of an active verb may be converted to the subject.

Subject	Verb	Object
Cats	drink	milk.
Milk	is drunk	by cats.

5. Impersonal Pattern (SVO)

The real subject of the sentence follows the verb, while an "anticipatory" subject *(it, there)* precedes the verb.

Subject	Verb	Complement	Subject
It	is	unlikely	that they will process.
There	was		an echo.
There	will be		a good turnout

6. Imperative Pattern (VO!)

The subject, though not explicitly stated, is "understood" to be *you*.

Verb	Object or Complement
Stop.	
Answer	my question.
Do not start	any trouble.
Be	good.

Upon these six basic patterns most English sentences are built. An inversion such as *Him I don't like* (rather than the normal *I don't like him*) provides emphasis by its very irregularity or deviation from the norm. Questions also represent a variation of normal patterning, the most common being the inversion of subject and verb (used in conjunction with *be, have, shall, will, can, may, must, ought, need*):

Was she there?
Must I stay?

STRUCTURAL TYPES

Sentences may also be classified on the basis of their grammatical structure: simple, compound, complex, compound-complex.

Simple

A simple sentence contains only one subject and one predicate—that is, one main clause, with no subordinate clauses. Such a sentence may contain modifying phrases, however.

I decided to go home.
Tired and dejected, I decided to go home.

Compound

A compound sentence contains at least two subjects and two predicates—that is, two or more main clauses, with no subordinate clauses. A compound sentence is actually two independent sentences linked by a semicolon and/or by a coordinating conjunction (*and, but, for, or, nor, yet*) or conjunctive adverb (*however, therefore,* and so on).

She was a sophomore; he was a junior.
She wanted to leave the stage, but the audience would not stop applauding.
The reviews of the show were poor; however, the word-of-mouth reports were excellent.

The compound sentence is useful when you wish to express two thoughts that are of approximately equal value or that are contrasting or opposing aspects of a single idea. The pairing of independent clauses into a compound sentence provides a structure that clarifies the relationship between the clauses.

Complex

A complex sentence contains one main clause and one or more subordinate clauses.

Although the reviews of the show were poor, the word-of-mouth reports were excellent.

Use a complex sentence when you wish to show more precisely the relationship between ideas—specifically, when you wish to give greater stress or importance to one part of the sentence. In such cases it is advisable to subordinate grammatically that which is actually subordinate or less important. (See "Working Toward Emphasis," pages 572–74.)

Compound-Complex

A compound-complex sentence contains at least two main clauses and at least one subordinate clause.

When the flowers arrived, she placed them in a large vase; thus she enjoyed the rest of the afternoon, gazing at her fragrant gift.

BASIC PRINCIPLES OF SENTENCE CORRECTNESS

Agreement of Subject and Verb

1. **A verb should agree with its subject in person and number.**

   Many zoo animals [third person plural subject] live [plural verb] in crowded cages.
   She [third person singular subject] lives [third person singular verb] in the country.

2. **Two or more subjects connected by *and* require a plural verb.**

   A noun and a verb are necessary in a sentence.

Exception: When two singular subjects connected by *and* present a single idea, the verb may be singular.

   His pride and joy is his new car.
   Ham and eggs is my favorite breakfast.

3. **When two or more subjects are connected by *or*, *either ... or*, or *neither ... nor*, the verb agrees with the subject nearest to it.**

   Either the men or the woman is guilty.
   Neither Jim nor his brothers are guilty.

4. **A collective noun referring to a group as a unit requires a singular verb; a collective noun referring to individuals in a group acting separately requires a plural verb.**

> The class is attentive.
> The class are going their separate ways.
>
> The public is easy to reach.
> The public are writing letters to the radio station.

5. **Nouns plural in form but singular in meaning require a singular verb.**

> The news is bad.
> Economics is a popular subject.
> Politics is an art.
> Ethics, like politics, is not a science.
> *The Magnificent Ambersons* is a fine film.

6. **Words stating time, money, fractions, weight, and amount are generally singular and require a singular verb.**

> Thirty days is a long time.
> Five dollars is the price.
> Two-thirds of nine is six.
> Twenty pounds is not considered excessive.
> Twelve miles is a long walk.

7. **A prepositional phrase that follows a subject does not affect the number of the verb.**

> The size of the pictures in the album is small.
> The cost of his pranks was paid by his parents.

8. **A relative pronoun used as a subject may be either singular or plural, depending on the number of its antecedent.**

> John is one of those men who always complain. [antecedent of *who is men*]
> John is the only one of those men who always complains. [antecedent of *who* is *one*]

9. **Singular pronouns require singular verbs: *each, everyone, everybody, anyone, anybody, someone, somebody, no one, nobody, one, another, anything, either, neither.***

> Each of the boys is gifted.
> Neither of the candidates shows any promise.

The pronoun *none* is singular or plural according to context.

> None of the students was willing to reply.
> None of the students were able to attend.

10. **Since *every* and *many a* before a word or series of words are viewed as modifiers, they should be followed by singular verbs.**

> Every man, woman, and child in town is invited.
> Many a girl in this situation has given up.

11. A singular subject followed by *with*, *in addition to*, *as well as*, and *including* requires a singular verb.

> The woman, as well as the three men in the car, was injured.
> Jane, as well as Jim, is leaving for the weekend.

12. In *here is/here are* and *there is/there are* constructions, the noun following the verb is considered the real subject and therefore determines the person and number of the verb. A singular subject obviously requires a singular verb:

> Here is your coat.

Similarly, a plural subject requires a plural verb:

> There are thirty students in the class.

When the first element of a compound subject is singular, the choice between a singular or plural verb is a matter of taste:

> There was [or *were*] joy and tears in her eyes.

Agreement of Pronoun and Antecedent

1. **A pronoun should agree with its antecedent in person, number, and gender.**

> The chairman [third person, singular, masculine] submitted his [third person, singular, masculine] report.
> the women [third person, plural, feminine] left their [third person, plural] coats in the closet.
> Mary and John [compound subject] handed in their [plural] papers.
> The sales pitch for aspirin [third person, singular, neuter] emphasized its [third person, singular, neuter] pain-killing properties.

2. **Collective nouns that refer to a group as a unit require singular pronouns; those that refer to individuals in a group acting separately require plural pronouns.**

> The jury announced its verdict.
> The audience applauded their hero.
> As a finale, everyone threw their hats in the air.

3. **The words *each*, *either*, *neither*, *somebody*, *anybody*, *nobody*, *someone*, *anyone*, and *no one* require a singular pronoun; *everyone* and *everybody* take a singular or plural pronoun, depending on meaning.**

> No one knew where to find his or her coat.
> No one can call his or her judgment infallible.
> Everyone reported his and her grades.
> > or
> They all reported their grades.

Since English has no single pronoun to indicate both male and female, *he* has traditionally been used to refer to both genders. This usage is essentially inaccurate, however, because the reference may be to a woman as well as a man. One way to avoid this problem is to pluralize.

> All the members of the cast know their roles.

Another possibility is to say simply:

> Someone left his or her book in class.

4. The impersonal *one* may be followed by his or her.

> One should watch his or her manners.

An alternate and more conservative usage provides more consistency and accuracy:

> One should watch one's manners.

5. *Who* refers to persons, *which* to things, and *that* to persons or things. The importance of definite, unambiguous pronoun reference cannot be over-emphasized; for further discussion and illustrations, see "Working Toward Coherence," pages 562–68.

Pronoun Case Forms

Pronouns and—to a lesser extent—nouns undergo *inflection*, a change of form to indicate their specific meaning or grammatical function in the sentence. The inflectional form of a noun or pronoun is referred to as its *case*; a subject (except the subject of an infinitive or of a participle which is in the objective case) is required to be in the *subjective*, or nominative, case (*woman/she*); an object is required to be in the *objective* case (*woman/her*). The *possessive*, or genitive, case form is indicated in nouns by the use of an apostrophe and in pronouns by a change in form (*woman's/hers*).

Nouns and some indefinite pronouns vary their case form only to show possession:

> The *girl's* book was lost on the train.
> *Anybody's* mother would have felt the same way.

The following six pronouns require different and distinctive forms in all three cases:

Subjective	I	we	he, she	they	who
Possessive	my (mine)	our (ours)	his, her (hers)	their (theirs)	whose
Objective	me	us	him, her	them	whom

You should keep several other principles of case in mind:

1. The personal pronouns *it* and *you* are inflected only to show possession: *its*, *your*, *yours*.

2. A pronoun used in apposition should be in the same case as the noun or pronoun to which it is in apposition.

> They put the blame on the two of us, John and *me*.

3. **The case of a pronoun is determined by its function in its own clause.**

> She will invite *whoever* can come. [pronoun subject of clause]
> She will invite *whomever* she wants. [pronoun object of clause]
> I will talk to *whoever* is in the office. [pronoun subject of clause]

4. **The case of a pronoun following *than, as,* or *but* is determined by whether the pronoun is the subject or object of the verb that follows, whether that verb is explicitly stated or only implied.**

> She is older than *I* [am].
> They call her more often than [they call] *me.*
> Everyone applauded but *I* [did not applaud].

5. **In standard written English the pronoun *whom* is consistently used when its position in the sentence requires the objective case.**

> The student *whom* he advised has finally registered. [*Whom* is direct object of *advised.*]
> To *whom* are you addressing that question? [*Whom* is object of preposition *to.*]

Exceptions: In informal usage—in speech or when the pronoun opens the sentence (where the subjective case is normally the rule)—the use of *who* has become acceptable, indeed idiomatic.

> *Who* did I see you with last night?
> She is a student *who* I admire greatly.

In many instances it is possible to avoid the controversy and confusion that surround the use of *who/whom* by simply editing the pronoun out of the sentence.

> She is a student I admire greatly.
> Are you talking about any particular writer? [rather than the correct but awkward-sounding *Whom are you talking about?*]

On similar grounds, writers who object to the conventionally correct use of the subjective case for a pronoun used as subject complement of the linking verb *be* ("Can it be *they?*") can sidestep the issue by recasting the sentence ("Do you hear them coming?") "It's me" (as opposed to the grammatically pure "It is I") has already been established as an idiom.

Sentence Integrity

A standard English sentence contains a complete subject and predicate. Deviations from the standard confuse the reader and suggest that the writer has been careless and negligent. The three most common problems, with their corrected versions, are:

1. Careless or Indefensible Sentence Fragment

> a. Treating a participial phrase or verbal as if it were a whole sentence

> *Wrong:*   Calling frantically to the men on the pier, and pointing to the injured swimmer.

In this case the participial phrases should be replaced by at least one verb:

Composing Sentences

Correct: He called frantically to the men on the pier, pointing to the injured swimmer.

or

Calling frantically..., he pointed....

Wrong: She wanted to get A's in all her subjects. Being competitive and ambitious.

Being is a verbal; the participial phrase modifies *she.*

Correct: Being competitive and ambitious, she wanted to get A's in all her subjects.

b. Treating a subordinate clause like a main clause.

Wrong: They wanted to return home as quickly as possible. Where they knew they would be welcome.

The *where* clause is subordinate and should be joined to its main clause by a comma.

Correct: They wanted to return home as quickly as possible, where they knew they would be welcome.

2. Comma Splice

This violation of sentence integrity is committed when a comma (rather than a period, semicolon, or colon) is used between two main clauses, thereby "splicing" the sentence.

Wrong: She simply could not answer the question, it confused her completely.

Correct: She simply could not answer the question. It confused her completely.

or

She simply could not answer the question, for it confused her completely.

In some cases a comma splice is committed when a comma rather than a semicolon is used before a conjunctive adverb (*however, therefore, thus, nevertheless,* and so on).

Wrong: I wanted to go, however, I could not raise the fare.
Correct: I wanted to go; however, I could not raise the fare.

3. Fused Sentence

This violation of sentence integrity consists in writing two sentences with no punctuation between them (no period or semicolon) and no coordinating conjunction.

Wrong: She got to the game on time that kind of punctuality was unusual for her.

Correct: She got to the game on time. That kind of punctuality was unusual for her.

        or

She got to the game on time; that kind....

Exceptions

Divergence from the standard complete sentence is acceptable when you are trying to achieve some special effect, as in the following instances.

1. In the case of the imperative, where the subject is "understood."

   Don't go. [subject "understood" to be *you*]

2. An answer to a question.

   Was she angry? Not at all.

3. An exclamation.

   Never!
   What a joy!

4. Part of running dialogue.

   "They looked the other way. Didn't want to know the truth."

5. A descriptive word or phrase, set off for emphasis.

   The mountains were lofty and ice-capped. An awesome sight.

6. Part of a stream of consciousness in which the thought processes naturally flow in fragments.

   This late age of the world's experience had bred in them all, all men and women, a well of tears. Tears and sorrows; a perfectly upright and stoical bearing.

   —Virginia Woolf, *Mrs. Dalloway*

7. Appositional sentences, especially where they are used as transitions.

   No money, no food.
   To return to my original topic, racism.

COMPOSING SENTENCES: A GUIDE

A sentence is a sequence of separate words and word clusters—that is, phrases and clauses. How these words are arranged on paper determines what they mean. A careful and skillful arrangement in which the separate parts fit together to form a cohesive structure is clear; an arrangement in which the parts are loosely and haphazardly thrown together is unclear, perhaps incomprehensible. Working toward clarity, then, means constructing sentences in which meaning flows logically and smoothly from one sentence element to the next, thereby enabling the reader to follow and grasp the exact contour of the writer's thought as well as its bare substance.

Composing Sentences

Combining Sentences

No single skill will promote good writing more than the ability to condense and consolidate sentences which do not carry sufficient meaning to be set apart as separate sentences. This section examines ways to combine sentences that are loosely written and needlessly repetitive. Only after you have mastered this skill can you produce tight, well-constructed sentences that you can then (as we shall see in the next section) *creatively* expand; in other words, which you can expand not by mere verbiage but by the artful, weaving in of added meaning and modification.

Sentence combining involves the reduction of a full sentence to one of the following sentence elements:

1. RELATIVE CLAUSE

> *Example:* The fighting fish is small and quarrelsome.
> The fighting fish lives in the waters around the Malay Archipelago.
>
> *Improvement:* The fighting fish, which is small and quarrelsome, lives in the waters around the Malay Archipelago.

2. PREPOSITIONAL PHRASE

> *Example:* Benjamin Franklin was born in Boston, Massachusetts. His birthday was January 17, 1706.
>
> *Improvement:* Benjamin Franklin was born in Boston, Massachusetts, on January 17, 1706.

3. PARTICIPIAL PHRASE

> *Example:* The blizzard paralyzed the city. It piled up drifts as tall as houses. It blocked roads and highways. It kept residents indoors where they were safe and warm.
>
> *Improvement:* The blizzard paralyzed the city, piling up drifts as tall as houses, blocking roads and highways, and keeping residents indoors where they were safe and warm.

4. ABSOLUTE PHRASE

> *Example:* The dancer soared across the stage. Her head was held high. Her arms were raised. Her legs were extended like the wings of a bird.
>
> *Improvement:* The dancer soared across the stage, her head held high, her arms raised, her legs extended like the wings of a bird.

Absolutes help us to weave narrative and descriptive details into a sentence, thereby providing a full rather than a fragmented image. Absolutes also help us to move from a general subject (a dancer) to specific aspects of the subject (her head, arms, legs).

5. APPOSITIVES

Example:	My neighbor is Mrs. Jones. She is the oldest living resident of our town.
Improvement:	My neighbor, Mrs. Jones, is the oldest living resident of our town.

6. SUBORDINATE CLAUSE

Example:	Honor was important to both Stamm and Zodomirsky. As a result of it they were both hurt in a duel.
Improvement:	Because honor was important to both Stamm and Zodomirsky, they were both hurt in a duel.

Expanding Sentences

Like the paragraph, writing the sentence is a generative or "additive" process; that is, a building or adding on to a basic unit. In the paragraph, as we have seen, the basic unit is a topic or lead sentence; in a sentence, the basic unit is a main clause. Like a topic sentence, a main clause is generally stated in general or abstract terms to which the writer adds specific modifiers (subordinate clauses, adjective clusters, verb clusters, prepositional phrases) that expand and enrich the meaning of the predication.

EXPANDING A MINIMAL SENTENCE

There are six basic ways in which we may add to or expand a minimal sentence.

1. Compounding what is called the "head" term in a subject/verb/complement pattern:

   Example: Fresh fruit is good.
   Head word: fruit
   Expansion: Fresh fruit and vegetables are good.

2. Juxtaposing appositive phrases to the head term:

   Expansion: Fresh fruit, a rare treat in any season, is good.

3. Using verbals or verbal phrases (participles, gerunds, infinitives) in the subject/verb/complement pattern:

   Expansion: Oozing with natural juices, fresh fruit is good.

4. Using noun clauses to serve as the subject or complement in the subject/verb/complement pattern:

   Expansion: Whoever eats fresh fruit says that it is good.

5. Using an adjective or adjective clause to modify the head term of the subject or complement in the subject/verb/complement pattern:

> Expansion: Wherever it comes from, fresh fruit is good.

6. Using an adverb or adverb clause to modify the verb in the subject/verb/complement pattern:

> Expansion: Fresh fruit is always good.

LEVELS OF GENERALIZATION

Christensen points out that "What you wish to say is found not in the noun but in what you add to qualify the noun.... The noun, the verb, and the main clause serve merely as a base from which the meaning will rise. The modifier is the essential part of any sentence" (4). **The sentence, then, like the paragraph, frequently exhibits levels of generalization, as the following subordinate sequence illustrates:**

1 He dipped his hands in the bichloride solution and shook them, (main clause)

  2 a quick shake, (noun cluster)

    3 fingers down (absolute)

      4 like the fingers of a pianist above the keys. (prepositional phrase)
> —Sinclair Lewis (cited in Christensen, *Notes*, page 9)

Coordinate and mixed sequences—such as the following—illustrate further the many shapes that sentences, like paragraphs, may assume:

1 He could sail for hours,

  2 searching the blanched grasses below him with his telescopic eyes, (verb cluster)

  2 gaining height against the wind, (verb cluster)

  2 descending in mile-long, gently declining swoops when he curved and rode back, (verb cluster)

  2 never beating a wing. (verb cluster)
> —Walter Van Tilberg Clark (cited in Christensen, *Notes*, page 10)

1 Joad's lips stretched tight over his teeth for a moment, and

1 he licked his lips,

  2 like a dog, (prepositional phrase)

    3 two licks, (noun cluster)

      4 one in each direction from the middle. (noun cluster)
> —John Steinbeck (cited in Christensen, *Notes*, page 11)

1 It was as though someone, somewhere, had touched a lever and shifted gears, and

1 the hospital was set for night running,

   2 smooth and silent, (adjective and adjective)

2 its normal clatter and hum muffled, (absolute)

2 the only sounds heard in the whitewalled room distant and unreal: (absolute)

   3 a low hum of voices from the nurses' desk, (noun cluster)

      4 quickly stifled, (verb cluster)

   3 the soft squish of rubber-soled shoes on the tiled corridor, (noun cluster)

   3 starched white cloth rustling against itself, (noun cluster) and outside,

   3 the lonesome whine of wind in the country night (noun cluster) and

   3 the Kansas dust beating against the windows. (noun cluster)
> —Student (cited in Christensen, *Notes*, pages 11–12)

It may seem strange to see sentences laid out in this almost mathematical manner, but it is important to recognize that a well-constructed sentence lends itself to schematization, for any well-constructed sentence has a plan or design. The practiced writer frequently creates the design spontaneously as the product of a well-ordered and trained mind, accustomed to bending words to its will. Just as frequently, however, the design is a result of the careful reworking and polishing of a rough first draft.

In any case, it is well to keep Christensen's schema in mind, for it describes more accurately than the traditionally "diagrammed" sentence how we actually write: we accumulate information as we go along; word follows word on the page; these words unite into clusters, phrases, clauses; separate parts combine to form a total statement—a sentence.

IMPROVING SENTENCES

Working Toward Unity

A sentence, however elaborated by modifications and qualifications, should be essentially about *one thing*.

> For the very nature of a Sentence implies one proposition to be expressed. It may consist of parts, indeed; but these parts must be so closely bound together as to make the impression upon the mind of one object, not of many.
>> —Blair, Lecture XI

Composing Sentences

Thus the reader, who can accommodate only one idea at a time (this being a universal human limitation), can grasp the writer's one idea before moving on to the next. A sentence is unified, then, if it clearly conveys its one main idea; a sentence is not unified if it tries to crowd in so many details that no single idea emerges as *the* idea of the sentence. Similarly, a sentence is not unified if its parts are illogically arranged or if there is needless shifting within the sentence from one subject to another. Consider now each of these impediments to sentence unity.

AVOID OVERCROWDING

When we talk about unity, we are actually concerned with something inside the writer: his or her idea as it forms in the mind and takes shape on paper. Is it one unified idea that takes a clearly defined shape? Or do many ideas—only vaguely related and vaguely expressed—crowd into one another to form an amorphous mass that buries rather than exhibits its meaning, as in the following sentence?

> We think that there is footloose in society, in the enthusiasms with which people become missionaries for the various things in which they take a deep personal interest, a great capacity for helping the other fellow along, and we believe that any leisure-time service should consider its function not alone to the promotion of specific activities, such as athletics, or the arts, but that we should consider as a leisure-time field, in which a great many will find happy outlets for their energies, the pursuit of information or of intellectual culture, not as a matter of schooling but as a matter of post-school avocational interest, and that others can only be served by affording organized outlets for their own leisure enjoyment, in being helpfully identified with causes and movements which are appealing to them, in capacities of service to their group as individuals, or to society at large.
>
> —"Youth...Leisure for Living"

To convert this gibberish into well-formed phrases and clauses, we must first isolate the main point, focus it sharply, and state it clearly. Then we must organize the details so that they follow in an orderly sequence. At the same time, we must eliminate meaningless generalities ("post-school avocational interest"). Having done all this, we are ready to convert these "notes" into an intelligibly written statement. In this case we will need more than one sentence:

> *Improvement:*   Most people appear to enjoy helping other people: notice how enthusiasts (say, tennis players) try to convert others to their pastime. A leisure-time agency could easily utilize this natural missionary impulse by building a program of social service into its regular program of athletic and cultural activities. Such a program would provide an organized outlet for people who want to do good for individuals in their own communities or for society at large.

AVOID PILED-UP PHRASES

Like the overcrowded sentence (of which it is a variation), the sentence with too many prepositional phrases, one piled on top of the other, confuses the reader

because no single coherent idea emerges. There is no rule concerning the number of prepositional phrases that can comfortably be accommodated in a sentence. Suffice it to say that a long string of phrases generally produces a loose, rambling effect. In such cases the writer should eliminate some of the phrases and replace others with single adjectives or adverbs.

> *Example:*   Words are the efforts made by an individual to crystallize his or her ideas and thoughts in order to express them in manner suitable to the mind of a rational creature.
>
> *Improvement:*   Words represent an individual's effort to crystallize and express his or her ideas in a rational manner (or simply "rationally").

AVOID ILLOGICAL ARRANGEMENT

Long, rambling sentences are not the only violators of unity. The following short sentence also fails to convey meaning because the hodgepodge arrangement of words on paper simply does not add up to one unified, well-thought-out idea. Indeed, it is impossible to infer from the following exactly what the writer *meant*—or was trying to say.

> If one moves into the sentient, aware sense of intellectual self-development, here too are found barriers to attainment.

Meaningless, confused, sentences generally issue from one of two problems: either your thoughts are tangled, or they are not coming out on paper as clearly as you envisioned them. In either case you must work with the sentence itself, examining it critically word by word and asking, "Does it make the clear, logical, unified statement that I have in mind? If not, how can I make it say what I want it to say and not something else?" Only after you have answered these questions can you begin to revise your sentences so that they will convey meaning effectively, so that they will not fall apart in the reader's mind. The writer of the sentence cited above has to rethink the idea because the form it took on paper does not make a logical statement.

Another kind of illogical arrangement, classified as a violation of unity, grows out of a careless, illogical combination of subject and predicate. Rhetoricians call this "faulty predication," a very common problem, illustrated by the following:

> The first step in hiking is comfortable shoes and light clothing.

The writer of this sentence should have asked, as he or she critically reread the first draft, "Are shoes and clothing steps in hiking?" Of course not. The sentence should read:

> The first step in preparing for a hike is to get comfortable shoes and light clothing.
>   or
> Before setting out on a hike, one should put on comfortable shoes and light clothing.

Neither of the improved versions is a model of rhetorical splendor, but at least each states a simple idea clearly and accurately, whereas in the original sentence the predicate does not sensibly complete the meaning the subject initiated.

Composing Sentences

Working Toward Coherence

To begin working toward a coherent sentence in which the main clause and its added elements flow smoothly and logically into one another—you must avoid the pitfalls listed below, each of which involves carelessness or misplacement of an added element.

AVOID MISPLACED MODIFIERS

It was a misplaced modifier that created the amusing song title of some years ago, "Throw Mama from the Train a Kiss." Similarly, it was a misplaced modifier (plus a few missing words) that produced the inadvertently humorous letter written by a serviceman's wife to the welfare service at Lackland Air Force Base: "In accordance with your instructions, I have given birth to twins in the enclosed envelope."

Word order is the principal grammatical process of the English language (the difference in meaning between "Dog bites man" and "Man bites dog" is simply a matter of how identical words are positioned); therefore it is vital that the writer arrange words on paper so that they show accurate relationships. Modifiers should be near the terms they modify, and related ideas should be close together; otherwise they may latch on to some other sentence element where they will not make sense.

Notice how easily the following sentences—each containing a misplaced modifier—can be improved either by repositioning the modifier or by restructuring the sentence slightly so that the reader can readily see what words and word groups are intended to go together:

Example:	He saw an accident which he reported yesterday.
Problem:	What does "yesterday" modify—the accident or the time of the report?
Improvement:	He saw an accident yesterday, which he immediately reported.
	or
	He immediately reported the accident (which) he saw yesterday.

Example:	She was the kind of girl who could accept the fact that she was pigeon-toed with a smile.
Improvement:	She was the kind of girl who could accept with a smile the fact that she was pigeon-toed.

Example:	He was born while the Korean War was in progress in the United States.
Improvement:	He was born in the United States while the Korean War was in progress.

In improving sentences with a dangling modifier, the writer must either change the placement of the modifier or revise the syntax of the main clause in the sentence.

Example:	Having just returned from a long cruise, the city seemed unbearably hot.

Problem: In *A Dictionary of American-English Usage*, Margaret Nicholson cites this as an example of the often inadvertently funny dangling participle. "The city had not been on the cruise," Nicholson points out—thereby voicing the English teacher's classic protest. Participles must be attached to the noun responsible for the action or they will "dangle." On this ground she revises the sentence to read:

Improvement: Having just returned from a long cruise, we found the city unbearably hot.

A prohibitive attitude toward the dangling participle will be familiar to almost all students, for the construction has long been universally condemned—unfairly so, according to many contemporary writers on usage and style who point out that in most instances the so-called dangling modifier (it may be a gerund or an infinitive as well as a participle) is often modifying the entire main clause, not just the single noun subject. Thus, according to Bergen and Cornelia Evans in *A Dictionary of Contemporary American Usage* (New York: Random House, 1957), it is not misleading or unclear to say "Looking at the subject dispassionately, what evidence is there?" They claim that "this is the idiomatic way of making statements of this kind and any other construction would be unnatural and cumbersome."

The general principle to follow is simply this: if a dangling modifier makes the meaning obscure or absurd you should rewrite the sentence so that it makes immediate sense. The reader should never have to reread the sentence in order to get it right. Thus, in order to be absolutely free of ambiguity, a sentence such as "After finishing college, my family moved to New York" should be improved to read "After I finished college, my family moved.to New York."

AVOID MIXED CONSTRUCTIONS

Sometimes a writer begins a sentence with one construction in mind and then, somewhere along the way, carelessly shifts to another.

Example: Students know that by getting together to discuss a problem how they can avoid violence.

Improvement: Students know that by getting together to discuss a problem they can avoid violence.

The second version of this sentence is an improvement because the second half of the sentence fulfills the expectation raised in the first half—namely that the subordinating conjunction "that" will be followed by a new subject and predicate. These grammatical terms may mean little or nothing to the average reader who has either forgotten or never really understood grammatical terminology, but the reader nonetheless responds to structural signs.

Thus a reader unconsciously knows that in a sentence beginning "I believe that ... " a subject and predicate will follow.

I believe that someone is knocking at the door.
    or

I believe that Harry will call.

not

I believe that how hard you try is good.

In this last sentence, as in the example cited above, the subordinating conjunction "that" is followed by a second subordinating conjunction, "how." The result is momentary confusion in the reader's mind, for halfway along in the sentence the signals shift abruptly. The implied promise of the sentence has not been fulfilled; the reader's expectations have been thwarted.

It is important to avoid this kind of awkwardness in sentence construction. Actually, carelessness rather than ignorance creates such problems, for, as Lewis Carroll has shown us, all native speakers are unconsciously familiar with the basic structure of English.

AVOID OTHER KINDS OF SHIFTS

We have seen that any change in the pattern of a sentence that surprises and stops the reader—even for a fraction of a second—or that disappoints an expectation set up in the early part of the sentence is a violation of coherence, the "sticking together" of the parts that makes the sentence a sound, consistent, and easy-to-read unit. **In addition to shifts in the basic pattern of the sentence that produce hybrid constructions, there are other kinds of shifts. They are not as obviously bad as those described above, but equally unnecessary and undesirable because they break up the flow and therefore the coherence of the sentence. These are shifts in voice, tense, mood, and person; we shall consider each of them in turn.**

Shift in Voice

Example: When the townspeople heard that the mayor had resigned, a general meeting was called.

Problem: In the above sentence the writer has needlessly shifted from active to passive voice—and this, in turn, has involved a shift in subject from "townspeople" to "meeting." Both of these shifts interfere with the smooth, natural flow of the sentence.

Improvement: When the townspeople discovered that the mayor had resigned, they called a general meeting.

(See "Use Active Voice," page 575.)

Shift in Tense

Example: They come into the room and began opening up the books that are on the table.

Problem: The writer shifts carelessly from present to past to present tense.

Improvement: They come into the room and begin opening up the books that are on the table.

| | or |
| | They came into the room and began opening up the books that were on the table. |

Shift in Mood

Example:	First discuss the problem; then you should take action.
Problem:	A needless shift in mode or mood—from imperative, which issues a command or request, to subjunctive, which expresses obligation.
Improvement:	First discuss the problem; then take action.

Shift in Person

Example:	A student should know the provisions of the Civil Rights Act, for one cannot be a good citizen unless you keep up with current legislation.
Problem:	The writer shifts from "student" to "one" to "you."
Improvement:	A student should know the provisions of the Civil Rights Act, for he or she cannot be a good citizen unless he or she keeps up with current legislation.
	or
	You should know the provisions of the Civil Rights Act, for you cannot be a good citizen unless you keep up with current legislation.

Blair sums up the case against unnecessary shifts:

> During the course of the Sentence, the scene should be changed as little as possible. We should not be hurried by sudden transitions from person to person, nor from subject to subject. There is commonly, in every Sentence, some person or thing, which is the governing word. This should be continued so, if possible, from the beginning to the end.... Should I express myself thus:

> > After we came to anchor they put me on shore, where I was welcomed by all my friends who received me with the greatest kindness.

> In this Sentence, though the objects contained in it have a sufficient connexion with each other, yet by this manner of representing them, by shifting so often both the place and the person, *we* and *they* and *I* and *who*, they appear in such a disunited view that the sense of connexion is almost lost. The Sentence is restored to its proper unity...in...the following manner:

> > Having come to anchor, I was put on shore, where I was welcomed by all my friends and received with the greatest kindness.[1]

---

[1] Note the dangling modifier here. Do you find it offensive? Can a person ("I") "come to anchor"? See the discussion on pages 562–63.

Composing Sentences

AVOID UNCLEAR REFERENCE

Still another violation of sentence coherence grows out of unclear pronoun reference, a common flaw in student writing. **"Reference" suggests that the meaning of a pronoun depends on its antecedent. Strictly speaking, a pronoun is a word used in place of a noun; therefore unless the reader knows precisely what noun or noun clause, what overall idea the pronoun is replacing, the sentence will be neither clear nor coherent.**

Example: The women were stopped and questioned by company guards. They then went to the police who refused to protect them. This attitude has also been reported in other towns.

Problem: The direct antecedent of "they" in the second sentence is "guards." Yet (as we realize on a second reading) the pronoun is supposed to refer to "women." Still another problem: "This attitude" is not clear. Does the writer mean "this *hostile* attitude"—or what? The pronoun references do not provide a clear and definite guide to meaning because the writer has been careless about antecedents of the personal pronoun and has not supplied enough information to indicate precisely what the demonstrative adjective "this" refers to. It is up to the writer to say *specifically* what he or she means here. The reader should not be asked to fill in a noun and adjectives.

Improvement: After being stopped and questioned by company guards, the women went to the police, who refused to protect them. A similar indifference on the part of the police has been reported in other towns.

Another unclear, ambiguous reference:

Example: Jim's father was president of the college, which gave him considerable prestige.

Problem: Does "him" refer to Jim's father? Technically it does, but is that what the writer means? (The reference of "which" is also vague.)

Improvement: Because his father was president of the college, Jim enjoyed considerable prestige.

AVOID UNNECESSARY SPLITS

Sentence flow or coherence is impaired by the careless separation or splitting of words that belong together, as in the following examples:

Subject Split from Its Verb

Example: Zodomirsky, shocked and grieved at the death of Mariana, becomes a monk.

Improvement: Shocked and grieved at the death of Mariana, Zodomirsky becomes a monk.

Verb Split from Its Object

> *Example:* She sipped slowly and contentedly the warm cocoa.
> *Improvement:* Slowly and contentedly she sipped the warm cocoa.

Verb Split from Its Auxiliaries

> *Example:* He had long ago known the woman.
> *Improvement:* He had known the woman long ago.
> or
> Long ago he had known the woman.

It should be pointed out here that not all splits are bad. Sometimes, as in the following sentence, the writer deliberately suspends the predication—the signal of the sentence's direction—without losing the flow or continuity of thought.

> "Alienation," a term once confined to philosophy, law, psychiatry, and advanced literary criticism, has entered the daily vocabulary.

AVOID WEAK CONNECTIVES

Avoid small, loose connectives that detract from the impact of a statement. As an example, we may look at Wilson Follett's observation in *Modern American Usage* on the use of "as."

> The novice's resort to *as* with the meaning *since* or *because* is always feeble. It makes trivial what follows. Webster (1934 edition) remarks: "*As* assigns a reason even more casually than *since*." What is worse, the untrained or heedless writer turns to this weak subordinating link to introduce a co-ordinate clause or what should be his main clause. In either case he ruins emphasis. *It was a comparatively unproductive year, as he was dogged by ill health and domestic worries.*

As Wilson Follett concluded, in place of *as* we should substitute the word *for*.

Similarly, the word "so" is a loose connective, more suited to rambling conversation than to writing.

> *So* I told him I was *so* angry I could barely contain myself. And *so* he finally admitted he was *so* sorry he could hardly stand it. And *so* I said "forget it." *So* we made up and *so* I'm seeing him again tonight.

Where "so" is used as an intensifier ("I was *so* happy") it can usually be eliminated without loss, for like most so-called intensifiers ("I really was happy," "I truly was so very happy") it does not work. In fact, it may produce a reverse effect by creating uneasiness and suspicion. "Exactly how happy is *so* happy?" the reader may wonder. "Why is the writer being vague and seemingly inarticulate and insistent?"

The use of "so" to introduce a clause of purpose or a clause of result is equally ineffective, although the usage is clearly established in informal conversation.

> I wanted to see the town so I asked them to take me along.
> The glass was broken so I had to get another.

Even here the link provided by "so" is weak and can be made more emphatic by using "so that."

The glass was broken so that I had to get another.

Better still, the first half of the sentence can be subordinated.

Because (or since) the glass was broken, I had to get another.

Working Toward Economy

Loose writing is often said to be a reflection of loose thinking; if so, verbosity is a root flaw. Frequently, however, loose writing is a sign not so much of loose thinking as of not enough work, specifically not enough reworking and revising of the original sentence. That first spontaneous overflow simply cannot convey meaning in a clear, concise, and effective manner. "With years of practice," as editor Norman Cousins has observed, "a man may be able to put down words swiftly and expertly. But it is the same kind of swiftness that enables a cellist, after having invested years of effort, to negotiate an intricate passage from Haydn" (479).

Those of us who are not experts will probably need more than one try at most sentences, for people are naturally wordy. Indeed, as George Orwell observed in "Politics and the English Language," "It is easier—even quicker once you have the habit—to say *In my opinion it is not an unjustifiable assumption that* than to say *I think.*"

We cannot very well trim our conversation as we go along, nor can we go back and edit it. When we write, however, we can and must do exactly that: we must return to the sentences we have written and rework, recast, rewrite them until they are lean, crisp, and concise, free of what Flaubert so justifiably deplored as fatty deposits. Such "tight" sentences have far more impact on the reader: "'Beware the anger of a quiet man' is superior to 'A quiet man's anger is especially to be feared,' for the same reasons and in the same way that a short, straight shaft is better than a long, crooked one in most machine operations" (Burgess).

Admittedly it is always harder to condense than to write; still there are concrete ways to go about the "boiling down" process. As we have seen, we can combine sentences and thereby eliminate unnecessary words as well as condense full sentences into sentence elements and long sentence elements into shorter ones. Let us consider each of these processes in some depth.

ELIMINATE UNNECESSARY WORDS

Avoid Indirect Expressions

Example: Probably the *Encyclopaedia Britannica* would provide one with the choicest information since it spends almost five pages expounding upon Shelley. (20 words)

Improvement: The *Encyclopaedia Britannica*, with five full pages on Shelley, is probably the best source. (14 words)

Example:	Without words and what they communicate both connotatively and denotatively, human beings would be reduced to the level of lower primates. (21 words)
Improvement:	Without language human beings would be reduced to the level of the lower primates. (14 words)

Example:	The agnostic is one who holds that he has no knowledge of God; indeed that the human mind is incapable of knowing whether there is or is not a God. (30 words)
Improvement:	An agnostic maintains that the human mind cannot know whether or not God exists. (14 words)

Avoid Useless Repetition

Example:	He sees not only the world of man, but instead he also sees the world of God. (17 words)
Improvement:	He sees both the world of man and the world of God. (12 words)

Example:	The main portion of the story dealt with Robert Peel's political life, an aspect of his life that was very active. (21 words)
Improvement:	The main portion of the story dealt with Robert Peel's very active political life. (14 words)

Example:	The average person in high school is a combination of both of these types, having a balance of both of these types of characteristics. (24 words)
Improvement:	The average high school student combines the characteristics of both types. (11 words)

Avoid Negative Phrasing

Example:	I find myself not in complete agreement with you. (9 words)
Improvement:	I disagree with you. (4 words)

Example:	I do not have much faith in his honesty. (9 words)
Improvement:	I distrust him. (3 words)

Example:	She was not very often on time. (7 words)
Improvement:	She usually arrived late. (4 words)
	or
	She usually was late. (4 words)

Example:	I do not expect to be misunderstood. (7 words)
Improvement:	I expect to be understood. (5 words)

Avoid Loose, Inexact Verbs

Example: He felt that the best way to avoid temptation was to get her to leave. (15 words)

Improvement: He felt that the best way to avoid temptation was to make her leave. (14 words)

Avoid Ineffective Intensifiers ("Really") and Qualifiers ("Rather")

Example: *A Farewell to Arms* was the novel which really first made Hemingway a commercial success. (15 words)

Improvement: *A Farewell to Arms* was Hemingway's first commercially successful novel. (10 words)

Example: The most powerful force in all the world is love. (10 words)
Improvement: The most powerful force in the world is love. (9 words)

Example: He was a somewhat quiet man. (6 words)
Improvement: He was a quiet man. (5 words)

Avoid Anticipatory Phrases Such as "It is," "There Was"[2]

Example: It is for the above-mentioned reasons that I abandoned the project. (11 words)

Improvement: For the above-mentioned reasons I abandoned the project. (8 words)

Example: There were crowds of people milling about. (7 words)
Improvement: Crowds of people were milling about. (6 words)

Example: The reason that he voted for the independent candidate was that she had an antiwar record. (16 words)

Improvement: He voted for the independent candidate because she had an antiwar record. (12 words)

Avoid Redundance

Example: Her dress was pink in color. (6 words)
Improvement: Her dress was pink. (4 words)

Example: The professor introduced a new innovation. (6 words)
Improvement: The professor introduced an innovation. (5 words)

---

[2] This principle generally applies, although with notable exceptions: specifically when the extra words contribute to the rhythm of the sentence or when they help to build the sentence toward an appropriately emphatic climax.

Avoid Deadwood (Words That Carry No Meaning)

Example:	In many cases students are now working along the lines of discussing controversial issues with the administration. (17 words)
Improvement:	Many students are now discussing controversial issues with the administration. (10 words)

Example:	He is working in the interest of political unity. (9 words)
Improvement:	He is working toward political unity. (6 words)

Example:	That society is an interesting one. (6 words)
Improvement:	That society is interesting. (4 words)

Example:	She was aware of the fact that he had not returned her paper. (13 words)
Improvement:	She was aware that he had not returned her paper. (10 words)

Here is a list of common deadwood expressions that pad rather than add to the meaning of a sentence:

along the lines of	in the interest of
to the extent that	of the nature of
the fact that	owing to the fact that
seems to me to be	with reference to
of the character that	tends to be
on the level of	may be said to be

Note how easily many such useless and cumbersome expressions can be abbreviated.

at that time	then
at some future time	after
in the event that	if
is aware of	knows
by virtue of	through
owing to the fact that	because
in spite of the fact that	despite
he is a man who	he
is likely to	may
was of the opinion that	believed
the question as to whether	whether
to be desirous of	to want
the great percentage of	most
to be deficient in	to lack
in a slow manner	slowly
there is no doubt that	undoubtedly
it may be assumed that	supposedly
as an example	
or	for example
an example is	
to take into consideration	to consider

CONDENSE LONG SENTENCE ELEMENTS

Reduce Clause to Phrase

Example: If we follow such a policy it may have the desired effect of convincing the U.S.S.R. that we mean business. (20 words)

Improvement: Following this policy may convince the U.S.S.R. that we mean business. (11 words)

Reduce Clause to Appositive

Example: Einstein, who was one of the most brilliant men of all time, behaved in a manner that was warm and human. (21 words)

Improvement: Einstein, one of the most brilliant men of all time, was a warm human being. (15 words)

Reduce Clause to Adjective

Example: He was introducing considerations which had nothing to do with the case. (12 words)

Improvement: He was introducing extraneous considerations. (5 words)

In summary, we should aspire to spareness and leanness of style, taking care not to go to the other extreme of making our style so spare as to be telegraphic:

> We shall always find our Sentences acquire more vigour and energy when... retrenched: provided always that we run not into the extreme of pruning so very close, as to give a hardness and dryness to style. For here, as in all other things, there is a due medium. Some regard, though not the principal, must be had to fullness and swelling of sound. Some leaves must be left to surround and shelter the fruit.
>
> —Blair, Lecture XII

Working Toward Emphasis

In a properly emphatic sentence every word and every group of words are given what Blair calls "due weight and force." To some extent you can build the clues as to what is most important in the sentence and what is less important into the grammatical construction of the sentence.

PUT MAIN IDEA IN MAIN CLAUSE

It is an oversimplification to say that you should always place the main idea in the main clause, and subordinate points in the subordinate clause, but it represents a helpful technique. If, for example, you have two points of information to present in a sentence—(1) that you were walking in the park, and (2) that you saw a thief steal a woman's purse—you certainly would want to emphasize the second point for that is clearly the *news* of the sentence: that you were witness to a theft. **Thus you would be wise to subordinate the background information by placing it in a subordinate rather than in a coordinate position:**

Example:	I was walking in the park and I saw a man snatch a woman's purse.
Problem:	This coordinate construction distributes importance equally to both halves of the sentence. Actually, however, the two halves are not equal and should not be made to seem so. The first clause should be made subordinate.
Improvement:	As I was walking in the park, I saw a man snatch a woman's purse.

USE EMPHATIC POSITIONS

You can also achieve proper emphasis in a sentence by positioning important elements. The beginning of the sentence and, especially, the end are the emphatic positions. In the unfolding of a sentence, as in the unfolding of an essay, the last words stand out and impress themselves most forcibly on the reader. To fail to take advantage of this, to allow a sentence to trail off with empty qualifying phrases, insignificant afterthoughts, or weak monosyllables such as "it," "was," "done," "is," "etc.," is not only to ignore an extremely important psychological resource but also to create a sense of anticlimax, of a sentence continuing past its natural and proper end.

Example:	The advances of the future must be made in the moral as well as the technological sphere, according to the commencement speaker.
Improvement:	According to the commencement speaker, the advances of the future must be made in the moral as well as the technological sphere.
Example:	Hawthorne was haunted throughout his life by the evil deeds his ancestors had done.
Improvement:	Hawthorne was haunted throughout his life by the evil deeds of his ancestors.
Example:	The word is the basic unit of language and what we communicate with.
Improvement:	The word is the basic unit of language with which we communicate.

Note that in the last example the final preposition has been moved to a less prominent middle position. This was done not because the final preposition is in itself bad, as the old rule proclaims ("Never end a sentence with a preposition"), but rather because it is an unemphatic word that ends the sentence weakly. Actually, where idiom demands it, a final preposition is acceptable:

I did not know what to put it in.

Where idiom does not demand a final preposition, however, it should be avoided, along with all small "inconsiderable words" as Blair terms them, referring to adverbs, participles, conjunctions.

> For besides the want of dignity which arises from those monosyllables at the end, the imagination cannot avoid resting for a little on the import of the word which closes the sentence; and as those prepositions [and other weak words] have no impact of their own but only serve to point out the relations of other words, it is disagreeable for the mind to be left pausing on a word which does not by itself produce any idea nor form any picture in the fancy.
>
> —Blair, Lecture XII

VARY NORMAL WORD ORDER

Because the normal and familiar pattern of the English sentence is subject/verb/object ("I don't like him"), any variation in this pattern calls attention to itself and thereby emphasizes the point being expressed ("Him I don't like"). The second sentence intensifies the predication because it wrenches subject and object out of their expected positions. The subject no longer opens the sentence; the object no longer follows the verb. Instead the word "him" opens the sentence—an unusual location for a pronoun in the objective case. Clearly, then, this sentence informs the reader that this is no ordinary dislike, just as this is no ordinary sentence. The inexperienced writer might try to get the point across by using weak intensifiers ("I really dislike him very much"); the simple transposition of pronouns is far more economical and successful.

Achieving emphasis through transposition is not necessarily a conscious process. The strength of our feelings often dictates a spontaneous switching of terms:

> That I cannot believe!
> Oh, the troubles I've had!
> Never will I do that again!

We can also make conscious use of this device in such simple transpositions as the ones listed below, all of them effective as emphasizers of what might otherwise be mundane observations.

> Cold was the night.
> Come winter and we'll see the fall of snow.
> Of this plan, he knew nothing.

> First a warning, musical; then the hour, irrevocable. [referring to Big Ben striking]
> —Virginia Woolf, *Mrs. Dalloway*

Working Toward Vigor

Closely allied to economy and emphasis is vigor: a lean, tightly constructed sentence with movement and energy built into its structure. Such a sentence, as Bishop Whately wrote long ago, will "stimulate attention, excite the Imagination, and . . .

arouse the feelings" (*Elements*). You will probably write a vigorous sentence in the active rather than in the passive voice and will choose a strong, substantial verb rather than a weak, colorless verb such as "is," "was," "does," or "has."

USE ACTIVE VOICE

"Voice" indicates whether the subject of a sentence acts or is acted upon, whether the subject is the doer of the action or the receiver.

> I hit the ball.

This is active voice because the subject, "I," is the actor or doer.

> The ball was hit.

This is passive voice because the subject, "ball," receives the action of being hit.

Once we are aware of the distinction between active and passive voice, we cannot fail to see that in general the active voice is more lively and assertive than the passive, which tends—as the term "passive" suggests—to lack immediacy.

> *Example:* The test was taken by the students.
> *Improvement:* The students took the test.

> *Example:* College students were recruited by the township and a new project was begun.
> *Improvement:* The township recruited college students and set up a new project

Sentences in the active voice are stronger and more emphatic for two reasons. First, they are more economical: the active voice generally requires fewer words. Second, use of the active voice emphasizes the *real* subject because the *real* subject is also the *grammatical* subject: "students" in the first example above is the *real* subject of the sentence, not "test." But we should also recognize that in some cases the passive voice is preferable: when the doer of the action is unknown ("The house was robbed"); when the receiver of the action, rather than the doer, has to be emphasized ("Shoplifters will be prosecuted"); and in formal report writing, where it is conventional for a writer to be anonymous ("The test was run and the following results obtained").

Despite these important exceptions, you should try, whenever possible, to strengthen and enliven your sentences by converting unnecessary and awkward passives into the active voice.

CONCENTRATE ACTIVITY IN VERBS

Another way to invigorate and at the same time tighten a sentence is to concentrate its action in substantial, well-chosen verbs, avoiding wherever possible weak verbs, such as "is," "was," "has," and "does." Shakespeare habitually used strong verbs rather than the weak state-of-being forms ("is" and "was"). When he did use them, he exacted from them their deepest existential meaning: "To be or not to be, that is the question."

The careless writer often uses a weak, roundabout verb form or inadvertently wastes the action of the sentence on a noun.

Example: He felt an obvious hatred for the new recruit.
Improvement: He obviously hated the new recruit.

Example: Thoreau became a complete recluse from society in his shack at Walden Pond.
Improvement: Thoreau secluded himself in his shack at Walden Pond.

Example: In this anthology are some of the best haiku and tanka verse ever written.
Improvement: This anthology contains some of the best haiku and tanka verse ever written.

Example: There were two contributing factors to this situation.
Improvement: Two factors contributed to this situation.

Example: There was a car moving in circles around the speedway.
Improvement: A car circled the speedway.

Note that when we exploit the peculiar power of the verb to invigorate a sentence, we have at the same time tightened the sentence by reducing the number of words and phrases. We have also pinpointed the action of the sentence on one vivid verb, instead of wasting it on a noun ("Thoreau became a recluse") or a participle ("a car moving").

CHOOSE SPECIFIC, CONCRETE WORDS

A third way to promote vigor in the sentence is to use words that are specific and concrete rather than general and abstract ("the tall, red-haired soldier at the end of the line" rather than "that man over there"). (See "Choosing Words.")

Working Toward Rhythm

Although rhythm is usually associated with poetry, it is a feature of prose writing as well. Indeed, anyone who has ever listened to a sentence read aloud knows that it is a unit not only of meaning but also of rhythm and sound. There is no better guide to good writing than the ear, because what sounds good usually reads well. Conversely, what is jarring, overly intricate, or unpronounceable is usually hard to read and just as hard to understand. Thus it is wise to test your sentences on your ear, to *listen* to the sound of the words—both individually and in combination—and to *feel* their rising and falling action. As one writer has noted, an author who would please or move his readers will often wish to do so by sound as well as sense. Here rhythm becomes important. Feeling tends to produce rhythm; and rhythm, feeling. Further, a strong rhythm may have a hypnotic effect, which holds the reader, as the Ancient Mariner held the wedding guest; prevents his attention from wandering; and makes him more suggestible. (Lucas, 215)

Basically, prose rhythm defies strict analysis and is probably "dictated by some inner pressure, hardly felt at the time, just as the rhythms of poetry seem to come into the head almost unbidden" (Boulton, 68). We may speculate that rhythm is associated with physical sensations: the writer's rate of breathing, heartbeat, pulse, metabolism. Similarly for the reader, a good sentence meets what Flaubert called "the needs of respiration." The sentence must "breathe" correctly—provide pauses where needed, change of pace, slowing down, speeding up. "A good sentence," Flaubert concluded, "should be like a good line of poetry, *unchangeable*, just as rhythmic, just as resonant."

Certainly the musical quality of the sentence cannot be denied, but neither can it be described easily in a short space. It will suffice to quote Blair once again, for his observations on "harmony"—though brief—are germane.

Let us consider agreeable sound, in general, as the property of a well-constructed Sentence.... This beauty of musical construction in prose, it is plain, will depend upon two things; the choice of words, and the arrangement of them.

I begin with the choice of words; on which head, there is not much to be said, unless I were to descend into a tedious and frivolous detail concerning the powers of the several letters, or simple sounds, of which Speech is composed. It is evident, that words are most agreeable to the ear which are composed of smooth and liquid sounds, where there is a proper intermixture of vowels and consonants; without too many harsh consonants rubbing against each other; or too many open vowels in succession, to cause a hiatus, or disagreeable aperture of the mouth. It may always be assumed as a principle, that whatever sounds are difficult in pronunciation, are, in the same proportion, harsh and painful to the ear. Vowels give softness; consonants strengthen the sound of words. The music of Language requires a just proportion of both; and will be hurt, will be rendered either grating or effeminate by an excess of either. Long words are commonly more agreeable to the ear than monosyllables. They please it by composition, or succession of sounds which they present to it: and, accordingly, the most musical languages abound most in them. Among words of any length, those are the most musical which do not run wholly either upon long or short syllables, but are composed of an intermixture of them; such as, *repeat, produce, velocity, celerity, independent, impetuosity.*

The next head, respecting the Harmony which results from a proper arrangement of the words and members of a period, is more complex, and of greater nicety. For, let the words themselves be ever so well chosen, and well sounding, yet, if they be ill disposed, the music of the Sentence is utterly lost.... In English, we may take, for an instance of a musical Sentence, the following from Milton, in his Treatise on Education:

We shall conduct you to a hill-side, laborious indeed, at the first ascent; but else, so smooth, so green, so full of goodly prospects, and melodious sounds on every side, that the harp of Orpheus was not more charming.

Every thing in this Sentence conspires to promote the Harmony. The words are happily chosen; full of liquid and soft sounds; *laborious, smooth, green, goodly, melodious, charming*: and these words so artfully arranged, that were we to alter the collocation of any one of them, we should, presently, be sensible of the melody suffering. For, let us observe, how finely the members of the period swell one above another. "So smooth, so green,"—"so full of goodly prospects, and melodious sounds on every side;"—till the ear, prepared by this gradual rise, is conducted to that full close on which it rests with pleasure;—"that the harp of Orpheus was not more charming."

—Blair, Lecture XIII

Rhythm and harmony are matters too complex to contemplate here with any thoroughness. We shall simply consider four basic rhetorical devices that contribute to the rhythmic and euphonious arrangement of sentence elements: (1) parallel construction; (2) balanced antithesis; (3) order of climax; (4) variation in sentence length, pattern, and type.

PARALLEL CONSTRUCTION

More than any other single resource available to the writer, parallel construction—repetition of sentence elements ("I came, I saw, I conquered")—provides a basis for rhythm in prose. Listen to these familiar words from Lincoln's Gettysburg Address: "…we cannot dedicate, we cannot consecrate, we cannot hallow this ground." Rhythmically, this sentence approaches poetry, as we can hear by noting the measured beat in each clause:

we cannot dedicate,

we cannot consecrate,

we cannot hallow this ground.

Or, if you wish to stress different syllables:

we cannot dedicate,

we cannot consecrate,

we cannot hallow this ground.

The casting of like ideas in like grammatical form improves a sentence on almost every count. It tightens, enlivens, and unifies. It also makes the sentence more emphatic and coherent, because likeness of form enables the reader to recognize more readily likeness of content: each item in a parallel series announces itself as a companion to the others—a comparable action:

They were walking, running, leaping. (three participles)

Because the meaning of such a sentence is reinforced by its structure and rhythm, a direction issued in parallel form is easier to grasp:

Walk, do not run, to the nearest exit. (two imperative verbs)

Similarly, a longer sentence that contains a series of observations or many details and qualifications is held together by a framework of parallelism.

> The only advice...that one person can give another about reading is to take no advice, to follow your own instincts, to use your own reason, to come to your own conclusions.
>
> —Virginia Woolf, *The Second Common Reader*

(Note the series of four infinitives: "to take...to follow...to use...to come....")

> Jealousy of Mr. Elliot had been the retarding weight, the doubt, the torment. That had begun to operate in the very hour of first meeting her in Bath; that had returned, after a short suspension, to ruin the concert; and that had influenced him in every thing he had said and done, or omitted to say and do, in the last four-and-twenty hours.
>
> —Jane Austen, *Persuasion*

(Note that in the first sentence above the three complements of "had been" are nouns presented in order of rising intensity: "weight," "doubt," "torment." In the second, longer sentence Austin holds the parts in place with the three long "that" clauses, in the last of which there is parallelism within the parallel: "every thing he had said and done, or omitted to say and do....")

Parallelism combined with repetition of key words produces an especially tight and emphatic rhythmic unit.

> No fact, however interesting, no image, however vivid, no phrase, however striking, no combination of sounds, however resonant, is of any use to a poet unless it fits: unless it appears to spring inevitably out of its context.
>
> —Northrop Frye, "New Directions from Old"

The careless and inexperienced writer is apt to overlook both the semantic and rhythmic significance of arranging like ideas in parallel form. He or she does not realize that when the items themselves correspond to one another, the reader expects to find the words in corresponding form and is disappointed if they are not.

Example:	They liked to go to the movies, hiking in the mountains, and on long rainy days they would sleep the whole afternoon.
Problem:	The writer has expressed three comparable activities in three different grammatical forms: an infinitive phrase, a participial phrase, and a clause.
Improvement:	They liked to go to the movies, to hike in the mountains, and on long rainy days to sleep the whole afternoon.
	or
	They liked going to the movies, hiking in the mountains, and—on long rainy days—sleeping the whole afternoon.

Example:	The course grade is based on three factors: what you do in the final examination, writing a term paper, and classwork.
Problem:	Here again, three ideas of equal importance are expressed in three different grammatical forms: a relative clause, a participial phrase, and a single noun.

Improvement: The course grade is based on three factors: a final examination, a term paper, and classwork.

BALANCED ANTITHESIS

When two ideas stand in opposition to each other (the "either ... or"), you can emphasize the contrast or tension between them by setting them forth in a form of parallelism called *balanced antithesis.*

> Either we live by accident and die by accident; or we live by plan and die by plan.
> —Thornton Wilder, *The Bridge of San Luis Rey*

> The tragedy of life is not that man loses but that he almost wins.
> —Heywood Broun

> Talent, Mr. Micawber has; money, Mr. Micawber has not.
> —Charles Dickens, *David Copperfield*

(Note that Dickens has achieved further emphasis by inverting normal word order.)

The force and binding power of balanced antithesis rest basically on parallel constructions in which the writer repeats key words in an opposite context. Note the impact, for example, of President John F. Kennedy's famous statement.

> Ask not what your country can do for you; ask what you can do for your country.

One way to emphasize a balanced antithesis is to pair words through alliteration:

> Both poems are didactic: one preaches, one praises.

> Yonder is one whose years have calmed his passions but not clouded his reason.
> —Samuel Johnson, *Rasselas*

Balanced antithesis should not, however, be overused. Herbert Read noted, "used with discretion [balanced antithesis] adds point and vivacity to expression; but when abused it becomes tedious and artificial." (40)

ORDER OF CLIMAX

> But in a larger sense we cannot dedicate, we cannot consecrate, we cannot hallow this ground.

Note that, in addition to casting this sentence in a parallel construction, Lincoln carefully organized its three verbs in climactic order, moving from the least commitment ("to dedicate" is to set aside ground); to a deeper commitment ("to consecrate" is to declare the ground sacred); to the very deepest commitment ("to hallow" is to perpetually honor the ground as holy). Thus, Lincoln fulfilled the requirements of a rhythmic as well as a properly emphatic statement; he did not allow his sentence to fall off at the end. Indeed, he arranged the verbs so that they would grow both in meaning and in rhythmic impact. **Rising action is so important because it rests on the natural human expectation that items in a series will intensify as they progress.** Surely it was this recognition that led Jane Austen in the sentence cited earlier to describe jealousy in progressively more oppressive terms: first as a "retard-ing weight," then as a "doubt," and finally as a "torment." To reverse the order (a "torment," a "doubt," a "retarding weight") would create an anticlimax—a letdown instead of buildup. Thus, as Blair wrote, the writer should always make certain that the "members" of a sentence

> go on rising and growing in their importance above one another. This sort of arrangement.... is always a beauty in composition. From what cause it pleases is abundantly evident. In all things we naturally love to ascend to what is more and more beautiful, rather than to follow the retrograde order. Having had once some considerable object set before us, it is with pain we are pulled back to attend to an inferior circumstance.... The same holds in melody...: that a falling off at the end always hurts greatly. For this reason particles, pronouns, and little words, are as ungracious to the ear, at the conclusion, as I formerly showed they were inconsistent with strength of expression. It is more than probable that the sense and sound here have a mutual influence on each. That which hurts the ear seems to mar the strength of meaning; and that which really degrades the sense, in consequence of this primary effect appears also to have a bad sound.
>
> —Blair, Lecture XIII

VARIATION IN SENTENCE LENGTH, PATTERN, AND TYPE

A succession of declarative sentences written in the conventional subject/verb/object order, with an average length of fourteen to twenty words, or two lines apiece, would produce a droning monotone. After a while the sameness of rhythm and pattern, the lack of emphasis, would dull the reader's senses and send his or her attention elsewhere. Note the tiresome succession of short, choppy sentences in the following paragraph:

> Hemingway's works abound in war, violence, and death. Hemingway had first-hand experience with all three. He took in two world wars. He also participated in smaller wars. They made him see death without disguise. He had no heroic illusions. [Note gap in thought here.] Life and death were intermingled in the minds of his characters.

Most writers intuitively vary sentence length because the mind in the process of composition tends to express itself in unequal "waves" of thought. Note in the following paragraph, for example, how John Steinbeck's sentences range in length from three words to forty-two:

Sentence Length

Average (27 words)	When I was very young and the urge to be someplace else was on me, I was assured by mature people that maturity would cure this itch.
Short (12 words)	When years described me as mature, the remedy prescribed was middle age.
Average (25 words)	In middle age I was assured that greater age would calm my fever and now that I am fifty-eight perhaps senility will do the job.
Short (3 words)	Nothing has worked.

Composing Sentences

Average (20 words)	Four hoarse blasts of a ship's whistle still raise the hair on my neck and set my feet to tapping.
Long (42 words)	The sound of a jet, an engine warming up, even the clopping of shod hooves on pavement brings on the ancient shudder, the dry mouth and vacant eye, the hot palms and the churn of stomach high up under the rib cage.
Average (15 words)	In other words, I don't improve; in further words, once a bum always a bum.
Short (6 words)	I fear the disease is incurable.

—John Steinbeck, *Travels with Charley*

Similarly, most writers tire of the typical declarative sentence and vary the pattern of their prose with the addition of a rhetorical question, an imperative, an exclamation.

> I hate to hear people saying, "He is young, he must wait; he will get plenty of chances." How do they know? Could Keats have waited, or Shelley, or Byron, or Burns?
> —J. A. Spender, *The Comments of Bagshot*

Writers also tire of the usual subject/verb/object pattern and automatically alter it so that sentences open differently—sometimes with the subject, other times with a prepositional phrase, an adverb, a subordinate clause.

> Sometimes in history, a nation collapses not because of its own flaws but because of the attacking nation's tremendous strength. Was this but the latest example? For years, from Berlin, I had watched Nazi Germany's mercurial rise in military might, which the sleeping democracies in the West did little to match. I had followed, too, at firsthand, Hitler's cynical but amazingly successful diplomacy, which had so easily duped the West and paved the way for one quick military conquest after another. But still the French debacle was quite incomprehensible. Not even the German generals I had talked with in Berlin expected it.
> —William Shirer, *The Collapse of the Third Republic*

The most dramatic wrenching of normal word order occurs in the periodic or suspended sentence, wherein the writer postpones the prediction to the end of the sentence, thereby achieving a kind of "suspense."

> The fighter who stays in the ring as long as he can stand on his feet, the man who keeps his business alive while his clothes are threadbare and his stomach empty, the captain who clings to his ship while there is a plank left afloat—that is Washington.
> —W. E. Woodward, *George Washington, the Image and the Man*

Because the reader does not know what a suspended sentence is about until the end, he or she will surely get lost or simply give up along the way unless the writer establishes a rhythmic unity that holds the sentence together and moves it toward its climax. This can be achieved only by observing strict parallelism, as in the following example:

> How is it that I, who had the biggest Big League Gum collection in the East, who can still recite the lineup of the 1931 World Series (though there isn't much demand for it), who missed supper rather than miss the ball scores on WOR at 7 P.M., who never read the great novels because of a boyhood spent reading baseball news and "The Baseball Magazine" instead—how is it that I, the despair of my parents for an addiction that shut

out almost every other field of knowledge, the bane of my sisters for the simulated major league doubleheaders that I played against the side of the house every day with a rubber ball, can hardly bring myself to follow the game today?
—William Zinsser, *Pop Goes America*

Sentences like these gain enormously in emphasis and vigor by virtue of their suspension—the "long and steady climb upward over successive terraces of clauses" (Potter)—followed by the final swift descent to the point of the sentence, its predication. Certainly the cadence of such a sentence captures the reader, so that it can elicit a whole new dimension of rhythmic as well as mental response.

Not all sentences are as dramatically suspended as the preceding examples. Frequently the writer introduces a short delay, using words that may seem unnecessary but that serve a rhythmic purpose.

> It was not until the other day, when I returned on a visit to Coney Island, that I recalled an important episode of my youth which had been buried all these years.
> —Isaac Rosenfeld, in "Coney Island Revisited"

At first we might deplore the seemingly useless "It was" opening of the preceding sentence. But if we study it more carefully, we will see that this normally poor construction works here; it enables the writer to build a short rhythmic suspense that has more impact that the direct and economical and flat alternative:

> I recalled an important, long-buried episode of my youth the other day when I returned on a visit to Coney Island.

To some extent it is true that a series of short, simple sentences conveys an impression of speed, whereas longer sentences, as Herbert Read noted, "give an air of solemnity and deliberation to writing" (35). Actually, long sentences may move swiftly, provided they are well constructed and flow smoothly and harmoniously from one word group to another. Take the two virtuoso examples that follow:

1. This sentence closes Lytton Strachey's biography of Queen Victoria:

> Perhaps her fading mind called up once more the shadows of the past to float before it, and retraced, for the last time, the vanished visions of that long history—passing back and back, through the cloud of years, to older and ever older memories—to the spring woods of Osborne, so full of primroses for Lord Beaconsfield—to Lord Palmerston's queer clothes and high demeanor; and Albert's face under the green lamp, and Albert's first stag at Balmoral, and Albert in his blue and silver uniform, and the Baron coming in through a doorway, and Lord M. dreaming at Windsor with the rooks cawing in the elmtrees, and the Archbishop of Canterbury on his knees in the dawn, and the old King's turkeycock ejaculations, and Uncle Leopold's soft voice at Claremont, and Lehzen with the globes, and her mother's feathers sweeping down towards her, and a great old repeater-watch of her father's in its tortoise-shell case, and a yellow rug, and some friendly flounces of sprigged muslin, and the trees and the grass at Kensington.
> —Lytton Strachey, *Queen Victoria*

This long sentence moves back steadily in time, as the writer imagines the queen's "fading mind" moving back through memory to retrace the "vanished visions" of her long life. As her memories pass "back and back, through the cloud of years," so this single sentence moves back and back in a continuous flow of images. Thus the writer encompasses one long life in one long tightly organized sentence that captures in its unity the unity and rhythm of the life it describes.

2. Here is another seemingly endless descriptive sentence, this one suspended:

> If the eyes are too big, and they are twice too big, and if they surround a nose that cannot be subdivided, and if the body parts might have been assembled by a weary parent on Christmas Eve, and if the teeth are borrowed from a rabbit soliciting carrots, and if the voice could summon sentry dogs, and if she does not walk so much as lurch, glide and jerk in continuing peril of collapsing like a rag doll dismissed by a bored child, and if on top of that she is saddled with being Judy Garland's first of three children by her second of five marriages, then how can the bearer of these oddments, how can this girl put together in the Flea Market, how can Liza Minnelli, at 23, threaten to become the major entertainment figure that she is becoming? (Thompson)

This sentence is clearly playful as well as descriptive. By piling *if*-clause upon *if*-clause, the writer has tried to intensify the mystery ("Who is this strange creature?" we wonder), and by building on a repetitive "and if . . . and if," he has established an almost breathless musical refrain, moving us, we are led to expect, to some sort of crescendo. Instead, the sentence falls off at the end, contrary to conventional principles of emphasis and harmony. Nonetheless, the sentence succeeds almost despite itself, for it brings us down to earth, again rhythmically. The subject, after all, is not of momentous import (note that most of the words are short and simple); the writer's weak ending seems to tell us that he knows he has been a bit overdramatic, but he has been writing in a spirit of fun. There is clearly a tongue-in-cheek element in this sentence. It is in itself a little essay, light and playful in tone.

FORGING A BETTER STYLE

As Blair points out in the following passage, the best way to forge a better style is to write slowly and carefully, never aiming directly for speed. At the same time, we must not be too plodding.

> Many rules concerning style I have delivered, but no rules will answer the end, without exercise and habit. At the same time, it is not every sort of composing that will improve style. This is so far from being the case, that by frequent, careless, and hasty composition, we shall acquire certainly a very bad style; we shall have more trouble afterwards in unlearning faults, and correcting negligences, than if we had not been accustomed to composition at all. In the beginning, therefore, we ought to write slowly and with much care. Let the facility and speed of writing, be the fruit of longer practice. Says Quintilian, with the greatest reason, "I enjoin, that such as are beginning the practice of composition, write slowly and with anxious deliberation. Their great object at first should be, to write as well as possible; practice will enable them to write speedily. By degrees, matter will offer itself still more readily; words will be at hand; composition will flow; every thing as in the arrangement of a well-ordered family, will present itself in its proper place. The sum of the whole is this; by hasty composition, we shall never acquire the art of composing well; by writing well, we shall come to write speedily."

> We must observe, however, that there may be an extreme, in too great and anxious care about words. We must not retard the course of thought, nor cool the heat of

imagination, by pausing too long on every word we employ. There is, on certain occasions, a glow of composition which should be kept up, if we hope to express ourselves happily, though at the expense of allowing some inadvertencies to pass. A more severe examination of these must be left to be the work of correction. For, if the practice of composition be useful, the laborious work of correcting is no less so: it is indeed absolutely necessary to our reaping any benefit from the habit of composition. What we have written, should be laid by for some little time, till the ardour of composition be past, till the fondness for the expressions we have used be worn off, and the expressions themselves be forgotten; and then, reviewing our work with a cool and critical eye, as if it were the performance of another we shall discern many imperfections which at first escaped us. Then is the season for pruning redundances; for weighing the arrangement of sentences; for attending to the juncture and connecting particles; and bringing style into a regular, correcting and supported form. This "*Limoe Labor*," must be submitted to by all who would communicate their thoughts with proper advantage to others; and some practice in it will soon sharpen their eye to the most necessary objects of attention, and render it a much more easy and practicable work than might at first be imagined.

—Blair, Lecture XIX

DISCUSSION AND EXERCISES

Grammar Quiz

Read the following sentences carefully and determine which ones are grammatically correct and what errors have been committed in the incorrect sentences. How *should* they read? (No rephrasing is necessary.)

1. He looked much stronger than me.
2. Each person in the class has their own preconceptions.
3. Stealing someone else's lines are plagiarism.
4. If I were more certain of the results, I would try out.
5. Turkey and stuffing are a traditional Thanksgiving treat.
6. The orchestra leader. said that neither the violin nor the viola were properly tuned.
7. I objected to him playing the piano at 3 A.M.
8. At the end of the road stands a large red maple tree and a gnarled oak.
9. Since her vacation she looks good.
10. The president, along with his aides, was going to appear at the bicentenary celebration.
11. The tickets are being saved for whoever wants them.
12. Each of the students were competent.
13. The engineer handed the blueprint to John and I.
14. We must remain here as long as they.
15. Each of us takes a turn.
16. My brother is one of those athletes whom is always in trim.
17. She got to the game late she was never on time.
18. There are more than one way to solve the problem.
19. It is important that she be allowed to remain onstage with the orchestra.
20. He tried his best, it was too difficult though.
21. Just ahead of me are the rest of the class.
22. It is up to we students to organize the debate.

23. The job of the jury is to make up their mind.
24. She took her work in the theater very serious.
25. Twenty dollars is a lot of money for a magazine subscription.

Sentence Exercises

1. Combine the following groups of sentences by reducing some of them to relative clauses, subordinate clauses, prepositional or participial phrases, absolutes, or appositives.

   a. Football is one of the most popular and colorful sports in America. Football attracts millions of spectators on fall weekends.

   b. Benjamin Franklin came from a large family. There were seventeen children in the family. He was the fifteenth child and the youngest son.

   c. The speaker mesmerized the audience. He gazed at them with his electric-blue eyes. He spoke in a rhythmic chant. He raised his arms repeatedly. He looked as if he wanted to supplicate the heavens.

   d. The city was in shambles. Telephone lines were down everywhere. The streets were littered with debris. Some of the debris consisted of fallen branches, pieces of glass from shattered windows, and assorted objects. They had detached themselves from roofs of houses and parked cars.

   e. Calypso is the official name for the dialect spoken in the Caribbean Islands. It is characterized by the sing-song and shortened words. The words often run together.

   f. During a recent conversation with a friend the term "intelligence" was used. It was used in a manner which made me reflect. I was reflecting on its meaning.

   g. Planets are heavenly bodies. They seem to have a motion of their own. They revolve around the sun.

   h. F. Scott Fitzgerald was an American novelist and short story writer. He was sometimes called "the laureate of the jazz age."

   i. It has been shown throughout history that some people are ahead of their time. Such is the case with Galileo and Newton.

   j. In the second section complications are introduced by Mariana. She begs Zodomirsky not to duel. This begging causes Zodomirsky to face a conflict between his honor as a man and his love for Mariana.

2. Expand the following sentences in the six basic ways a minimal sentence may be expanded. See illustration on page 557 under heading "Expanding Sentences."

   a. Cool evenings are comfortable.
   b. Healthy children are creative.
   c. Great art is exciting.
   d. Clothes make the man.
   e. Women are asserting their Selves.

3. Generate your own sentences according to the pattern illustrated on pages 557–58, under the heading "Levels of Generalization." Substitute the following main clauses:

   a. He raised his hand in the air and held it...
      (follow a 1, 2, 3, 4 subordinate sequence)
   b. He could write for hours...
      (follow a 1, 2, 2, 2, 2 coordinate sequence)
   c. Her lips tightened over her white teeth for a moment, and...
      (follow a 1, 1, 2, 3, 4 sequence here)

d. It was as though someone had pulled a lever at midnight and suddenly the campus was awake and running...
(follow a 1, 2, 2, 2, 3, 3, 3, 3, 3 mixed coordinate sequence)

4. Locate the weaknesses in the following sentences, and rewrite each sentence to improve it.

   a. Just as scientific progress has dispelled the belief that an "evil spirit" causes the headache, so has it replaced the former cure of boring holes in the skull with aspirin.
   b. There are more single women than men in the United States, according to the Census Bureau.
   c. Most of the churches have large congregations that are rather wealthy.
   d. In 1870 Pavlov conducted an investigation of the pancreatic nerves and was awarded a gold medal for it.
   e. One old cottage in particular attracted my attention. It was a huge white structure with four gables, one at each corner.
   f. Milton, who was one of the most scholarly men of all time, devoted a good part of his life to activities in the sphere of politics.
   g. She began singing in a coffeehouse in Boston at the age of nineteen.
   h. The author's central purpose is a view of human behavior.
   i. It is important to keep in mind what sin and guilt meant in Hawthorne's use.
   j. He was a man of heroic soul, keen intellect, and quiet wit.
   k. There is a noticeable lack of friends in his life.
   l. On returning to the deck, the sea became dark and turbulent.
   m. The French engineers proposed an alternative plan. Their plan called for the construction of a semicircular dam two hundred fifty feet wide which cost eighty million dollars.
   n. There are two basic means of communication of which one is speaking and the other is the use of the written word.
   o. The English hate frogs, but the French love frogs and hate the English, and cut off their hind legs and consider them a great delicacy.
   p. The next morning he was found lying on the floor by a cleaning woman.

5. Comment on the following passages and indicate what factors contribute to their rhetorical effectiveness.

   a. When youth is gone, every man will look back upon that period of life with infinite sorrow and regret. It is the bitter sorrow and regret of a man who knows that once he had a great talent and wasted it, of a man who knows that once he had a great treasure and got nothing from it, of a man who knows that he had strength enough for everything and never used it.

   —Thomas Wolfe

   b. The world of Homer is unbearably sad because it never transcends the immediate moment; one is happy, one is unhappy, one wins, one loses, finally one dies. That is all. Joy and suffering are simply what one feels at the moment; they have no meaning beyond that; they pass away as they came; they point in no direction; they change nothing. It is a tragic world but a world without guilt for its tragic flaw is not a flaw in human nature, still less in an individual character, but a flaw in the nature of existence.

   —W. H. Auden, Introduction to
   The Portable Greek Reader

   c. I who am blind can give one hint to those who see—one admonition to those who would make full use of the gift of sight: Use your eyes as if tomorrow you would be stricken blind. And the same method can be applied to the other senses. Hear the music of voices, the song of a bird, the mighty strains of an orchestra, as if you would be stricken deaf tomorrow. Touch each object you want to touch as if tomorrow your tactile sense would fail. Smell the perfume of flowers, taste with relish each morsel, as if tomorrow you could never smell and taste again. Make the most of every sense; glory in all the facets of pleasure and beauty which the world reveals to you through the several means of contact which Nature provides. But of all the senses, I am sure that sight must be the most delightful.

—Helen Keller, *Three Days to See*

d. They went down to the camp in black, but they came back to the town in white; they went down to the camp in ropes, they came back in chains of gold; they went down to the camp with their feet in fetters, but came back with their steps enlarged under them; they went also to the camp looking for death, but they came back from thence with assurance of life; they went down to the camp with heavy hearts, but came back with pipe and tabor playing before them.

—John Bunyan, *Life and Death of Mr. Badman*

e. We sailed early in January, and for nearly a year we wandered from country to country. I saw Egypt. I saw the Pyramids, at noon and at sunset, by moonlight, and at sunrise. I saw the Tombs of the Kings, and the great Temple at Karnak. I saw the lovely vanished Temple of Philae. I saw the coast of Asia Minor, and the harbor of Smyrna. I sailed on the Aegean Sea. I saw the Isles of Greece, and the Acropolis. I saw the Golden Horn in the sunrise, and the minarets and the cypresses of Constantinople. I saw Italy. I saw Switzerland. I saw Paris. I saw London. I saw England in summer. I saw the frozen lakes of Norway, and the midnight sun over the ice fields.

—Ellen Glasgow, *The Woman Within*

Punctuation Review

FOUR MAIN FUNCTIONS

*T*he following chart demonstrates at a glance the fundamental principles of sentence punctuation; it is followed by a brief summary of the main points of punctuation usage.

Punctuation Chart

1. Sentence. Sentence.
2. Main clause; main clause.
3. Main clause: main clause.
4. Main clause, { and / or / but / for / nor } main clause.
5. Main clause; { so that / therefore / however / then } main clause.
6. Main clause subordinate clause.
7. Subordinate clause, main clause.
8. Introductory word or phrase, main clause.
9. Main clause subordinate clause; main clause.
10. Main clause; subordinate clause, main clause.

As you can see, the rules of punctuation are neither numerous nor complicated. They must be adhered to *with exactness*, however, for as linguist Harold Whitehall has pointed out, "The traditional purpose of punctuation is to symbolize by means of visual signs the patterns heard in speech" (119). In other words, punctuation marks do the work of vocal inflections in conveying critical distinctions in meaning, as between "He's a great guy!" and "He's a great guy?"

Punctuation marks serve readers in much the same way that road signs serve drivers: they let readers know where they are and keep them moving in the right direction. Whitehall has noted (119) that the most important function of punctuation is "to make grammar graphic" and that it fulfills this function in four ways:

1. by *linking* parts of sentences and words

semicolon
colon
dash
hyphen

2. by *separating* sentences and parts of sentences

> period
> question mark
> exclamation point
> comma

3. by *enclosing* parts of sentences

> paired commas
> paired dashes
> paired parentheses
> paired brackets
> paired quotation marks

4. by *indicating* omissions

> apostrophe
> omission period or dot
> triple periods or dots

Let us consider each of these marks in its turn.

Linking Punctuation

USE A SEMICOLON (;)

1. **To link main clauses that could otherwise occur as separate sentences, especially if they are parallel in structure and emphasis:**

> I insisted on a camping trip; no other vacation interested me.

2. **To link word groups containing heavy internal punctuation:**

> My department chairman, John Webster, plans to travel through most of southern Europe; through all of the Near East; and, if he has the time, along the northern, western, and southern coasts of Africa.

3. **To link main clauses joined by a conjunctive adverb (for example, *moreover, therefore, indeed, also, instead, likewise, meanwhile, hence, nevertheless, consequently*):**

> I mailed in a deposit; however, I received no reply.

4. **To precede words, phrases, or abbreviations such as *namely, for instance, i.e., e.g.*, which provide a summary or explanation of what has gone before in the sentence:**

> A writer should follow a specific principle of organization; for example, time order, space order, order of climax.

According to Whitehall, the semicolon distributes emphasis more or less equally between the preceding and following statements; whereas the colon throws emphasis forward toward the following statement.

Punctuation Review

USE A COLON (:)

1. **To introduce a summary or a list; generally the introductory clause should be a main clause** (see page 546):

   He carried a suitcase filled with books: the plays of Shakespeare, the novels of George Eliot, the poems of Keats, the essays of Montaigne, and the collected cartoon strips of Charles Schulz.

2. **To introduce an extended quotation (use a comma if the quotation is a single sentence or part of a sentence):**

   He said: "I cannot begin to think about returning home. My work is barely under way; in fact, today I had my first chance to examine the data. The preliminary findings are certainly promising."

3. **To introduce a formal statement or question:**

   The committee met to consider a sobering question: What shall we do if the president resigns?

Whitehall explains that the dash, unlike the anticipatory colon, throws the reader's attention back to the original statement.

USE A DASH (--; TYPED AS A DOUBLE HYPHEN WITH NO SPACING)

1. **To introduce a final clause that summarizes, explains, amplifies, or provides an unexpected addition to what has gone before.**

   Freedom of speech, freedom of worship, freedom from want, freedom from fear--these form the foundation of a democratic state.

   He was modest, shy, simply dressed--and absolutely obsessed with the subject of sex.

2. **To indicate a break in thought or in speech:**

   Periodically--I'd say about every two months--he writes me to ask for a loan. I--I don't know what to say.

3. **To stress or reinforce an idea:**

   She was good--too good.

USE A HYPHEN (-)

1. **To designate compound words or to separate certain prefixes and suffixes from their root words:**

brother-in-law	self-government
six-year-old	ex-governor
five-story	governor-elect
soft-spoken	great-grandfather

   Since usage varies and is often divided, consult a current dictionary of your choice. Also let your ear be a guide.

2. To indicate continuation of a word divided at the end of a line. (Always check the dictionary to make certain you are dividing the word where the syllables break.)

3. To link the elements of compound numbers from twenty-one to ninety-nine and to link the elements of fractions:

> sixty-eight dollars
> two-thirds of a nation

4. To link nouns or modifiers which are being used in a compound sense:

> It was a well-run school.
> The year-end dinner-dance was a great success.
> There were cradle-to-grave benefits.
> Her reasons were all-too-human.

Many formerly hyphenated words have become fused into single units, such as *seaweed* and *bookkeeper*. Where there is no precedent, the best policy is to hyphenate when you feel that hyphenation will make your meaning clearer.

Separating Punctuation

USE A PERIOD (.)

1. To separate declarative subject-predicate sentences (including mild commands) from sentences which follow. One can *hear* the end of a declarative sentence, for there is a distinct drop in the voice from high to low pitch:

> The lake is light blue.
> Do not be late.

2. To conclude a statement which may not be in conventional subject-predicate form but which clearly falls in pitch and thereby generates a pause:

> The more, the merrier.

USE A QUESTION MARK (?)

1. To separate questions and quoted questions from their following context. Because the grammatical meaning of the question mark is "answer needed," it should be used to indicate all forms of query:

> Did she say that?
> She said what?
> Can you pass the course? is the main question.
> He asked me, "Are you leaving tonight?"

2. To express more than one query in the same sentence:

> Did she say that? or you? or who?

USE AN EXCLAMATION POINT (!)

1. **To separate exclamatory sentences expressing surprise, incredulity, admiration, or other strong emotion from their following context:**

   How lovely!
   What a surprise!
   I can't believe it!
   O Lord, save thy people!

USE A COMMA (,)

1. **To separate elements in a sentence that might cause confusion or fail to make sense if considered in combination:**

   Instead of hundreds, thousands came.
   To Mary, Clark was very friendly.
   What the answer is, is hard to say.
   Out of every hundred, fifty were rejected.

2. **To separate main clauses that are joined by a coordinating conjunction (*and, but, or, nor, for*):**

   She attended all the lectures, but she could not get to the laboratory sessions.

3. **To separate introductory words, phrases, or dependent clauses from the main clause and thereby to facilitate reading:**

   Luckily, she arrived in time.
   Up to that time, she had never taken a math course.
   Before gathering shells, we went for a swim.
   Although he intended no harm, his behavior created chaos in the classroom.

4. **To separate words, phrases, or clauses in a series:**

   The blonde, pretty, somewhat plump girl said her name was Nancy.
   They wanted bread, cheese, salami, and wine.
   He looked after the baby, cleaned, and cooked.
   After looking through my desk, after phoning the lost and found office, after questioning everyone in the building, I finally found my notebook.
   I came, I saw, I conquered.[1]

5. **To set off nonrestrictive[2] or parenthetical words, phrases, or clauses in a sentence:**

   The financial risk, he reported, was enormous.

---

[1] When a complete predication is made in two or three words, or when the predications form a unit of expression (such as a proverb or familiar saying), commas may be used in place of periods or semicolons.

[2] Restrictive modifiers are those which are essential to the meaning of a sentence ("The woman *who snatched the purse* was arrested"). Nonrestrictive modifiers are not essential but merely elaborative; they could be eliminated without altering the basic meaning of the sentence ("The woman who snatched the purse was arrested, *while her husband stood by, unable to help*").

Chapter One, which deals with definition, serves as an introduction to all forms of discourse.
but: The chapter which deals with definition serves as an introduction to all forms of discourse. [No comma is necessary here because the clause *which deals with definition* is restrictive—that is, essential to identify the chapter being referred to.]

6. **To set off words or phrases in apposition:**

That man, the owner of the bookstore, will never reduce his prices.

7. **To set off words or phrases in contrast:**

He needs sympathy, not anger.

8. **To set off absolute expressions:**

The course having ended, the students prepared to leave the campus. [nominative absolute]
Indoors or out, tennis is a healthful sport. [absolute phrase]
Well, let's get started. [mild interjection]
We don't have a chance, do we? [echo question]

9. **To indicate the omission of an "understood" verb in a compound sentence:**

Byron was a poet; Beethoven, a composer.
My brother lives in New Jersey; my sister, in New York.

10. **To set off a noun or phrase in direct address:**

Madame President, the vote has been counted.

11. **To set off *Yes* and *No* when used at the beginning of a sentence:**

No, I cannot leave the building.

12. **To separate a direct quotation from its context:**

"I cannot go," she told him.

13. **To separate elements in dates and place names:**

She was born December 15, 1954, in Sioux City, Iowa, and lived there for ten years.

14. **To separate initials or the abbreviations of academic degrees from the rest of a sentence:**

Brown, J. S., and Jones, B. D., are listed in the student directory.
Thomas Hale, M. D., and James Hale, D. D. S., will open their clinic next week.

DO *NOT* USE A COMMA

1. **To separate compound predicates or pairs of words, phrases, or dependent clauses joined by a coordinating conjunction:**

She was born in Sioux City and lived there for ten years.
Do you want cake or pie?
I tried to call or to come as quickly as possible.
Students who want to pass the course but who are unable to grasp basic concepts must attend review sessions.

2. **To separate main clauses** (see comma splice, page 554).
3. **To separate two nouns, one of which identifies the other; in such cases the appositive is so closely related to the noun as to be considered a part of it:**

The booklet "Fixing Furniture" is on the coffee table.
My sister Jane leaves for school on Monday.
Carter's boat *The Nautilus* will be ready in June.

4. **To separate an appositive which is part of a name:**

I remember reading about Richard the Lion-Hearted.

5. **To separate an appositive which contains several words in a series, punctuated by commas; in such instances use dashes instead:**

We looked for them—John, Harry, Jim, and Kate—for almost four hours.

6. **To separate the month and year in a date:**

The bridge was opened in June 1960.

Enclosing Punctuation

Enclosing punctuation consists of paired commas, dashes, parentheses, brackets, and quotation marks, all of which "are used to enclose elements outside the main structure of a sentence. They represent a triple scale of enclosure, in which paired commas enclose elements most closely related to the main thought of the sentence and parentheses those elements least closely related" (Whitehall, 128). Paired dashes enclose elements whose connection falls between the two extremes of closeness. Brackets are essentially a special kind of parentheses, and quotation marks are used mainly to enclose direct reports of spoken words.

USE PAIRED COMMAS (,...,)

1. **To enclose nonrestrictive sentence elements—that is, elements that are not essential because they do not identify the word they modify, but merely add information about it:**

The boat, which was red, sank under the first wave.
but: The boat which we built ourselves sank under the first wave.

2. **To enclose interpolated or transitional words or phrases:**

The truth, as a matter of fact, is none of your business.
Your report, I conclude, is based on secondary sources.
That notion, however, has no basis in fact.

USE PAIRED DASHES (-- . . . --)

1. To enclose elements that are not as closely related to the main thought of the sentence as are those contained within paired commas, but not as incidental to the main thought as are those within parentheses:

   My subject--related to anthropology, yet not strictly anthropological--concerns a tribe of New Zealanders now almost extinct.

2. To provide emphasis or suspense:

   She said--and she must have known it all along--that he had won first prize.

3. To mark a sudden break or abrupt change in thought:

   If I fail the boards--which heaven forbid!--I will have to take them again next year.
   He said--and no one could contradict him--that the dates had been miscalculated.

4. To replace paired commas when the enclosed word group contains heavy comma punctuation:

   A representative from each department--English, History, Zoology, Political Science, Anthropology, and Psychology--attended the meeting.

USE PARENTHESIS (. . .)

1. To enclose material clearly not part of the main thought of the sentence, and not a grammatical element of the sentence, yet important enough to be included:

   The standard Austen text (based on a collation of the early editions by R. W. Chapman) should be cited in the footnotes.

2. To enclose an explanatory word or phrase that is not part of the main statement:

   The unconscious (not to be confused with the subconscious) was definitively explored by Sigmund Freud.

3. To enclose references and directions:

   The data (see Chart 13) indicate that the incidence of polio is decreasing.

4. To enclose the numbering elements of a series:

   The aims of the new party were (1) to gather together local dissidents; (2) to formulate common goals; and (3) to promote these goals through political activism.

5. To enclose figures repeated to ensure accuracy:

   Enclosed is fifty dollars ($50.00) to cover the cost of our tickets.

Punctuation Review

USE BRACKETS [. . .]

1. **To insert additions or comments in a quoted passage:**

   "She [Edith Wharton] addressed herself to the novel of manners." She testified that she had, as she put it, "never seen the man in her life [I actually saw them together in the cafeteria last week] nor even heard his name spoken."

2. **To enclose *sic*, indicating that an error in a quotation has been noted but not changed:**

   "Zelda Fitzgerald's *Save Me the Waltz* was published in 1934 [*sic*]."

USED PAIRED QUOTATION MARKS (". . .")

1. **To enclose direct quotations (use paired single quotation marks to enclose a quotation within a quotation):**

   The reply was a firm "Yes."
   Jim said, "I am leaving," but she refused to believe him.
   "When I asked her to come home," he explained, "she told me, 'Never again.'"

2. **To enclose technical terms used in a nontechnical context:**

   His tendency to "disassociate" suggested a possible psychological disorder.

3. **To enclose terms used in an idiomatic or deprecatory sense, such as hackneyed expressions, slang, sarcasm (such usage should be sparing):**

   The "reward" was a ten-dollar fine.
   She appeared to think it was "the thing to do."

4. **To enclose words used as words (an alternative is to italicize such words; see page 603):**

   How hot is "hot"?

5. **To enclose titles of essays, short stories, short poems, chapters of a book, newspaper and magazine articles:**

   I suggest that you read Milton's "Lycidas."
   Is Dorothy Parker's "The Waltz" really about a waltz?

Remember the proper positioning of quotation marks:

1. **Quotation marks are always used *in pairs*; for every opening quotation mark, there must be a closing one.**
2. **Quotation marks always go outside commas and periods:**

   She said, "Let's go now," and then I heard a crash.
   She heard someone say, "The party is over."

3. **Quotation marks always go inside semicolons and colons:**

   He told me plainly, "It was all your fault"; but I knew better.
   She wanted to "pack them all up": the books, the furniture, the equipment.

4. Quotation marks may go inside or outside the question marks and exclamation points, depending on the intended meaning:

> He asked me, "Where are my books?" [The question mark applies only to the quotation.]
> Did he really say, "Those are my books"? [The question mark does not apply to the quotation, but rather to the whole sentence.]
> *but*: Did he really ask you, "Where are my books?" [A second question mark is not used after the quotation mark.]
> He said, "What a great book!" [The exclamation point applies only to the quotation.]
> How wonderful it was to hear him say, "You have passed the course"! [The exclamation point does not apply to the quotation, but rather to the whole sentence.]

Punctuation Indicating Omissions

USE AN APOSTROPHE (')

1. To indicate contractions or omitted letters:

> you've (you have)
> o'clock (of the clock)
> it's (it is)

2. To form plurals of letters, figures, symbols, and words used as words:

> She received three *A*'s.
> Her *e*'s and *l*'s look alike.
> The beginning writer has trouble making *8*'s.
> His *and*'s are usually *&*'s.

3. To indicate the possessive case of nouns and pronouns:
   a. Add *'s* to form the possessive case of all singular nouns:

> cat's, girl's, man's, lady's, Jones's, Keats's, Dickens's

When a noun ends in an *s* sound, the option exists of adding only an apostrophe, omitting the second *s*. In such instances be sure to place the apostrophe *after* the *s* that is part of the noun:

> Keats' *or* Keats's [not *Keat's*]
> Jones' *or* Jones's [not *Jone's*]
> James' *or* James's [not *Jame's*]

The choice of which form to use depends on how it sounds (does "Dickens's novels" *sound* better to your ear than "Dickens' novels"?) Whenever the addition of an *s* creates real difficulty in pronunciation, add only the apostrophe:

> Aristophanes', Mars', mistress'

b. **Add an apostrophe alone to form the possessive of most plural nouns:**

>   boys', hats', sailors', musicians'

Nouns that end in *s* in the singular must add *es* for the plurals; to form the possessive, place the apostrophe after the final *s*:

>   The Joneses' books are for sale.
>   Ladies' hats are on the fourth floor.

The relatively few plurals which do not end in *s* must add *s* to form the possessive:

>   people's, men's, women's, children's, oxen's, mice's

c. **Add *'s* to the final word of compound nouns:**

>   secretary-treasurer's report
>   brother-in-law's room [singular possessive]
>   brothers-in-law's rooms [plural possessive]

d. **Add *'s* only to the last noun to show joint possession in a series of nouns:**

>   soldiers and sailors' home
>   Tom, Dick, and Harry's apartment

e. **Add *'s* to each noun to show separate possession in a series of nouns:**

>   Tom's, Dick's, and Harry's apartments

f. **Add an apostrophe or *'s* to the last component of an indefinite pronoun:**

>   somebody else's desk
>   others' classes

4. **To indicate the omission of initial centuries in dates:**

>   the class of '45

DO *NOT* USE AN APOSTROPHE

1. **To form the possessive of personal pronouns:**

>   his, hers, theirs, its, whose

Do not confuse the possessive pronoun *its* with the contraction *it's* ("it is"):

>   Its wing is broken.
>   It's a broken wing.

Similarly, do not confuse the possessive pronoun *whose* with the contraction *who's* ("who is"):

>   Who's on the telephone?
>   Whose telephone should I use?

2. To form plurals of spelled-out numbers and of words that already contain an apostrophe:

> threes and fours
> a list of don'ts

Do add *'s*, however, if it makes the plural easier to read:

> *which*'s and *that*'s

3. After words ending in *s*, such as names of countries and other organized bodies that are more descriptive than possessive:

> United Nations Assembly
> United States policy
> merchants market

4. To form the simple plural of a noun:

> The Smiths and Joneses arrived late. [*not* The Smith's and Jones's arrived late.]

5. To show possessive case of an inanimate object:

> the woman's leg
> *but*: the leg of the chair

Some idioms have been established in the possessive (*a hair's breadth*); some organizations composed of people may be referred to in the possessive (*the company's retirement plan, the city's streets*); and some expressions of time may be cast in the *'s* possessive (*a week's work, a month's salary, today's paper*). But general usage dictates that the possessive case should not be cast in the *'s* form for inanimate objects. Thus *the door of the car* is preferable to *the car's door*; *the emblem on his shirt to the shirt's emblem*; *the living room of the house to the house's living room*.

USE AN OMISSION PERIOD OR DOT (.)

1. To indicate abbreviation:

> Mr. L. B. Matthews
> B.A., M.S., M.D., Ph.D.
> R.F.D.
> U.S.

When a sentence ends with an abbreviated word, use only one period to punctuate both the abbreviation and the sentence:

> Please send my packages C.O.D.

DO *NOT* USE AN OMISSION PERIOD

1. After Roman numerals:

> III   IV   XXX

2. After the word *percent* (for *per centum*).
3. With abbreviated names of well-known government agencies, labor organizations, and the like:

> NIH (National Institute of Health)
> UMW (United Mine Workers)
> OPEC (Organization of Petroleum Exporting Countries)

USE TRIPLE PERIODS OR DOTS, CALLED ELLIPSES (…)

1. To indicate omission of words or phrases from a quoted text:

> "On the other hand, when Marx the reformer spoke,…we get a wholly different conception of the function of the theory and of its claim to truth." "The ultimate aim is to bring about a more intelligent use of language…." [The first period punctuates the sentence, and the last three periods indicate the omission of the words that followed in the original text.]

2. To indicate omission in content, in order to leave something to the reader's imagination or to create an atmosphere (use sparingly to avoid a mannered effect):

> They rowed on … past the meadow … past the old decaying castle … on and on they rowed.

GENERAL MECHANICS

Capitalization

1. Capitalize the first word of every sentence of a direct quotation, and, generally, of each line of a poem.
2. Capitalize all proper nouns—the names of persons, places, and official organizations:

> Abraham Lincoln
> Paris, France
> Union Station [but: *the railroad station in Washington*]
> British Commonwealth: the Commonwealth [but not when used in a general sense: *a commonwealth of nations*]
> Bureau of the Census; the Census Bureau [but not when used in a general sense: *the census bureau in Laurel*]

3. Capitalize the names of specific geographic locations and features:

> the North Atlantic states, the East, the South [but not when used merely to indicate direction or position: *north, south, east, west*]
> the Promised Land
> the Continent [but not when merely descriptive: *continental boundaries*]

4. Capitalize days, months, holidays, historic events (but not seasons):

> Monday, January, Fourth of July, War of 1812, spring, summer, fall, winter

5. Capitalize titles of all books—literary works, official publications, documents, formal acts and treaties:

> *The Oxford Companion to English Literature* [do not capitalize prepositions, conjunctions, or articles within a title]
> *American Journal of Science*
> Treaty of Ghent

6. Capitalize specific school courses and all language courses or references to languages (but not general subject areas: *math, science, literature*):

> Survey of English Literature

7. Capitalize titles preceding names and the names of offices when they are used as titles:

> Doctor Smith [but not an occupation itself: *doctor, engineer, chemist*] Ambassador George [but not when used in a general sense: *ambassador-at-large*] President Lincoln [*President* and *Presidency* are always capitalized when they refer to the office of President of the United States; the term is *not* capitalized when used in a general sense: *the president of a college*]

Italics

Use italics (underline)

1. To indicate the titles of books, plays, newspapers, magazines, paintings, sculpture, the names of ships and aircraft:

> *Madame Bovary, Othello,* the *Boston Globe, The New Yorker,* the *Mona Lisa,* the *Queen Mary,* the *Spirit of St. Louis*

2. To indicate foreign words and phrases:

> *ad hoc*
> *ad infinitum*
> *madre*
> *bonjour*
> *savoir-faire*
> *Zeitgeist*

Many foreign words and phrases become completely assimilated into English and may be printed roman, rather than italic.

> papier-mâché
> en route
> ibid.

3. To indicate words or phrases used as words or phrases (quotation marks may be used instead of underlining, but whichever form you use, be consistent throughout):

> How hot is *hot?*
> He said *honey* so many times that it began to sound like a nonsense word.

Abbreviations and Contractions

Abbreviations should be avoided except where convention specifically dictates their usage. Contractions, a form of abbreviation whereby an apostrophe replaces an omitted letter (*you're* for *you are*), should also be avoided except in dialog or in informal essays, where contractions provide the more relaxed and natural tone suitable for such writing.

Abbreviations may be used to designate

1. **Established titles and degrees:**

   Mr., Mrs., Ms., B.A., Ph.D.

2. **Time:**

   It was 4:30 A.M.

3. **Established organizations or agencies:**

   UNESCO, CIA, CARE

4. **Certain standard foreign phrases:**

   i.e. (that is)
   e.g. (for example)
   etc. (and so on)

DO *NOT* ABBREVIATE

1. Professional titles:

   Professor [not *Prof.*]
   President [not *Pres.*]

2. Names of days, months, or periods of time:

   Tuesday [not *Tues.*]
   February [not *Feb.*]
   years [not *yrs.*]

3. Names of nations, states, streets, avenues, and so on:

   United States [not *U.S.*]
   12 Selma Drive [not *Dr.*]

4. Holidays

   Christmas [not *Xmas*]

5. Weights and measures

   pounds [not *lbs.*]
   feet [not *ft.*]

Numbers

Although usage varies somewhat, the following is a reasonably reliable guide to the use of numbers.

1. **Use numbers for dates, street addresses, telephone and social security numbers and the like, chapters of a book, decimals, percentages, and fractions (in a mathematical context; see item 5, below):**

   January 22, 1970 [not *January 22nd*]
   Chapter 14
   .12
   12 percent
   ¼, ⅓ [not *¼th, ⅓rd*]

2. **Use numbers to indicate measurement or weight:**

   The room was 14 × 12 feet.
   She weighed 115 pounds.

3. **Use numbers in a sentence containing a series of figures:**

   He calculated the following totals: 18, 14, 12, 19, and 15.

4. **Use numbers to indicate time, always adding** A.M. **or** P.M.:

   The meeting adjourned at 4:15 P.M.

5. **Use words when no more than two words are required to pronounce a figure:**

   twelve, forty-two, nine thousand, one-half, ten million
   Jane is twenty years old.

6. **Use numbers when more than two words are required to pronounce a figure:**

   $10.86; 9,842; 354

7. **Never begin a sentence with a number:**

   Twelve students were reported missing. [not *12 students* ...]
   In 1912 he had his first success. [not *1912 marked* ...]

Spelling

Because English spelling is not only not phonetic but also exasperatingly irregular, we must trust to memory and to the clear mental picture of words that most of us gain during our many years of schooling and independent reading. There are many intelligent people, however, who simply cannot retain the image of the correct spelling of a word. Whatever the reason for this inability, a simple prescription is in order: **A dictionary or comparable word guide must always be kept within easy reach. There is no overemphasizing the importance of accurate spelling.** Anything less than complete accuracy tends to brand the writer as careless and unreliable, if not subliterate: so strong is the concern about spelling in American schools and in the society at large.

In addition to consulting a dictionary regularly, you may find it helpful to study the following list of commonly misspelled words in order to check your memory and reinforce correct practice.

101 COMMONLY MISSPELLED WORDS

absence	governor	peculiar
all right	grammar	persistent
already	grievous	persuade
analogous	guarantee	polluted
appalled		possession
apparatus	harass	preceding
argument	height	preferable
ascendance		preferred
	independent	prejudice
balance	ingenious	principal (compare *principle*)
believe	interpretation	privilege
benefited	interruption	
breath (compare *breathe*)	irresistible	questionnaire
	its (compare *it's*)	quite (compare *quiet*)
cemetery		
changeable	judgment	receive
choose (compare *chose*)		recommend
committed	likable	recurrence
consensus	loneliness	referring
correspondent	lose	relevant
		repetition
defensible	maintenance	resemblance
definite	mathematics	reverence
dependent	miscellaneous	rhyme
desirable	mischievous	
development	misspell	seize (compare *siege*)
devise (compare *device*)	movable	separate
disappearance		similar
disastrous	necessary	stationary (compare *stationery*)
dissension	neighbor	succeed
	ninety	
effect (compare *affect*)	noticeable	than (compare *then*)
embarrass		their (compare *there*)
environment	occasionally	tyranny
exaggerate	occurrence	
exhilarate	occurred	whose (compare *who's*)
existence	offense	
exorbitant	omitted	your (compare *you're*)
friend	parallel	
fulfilled	parceled	

EXERCISES

1. Revise the following opening paragraphs taken from narrative essays. Tighten sentences by combining them and by getting rid of excess verbiage.

   a. It was a cool, refreshing evening, and highly welcomed after a long, tedious day of sightseeing in the humid city of Budapest. The sky was cloudy and a sweet fragrance of rain was in the air. The city was calm and peaceful.

   b. It was a typical late August day, the sun was shining bright but the air was dry. You could almost sense Autumn was coming and with Autumn, another school year. For me, it was my first, as I was going into first grade. I was excited about starting school and I couldn't stop talking about it. I needed many things for school: pencils, paper and erasers. Since I was going to be a student, I needed a pair of nice shoes. My birthday was in a few days so my Grandmother bought me an early present. The shoes were Hushpuppy loafers, the kind that didn't have any laces. I was so proud of them that I wanted to show all my friends the shoes as soon as we got home from the store.

   c. It was a very dark and rainy night when we set out to a destination unknown. We had heard that there was to be a very big party near one of our neighboring schools. My two friends and myself got off to a late start from home. It was about 11:30 when we finally started out for the party. We only had a general idea of where the party was being held. One of my friends was driving, I was in the passenger seat, and my other friend was in the back seat. The car was a yellow Fiat.

2. Edit the following paper, written by a student at Drew University, focusing on such specific features as title, introduction and conclusion, over-all organization, paragraph division and organization, paragraph development, sentence structure, and choice of words. Is the essay clear? Unified? Coherent? Does it flow smoothly and gracefully? What needs to be deleted, added, or repositioned? Try to assess the strengths of this paper; then note and diagnose weaknesses. Finally, revise and rewrite so as to produce a distinctly improved piece.

Teenage Suicide

The teenage years present considerable stress, due to the adolescent's search for psychological identity and independence. Preparation for a new social role as an adult also heightens his/her vulnerability to suicidal tendencies which are manifested in depression.

Adolescents may not recognize feelings of unhappiness in themselves. Signs of depression can go unnoticed "until matters erupt in some acute, overcrisis," according to Adele D. Hoffman, M.D. Even if depression is recognized, it can be difficult to help. Few resources exist where young people can seek guidance when they cannot confide in their parents. It is also difficult for teenagers to ask for help because they would be admitting to personal weaknesses or deficiencies.

Contributing factors to adolescent suicide include conflicts involving the family. As teenagers become more independent from their parents, they take on more demanding responsibilities which they may not be able to cope with. Lack of communication leads to frustration because the teen has not voiced his opinion or has not been understood. Moreover, the loss of a family member, through death or even divorce, may also cause a great deal of hardship. The home may be an unhappy place altogether, and it may place burdens on the adolescent, leading to suicide.

Boredom also leads to suicide. The adolescent may be unhappy with his lifestyle especially when he cannot find ways to improve it. The youth must have a willingness to try new things, otherwise the boredom will lead to desperate and helpless feelings.

Punctuation Review

School places academic and social pressures on the troubled adolescent with which he may not be able to cope with. Since school is such an integral part of a teenager's life, the teenager must be able to face these pressures. Classmates cause problems for the adolescent, in and out of school. If a teen is turned on to drugs by his friends, his physical well-being will suffer for it. If the adolescent is involved in a relationship that breaks up, feelings of guilt and rejection will he hard to handle effectively. These mental pressures could lead to suicide.

In general, suicide is a very complex and important problem. The pressures caused by today's society have increased the number of teenage suicides. In order to correct this, people have to recognize the anguish of adolescents and try to understand them. In turn, adolescents need to be more open with their problems with the people who can help them.

3. Punctuation Quiz: Copy over the following sentences, providing appropriate punctuation and capitalization.

1. After listening to Ellen David and June I decided to vote for the proposition.
2. Your insurance premium has been overdue for three months consequently we are forced to cancel your policy.
3. Blake walked up to the soldier and said. What do you think you are doing in my garden?
4. On May 22 1978 he wrote that threatening letter.
5. The book is neither Fredericks nor mine. Could it be Betsys?
6. Do you agree that Dostoevsky is the greatest Russian novelist
7. Put quotation marks around the word questionable if you want to emphasize it.
8. Jane Carlyle the wife of Thomas Carlyle was one of the greatest letter writers of the nineteenth century.
9. I am going to drop the economics course in order to take english 101.
10. Nothing is going to be gained by arguing with him in fact the situation can only be worsened by doing so.
11. Walking down the street with Professor Alden I told him of my plans for graduate school.
12. The diversity of aesthetic theories however makes the task of the historian difficult.
13. If you arrive after eight o'clock you will not be admitted.
14. The title of that book is the psychology of learning.
15. They planned this trip long and carefully but there was no way to anticipate all the dangers.
16. Doesnt Mr. Jones refusal to pay his rent strengthen the landlords case for evicting him?
17. Mr. Lodge drove down the street slowly hesitantly as if someone were going to jump out in front of the car at any minute.
18. Winning it seems is knowing when to quit losing is more a matter of overstaying your luck.
19. Send the package to Box 705 Drew University Madison New Jersey 07940.
20. Naomi Wood was born in England educated at Cambridge University and is now Professor of Geology at the University of Wisconsin.
21. It is one of the wittiest books I've ever read which is why I recommend it so highly.
22. John you cannot expect that letter to arrive before Tuesday.
23. Because no one else seemed willing Cameron said that he would finish the inventory.
24. The spanish members of the community sent their congratulations to senator Perez.
25. The drug provided him relief from physical pain however, he never claimed that it increased his creative powers.

Copyrights and Acknowledgments

228 HERE IS THE JERSEY TOMATO from "The Jersey Tomato" by Deborah A. Boerner. *New Jersey Outdoors*, Summer 1983. Reprinted by permission of the author and *New Jersey Outdoors* Magazine.

231 SWEET TRUTHS ABOUT SUGAR from *The One Hundred Percent Natural, Purely Organic, Cholesterol-free, Megavitamin, Low-Carbohydrate Nutrition Hoax* by Elizabeth M. Whelan and Frederick J. Stare, M.D. Copyright © 1983 Elizabeth M. Whelan and Frederick J. Stare. Reprinted with the permission of Atheneum Publishers.

233 MARRYING ABSURD from *Slouching Toward Bethlehem* by Joan Didion. Copyright © 1967 by Joan Didion. Reprinted by permission of Farrar, Straus & Giroux, Inc.

240 THE TACTICS AND STRATEGY OF SCIENCE from *On Understanding Science* by James B. Conant. Copyright © 1947 by Yale University Press. Used by permission.

246 THE PARADOX OF THE SIXTIES from the *New York Times*, 21 December 1969. © 1969 by The New York Times Company. Reprinted by permission.

250 A DEFINITION OF PHILOSOPHY from *A History of Western Philosophy* by Bertrand Russell. Copyright © 1945, 1972 by Bertrand Russell. Reprinted by permission of Simon & Schuster, Inc.

253 THREE MEANINGS OF GRAMMAR from "Revolution in Grammar" by W. Nelson Francis. Reprinted from *The Quarterly Journal of Speech*, October 1954, by permission of W. Nelson Francis and Speech Communication Association.

254 WHAT IS HISTORY? from *The Gateway to History* by Allan Nevins (Lexington, MA: D. C. Heath and Company, 1938). Reprinted by permission of the publisher.

255 "UNIVERSE" AND "UNIVERSITY" from *Words of Science and the History Behind Them* by Isaac Asimov, published by Houghton Mifflin Company. Copyright © 1959 by Isaac Asimov. Reprinted by permission of the publisher.

255 THE SECURITY OF DISCIPLINE from *Mental Hygiene*, 36, No. 3 (July 1952), pages 353–72. Reprinted by permission.

257 THE MEANING OF "NEGRO" from Negro History Bulletin (February 1971). Reprints with permission of the Negro History Bulletin, a publication for the Study of Afro-American Life & History, Inc. Washington, D.C.

260 WHAT MAKES A "JERK" A JERK? from *Last Things First* (Boston: Houghton Mifflin) Copyright © 1957, 1958, 1959, 1960 by The Chicago Daily News and General Features Corporation; copyright 1961 by Sidney J. Harris.

261 DEMOCRACY from *The Wild Flag* by E. B. White. Copyright by E. B. White, 1943–46. First appeared as an editorial in *The New Yorker*. Reprinted by permission of the author.

262 THE NATURE OF PREJUDICE from "Reading the Nature of Prejudice" by Gordon W. Allport in the *Claremont College Reading Conference 17th Yearbook*. Reprinted by permission of the Claremont College Curriculum Laboratory.

268 WHAT IS THE FUNCTION OF A CRITIC? from *The Dyer's Hand and Other Essays* by W. H. Auden. © 1962 by W. H. Auden. Reprinted by permission of Random House, Inc.

270 ANOTHER SCHOOL YEAR—WHAT FOR? by John Ciardi from the *Rutgers Alumni Monthly*, November 1954. Reprinted by permission.

272 THE TUCSON ZOO from *The Medusa and the Snail* by Lewis Thomas (New York: The Viking Press, 1979), pages 7–11. Copyright © 1974–79 by Lewis Thomas. Originally appeared in *The New England Journal of Medicine*. Reprinted by permission of Viking Penguin, Inc.

274 THE TEDDY BEAR—SOLACE FOR LIFE by Glenn Collins. Copyright © by The New York Times Company. Reprinted by permission.

275 THE POSTCARD: COUNT YOUR MISERIES by Russell Baker. Copyright © 1983 by The New York Times Company. Reprinted by permission.

281 THE COMPOSITION OF BLOOD from "The Life Stream: What Blood Is and What It Does" by Louis Faugeres Bishop in *The Book of Popular Science*, III (Canada: The Grolier Society, 1971), pages 325–31.

Illustration Credits

List of Works Cited

Adamic, Louis. *Dynamite: The Story of Class Violence in America*. Gloucester: Peter Smith, 1963.

Addison, Joseph. "Recreation." *The Spectator*, No. 115, 12 July 1711.

Agee, James, and Walker Evans. "Shady Grove, Alabama, July 1936." *Let Us Now Praise Famous Men*. Boston: Houghton, 1969.

Allport, Gordon W. "The Nature of Prejudice." "Reading the Nature of Prejudice." *Claremont College Reading Conference 17th Yearbook*.

Angell, Roger. "The Baseball." *Five Seasons*. New York: Popular, 1977.

Asimov, Isaac. "Universe and University." *Words of Science and the History Behind Them*. Boston: Houghton, 1959.

Auden, W. H. "What Is the Function of a Critic?" From "Let Him Not Dare to Lay Down the Law." *The Dyer's Hand and Other Essays*. New York: Random, 1962.

Baker, Russell. "The Prim Mr. Fleagle." *Growing Up*. New York: Congdon, 1982. 186–89.

_____. "The Postcard: Count Your Miseries." *New York Times* 27 Aug. 1983: 21.

Barton, Mary Neill, and Marion V. Bell. *Reference Books: A Brief Guide for Students and Other Uses of the Library*. 6th ed. Baltimore: Enoch Pratt Free Library, 1966.

Bass, Paul B. *A Complete Critical Outline of Don Quixote*. Boston: Student Outlines, 1957. 32–33.

Beardsley, Monroe C. *Thinking Straight*. 3rd ed. Englewood Cliffs, NJ: Prentice, 1966.

Bernstein, Theodore. *The Careful Writer*. New York: Atheneum, 1965.

Bishop, Louis Faugeres. "The Composition of Blood." From "The Life Stream: What Blood Is and What It Does." *Book of Popular Science III*. Toronto: Grolier Society, 1971.

Blair, Hugh. *Lectures on Rhetoric and Belles Lettres*. Brooklyn: Printed by Thomas Kirk, 1812.

Bliven, Bruce. "Why Is the Sky Dark at Night?" *Reader's Digest* July 1963.

Bly, Carol. "Great Snows." *Letters from the Country*. New York: Penguin, 1982. 40–45.

Boerner, Deborah H. "Here Is the Jersey Tomato." *New Jersey Outdoors* Summer 1983: 22–23.

Boulton, Majorie. *The Anatomy of Prose*. London: Routledge and Kegan Paul, 1954.

Brautigan, Richard. "Your Departure Versus the Hindenburg." *The Pill Versus the Springhill Mine Disaster*. New York: Dell, 1973.

Bridgeman, P. W. "The Way Things Are." *The Limits of Language*. Ed. Walker Gibson. New York: Hill and Wang, 1962.

Broehl, Wayne G., Jr. *The Molly Maguires*. Cambridge: Harvard UP, 1964.

Brooks, Thomas R. *Toil and Trouble: A History of American Labor*. New York: Delacorte, 1964.

Brown, Claude. "The Day I Got Shot." *Manchild in the Promised Land*. New York: Macmillan, 1965.

Burke, Kenneth. *A Grammar of Motives and a Rhetoric of Motives*. Cleveland: World, 1962.

Cameron, Peter. "Memorial Day." *New Yorker* 30 May 1983.

Carnegie, Dale. "How to Stop Worrying." *How to Stop Worrying and Start Living*. New York: Simon, 1975.

Carr, Emily. *Fresh Seeing*. Toronto, Vancouver: Clark Irwin, 1972.

Catton, Bruce. "Grant and Lee: A Study in Contrasts." *The American Story*. Ed. Earl S. Miers. New York: Broadcast Music, 1956.

Chapman, R. L. "Timor Mortis Conturbat Me." *The Nation*. 5 April 1975: 414.

Charlton, James, ed. *The Writer's Quotation Book: A Literary Companion*. New York: Penguin, 1981.

Chesterton, G. K. "On Running After One's Hat." *All Things Considered*. Folcroft, 1978.

Cheyney, Edward P. "Migrating to England." *A Short History of England*. Lexington, MA: Ginn and Company, 1904.

Christensen, Francis. "A Generative Rhetoric of the Sentence." *Notes Toward a New Rhetoric*. New York: Harper, 1967.

———. "Symposium on the Paragraph." *College Composition and Communication* 17 (1966): 60–88.

———. *Notes Toward a New Rhetoric*. New York: Harper, 1967.

———, and Bonniejean Christensen. *A New Rhetoric*. New York: Harper, 1976.

Churchill, Sir Winston. "In the Battle of Hastings." *A History of the English-Speaking Peoples: The Birth of Britain*. New York: Dodd, 1957.

Ciardi, John. "Another School Year—What For?" *Rutgers Alumni Monthly* Nov. 1954.

Cohen, Bernard I. "Isaac Newton." *Scientific American* Dec. 1955.

Collins, Glenn. "The Teddy Bear—Solace for Life." *New York Times*.

Compaine, Benjamin. "Computers and the New Literacy." From "The New Literacy." *Science Digest* March 1983.

Conant, James B. "The Tactics and Strategy of Science." *On Understanding Science*. New Haven: Yale UP, 1947.

Cousins, Norman. *Present Tense: An American Editor's Odyssey*. New York: McGraw, 1967.

Cummings, E. E. "anyone lived in a pretty how town." *Complete Poems 1913–1962*. New York: Harcourt, 1968.

———. "My Father." *i: Six Nonlectures*. Cambridge: Harvard UP, 1953.

Darley, John M., and Bibb Latané. "Unresponsive Bystanders: Why Don't They Help?" *Psychology Today* Dec. 1968.

Davis, Robert Gorham. "Logic and Logical Fallacies." *Harvard Handbook for English*. Cambridge: Harvard UP, 1947.

de Beauvoir, Simone. "Why I Decided to Be a Writer." *Memoirs of a Dutiful Daughter*. New York: Harper, 1974.

del Castillo, Michel. *Child of Our Time*. New York: Knopf, 1958.

DeMille, Agnes. "Composing a Ballet." *Dance to the Piper*. Boston: Little, 1951.

DeWees, F. P. *The Molly Maguires*. Philadelphia: Lippincott, 1877.

Didion, Joan. "Marrying Absurd." *Slouching Towards Bethlehem*. New York: Farrar, 1967.

———. "At the Dam." *The White Album*. New York: Simon, 1979.

Dillard, Annie. *Pilgrim at Tinker's Creek*. New York: Harper's Magazine Press, 1974.

Dinesen, Isak. *Out of Africa*. New York: Random, 1937.

Dionne, E. J. "Review of *The Nazi Question* by Pierre Ayçoberry." *New York Times Book Review* 29 Aug. 1981.

Du Bois, Franklin S., M.D. "The Security of Discipline." *Mental Hygiene* 36. 3 (1952): 353–72.

Elbow, Peter. *Writing Without Teachers*. New York: Oxford UP, 1973.

Esslin, Martin. *The Theatre of the Absurd*. New York: Doubleday, 1969.

Foner, Philip S. *History of the Labor Movement in the United States*. New York: International, 1965. Vol. 4.

Ford, George, and Sylvere Monod, eds. *Hard Times*. New York: Norton, 1966.

Fordham, Frieda. "Jung's Psychological Types." *An Introduction to Jung's Psychology*. Baltimore: Pelican, 1966.

Forster, E. M. "My Wood." *Abinger Harvest*. New York: Harcourt, 1964.

Francis, Nelson W. "Revolution in Grammar." *Quarterly Journal of Speech* Oct. 1954.

_____. "Three Meanings of Grammar." From "Revolution in Grammar." *The Quarterly Journal of Speech* Oct. 1954.

Franklin, Benjamin. Letter to David Hume. 24 Jan. 1792.

_____. "A Rule to Forbear All Direct Contradictions." *Autobiography*.

Froude, James Anthony. "The Execution of Mary, Queen of Scots." *History of England from the Fall of Wolsey to the Defeat of the Spanish Armada*. New York: AMS Press, 1969.

Frye, Northrop. "Myth and Folk Tale." From "Myth, Fiction, and Displacement." *Daedalus* 90.1.

Gale, Mary. "A Case for Senior Theatergoers." *New York Times* 30 Dec. 1979.

Gardner, John. *Excellence*. New York: Harper, 1961.

Geisel, Theodor Seuss. "The Kingdom of Didd." *The 500 Hats of Bartholomew Cubbins*. New York: Vanguard, 1938.

Gilbert, Allan H. "College Lectures Are Obsolete." *CEA Critic* Oct. 1967.

Gilliatt, Penelope. "Review of Federico Fellini's *8 1/2*." *Unholy Fools*. n.p., 1973.

Girsdansky, Michael. *The Adventures of Language*. Rev. and ed. by Mario Pei. New York: Fawcett, 1967.

"Give the Trains a Chance." Editorial. *Life* 3 Dec. 1971.

Golding, William. "Swiss Family Robinson." *The Hot Gates*. New York: Harcourt, 1966. 106–108.

Gowers, Sir Ernest. *The Complete Plain Words*. Rev. Sir Bruce Fraser. London: Her Majesty's Stationary Office, 1973.

Gregory, Dick. "Not Poor, Just Broke." *nigger: An Autobiography*. New York: Dutton, 1964.

Hall, Donald. *Writing Well*. Boston, Toronto: Little, 1976.

Hamill, Pete. "Boy Meets Girl, Boy Loses Girl, Man Gets Woman." New York *Daily News*, 24 April 1978.

Harris, Sidney J. "What Makes a 'Jerk' a Jerk?" *Last Things First*. Boston: Houghton, 1961.

Holt, John "Three Kinds of Discipline." *Freedom and Beyond*. New York: Dutton, 1972.

Hudson, W. H. *Birds and Man*. New York: Knopf, 1923.

Hughes, Langston. "Dream Deferred." *The Panther and the Lash: Poems of Our Times*. New York: Knopf, 1951.

Huppe, Bernard F., and Jack Kiminsky. *Logic and Language*. New York: Knopf, 1956. 204.

"Hurricanes." *Hurricane*. United States Department of Commerce, n.d.

Huxley, Thomas Henry. "Thinking Scientifically." *Collected Essays*. Westport: Greenwood, 1966.

Jacoby, Susan. "The First Girl at Second Base." *New York Times*, 1979.

Jones, W. T. "Marxism." *A History of Western Philosophy*. New York: Harcourt, 1952.

Jordan, Susan Britt. "That Lean and Hungry Look." *Newsweek* 9 Oct. 1978.

Joyce, James. "Clay." *Dubliners.* 1916. New York: Viking, 1967.

Kaplan, Norman, M.D. "How to Lose Weight Sensibly and Successfully and Permanently." From "The Bottom Line about Fat." *Saturday Evening Post* Oct. 1983: 17–23.

Kazantzakis, Nikos. "A Night in a Calabrian Village." *A Report to Greco.* Trans. P. A. Bien. New York: Simon, 1965.

Kennedy, John F. Inaugural Address. 20 Jan. 1961.

Kennedy, Richard. *A Boy at the Hogarth Press.* New York: Penguin, 1978.

King, Martin Luther, Jr. "Letter from Birmingham Jail, April 16, 1963." *Why We Can't Wait.* New York: Harper, 1964.

———. "Three Types of Resistance to Oppression." *Stride Toward Freedom.* New York: Harper, 1958. 211–15.

Kingston, Maxine Hong. "Uncle Bun." *China Men.* New York: Knopf, 1980.

Kitzhaber, Albert. *Themes, Theories, and Therapy.* New York: McGraw, 1967.

Kleinfield, Sonny. "Dwarfs." *Atlantic Monthly* Sept. 1975.

Korzybski, Alfred. *Science and Sanity.* 3rd ed. Lakeville, Conn.: Institute of General Semantics, 1948.

Lask, Thomas. "Publishing." *New York Times* 21 Dec. 1979.

Lee, Laurie. "The Village School." *The Edge of Day: A Boyhood in the West of England.* New York: William Morrow, 1959.

Lens, Sidney. *The Labor Wars.* New York: Doubleday, 1973.

Leonard, John. "Review of *A Weave of Women* by E. M. Broner." *New York Times* 6 July 1978.

Lobsenz, Norman. *Writing as a Career.* New York: Henry Z. Walck, 1963.

Lockard, Duane. "Life, and Death, in the Coal Mines." *New York Times* 21 June 1969.

Lord, John. *Experiments in Diction, Rhetoric, Style.* New York: Holt, 1960.

———. *The Paragraph: Structure and Style.* New York: Holt, 1964.

Lucas, F. L. *Style.* New York: Macmillan, 1962.

Macdonald, Dwight. *Against the American Grain.* New York: Random, 1962.

MacKenzie, Robert. "Review: Thicke of the Night." *TV Guide* 29 Oct. 1983.

Matson, Katinka. "Sylvia Plath: A Short Life." *Short Lives: Portraits of Writers, Painters, Poets, Actors, Musicians, and Performers in Pursuit of Death.* London: Picador, Pan Books, 1981. 253–62.

"The Meaning of 'Negro.'" *Negro History Bulletin* Feb. 1971.

Millikan, Robert Andrew. "The Spirit of Modern Science." *Science in Literature.* Ed. Federick H. Law. New York: Harper, 1929.

Moffett, James. "Writing, Inner Speech and Meditation." *College English,* 14, No. 3 (1982): 231.

"Molly Maguires." *Encyclopaedia Britannica.* 1951 ed.

Morris, Jan. "The Latest Fashion in Travel." *Vanity Fair,* April 1981.

Mortimer, Penelope. "In the First Place." *About Time: An Aspect of an Autobiography.* New York: Doubleday, 1979.

Muggeridge, Malcolm. "Review of *Tolstoy and Gandhi, Men of Peace.*" *New York Times Book Review* 28 Aug. 1963.

Murphy, Robert W. *How and Where to Look It Up.* New York: McGraw, 1958.

Neill, Thomas P. "What Is An Intellectual?" *Thought* 32.125. New York: Fordham UP, 1957. 200–201.

Nevins, Allan. "What Is History?" *The Gateway to History*. Lexington: Heath, 1938.

Orwell, George. *Shooting an Elephant and Other Essays*. New York: Harcourt, 1950.

———. "Such, Such Were the Joys." *Such, Such Were the Joys*. New York: Harcourt, 1953.

———. "A Hanging." *Shooting an Elephant and Other Essays*. New York: Harcourt, 1950.

———. "Some Thoughts on the Common Toad." *Shooting an Elephant and Other Essays*. New York: Harcourt, 1950.

Panofsky, Erwin. *Meaning in the Visual Arts*. New York: Doubleday, 1955.

Partridge, Eric. *A Dictionary of Clichés*. New York: Dutton, 1963.

Pinkerton, Allan. *The Molly Maguires and the Detectives*. New York: G. W. Dillingham, 1877.

Plath, Sylvia. "Winter Trees." *Winter Trees*. New York: Harper, 1972.

Podhoretz, Norman. *Making It*. New York: Random, 1968.

Potter, Stephen. *Our Language*. London: Books, Ltd. 1950.

"The Process of Riveting." From "Riveting a Skyscraper." *Fortune*. Oct. 1930.

Progoff, Ira. *Depth Psychology and Modern Man*. New York: Julian Press, 1959.

Rammel, Melody. "The Molly Maguire Movement." By Wayne G. Broehl, Jr. Cambridge: Harvard UP, 1964.

Randolph, David. "Five Basic Elements of Music." *This Is Music: A Guide to the Pleasures of Listening*. New York: Cornerstone, 1964.

Rayback, Joseph G. *A History of American Labor*. New York: Macmillan, 1959.

Read, Herbert. *English Prose Style*. Boston: Beacon, 1955.

———. *Modern Prose Style*. Boston: Beacon, 1952.

The Reader's Digest of Books. Helen Rex Keller, ed. New York: Macmillan, 1929.

"Real Work for Real Money in Prison." Editorial. *New York Times* 22 June 1983: A26.

Reston, James. "The Paradox of the Sixties." *New York Times*, 21 Dec. 1969.

Rico, Gabriele L. *Writing the Natural Way: Using Right-Brain Techniques to Release Your Expressive Powers*. Los Angeles: Tarcher, 1983.

Rodgers, Paul C., Jr. "A Discourse-Centered Rhetoric of the Paragraph." *College Composition and Communication* 17 (1966): 5.

Rogers, Carl R. "Communication: Its Blocking and Its Facilitation." *Et cetera* IX, 2.

Rooney, Andrew A. *A Few Minutes with Andy Rooney*. New York: Warner, 1981.

Rosenthal, A. M. "No News from Auschwitz." *New York Times*, 1958.

Ruby, Lionel. *The Art of Making Sense*. Philadelphia: Lippincott, 1968.

Russell, Bertrand. "A Definition of Philosophy." *A History of Western Philosophy*. New York: Simon, 1972.

Schell, Jonathan. "Our Strange Indifference to Nuclear Peril." *The Fate of the Earth*. New York: Knopf, 1982.

Schulz, Charles M. "But a Comic Strip Has to *Grow*." *Saturday Review*, 12 April 1969: 73–74.

Shankar, Ravi. "Studying Music in India." *My Music, My Life*. Kinnara School of Indian Music, 1968.

Sondel, Bess. *The Humanity of Words*. New York: World, 1958.

Sorensen, Theodore. *Kennedy*. New York: Harper, 1965.

Spence, Jonathan. *The Death of Woman Wang*. Hammondsworth, Middlesex, England: Penguin, 1978.

Stade, George. "Football—the Game of Aggression." From "Game Theory." *Columbia Forum* IV, 4.

Stallman, R. W. "An Interpretation of E. E. Cumming's 'anyone lived in a pretty how town.'" *The Creative Reader*, 2nd ed. New York: Ronald, 1962.

Steinbeck, John. "A Night in a Maine Motel." *Travels with Charley in Search of America*. New York: Viking, 1962.

Stevens, Wallace. "The Idea of Order at Key West." *The Collected Poems of Wallace Stevens*. 1934. New York: Knopf, 1964.

Stout, Hilary. "Why College Students Take a 'Sabbatical.'" *New York Times*, 14 Nov. 1982.

Syfers, Judy. "Why I Want a Wife." *Ms.* Dec. 1979.

Thesaurus of Book Digests. Ed. Hiram Haydn and Edmund Fuller. New York: Crown. 1949.

Thomas, Dylan. "Do Not Go Gentle into That Good Night." *Collected Poems*. New York: New Directions, 1952.

Thomas, Henry, and Dana Lee Thomas. *Living Biographies of Great Scientists*. New York: Doubleday, 1941.

Thomas, Lewis. "The Tucson Zoo." *The Medusa and the Snail*. New York: Viking, 1979. 7–11.

Thomas, Richard L. "How to Dismount from an Elephant." *Harper's* May 1967.

Thompson, Thomas. "Judy's Daughter Wants to Be Liza." *Life* 17 Oct. 1969.

"Time to Start Saving the Soil." *New York Times* 2 Sept. 1977.

Updike, John. "Central Park." *Assorted Prose*. New York: Knopf, 1965.

Walzl, Florence. "Interpretation of Joyce's 'Clay.'" *Explicator* Feb. 1962.

Weissenborn, Shirley. "How to Run for Office in a Very Small Town." n.p., n.d.

Whately, Richard. *Elements of Rhetoric*. Boston and Cambridge: James Monroe, 1854.

Whelan, Elizabeth M., and Frederick J. Stare, M.D. "Sweet Truths About Sugar." *The One Hundred Percent Natural, Purely Organic, Cholesterol-free, Megavitamin, Low-Carbohydrate Nutrition Hoax*. New York: Atheneum, 1983.

White, E. B. "Democracy." *The Wild Flag*. Boston: Houghton, 1946.

————. "An Approach to Style." *The Elements of Style*. By William Strunk, Jr. and E. B. White. 3rd ed. New York: Macmillan, 1979.

White, William Allen. "Mary White." *America Is West*. Ed. John T. Flanagan. Minneapolis: U of Minnesota P, 1945.

Whitehall, Harold. *Structural Essentials of English*. New York: Harcourt, 1956.

Wicker, Tom. *JFK and LBJ: The Influence of Personality Upon Politics*. New York: Morrow, 1968.

————. *Kennedy Without Tears: The Man Beneath the Myth*. New York: Morrow, 1964.

Williams, Craig B., and Allan H. Stevenson. *A Research Manual*. New York: Harper, 1963.

Wolfe, Thomas. "The Quality of Memory." *The Story of a Novel*. New York: Scribner's, 1936.

"Write Before Writing." *College Composition and Communication* 29 (Dec. 1978): 375–81.

Yeats, William Butler. "Grandfather." *Autobiographies*. New York: Macmillan, 1936.

Young, John V. "Moonrise Over Monument Valley." *When the Full Moon Shines Its Magic Light Over Monument Valley*. New York: New York Times Company, 1965.

Young, Richard. *Rhetoric: Discovery and Change*. New York: Harcourt, 1970.

Young, Richard E., Alton L. Becker, and Kenneth L. Pike. *Rhetoric: Discovery and Change*. New York: Harcourt, 1970.

Index